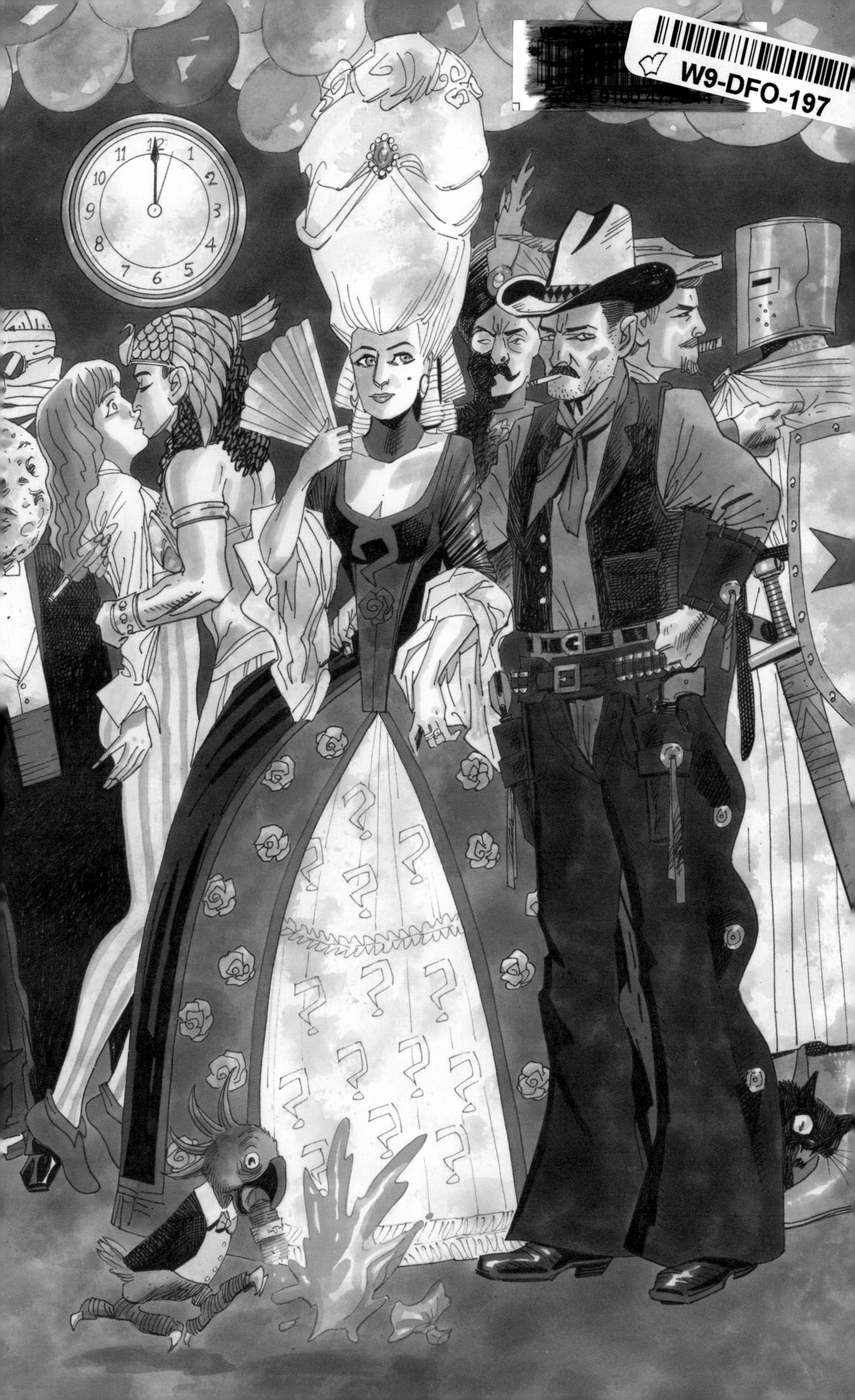

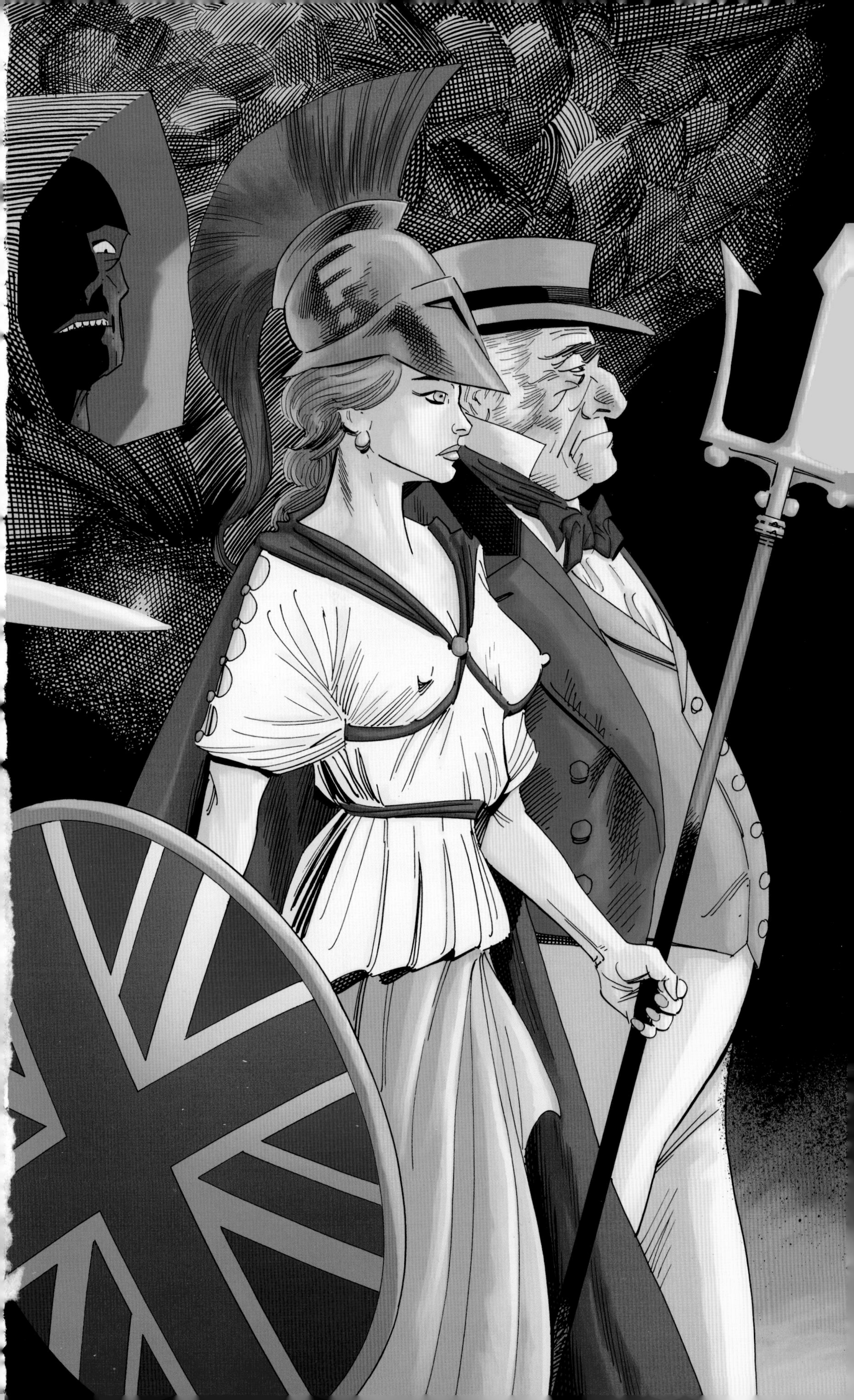

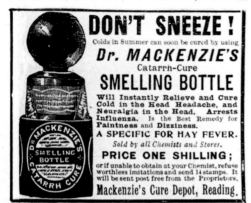
Some of the lyrics in this work were inspired by songs from The Threepenny Opera. We extend our thanks to the heirs of Bertolt Brecht and the Kurt Weill Foundation for Music, Inc. for their kind permission. Songs from The Threepenny Opera (Die Dreigroschenoper) Music by Kurt Weill, Lyrics by Bertolt Brecht. Original copyright © 1928 by Universal Edition, © renewed 1955. "The Threepenny Opera" ("Die Dreigroschenoper"), including all authorized translations of the musical compositions from that work, is fully protected by international copyright and is used by permission of WB Music Corp., European American Music Corporation, Universal Edition (London) Ltd. and Universal Edition AG on behalf of all copyright proprietors.

The League of Extraordinary Gentlemen Volume III: Century © & ™ 2014 Alan Moore & Kevin O'Neill. Co-Published by Top Shelf Productions, PO Box 1282, Marietta, GA 30061-1282, USA & Knockabout Comics, 42c Lancaster Road, London, W11 1QR, United Kingdom. Top Shelf Productions® and the Top Shelf logo are registered trademarks of Top Shelf Productions, Inc. All Rights Reserved. Originally published in magazine form as LEAGUE OF EXTRAORDINARY GENTLEMEN: CENTURY #1 1910, #2 1969, #3 2009. This is a work of fiction. Names, characters, places, and incidents are the products of the author's imagination or are used fictitiously. Any resemblance to actual events, locales, or persons, living or dead, is entirely coincidental. No part of this publication may be reproduced without permission, except for small excerpts for purposes of review. First printing, June, 2014. Printed in Hong Kong.

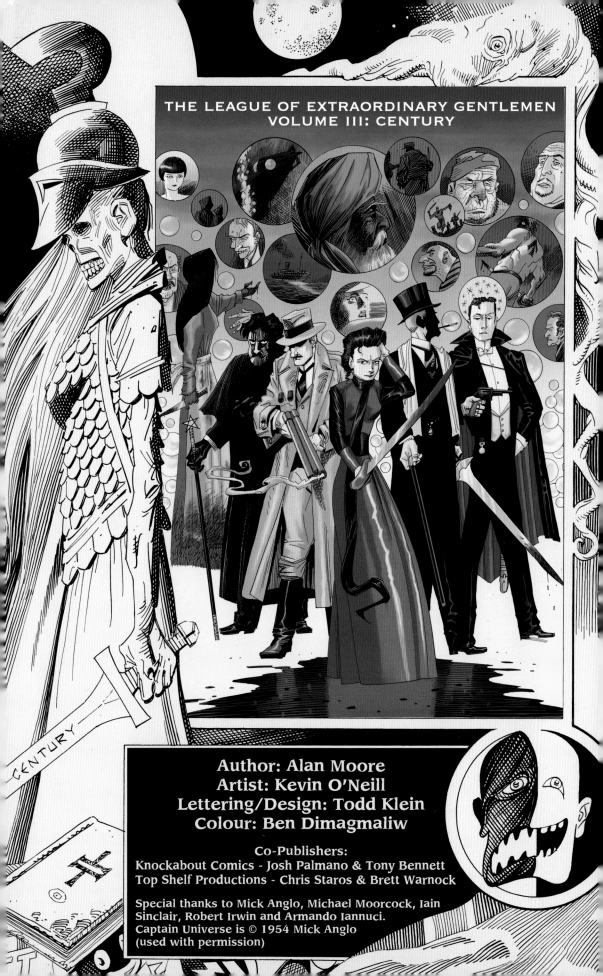

THE LEAGUE OF EXTRAORDINARY GENTLEMEN
VOLUME III: CENTURY

Author: Alan Moore
Artist: Kevin O'Neill
Lettering/Design: Todd Klein
Colour: Ben Dimagmaliw

Co-Publishers:
Knockabout Comics - Josh Palmano & Tony Bennett
Top Shelf Productions - Chris Staros & Brett Warnock

Special thanks to Mick Anglo, Michael Moorcock, Iain
Sinclair, Robert Irwin and Armando Iannuci.
Captain Universe is © 1954 Mick Anglo
(used with permission)

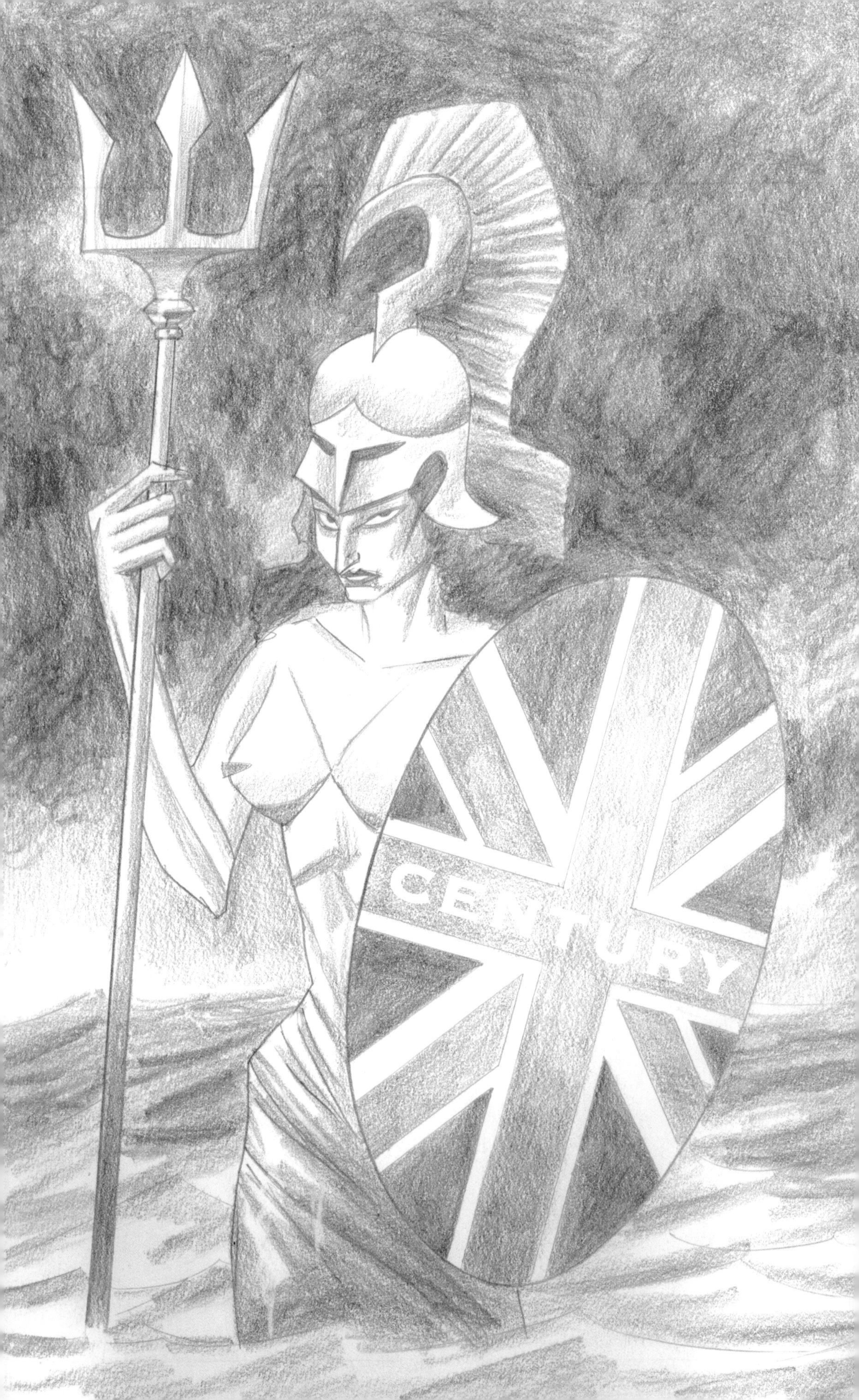
CENTURY

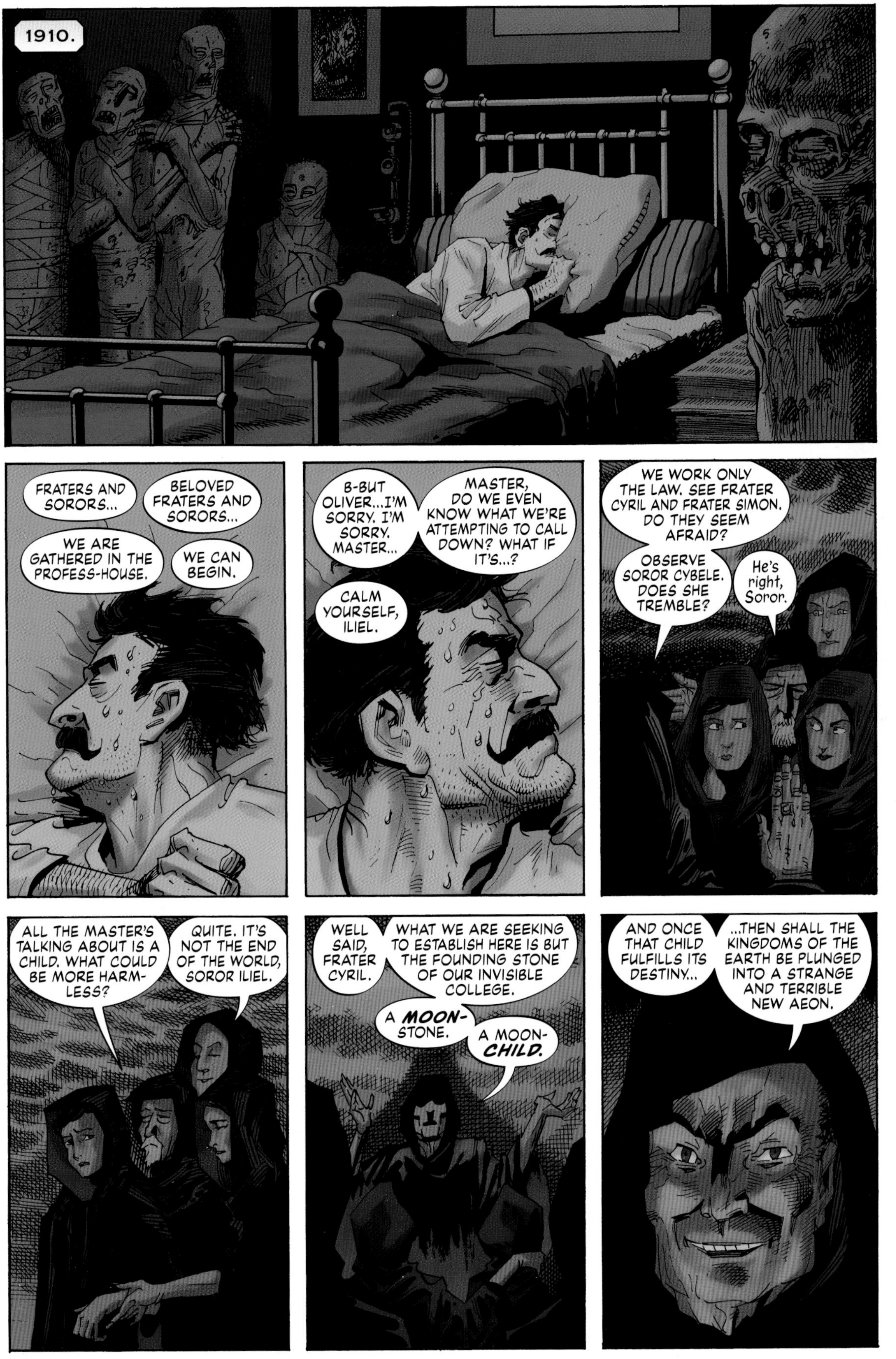
1910.
FRATERS AND SORORS...
BELOVED FRATERS AND SORORS...
WE ARE GATHERED IN THE PROFESS-HOUSE.
WE CAN BEGIN.
B-BUT OLIVER...I'M SORRY. I'M SORRY. MASTER...
MASTER, DO WE EVEN KNOW WHAT WE'RE ATTEMPTING TO CALL DOWN? WHAT IF IT'S...?
CALM YOURSELF, ILIEL.
WE WORK ONLY THE LAW. SEE FRATER CYRIL AND FRATER SIMON. DO THEY SEEM AFRAID?
OBSERVE SOROR CYBELE. DOES SHE TREMBLE?
He's right, Soror.
ALL THE MASTER'S TALKING ABOUT IS A CHILD. WHAT COULD BE MORE HARMLESS?
QUITE. IT'S NOT THE END OF THE WORLD, SOROR ILIEL.
WELL SAID, FRATER CYRIL.
WHAT WE ARE SEEKING TO ESTABLISH HERE IS BUT THE FOUNDING STONE OF OUR INVISIBLE COLLEGE.
A MOON-STONE.
A MOON-CHILD.
AND ONCE THAT CHILD FULFILLS ITS DESTINY...
...THEN SHALL THE KINGDOMS OF THE EARTH BE PLUNGED INTO A STRANGE AND TERRIBLE NEW AEON.

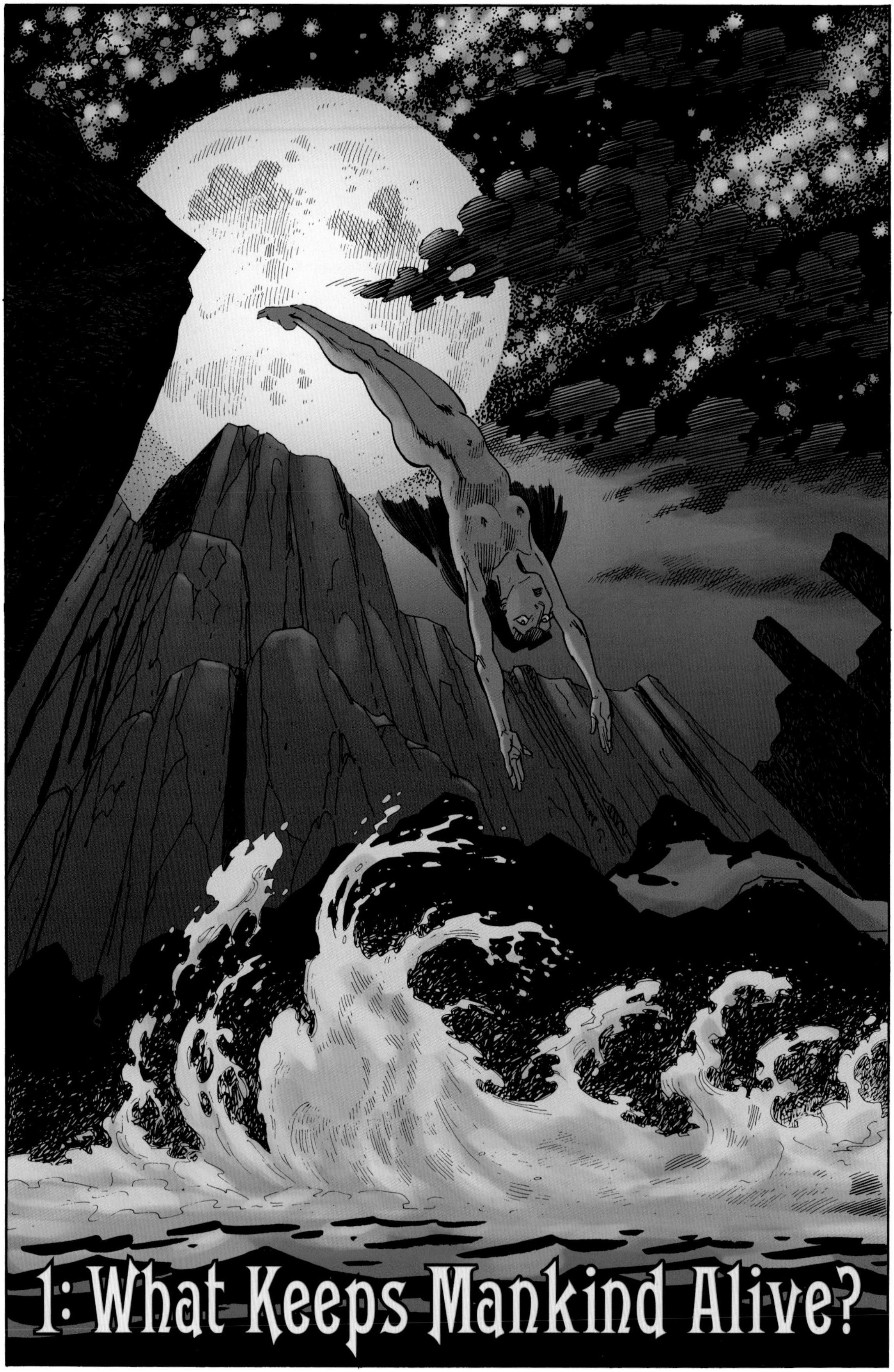
1: What Keeps Mankind Alive?

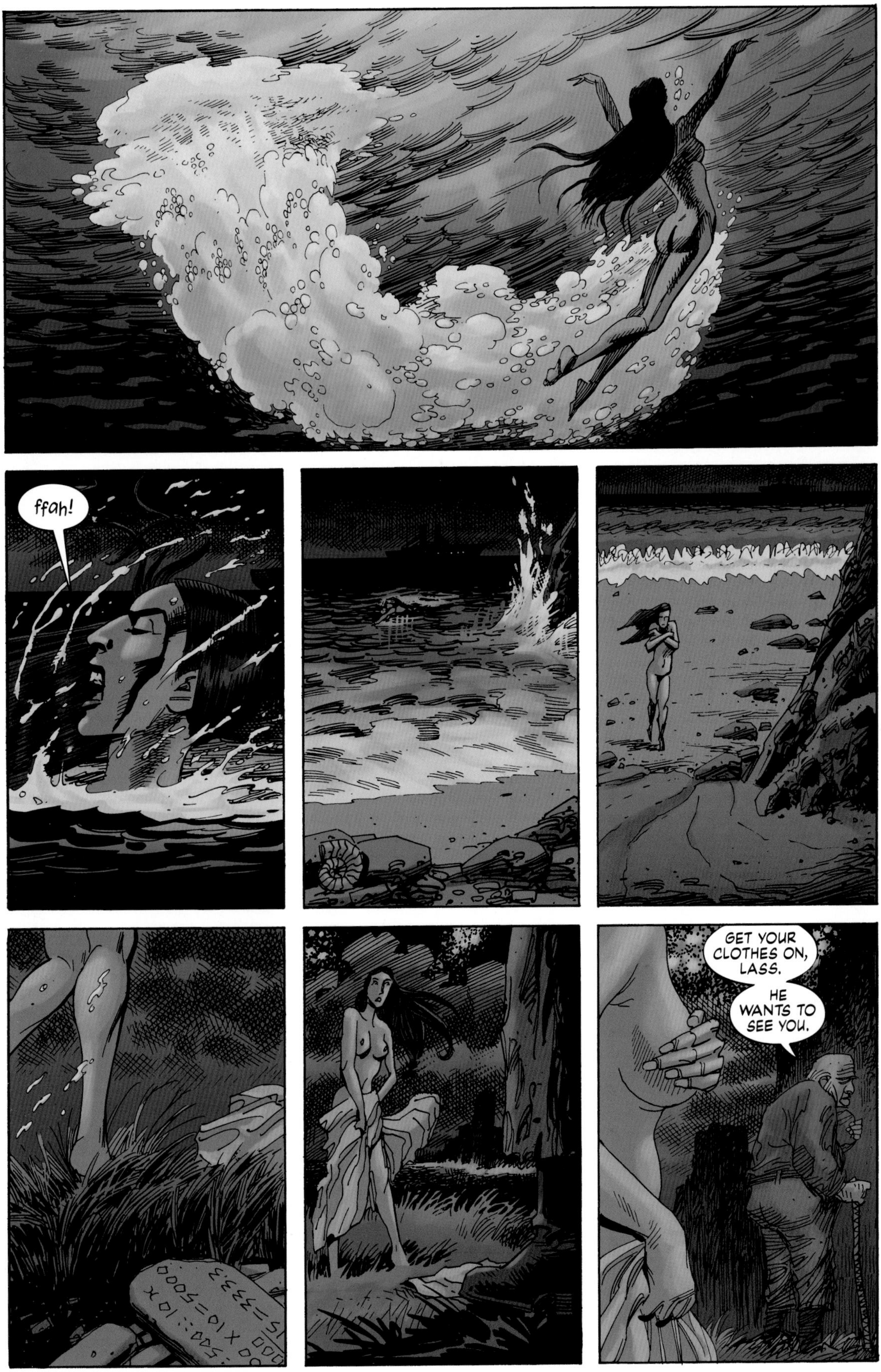
ffah!
GET YOUR CLOTHES ON, LASS.
HE WANTS TO SEE YOU.

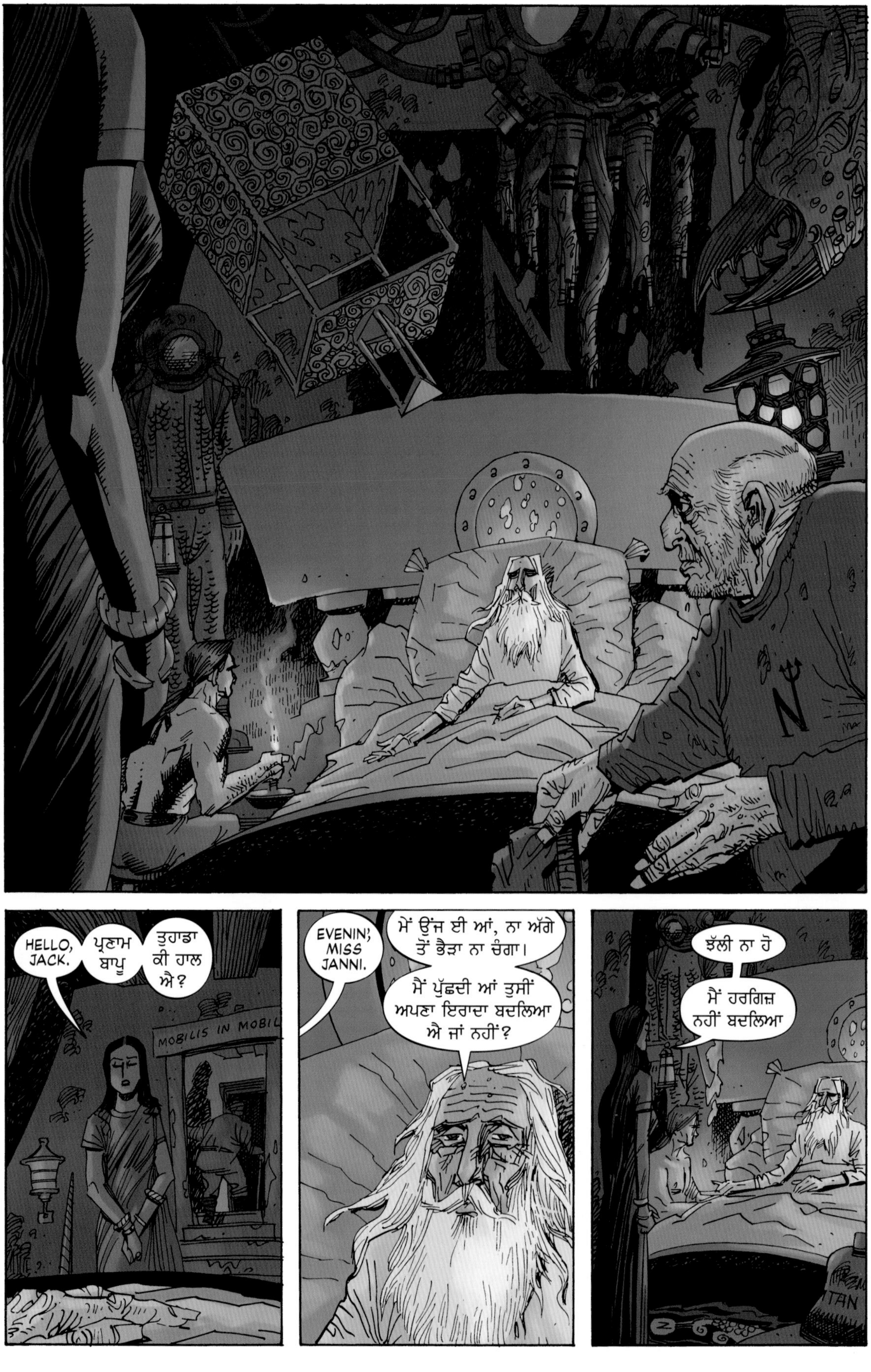
HELLO, JACK.
ਪ੍ਰਣਾਮ ਬਾਪੂ
ਤੁਹਾਡਾ ਕੀ ਹਾਲ ਐ?
MOBILIS IN MOBIL
EVENIN', MISS JANNI.
ਮੈਂ ਉਂਜ ਈ ਆਂ, ਨਾ ਅੱਗੇ ਤੋਂ ਭੈੜਾ ਨਾ ਚੰਗਾ।
ਮੈਂ ਪੁੱਛਦੀ ਆਂ ਤੁਸੀਂ ਅਪਣਾ ਇਰਾਦਾ ਬਦਲਿਆ ਐ ਜਾਂ ਨਹੀਂ?
ਝੱਲੀ ਨਾ ਹੋ
ਮੈਂ ਹਰਗਿਜ਼ ਨਹੀਂ ਬਦਲਿਆ

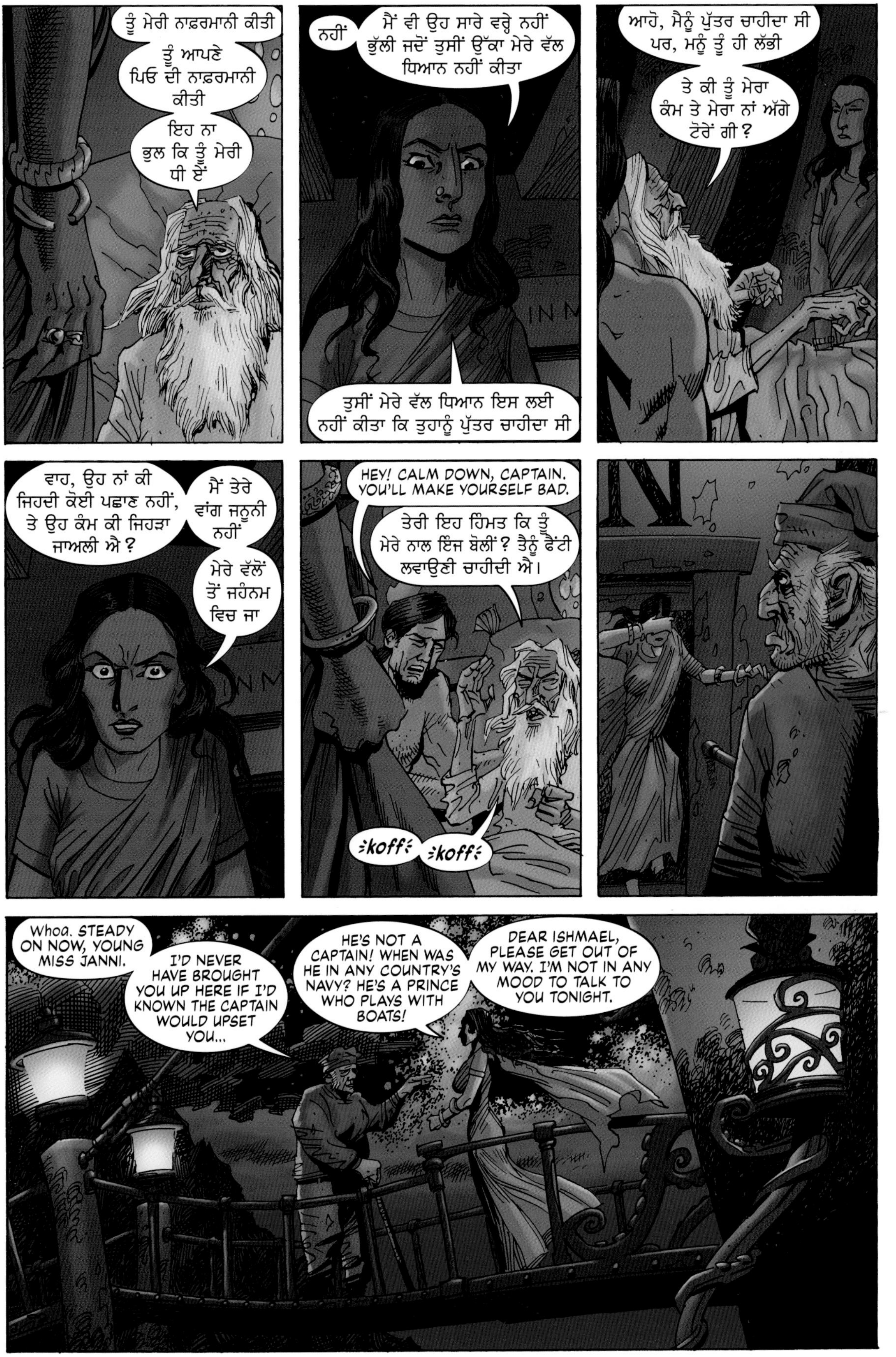
ਤੂੰ ਮੇਰੀ ਨਾਫ਼ਰਮਾਨੀ ਕੀਤੀ
ਤੂੰ ਆਪਣੇ ਪਿਓ ਦੀ ਨਾਫ਼ਰਮਾਨੀ ਕੀਤੀ
ਇਹ ਨਾ ਭੁਲ ਕਿ ਤੂੰ ਮੇਰੀ ਧੀ ਏਂ
ਨਹੀਂ
ਮੈਂ ਵੀ ਉਹ ਸਾਰੇ ਵਰ੍ਹੇ ਨਹੀਂ ਭੁੱਲੀ ਜਦੋਂ ਤੁਸੀਂ ਉੱਕਾ ਮੇਰੇ ਵੱਲ ਧਿਆਨ ਨਹੀਂ ਕੀਤਾ
ਤੁਸੀਂ ਮੇਰੇ ਵੱਲ ਧਿਆਨ ਇਸ ਲਈ ਨਹੀਂ ਕੀਤਾ ਕਿ ਤੁਹਾਨੂੰ ਪੁੱਤਰ ਚਾਹੀਦਾ ਸੀ
ਆਹੋ, ਮੈਨੂੰ ਪੁੱਤਰ ਚਾਹੀਦਾ ਸੀ ਪਰ, ਮਨੂੰ ਤੂੰ ਹੀ ਲੱਭੀ
ਤੇ ਕੀ ਤੂੰ ਮੇਰਾ ਕੰਮ ਤੇ ਮੇਰਾ ਨਾਂ ਅੱਗੇ ਟੋਰੇਂ ਗੀ ?
ਵਾਹ, ਉਹ ਨਾਂ ਕੀ ਜਿਹਦੀ ਕੋਈ ਪਛਾਣ ਨਹੀਂ, ਤੇ ਉਹ ਕੰਮ ਕੀ ਜਿਹੜਾ ਜਾਅਲੀ ਐ ?
ਮੈਂ ਤੇਰੇ ਵਾਂਗ ਜਨੂਨੀ ਨਹੀਂ
ਮੇਰੇ ਵੱਲੋਂ ਤੋਂ ਜਹੰਨਮ ਵਿਚ ਜਾ
HEY! CALM DOWN, CAPTAIN. YOU'LL MAKE YOURSELF BAD.
ਤੇਰੀ ਇਹ ਹਿੰਮਤ ਕਿ ਤੂੰ ਮੇਰੇ ਨਾਲ ਇੰਜ ਬੋਲੀਂ ? ਤੈਨੂੰ ਫੈਂਟੀ ਲਵਾਉਣੀ ਚਾਹੀਦੀ ਐ।
koff koff
Whoa. STEADY ON NOW, YOUNG MISS JANNI.
I'D NEVER HAVE BROUGHT YOU UP HERE IF I'D KNOWN THE CAPTAIN WOULD UPSET YOU...
HE'S NOT A CAPTAIN! WHEN WAS HE IN ANY COUNTRY'S NAVY? HE'S A PRINCE WHO PLAYS WITH BOATS!
DEAR ISHMAEL, PLEASE GET OUT OF MY WAY. I'M NOT IN ANY MOOD TO TALK TO YOU TONIGHT.

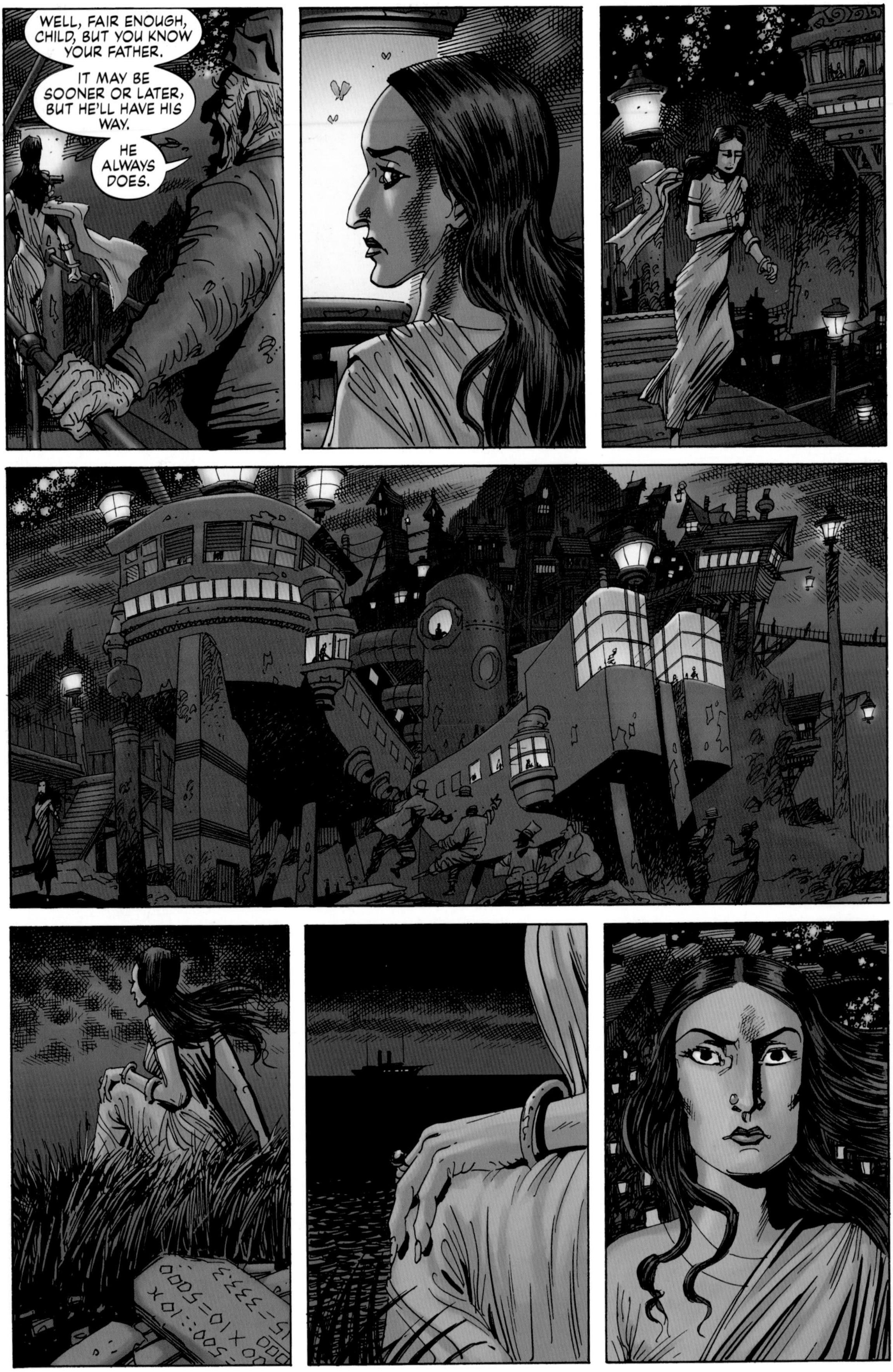
WELL, FAIR ENOUGH, CHILD, BUT YOU KNOW YOUR FATHER.
IT MAY BE SOONER OR LATER, BUT HE'LL HAVE HIS WAY.
HE ALWAYS DOES.

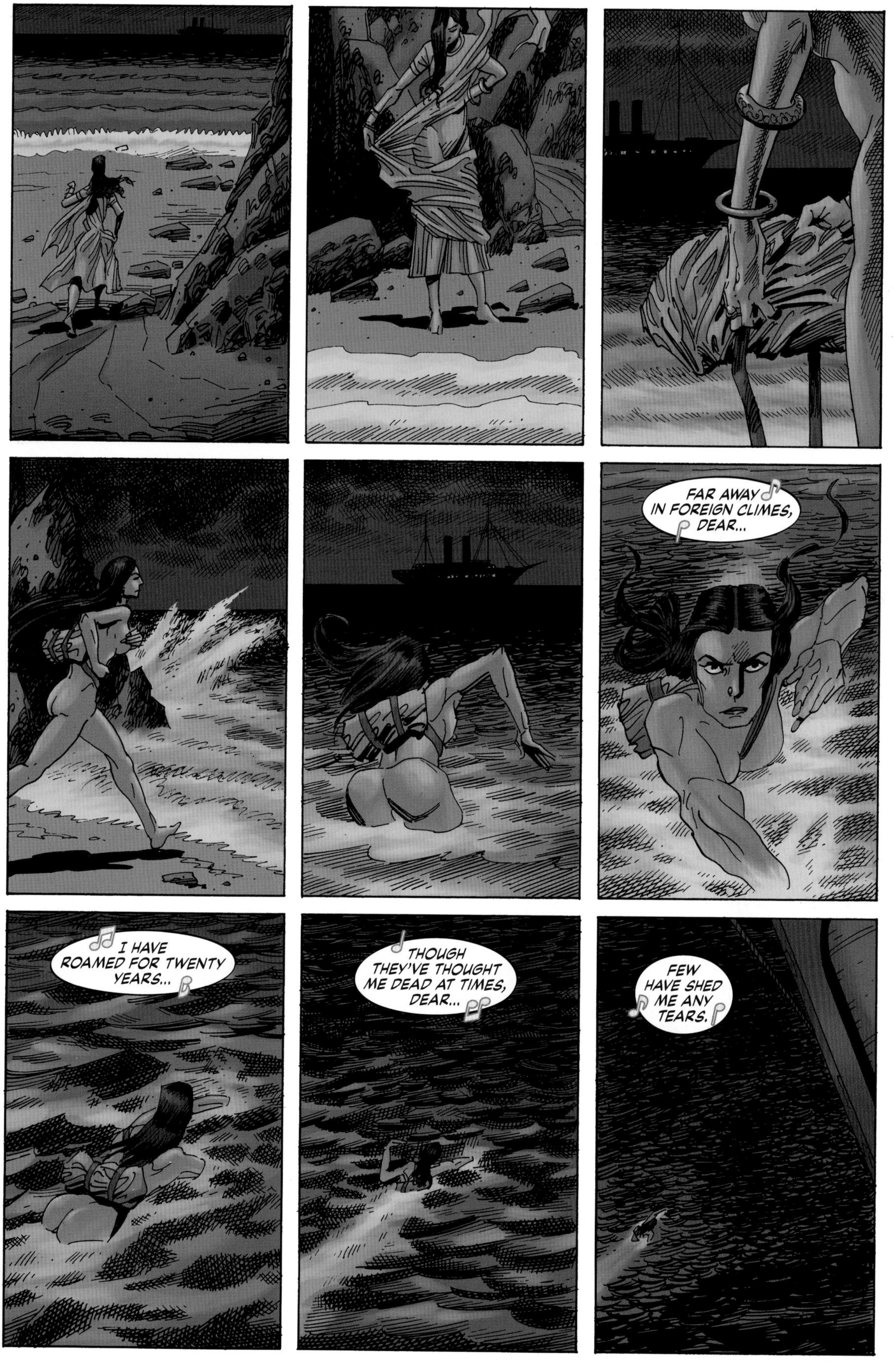
FAR AWAY IN FOREIGN CLIMES, DEAR...
I HAVE ROAMED FOR TWENTY YEARS...
THOUGH THEY'VE THOUGHT ME DEAD AT TIMES, DEAR...
FEW HAVE SHED ME ANY TEARS.

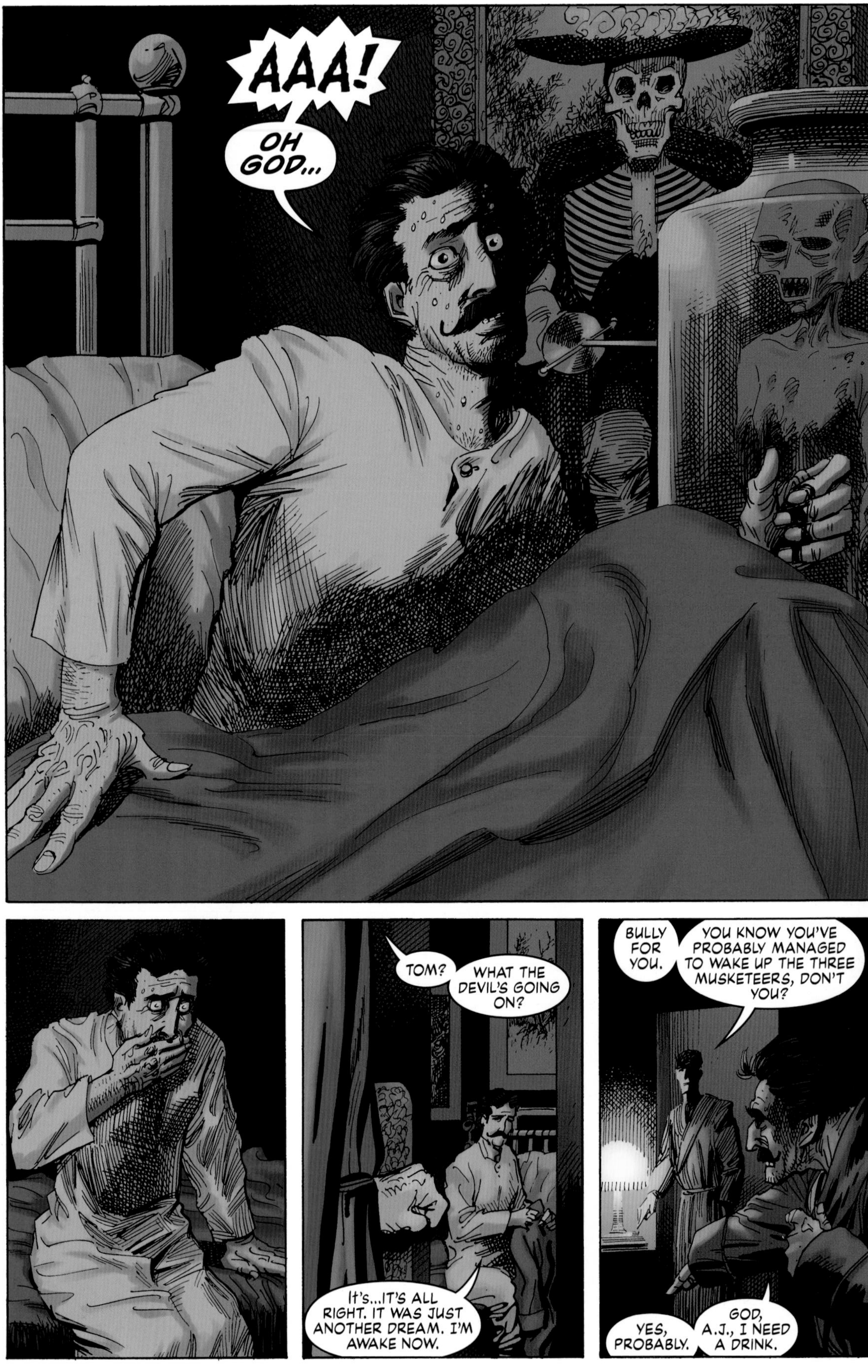
AAA!
OH GOD...
TOM?
WHAT THE DEVIL'S GOING ON?
IT'S...IT'S ALL RIGHT. IT WAS JUST ANOTHER DREAM. I'M AWAKE NOW.
BULLY FOR YOU.
YOU KNOW YOU'VE PROBABLY MANAGED TO WAKE UP THE THREE MUSKETEERS, DON'T YOU?
YES, PROBABLY.
GOD, A.J., I NEED A DRINK.

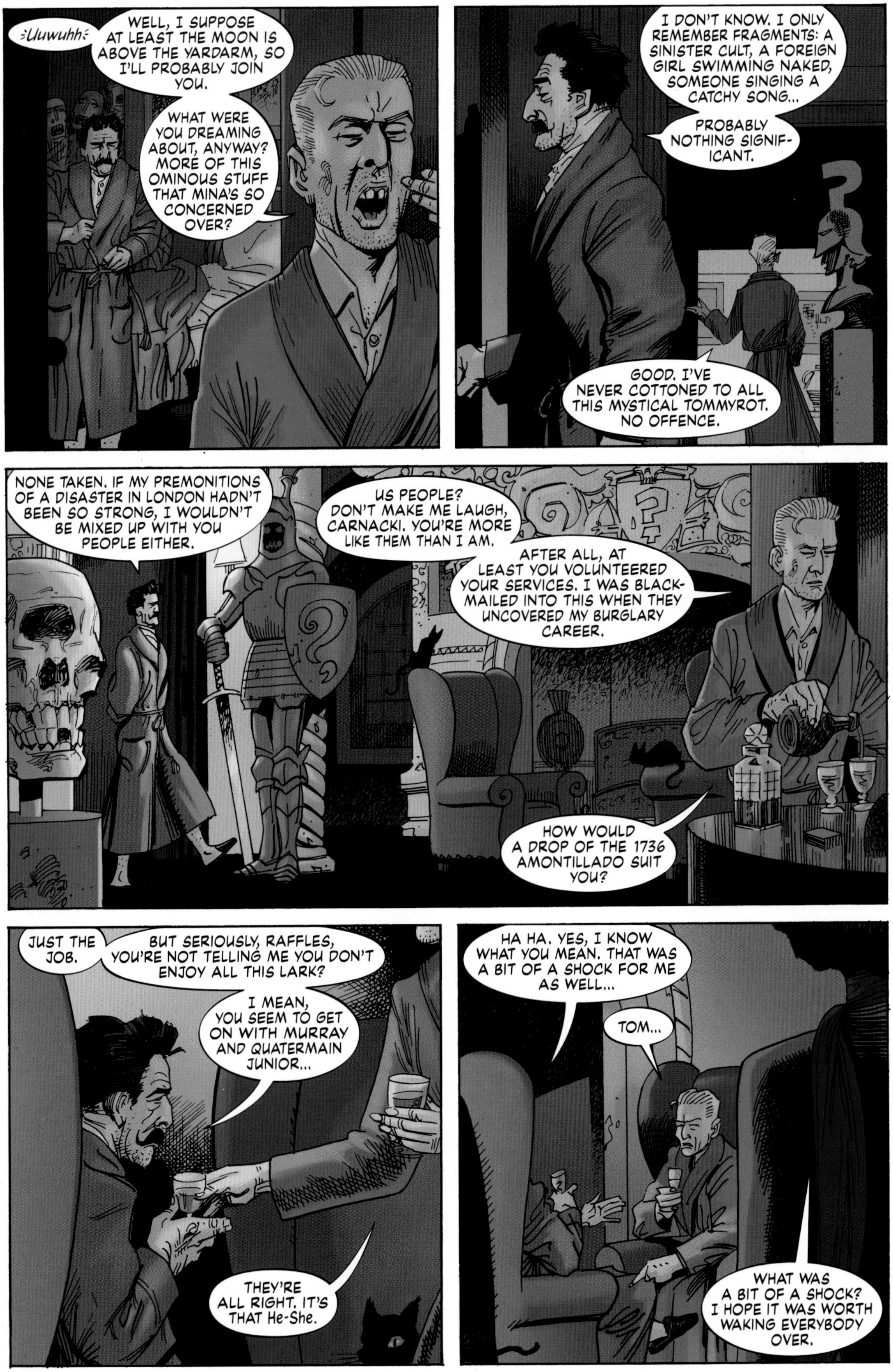

Uuwuhh
WELL, I SUPPOSE AT LEAST THE MOON IS ABOVE THE YARDARM, SO I'LL PROBABLY JOIN YOU.
WHAT WERE YOU DREAMING ABOUT, ANYWAY? MORE OF THIS OMINOUS STUFF THAT MINA'S SO CONCERNED OVER?
I DON'T KNOW. I ONLY REMEMBER FRAGMENTS: A SINISTER CULT, A FOREIGN GIRL SWIMMING NAKED, SOMEONE SINGING A CATCHY SONG...
PROBABLY NOTHING SIGNIFICANT.
GOOD. I'VE NEVER COTTONED TO ALL THIS MYSTICAL TOMMYROT. NO OFFENCE.
NONE TAKEN. IF MY PREMONITIONS OF A DISASTER IN LONDON HADN'T BEEN SO STRONG, I WOULDN'T BE MIXED UP WITH YOU PEOPLE EITHER.
US PEOPLE? DON'T MAKE ME LAUGH, CARNACKI. YOU'RE MORE LIKE THEM THAN I AM.
AFTER ALL, AT LEAST YOU VOLUNTEERED YOUR SERVICES. I WAS BLACKMAILED INTO THIS WHEN THEY UNCOVERED MY BURGLARY CAREER.
HOW WOULD A DROP OF THE 1736 AMONTILLADO SUIT YOU?
JUST THE JOB.
BUT SERIOUSLY, RAFFLES, YOU'RE NOT TELLING ME YOU DON'T ENJOY ALL THIS LARK?
I MEAN, YOU SEEM TO GET ON WITH MURRAY AND QUATERMAIN JUNIOR...
THEY'RE ALL RIGHT. IT'S THAT He-She.
HA HA. YES, I KNOW WHAT YOU MEAN. THAT WAS A BIT OF A SHOCK FOR ME AS WELL...
TOM...
WHAT WAS A BIT OF A SHOCK? I HOPE IT WAS WORTH WAKING EVERYBODY OVER.

Oh, CARNACKI JUST HAD ONE OF HIS NIGHTMARES. ISN'T THAT RIGHT, TOM?

Really? AND DID IT YIELD ANY CLUES TO OUR FORTHCOMING DISASTER, MR. CARNACKI?

I'M AFRAID NOT...ALTHOUGH THERE WAS SOME STUFF ABOUT A CULT OR SECT OF SOME KIND.

ACTUALLY, THINKING ABOUT IT, ONE OF THE CHAPS I DREAMED OF SEEMED TERRIBLY FAMILIAR...

WHAT A BORE. ALL THE CHAPS I DREAM OF ARE TERRIBLY *OVER*-FAMILIAR.

Oh, LANDO, DO SHUT UP.

SO, MR. CARNACKI, WHERE DID YOU RECOGNISE THE MAN IN YOUR DREAM FROM? SOME FORMER ENEMY, PERHAPS?

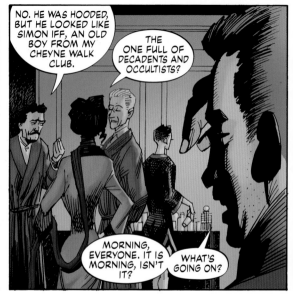

NO. HE WAS HOODED, BUT HE LOOKED LIKE SIMON IFF, AN OLD BOY FROM MY CHEYNE WALK CLUB.

THE ONE FULL OF DECADENTS AND OCCULTISTS?

MORNING, EVERYONE. IT IS MORNING, ISN'T IT?

WHAT'S GOING ON?

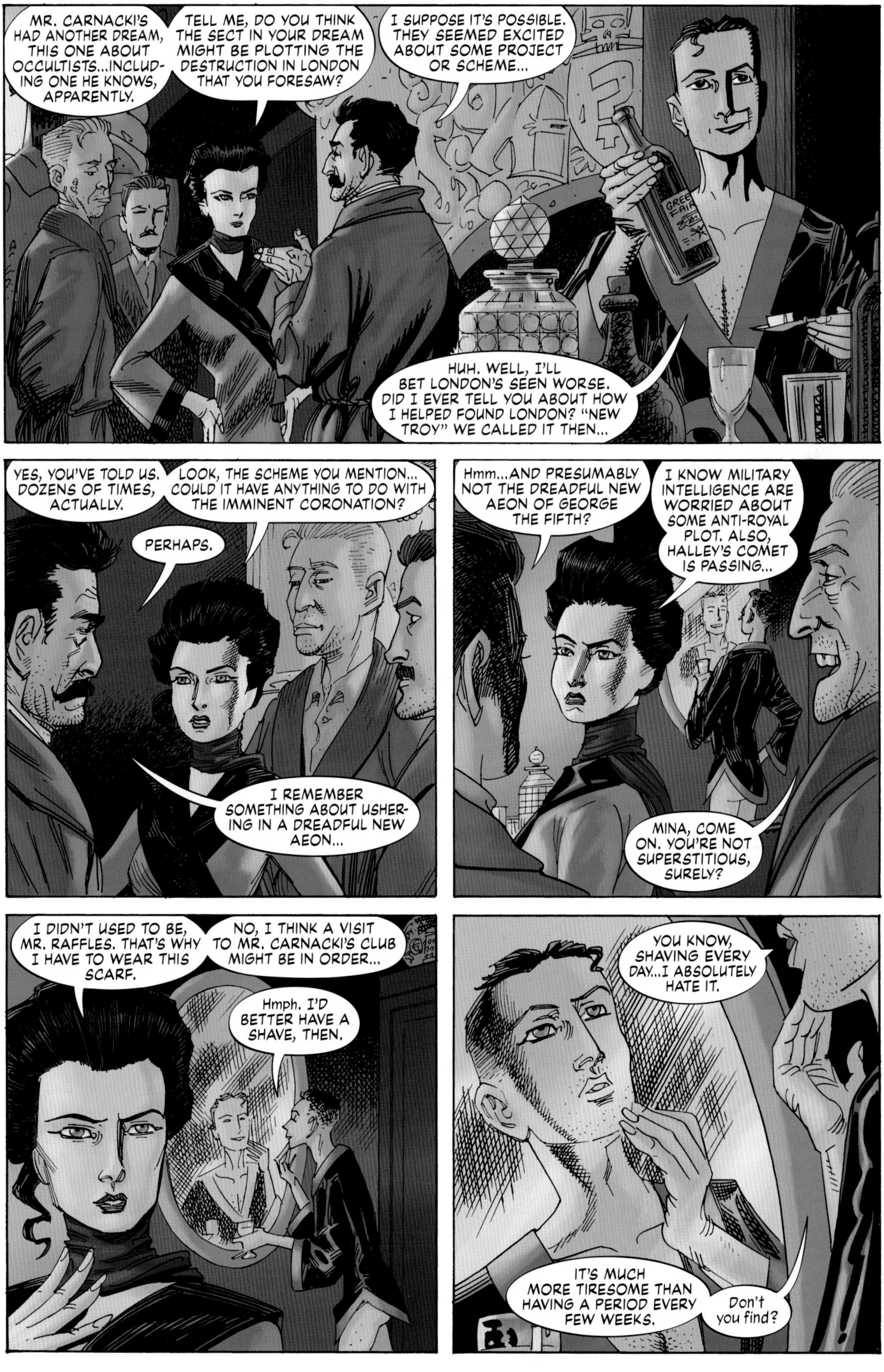
MR. CARNACKI'S HAD ANOTHER DREAM, THIS ONE ABOUT OCCULTISTS...INCLUDING ONE HE KNOWS, APPARENTLY.
TELL ME, DO YOU THINK THE SECT IN YOUR DREAM MIGHT BE PLOTTING THE DESTRUCTION IN LONDON THAT YOU FORESAW?
I SUPPOSE IT'S POSSIBLE. THEY SEEMED EXCITED ABOUT SOME PROJECT OR SCHEME...
HUH. WELL, I'LL BET LONDON'S SEEN WORSE. DID I EVER TELL YOU ABOUT HOW I HELPED FOUND LONDON? "NEW TROY" WE CALLED IT THEN...
YES, YOU'VE TOLD US. DOZENS OF TIMES, ACTUALLY.
LOOK, THE SCHEME YOU MENTION... COULD IT HAVE ANYTHING TO DO WITH THE IMMINENT CORONATION?
PERHAPS.
I REMEMBER SOMETHING ABOUT USHERING IN A DREADFUL NEW AEON...
Hmm...AND PRESUMABLY NOT THE DREADFUL NEW AEON OF GEORGE THE FIFTH?
I KNOW MILITARY INTELLIGENCE ARE WORRIED ABOUT SOME ANTI-ROYAL PLOT. ALSO, HALLEY'S COMET IS PASSING...
MINA, COME ON. YOU'RE NOT SUPERSTITIOUS, SURELY?
I DIDN'T USED TO BE, MR. RAFFLES. THAT'S WHY I HAVE TO WEAR THIS SCARF.
NO, I THINK A VISIT TO MR. CARNACKI'S CLUB MIGHT BE IN ORDER...
Hmph. I'D BETTER HAVE A SHAVE, THEN.
YOU KNOW, SHAVING EVERY DAY...I ABSOLUTELY HATE IT.
IT'S MUCH MORE TIRESOME THAN HAVING A PERIOD EVERY FEW WEEKS.
Don't you find?

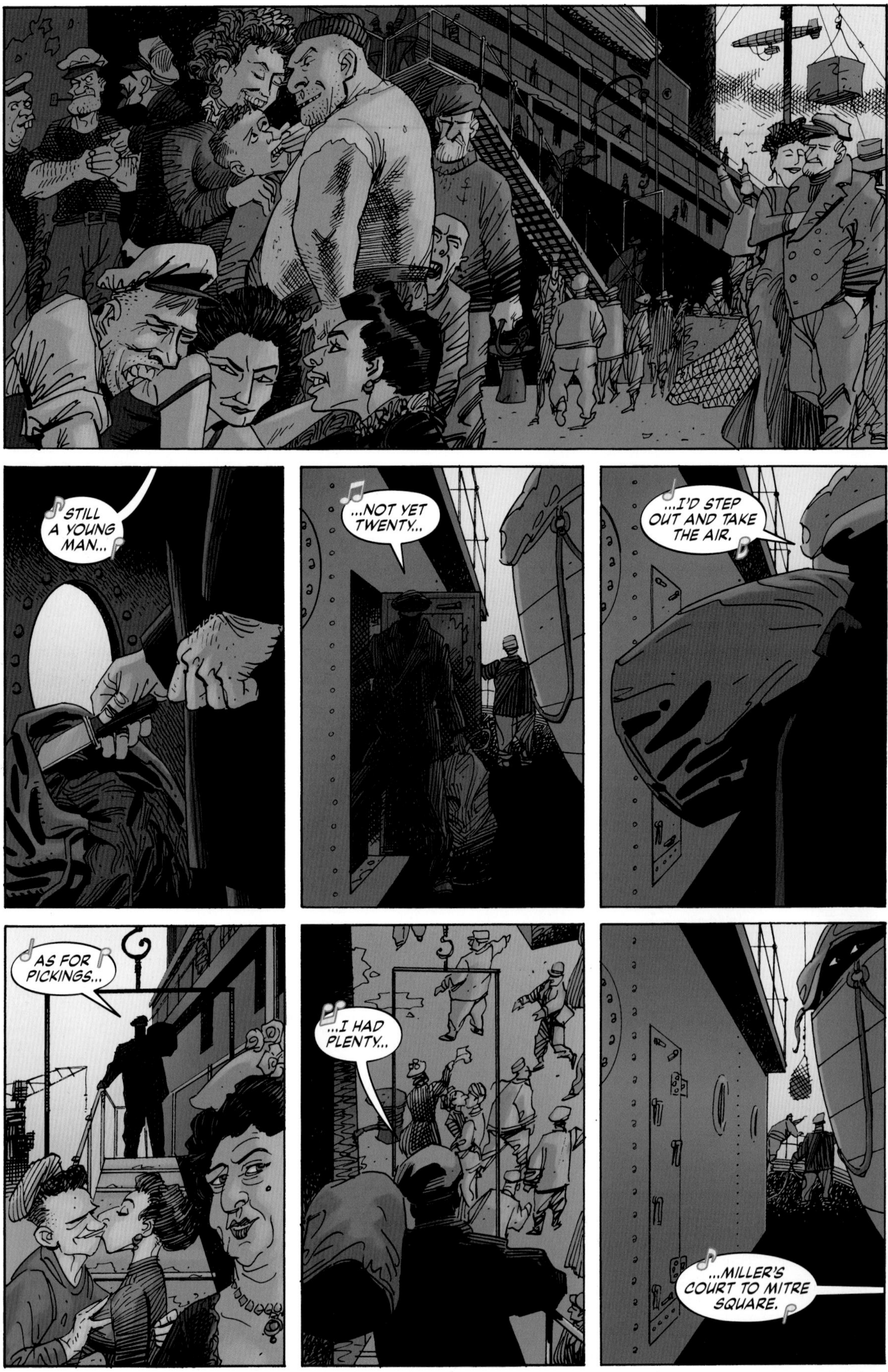
STILL A YOUNG MAN...
...NOT YET TWENTY...
...I'D STEP OUT AND TAKE THE AIR.
AS FOR PICKINGS...
...I HAD PLENTY...
...MILLER'S COURT TO MITRE SQUARE.

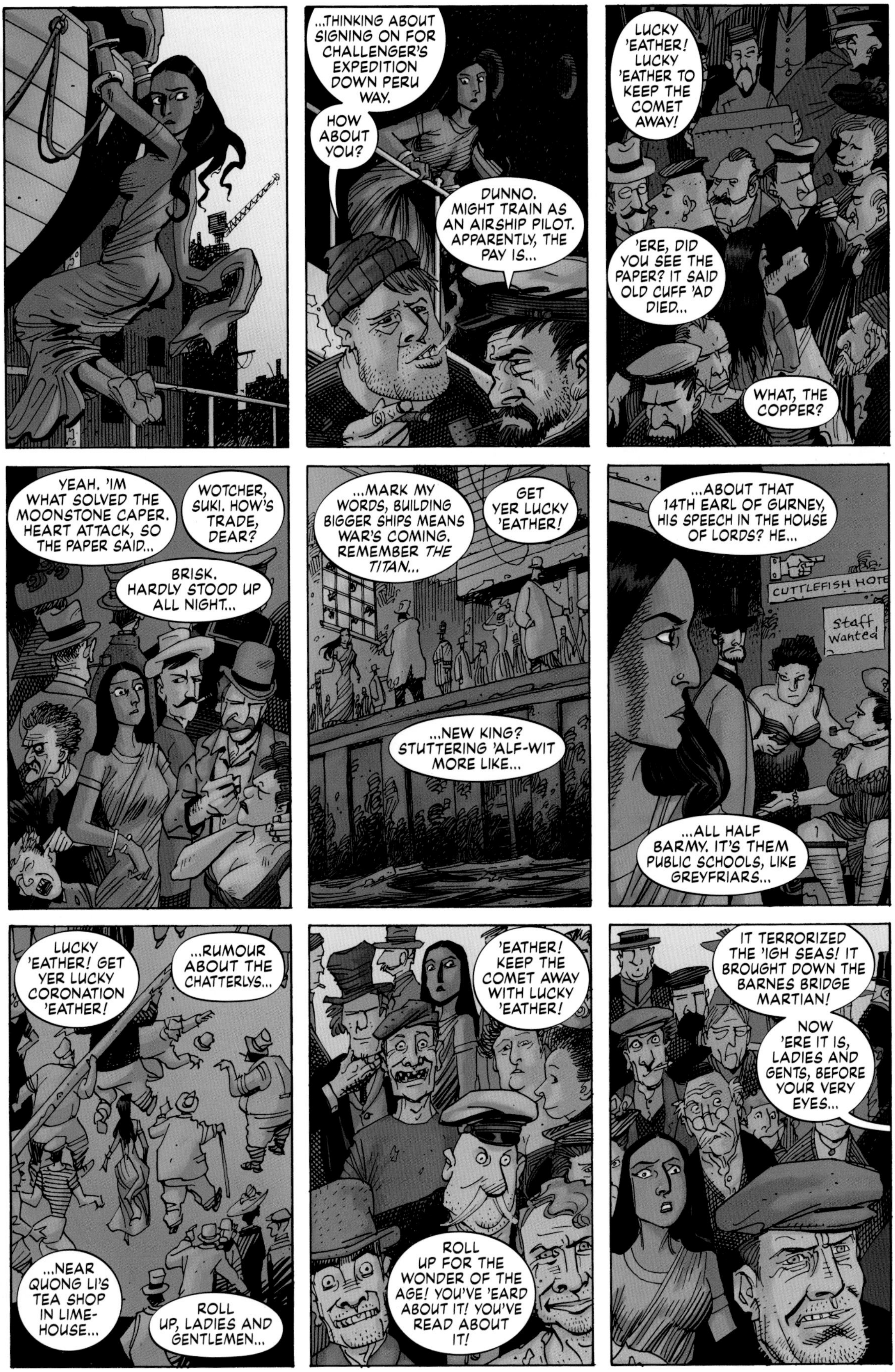
...THINKING ABOUT SIGNING ON FOR CHALLENGER'S EXPEDITION DOWN PERU WAY.
HOW ABOUT YOU?
DUNNO. MIGHT TRAIN AS AN AIRSHIP PILOT. APPARENTLY, THE PAY IS...
LUCKY 'EATHER! LUCKY 'EATHER TO KEEP THE COMET AWAY!
'ERE, DID YOU SEE THE PAPER? IT SAID OLD CUFF 'AD DIED...
WHAT, THE COPPER?
YEAH. 'IM WHAT SOLVED THE MOONSTONE CAPER. HEART ATTACK, SO THE PAPER SAID...
WOTCHER, SUKI. HOW'S TRADE, DEAR?
BRISK. HARDLY STOOD UP ALL NIGHT...
...MARK MY WORDS, BUILDING BIGGER SHIPS MEANS WAR'S COMING. REMEMBER *THE TITAN*...
GET YER LUCKY 'EATHER!
...NEW KING? STUTTERING 'ALF-WIT MORE LIKE...
...ABOUT THAT 14TH EARL OF GURNEY, HIS SPEECH IN THE HOUSE OF LORDS? HE...
CUTTLEFISH HOTE
Staff Wanted
...ALL HALF BARMY. IT'S THEM PUBLIC SCHOOLS, LIKE GREYFRIARS...
LUCKY 'EATHER! GET YER LUCKY CORONATION 'EATHER!
...RUMOUR ABOUT THE CHATTERLYS...
...NEAR QUONG LI'S TEA SHOP IN LIME-HOUSE...
ROLL UP, LADIES AND GENTLEMEN...
'EATHER! KEEP THE COMET AWAY WITH LUCKY 'EATHER!
ROLL UP FOR THE WONDER OF THE AGE! YOU'VE 'EARD ABOUT IT! YOU'VE READ ABOUT IT!
IT TERRORIZED THE 'IGH SEAS! IT BROUGHT DOWN THE BARNES BRIDGE MARTIAN!
NOW 'ERE IT IS, LADIES AND GENTS, BEFORE YOUR VERY EYES...

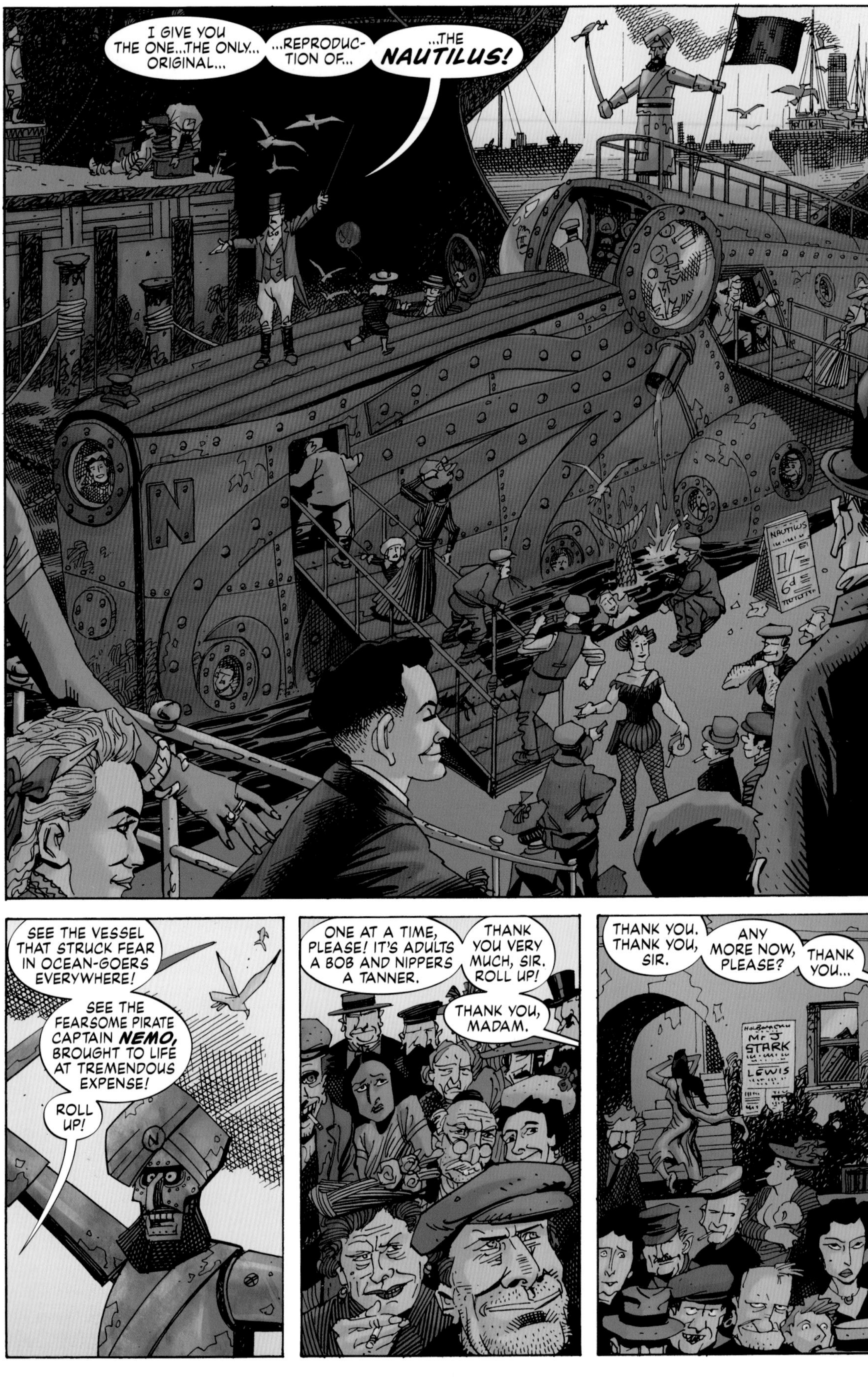
I GIVE YOU THE ONE...THE ONLY... ORIGINAL...
...REPRODUCTION OF...
...THE *NAUTILUS!*
NAUTILUS
SEE THE VESSEL THAT STRUCK FEAR IN OCEAN-GOERS EVERYWHERE!
SEE THE FEARSOME PIRATE CAPTAIN *NEMO,* BROUGHT TO LIFE AT TREMENDOUS EXPENSE!
ROLL UP!
ONE AT A TIME, PLEASE! IT'S ADULTS A BOB AND NIPPERS A TANNER.
THANK YOU VERY MUCH, SIR. ROLL UP!
THANK YOU, MADAM.
THANK YOU. THANK YOU, SIR.
ANY MORE NOW, PLEASE?
THANK YOU...
Mr J STARK
LEWIS

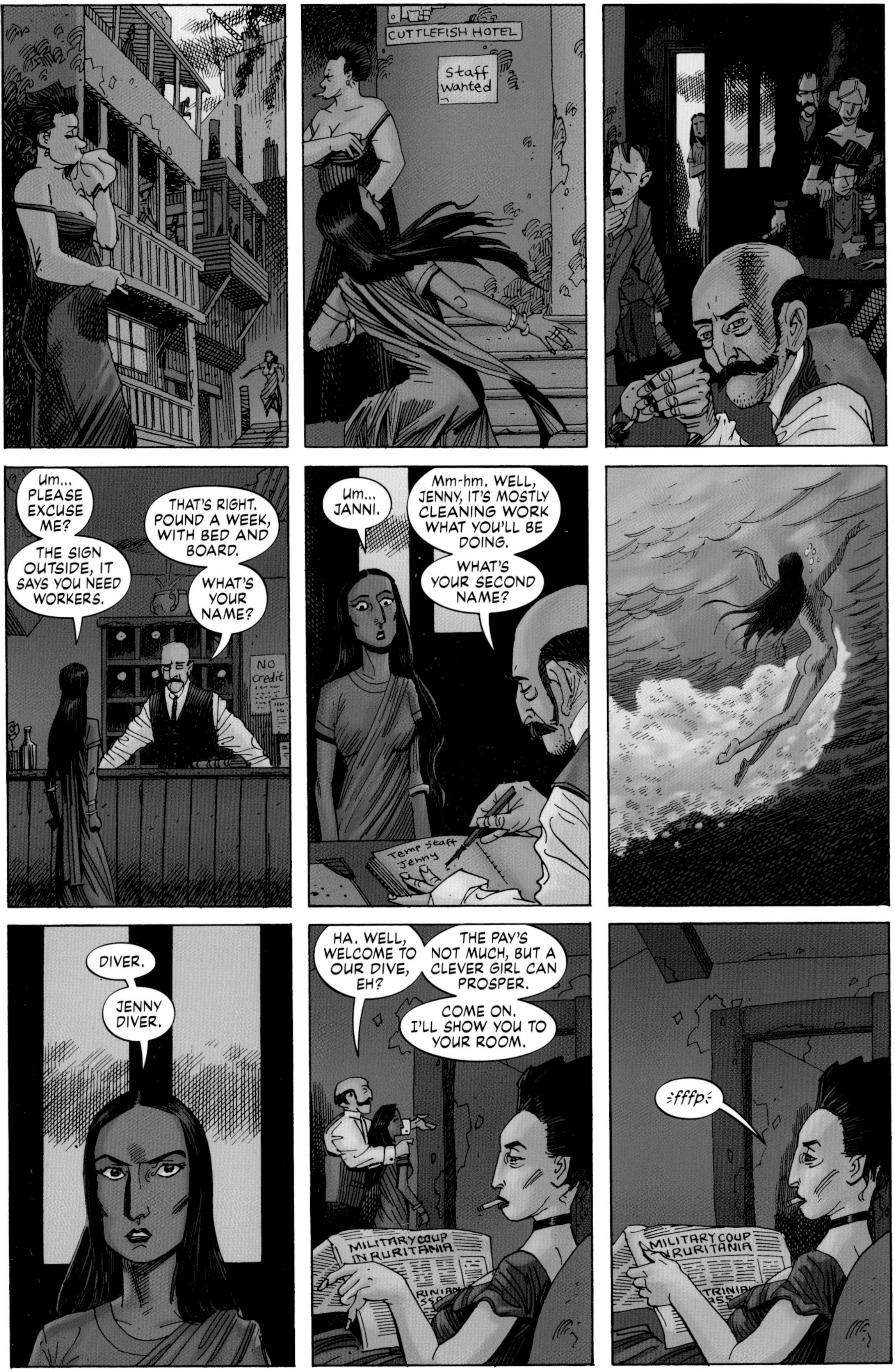
CUTTLEFISH HOTEL
Staff wanted
Um... PLEASE EXCUSE ME?
THE SIGN OUTSIDE, IT SAYS YOU NEED WORKERS.
THAT'S RIGHT. POUND A WEEK, WITH BED AND BOARD.
WHAT'S YOUR NAME?
NO Credit
Um... JANNI.
Mm-hm. WELL, JENNY, IT'S MOSTLY CLEANING WORK WHAT YOU'LL BE DOING.
WHAT'S YOUR SECOND NAME?
Temp Staff Jenny
DIVER.
JENNY DIVER.
HA. WELL, WELCOME TO OUR DIVE, EH?
THE PAY'S NOT MUCH, BUT A CLEVER GIRL CAN PROSPER.
COME ON. I'LL SHOW YOU TO YOUR ROOM.
MILITARY COUP IN RURITANIA
fffp
MILITARY COUP IN RURITANIA

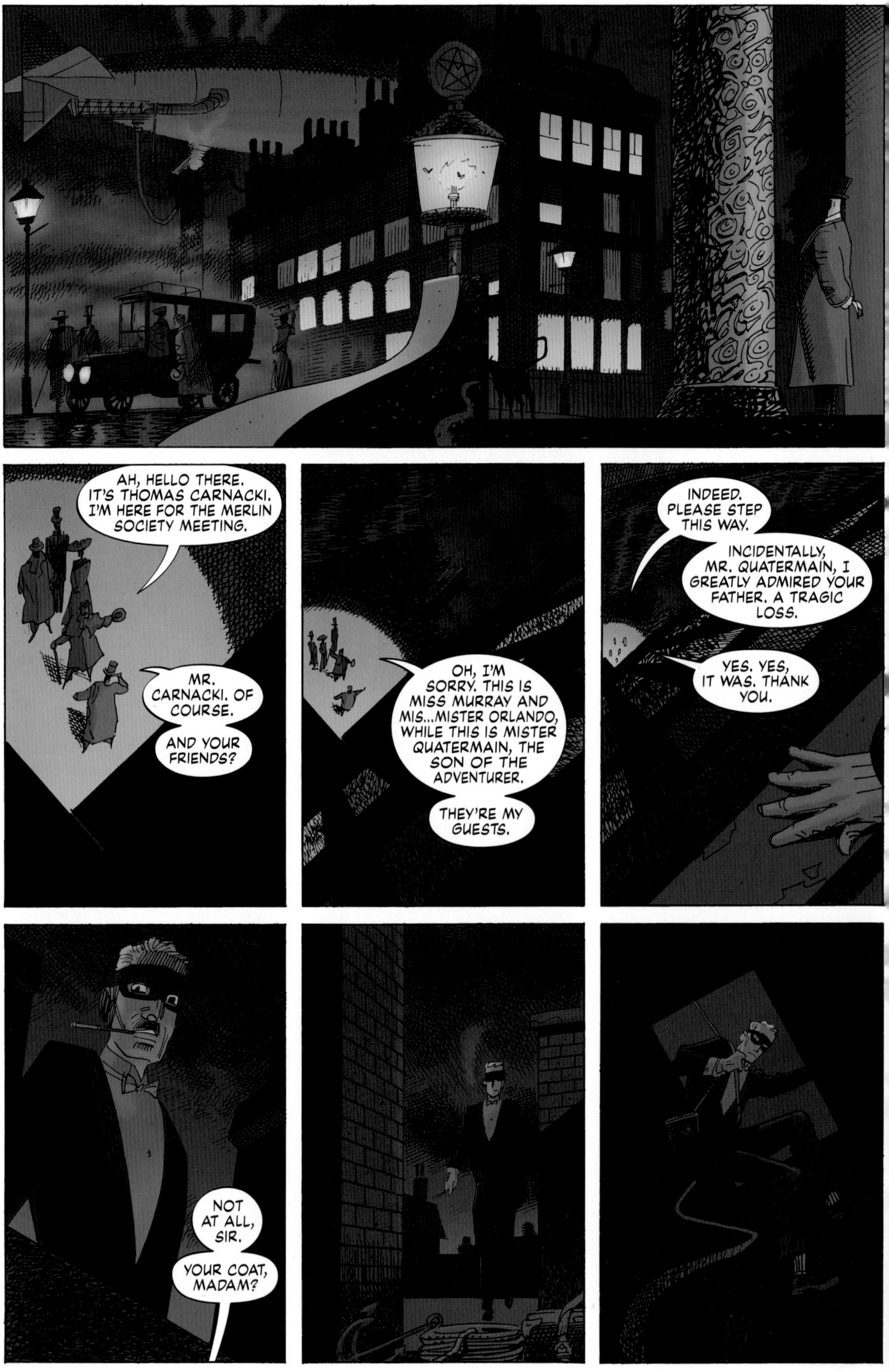

AH, HELLO THERE. IT'S THOMAS CARNACKI. I'M HERE FOR THE MERLIN SOCIETY MEETING.
MR. CARNACKI. OF COURSE.
AND YOUR FRIENDS?
OH, I'M SORRY. THIS IS MISS MURRAY AND MIS...MISTER ORLANDO, WHILE THIS IS MISTER QUATERMAIN, THE SON OF THE ADVENTURER.
THEY'RE MY GUESTS.
INDEED. PLEASE STEP THIS WAY.
INCIDENTALLY, MR. QUATERMAIN, I GREATLY ADMIRED YOUR FATHER. A TRAGIC LOSS.
YES. YES, IT WAS. THANK YOU.
NOT AT ALL, SIR.
YOUR COAT, MADAM?

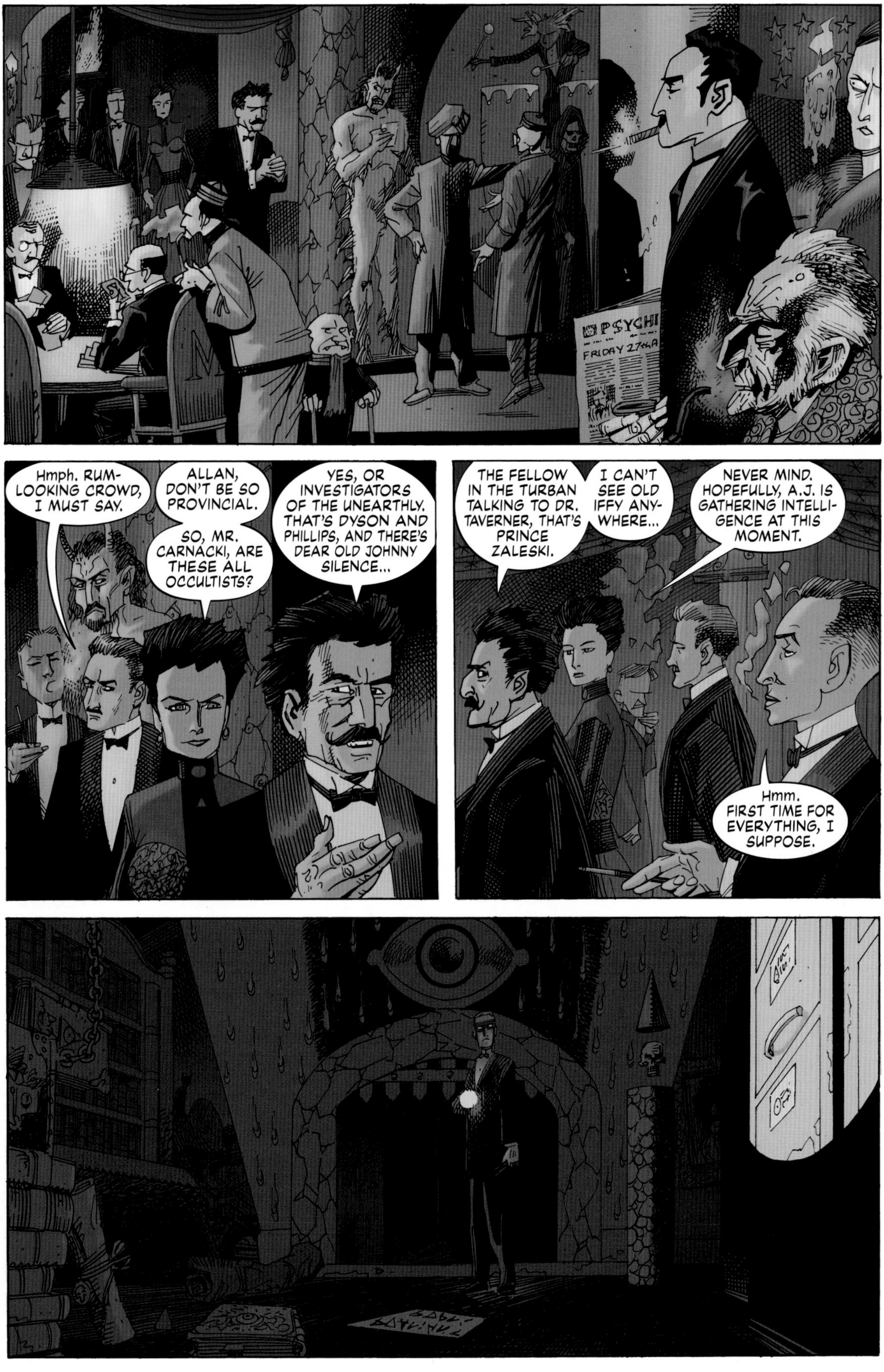
PSYCHI
FRIDAY 27th A
Hmph. RUM-LOOKING CROWD, I MUST SAY.
ALLAN, DON'T BE SO PROVINCIAL.
SO, MR. CARNACKI, ARE THESE ALL OCCULTISTS?
YES, OR INVESTIGATORS OF THE UNEARTHLY. THAT'S DYSON AND PHILLIPS, AND THERE'S DEAR OLD JOHNNY SILENCE...
THE FELLOW IN THE TURBAN TALKING TO DR. TAVERNER, THAT'S PRINCE ZALESKI.
I CAN'T SEE OLD IFFY ANYWHERE...
NEVER MIND. HOPEFULLY, A.J. IS GATHERING INTELLIGENCE AT THIS MOMENT.
Hmm. FIRST TIME FOR EVERYTHING, I SUPPOSE.

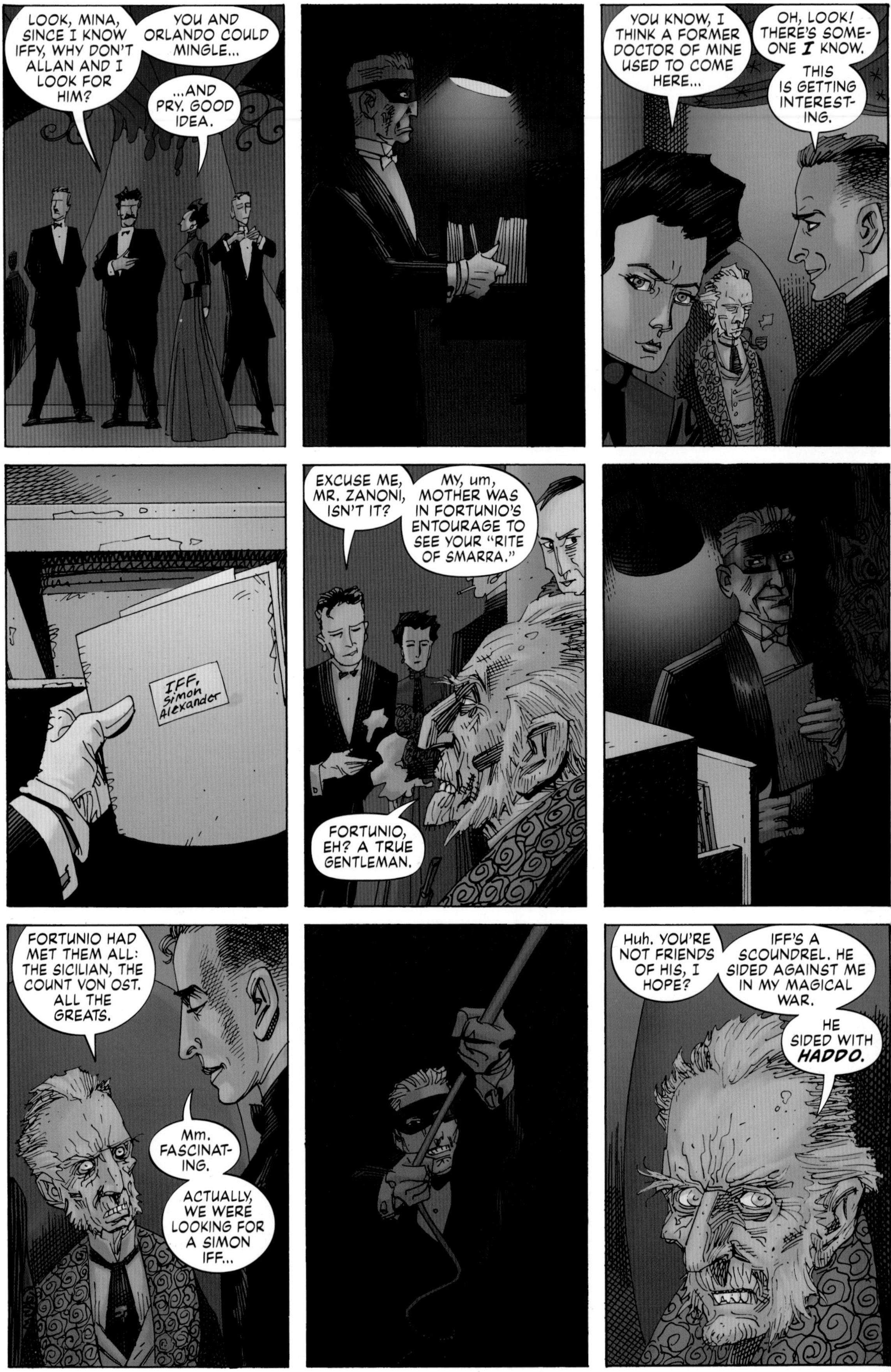
LOOK, MINA, SINCE I KNOW IFFY, WHY DON'T ALLAN AND I LOOK FOR HIM?
YOU AND ORLANDO COULD MINGLE...
...AND PRY. GOOD IDEA.
YOU KNOW, I THINK A FORMER DOCTOR OF MINE USED TO COME HERE...
OH, LOOK! THERE'S SOMEONE *I* KNOW.
THIS IS GETTING INTERESTING.
IFF, Simon Alexander
EXCUSE ME, MR. ZANONI, ISN'T IT?
MY, um, MOTHER WAS IN FORTUNIO'S ENTOURAGE TO SEE YOUR "RITE OF SMARRA."
FORTUNIO, EH? A TRUE GENTLEMAN.
FORTUNIO HAD MET THEM ALL: THE SICILIAN, THE COUNT VON OST. ALL THE GREATS.
Mm. FASCINATING.
ACTUALLY, WE WERE LOOKING FOR A SIMON IFF...
Huh. YOU'RE NOT FRIENDS OF HIS, I HOPE?
IFF'S A SCOUNDREL. HE SIDED AGAINST ME IN MY MAGICAL WAR.
HE SIDED WITH **HADDO.**

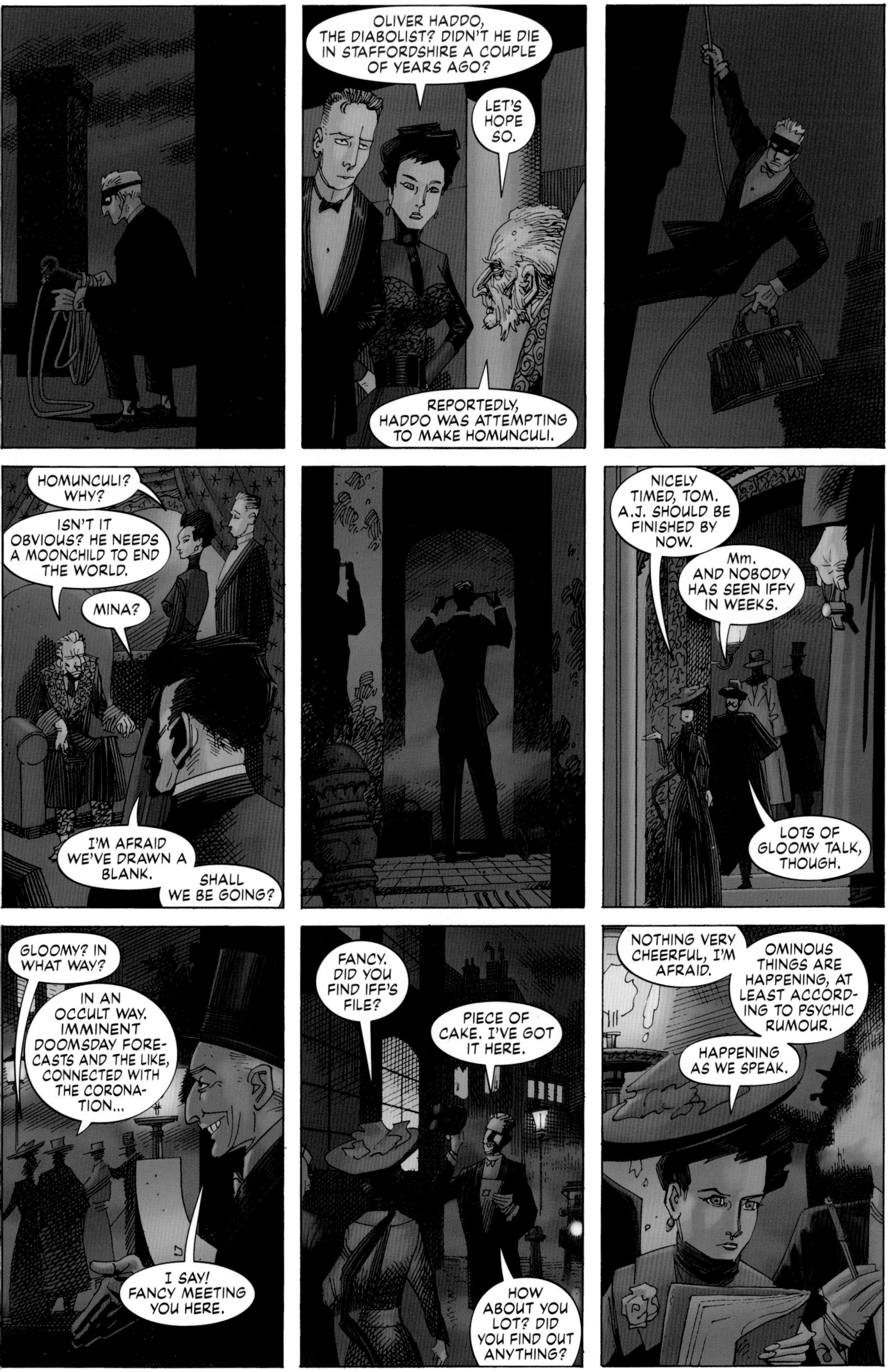
OLIVER HADDO, THE DIABOLIST? DIDN'T HE DIE IN STAFFORDSHIRE A COUPLE OF YEARS AGO?
LET'S HOPE SO.
REPORTEDLY, HADDO WAS ATTEMPTING TO MAKE HOMUNCULI.
HOMUNCULI? WHY?
ISN'T IT OBVIOUS? HE NEEDS A MOONCHILD TO END THE WORLD.
MINA?
I'M AFRAID WE'VE DRAWN A BLANK.
SHALL WE BE GOING?
NICELY TIMED, TOM. A.J. SHOULD BE FINISHED BY NOW.
Mm. AND NOBODY HAS SEEN IFFY IN WEEKS.
LOTS OF GLOOMY TALK, THOUGH.
GLOOMY? IN WHAT WAY?
IN AN OCCULT WAY. IMMINENT DOOMSDAY FORE-CASTS AND THE LIKE, CONNECTED WITH THE CORONA-TION...
I SAY! FANCY MEETING YOU HERE.
FANCY. DID YOU FIND IFF'S FILE?
PIECE OF CAKE. I'VE GOT IT HERE.
HOW ABOUT YOU LOT? DID YOU FIND OUT ANYTHING?
NOTHING VERY CHEERFUL, I'M AFRAID.
OMINOUS THINGS ARE HAPPENING, AT LEAST ACCORD-ING TO PSYCHIC RUMOUR.
HAPPENING AS WE SPEAK.

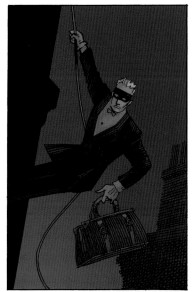

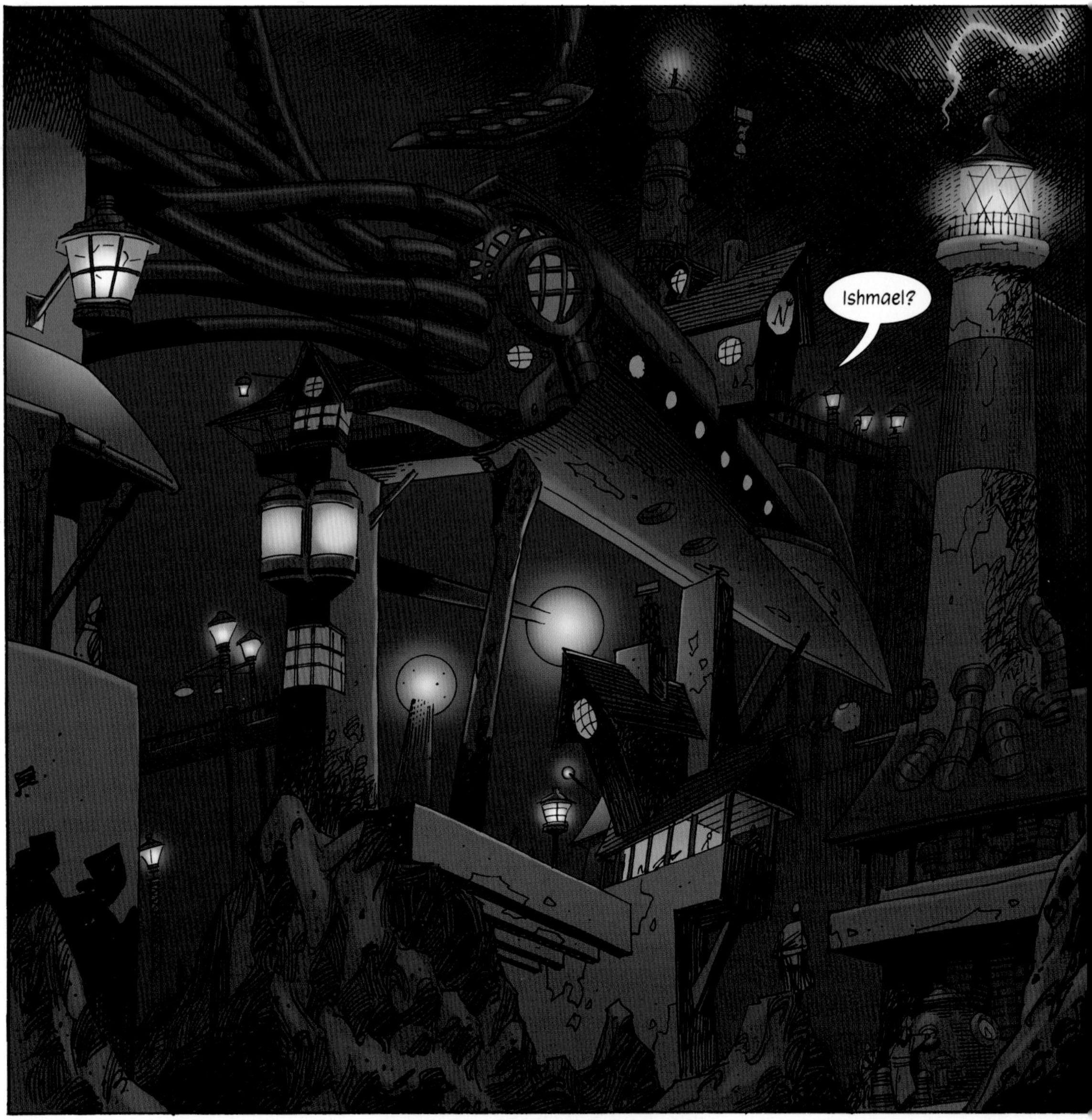
Ishmael?

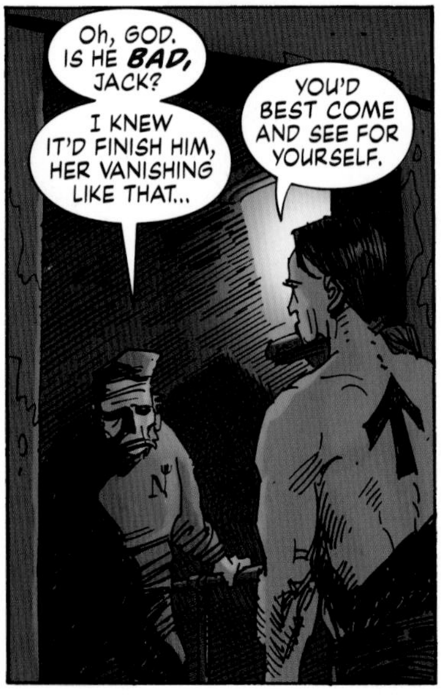
Oh, GOD. IS HE ***BAD,*** JACK?
I KNEW IT'D FINISH HIM, HER VANISHING LIKE THAT...
YOU'D BEST COME AND SEE FOR YOURSELF.

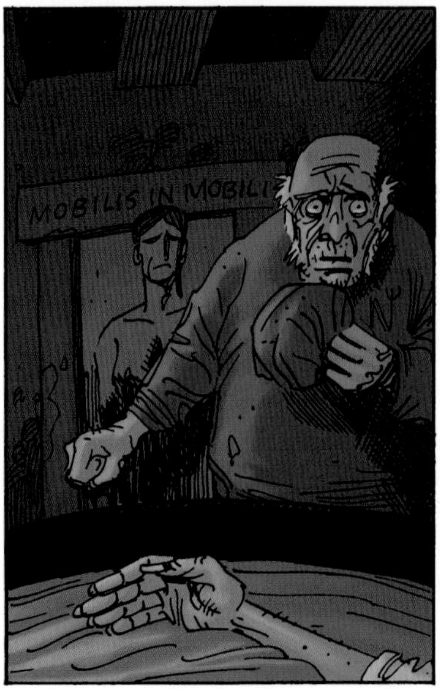
MOBILIS IN MOBILI

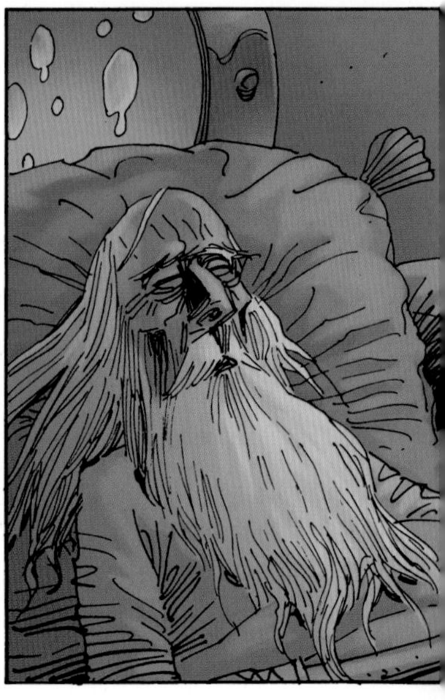

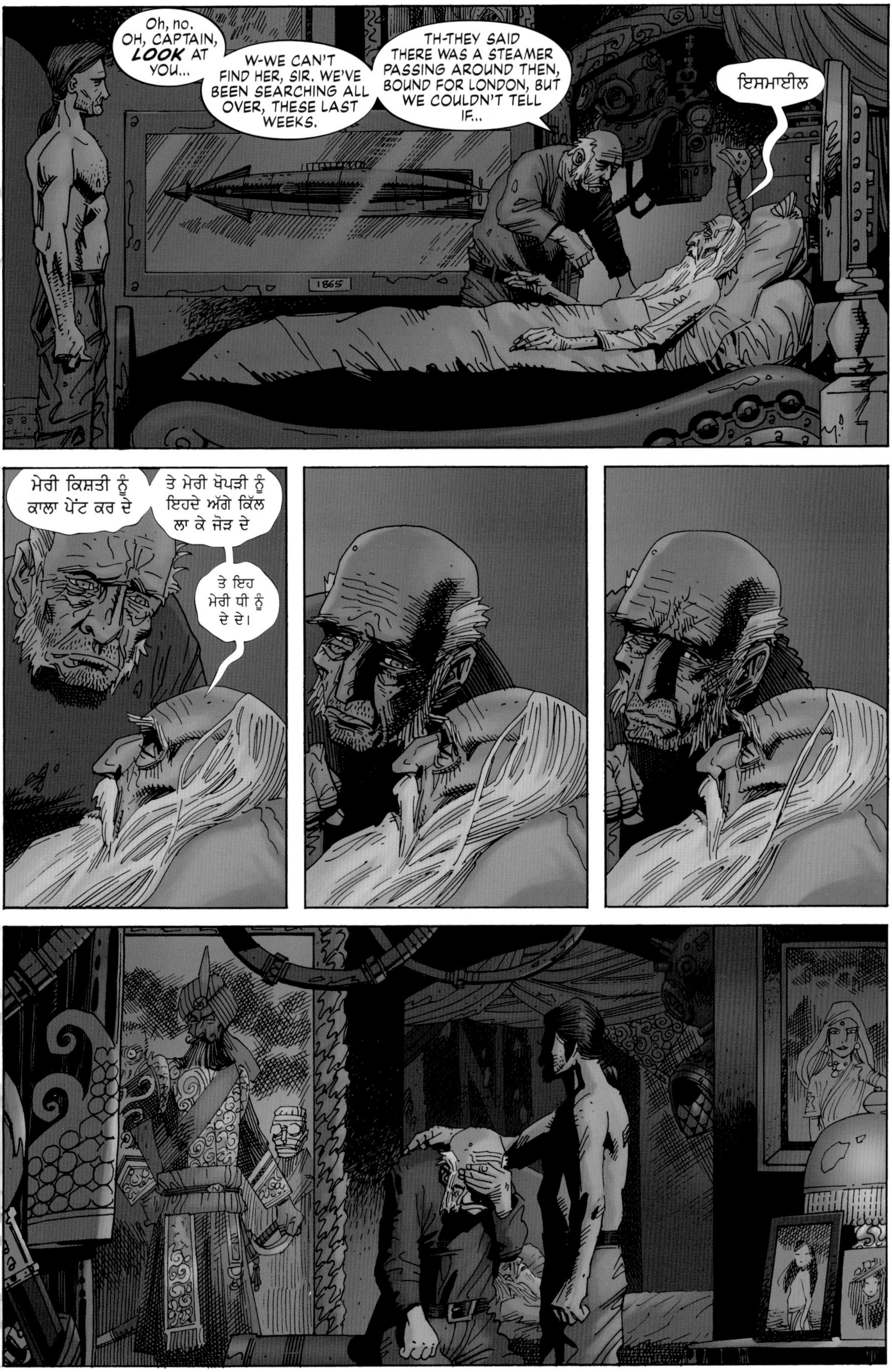
Oh, no. OH, CAPTAIN, LOOK AT YOU...
W-WE CAN'T FIND HER, SIR. WE'VE BEEN SEARCHING ALL OVER, THESE LAST WEEKS.
TH-THEY SAID THERE WAS A STEAMER PASSING AROUND THEN, BOUND FOR LONDON, BUT WE COULDN'T TELL IF...
ਇਸਮਾਈਲ
1865
ਮੇਰੀ ਕਿਸ਼ਤੀ ਨੂੰ ਕਾਲਾ ਪੇਂਟ ਕਰ ਦੇ
ਤੇ ਮੇਰੀ ਖੋਪੜੀ ਨੂੰ ਇਹਦੇ ਅੱਗੇ ਕਿੱਲ ਲਾ ਕੇ ਜੋੜ ਦੇ
ਤੇ ਇਹ ਮੇਰੀ ਧੀ ਨੂੰ ਦੇ ਦੇ।

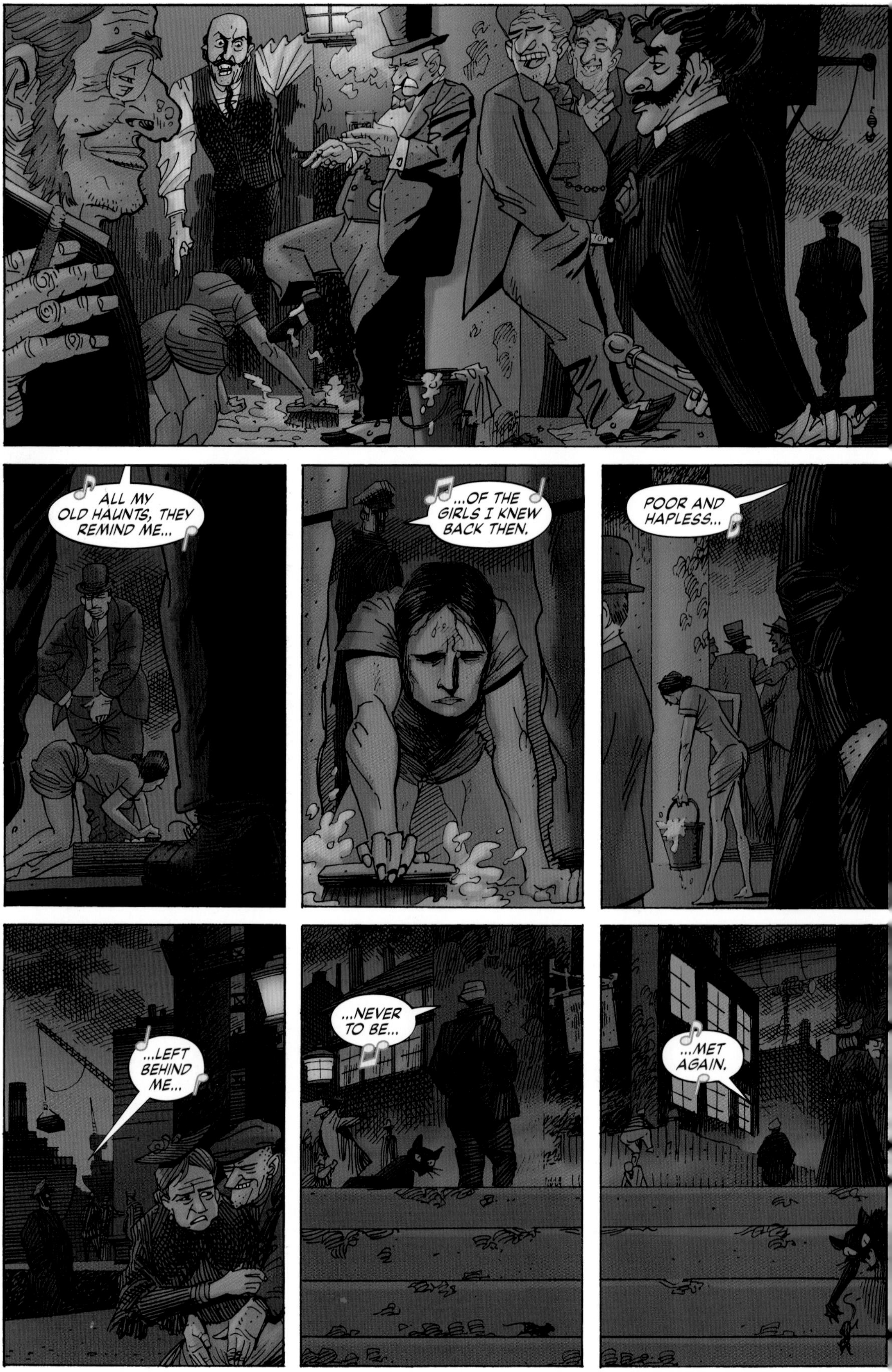
ALL MY OLD HAUNTS, THEY REMIND ME...
...OF THE GIRLS I KNEW BACK THEN.
POOR AND HAPLESS...
...LEFT BEHIND ME...
...NEVER TO BE...
...MET AGAIN.

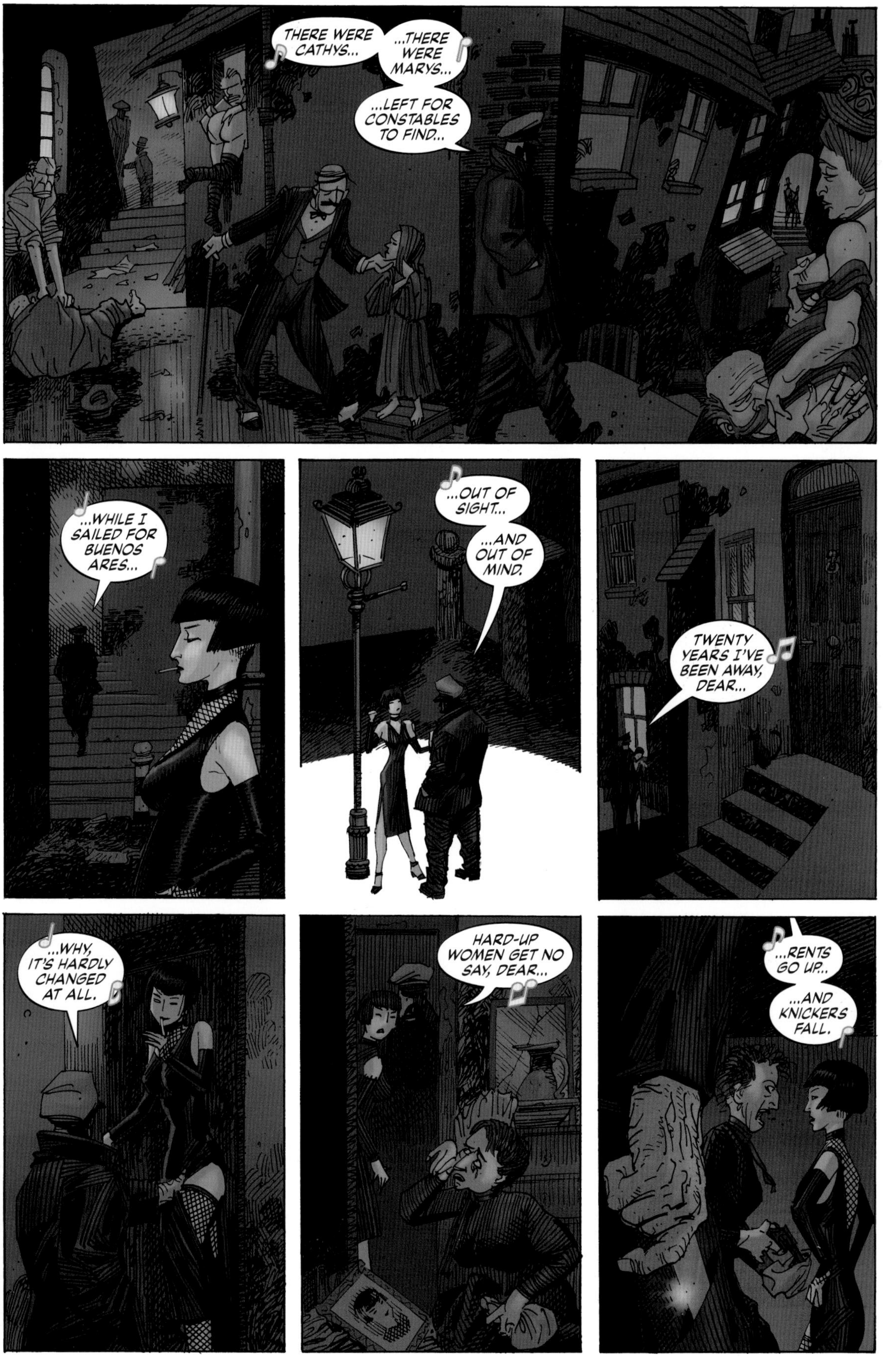
THERE WERE CATHYS...
...THERE WERE MARYS...
...LEFT FOR CONSTABLES TO FIND...
...WHILE I SAILED FOR BUENOS ARES...
...OUT OF SIGHT...
...AND OUT OF MIND.
TWENTY YEARS I'VE BEEN AWAY, DEAR...
...WHY, IT'S HARDLY CHANGED AT ALL.
HARD-UP WOMEN GET NO SAY, DEAR...
...RENTS GO UP...
...AND KNICKERS FALL.

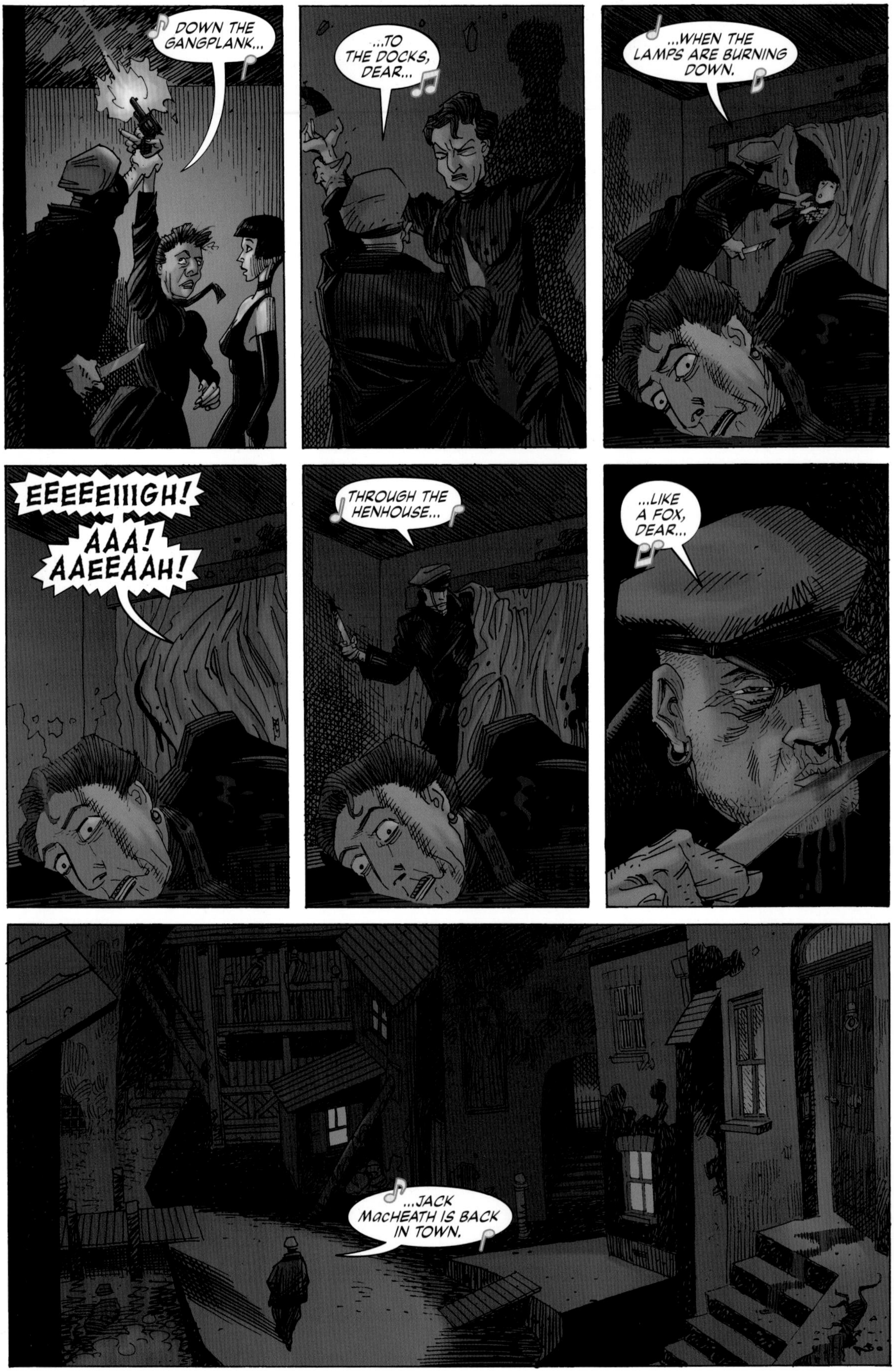
DOWN THE GANGPLANK...
...TO THE DOCKS, DEAR...
...WHEN THE LAMPS ARE BURNING DOWN.
EEEEEIIIGH!
AAA! AAEEAAH!
THROUGH THE HENHOUSE...
...LIKE A FOX, DEAR...
...JACK MacHEATH IS BACK IN TOWN.

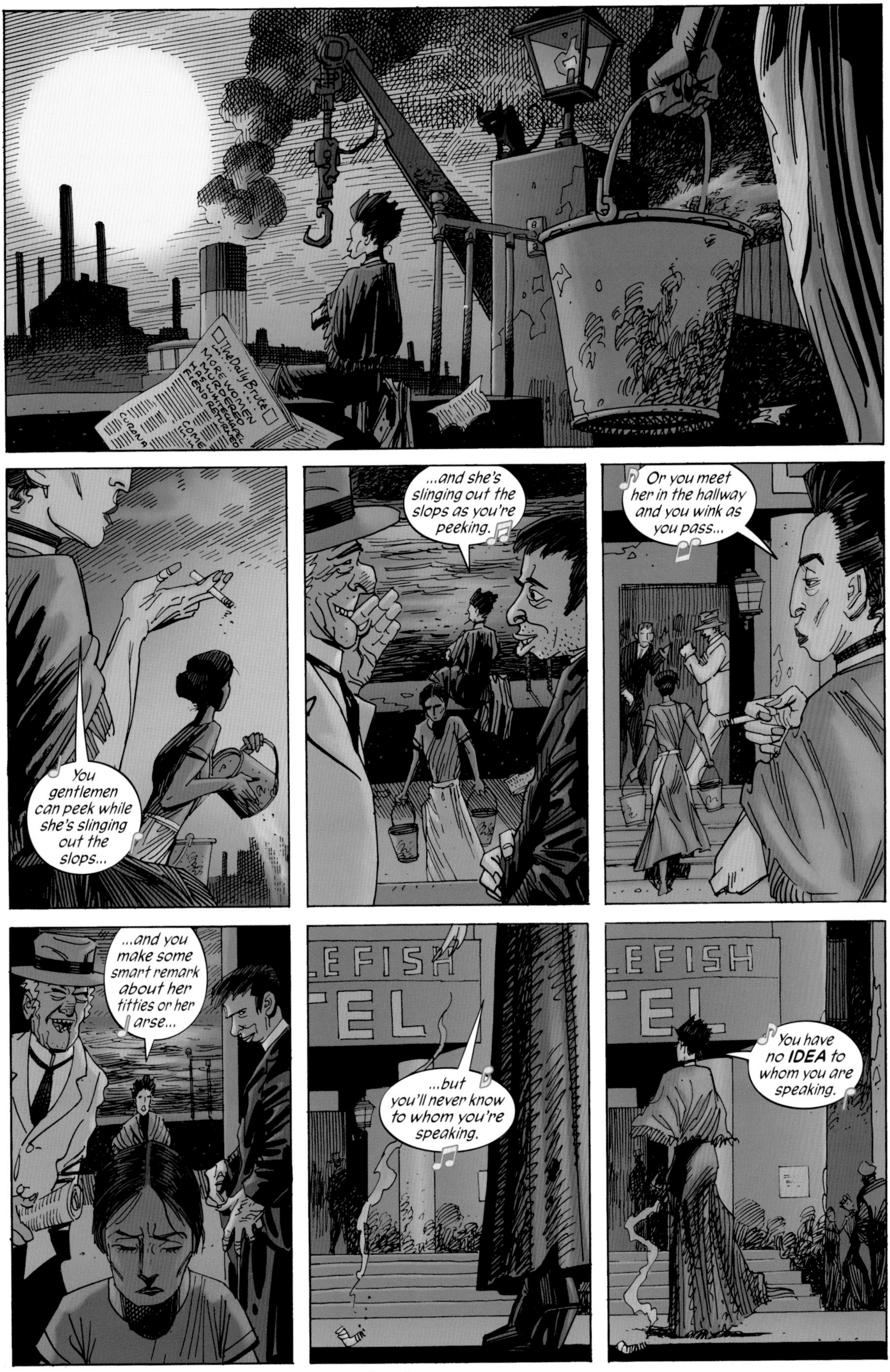

The Daily Brute
MORE WOMEN MURDERED
HAS WHITECHAPEL FIEND RETURNED
COME
CURONA
You gentlemen can peek while she's slinging out the slops...
...and she's slinging out the slops as you're peeking.
Or you meet her in the hallway and you wink as you pass...
...and you make some smart remark about her titties or her arse...
LEFISH
EL
...but you'll never know to whom you're speaking.
LEFISH
EL
You have no **IDEA** to whom you are speaking.

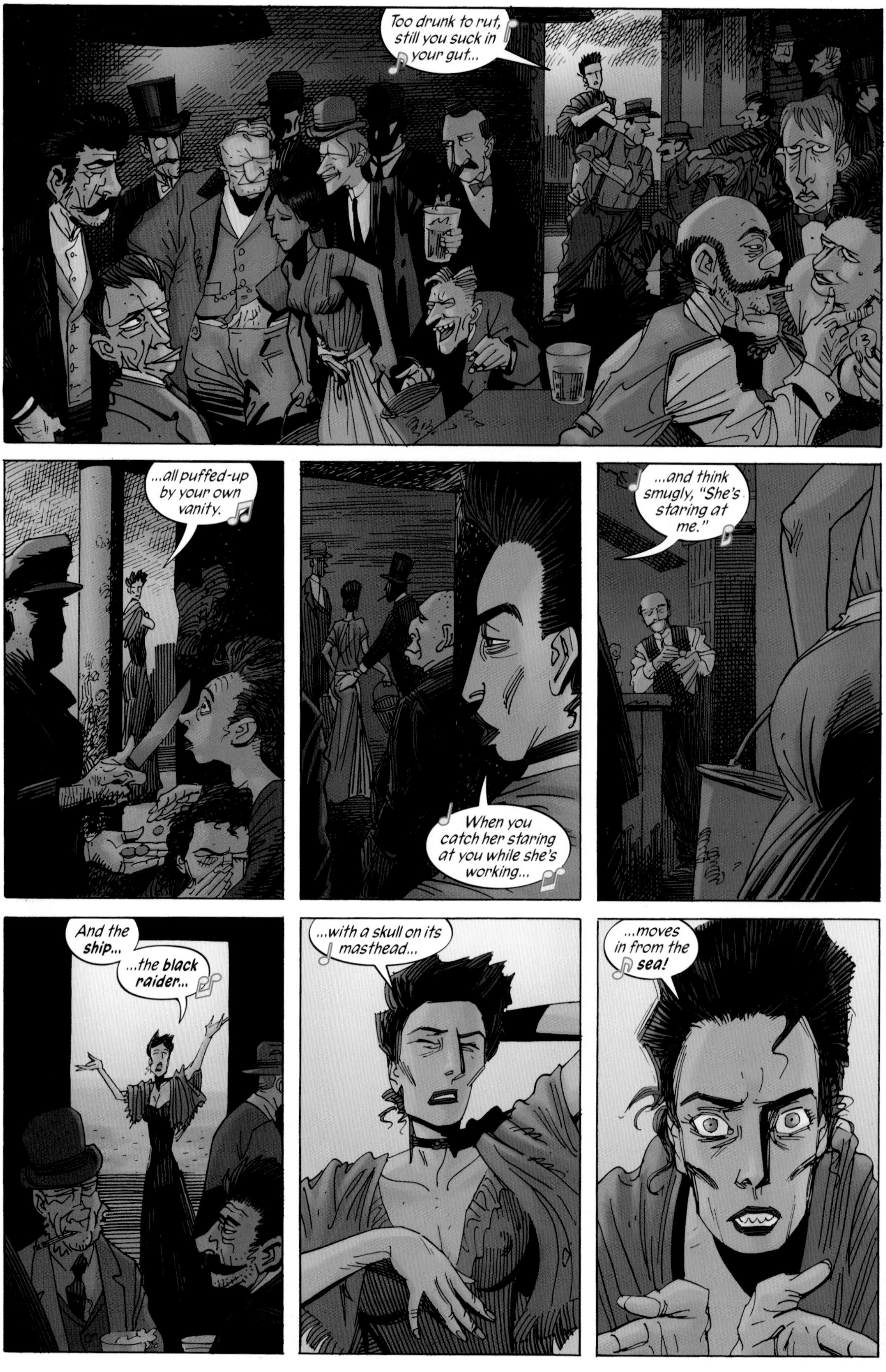
Too drunk to rut, still you suck in your gut...
...all puffed-up by your own vanity.
When you catch her staring at you while she's working...
...and think smugly, "She's staring at me."
And the ship...
...the black raider...
...with a skull on its masthead...
...moves in from the sea!

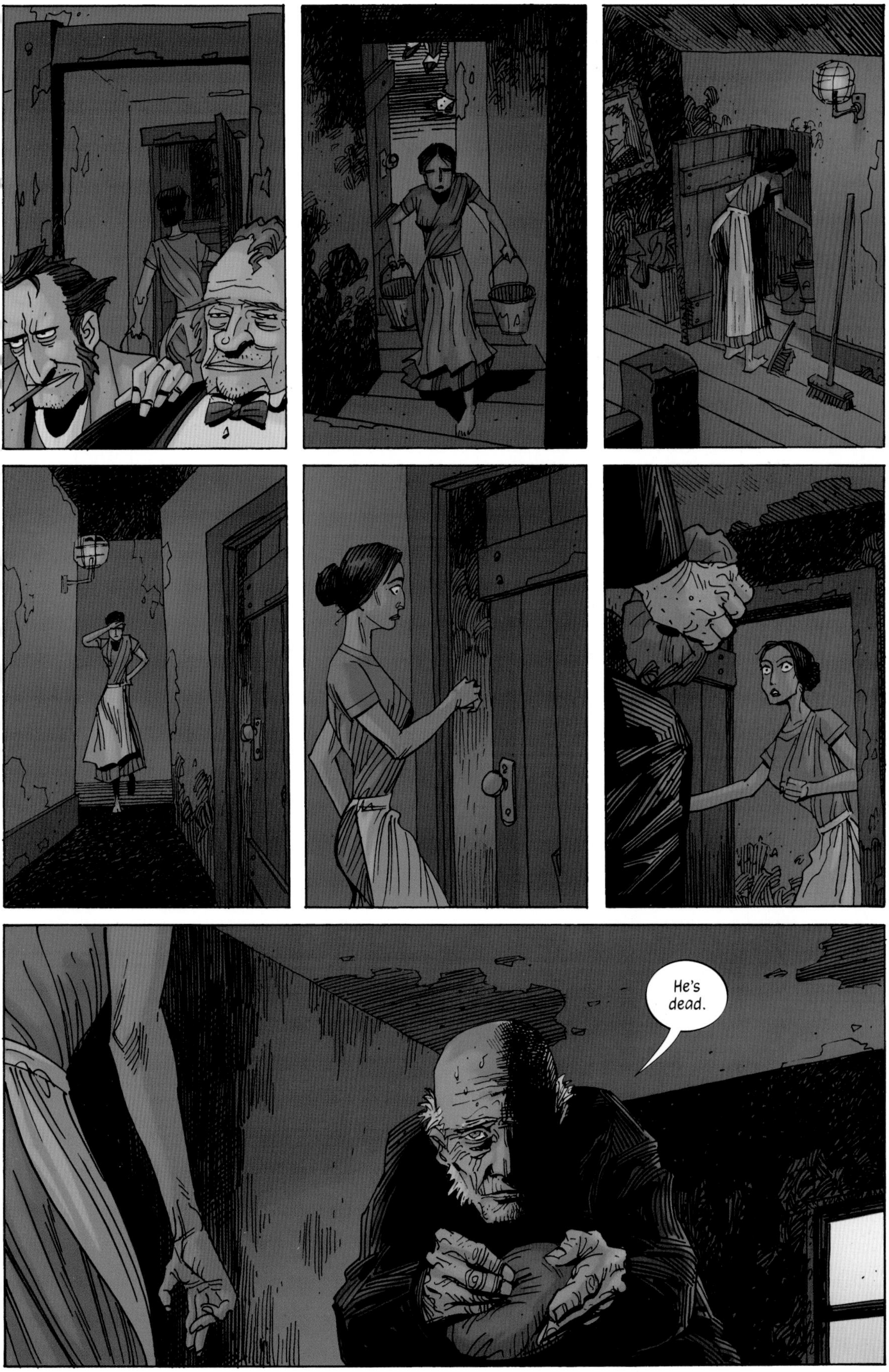
He's dead.

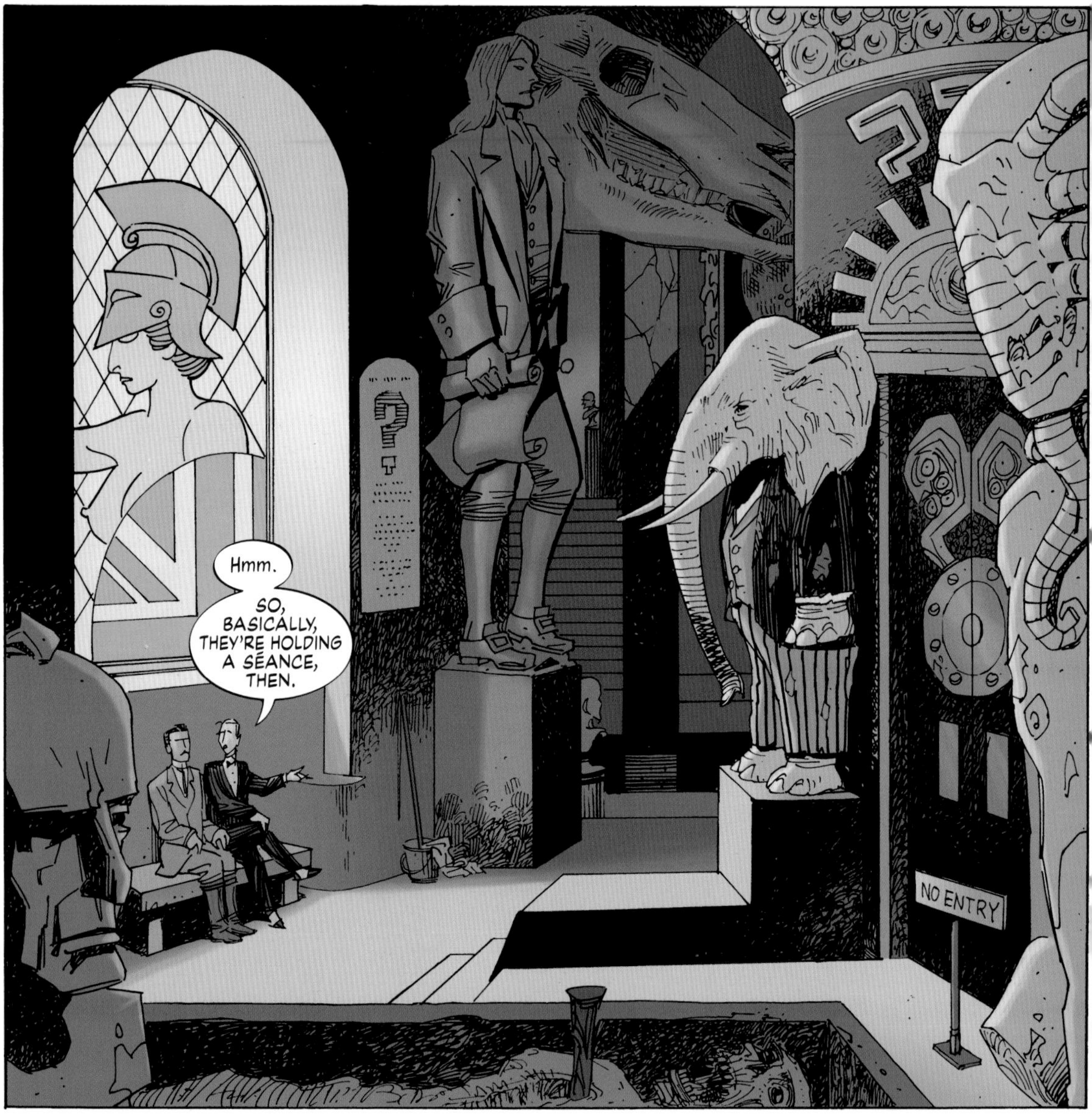
Hmm.
SO, BASICALLY, THEY'RE HOLDING A SÉANCE, THEN.
NO ENTRY

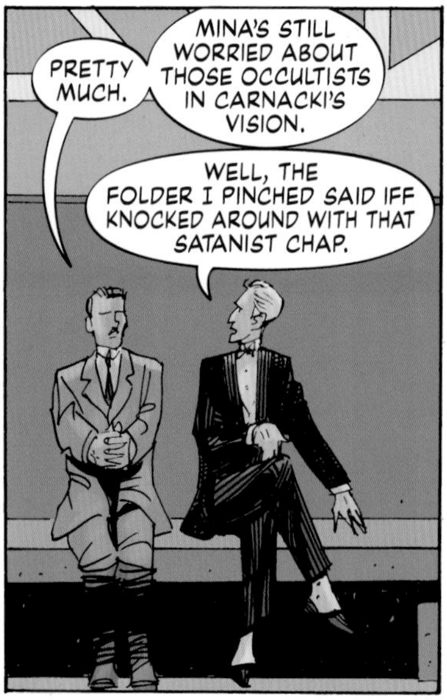
PRETTY MUCH.
MINA'S STILL WORRIED ABOUT THOSE OCCULTISTS IN CARNACKI'S VISION.
WELL, THE FOLDER I PINCHED SAID IFF KNOCKED AROUND WITH THAT SATANIST CHAP.

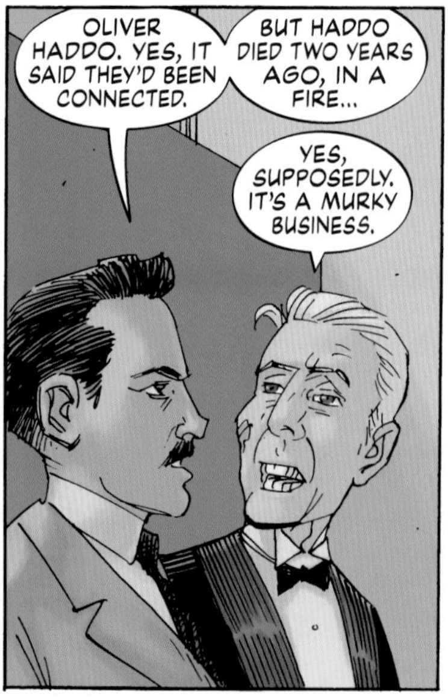
OLIVER HADDO. YES, IT SAID THEY'D BEEN CONNECTED.
BUT HADDO DIED TWO YEARS AGO, IN A FIRE...
YES, SUPPOSEDLY. IT'S A MURKY BUSINESS.

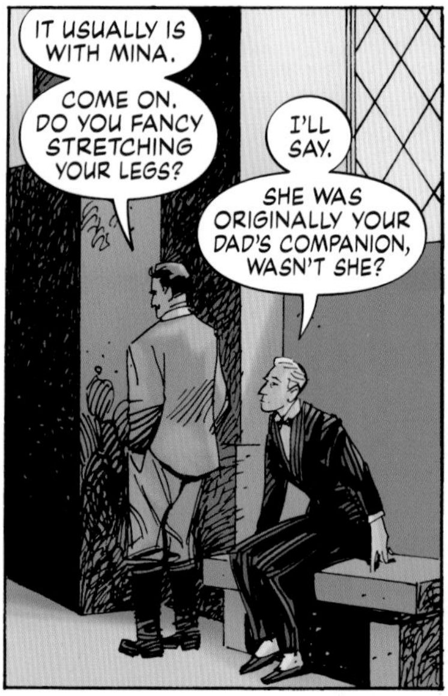
IT USUALLY IS WITH MINA.
COME ON. DO YOU FANCY STRETCHING YOUR LEGS?
I'LL SAY.
SHE WAS ORIGINALLY YOUR DAD'S COMPANION, WASN'T SHE?

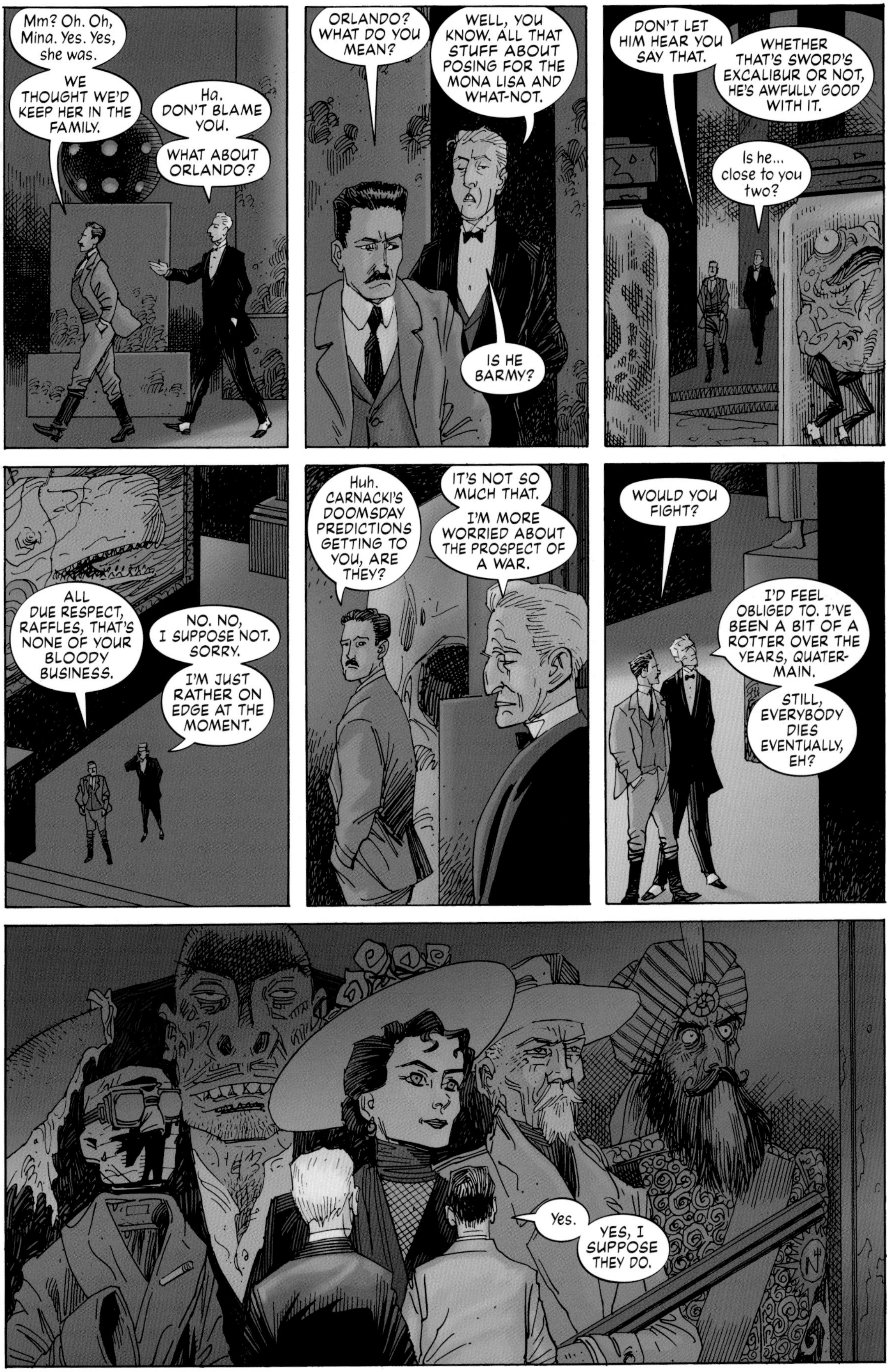
Mm? Oh. Oh, Mina. Yes. Yes, she was.
WE THOUGHT WE'D KEEP HER IN THE FAMILY.
Ha. DON'T BLAME YOU.
WHAT ABOUT ORLANDO?
ORLANDO? WHAT DO YOU MEAN?
WELL, YOU KNOW. ALL THAT STUFF ABOUT POSING FOR THE MONA LISA AND WHAT-NOT.
IS HE BARMY?
DON'T LET HIM HEAR YOU SAY THAT.
WHETHER THAT'S SWORD'S EXCALIBUR OR NOT, HE'S AWFULLY GOOD WITH IT.
Is he... close to you two?
ALL DUE RESPECT, RAFFLES, THAT'S NONE OF YOUR BLOODY BUSINESS.
NO. NO, I SUPPOSE NOT. SORRY.
I'M JUST RATHER ON EDGE AT THE MOMENT.
Huh. CARNACKI'S DOOMSDAY PREDICTIONS GETTING TO YOU, ARE THEY?
IT'S NOT SO MUCH THAT.
I'M MORE WORRIED ABOUT THE PROSPECT OF A WAR.
WOULD YOU FIGHT?
I'D FEEL OBLIGED TO. I'VE BEEN A BIT OF A ROTTER OVER THE YEARS, QUATER-MAIN.
STILL, EVERYBODY DIES EVENTUALLY, EH?
Yes.
YES, I SUPPOSE THEY DO.

WELL, MR. CARNACKI? ARE YOU GETTING ANY INFORMATION ABOUT IFF OR HADDO FROM YOUR... WHAT DID YOU CALL IT?

IT'S A SCRYING GLASS, A BLACK MIRROR MADE OF OBSIDIAN.

IT'S FROM THE MUSEUM'S COLLECTION. IT USED TO BELONG TO GLORIANA'S ALCHEMIST, JOHN SUBTLE.

OH, HONESTLY! SUBTLE WAS JUST A CODE-NAME THAT QUEEN GLORY GAVE TO DUKE PROSPERO OF MILAN. I WAS THERE.

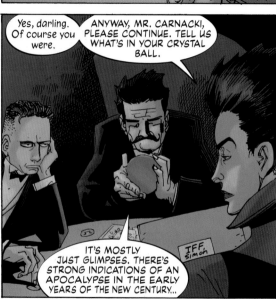

Yes, darling. Of course you were.

ANYWAY, MR. CARNACKI, PLEASE CONTINUE. TELL US WHAT'S IN YOUR CRYSTAL BALL.

IT'S MOSTLY JUST GLIMPSES. THERE'S STRONG INDICATIONS OF AN APOCALYPSE IN THE EARLY YEARS OF THE NEW CENTURY...

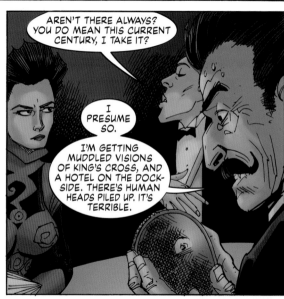

AREN'T THERE ALWAYS? YOU DO MEAN THIS CURRENT CENTURY, I TAKE IT?

I PRESUME SO.

I'M GETTING MUDDLED VISIONS OF KING'S CROSS, AND A HOTEL ON THE DOCK-SIDE. THERE'S HUMAN HEADS PILED UP. IT'S TERRIBLE.

I SEE. AND ARE SIMON IFF OR OLIVER HADDO INVOLVED IN ANY OF THIS?

YES. YES, I SENSE THEY'RE MIXED UP IN THE APOCALYPSE PART OF THE VISION.

I ALSO CONNECT THEM WITH KING'S CROSS.

"KING'S CROSS." THAT IS THE RAILWAY STATION, I SUPPOSE, AND NOT AN OBLIQUE REFERENCE TO THE IMMINENT CORONATION?

HM. I HADN'T THOUGHT OF THAT. THE WAY DIVINATION WORKS, IT COULD BE ALLUD-ING TO BOTH THINGS.

THAT SOUNDS OMINOUS.

WHAT ABOUT THIS HOTEL ON THE DOCKS YOU MENTIONED?

THAT'S MORE INDISTINCT.

I SENSE SOME THREAT...A RUTHLESS KILLER RECENTLY ARRIVED IN ENGLAND...SOME CRISIS ERUPTING ON CORONATION DAY. NOTHING SPECIFIC, THOUGH.

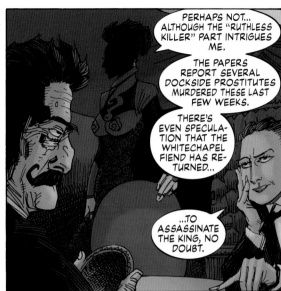

PERHAPS NOT... ALTHOUGH THE "RUTHLESS KILLER" PART INTRIGUES ME.

THE PAPERS REPORT SEVERAL DOCKSIDE PROSTITUTES MURDERED THESE LAST FEW WEEKS.

THERE'S EVEN SPECULA-TION THAT THE WHITECHAPEL FIEND HAS RE-TURNED...

...TO ASSASSINATE THE KING, NO DOUBT.

WELL, WHY NOT? IT'S SCARCELY MORE RIDICULOUS THAN YOU HAVING HIGH TEA WITH PROSPERO AND QUEEN GLORIANA.

OH, COME ON! IT'S A BIT ELABORATE, SURELY? AND WHERE DO THESE KING'S CROSS BLACK MAGICIANS FIT IN?

THEY MAY NOT FIT IN AT ALL. ON THE OTHER HAND, THEIR RITUALS MAY BE CAUSING ALL OF THESE EVENTS.

THANK YOU, MR. CARNACKI.

I PROPOSE WE INVESTIGATE KING'S CROSS...AFTER INFORMING MILITARY INTELLIGENCE, NATURALLY.

OH, BLAST! DOES THAT MEAN WE HAVE TO SIT THROUGH A MEETING WITH FATTY HOLMES?

WELL, NOT ALL OF US, SURELY?

BESIDES, HOLMES MIGHT HAVE USEFUL INFORMATION. ONE MEETING'S HARDLY THE END OF THE WORLD.

Hm.

YES, WELL.

LET'S HOPE NOT, ANYWAY.

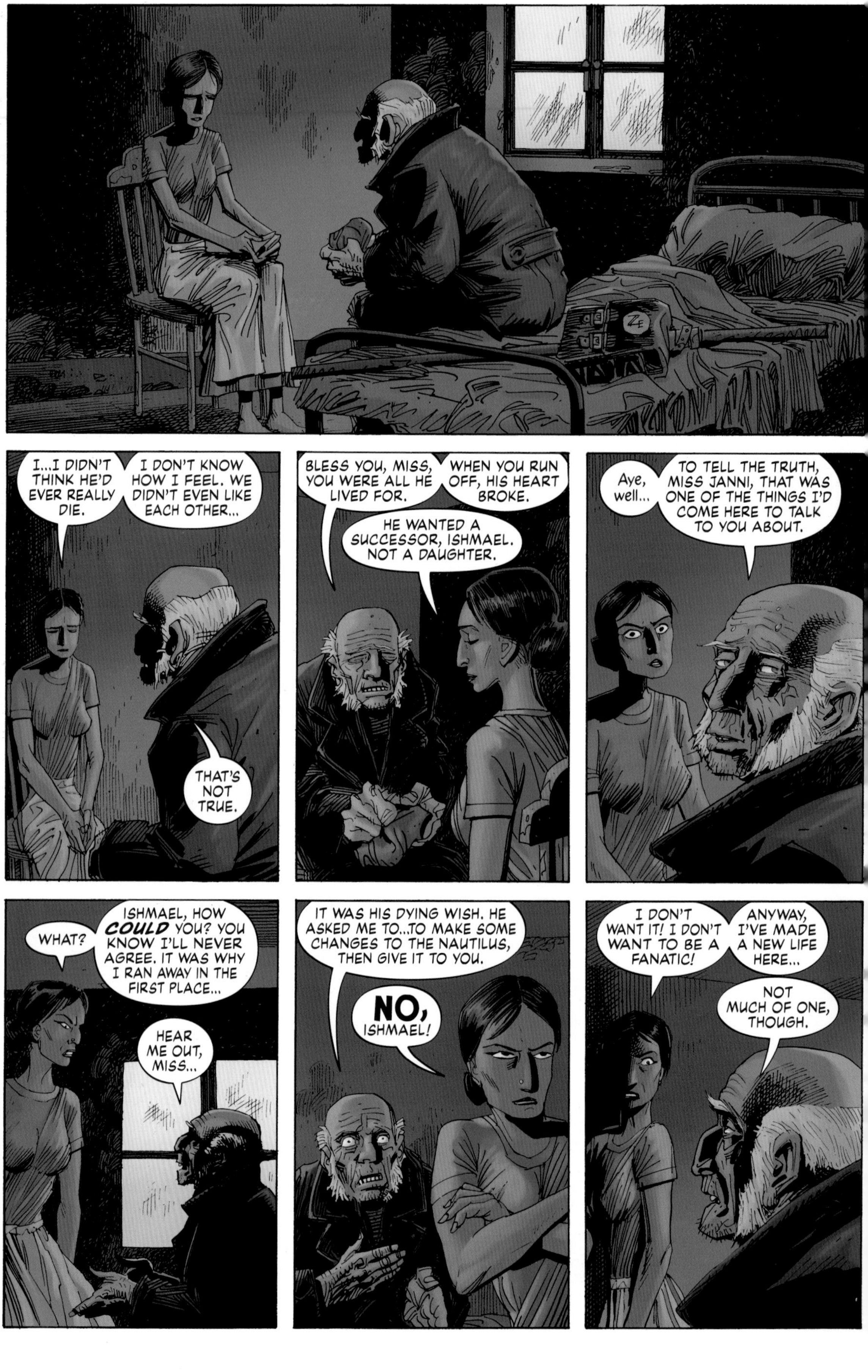

I...I DIDN'T THINK HE'D EVER REALLY DIE.
I DON'T KNOW HOW I FEEL. WE DIDN'T EVEN LIKE EACH OTHER...
THAT'S NOT TRUE.
BLESS YOU, MISS, YOU WERE ALL HE LIVED FOR.
WHEN YOU RUN OFF, HIS HEART BROKE.
HE WANTED A SUCCESSOR, ISHMAEL. NOT A DAUGHTER.
Aye, well...
TO TELL THE TRUTH, MISS JANNI, THAT WAS ONE OF THE THINGS I'D COME HERE TO TALK TO YOU ABOUT.
WHAT?
ISHMAEL, HOW COULD YOU? YOU KNOW I'LL NEVER AGREE. IT WAS WHY I RAN AWAY IN THE FIRST PLACE...
HEAR ME OUT, MISS...
IT WAS HIS DYING WISH. HE ASKED ME TO...TO MAKE SOME CHANGES TO THE NAUTILUS, THEN GIVE IT TO YOU.
NO, ISHMAEL!
I DON'T WANT IT! I DON'T WANT TO BE A FANATIC!
ANYWAY, I'VE MADE A NEW LIFE HERE...
NOT MUCH OF ONE, THOUGH.

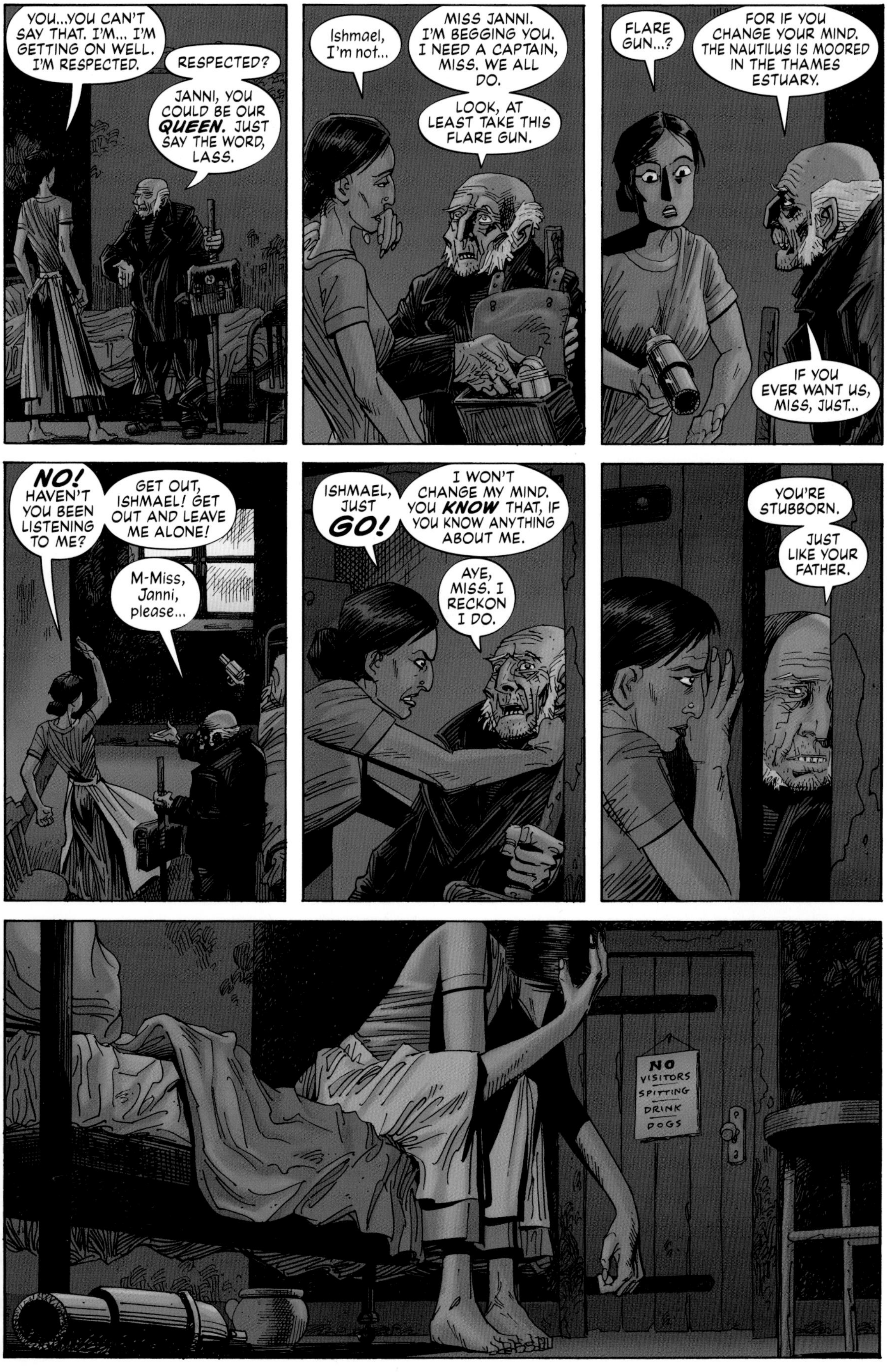

YOU...YOU CAN'T SAY THAT. I'M... I'M GETTING ON WELL. I'M RESPECTED.
RESPECTED?
JANNI, YOU COULD BE OUR **QUEEN**. JUST SAY THE WORD, LASS.
Ishmael, I'm not...
MISS JANNI. I'M BEGGING YOU. I NEED A CAPTAIN, MISS. WE ALL DO.
LOOK, AT LEAST TAKE THIS FLARE GUN.
FLARE GUN...?
FOR IF YOU CHANGE YOUR MIND. THE NAUTILUS IS MOORED IN THE THAMES ESTUARY.
IF YOU EVER WANT US, MISS, JUST...
NO! HAVEN'T YOU BEEN LISTENING TO ME?
GET OUT, ISHMAEL! GET OUT AND LEAVE ME ALONE!
M-Miss, Janni, please...
ISHMAEL, JUST **GO!**
I WON'T CHANGE MY MIND. YOU **KNOW** THAT, IF YOU KNOW ANYTHING ABOUT ME.
AYE, MISS. I RECKON I DO.
YOU'RE STUBBORN.
JUST LIKE YOUR FATHER.
NO
VISITORS
SPITTING
DRINK
DOGS

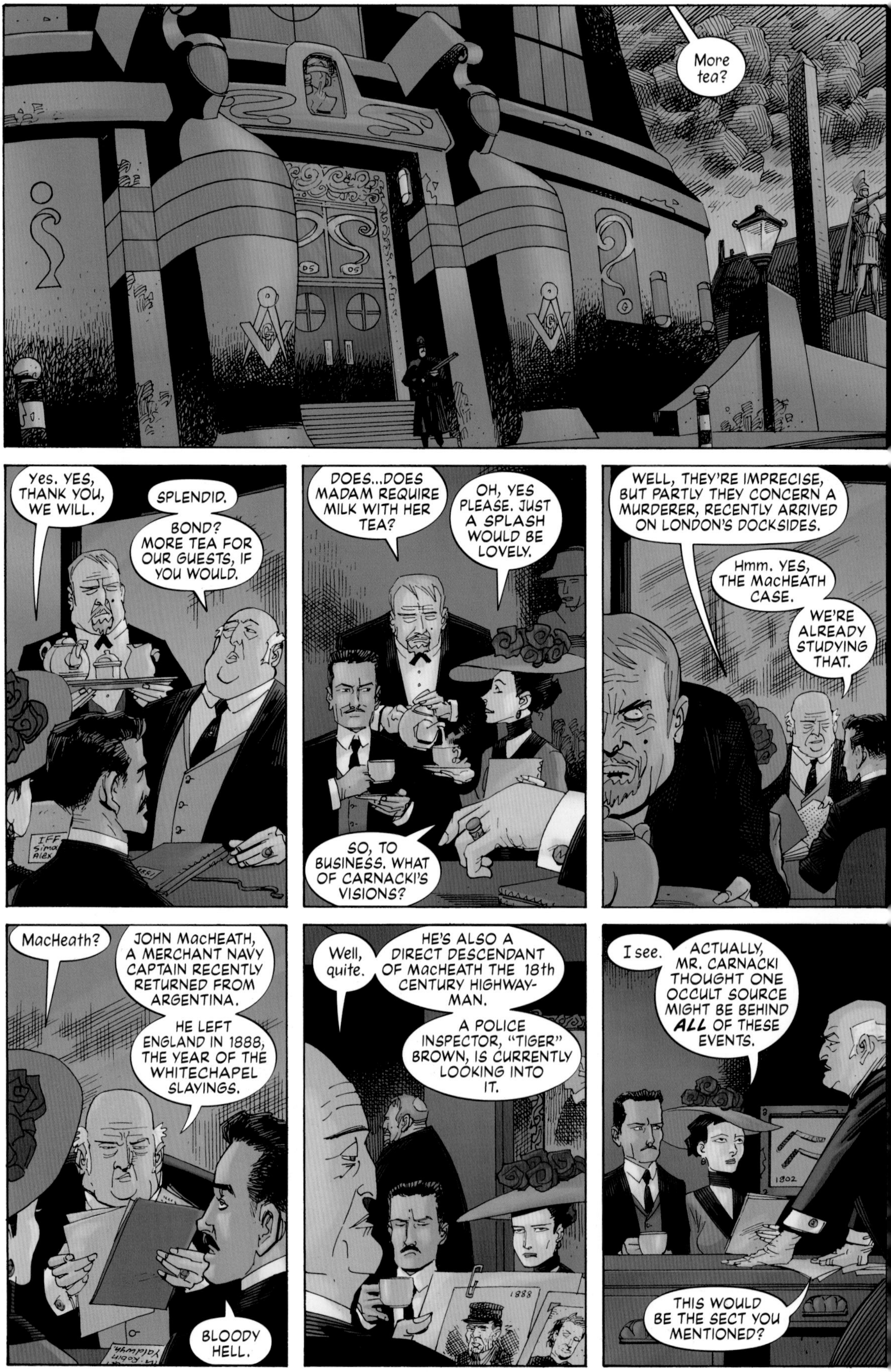
More tea?
Yes. YES, THANK YOU, WE WILL.
SPLENDID.
BOND? MORE TEA FOR OUR GUESTS, IF YOU WOULD.
DOES...DOES MADAM REQUIRE MILK WITH HER TEA?
OH, YES PLEASE. JUST A SPLASH WOULD BE LOVELY.
SO, TO BUSINESS. WHAT OF CARNACKI'S VISIONS?
WELL, THEY'RE IMPRECISE, BUT PARTLY THEY CONCERN A MURDERER, RECENTLY ARRIVED ON LONDON'S DOCKSIDES.
Hmm. YES, THE MacHEATH CASE.
WE'RE ALREADY STUDYING THAT.
MacHeath?
JOHN MacHEATH, A MERCHANT NAVY CAPTAIN RECENTLY RETURNED FROM ARGENTINA.
HE LEFT ENGLAND IN 1888, THE YEAR OF THE WHITECHAPEL SLAYINGS.
BLOODY HELL.
Well, quite.
HE'S ALSO A DIRECT DESCENDANT OF MacHEATH THE 18th CENTURY HIGHWAY-MAN.
A POLICE INSPECTOR, "TIGER" BROWN, IS CURRENTLY LOOKING INTO IT.
1888
I see.
ACTUALLY, MR. CARNACKI THOUGHT ONE OCCULT SOURCE MIGHT BE BEHIND ***ALL*** OF THESE EVENTS.
1802
THIS WOULD BE THE SECT YOU MENTIONED?

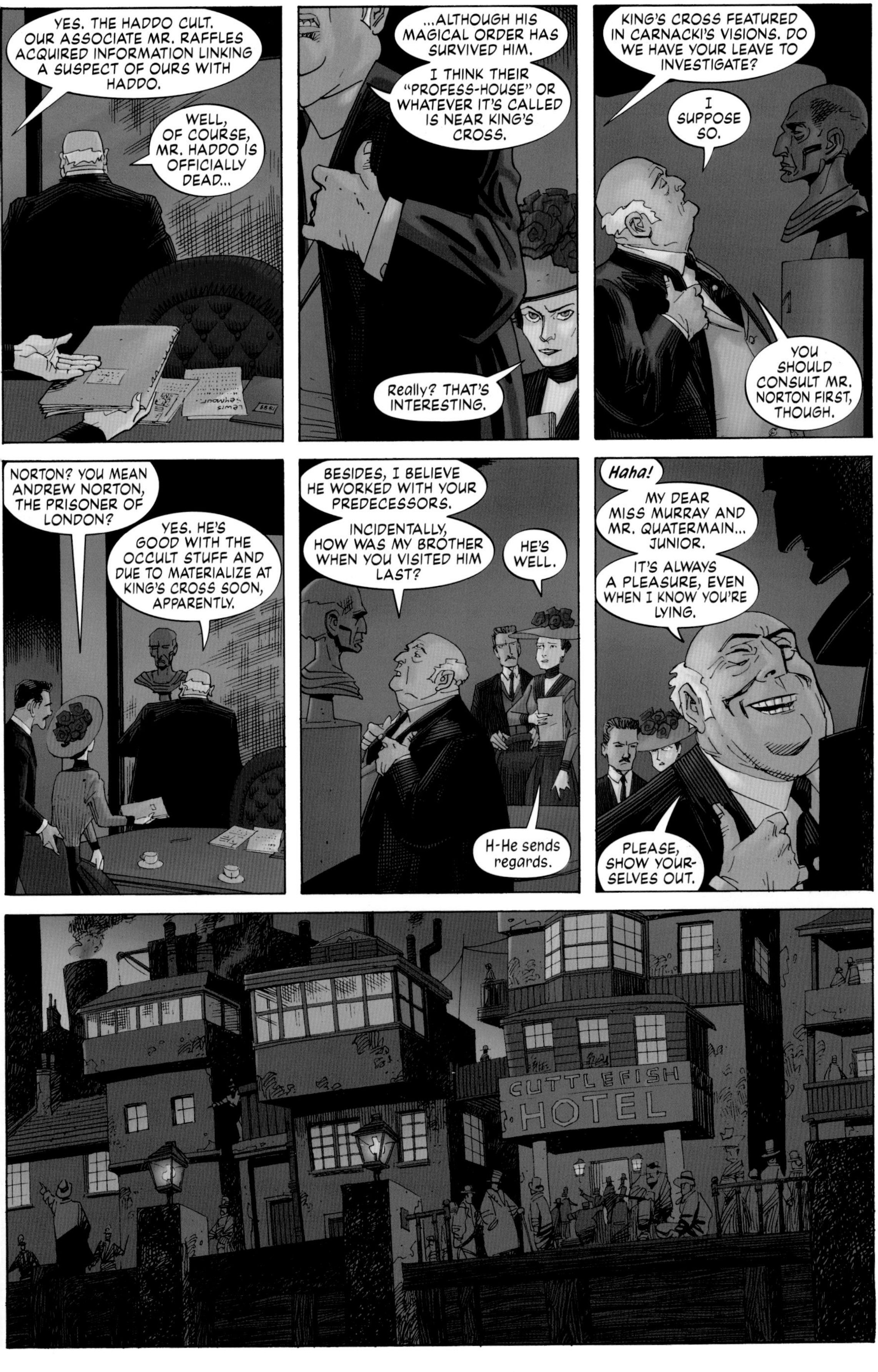
YES. THE HADDO CULT. OUR ASSOCIATE MR. RAFFLES ACQUIRED INFORMATION LINKING A SUSPECT OF OURS WITH HADDO.
WELL, OF COURSE, MR. HADDO IS OFFICIALLY DEAD...
...ALTHOUGH HIS MAGICAL ORDER HAS SURVIVED HIM.
I THINK THEIR "PROFESS-HOUSE" OR WHATEVER IT'S CALLED IS NEAR KING'S CROSS.
Really? THAT'S INTERESTING.
KING'S CROSS FEATURED IN CARNACKI'S VISIONS. DO WE HAVE YOUR LEAVE TO INVESTIGATE?
I SUPPOSE SO.
YOU SHOULD CONSULT MR. NORTON FIRST, THOUGH.
NORTON? YOU MEAN ANDREW NORTON, THE PRISONER OF LONDON?
YES. HE'S GOOD WITH THE OCCULT STUFF AND DUE TO MATERIALIZE AT KING'S CROSS SOON, APPARENTLY.
BESIDES, I BELIEVE HE WORKED WITH YOUR PREDECESSORS.
INCIDENTALLY, HOW WAS MY BROTHER WHEN YOU VISITED HIM LAST?
HE'S WELL.
H-He sends regards.
Haha!
MY DEAR MISS MURRAY AND MR. QUATERMAIN... JUNIOR.
IT'S ALWAYS A PLEASURE, EVEN WHEN I KNOW YOU'RE LYING.
PLEASE, SHOW YOURSELVES OUT.
CUTTLEFISH HOTEL

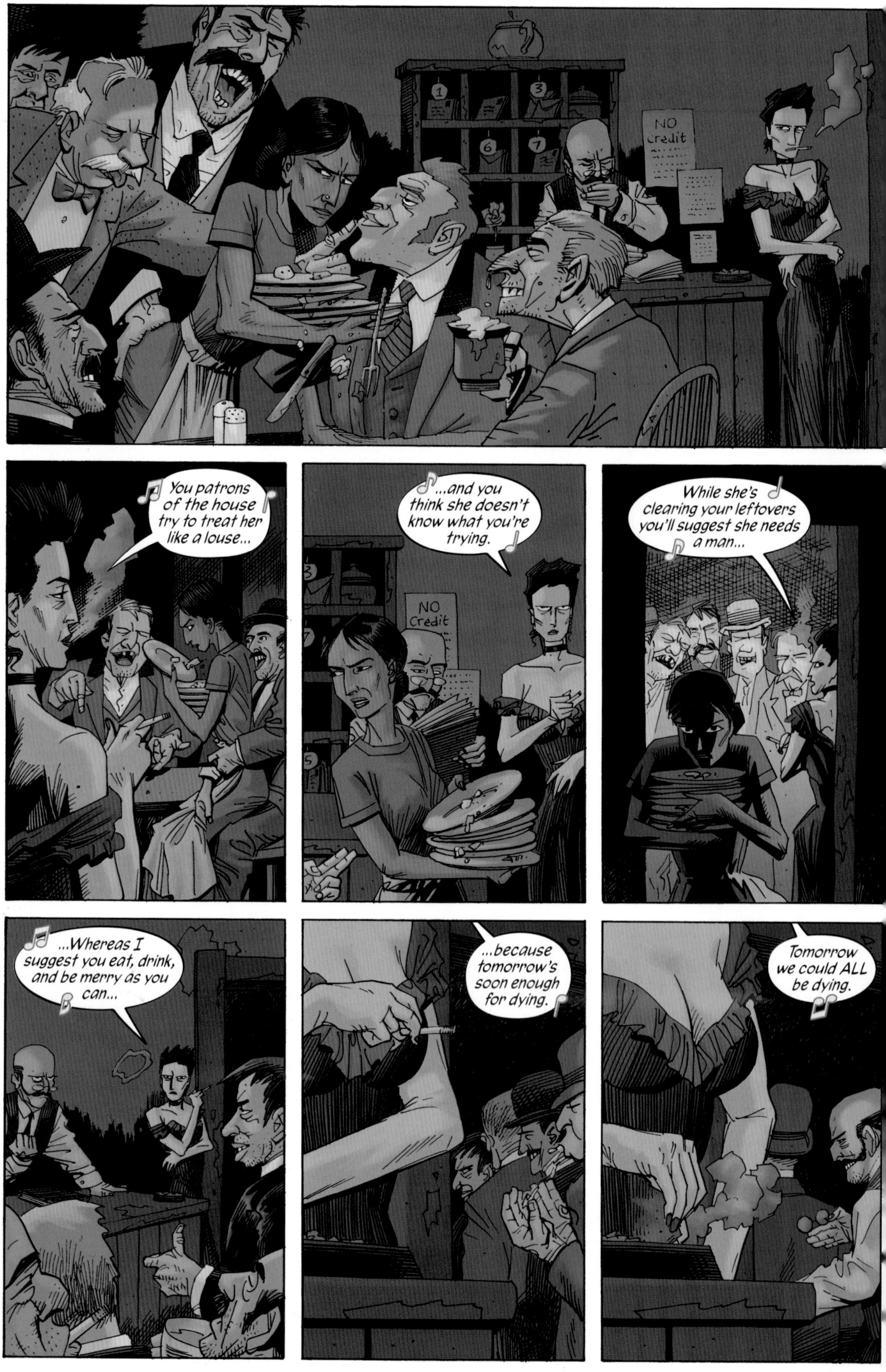
NO credit
You patrons of the house try to treat her like a louse...
...and you think she doesn't know what you're trying.
NO Credit
While she's clearing your leftovers you'll suggest she needs a man...
...Whereas I suggest you eat, drink, and be merry as you can...
...because tomorrow's soon enough for dying.
Tomorrow we could ALL be dying.

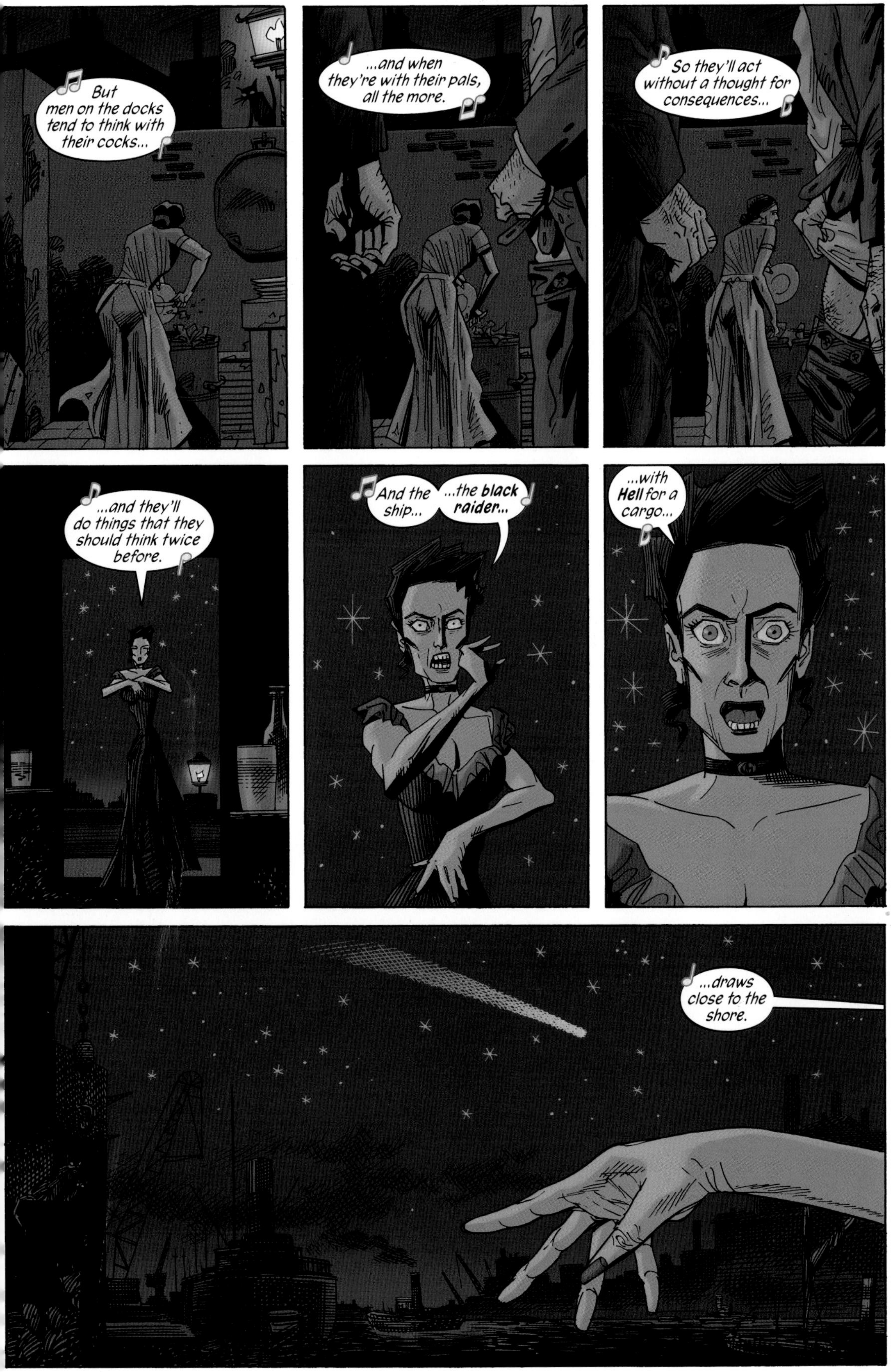
But men on the docks tend to think with their cocks...
...and when they're with their pals, all the more.
So they'll act without a thought for consequences...
...and they'll do things that they should think twice before.
And the ship...
...the **black raider**...
...with **Hell** for a cargo...
...draws close to the shore.

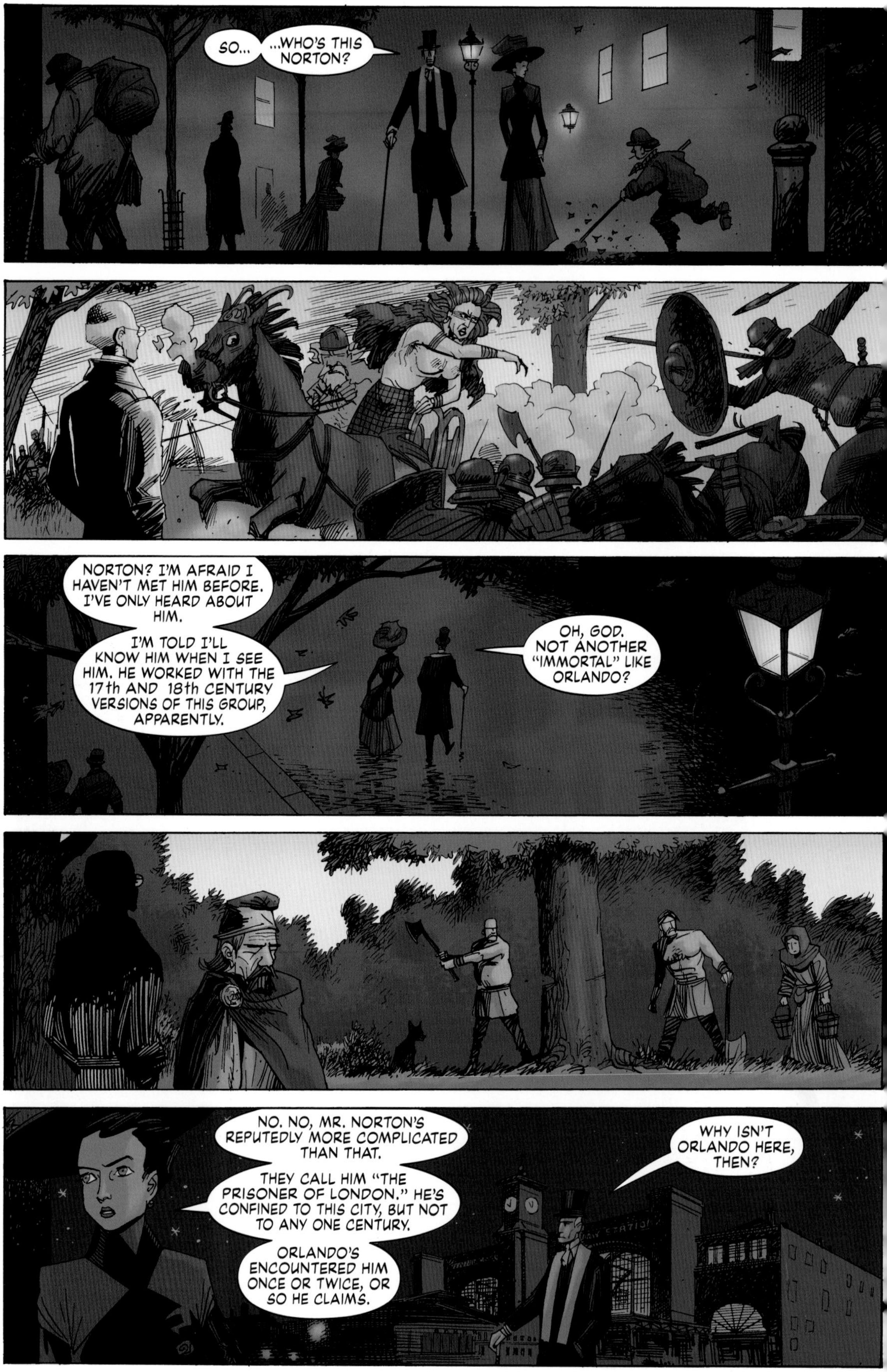
SO...
...WHO'S THIS NORTON?
NORTON? I'M AFRAID I HAVEN'T MET HIM BEFORE. I'VE ONLY HEARD ABOUT HIM.
I'M TOLD I'LL KNOW HIM WHEN I SEE HIM. HE WORKED WITH THE 17th AND 18th CENTURY VERSIONS OF THIS GROUP, APPARENTLY.
OH, GOD. NOT ANOTHER "IMMORTAL" LIKE ORLANDO?
NO. NO, MR. NORTON'S REPUTEDLY MORE COMPLICATED THAN THAT.
THEY CALL HIM "THE PRISONER OF LONDON." HE'S CONFINED TO THIS CITY, BUT NOT TO ANY ONE CENTURY.
ORLANDO'S ENCOUNTERED HIM ONCE OR TWICE, OR SO HE CLAIMS.
WHY ISN'T ORLANDO HERE, THEN?

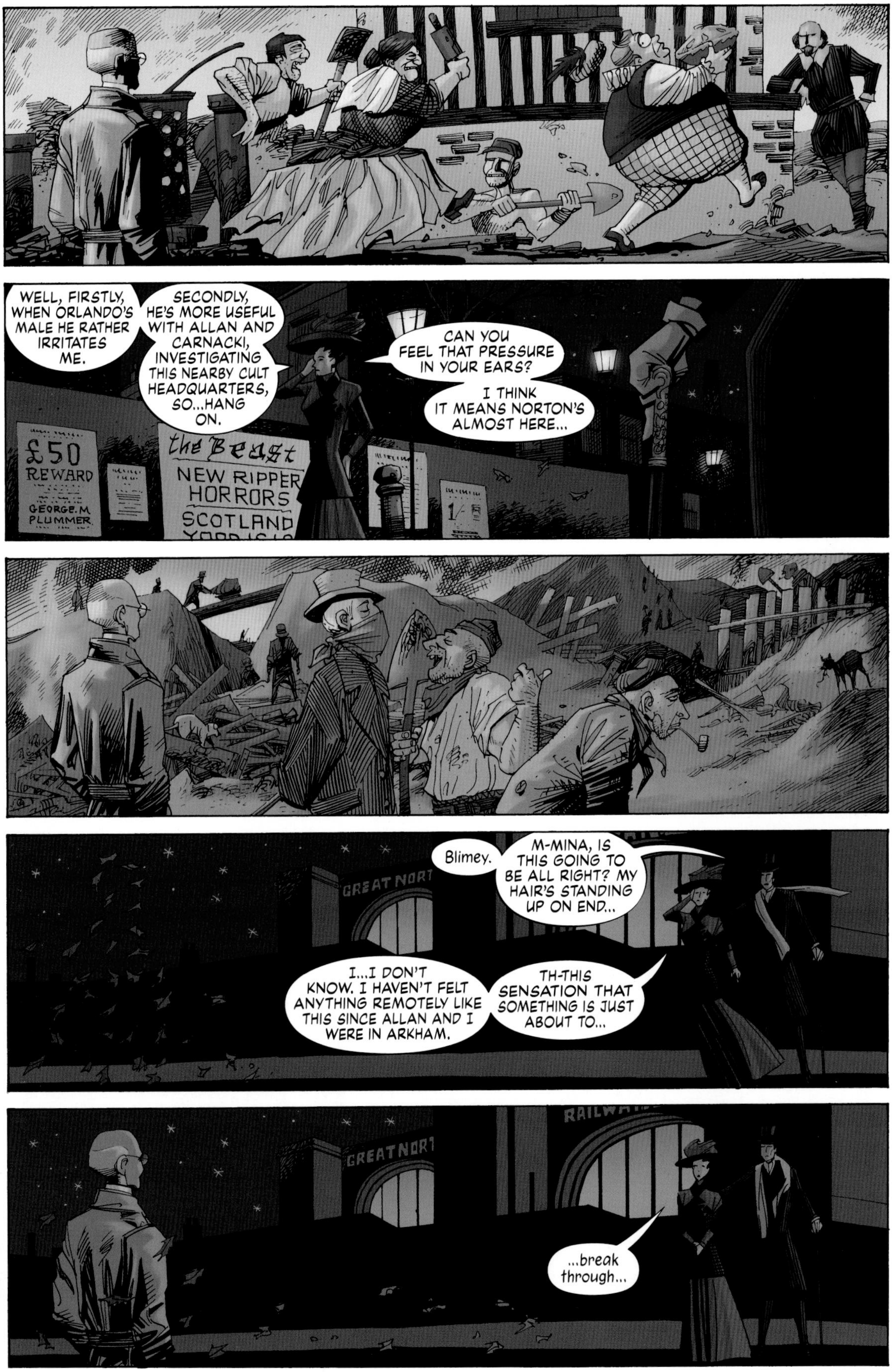
WELL, FIRSTLY, WHEN ORLANDO'S MALE HE RATHER IRRITATES ME.
SECONDLY, HE'S MORE USEFUL WITH ALLAN AND CARNACKI, INVESTIGATING THIS NEARBY CULT HEADQUARTERS, SO...HANG ON.
CAN YOU FEEL THAT PRESSURE IN YOUR EARS?
I THINK IT MEANS NORTON'S ALMOST HERE...
£50 REWARD
GEORGE.M PLUMMER
the Beast
NEW RIPPER HORRORS
SCOTLAND
1/-
GREAT NORT
Blimey.
M-MINA, IS THIS GOING TO BE ALL RIGHT? MY HAIR'S STANDING UP ON END...
I...I DON'T KNOW. I HAVEN'T FELT ANYTHING REMOTELY LIKE THIS SINCE ALLAN AND I WERE IN ARKHAM.
TH-THIS SENSATION THAT SOMETHING IS JUST ABOUT TO...
RAILWA
GREAT NORT
...break through...

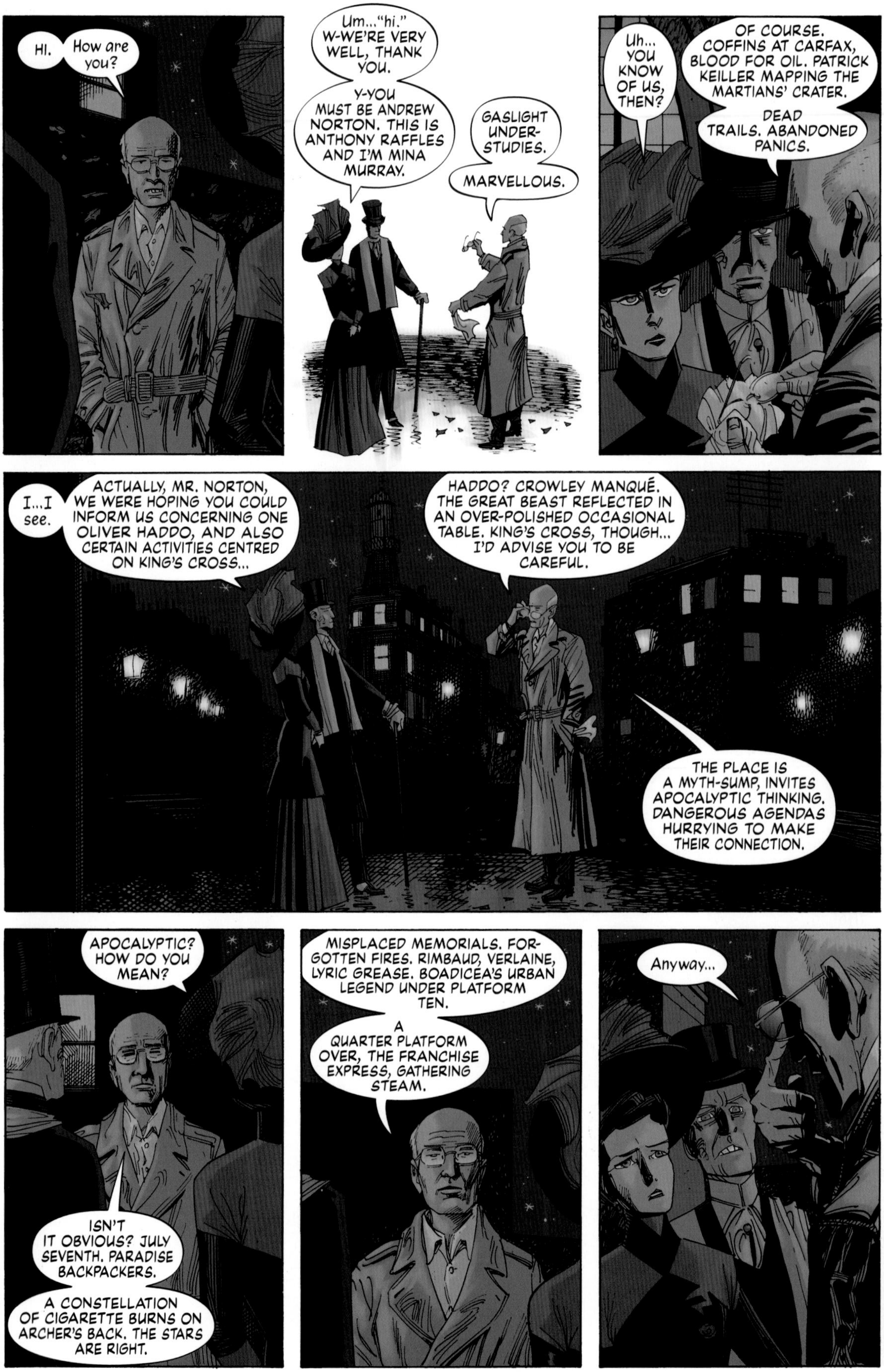
HI.
How are you?
Um..."hi." W-WE'RE VERY WELL, THANK YOU.
Y-YOU MUST BE ANDREW NORTON. THIS IS ANTHONY RAFFLES AND I'M MINA MURRAY.
GASLIGHT UNDER-STUDIES.
MARVELLOUS.
Uh... YOU KNOW OF US, THEN?
OF COURSE. COFFINS AT CARFAX, BLOOD FOR OIL. PATRICK KEILLER MAPPING THE MARTIANS' CRATER.
DEAD TRAILS. ABANDONED PANICS.
I...I see.
ACTUALLY, MR. NORTON, WE WERE HOPING YOU COULD INFORM US CONCERNING ONE OLIVER HADDO, AND ALSO CERTAIN ACTIVITIES CENTRED ON KING'S CROSS...
HADDO? CROWLEY MANQUÉ. THE GREAT BEAST REFLECTED IN AN OVER-POLISHED OCCASIONAL TABLE. KING'S CROSS, THOUGH... I'D ADVISE YOU TO BE CAREFUL.
THE PLACE IS A MYTH-SUMP, INVITES APOCALYPTIC THINKING. DANGEROUS AGENDAS HURRYING TO MAKE THEIR CONNECTION.
APOCALYPTIC? HOW DO YOU MEAN?
ISN'T IT OBVIOUS? JULY SEVENTH. PARADISE BACKPACKERS.
A CONSTELLATION OF CIGARETTE BURNS ON ARCHER'S BACK. THE STARS ARE RIGHT.
MISPLACED MEMORIALS. FOR-GOTTEN FIRES. RIMBAUD, VERLAINE, LYRIC GREASE. BOADICEA'S URBAN LEGEND UNDER PLATFORM TEN.
A QUARTER PLATFORM OVER, THE FRANCHISE EXPRESS, GATHERING STEAM.
Anyway...

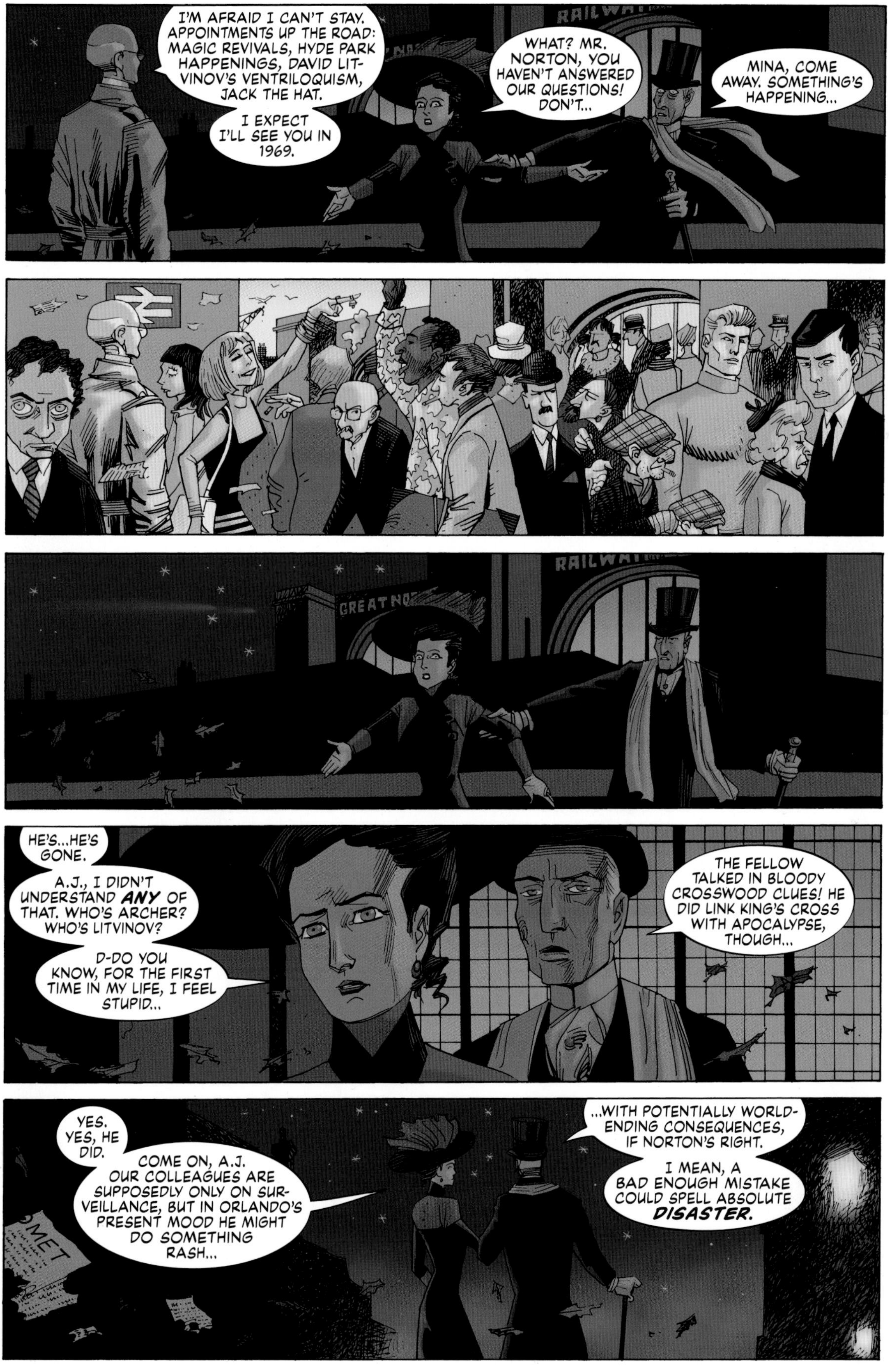
I'M AFRAID I CAN'T STAY. APPOINTMENTS UP THE ROAD: MAGIC REVIVALS, HYDE PARK HAPPENINGS, DAVID LITVINOV'S VENTRILOQUISM, JACK THE HAT.
I EXPECT I'LL SEE YOU IN 1969.
WHAT? MR. NORTON, YOU HAVEN'T ANSWERED OUR QUESTIONS! DON'T...
MINA, COME AWAY. SOMETHING'S HAPPENING...
HE'S...HE'S GONE.
A.J., I DIDN'T UNDERSTAND ANY OF THAT. WHO'S ARCHER? WHO'S LITVINOV?
D-DO YOU KNOW, FOR THE FIRST TIME IN MY LIFE, I FEEL STUPID...
THE FELLOW TALKED IN BLOODY CROSSWOOD CLUES! HE DID LINK KING'S CROSS WITH APOCALYPSE, THOUGH...
YES. YES, HE DID.
COME ON, A.J. OUR COLLEAGUES ARE SUPPOSEDLY ONLY ON SURVEILLANCE, BUT IN ORLANDO'S PRESENT MOOD HE MIGHT DO SOMETHING RASH...
...WITH POTENTIALLY WORLD-ENDING CONSEQUENCES, IF NORTON'S RIGHT.
I MEAN, A BAD ENOUGH MISTAKE COULD SPELL ABSOLUTE DISASTER.

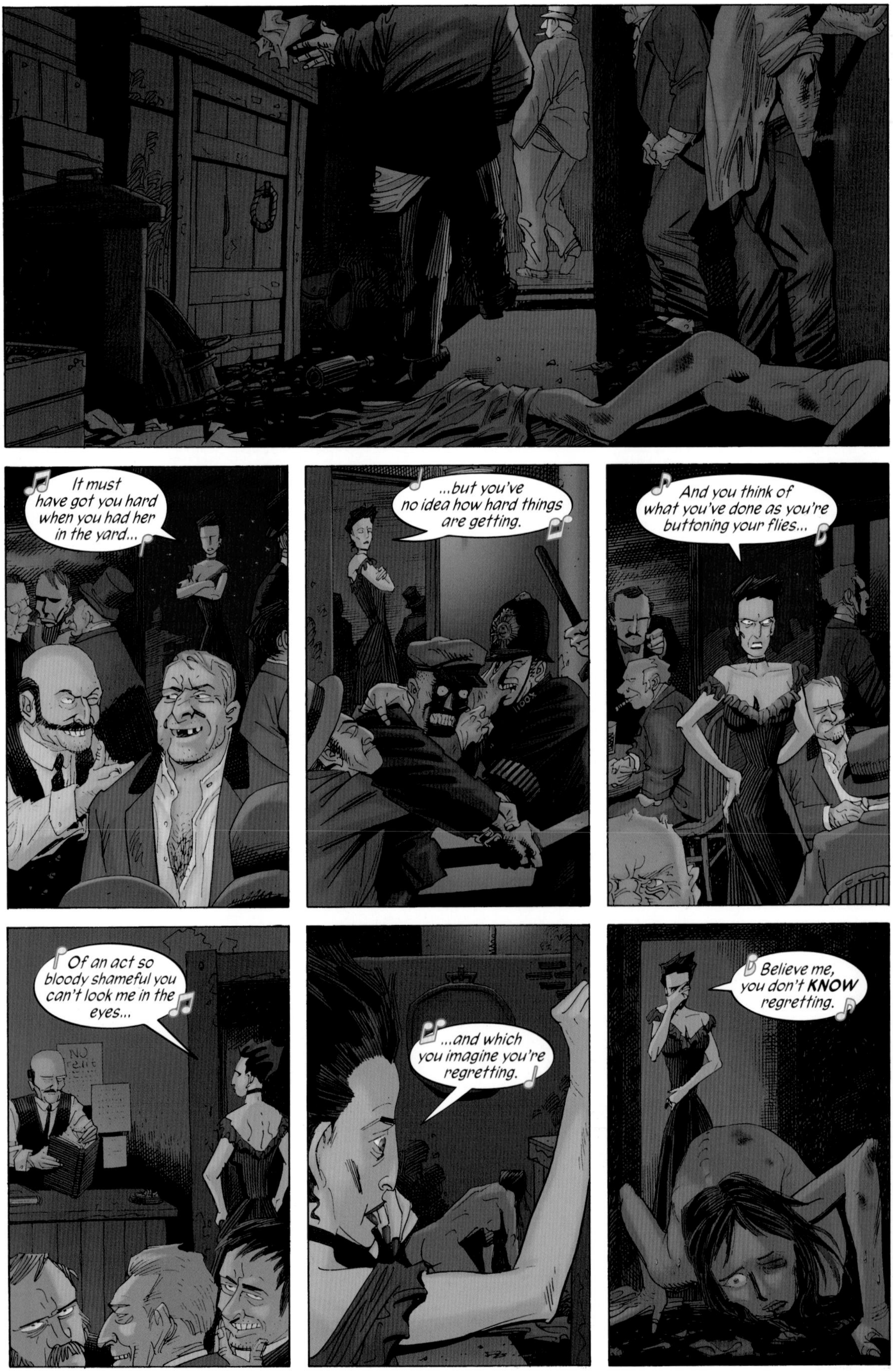
It must have got you hard when you had her in the yard...
...but you've no idea how hard things are getting.
And you think of what you've done as you're buttoning your flies...
Of an act so bloody shameful you can't look me in the eyes...
...and which you imagine you're regretting.
Believe me, you don't KNOW regretting.

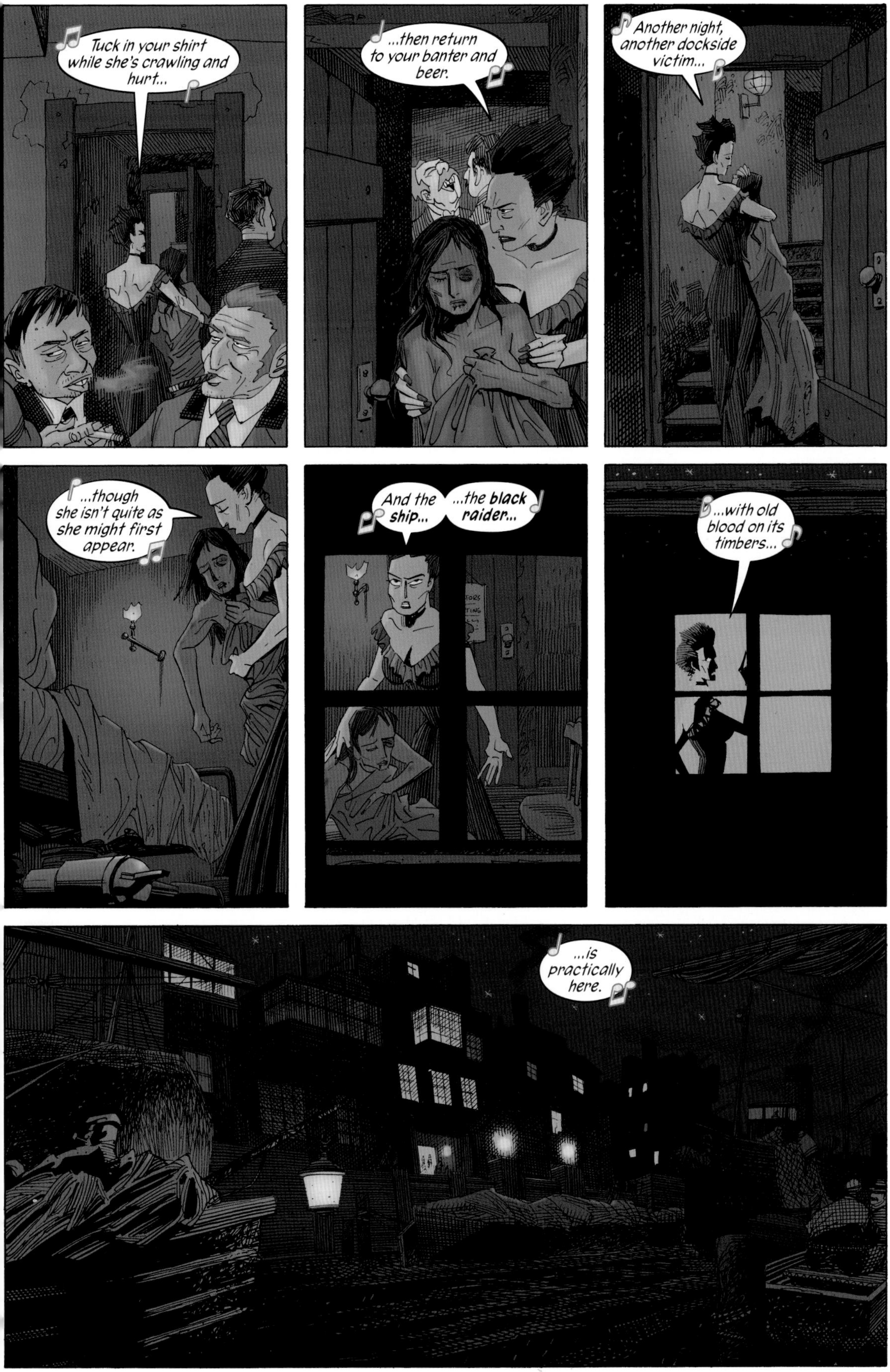
Tuck in your shirt while she's crawling and hurt...
...then return to your banter and beer.
Another night, another dockside victim...
...though she isn't quite as she might first appear.
And the ship...
...the black raider...
...with old blood on its timbers...
...is practically here.

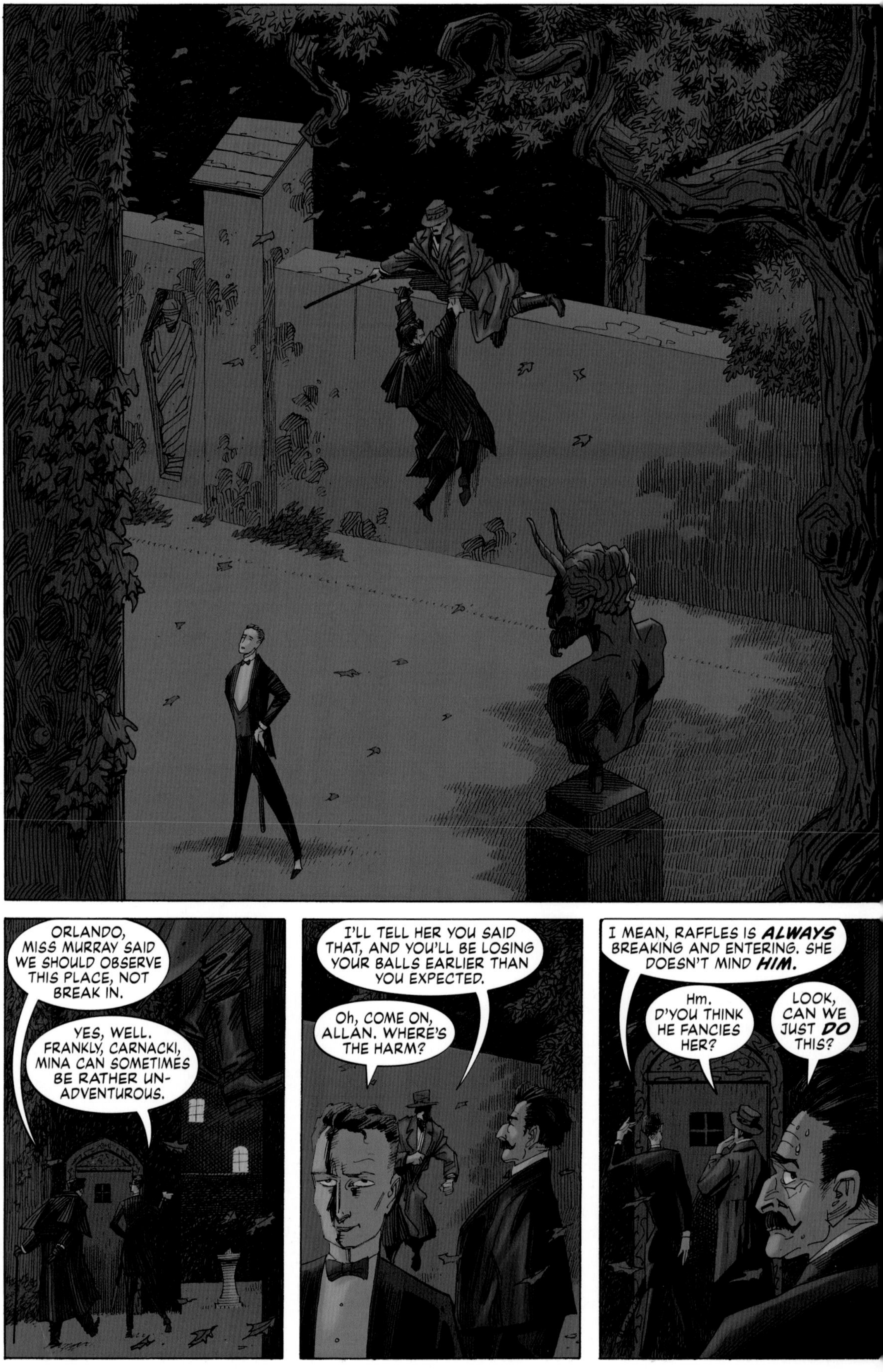
ORLANDO, MISS MURRAY SAID WE SHOULD OBSERVE THIS PLACE, NOT BREAK IN.
YES, WELL. FRANKLY, CARNACKI, MINA CAN SOMETIMES BE RATHER UN-ADVENTUROUS.
I'LL TELL HER YOU SAID THAT, AND YOU'LL BE LOSING YOUR BALLS EARLIER THAN YOU EXPECTED.
Oh, COME ON, ALLAN. WHERE'S THE HARM?
I MEAN, RAFFLES IS ***ALWAYS*** BREAKING AND ENTERING. SHE DOESN'T MIND ***HIM.***
Hm. D'YOU THINK HE FANCIES HER?
LOOK, CAN WE JUST ***DO*** THIS?

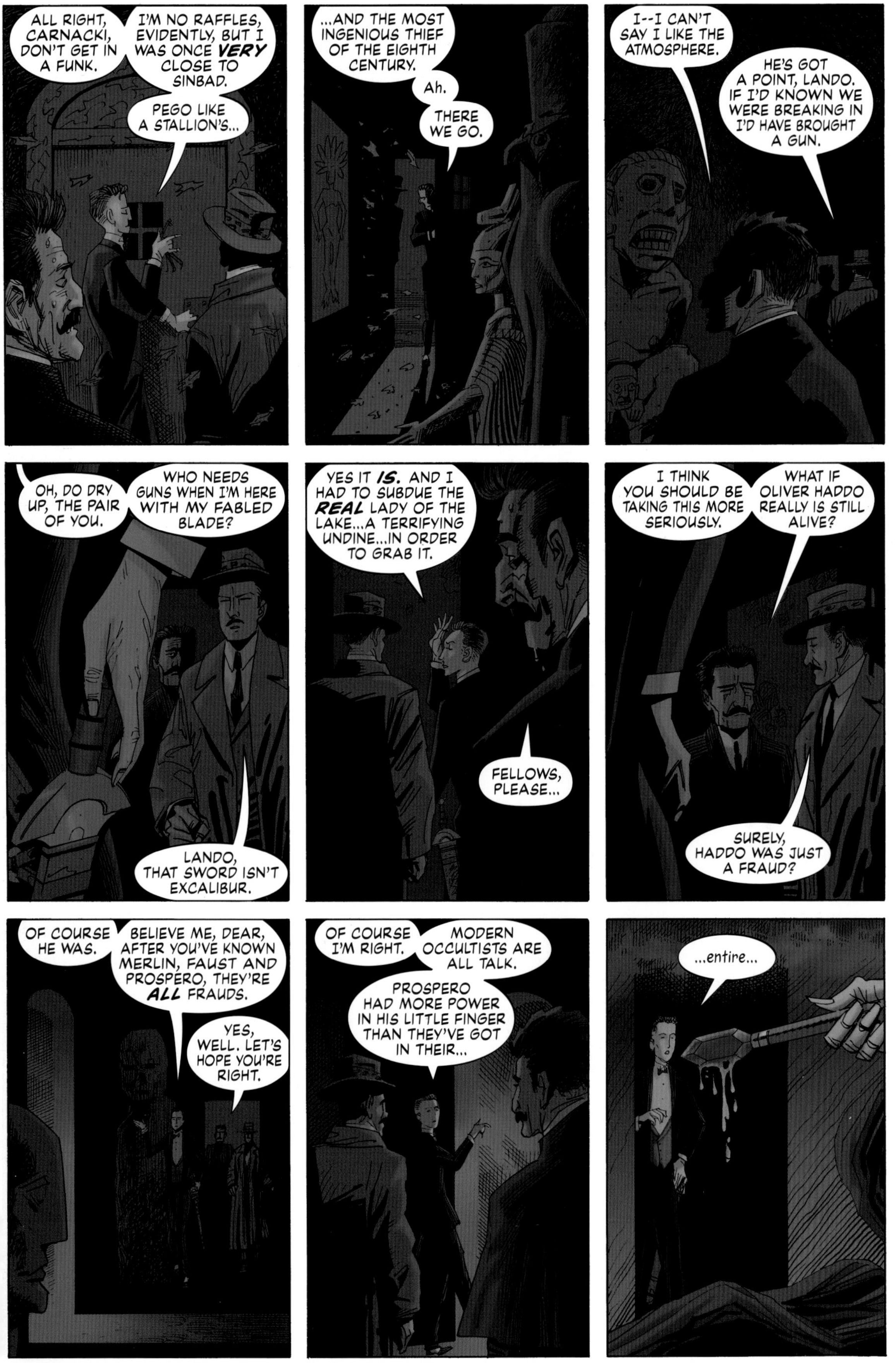
ALL RIGHT, CARNACKI, DON'T GET IN A FUNK.
I'M NO RAFFLES, EVIDENTLY, BUT I WAS ONCE VERY CLOSE TO SINBAD.
PEGO LIKE A STALLION'S...
...AND THE MOST INGENIOUS THIEF OF THE EIGHTH CENTURY.
Ah.
THERE WE GO.
I--I CAN'T SAY I LIKE THE ATMOSPHERE.
HE'S GOT A POINT, LANDO. IF I'D KNOWN WE WERE BREAKING IN I'D HAVE BROUGHT A GUN.
OH, DO DRY UP, THE PAIR OF YOU.
WHO NEEDS GUNS WHEN I'M HERE WITH MY FABLED BLADE?
LANDO, THAT SWORD ISN'T EXCALIBUR.
YES IT IS. AND I HAD TO SUBDUE THE REAL LADY OF THE LAKE...A TERRIFYING UNDINE...IN ORDER TO GRAB IT.
FELLOWS, PLEASE...
I THINK YOU SHOULD BE TAKING THIS MORE SERIOUSLY.
WHAT IF OLIVER HADDO REALLY IS STILL ALIVE?
SURELY, HADDO WAS JUST A FRAUD?
OF COURSE HE WAS.
BELIEVE ME, DEAR, AFTER YOU'VE KNOWN MERLIN, FAUST AND PROSPERO, THEY'RE ALL FRAUDS.
YES, WELL. LET'S HOPE YOU'RE RIGHT.
OF COURSE I'M RIGHT.
MODERN OCCULTISTS ARE ALL TALK.
PROSPERO HAD MORE POWER IN HIS LITTLE FINGER THAN THEY'VE GOT IN THEIR...
...entire...

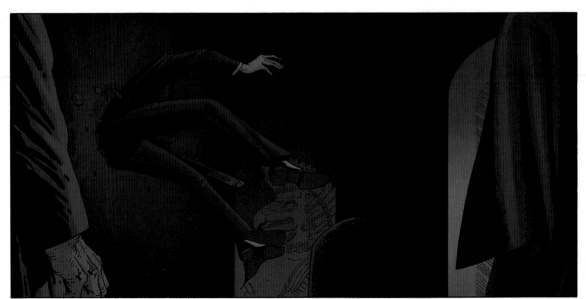

Gentlemen...

...WON'T YOU COME IN?

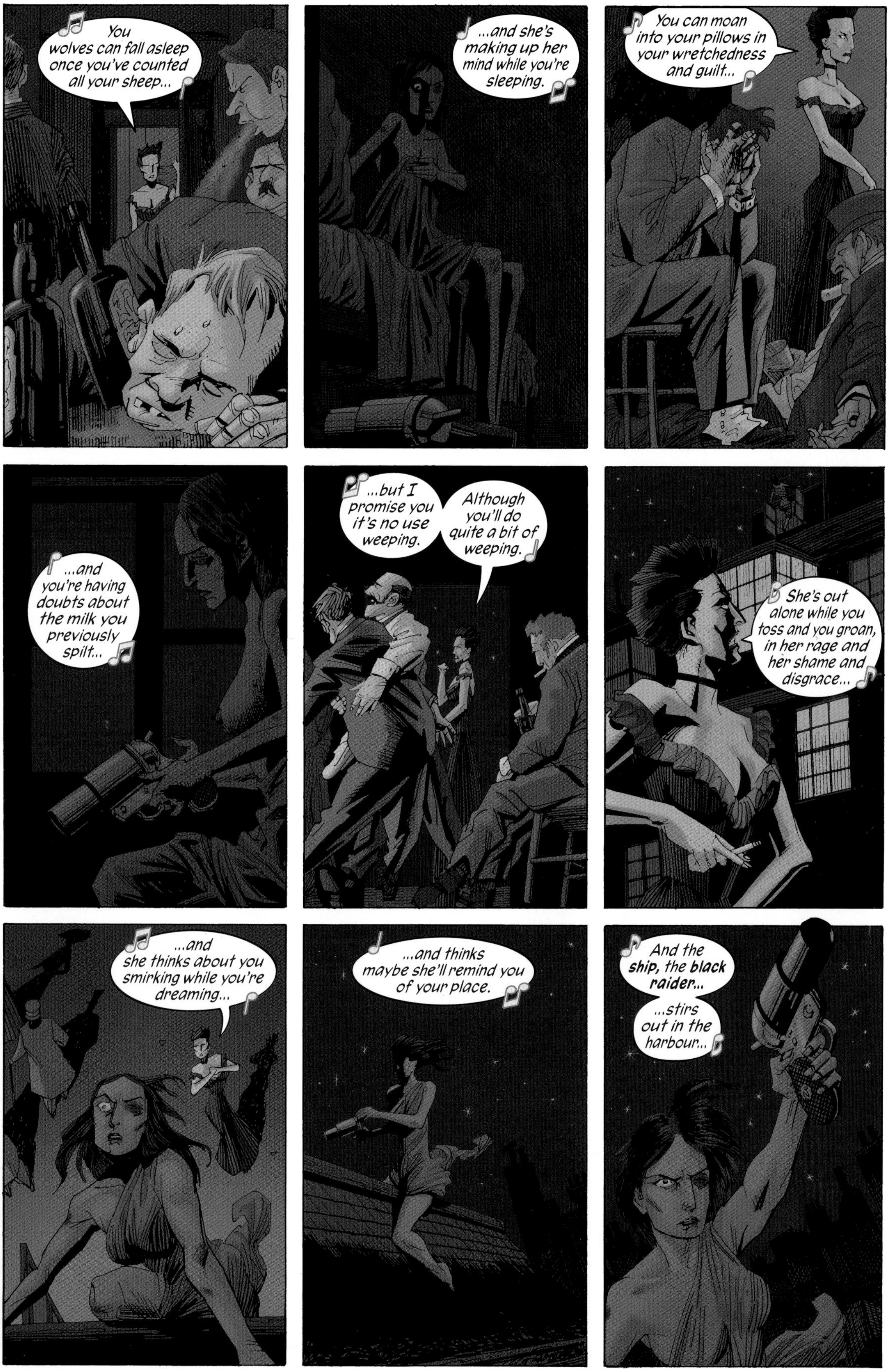
You wolves can fall asleep once you've counted all your sheep...
...and she's making up her mind while you're sleeping.
You can moan into your pillows in your wretchedness and guilt...
...and you're having doubts about the milk you previously spilt...
...but I promise you it's no use weeping.
Although you'll do quite a bit of weeping.
She's out alone while you toss and you groan, in her rage and her shame and disgrace...
...and she thinks about you smirking while you're dreaming...
...and thinks maybe she'll remind you of your place.
And the **ship**, the **black raider**...
...stirs out in the harbour...

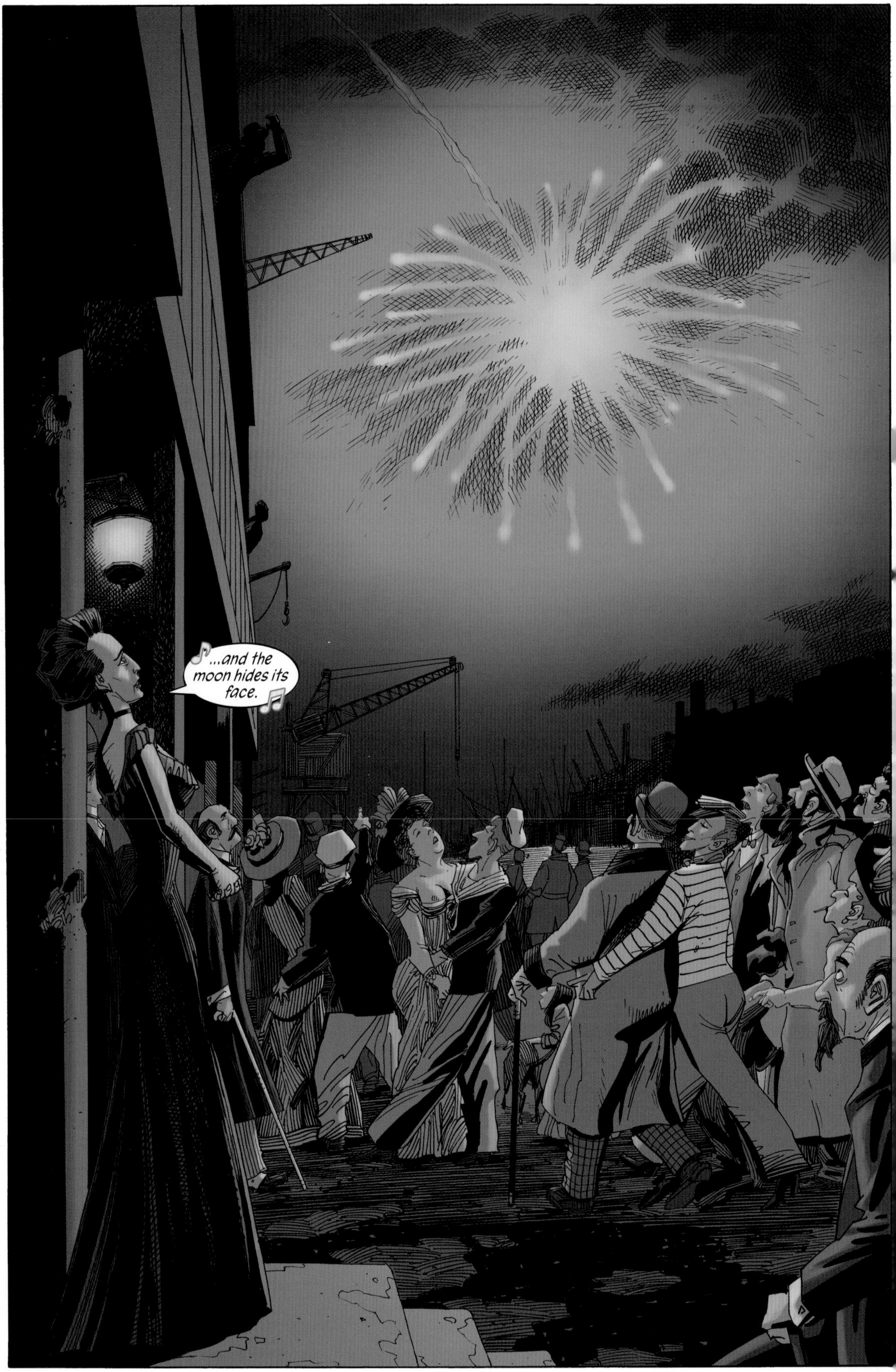
...and the moon hides its face.

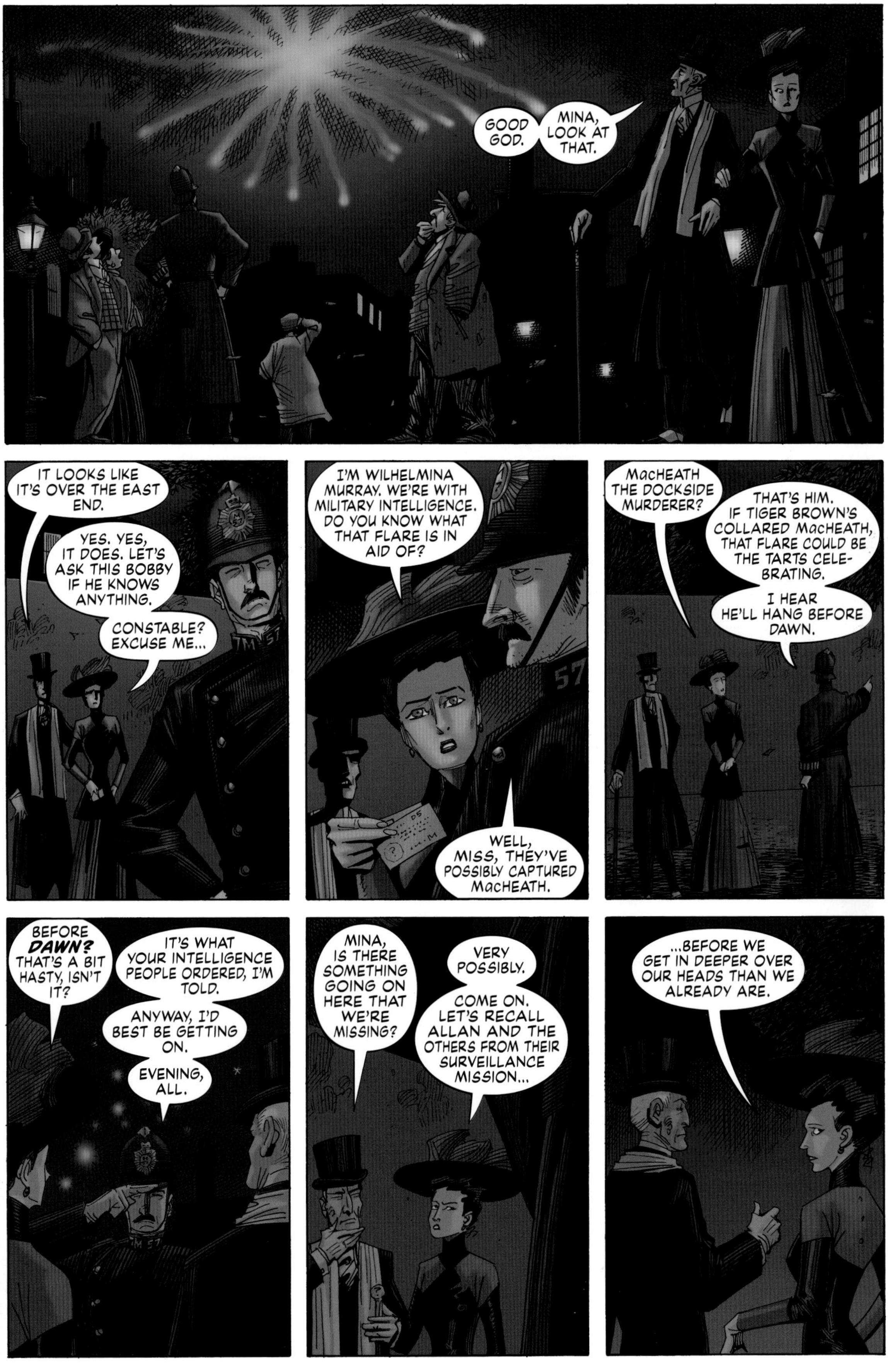
MINA, LOOK AT THAT.
GOOD GOD.
IT LOOKS LIKE IT'S OVER THE EAST END.
YES. YES, IT DOES. LET'S ASK THIS BOBBY IF HE KNOWS ANYTHING.
CONSTABLE? EXCUSE ME...
I'M WILHELMINA MURRAY. WE'RE WITH MILITARY INTELLIGENCE. DO YOU KNOW WHAT THAT FLARE IS IN AID OF?
WELL, MISS, THEY'VE POSSIBLY CAPTURED MacHEATH.
MacHEATH THE DOCKSIDE MURDERER?
THAT'S HIM. IF TIGER BROWN'S COLLARED MacHEATH, THAT FLARE COULD BE THE TARTS CELE-BRATING.
I HEAR HE'LL HANG BEFORE DAWN.
BEFORE *DAWN?* THAT'S A BIT HASTY, ISN'T IT?
IT'S WHAT YOUR INTELLIGENCE PEOPLE ORDERED, I'M TOLD.
ANYWAY, I'D BEST BE GETTING ON.
EVENING, ALL.
MINA, IS THERE SOMETHING GOING ON HERE THAT WE'RE MISSING?
VERY POSSIBLY.
COME ON. LET'S RECALL ALLAN AND THE OTHERS FROM THEIR SURVEILLANCE MISSION...
...BEFORE WE GET IN DEEPER OVER OUR HEADS THAN WE ALREADY ARE.

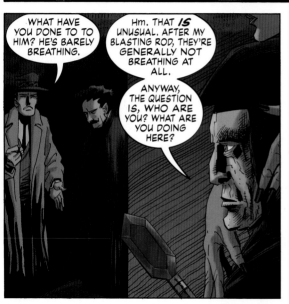

WHAT HAVE YOU DONE TO TO HIM? HE'S BARELY BREATHING.

Hm. THAT *IS* UNUSUAL. AFTER MY BLASTING ROD, THEY'RE GENERALLY NOT BREATHING AT ALL.

ANYWAY, THE QUESTION IS, WHO ARE YOU? WHAT ARE YOU DOING HERE?

I KNOW THE OLDER FELLOW FROM MY CLUB, MASTER. HE'S CARNACKI. CARNACKI THE GHOST FINDER.

OH...THE WHISTLING ROOM CAPER? I'VE HEARD OF YOU.

AND I OF YOU.

YOU ARE OLIVER HADDO, I TAKE IT?

WHAT? ME? OF COURSE NOT. HADDO'S DEAD. HADN'T YOU HEARD?

I'M DR. KARSWELL TRELAWNEY, VARIOUSLY OF STONEDENE, AND LUFFORD IN WARWICKSHIRE.

FRATER SIMON YOU APPARENTLY KNOW ALREADY. THIS IS SOROR CYBELE, AND THERE'S FRATER CYRIL.

YES. YES, IT'S EXACTLY AS IT WAS IN MY DREAM, EXCEPT...

EXCEPT THERE WAS ANOTHER WOMAN. SOME-ONE CALLED "ILIEL."

NEVER HEARD OF HER.

ILIEL, THOUGH... THE NAME ADDS UP TO EIGHTY-ONE. A LUNAR NUMBER.

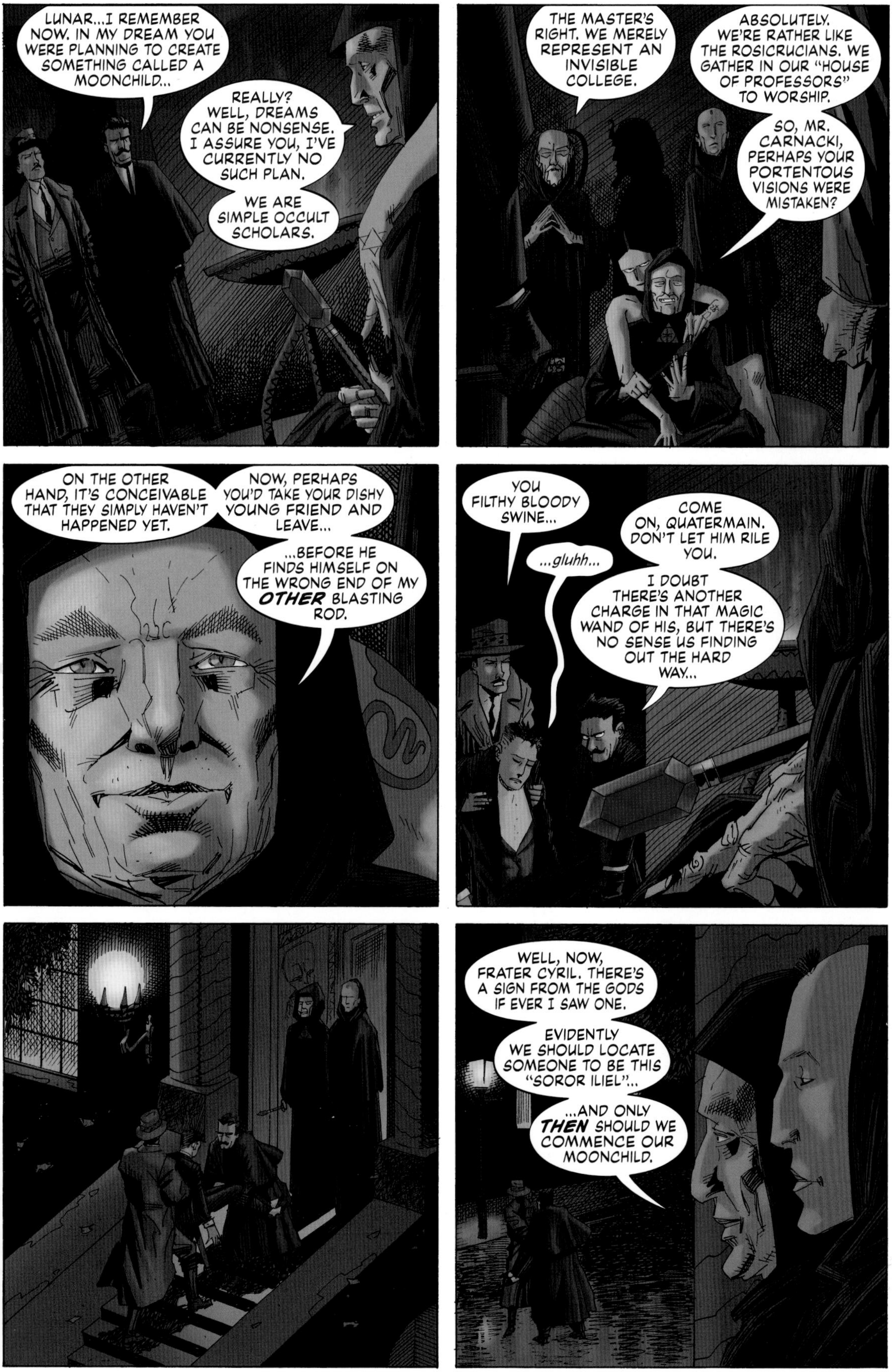
LUNAR...I REMEMBER NOW. IN MY DREAM YOU WERE PLANNING TO CREATE SOMETHING CALLED A MOONCHILD...
REALLY? WELL, DREAMS CAN BE NONSENSE. I ASSURE YOU, I'VE CURRENTLY NO SUCH PLAN.
WE ARE SIMPLE OCCULT SCHOLARS.
THE MASTER'S RIGHT. WE MERELY REPRESENT AN INVISIBLE COLLEGE.
ABSOLUTELY. WE'RE RATHER LIKE THE ROSICRUCIANS. WE GATHER IN OUR "HOUSE OF PROFESSORS" TO WORSHIP.
SO, MR. CARNACKI, PERHAPS YOUR PORTENTOUS VISIONS WERE MISTAKEN?
ON THE OTHER HAND, IT'S CONCEIVABLE THAT THEY SIMPLY HAVEN'T HAPPENED YET.
NOW, PERHAPS YOU'D TAKE YOUR DISHY YOUNG FRIEND AND LEAVE...
...BEFORE HE FINDS HIMSELF ON THE WRONG END OF MY OTHER BLASTING ROD.
YOU FILTHY BLOODY SWINE...
...gluhh...
COME ON, QUATERMAIN. DON'T LET HIM RILE YOU.
I DOUBT THERE'S ANOTHER CHARGE IN THAT MAGIC WAND OF HIS, BUT THERE'S NO SENSE US FINDING OUT THE HARD WAY...
WELL, NOW, FRATER CYRIL. THERE'S A SIGN FROM THE GODS IF EVER I SAW ONE.
EVIDENTLY WE SHOULD LOCATE SOMEONE TO BE THIS "SOROR ILIEL"...
...AND ONLY THEN SHOULD WE COMMENCE OUR MOONCHILD.

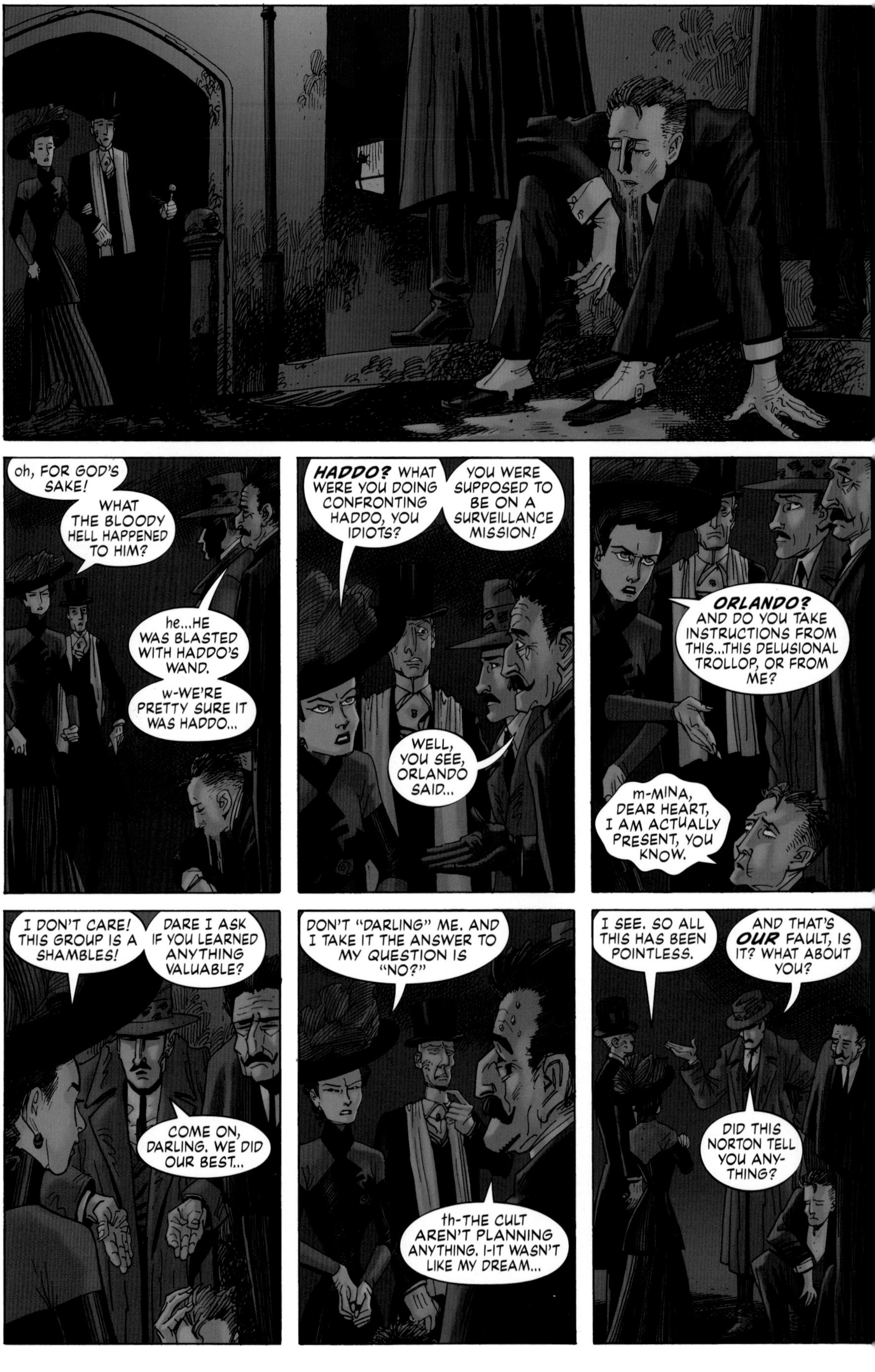
oh, FOR GOD'S SAKE!
WHAT THE BLOODY HELL HAPPENED TO HIM?
he...HE WAS BLASTED WITH HADDO'S WAND.
w-WE'RE PRETTY SURE IT WAS HADDO...
HADDO? WHAT WERE YOU DOING CONFRONTING HADDO, YOU IDIOTS?
YOU WERE SUPPOSED TO BE ON A SURVEILLANCE MISSION!
WELL, YOU SEE, ORLANDO SAID...
ORLANDO? AND DO YOU TAKE INSTRUCTIONS FROM THIS...THIS DELUSIONAL TROLLOP, OR FROM ME?
m-MINA, DEAR HEART, I AM ACTUALLY PRESENT, YOU KNOW.
I DON'T CARE! THIS GROUP IS A SHAMBLES!
DARE I ASK IF YOU LEARNED ANYTHING VALUABLE?
COME ON, DARLING. WE DID OUR BEST...
DON'T "DARLING" ME. AND I TAKE IT THE ANSWER TO MY QUESTION IS "NO?"
th-THE CULT AREN'T PLANNING ANYTHING. I-IT WASN'T LIKE MY DREAM...
I SEE. SO ALL THIS HAS BEEN POINTLESS.
AND THAT'S OUR FAULT, IS IT? WHAT ABOUT YOU?
DID THIS NORTON TELL YOU ANYTHING?

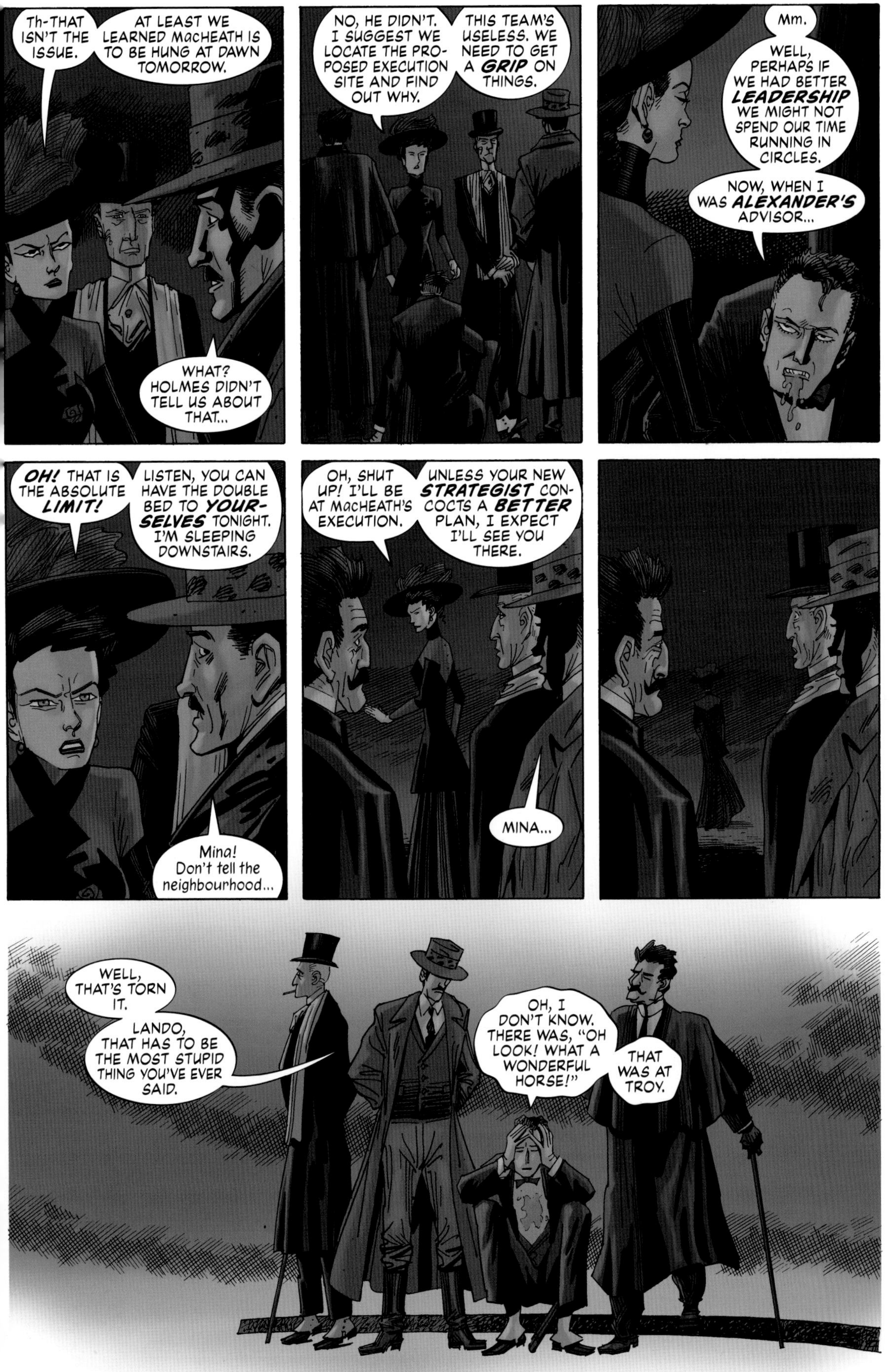
Th-THAT ISN'T THE ISSUE.
AT LEAST WE LEARNED MacHEATH IS TO BE HUNG AT DAWN TOMORROW.
WHAT? HOLMES DIDN'T TELL US ABOUT THAT...
NO, HE DIDN'T. I SUGGEST WE LOCATE THE PROPOSED EXECUTION SITE AND FIND OUT WHY.
THIS TEAM'S USELESS. WE NEED TO GET A GRIP ON THINGS.
Mm.
WELL, PERHAPS IF WE HAD BETTER LEADERSHIP WE MIGHT NOT SPEND OUR TIME RUNNING IN CIRCLES.
NOW, WHEN I WAS ALEXANDER'S ADVISOR...
OH! THAT IS THE ABSOLUTE LIMIT!
LISTEN, YOU CAN HAVE THE DOUBLE BED TO YOURSELVES TONIGHT. I'M SLEEPING DOWNSTAIRS.
Mina! Don't tell the neighbourhood...
OH, SHUT UP! I'LL BE AT MacHEATH'S EXECUTION.
UNLESS YOUR NEW STRATEGIST CONCOCTS A BETTER PLAN, I EXPECT I'LL SEE YOU THERE.
MINA...
WELL, THAT'S TORN IT.
LANDO, THAT HAS TO BE THE MOST STUPID THING YOU'VE EVER SAID.
OH, I DON'T KNOW. THERE WAS, "OH LOOK! WHAT A WONDERFUL HORSE!"
THAT WAS AT TROY.

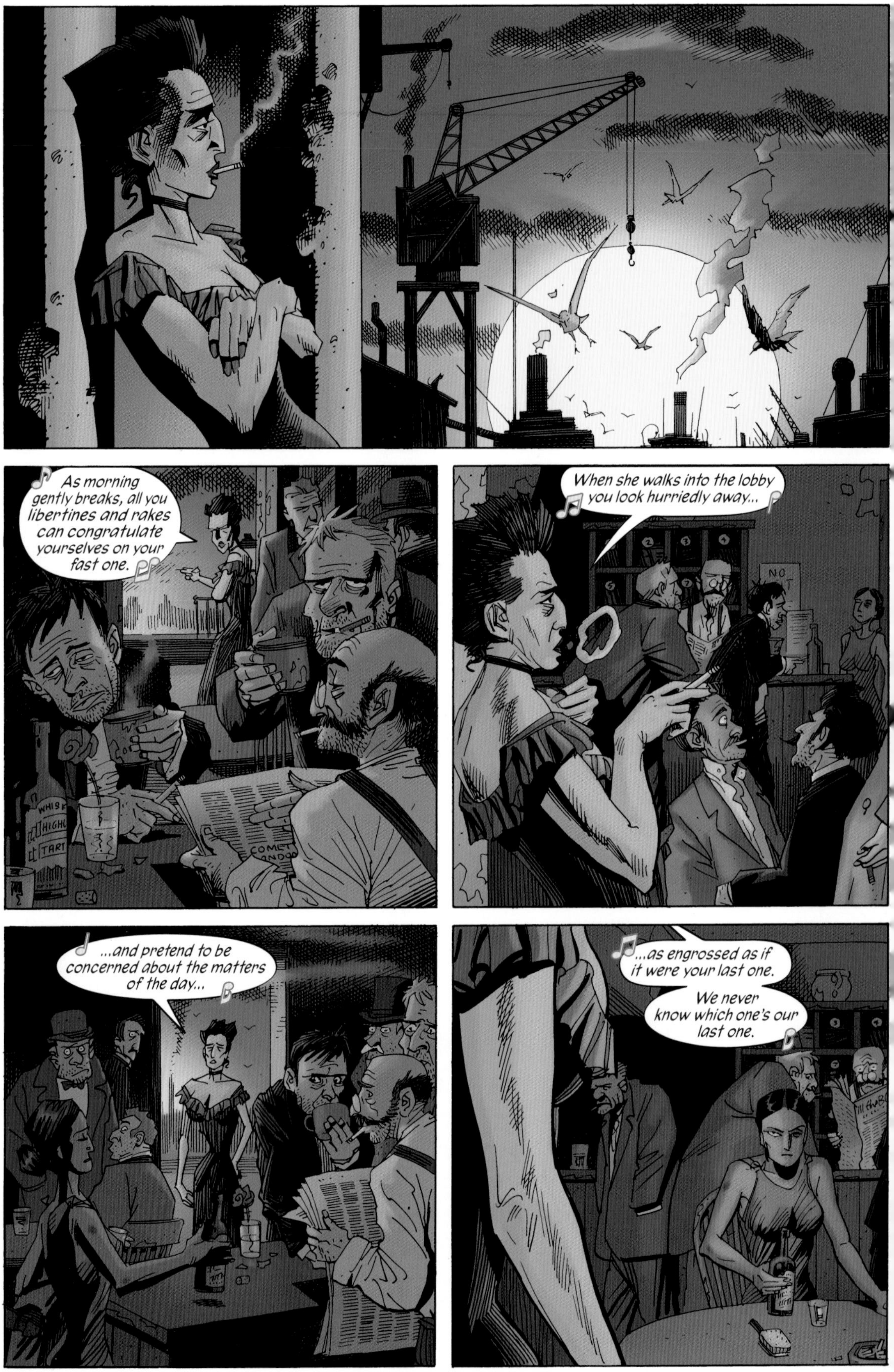

As morning gently breaks, all you libertines and rakes can congratulate yourselves on your fast one.
When she walks into the lobby you look hurriedly away...
...and pretend to be concerned about the matters of the day...
...as engrossed as if it were your last one.
We never know which one's our last one.

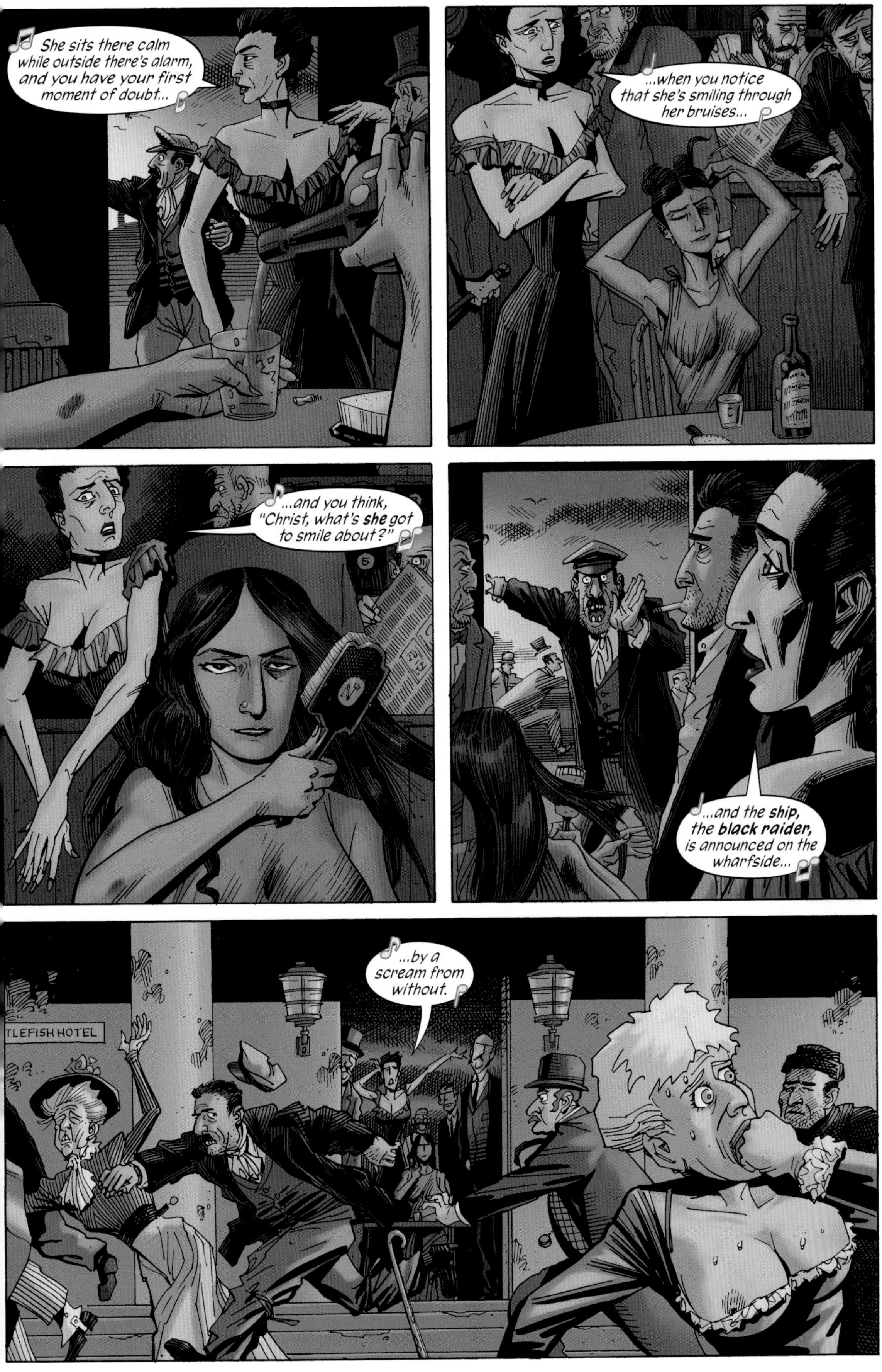

She sits there calm while outside there's alarm, and you have your first moment of doubt...
...when you notice that she's smiling through her bruises...
...and you think, "Christ, what's **she** got to smile about?"
...and the **ship**, the **black raider**, is announced on the wharfside...
...by a scream from without.
TLEFISH HOTEL

MR. HOLMES. THERE YOU ARE.

WOULD YOU MIND TELLING ME WHAT'S GOING ON?

NOT AT ALL. IT'S AN EXECUTION. WE'RE HANGING MacHEATH.

WITH RESPECT, SIR, I KNOW THAT. BUT WHY SO HURRIEDLY? IS THERE TO BE NO TRIAL?

OF COURSE NOT. IT MIGHT EMBARRASS THE ARISTOCRACY.

THE ARISTOCRACY? WHAT DO THEY HAVE TO DO WITH ANYTHING?

MY DEAR LADY, THIS IS ENGLAND. THEY HAVE TO DO WITH EVERYTHING...

...ESPECIALLY 1888'S NOTORIOUS WHITECHAPEL MURDERS.

YOU SEE, MacHEATH ABSCONDED FOR ARGENTINA IN EARLY DECEMBER THAT YEAR.

THE LAST MURDER HAPPENED ON BOXING DAY.

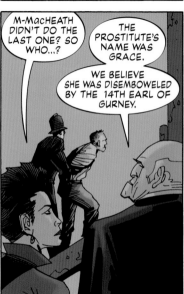

M-MacHEATH DIDN'T DO THE LAST ONE? SO WHO...?

THE PROSTITUTE'S NAME WAS GRACE.

WE BELIEVE SHE WAS DISEMBOWELED BY THE 14TH EARL OF GURNEY.

BETTER EVERYONE THINKS MacHEATH DID THEM ALL, EH? A TRIAL WOULD ONLY RAISE AWKWARD QUESTIONS.

INCIDENTALLY, HOW DID YOUR PREDICTED ARMAGEDDON TURN OUT?

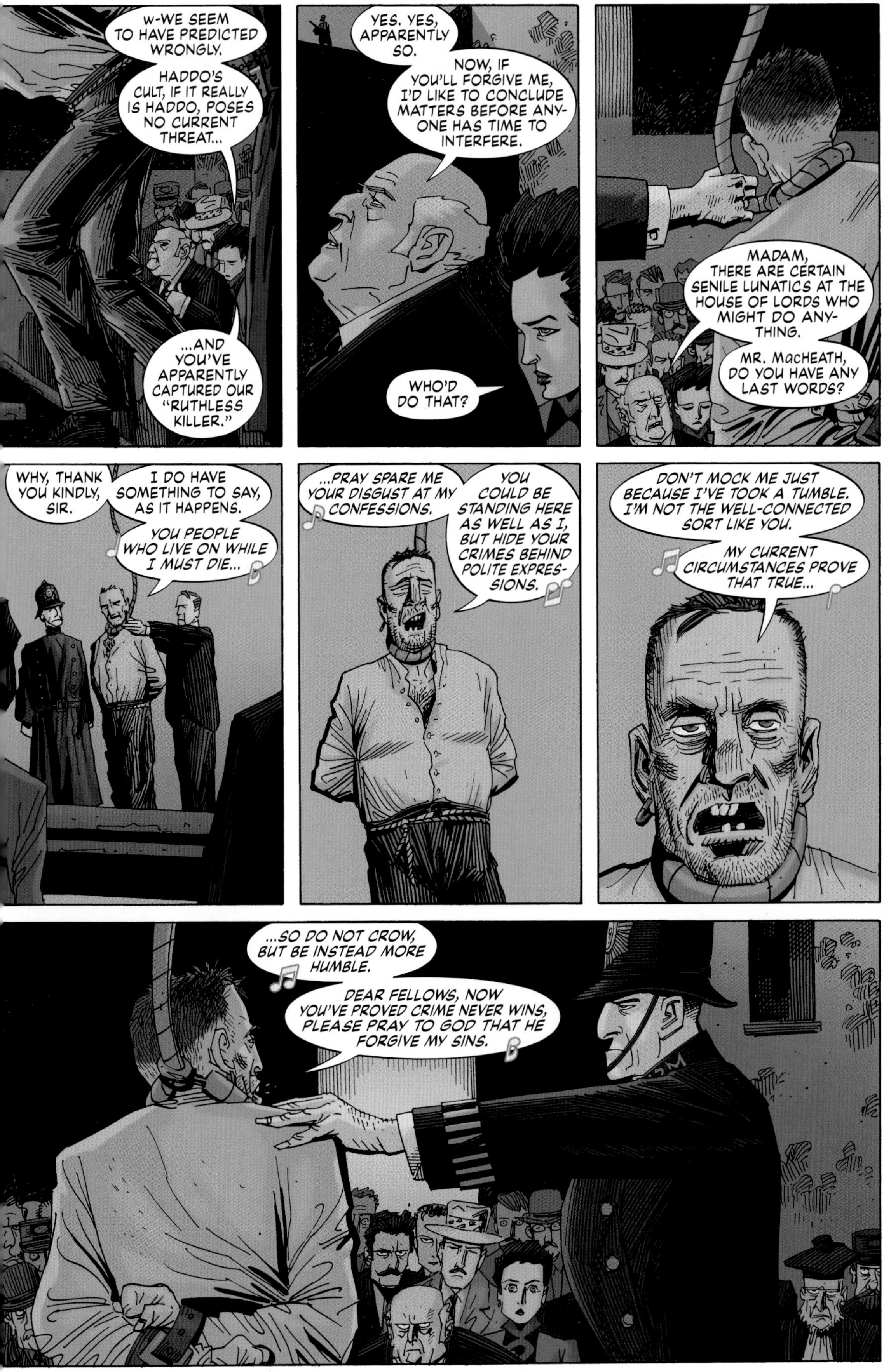
W-WE SEEM TO HAVE PREDICTED WRONGLY.
HADDO'S CULT, IF IT REALLY IS HADDO, POSES NO CURRENT THREAT...
...AND YOU'VE APPARENTLY CAPTURED OUR "RUTHLESS KILLER."
YES. YES, APPARENTLY SO.
NOW, IF YOU'LL FORGIVE ME, I'D LIKE TO CONCLUDE MATTERS BEFORE ANYONE HAS TIME TO INTERFERE.
WHO'D DO THAT?
MADAM, THERE ARE CERTAIN SENILE LUNATICS AT THE HOUSE OF LORDS WHO MIGHT DO ANYTHING.
MR. MacHEATH, DO YOU HAVE ANY LAST WORDS?
WHY, THANK YOU KINDLY, SIR.
I DO HAVE SOMETHING TO SAY, AS IT HAPPENS.
YOU PEOPLE WHO LIVE ON WHILE I MUST DIE...
...PRAY SPARE ME YOUR DISGUST AT MY CONFESSIONS.
YOU COULD BE STANDING HERE AS WELL AS I, BUT HIDE YOUR CRIMES BEHIND POLITE EXPRESSIONS.
DON'T MOCK ME JUST BECAUSE I'VE TOOK A TUMBLE. I'M NOT THE WELL-CONNECTED SORT LIKE YOU.
MY CURRENT CIRCUMSTANCES PROVE THAT TRUE...
...SO DO NOT CROW, BUT BE INSTEAD MORE HUMBLE.
DEAR FELLOWS, NOW YOU'VE PROVED CRIME NEVER WINS, PLEASE PRAY TO GOD THAT HE FORGIVE MY SINS.

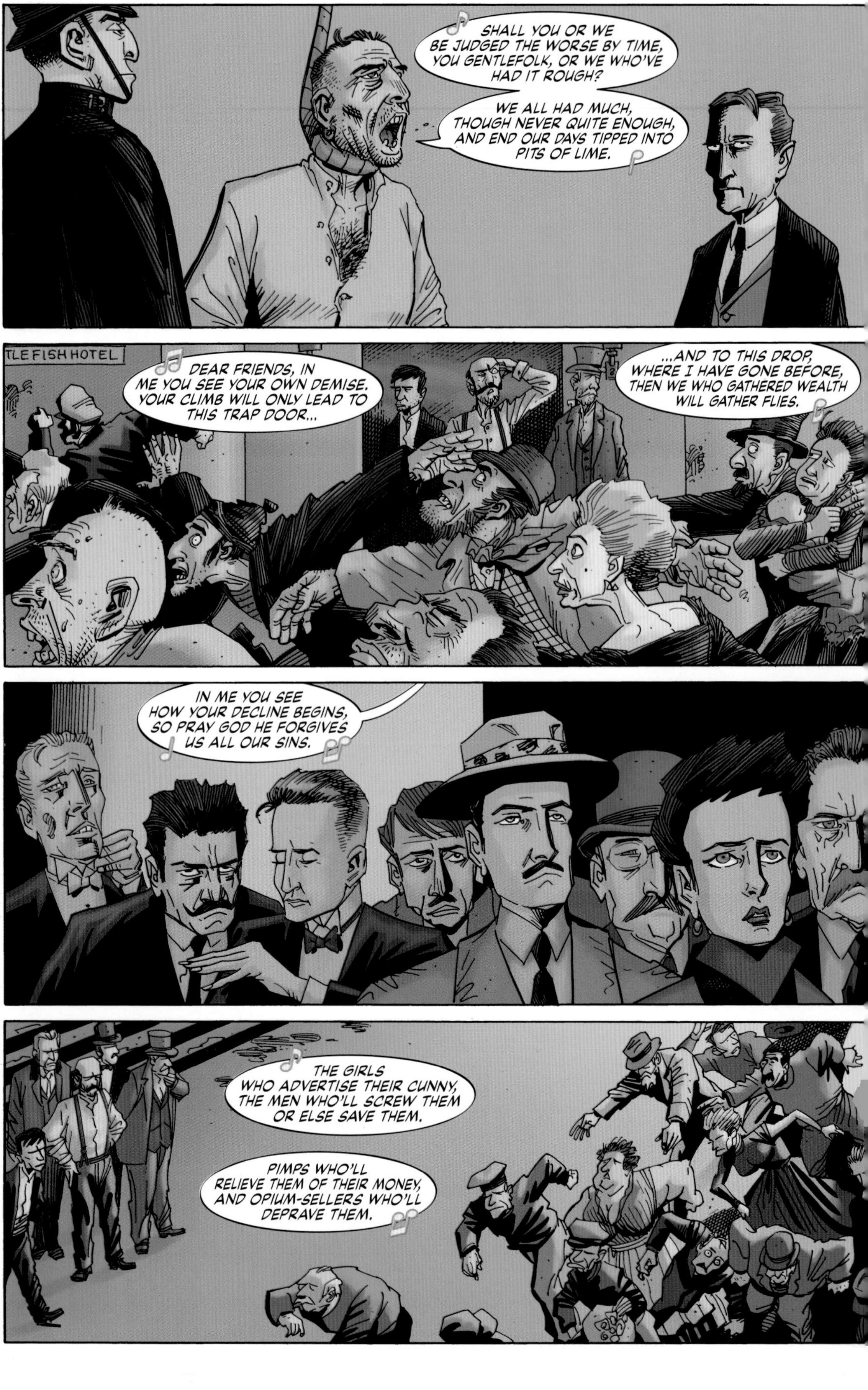
SHALL YOU OR WE BE JUDGED THE WORSE BY TIME, YOU GENTLEFOLK, OR WE WHO'VE HAD IT ROUGH?
WE ALL HAD MUCH, THOUGH NEVER QUITE ENOUGH, AND END OUR DAYS TIPPED INTO PITS OF LIME.
TLE FISH HOTEL
DEAR FRIENDS, IN ME YOU SEE YOUR OWN DEMISE. YOUR CLIMB WILL ONLY LEAD TO THIS TRAP DOOR...
...AND TO THIS DROP, WHERE I HAVE GONE BEFORE, THEN WE WHO GATHERED WEALTH WILL GATHER FLIES.
IN ME YOU SEE HOW YOUR DECLINE BEGINS, SO PRAY GOD HE FORGIVES US ALL OUR SINS.
THE GIRLS WHO ADVERTISE THEIR CUNNY, THE MEN WHO'LL SCREW THEM OR ELSE SAVE THEM.
PIMPS WHO'LL RELIEVE THEM OF THEIR MONEY, AND OPIUM-SELLERS WHO'LL DEPRAVE THEM.

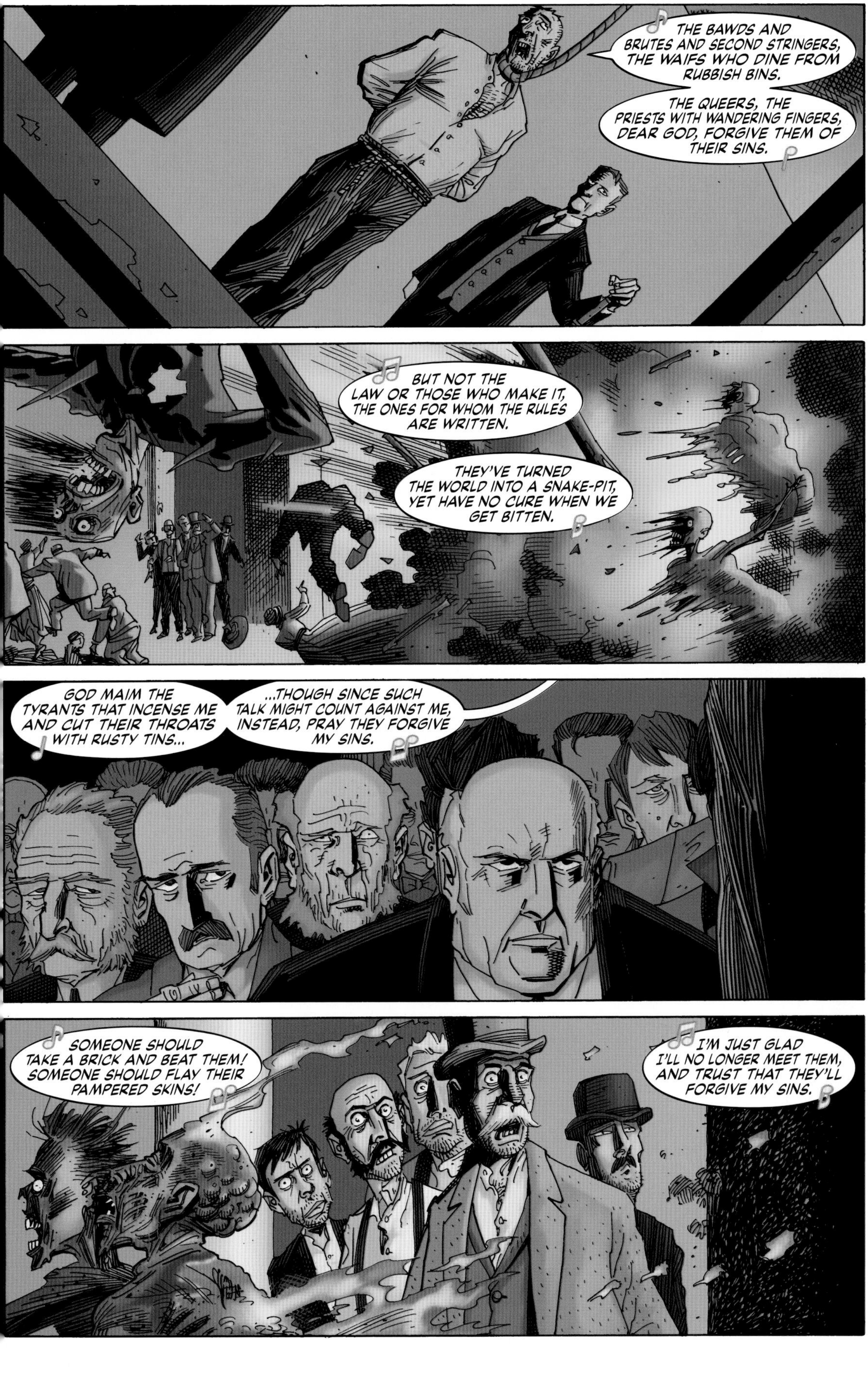
THE BAWDS AND BRUTES AND SECOND STRINGERS, THE WAIFS WHO DINE FROM RUBBISH BINS.
THE QUEERS, THE PRIESTS WITH WANDERING FINGERS, DEAR GOD, FORGIVE THEM OF THEIR SINS.
BUT NOT THE LAW OR THOSE WHO MAKE IT, THE ONES FOR WHOM THE RULES ARE WRITTEN.
THEY'VE TURNED THE WORLD INTO A SNAKE-PIT, YET HAVE NO CURE WHEN WE GET BITTEN.
GOD MAIM THE TYRANTS THAT INCENSE ME AND CUT THEIR THROATS WITH RUSTY TINS...
...THOUGH SINCE SUCH TALK MIGHT COUNT AGAINST ME, INSTEAD, PRAY THEY FORGIVE MY SINS.
SOMEONE SHOULD TAKE A BRICK AND BEAT THEM! SOMEONE SHOULD FLAY THEIR PAMPERED SKINS!
I'M JUST GLAD I'LL NO LONGER MEET THEM, AND TRUST THAT THEY'LL FORGIVE MY SINS.

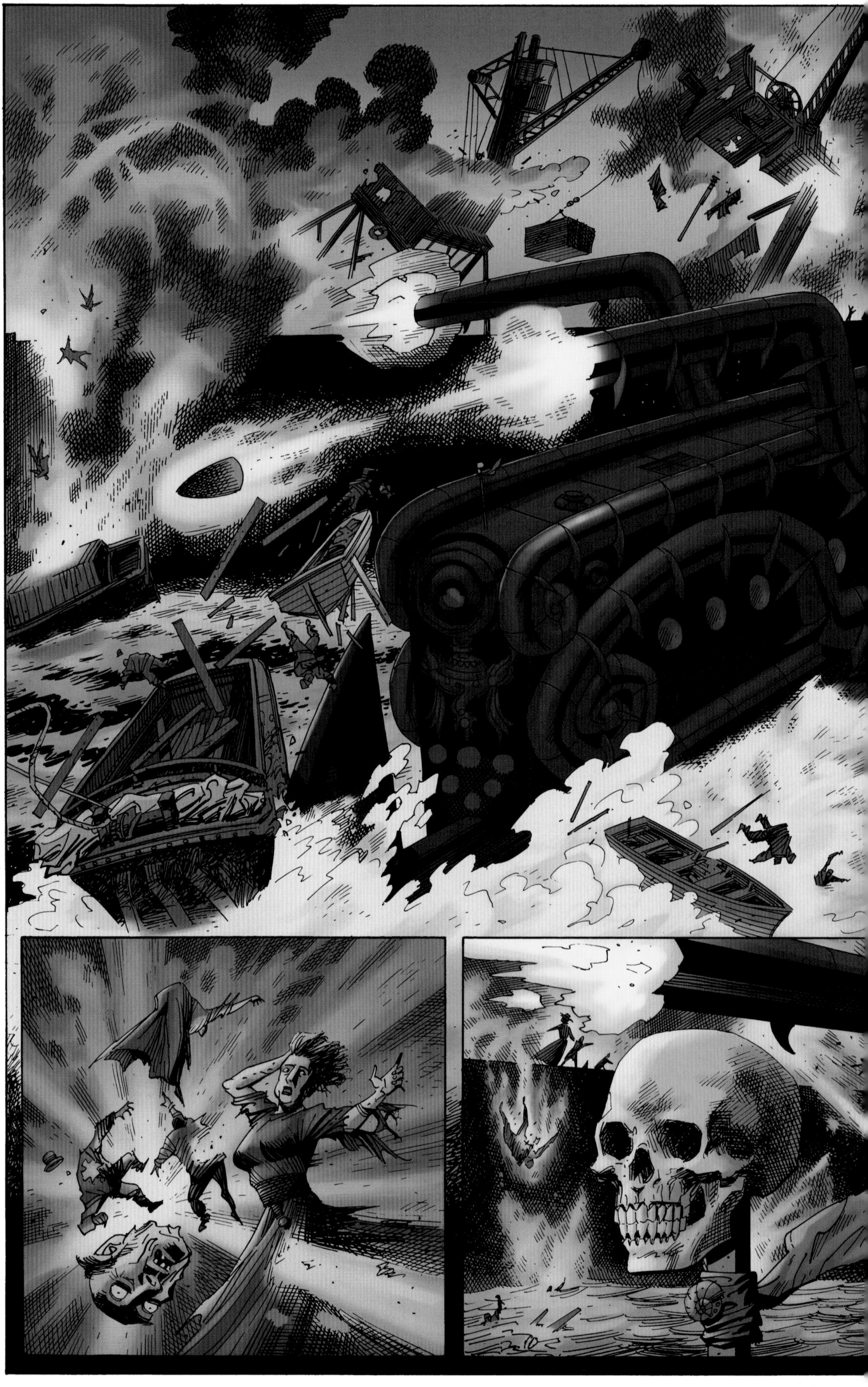

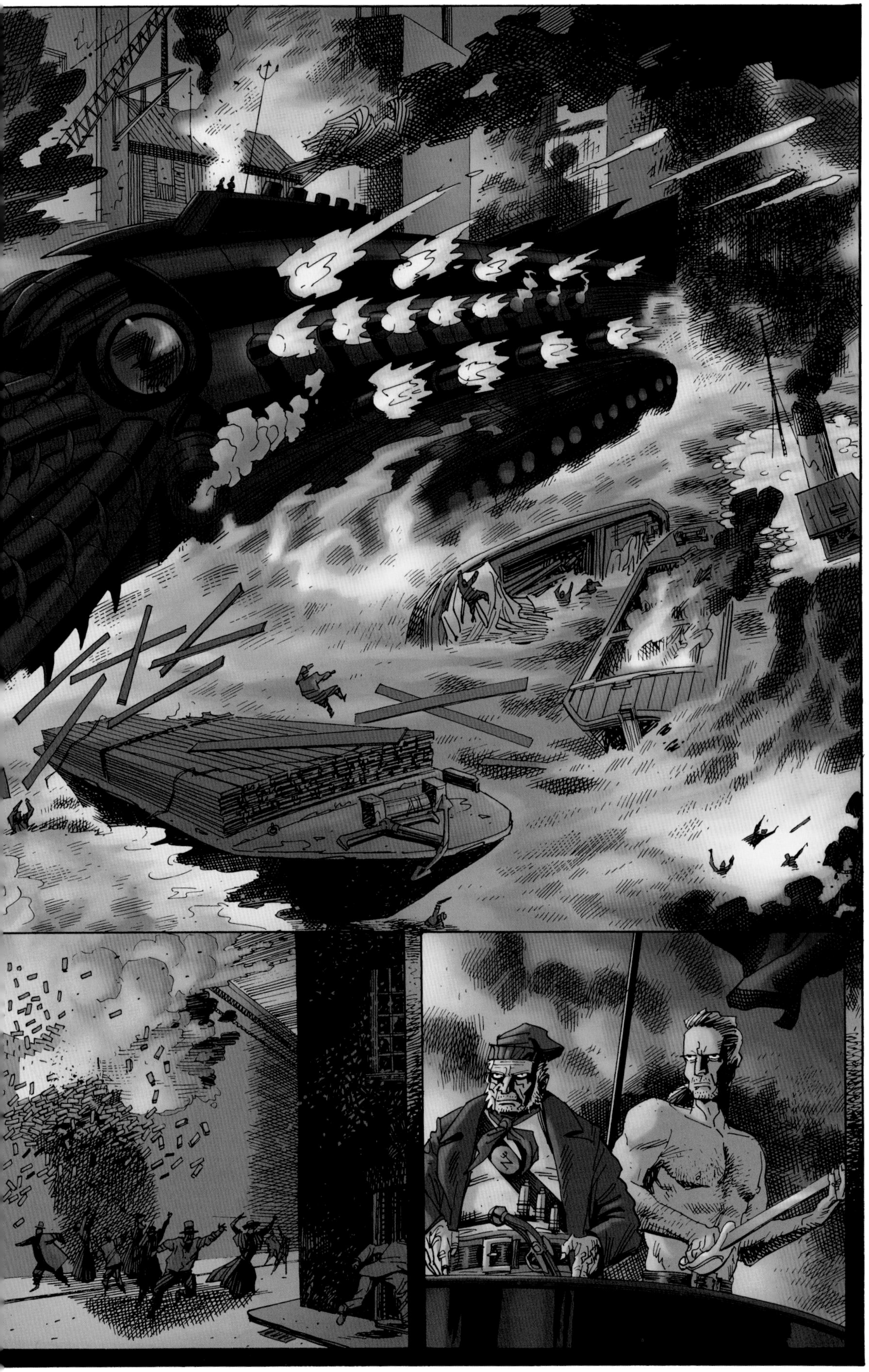

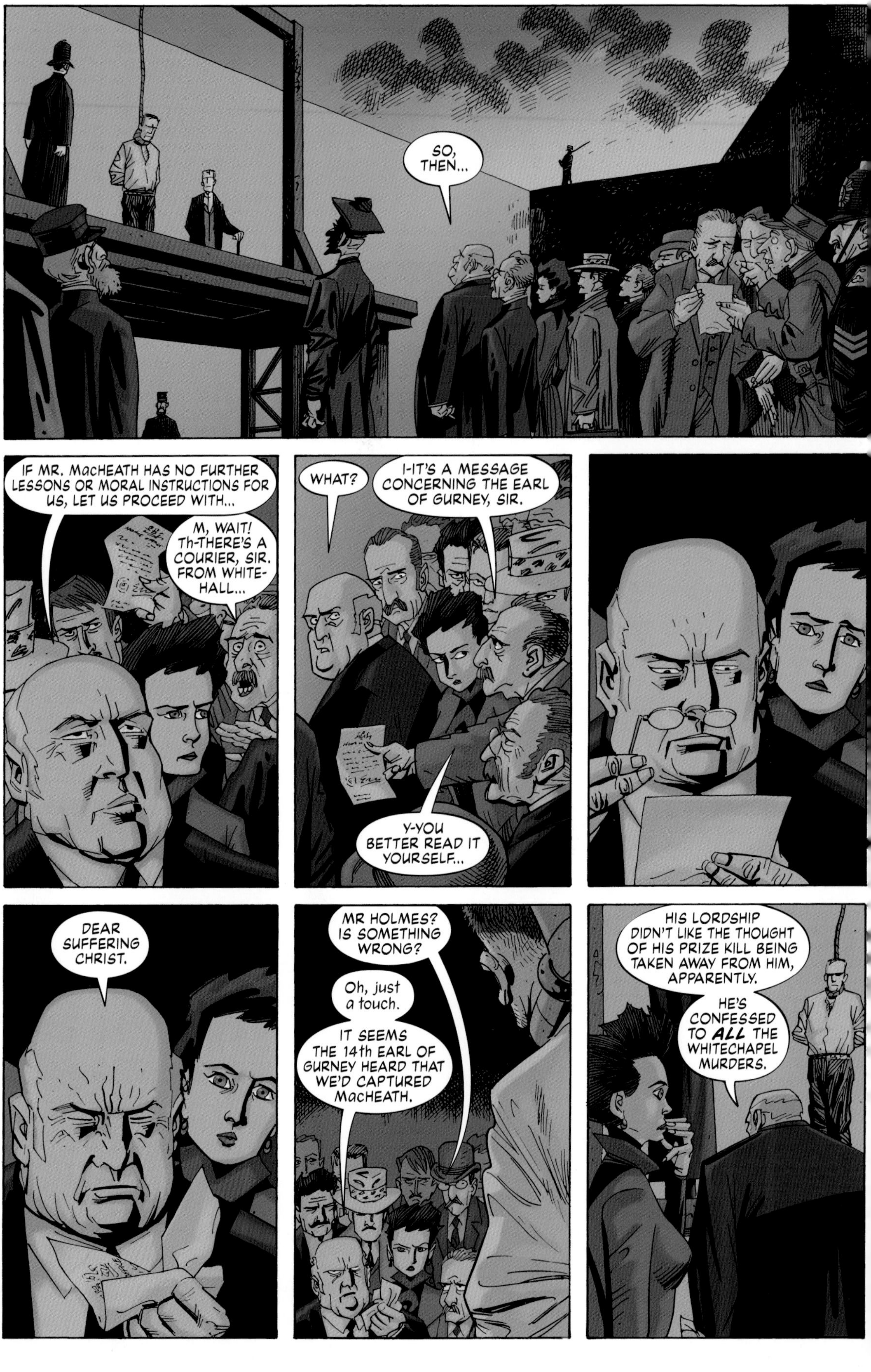
SO, THEN...
IF MR. MacHEATH HAS NO FURTHER LESSONS OR MORAL INSTRUCTIONS FOR US, LET US PROCEED WITH...
M, WAIT! Th-THERE'S A COURIER, SIR. FROM WHITE-HALL...
WHAT?
I-IT'S A MESSAGE CONCERNING THE EARL OF GURNEY, SIR.
Y-YOU BETTER READ IT YOURSELF...
DEAR SUFFERING CHRIST.
MR HOLMES? IS SOMETHING WRONG?
Oh, just a touch.
IT SEEMS THE 14th EARL OF GURNEY HEARD THAT WE'D CAPTURED MacHEATH.
HIS LORDSHIP DIDN'T LIKE THE THOUGHT OF HIS PRIZE KILL BEING TAKEN AWAY FROM HIM, APPARENTLY.
HE'S CONFESSED TO ALL THE WHITECHAPEL MURDERS.

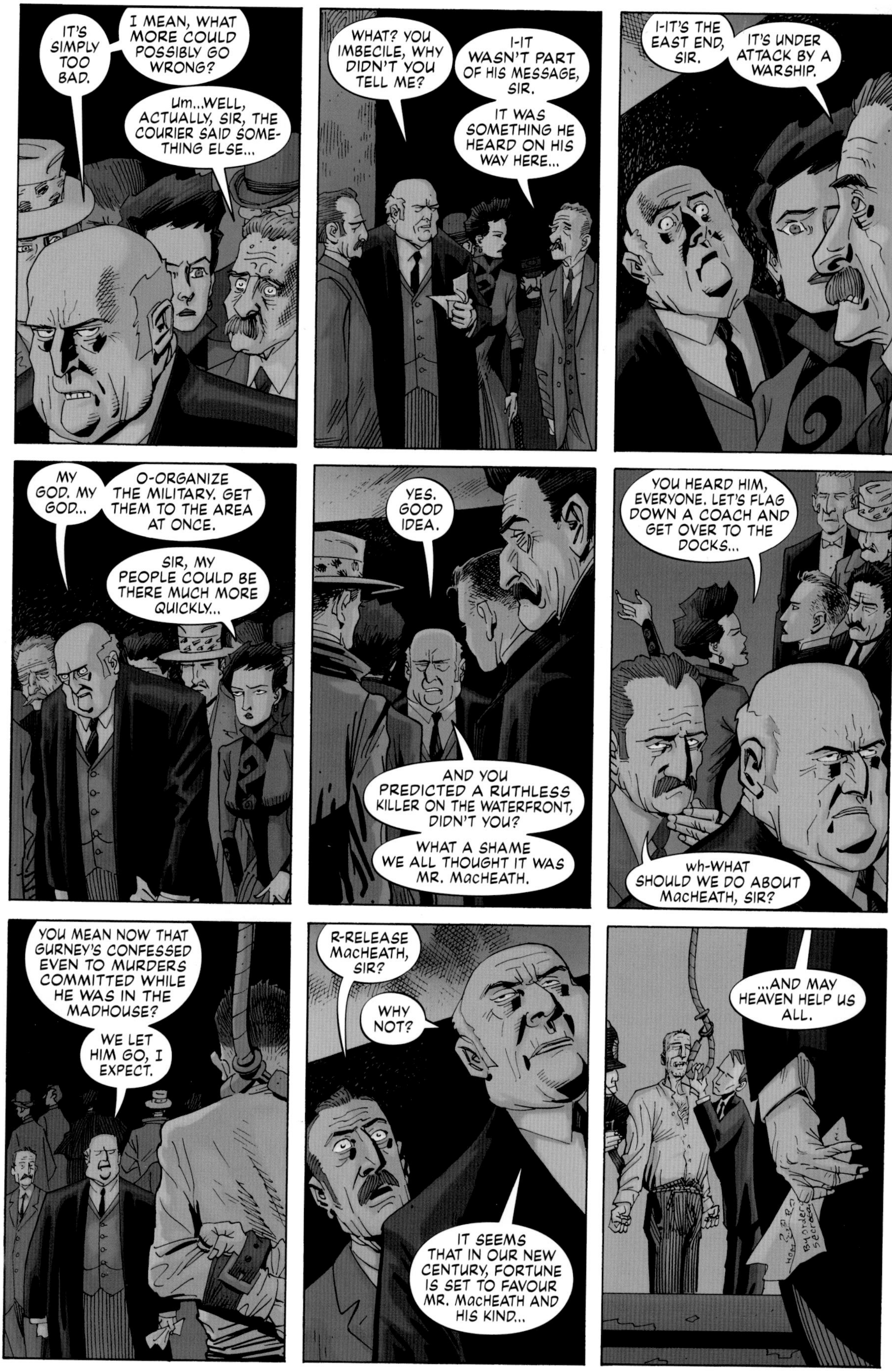
IT'S SIMPLY TOO BAD.
I MEAN, WHAT MORE COULD POSSIBLY GO WRONG?
Um...WELL, ACTUALLY, SIR, THE COURIER SAID SOME-THING ELSE...
WHAT? YOU IMBECILE, WHY DIDN'T YOU TELL ME?
I-IT WASN'T PART OF HIS MESSAGE, SIR.
IT WAS SOMETHING HE HEARD ON HIS WAY HERE...
I-IT'S THE EAST END, SIR.
IT'S UNDER ATTACK BY A WARSHIP.
MY GOD. MY GOD...
O-ORGANIZE THE MILITARY. GET THEM TO THE AREA AT ONCE.
SIR, MY PEOPLE COULD BE THERE MUCH MORE QUICKLY...
YES. GOOD IDEA.
AND YOU PREDICTED A RUTHLESS KILLER ON THE WATERFRONT, DIDN'T YOU?
WHAT A SHAME WE ALL THOUGHT IT WAS MR. MacHEATH.
YOU HEARD HIM, EVERYONE. LET'S FLAG DOWN A COACH AND GET OVER TO THE DOCKS...
wh-WHAT SHOULD WE DO ABOUT MacHEATH, SIR?
YOU MEAN NOW THAT GURNEY'S CONFESSED EVEN TO MURDERS COMMITTED WHILE HE WAS IN THE MADHOUSE?
WE LET HIM GO, I EXPECT.
R-RELEASE MacHEATH, SIR?
WHY NOT?
IT SEEMS THAT IN OUR NEW CENTURY, FORTUNE IS SET TO FAVOUR MR. MacHEATH AND HIS KIND...
...AND MAY HEAVEN HELP US ALL.

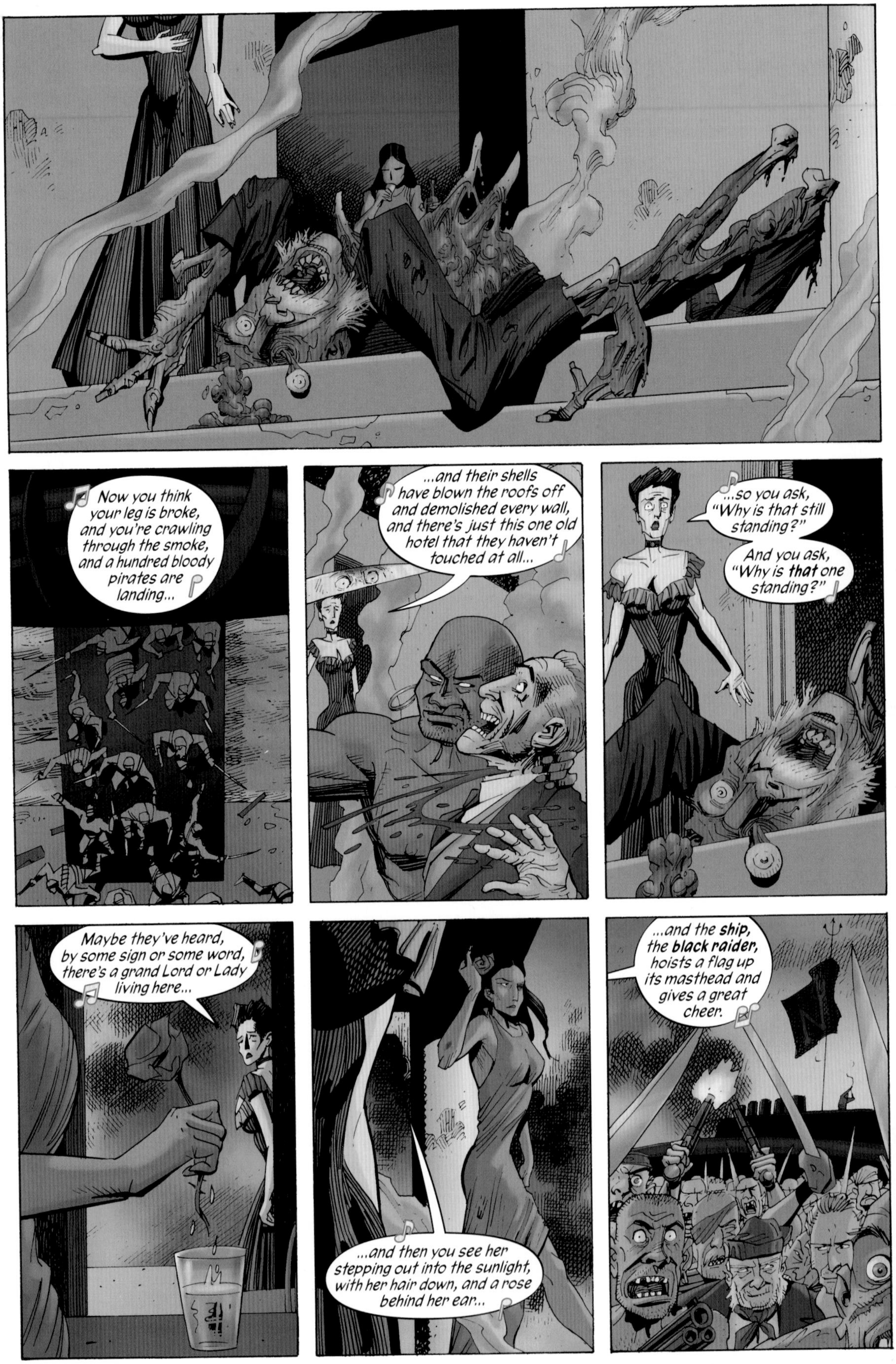
Now you think your leg is broke, and you're crawling through the smoke, and a hundred bloody pirates are landing...
...and their shells have blown the roofs off and demolished every wall, and there's just this one old hotel that they haven't touched at all...
...so you ask, "Why is that still standing?"
And you ask, "Why is **that** one standing?"
Maybe they've heard, by some sign or some word, there's a grand Lord or Lady living here...
...and then you see her stepping out into the sunlight, with her hair down, and a rose behind her ear...
...and the **ship**, the **black raider**, hoists a flag up its masthead and gives a great cheer.

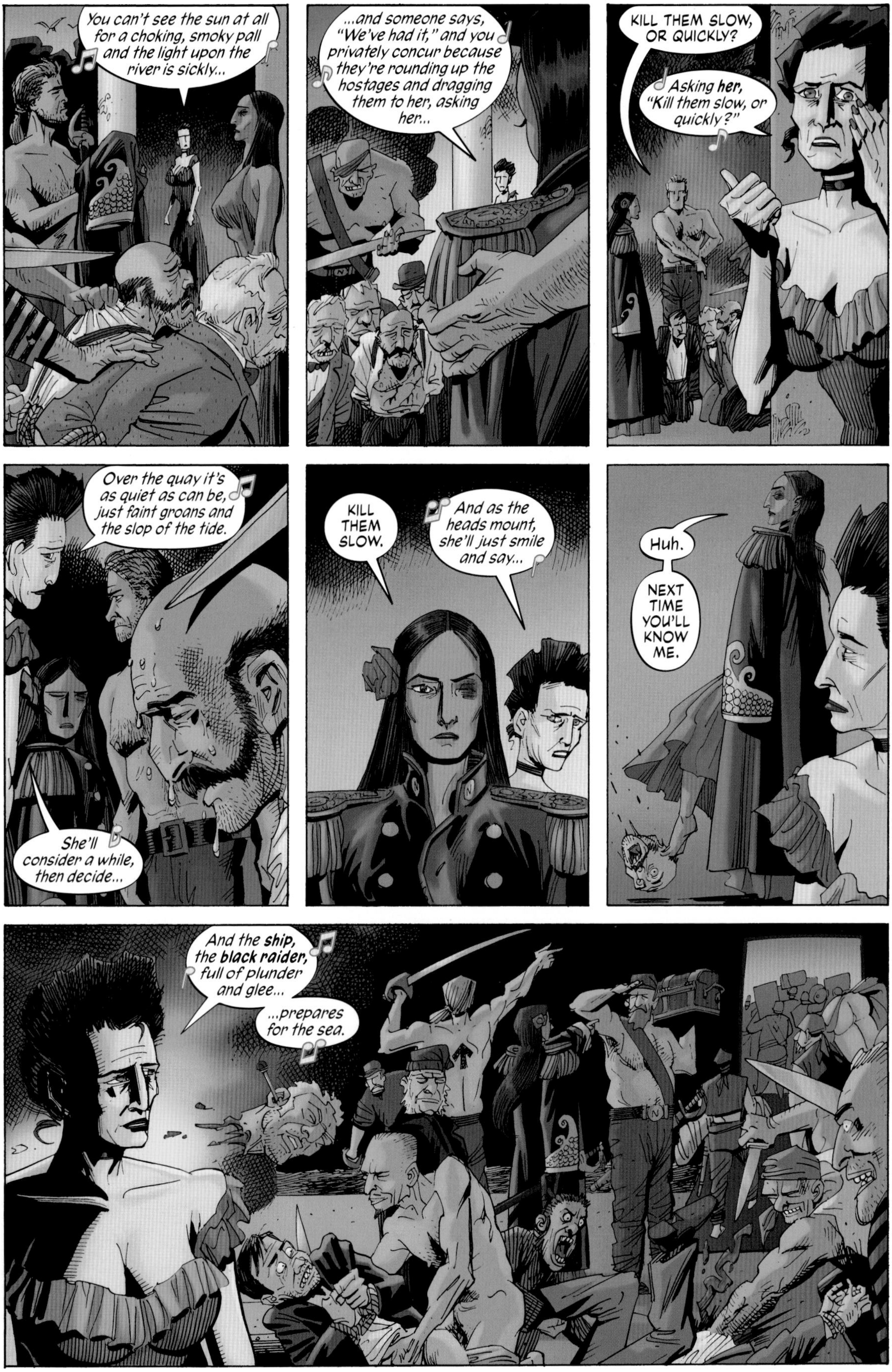
You can't see the sun at all for a choking, smoky pall and the light upon the river is sickly...
...and someone says, "We've had it," and you privately concur because they're rounding up the hostages and dragging them to her, asking her...
KILL THEM SLOW, OR QUICKLY?
Asking **her,** "Kill them slow, or quickly?"
Over the quay it's as quiet as can be, just faint groans and the slop of the tide.
She'll consider a while, then decide...
KILL THEM SLOW.
And as the heads mount, she'll just smile and say...
Huh.
NEXT TIME YOU'LL KNOW ME.
And the **ship,** the **black raider,** full of plunder and glee...
...prepares for the sea.

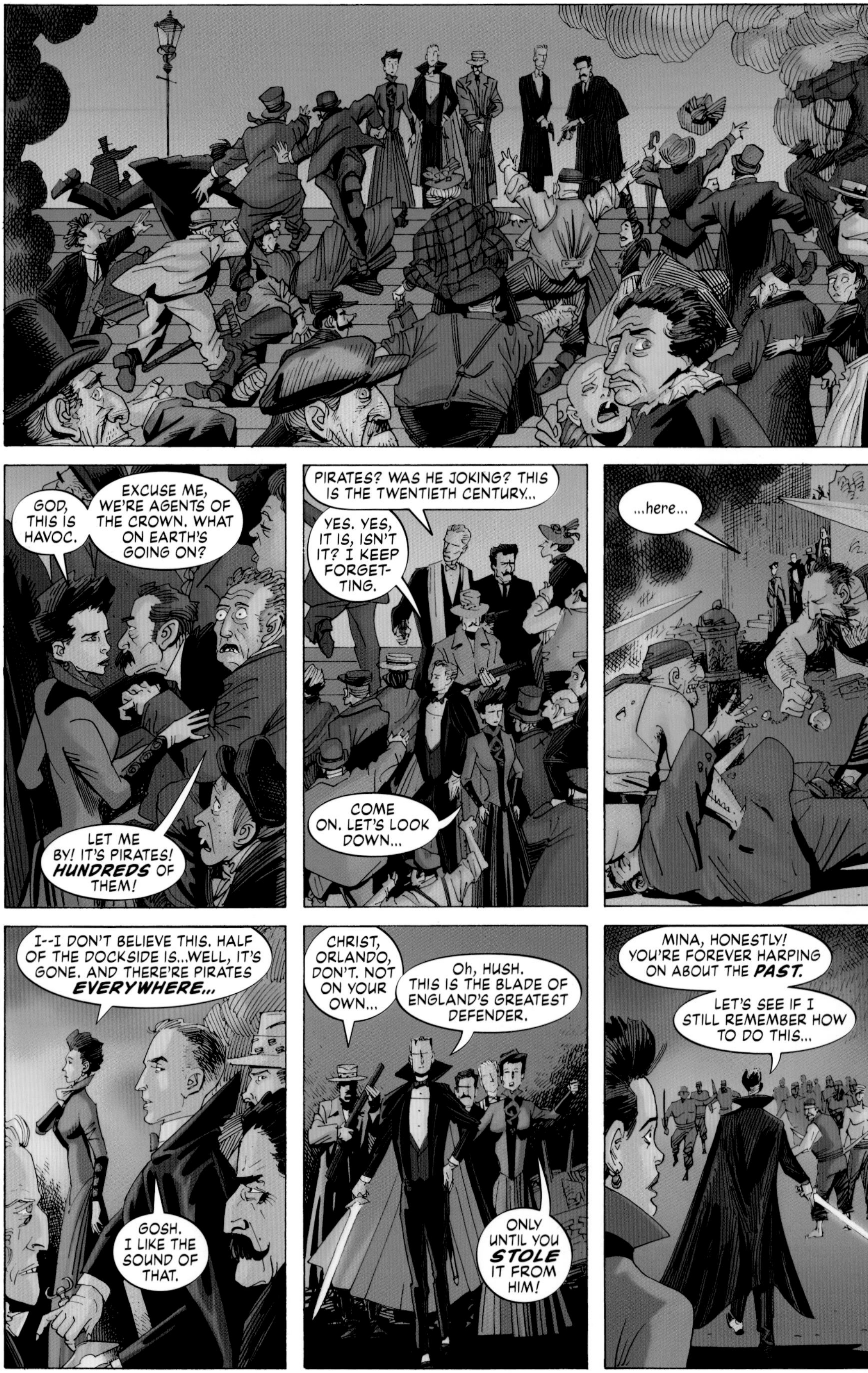

GOD, THIS IS HAVOC.
EXCUSE ME, WE'RE AGENTS OF THE CROWN. WHAT ON EARTH'S GOING ON?
LET ME BY! IT'S PIRATES! **HUNDREDS** OF THEM!
PIRATES? WAS HE JOKING? THIS IS THE TWENTIETH CENTURY...
YES. YES, IT IS, ISN'T IT? I KEEP FORGET-TING.
COME ON. LET'S LOOK DOWN...
...here...
I--I DON'T BELIEVE THIS. HALF OF THE DOCKSIDE IS...WELL, IT'S GONE. AND THERE'RE PIRATES **EVERYWHERE...**
GOSH. I LIKE THE SOUND OF THAT.
CHRIST, ORLANDO, DON'T. NOT ON YOUR OWN...
Oh, HUSH. THIS IS THE BLADE OF ENGLAND'S GREATEST DEFENDER.
ONLY UNTIL YOU **STOLE** IT FROM HIM!
MINA, HONESTLY! YOU'RE FOREVER HARPING ON ABOUT THE **PAST.**
LET'S SEE IF I STILL REMEMBER HOW TO DO THIS...

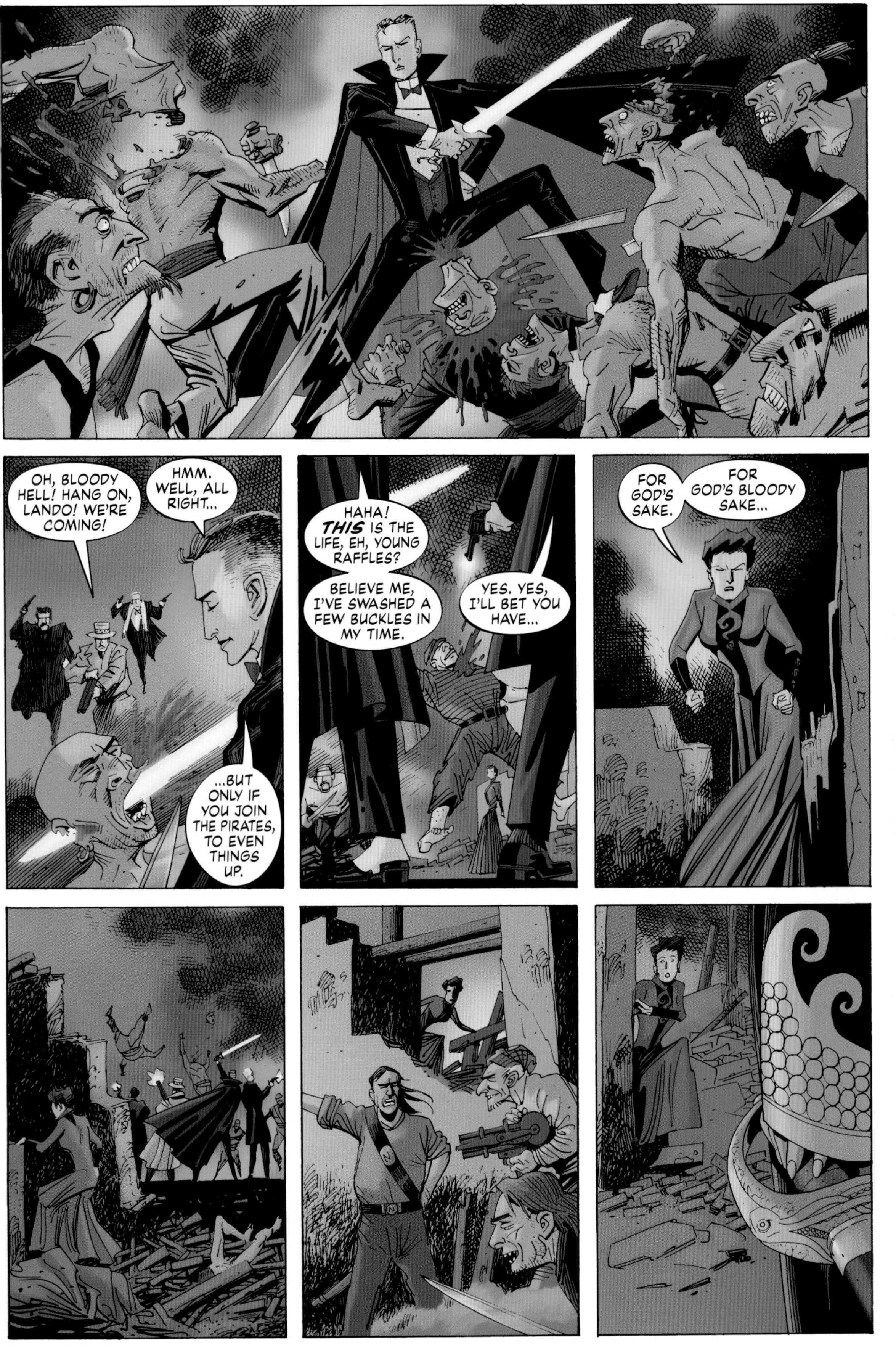
OH, BLOODY HELL! HANG ON, LANDO! WE'RE COMING!
HMM. WELL, ALL RIGHT...
...BUT ONLY IF YOU JOIN THE PIRATES, TO EVEN THINGS UP.
HAHA! THIS IS THE LIFE, EH, YOUNG RAFFLES?
BELIEVE ME, I'VE SWASHED A FEW BUCKLES IN MY TIME.
YES. YES, I'LL BET YOU HAVE...
FOR GOD'S SAKE.
FOR GOD'S BLOODY SAKE...

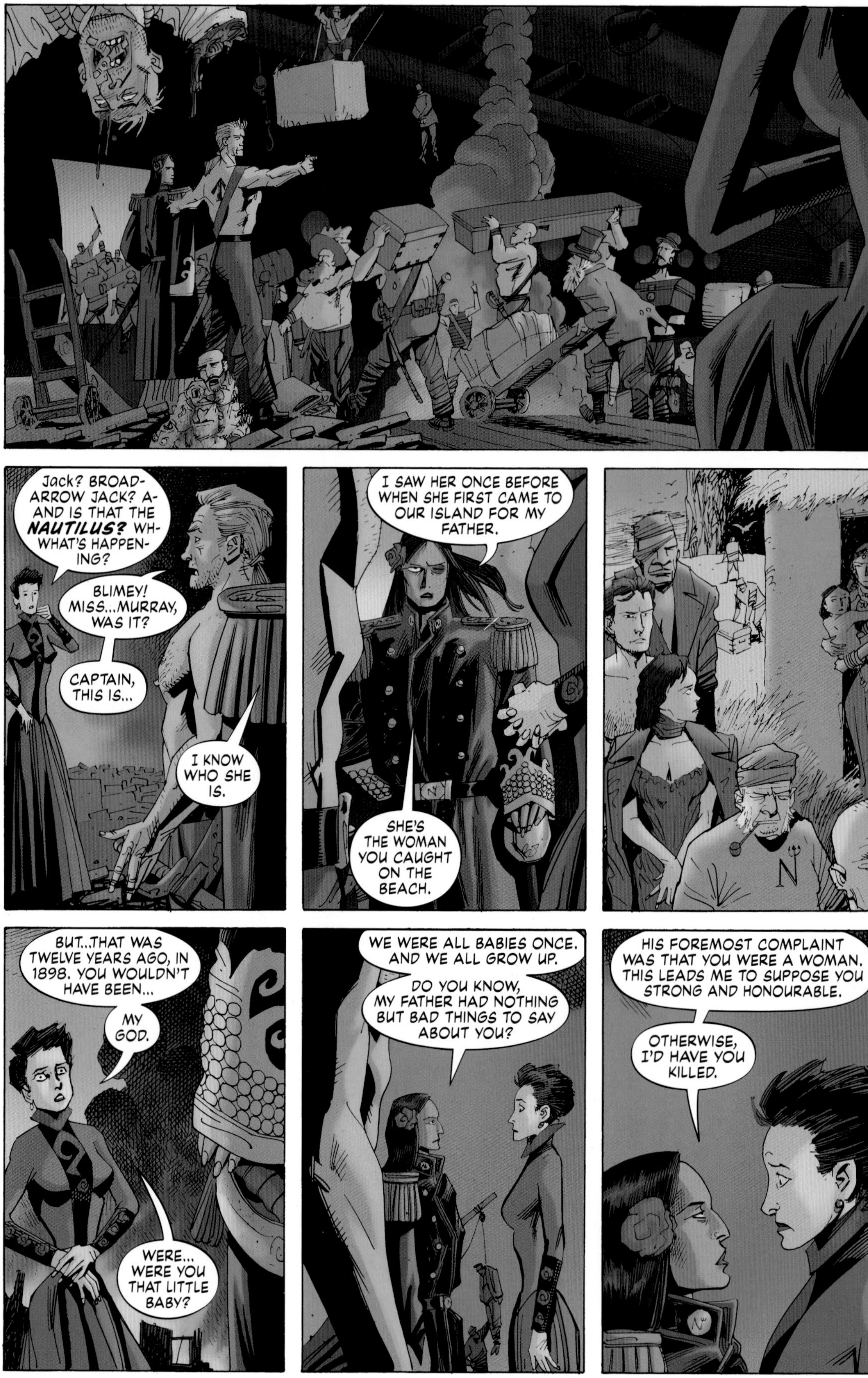
Jack? BROAD-ARROW JACK? A-AND IS THAT THE ***NAUTILUS?*** WH-WHAT'S HAPPEN-ING?
BLIMEY! MISS...MURRAY, WAS IT?
CAPTAIN, THIS IS...
I KNOW WHO SHE IS.
I SAW HER ONCE BEFORE WHEN SHE FIRST CAME TO OUR ISLAND FOR MY FATHER.
SHE'S THE WOMAN YOU CAUGHT ON THE BEACH.
BUT...THAT WAS TWELVE YEARS AGO, IN 1898. YOU WOULDN'T HAVE BEEN...
MY GOD.
WERE... WERE YOU THAT LITTLE BABY?
WE WERE ALL BABIES ONCE. AND WE ALL GROW UP.
DO YOU KNOW, MY FATHER HAD NOTHING BUT BAD THINGS TO SAY ABOUT YOU?
HIS FOREMOST COMPLAINT WAS THAT YOU WERE A WOMAN. THIS LEADS ME TO SUPPOSE YOU STRONG AND HONOURABLE.
OTHERWISE, I'D HAVE YOU KILLED.

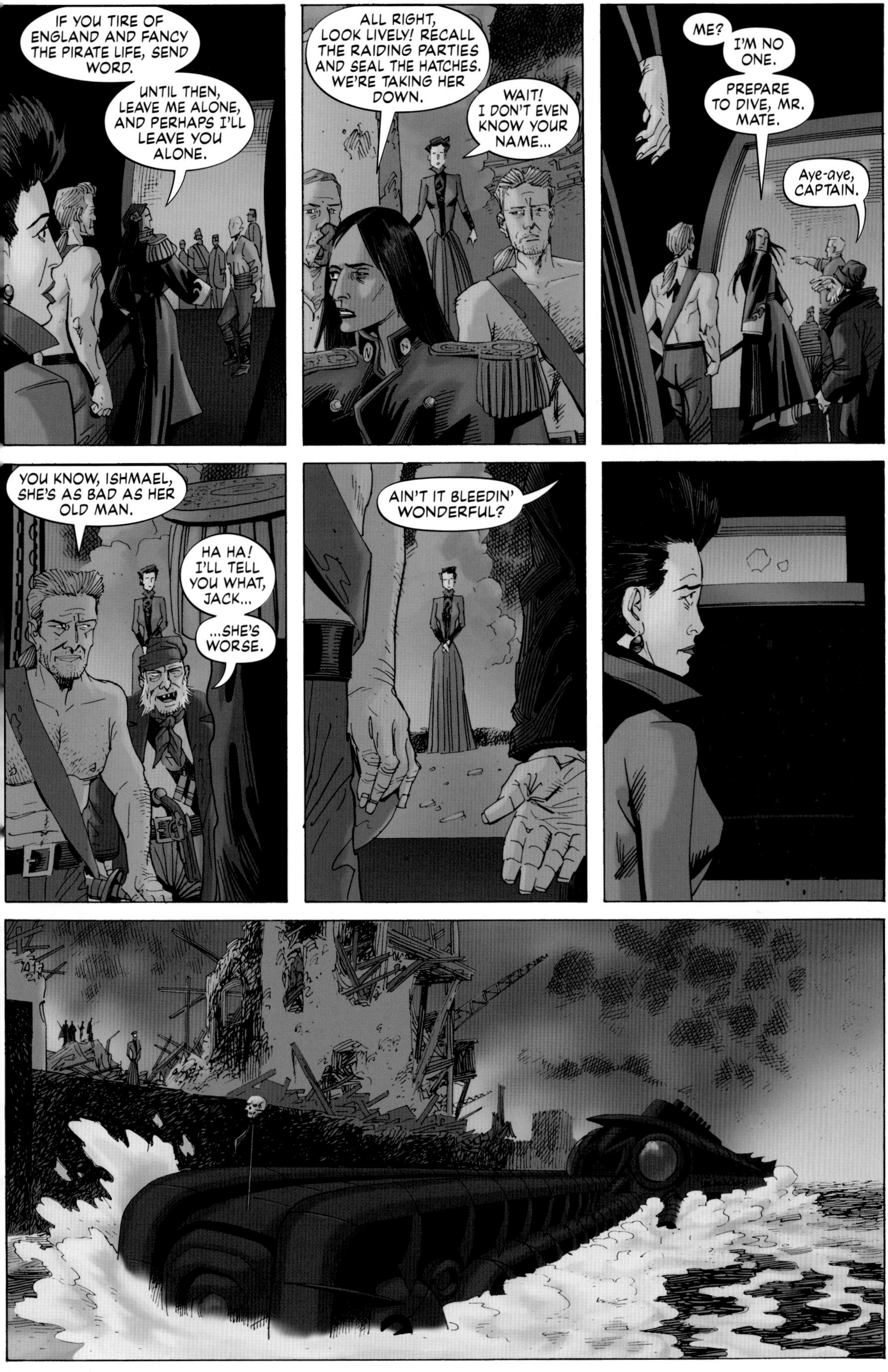
IF YOU TIRE OF ENGLAND AND FANCY THE PIRATE LIFE, SEND WORD.
UNTIL THEN, LEAVE ME ALONE, AND PERHAPS I'LL LEAVE YOU ALONE.
ALL RIGHT, LOOK LIVELY! RECALL THE RAIDING PARTIES AND SEAL THE HATCHES. WE'RE TAKING HER DOWN.
WAIT! I DON'T EVEN KNOW YOUR NAME...
ME?
I'M NO ONE.
PREPARE TO DIVE, MR. MATE.
Aye-aye, CAPTAIN.
YOU KNOW, ISHMAEL, SHE'S AS BAD AS HER OLD MAN.
HA HA! I'LL TELL YOU WHAT, JACK...
...SHE'S WORSE.
AIN'T IT BLEEDIN' WONDERFUL?

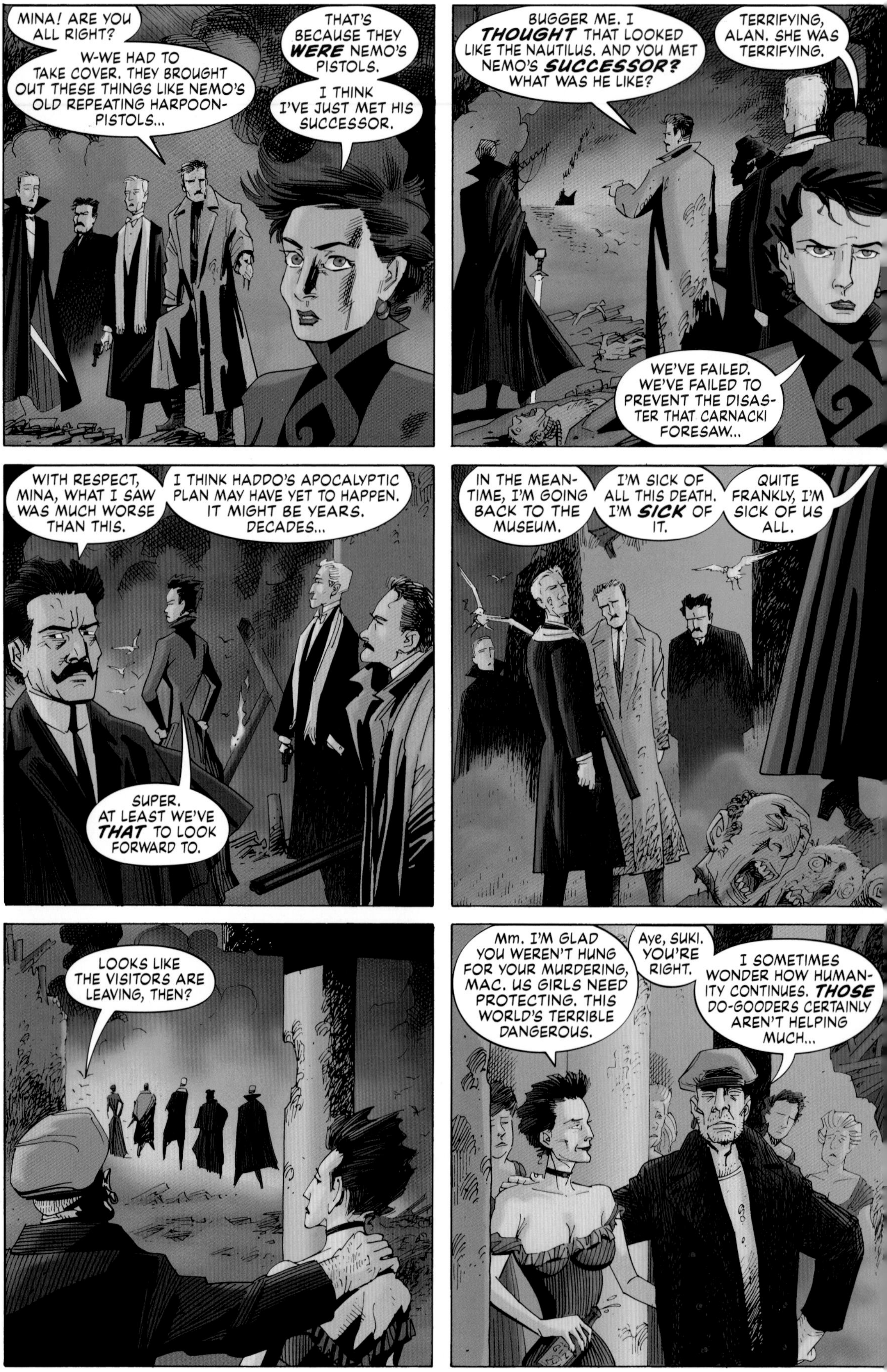
MINA! ARE YOU ALL RIGHT?
W-WE HAD TO TAKE COVER. THEY BROUGHT OUT THESE THINGS LIKE NEMO'S OLD REPEATING HARPOON-PISTOLS...
THAT'S BECAUSE THEY WERE NEMO'S PISTOLS.
I THINK I'VE JUST MET HIS SUCCESSOR.
BUGGER ME. I THOUGHT THAT LOOKED LIKE THE NAUTILUS. AND YOU MET NEMO'S SUCCESSOR? WHAT WAS HE LIKE?
TERRIFYING, ALAN. SHE WAS TERRIFYING.
WE'VE FAILED. WE'VE FAILED TO PREVENT THE DISASTER THAT CARNACKI FORESAW...
WITH RESPECT, MINA, WHAT I SAW WAS MUCH WORSE THAN THIS.
I THINK HADDO'S APOCALYPTIC PLAN MAY HAVE YET TO HAPPEN. IT MIGHT BE YEARS. DECADES...
SUPER. AT LEAST WE'VE THAT TO LOOK FORWARD TO.
IN THE MEANTIME, I'M GOING BACK TO THE MUSEUM.
I'M SICK OF ALL THIS DEATH. I'M SICK OF IT.
QUITE FRANKLY, I'M SICK OF US ALL.
LOOKS LIKE THE VISITORS ARE LEAVING, THEN?
Mm. I'M GLAD YOU WEREN'T HUNG FOR YOUR MURDERING, MAC. US GIRLS NEED PROTECTING. THIS WORLD'S TERRIBLE DANGEROUS.
Aye, SUKI. YOU'RE RIGHT.
I SOMETIMES WONDER HOW HUMANITY CONTINUES. THOSE DO-GOODERS CERTAINLY AREN'T HELPING MUCH...

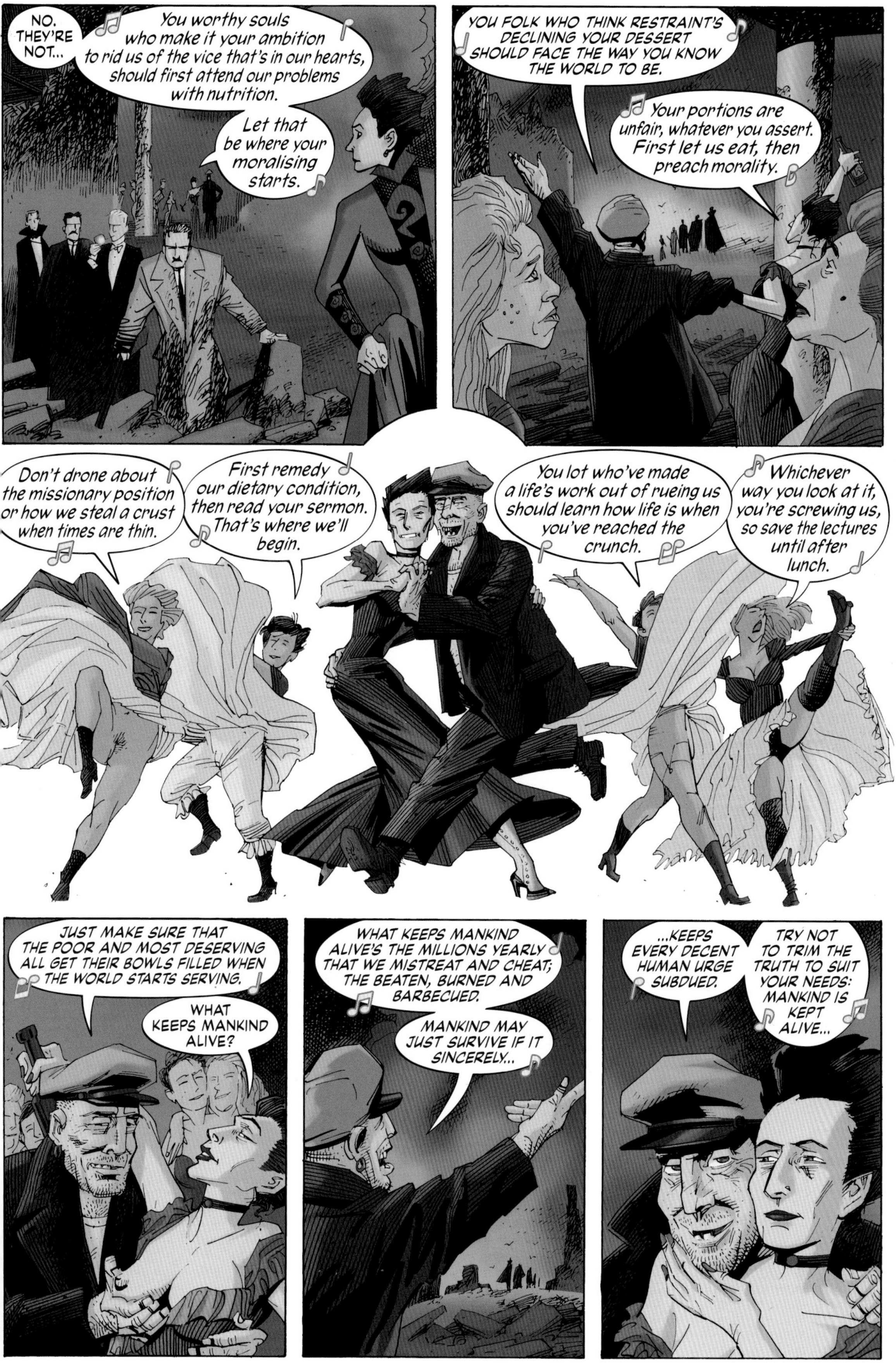
NO. THEY'RE NOT...
You worthy souls who make it your ambition to rid us of the vice that's in our hearts, should first attend our problems with nutrition.
Let that be where your moralising starts.
YOU FOLK WHO THINK RESTRAINT'S DECLINING YOUR DESSERT SHOULD FACE THE WAY YOU KNOW THE WORLD TO BE.
Your portions are unfair, whatever you assert. First let us eat, then preach morality.
Don't drone about the missionary position or how we steal a crust when times are thin.
First remedy our dietary condition, then read your sermon. That's where we'll begin.
You lot who've made a life's work out of rueing us should learn how life is when you've reached the crunch.
Whichever way you look at it, you're screwing us, so save the lectures until after lunch.
JUST MAKE SURE THAT THE POOR AND MOST DESERVING ALL GET THEIR BOWLS FILLED WHEN THE WORLD STARTS SERVING.
WHAT KEEPS MANKIND ALIVE?
WHAT KEEPS MANKIND ALIVE'S THE MILLIONS YEARLY THAT WE MISTREAT AND CHEAT; THE BEATEN, BURNED AND BARBECUED.
MANKIND MAY JUST SURVIVE IF IT SINCERELY...
...KEEPS EVERY DECENT HUMAN URGE SUBDUED.
TRY NOT TO TRIM THE TRUTH TO SUIT YOUR NEEDS: MANKIND IS KEPT ALIVE...

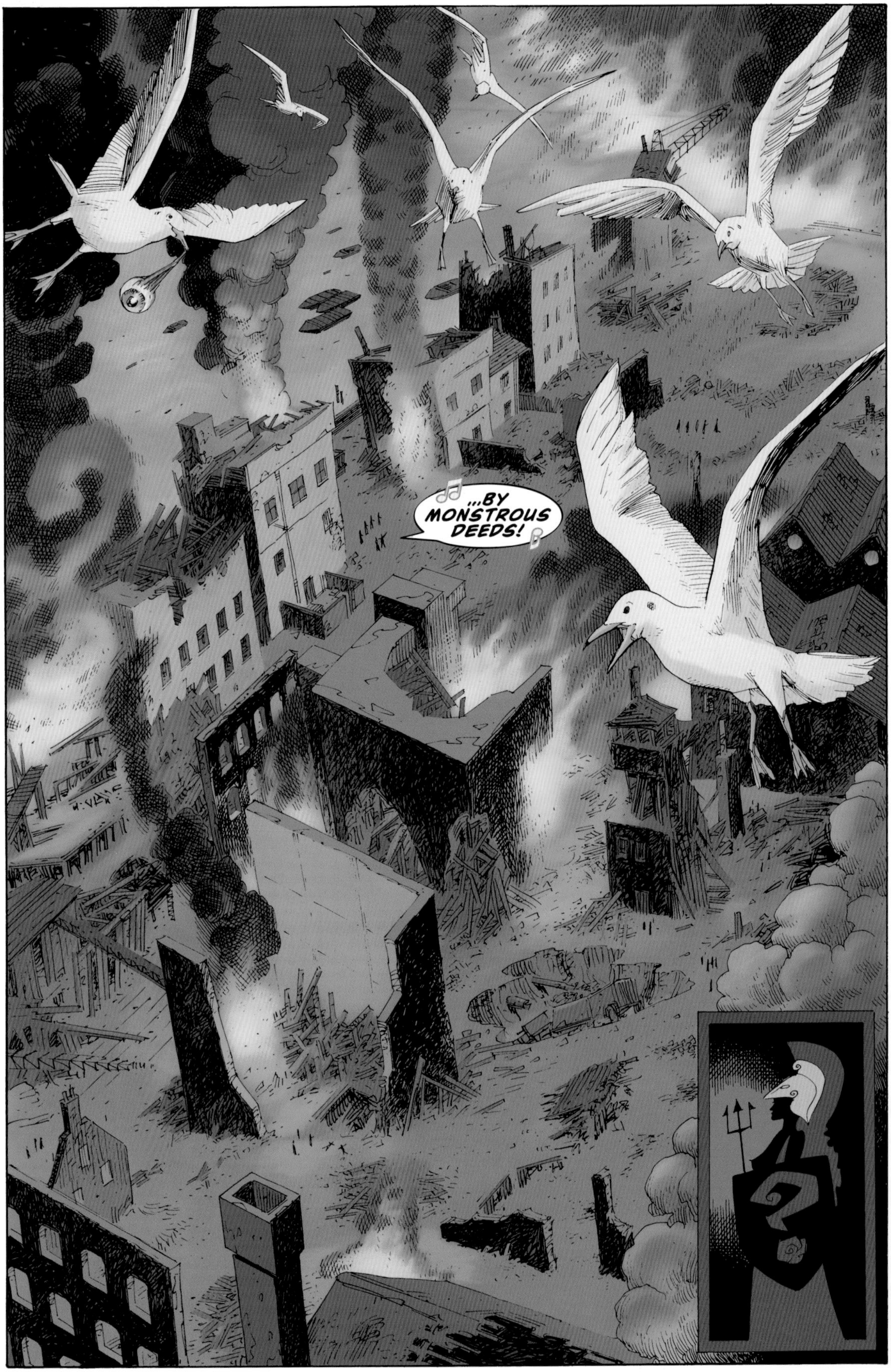
...BY MONSTROUS DEEDS!

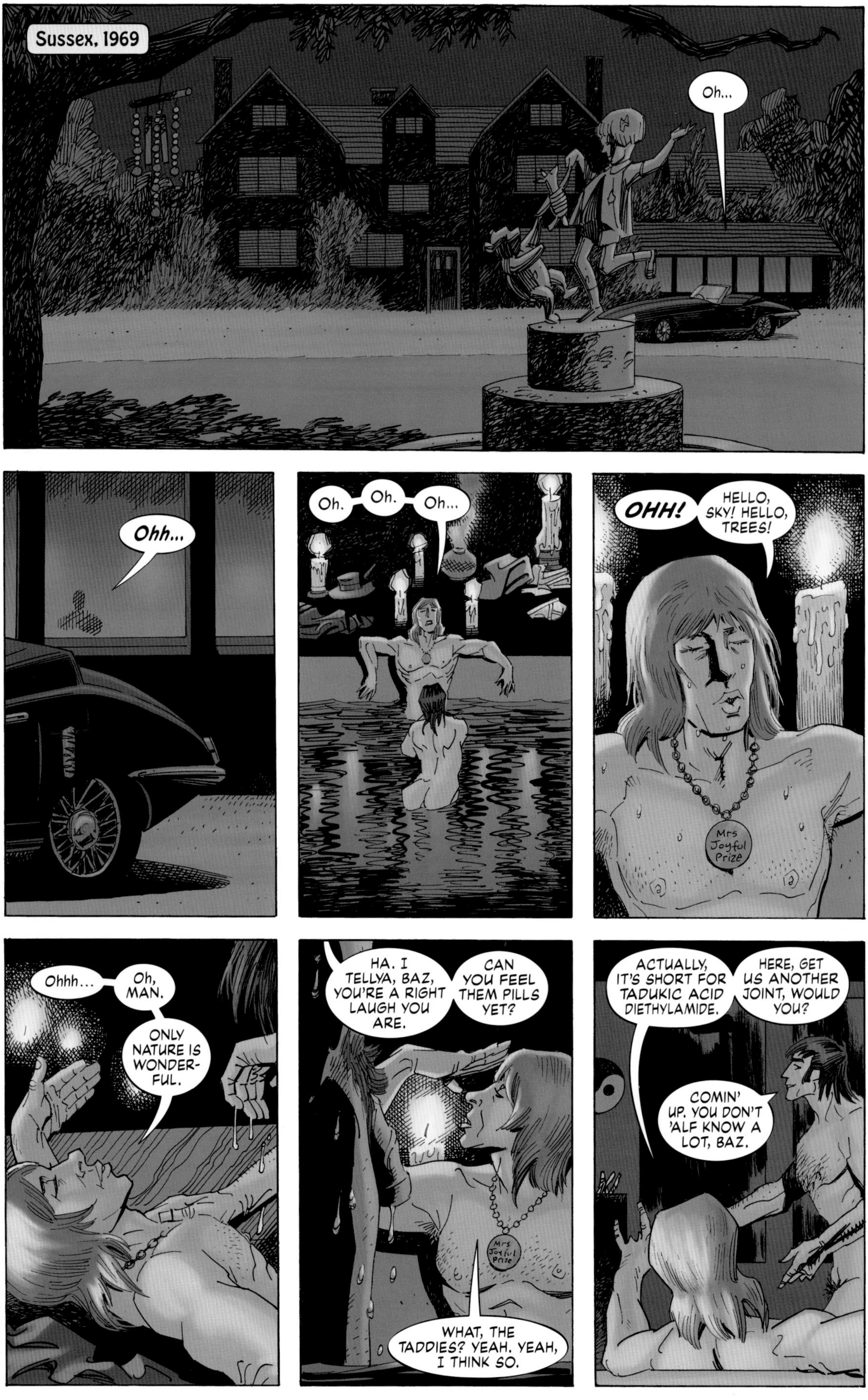
Sussex, 1969
Oh...
Ohh...
Oh.
Oh.
Oh...
OHH!
HELLO, SKY! HELLO, TREES!
Mrs Joyful Prize
Ohhh...
Oh, MAN.
ONLY NATURE IS WONDER-FUL.
HA. I TELLYA, BAZ, YOU'RE A RIGHT LAUGH YOU ARE.
CAN YOU FEEL THEM PILLS YET?
Mrs Joyful Prize
WHAT, THE TADDIES? YEAH. YEAH, I THINK SO.
ACTUALLY, IT'S SHORT FOR TADUKIC ACID DIETHYLAMIDE.
HERE, GET US ANOTHER JOINT, WOULD YOU?
COMIN' UP. YOU DON'T 'ALF KNOW A LOT, BAZ.

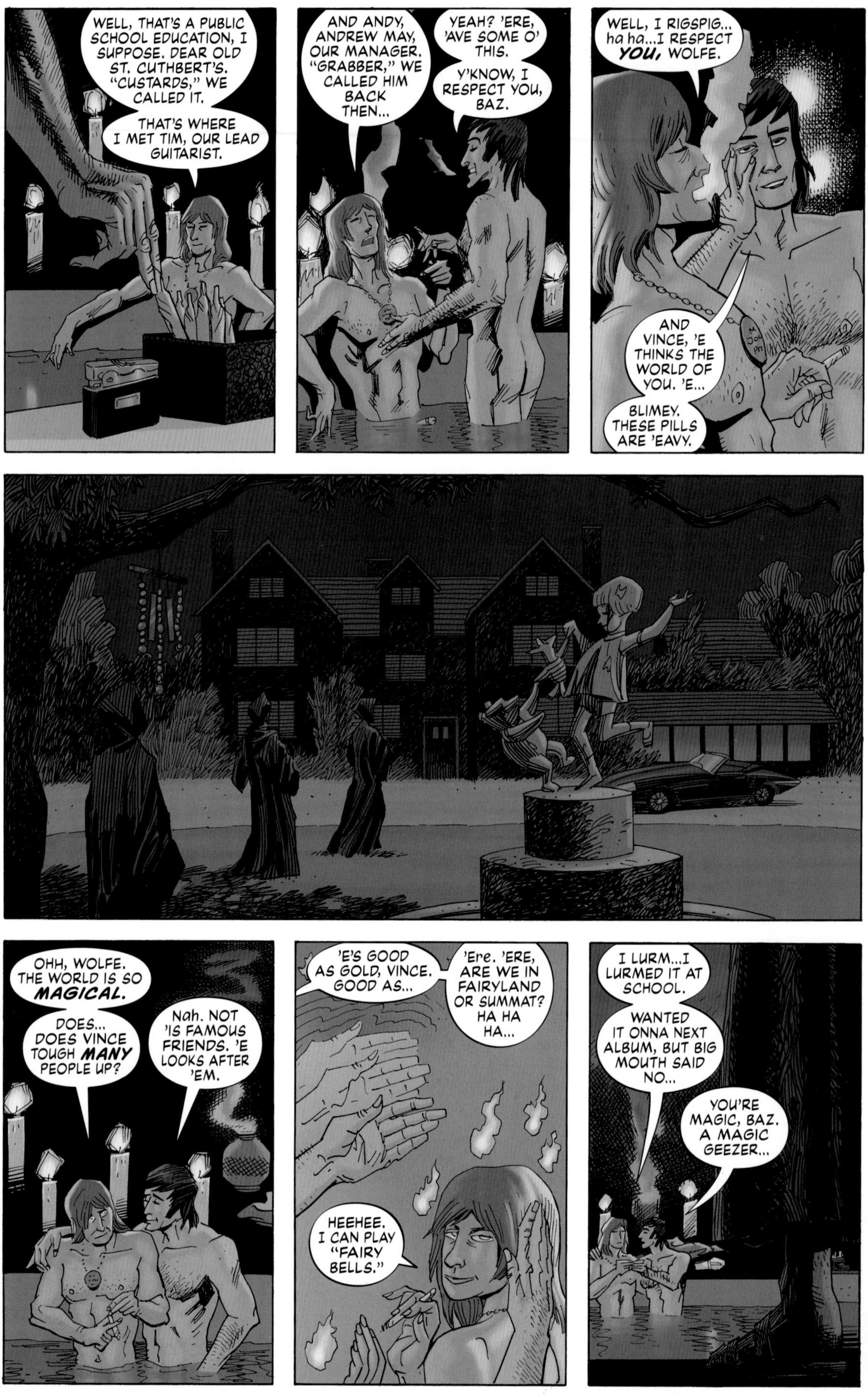
WELL, THAT'S A PUBLIC SCHOOL EDUCATION, I SUPPOSE. DEAR OLD ST. CUTHBERT'S. "CUSTARDS," WE CALLED IT.
THAT'S WHERE I MET TIM, OUR LEAD GUITARIST.
AND ANDY, ANDREW MAY, OUR MANAGER. "GRABBER," WE CALLED HIM BACK THEN...
YEAH? 'ERE, 'AVE SOME O' THIS.
Y'KNOW, I RESPECT YOU, BAZ.
WELL, I RIGSPIG... ha ha...I RESPECT YOU, WOLFE.
AND VINCE, 'E THINKS THE WORLD OF YOU. 'E...
BLIMEY. THESE PILLS ARE 'EAVY.
OHH, WOLFE. THE WORLD IS SO MAGICAL.
DOES... DOES VINCE TOUGH MANY PEOPLE UP?
Nah. NOT 'IS FAMOUS FRIENDS. 'E LOOKS AFTER 'EM.
'E'S GOOD AS GOLD, VINCE. GOOD AS...
'Ere. 'ERE, ARE WE IN FAIRYLAND OR SUMMAT? HA HA HA...
HEEHEE. I CAN PLAY "FAIRY BELLS."
I LURM...I LURMED IT AT SCHOOL.
WANTED IT ONNA NEXT ALBUM, BUT BIG MOUTH SAID NO...
YOU'RE MAGIC, BAZ. A MAGIC GEEZER...

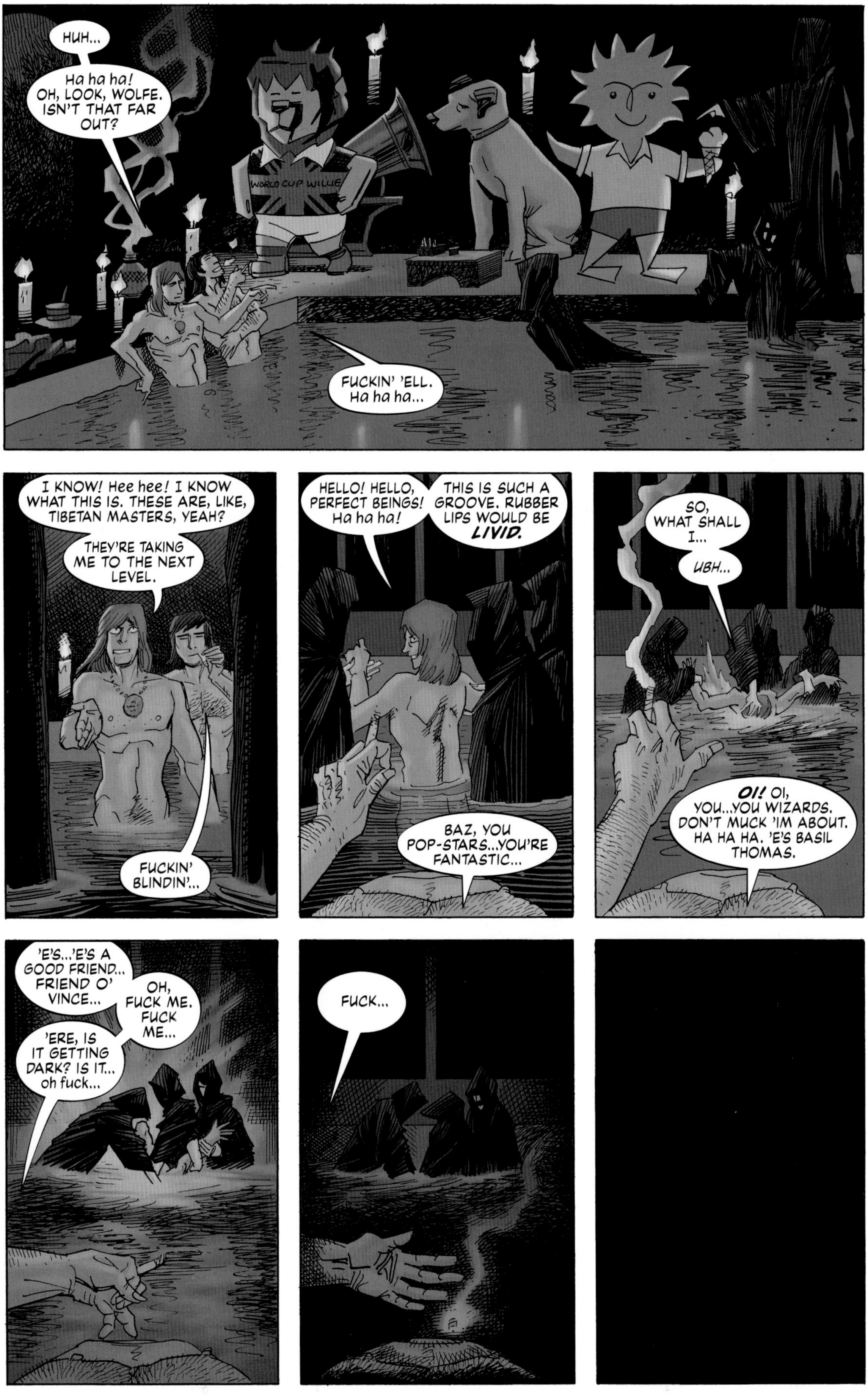
HUH...
Ha ha ha! OH, LOOK, WOLFE. ISN'T THAT FAR OUT?
WORLD CUP WILLIE
FUCKIN' 'ELL. Ha ha ha...
I KNOW! Hee hee! I KNOW WHAT THIS IS. THESE ARE, LIKE, TIBETAN MASTERS, YEAH?
THEY'RE TAKING ME TO THE NEXT LEVEL.
FUCKIN' BLINDIN'...
HELLO! HELLO, PERFECT BEINGS! Ha ha ha!
THIS IS SUCH A GROOVE. RUBBER LIPS WOULD BE LIVID.
BAZ, YOU POP-STARS...YOU'RE FANTASTIC...
SO, WHAT SHALL I...
UBH...
OI! OI, YOU...YOU WIZARDS. DON'T MUCK 'IM ABOUT. HA HA HA. 'E'S BASIL THOMAS.
'E'S...'E'S A GOOD FRIEND... FRIEND O' VINCE...
OH, FUCK ME. FUCK ME...
'ERE, IS IT GETTING DARK? IS IT... oh fuck...
FUCK...

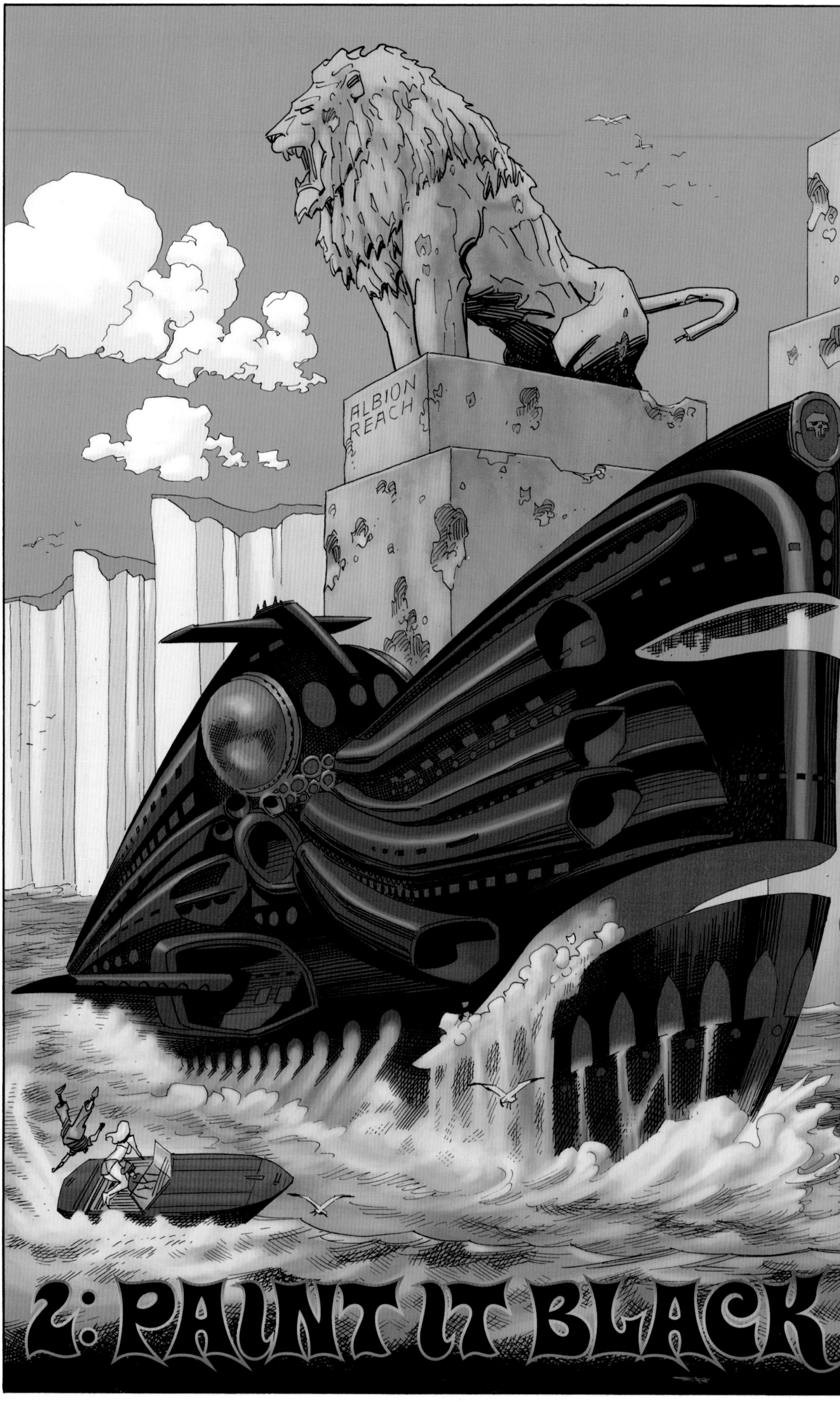
ALBION REACH
2: PAINT IT BLACK

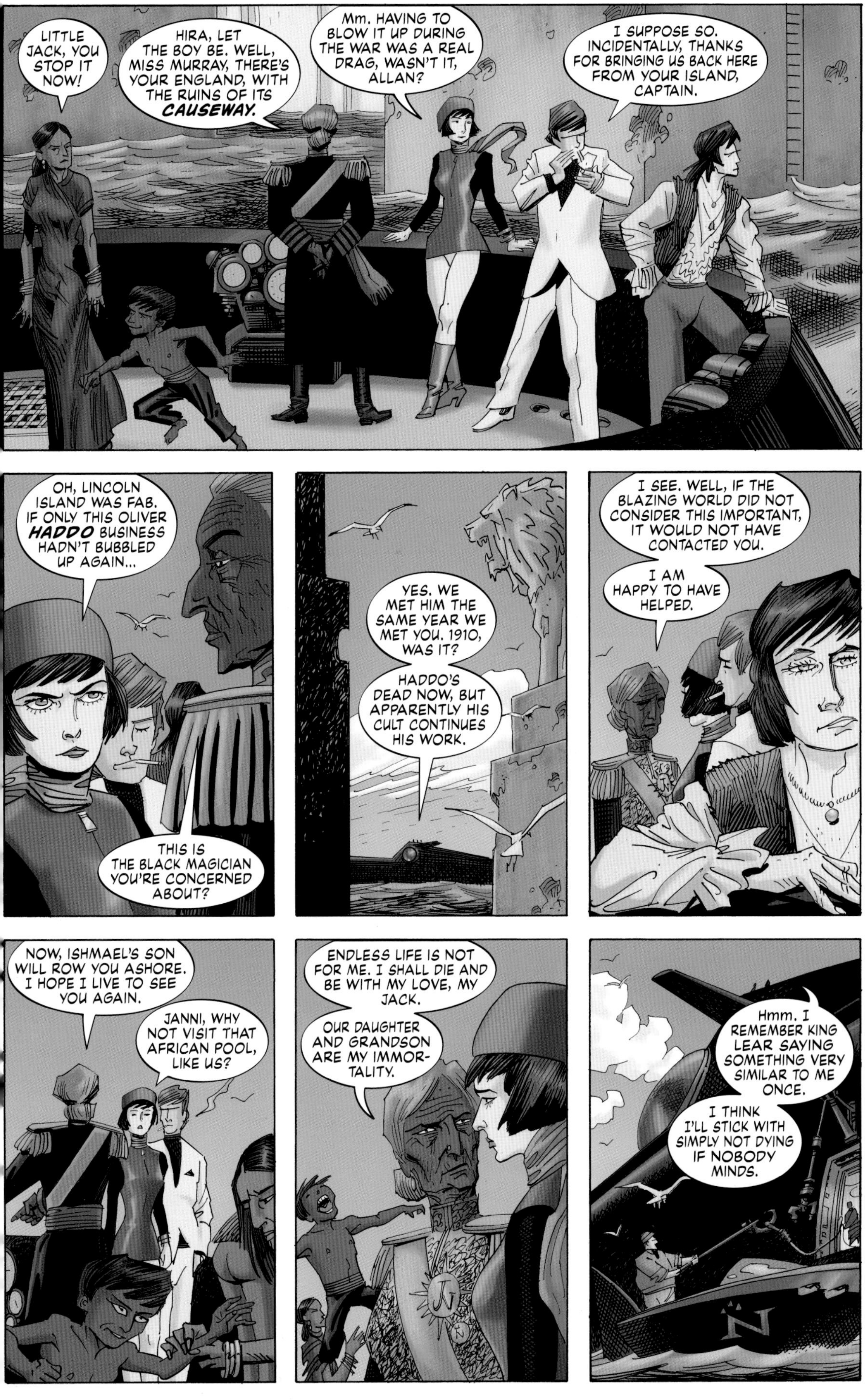
LITTLE JACK, YOU STOP IT NOW!
HIRA, LET THE BOY BE. WELL, MISS MURRAY, THERE'S YOUR ENGLAND, WITH THE RUINS OF ITS CAUSEWAY.
Mm. HAVING TO BLOW IT UP DURING THE WAR WAS A REAL DRAG, WASN'T IT, ALLAN?
I SUPPOSE SO. INCIDENTALLY, THANKS FOR BRINGING US BACK HERE FROM YOUR ISLAND, CAPTAIN.
OH, LINCOLN ISLAND WAS FAB. IF ONLY THIS OLIVER HADDO BUSINESS HADN'T BUBBLED UP AGAIN...
THIS IS THE BLACK MAGICIAN YOU'RE CONCERNED ABOUT?
YES. WE MET HIM THE SAME YEAR WE MET YOU. 1910, WAS IT?
HADDO'S DEAD NOW, BUT APPARENTLY HIS CULT CONTINUES HIS WORK.
I SEE. WELL, IF THE BLAZING WORLD DID NOT CONSIDER THIS IMPORTANT, IT WOULD NOT HAVE CONTACTED YOU.
I AM HAPPY TO HAVE HELPED.
NOW, ISHMAEL'S SON WILL ROW YOU ASHORE. I HOPE I LIVE TO SEE YOU AGAIN.
JANNI, WHY NOT VISIT THAT AFRICAN POOL, LIKE US?
ENDLESS LIFE IS NOT FOR ME. I SHALL DIE AND BE WITH MY LOVE, MY JACK.
OUR DAUGHTER AND GRANDSON ARE MY IMMOR-TALITY.
Hmm. I REMEMBER KING LEAR SAYING SOMETHING VERY SIMILAR TO ME ONCE.
I THINK I'LL STICK WITH SIMPLY NOT DYING IF NOBODY MINDS.

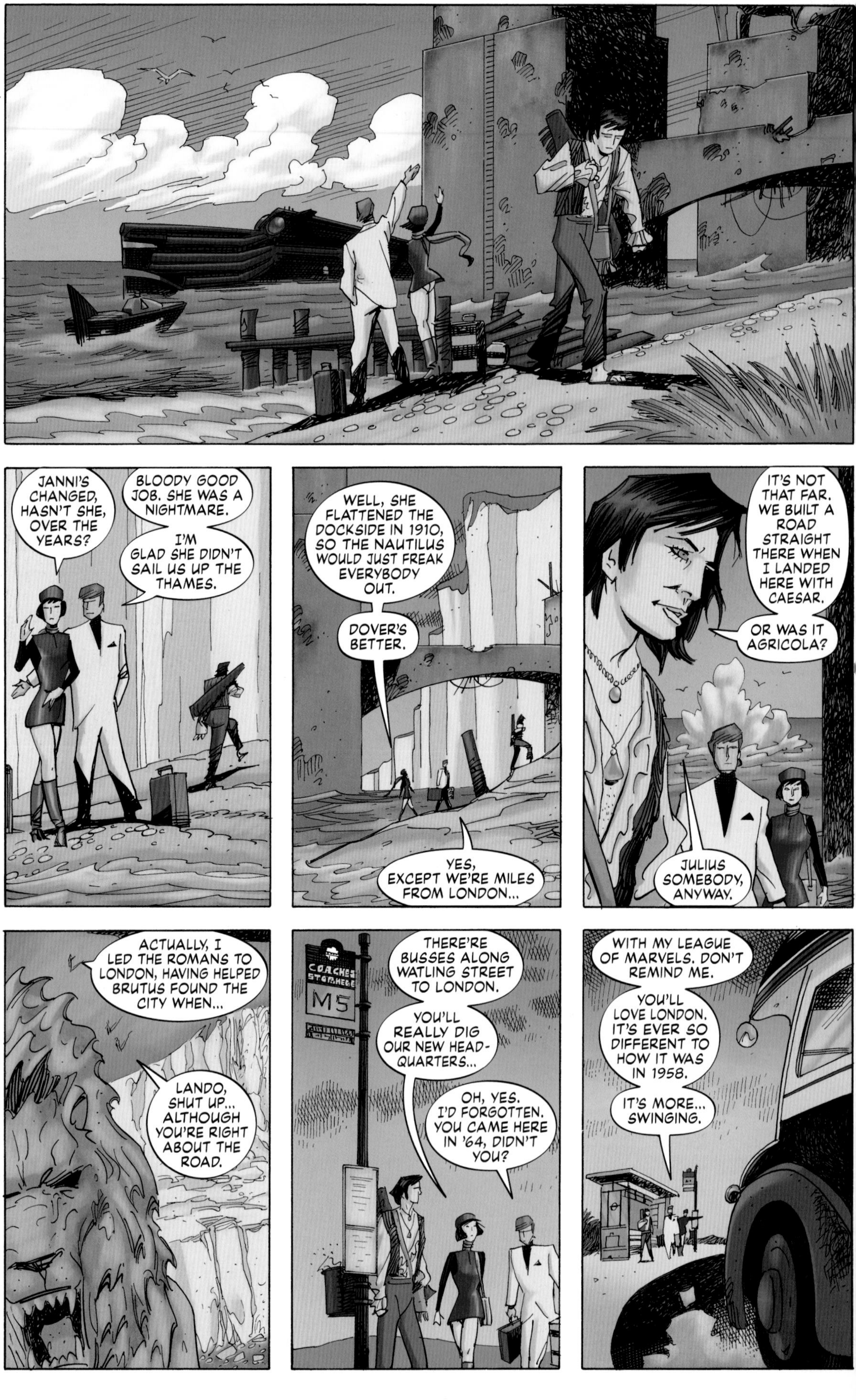
JANNI'S CHANGED, HASN'T SHE, OVER THE YEARS?
BLOODY GOOD JOB. SHE WAS A NIGHTMARE.
I'M GLAD SHE DIDN'T SAIL US UP THE THAMES.
WELL, SHE FLATTENED THE DOCKSIDE IN 1910, SO THE NAUTILUS WOULD JUST FREAK EVERYBODY OUT.
DOVER'S BETTER.
YES, EXCEPT WE'RE MILES FROM LONDON...
IT'S NOT THAT FAR. WE BUILT A ROAD STRAIGHT THERE WHEN I LANDED HERE WITH CAESAR.
OR WAS IT AGRICOLA?
JULIUS SOMEBODY, ANYWAY.
ACTUALLY, I LED THE ROMANS TO LONDON, HAVING HELPED BRUTUS FOUND THE CITY WHEN...
LANDO, SHUT UP... ALTHOUGH YOU'RE RIGHT ABOUT THE ROAD.
M5
THERE'RE BUSSES ALONG WATLING STREET TO LONDON.
YOU'LL REALLY DIG OUR NEW HEAD-QUARTERS...
OH, YES. I'D FORGOTTEN. YOU CAME HERE IN '64, DIDN'T YOU?
WITH MY LEAGUE OF MARVELS. DON'T REMIND ME.
YOU'LL LOVE LONDON. IT'S EVER SO DIFFERENT TO HOW IT WAS IN 1958.
IT'S MORE... SWINGING.

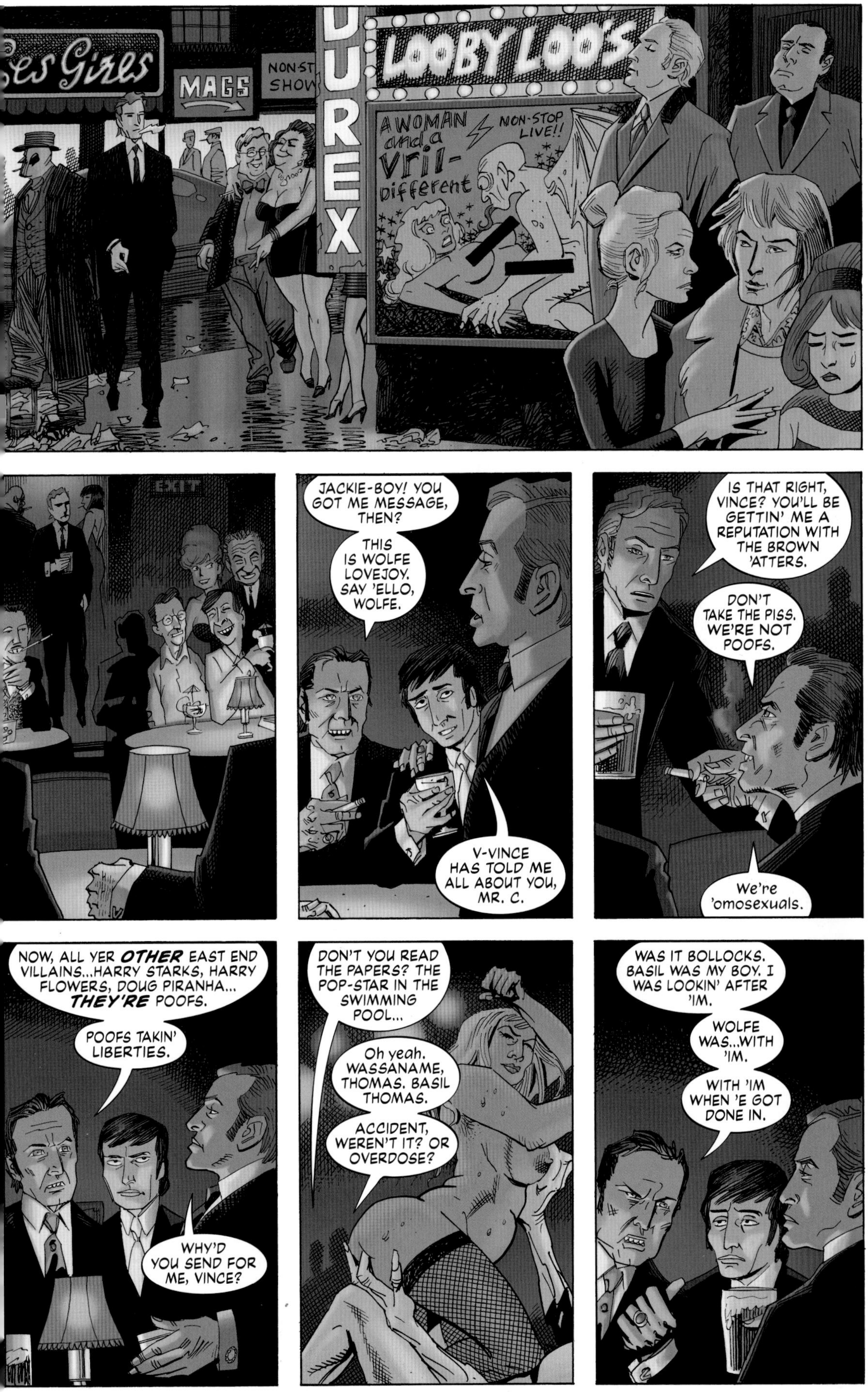
Les Girls
MAGS
NON-ST
SHOW
DUREX
LOOBY LOO'S
A WOMAN and a Vril-Different
NON-STOP LIVE!!
EXIT
JACKIE-BOY! YOU GOT ME MESSAGE, THEN?
THIS IS WOLFE LOVEJOY. SAY 'ELLO, WOLFE.
V-VINCE HAS TOLD ME ALL ABOUT YOU, MR. C.
IS THAT RIGHT, VINCE? YOU'LL BE GETTIN' ME A REPUTATION WITH THE BROWN 'ATTERS.
DON'T TAKE THE PISS. WE'RE NOT POOFS.
We're 'omosexuals.
NOW, ALL YER *OTHER* EAST END VILLAINS...HARRY STARKS, HARRY FLOWERS, DOUG PIRANHA... ***THEY'RE*** POOFS.
POOFS TAKIN' LIBERTIES.
WHY'D YOU SEND FOR ME, VINCE?
DON'T YOU READ THE PAPERS? THE POP-STAR IN THE SWIMMING POOL...
Oh yeah. WASSANAME, THOMAS. BASIL THOMAS.
ACCIDENT, WEREN'T IT? OR OVERDOSE?
WAS IT BOLLOCKS. BASIL WAS MY BOY. I WAS LOOKIN' AFTER 'IM.
WOLFE WAS...WITH 'IM.
WITH 'IM WHEN 'E GOT DONE IN.

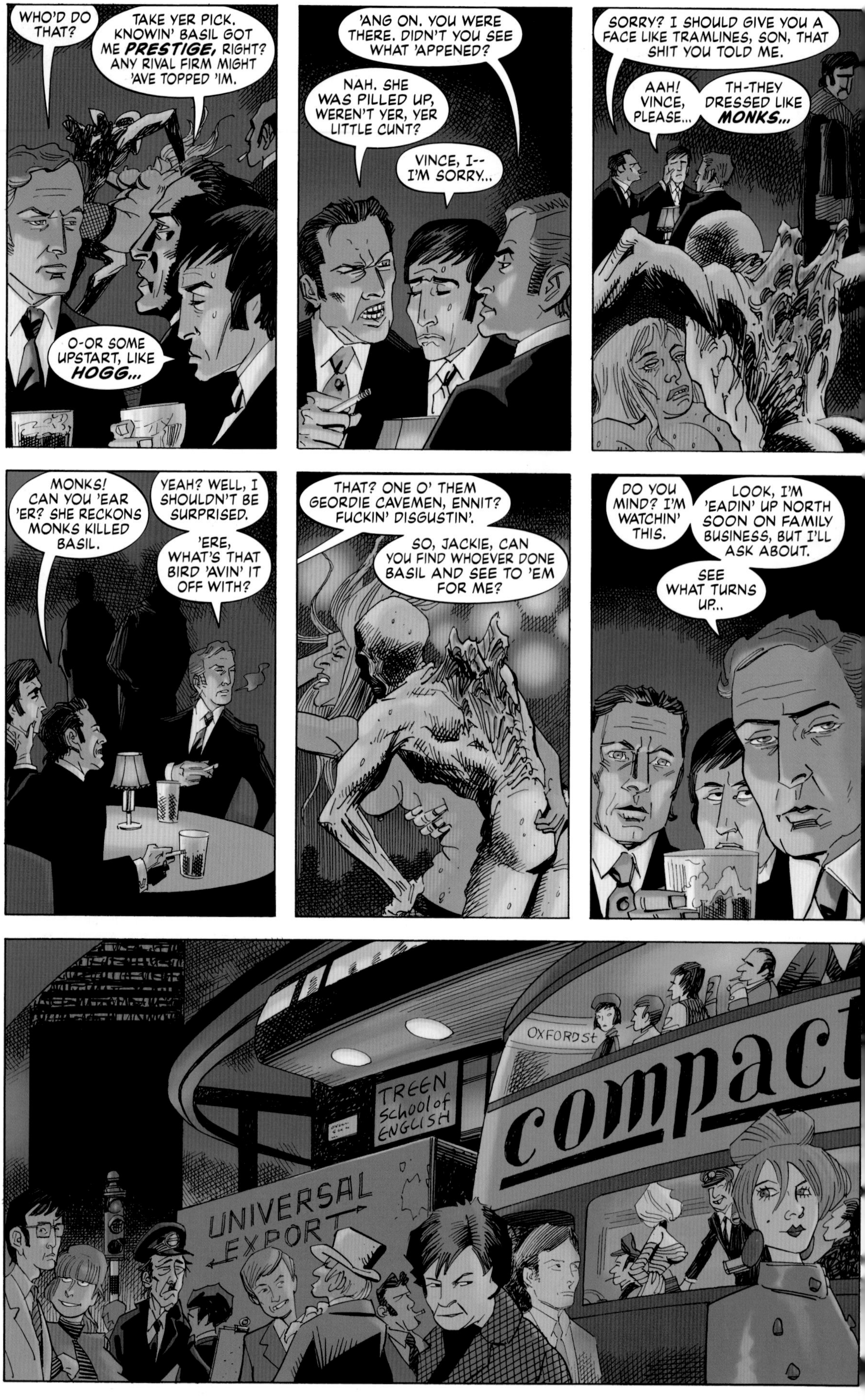
WHO'D DO THAT?
TAKE YER PICK. KNOWIN' BASIL GOT ME **PRESTIGE,** RIGHT? ANY RIVAL FIRM MIGHT 'AVE TOPPED 'IM.
O-OR SOME UPSTART, LIKE **HOGG...**
'ANG ON. YOU WERE THERE. DIDN'T YOU SEE WHAT 'APPENED?
NAH. SHE WAS PILLED UP, WEREN'T YER, YER LITTLE CUNT?
VINCE, I-- I'M SORRY...
SORRY? I SHOULD GIVE YOU A FACE LIKE TRAMLINES, SON, THAT SHIT YOU TOLD ME.
AAH! VINCE, PLEASE...
TH-THEY DRESSED LIKE **MONKS...**
MONKS! CAN YOU 'EAR 'ER? SHE RECKONS MONKS KILLED BASIL.
YEAH? WELL, I SHOULDN'T BE SURPRISED.
'ERE, WHAT'S THAT BIRD 'AVIN' IT OFF WITH?
THAT? ONE O' THEM GEORDIE CAVEMEN, ENNIT? FUCKIN' DISGUSTIN'.
SO, JACKIE, CAN YOU FIND WHOEVER DONE BASIL AND SEE TO 'EM FOR ME?
DO YOU MIND? I'M WATCHIN' THIS.
LOOK, I'M 'EADIN' UP NORTH SOON ON FAMILY BUSINESS, BUT I'LL ASK ABOUT.
SEE WHAT TURNS UP...
OXFORD St
TREEN School of ENGLISH
compact
UNIVERSAL
EXPORT

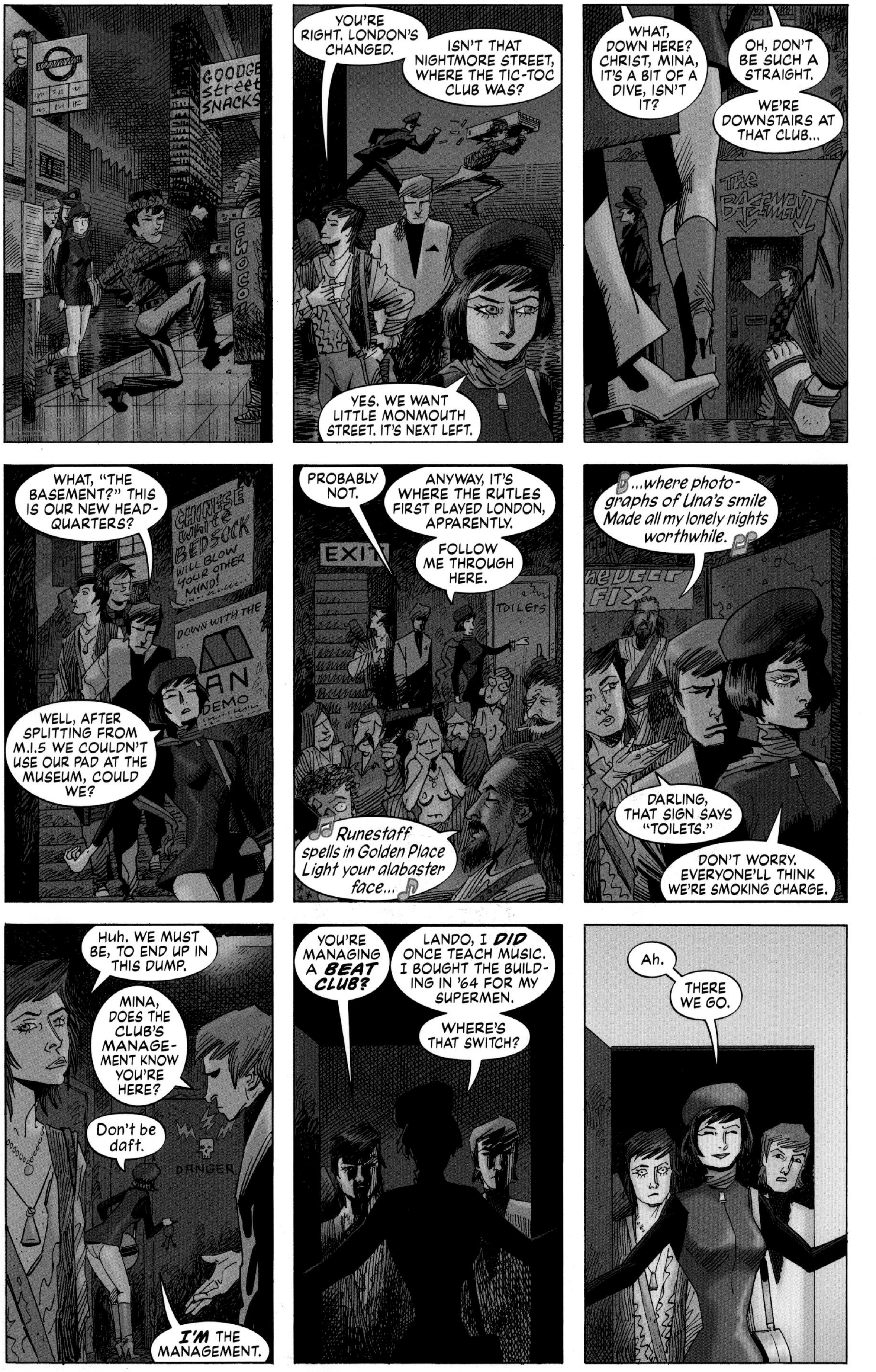
GOODGE street SNACKS
YOU'RE RIGHT. LONDON'S CHANGED.
ISN'T THAT NIGHTMORE STREET, WHERE THE TIC-TOC CLUB WAS?
YES. WE WANT LITTLE MONMOUTH STREET. IT'S NEXT LEFT.
WHAT, DOWN HERE? CHRIST, MINA, IT'S A BIT OF A DIVE, ISN'T IT?
OH, DON'T BE SUCH A STRAIGHT.
WE'RE DOWNSTAIRS AT THAT CLUB...
The BASEMENT
WHAT, "THE BASEMENT?" THIS IS OUR NEW HEAD-QUARTERS?
CHINESE White BEDSOCK WILL BLOW YOUR OTHER MIND!
DOWN WITH THE
DEMO
WELL, AFTER SPLITTING FROM M.I.5 WE COULDN'T USE OUR PAD AT THE MUSEUM, COULD WE?
PROBABLY NOT.
ANYWAY, IT'S WHERE THE RUTLES FIRST PLAYED LONDON, APPARENTLY.
FOLLOW ME THROUGH HERE.
EXIT
TOILETS
Runestaff spells in Golden Place Light your alabaster face...
...where photo-graphs of Una's smile Made all my lonely nights worthwhile.
FIX
DARLING, THAT SIGN SAYS "TOILETS."
DON'T WORRY. EVERYONE'LL THINK WE'RE SMOKING CHARGE.
Huh. WE MUST BE, TO END UP IN THIS DUMP.
MINA, DOES THE CLUB'S MANAGE-MENT KNOW YOU'RE HERE?
Don't be daft.
DANGER
I'M THE MANAGEMENT.
YOU'RE MANAGING A BEAT CLUB?
LANDO, I DID ONCE TEACH MUSIC. I BOUGHT THE BUILD-ING IN '64 FOR MY SUPERMEN.
WHERE'S THAT SWITCH?
Ah.
THERE WE GO.

BLOODY HELL.

TALK ABOUT SPACE-AGE.

WOOF WOOF ?

IT'S A BIT BRIGHT AND GLEAMING. NEVER MIND. I CAN GET SOME HANGINGS AND ASTRO-LAMPS AND THINGS.

IT RUNS STRAIGHT THROUGH TO NIGHTMORE STREET'S CELLARS, SO THERE'S PLENTY OF ROOM.

MAKE YOURSELVES AT HOME.

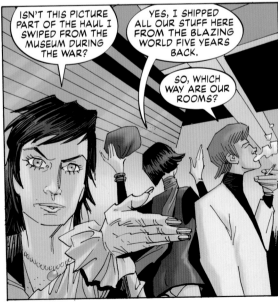

ISN'T THIS PICTURE PART OF THE HAUL I SWIPED FROM THE MUSEUM DURING THE WAR?

YES, I SHIPPED ALL OUR STUFF HERE FROM THE BLAZING WORLD FIVE YEARS BACK.

SO, WHICH WAY ARE OUR ROOMS?

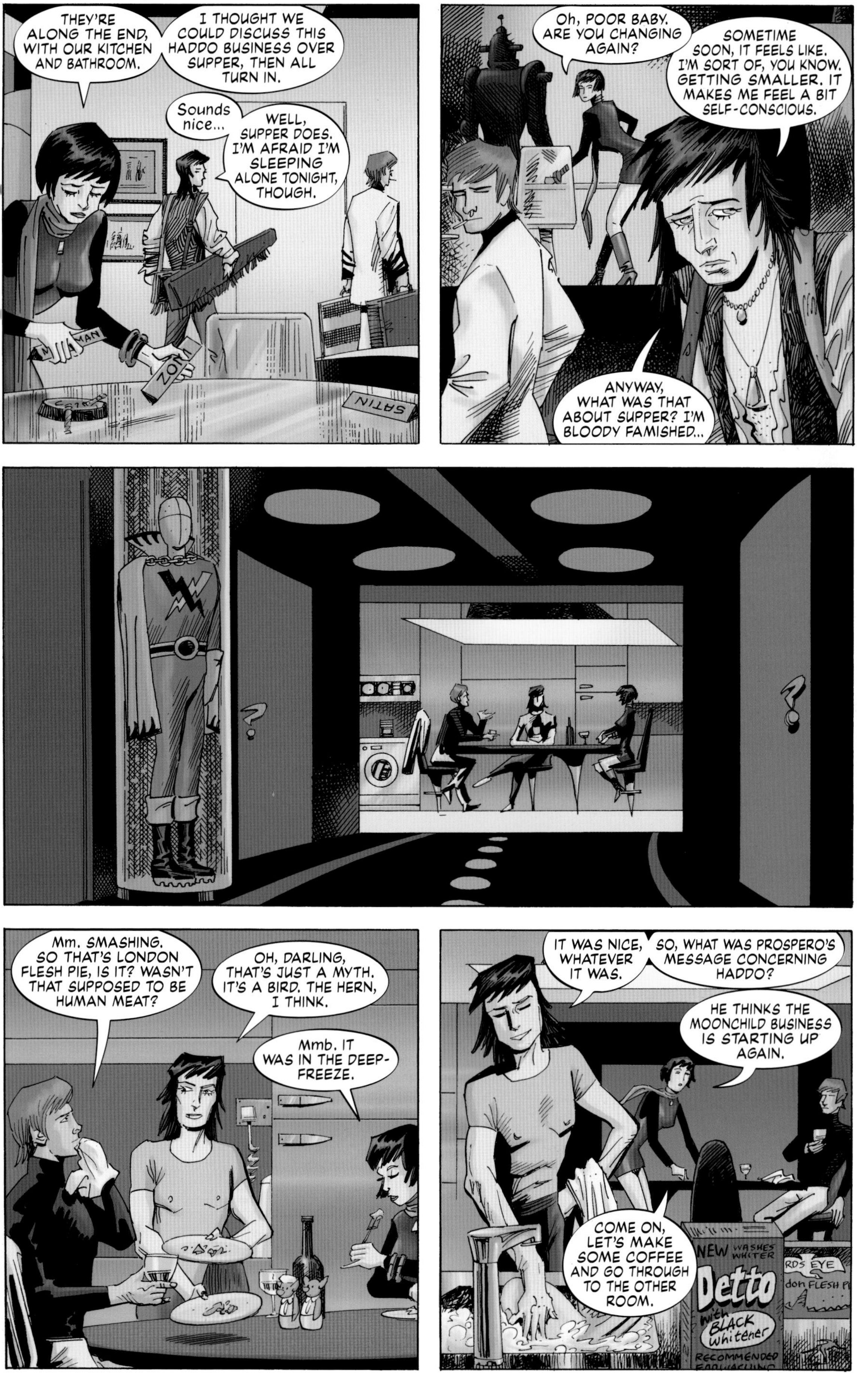
THEY'RE ALONG THE END, WITH OUR KITCHEN AND BATHROOM.
I THOUGHT WE COULD DISCUSS THIS HADDO BUSINESS OVER SUPPER, THEN ALL TURN IN.
Sounds nice...
WELL, SUPPER DOES. I'M AFRAID I'M SLEEPING ALONE TONIGHT, THOUGH.
SATIN
Oh, POOR BABY. ARE YOU CHANGING AGAIN?
SOMETIME SOON, IT FEELS LIKE. I'M SORT OF, YOU KNOW. GETTING SMALLER. IT MAKES ME FEEL A BIT SELF-CONSCIOUS.
ANYWAY, WHAT WAS THAT ABOUT SUPPER? I'M BLOODY FAMISHED...
Mm. SMASHING. SO THAT'S LONDON FLESH PIE, IS IT? WASN'T THAT SUPPOSED TO BE HUMAN MEAT?
OH, DARLING, THAT'S JUST A MYTH. IT'S A BIRD. THE HERN, I THINK.
Mmb. IT WAS IN THE DEEP-FREEZE.
IT WAS NICE, WHATEVER IT WAS.
SO, WHAT WAS PROSPERO'S MESSAGE CONCERNING HADDO?
HE THINKS THE MOONCHILD BUSINESS IS STARTING UP AGAIN.
COME ON, LET'S MAKE SOME COFFEE AND GO THROUGH TO THE OTHER ROOM.
NEW WASHES WHITER
Detto
with BLACK whitener
RECOMMENDED

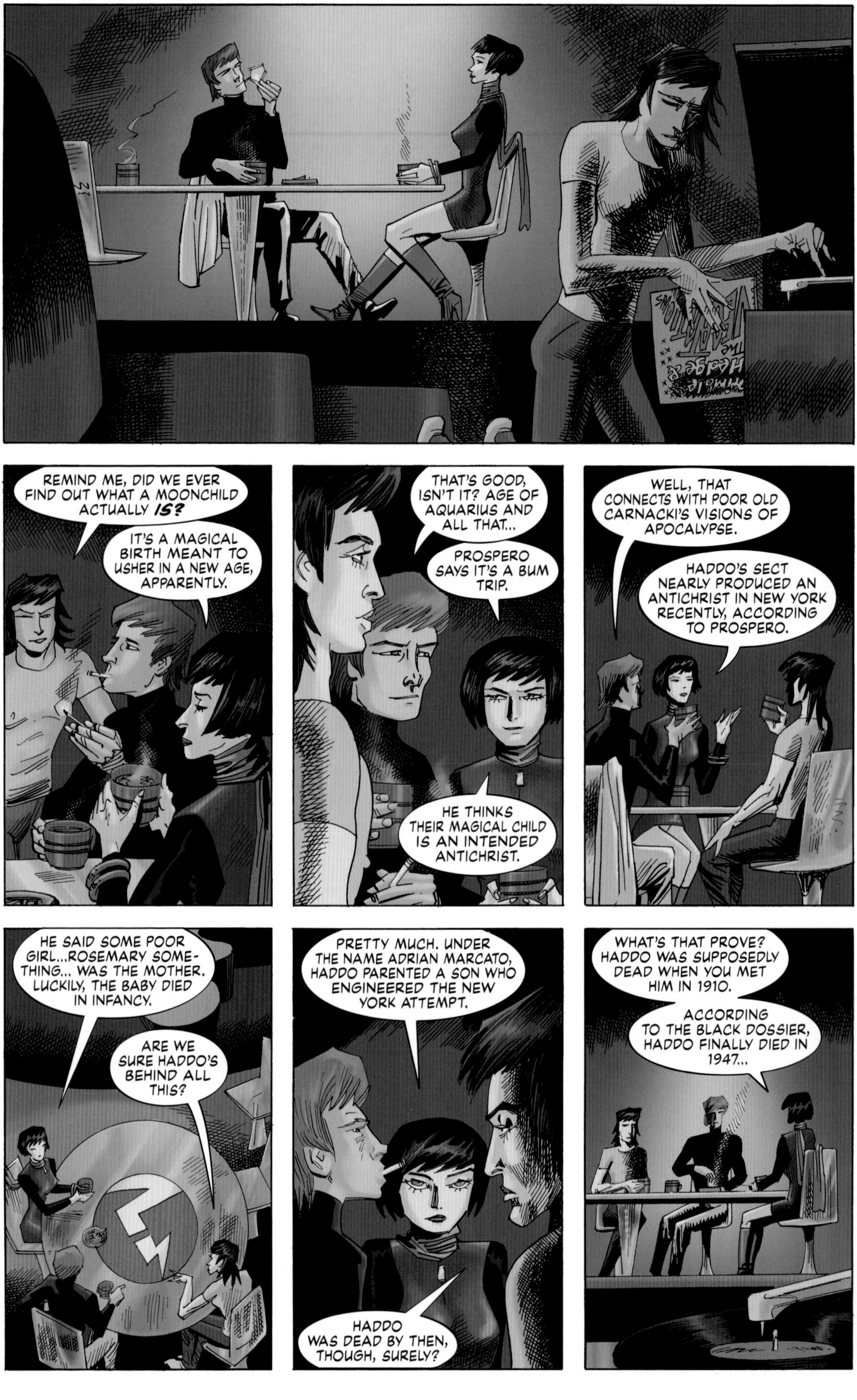
REMIND ME, DID WE EVER FIND OUT WHAT A MOONCHILD ACTUALLY *IS?*
IT'S A MAGICAL BIRTH MEANT TO USHER IN A NEW AGE, APPARENTLY.
THAT'S GOOD, ISN'T IT? AGE OF AQUARIUS AND ALL THAT...
PROSPERO SAYS IT'S A BUM TRIP.
HE THINKS THEIR MAGICAL CHILD IS AN INTENDED ANTICHRIST.
WELL, THAT CONNECTS WITH POOR OLD CARNACKI'S VISIONS OF APOCALYPSE.
HADDO'S SECT NEARLY PRODUCED AN ANTICHRIST IN NEW YORK RECENTLY, ACCORDING TO PROSPERO.
HE SAID SOME POOR GIRL...ROSEMARY SOME-THING... WAS THE MOTHER. LUCKILY, THE BABY DIED IN INFANCY.
ARE WE SURE HADDO'S BEHIND ALL THIS?
PRETTY MUCH. UNDER THE NAME ADRIAN MARCATO, HADDO PARENTED A SON WHO ENGINEERED THE NEW YORK ATTEMPT.
HADDO WAS DEAD BY THEN, THOUGH, SURELY?
WHAT'S THAT PROVE? HADDO WAS SUPPOSEDLY DEAD WHEN YOU MET HIM IN 1910.
ACCORDING TO THE BLACK DOSSIER, HADDO FINALLY DIED IN 1947...

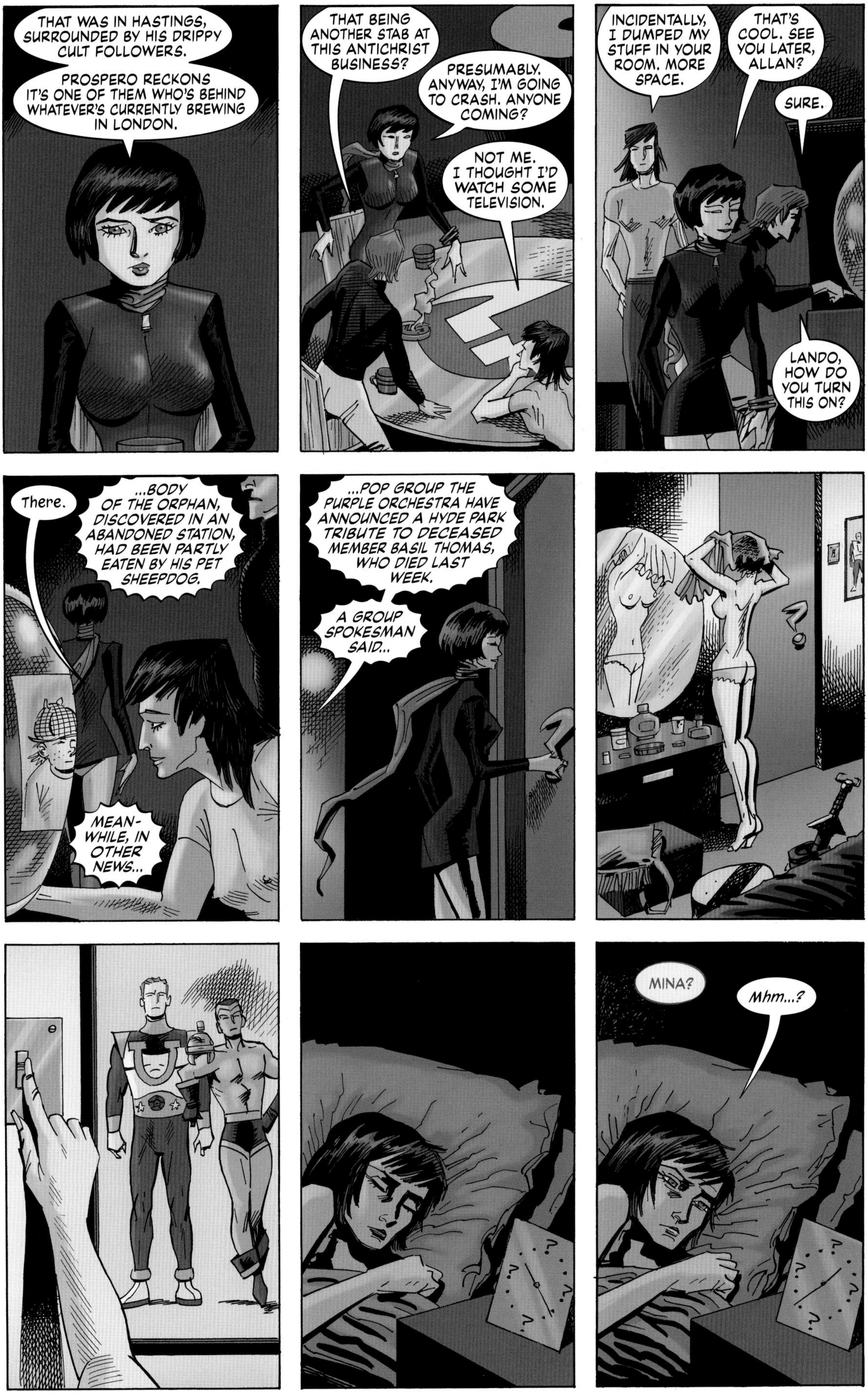
THAT WAS IN HASTINGS, SURROUNDED BY HIS DRIPPY CULT FOLLOWERS.
PROSPERO RECKONS IT'S ONE OF THEM WHO'S BEHIND WHATEVER'S CURRENTLY BREWING IN LONDON.
THAT BEING ANOTHER STAB AT THIS ANTICHRIST BUSINESS?
PRESUMABLY. ANYWAY, I'M GOING TO CRASH. ANYONE COMING?
NOT ME. I THOUGHT I'D WATCH SOME TELEVISION.
INCIDENTALLY, I DUMPED MY STUFF IN YOUR ROOM. MORE SPACE.
THAT'S COOL. SEE YOU LATER, ALLAN?
SURE.
LANDO, HOW DO YOU TURN THIS ON?
There.
...BODY OF THE ORPHAN, DISCOVERED IN AN ABANDONED STATION, HAD BEEN PARTLY EATEN BY HIS PET SHEEPDOG.
MEAN-WHILE, IN OTHER NEWS...
...POP GROUP THE PURPLE ORCHESTRA HAVE ANNOUNCED A HYDE PARK TRIBUTE TO DECEASED MEMBER BASIL THOMAS, WHO DIED LAST WEEK.
A GROUP SPOKESMAN SAID...
MINA?
Mhm...?

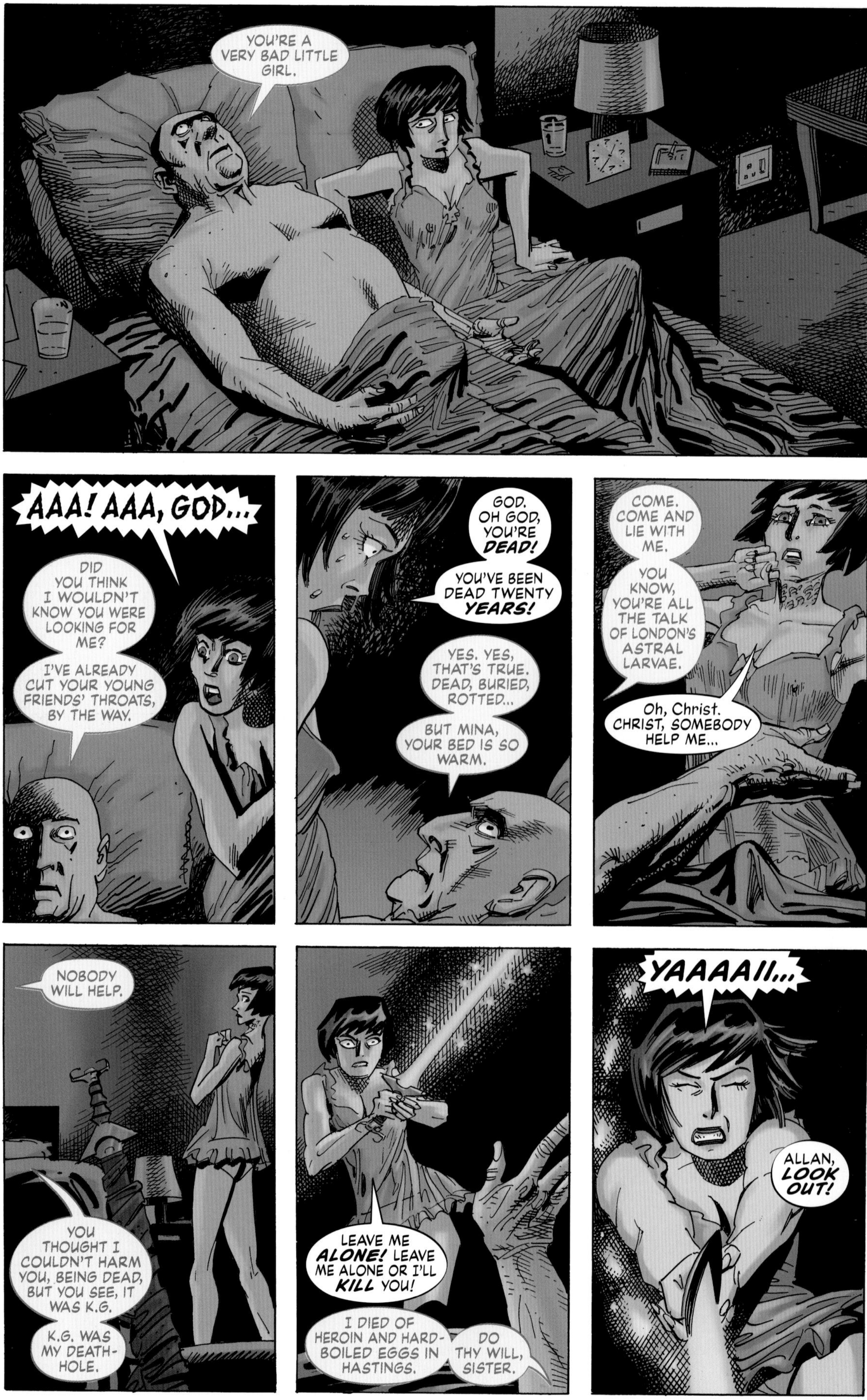
YOU'RE A VERY BAD LITTLE GIRL.
AAA! AAA, GOD...
DID YOU THINK I WOULDN'T KNOW YOU WERE LOOKING FOR ME?
I'VE ALREADY CUT YOUR YOUNG FRIENDS' THROATS, BY THE WAY.
GOD. OH GOD, YOU'RE DEAD!
YOU'VE BEEN DEAD TWENTY YEARS!
YES. YES, THAT'S TRUE. DEAD, BURIED, ROTTED...
BUT MINA, YOUR BED IS SO WARM.
COME. COME AND LIE WITH ME.
YOU KNOW, YOU'RE ALL THE TALK OF LONDON'S ASTRAL LARVAE.
Oh, Christ. CHRIST, SOMEBODY HELP ME...
NOBODY WILL HELP.
YOU THOUGHT I COULDN'T HARM YOU, BEING DEAD, BUT YOU SEE, IT WAS K.G.
K.G. WAS MY DEATH-HOLE.
LEAVE ME ALONE! LEAVE ME ALONE OR I'LL KILL YOU!
I DIED OF HEROIN AND HARD-BOILED EGGS IN HASTINGS.
DO THY WILL, SISTER.
YAAAAII...
ALLAN, LOOK OUT!

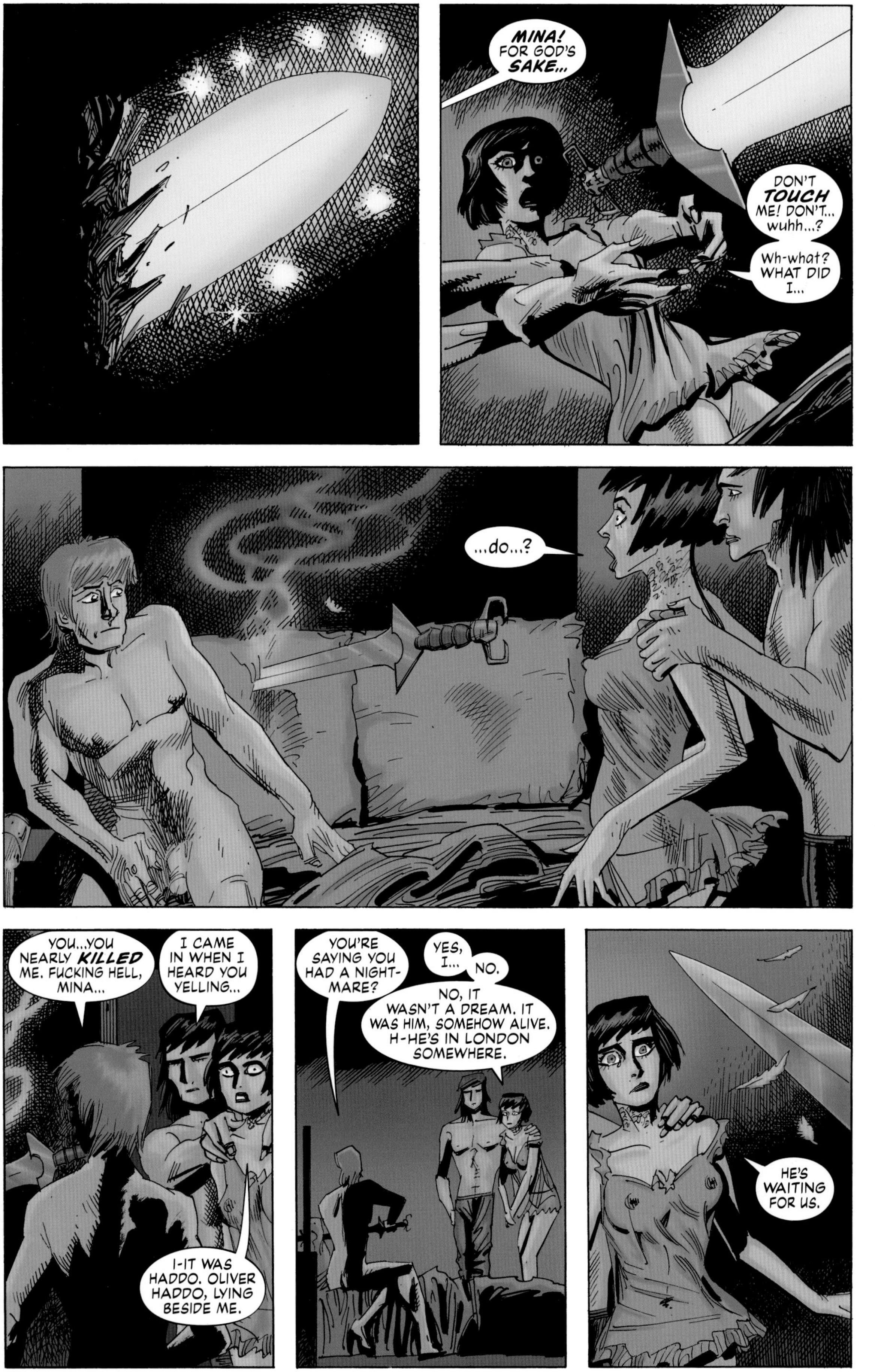
MINA! FOR GOD'S SAKE...
DON'T TOUCH ME! DON'T... wuhh...?
Wh-what? WHAT DID I...
...do...?
YOU...YOU NEARLY KILLED ME. FUCKING HELL, MINA...
I CAME IN WHEN I HEARD YOU YELLING...
I-IT WAS HADDO. OLIVER HADDO, LYING BESIDE ME.
YOU'RE SAYING YOU HAD A NIGHT-MARE?
YES, I...
NO.
NO, IT WASN'T A DREAM. IT WAS HIM, SOMEHOW ALIVE. H-HE'S IN LONDON SOMEWHERE.
HE'S WAITING FOR US.

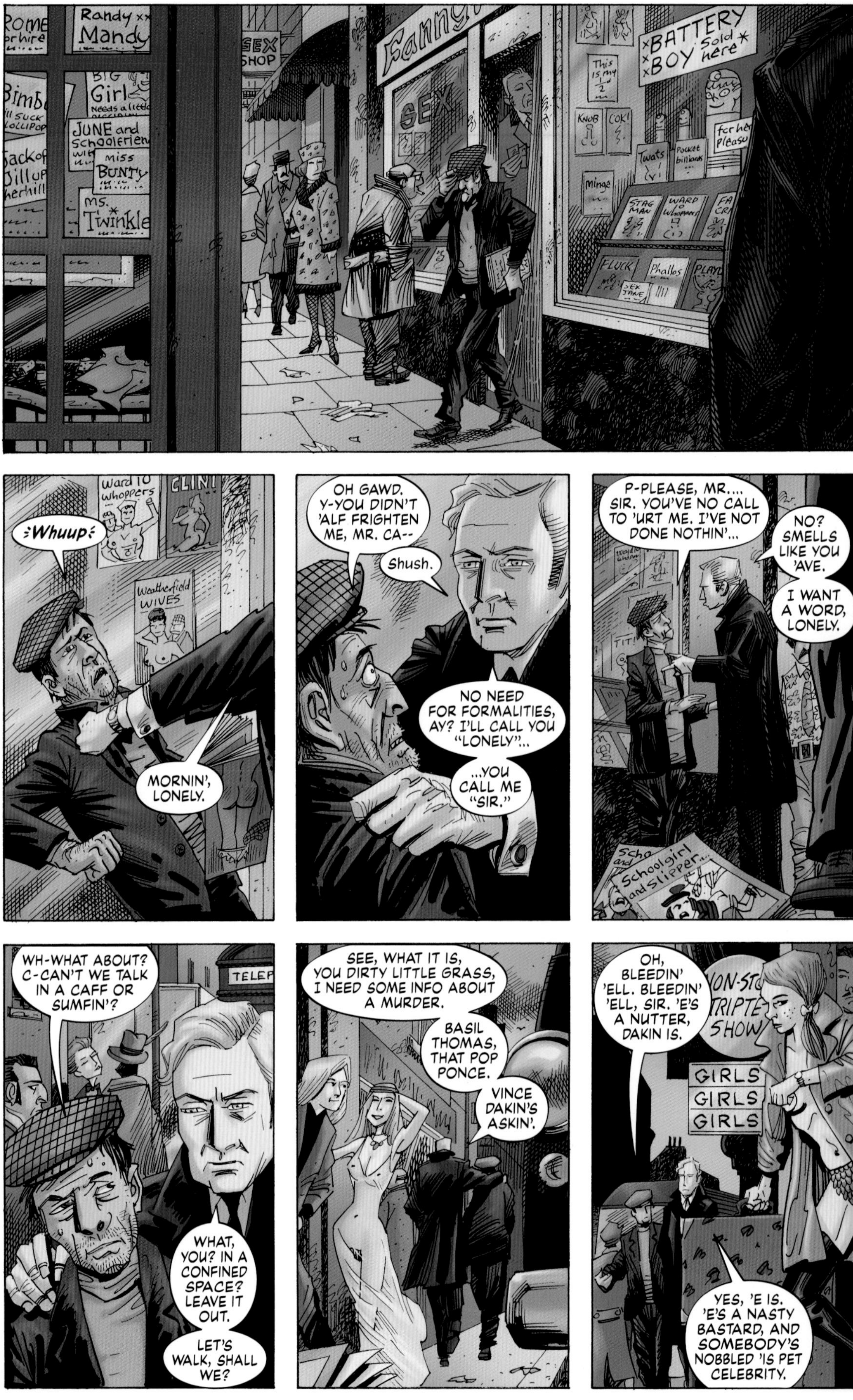
Whuup
MORNIN', LONELY.
OH GAWD. Y-YOU DIDN'T 'ALF FRIGHTEN ME, MR. CA--
Shush.
NO NEED FOR FORMALITIES, AY? I'LL CALL YOU "LONELY"...
...YOU CALL ME "SIR."
P-PLEASE, MR.... SIR. YOU'VE NO CALL TO 'URT ME. I'VE NOT DONE NOTHIN'...
NO? SMELLS LIKE YOU 'AVE.
I WANT A WORD, LONELY.
WH-WHAT ABOUT? C-CAN'T WE TALK IN A CAFF OR SUMFIN'?
WHAT, YOU? IN A CONFINED SPACE? LEAVE IT OUT.
LET'S WALK, SHALL WE?
SEE, WHAT IT IS, YOU DIRTY LITTLE GRASS, I NEED SOME INFO ABOUT A MURDER.
BASIL THOMAS, THAT POP PONCE.
VINCE DAKIN'S ASKIN'.
OH, BLEEDIN' 'ELL. BLEEDIN' 'ELL, SIR. 'E'S A NUTTER, DAKIN IS.
YES, 'E IS. 'E'S A NASTY BASTARD, AND SOMEBODY'S NOBBLED 'IS PET CELEBRITY.

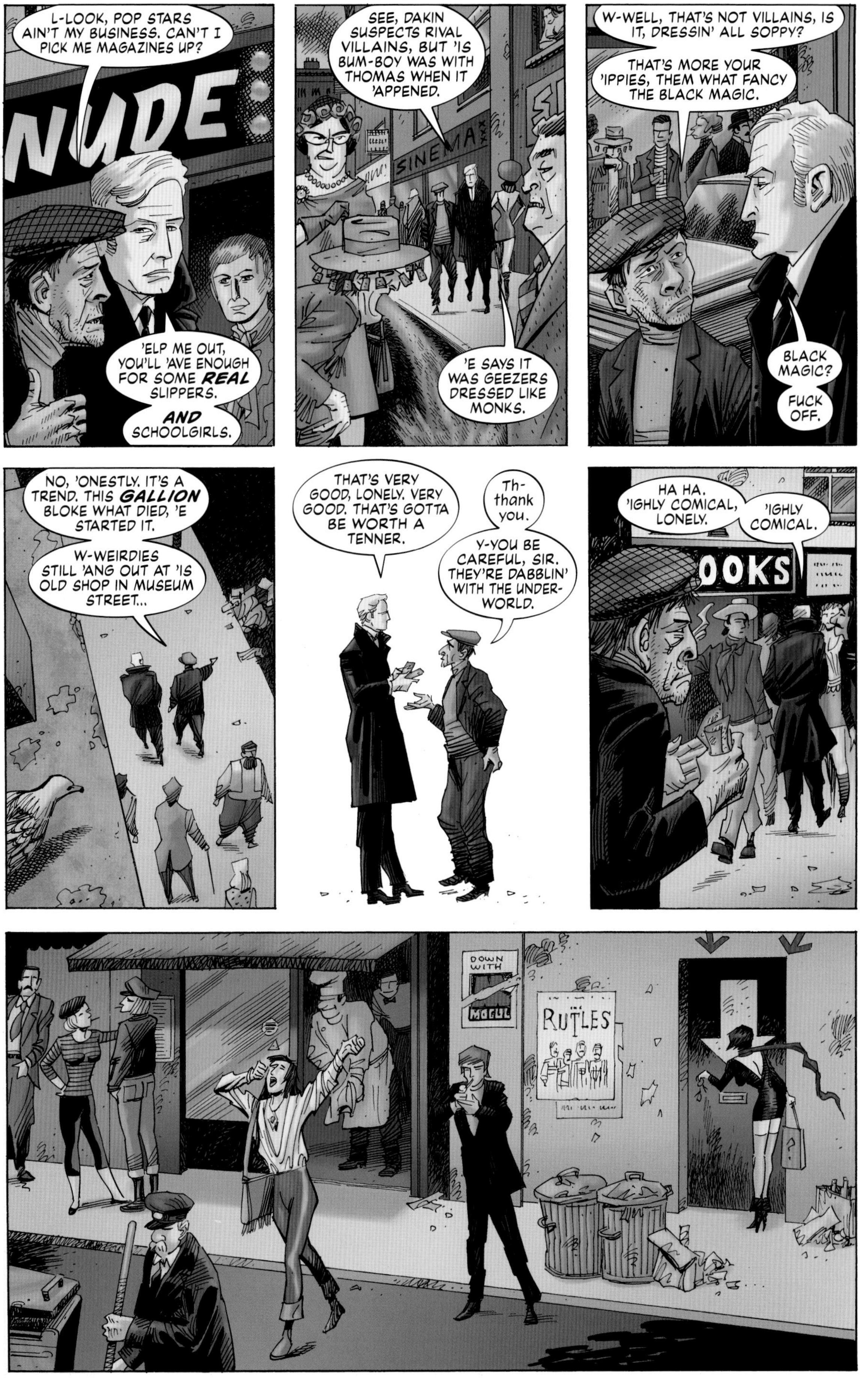
L-LOOK, POP STARS AIN'T MY BUSINESS. CAN'T I PICK ME MAGAZINES UP?
NUDE
'ELP ME OUT, YOU'LL 'AVE ENOUGH FOR SOME ***REAL*** SLIPPERS.
AND SCHOOLGIRLS.
SEE, DAKIN SUSPECTS RIVAL VILLAINS, BUT 'IS BUM-BOY WAS WITH THOMAS WHEN IT 'APPENED.
SINEMA
'E SAYS IT WAS GEEZERS DRESSED LIKE MONKS.
W-WELL, THAT'S NOT VILLAINS, IS IT, DRESSIN' ALL SOPPY?
THAT'S MORE YOUR 'IPPIES, THEM WHAT FANCY THE BLACK MAGIC.
BLACK MAGIC?
FUCK OFF.
NO, 'ONESTLY. IT'S A TREND. THIS ***GALLION*** BLOKE WHAT DIED, 'E STARTED IT.
W-WEIRDIES STILL 'ANG OUT AT 'IS OLD SHOP IN MUSEUM STREET...
THAT'S VERY GOOD, LONELY. VERY GOOD. THAT'S GOTTA BE WORTH A TENNER.
Th-thank you.
Y-YOU BE CAREFUL, SIR. THEY'RE DABBLIN' WITH THE UNDER-WORLD.
HA HA. 'IGHLY COMICAL, LONELY.
'IGHLY COMICAL.
OOKS
DOWN WITH
MOGUL
RUTLES

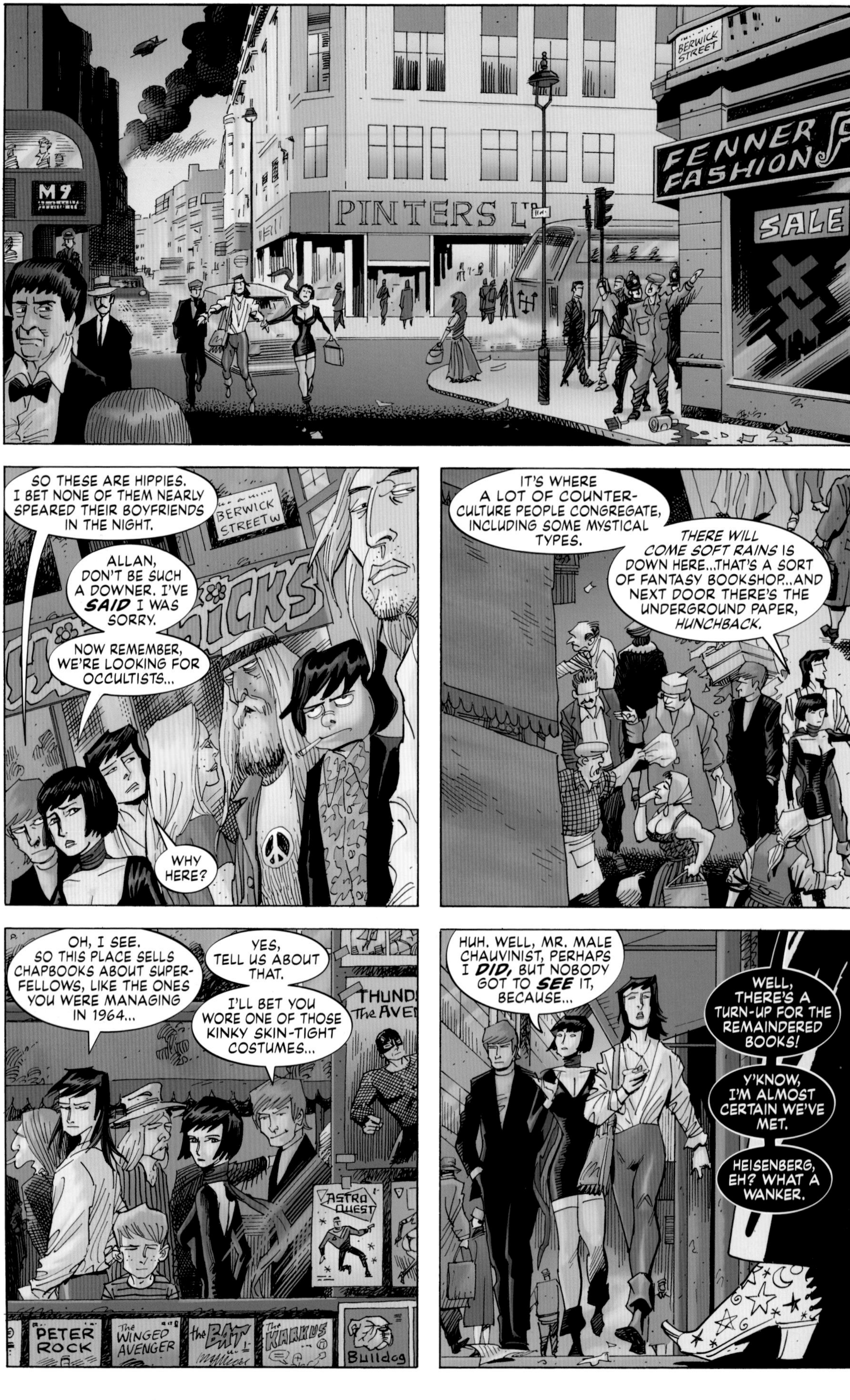

M9
PINTERS L
FENNER FASHION
BERWICK STREET
SALE
SO THESE ARE HIPPIES. I BET NONE OF THEM NEARLY SPEARED THEIR BOYFRIENDS IN THE NIGHT.
BERWICK STREET W
ALLAN, DON'T BE SUCH A DOWNER. I'VE *SAID* I WAS SORRY.
NOW REMEMBER, WE'RE LOOKING FOR OCCULTISTS...
WHY HERE?
IT'S WHERE A LOT OF COUNTER-CULTURE PEOPLE CONGREGATE, INCLUDING SOME MYSTICAL TYPES.
THERE WILL COME SOFT RAINS IS DOWN HERE...THAT'S A SORT OF FANTASY BOOKSHOP...AND NEXT DOOR THERE'S THE UNDERGROUND PAPER, *HUNCHBACK*.
OH, I SEE. SO THIS PLACE SELLS CHAPBOOKS ABOUT SUPER-FELLOWS, LIKE THE ONES YOU WERE MANAGING IN 1964...
YES, TELL US ABOUT THAT.
I'LL BET YOU WORE ONE OF THOSE KINKY SKIN-TIGHT COSTUMES...
THUND!
The AVE
ASTRO QUEST
PETER ROCK
The WINGED AVENGER
the BAT
The KARKUS
Bulldog
HUH. WELL, MR. MALE CHAUVINIST, PERHAPS I *DID*, BUT NOBODY GOT TO *SEE* IT, BECAUSE...
WELL, THERE'S A TURN-UP FOR THE REMAINDERED BOOKS!
Y'KNOW, I'M ALMOST CERTAIN WE'VE MET.
HEISENBERG, EH? WHAT A WANKER.

WHAT IN THE NAME OF MITHRAS...?

UH...HEY, BROTHER. I-I'M SORRY, BUT I DON'T...

YOU LODGED AT OUR OLD MUM'S, LATE FIFTIES. THE BIRTHDAY PARTY AND BAN THE BOMB. TASTY TIMES.

I'M JEREMIAH CORNELIUS.

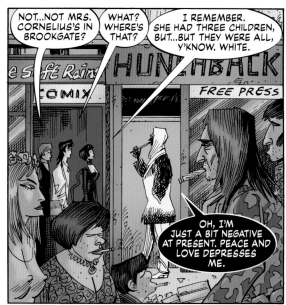

NOT...NOT MRS. CORNELIUS'S IN BROOKGATE?

WHAT? WHERE'S THAT?

I REMEMBER. SHE HAD THREE CHILDREN, BUT...BUT THEY WERE ALL, Y'KNOW. WHITE.

OH, I'M JUST A BIT NEGATIVE AT PRESENT. PEACE AND LOVE DEPRESSES ME.

OH, GOD. IS THAT OPIUM?

Allan, don't start.

SO, UH, WHAT ARE YOU DOING DOWN HERE, MR. CORNELIUS?

OH, CALL ME CORNY. I'M COLLECTING ROYALTIES ON MY HUNCHBACK COMIC STRIP. THEY'RE SERIALIZING MY EXPLOITS, APPARENTLY.

WHAT ABOUT YOU? RUNAWAY SPIES, WEREN'T YOU? I BET MISS BRUNNER WOULDN'T APPROVE OF YOU...

WE...WE LEFT M.I.5. WE'RE WORKING ON OUR OWN, NOW.

ACTUALLY, WE'RE INVESTIGATING THE OCCULT SCENE. YOU KNOW: OLIVER HADDO.

HADDO? HIS LAST APPRENTICE WAS KOSMO GALLION, RAN A BOOKSHOP IN MUSEUM STREET. DIED SOME YEARS BACK.

THE METATEMPORAL DETECTIVE MIGHT KNOW MORE. HE'S DUE TO MATERIALIZE NEAR KING'S CROSS TOMORROW.

Y-YOU MEAN ANDREW NORTON?

IF YOU LIKE. PERSONALLY, I'VE ALWAYS CALLED HIM TAFFY.

ANYWAY, GOOD LUCK WITH YOUR WITCH-HUNT. THOSE WERE THE DAYS, EH? NO FUEL CRISIS WHEN YOU'RE BURNING OLD WOMEN.

YOU KNOW, I DO MISS CROMWELL.

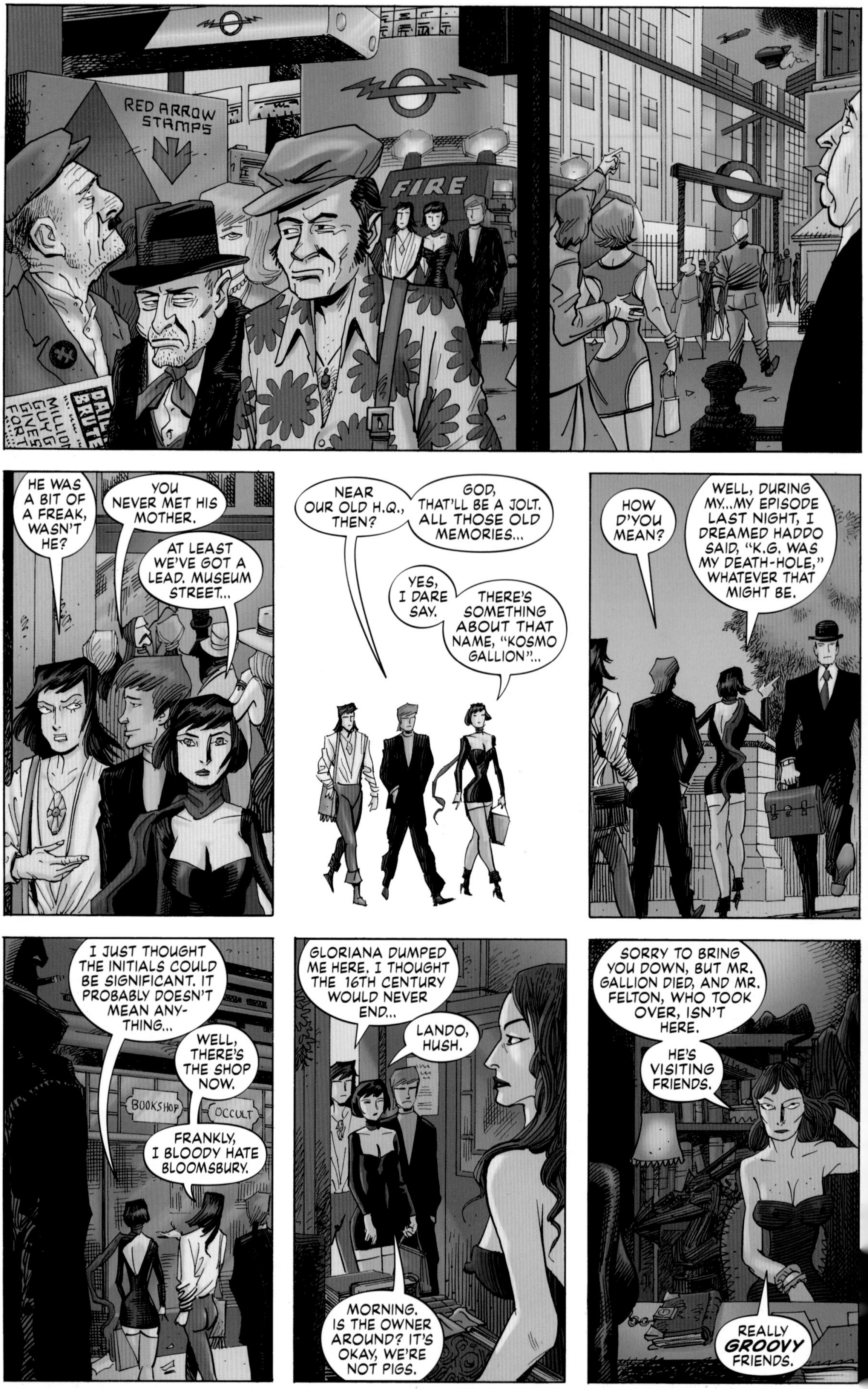

RED ARROW STAMPS
FIRE
DAILY BRUTE
HE WAS A BIT OF A FREAK, WASN'T HE?
YOU NEVER MET HIS MOTHER.
AT LEAST WE'VE GOT A LEAD. MUSEUM STREET...
NEAR OUR OLD H.Q., THEN?
GOD, THAT'LL BE A JOLT. ALL THOSE OLD MEMORIES...
YES, I DARE SAY.
THERE'S SOMETHING ABOUT THAT NAME, "KOSMO GALLION"...
HOW D'YOU MEAN?
WELL, DURING MY...MY EPISODE LAST NIGHT, I DREAMED HADDO SAID, "K.G. WAS MY DEATH-HOLE," WHATEVER THAT MIGHT BE.
I JUST THOUGHT THE INITIALS COULD BE SIGNIFICANT. IT PROBABLY DOESN'T MEAN ANY-THING...
WELL, THERE'S THE SHOP NOW.
BOOKSHOP
OCCULT
FRANKLY, I BLOODY HATE BLOOMSBURY.
GLORIANA DUMPED ME HERE. I THOUGHT THE 16TH CENTURY WOULD NEVER END...
LANDO, HUSH.
MORNING. IS THE OWNER AROUND? IT'S OKAY, WE'RE NOT PIGS.
SORRY TO BRING YOU DOWN, BUT MR. GALLION DIED, AND MR. FELTON, WHO TOOK OVER, ISN'T HERE.
HE'S VISITING FRIENDS.
REALLY GROOVY FRIENDS.

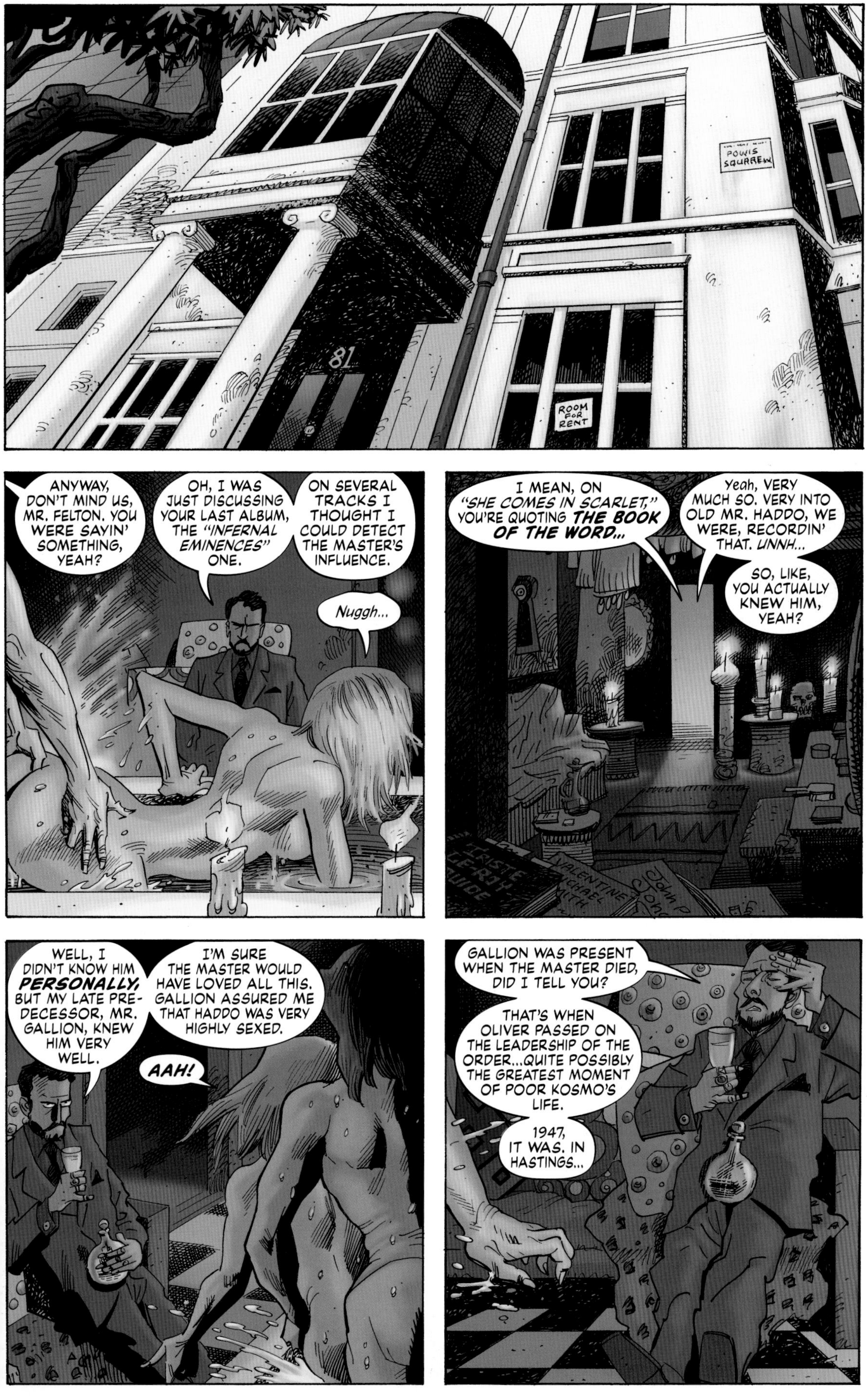
POWIS SQUARE
81
ROOM FOR RENT
ANYWAY, DON'T MIND US, MR. FELTON. YOU WERE SAYIN' SOMETHING, YEAH?
OH, I WAS JUST DISCUSSING YOUR LAST ALBUM, THE "INFERNAL EMINENCES" ONE.
ON SEVERAL TRACKS I THOUGHT I COULD DETECT THE MASTER'S INFLUENCE.
Nuggh...
I MEAN, ON "SHE COMES IN SCARLET," YOU'RE QUOTING **THE BOOK OF THE WORD...**
Yeah, VERY MUCH SO. VERY INTO OLD MR. HADDO, WE WERE, RECORDIN' THAT. UNNH...
SO, LIKE, YOU ACTUALLY KNEW HIM, YEAH?
WELL, I DIDN'T KNOW HIM **PERSONALLY,** BUT MY LATE PREDECESSOR, MR. GALLION, KNEW HIM VERY WELL.
I'M SURE THE MASTER WOULD HAVE LOVED ALL THIS. GALLION ASSURED ME THAT HADDO WAS VERY HIGHLY SEXED.
AAH!
GALLION WAS PRESENT WHEN THE MASTER DIED, DID I TELL YOU?
THAT'S WHEN OLIVER PASSED ON THE LEADERSHIP OF THE ORDER...QUITE POSSIBLY THE GREATEST MOMENT OF POOR KOSMO'S LIFE.
1947, IT WAS. IN HASTINGS...

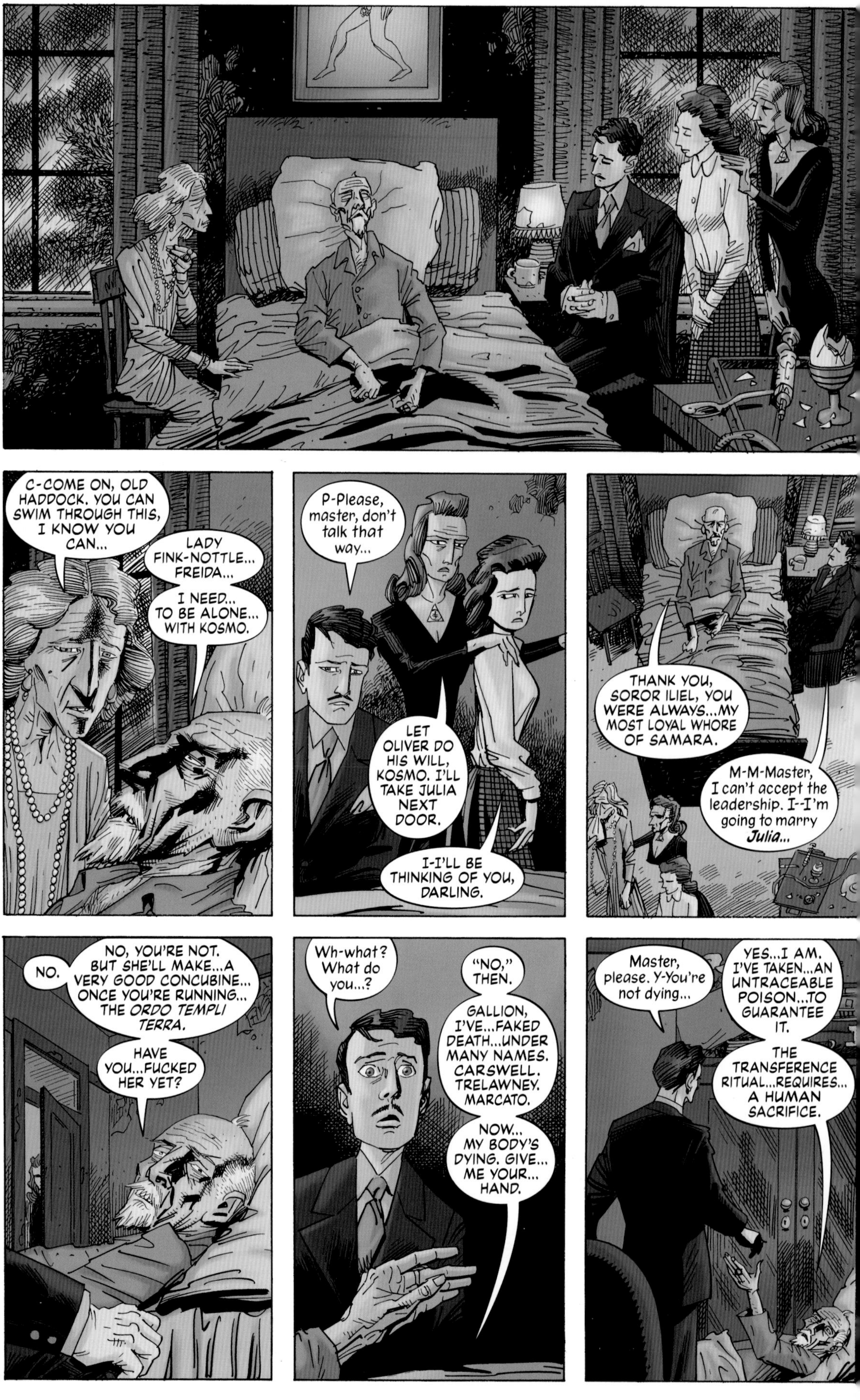
C-COME ON, OLD HADDOCK. YOU CAN SWIM THROUGH THIS, I KNOW YOU CAN...
LADY FINK-NOTTLE... FREIDA...
I NEED... TO BE ALONE... WITH KOSMO.
P-Please, master, don't talk that way...
LET OLIVER DO HIS WILL, KOSMO. I'LL TAKE JULIA NEXT DOOR.
I-I'LL BE THINKING OF YOU, DARLING.
THANK YOU, SOROR ILIEL, YOU WERE ALWAYS...MY MOST LOYAL WHORE OF SAMARA.
M-M-Master, I can't accept the leadership. I--I'm going to marry *Julia*...
NO.
NO, YOU'RE NOT. BUT SHE'LL MAKE...A VERY GOOD CONCUBINE... ONCE YOU'RE RUNNING... THE *ORDO TEMPLI TERRA*.
HAVE YOU...FUCKED HER YET?
Wh-what? What do you...?
"NO," THEN.
GALLION, I'VE...FAKED DEATH...UNDER MANY NAMES. CARSWELL. TRELAWNEY. MARCATO.
NOW... MY BODY'S DYING. GIVE... ME YOUR... HAND.
Master, please. Y-You're not dying...
YES...I AM. I'VE TAKEN...AN UNTRACEABLE POISON...TO GUARANTEE IT.
THE TRANSFERENCE RITUAL...REQUIRES... A HUMAN SACRIFICE.

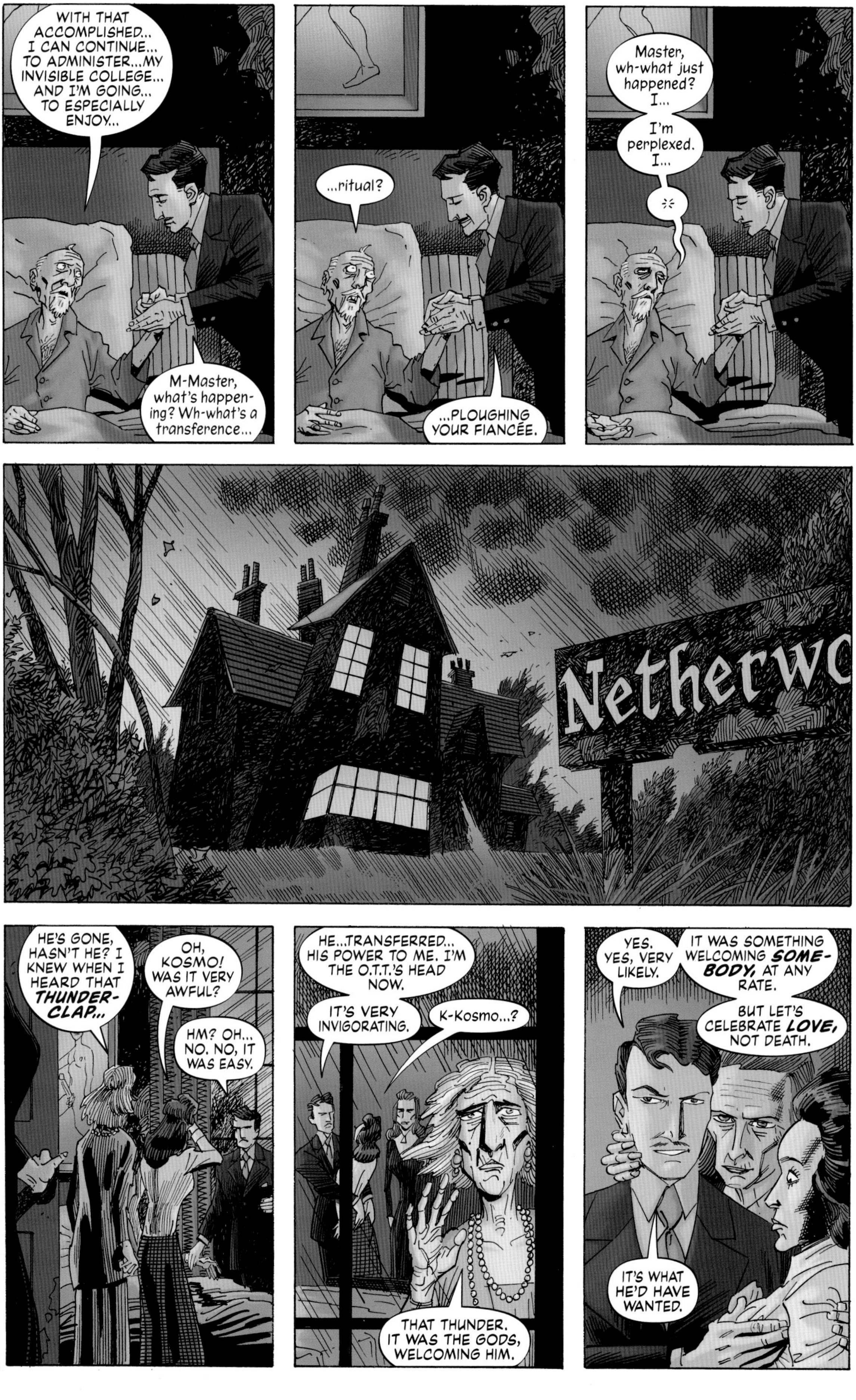
WITH THAT ACCOMPLISHED... I CAN CONTINUE... TO ADMINISTER...MY INVISIBLE COLLEGE... AND I'M GOING... TO ESPECIALLY ENJOY...
M-Master, what's happening? Wh-what's a transference...
...ritual?
...PLOUGHING YOUR FIANCÉE.
Master, wh-what just happened? I...
I'm perplexed. I...
Netherwo
HE'S GONE, HASN'T HE? I KNEW WHEN I HEARD THAT THUNDER-CLAP...
OH, KOSMO! WAS IT VERY AWFUL?
HM? OH... NO. NO, IT WAS EASY.
HE...TRANSFERRED... HIS POWER TO ME. I'M THE O.T.T.'S HEAD NOW.
IT'S VERY INVIGORATING.
K-Kosmo...?
THAT THUNDER. IT WAS THE GODS, WELCOMING HIM.
YES. YES, VERY LIKELY.
IT WAS SOMETHING WELCOMING SOME-BODY, AT ANY RATE.
BUT LET'S CELEBRATE LOVE, NOT DEATH.
IT'S WHAT HE'D HAVE WANTED.

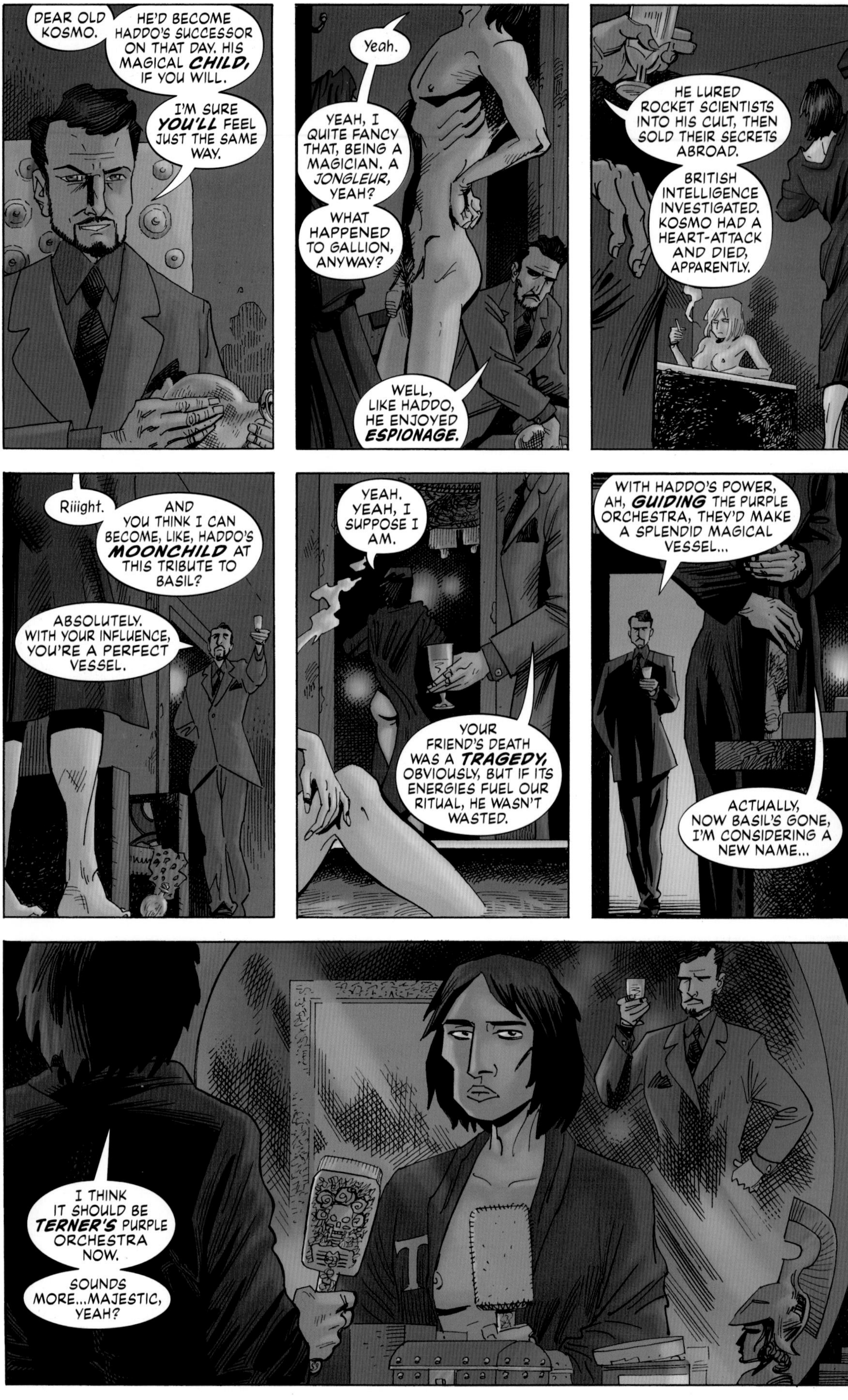
DEAR OLD KOSMO.
HE'D BECOME HADDO'S SUCCESSOR ON THAT DAY. HIS MAGICAL CHILD, IF YOU WILL.
I'M SURE YOU'LL FEEL JUST THE SAME WAY.
Yeah.
YEAH, I QUITE FANCY THAT, BEING A MAGICIAN. A JONGLEUR, YEAH?
WHAT HAPPENED TO GALLION, ANYWAY?
WELL, LIKE HADDO, HE ENJOYED ESPIONAGE.
HE LURED ROCKET SCIENTISTS INTO HIS CULT, THEN SOLD THEIR SECRETS ABROAD.
BRITISH INTELLIGENCE INVESTIGATED. KOSMO HAD A HEART-ATTACK AND DIED, APPARENTLY.
Riiight.
AND YOU THINK I CAN BECOME, LIKE, HADDO'S MOONCHILD AT THIS TRIBUTE TO BASIL?
ABSOLUTELY. WITH YOUR INFLUENCE, YOU'RE A PERFECT VESSEL.
YEAH. YEAH, I SUPPOSE I AM.
YOUR FRIEND'S DEATH WAS A TRAGEDY, OBVIOUSLY, BUT IF ITS ENERGIES FUEL OUR RITUAL, HE WASN'T WASTED.
WITH HADDO'S POWER, AH, GUIDING THE PURPLE ORCHESTRA, THEY'D MAKE A SPLENDID MAGICAL VESSEL...
ACTUALLY, NOW BASIL'S GONE, I'M CONSIDERING A NEW NAME...
I THINK IT SHOULD BE TERNER'S PURPLE ORCHESTRA NOW.
SOUNDS MORE...MAJESTIC, YEAH?

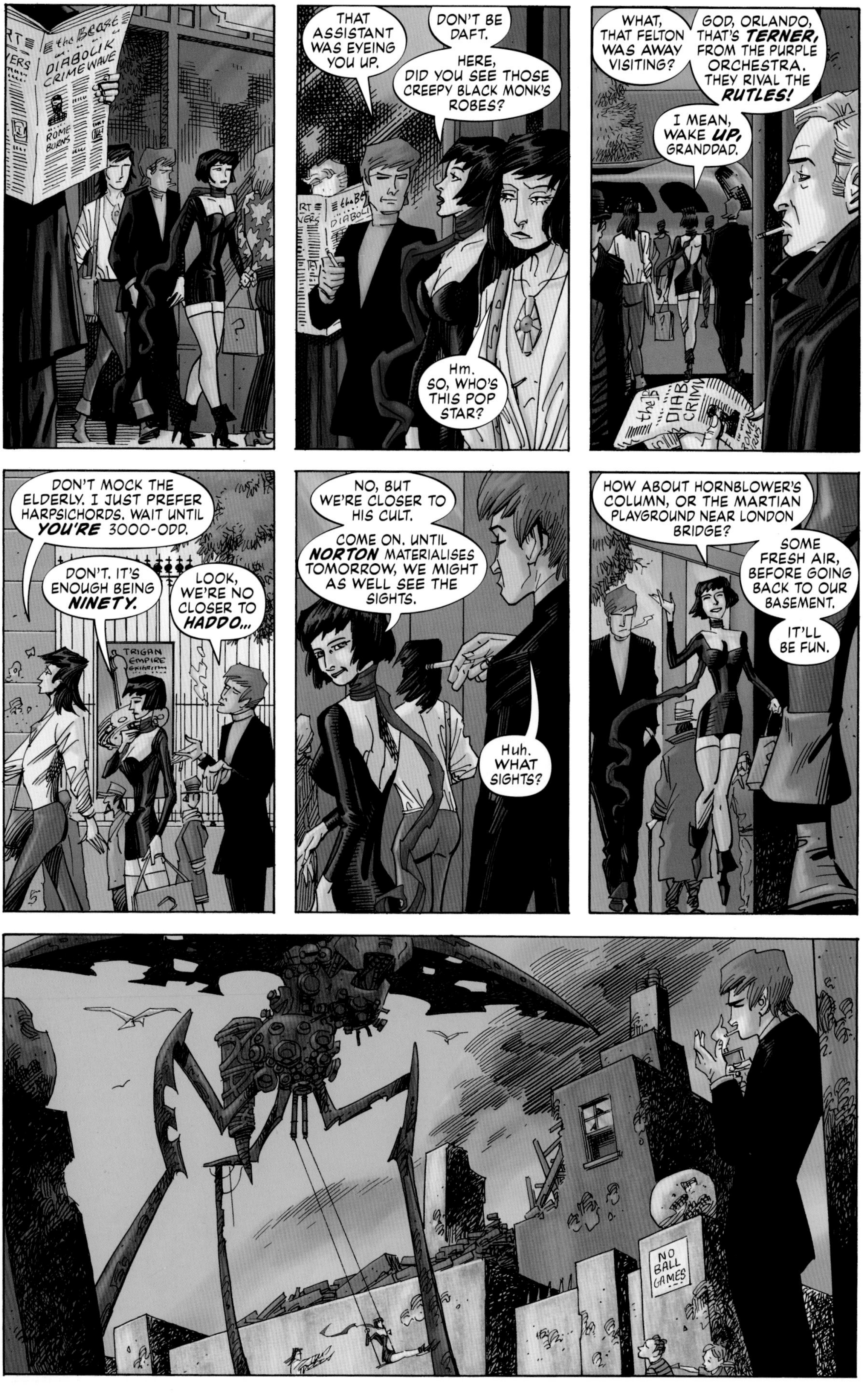
the BEAST
DIABOLIK CRIMEWAVE
ROME BURNS
THAT ASSISTANT WAS EYEING YOU UP.
DON'T BE DAFT.
HERE, DID YOU SEE THOSE CREEPY BLACK MONK'S ROBES?
Hm. SO, WHO'S THIS POP STAR?
WHAT, THAT FELTON WAS AWAY VISITING?
GOD, ORLANDO, THAT'S TERNER, FROM THE PURPLE ORCHESTRA. THEY RIVAL THE RUTLES!
I MEAN, WAKE UP, GRANDDAD.
DON'T MOCK THE ELDERLY. I JUST PREFER HARPSICHORDS. WAIT UNTIL YOU'RE 3000-ODD.
DON'T. IT'S ENOUGH BEING NINETY.
LOOK, WE'RE NO CLOSER TO HADDO...
TRIGAN EMPIRE
NO, BUT WE'RE CLOSER TO HIS CULT.
COME ON. UNTIL NORTON MATERIALISES TOMORROW, WE MIGHT AS WELL SEE THE SIGHTS.
Huh. WHAT SIGHTS?
HOW ABOUT HORNBLOWER'S COLUMN, OR THE MARTIAN PLAYGROUND NEAR LONDON BRIDGE?
SOME FRESH AIR, BEFORE GOING BACK TO OUR BASEMENT.
IT'LL BE FUN.
NO BALL GAMES

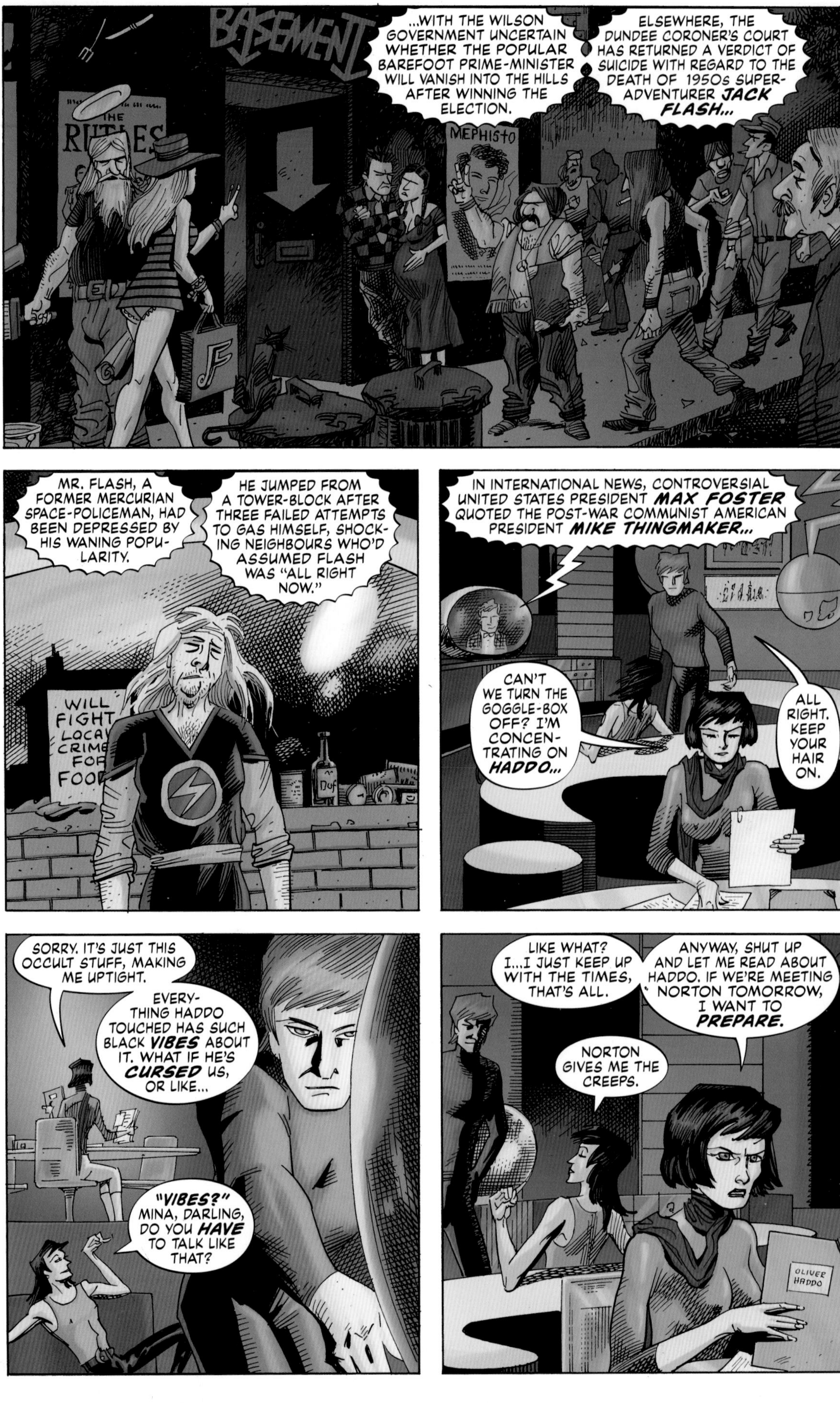
BASEMENT
THE RUTLES
MEPHISTO
...WITH THE WILSON GOVERNMENT UNCERTAIN WHETHER THE POPULAR BAREFOOT PRIME-MINISTER WILL VANISH INTO THE HILLS AFTER WINNING THE ELECTION.
ELSEWHERE, THE DUNDEE CORONER'S COURT HAS RETURNED A VERDICT OF SUICIDE WITH REGARD TO THE DEATH OF 1950s SUPER-ADVENTURER JACK FLASH...
MR. FLASH, A FORMER MERCURIAN SPACE-POLICEMAN, HAD BEEN DEPRESSED BY HIS WANING POPULARITY.
HE JUMPED FROM A TOWER-BLOCK AFTER THREE FAILED ATTEMPTS TO GAS HIMSELF, SHOCKING NEIGHBOURS WHO'D ASSUMED FLASH WAS "ALL RIGHT NOW."
WILL FIGHT LOCAL CRIME FOR FOOD
IN INTERNATIONAL NEWS, CONTROVERSIAL UNITED STATES PRESIDENT MAX FOSTER QUOTED THE POST-WAR COMMUNIST AMERICAN PRESIDENT MIKE THINGMAKER...
CAN'T WE TURN THE GOGGLE-BOX OFF? I'M CONCENTRATING ON HADDO...
ALL RIGHT. KEEP YOUR HAIR ON.
SORRY. IT'S JUST THIS OCCULT STUFF, MAKING ME UPTIGHT.
EVERYTHING HADDO TOUCHED HAS SUCH BLACK VIBES ABOUT IT. WHAT IF HE'S CURSED US, OR LIKE...
"VIBES?" MINA, DARLING, DO YOU HAVE TO TALK LIKE THAT?
LIKE WHAT? I...I JUST KEEP UP WITH THE TIMES, THAT'S ALL.
ANYWAY, SHUT UP AND LET ME READ ABOUT HADDO. IF WE'RE MEETING NORTON TOMORROW, I WANT TO PREPARE.
NORTON GIVES ME THE CREEPS.
OLIVER HADDO

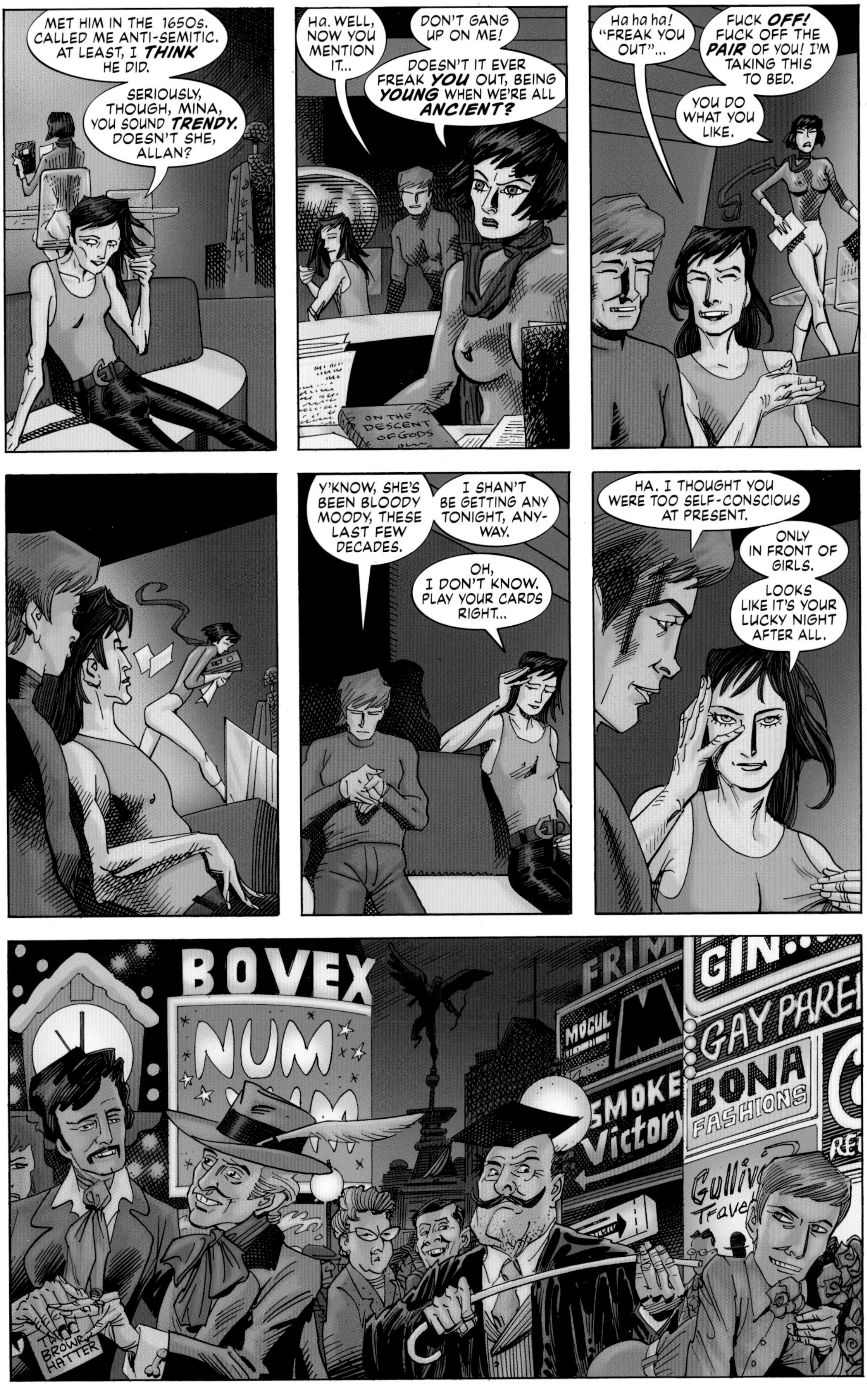
MET HIM IN THE 1650s. CALLED ME ANTI-SEMITIC. AT LEAST, I THINK HE DID.
SERIOUSLY, THOUGH, MINA, YOU SOUND TRENDY. DOESN'T SHE, ALLAN?
Ha. WELL, NOW YOU MENTION IT...
DON'T GANG UP ON ME!
DOESN'T IT EVER FREAK YOU OUT, BEING YOUNG WHEN WE'RE ALL ANCIENT?
ON THE DESCENT OF GODS
Ha ha ha! "FREAK YOU OUT"...
FUCK OFF! FUCK OFF THE PAIR OF YOU! I'M TAKING THIS TO BED.
YOU DO WHAT YOU LIKE.
Y'KNOW, SHE'S BEEN BLOODY MOODY, THESE LAST FEW DECADES.
I SHAN'T BE GETTING ANY TONIGHT, ANY-WAY.
OH, I DON'T KNOW. PLAY YOUR CARDS RIGHT...
HA. I THOUGHT YOU WERE TOO SELF-CONSCIOUS AT PRESENT.
ONLY IN FRONT OF GIRLS.
LOOKS LIKE IT'S YOUR LUCKY NIGHT AFTER ALL.
BOVEX
NUM
MOGUL
M
SMOKE Victory
GAY PAREE
BONA FASHIONS
BROWN HATTER

VINCE?

YOU GOT A MINUTE?

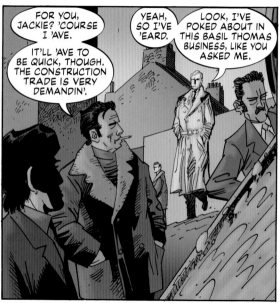

FOR YOU, JACKIE? 'COURSE I 'AVE.

IT'LL 'AVE TO BE QUICK, THOUGH. THE CONSTRUCTION TRADE IS VERY DEMANDIN'.

YEAH, SO I'VE 'EARD.

LOOK, I'VE POKED ABOUT IN THIS BASIL THOMAS BUSINESS, LIKE YOU ASKED ME.

YEAH? SO 'OO'S BEHIND IT, THEN? IT BETTER NOT BE FUCKIN' STARKS...

I DON'T THINK IT'S ANOTHER FIRM, VINCE.

I RECKON IT'S ONE OF THEM BLACK MAGIC OUTFITS YOU 'EAR ABOUT IN THE PAPERS.

THERE'S THIS TOP WIZARD OR WHAT-NOT. 'E'S GOT MONKS' ROBES LIKE MATEY 'ERE SAW. PLUS HE'S PALLY WITH THE SINGER FROM THOMAS'S POP GROUP.

YOU'RE PULLIN' MY PISSER.

BONEHEAD! WHERE'S THAT BACKFILL?

Comin', boss...

THAT'S WHAT I 'EARD, ANYWAY.

'ERE, WHAT'S UP WITH YOUR MUSH, DARLIN'? TRIP OVER COMIN' OUT THE LADIES?

I LOVE THIS BOY, JACKIE, BUT I 'AVE TO BE STRICT SOMETIMES.

SO, THESE DEVIL-WORSHIPPIN' BLEEDERS...

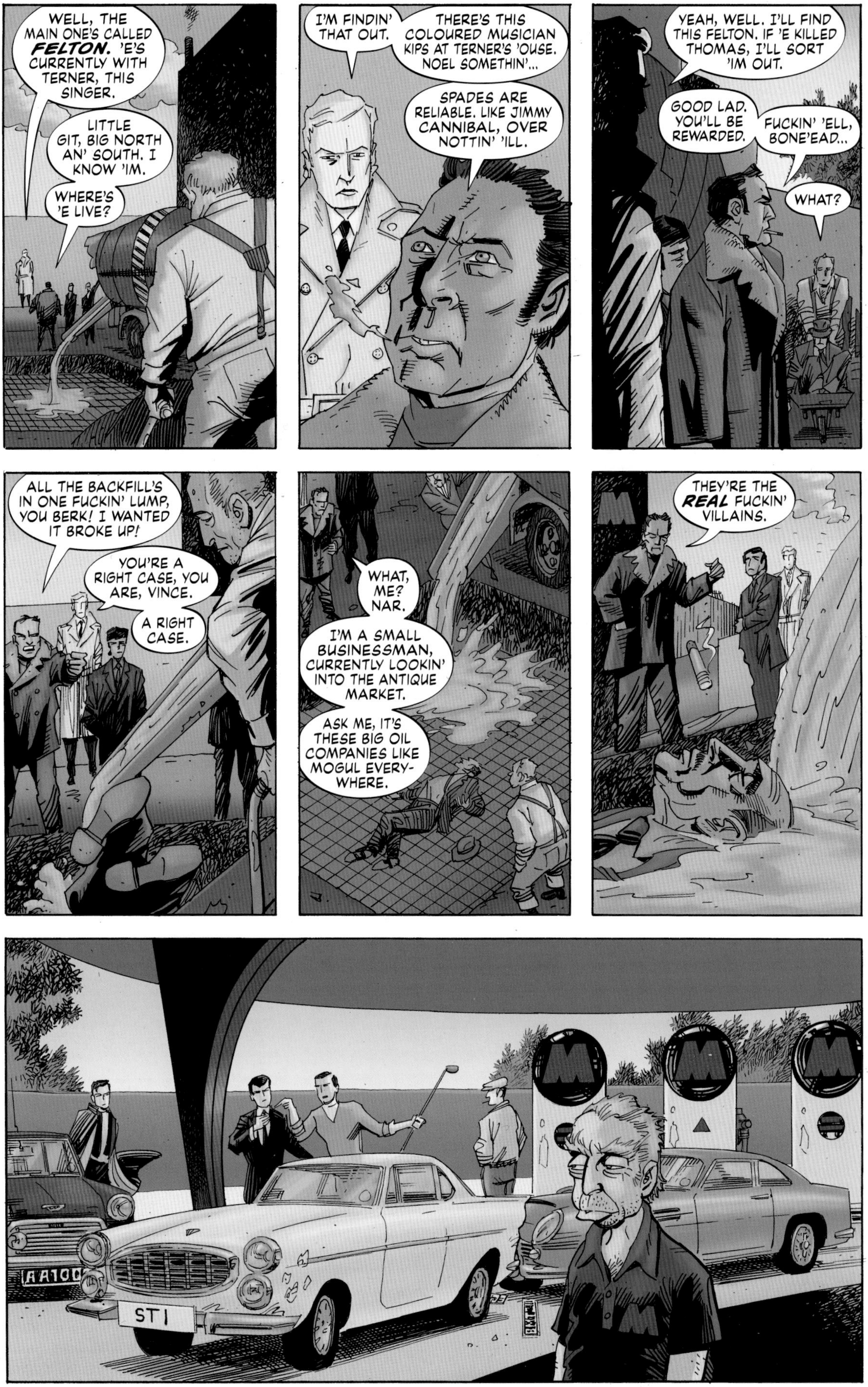
WELL, THE MAIN ONE'S CALLED FELTON. 'E'S CURRENTLY WITH TERNER, THIS SINGER.
LITTLE GIT, BIG NORTH AN' SOUTH. I KNOW 'IM.
WHERE'S 'E LIVE?
I'M FINDIN' THAT OUT.
THERE'S THIS COLOURED MUSICIAN KIPS AT TERNER'S 'OUSE. NOEL SOMETHIN'...
SPADES ARE RELIABLE. LIKE JIMMY CANNIBAL, OVER NOTTIN' 'ILL.
YEAH, WELL. I'LL FIND THIS FELTON. IF 'E KILLED THOMAS, I'LL SORT 'IM OUT.
GOOD LAD. YOU'LL BE REWARDED.
FUCKIN' 'ELL, BONE'EAD...
WHAT?
ALL THE BACKFILL'S IN ONE FUCKIN' LUMP, YOU BERK! I WANTED IT BROKE UP!
YOU'RE A RIGHT CASE, YOU ARE, VINCE.
A RIGHT CASE.
WHAT, ME? NAR.
I'M A SMALL BUSINESSMAN, CURRENTLY LOOKIN' INTO THE ANTIQUE MARKET.
ASK ME, IT'S THESE BIG OIL COMPANIES LIKE MOGUL EVERY-WHERE.
THEY'RE THE REAL FUCKIN' VILLAINS.
AA100
ST 1

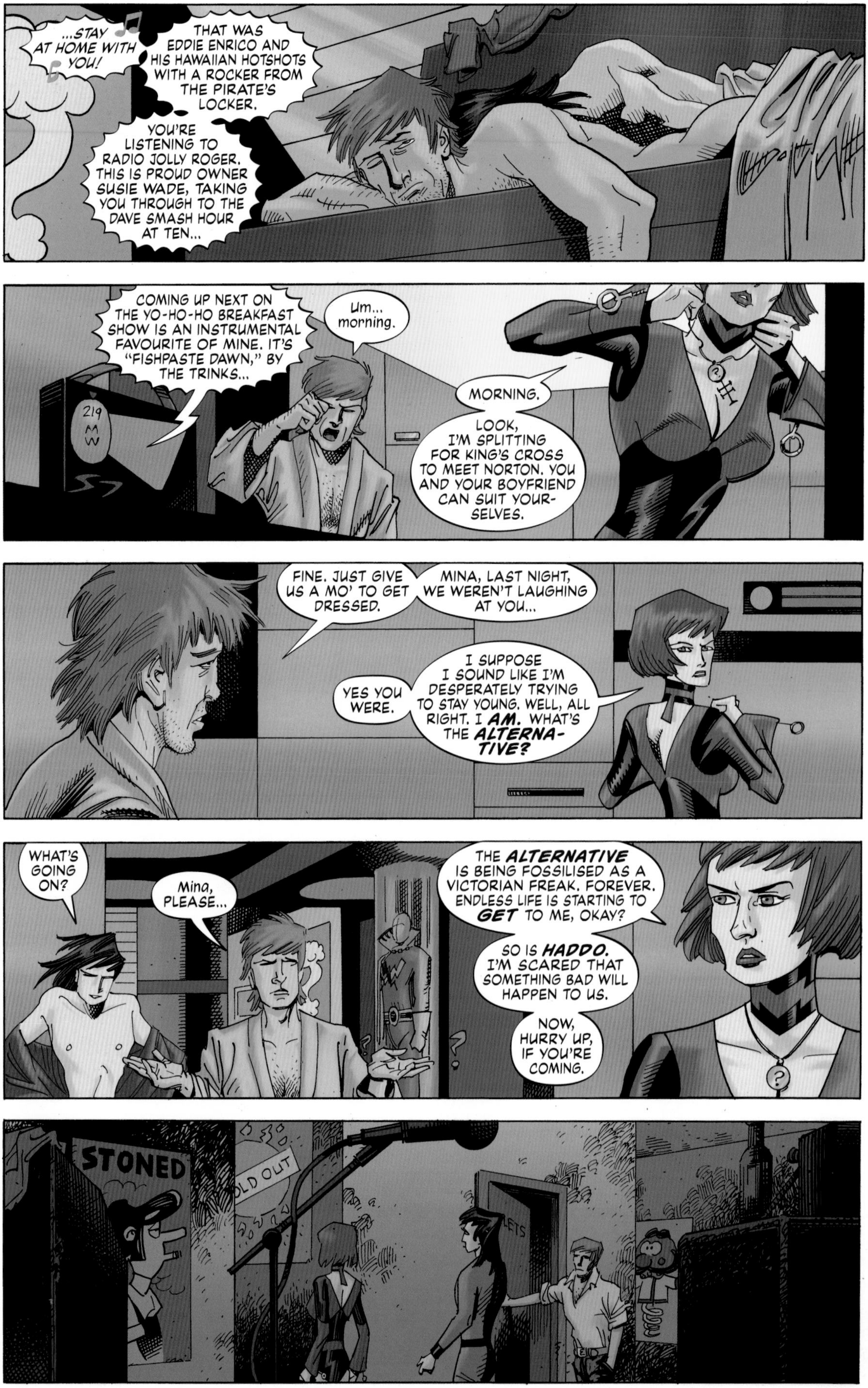
...STAY AT HOME WITH YOU!
THAT WAS EDDIE ENRICO AND HIS HAWAIIAN HOTSHOTS WITH A ROCKER FROM THE PIRATE'S LOCKER.
YOU'RE LISTENING TO RADIO JOLLY ROGER. THIS IS PROUD OWNER SUSIE WADE, TAKING YOU THROUGH TO THE DAVE SMASH HOUR AT TEN...
COMING UP NEXT ON THE YO-HO-HO BREAKFAST SHOW IS AN INSTRUMENTAL FAVOURITE OF MINE. IT'S "FISHPASTE DAWN," BY THE TRINKS...
Um... morning.
219 MW
MORNING.
LOOK, I'M SPLITTING FOR KING'S CROSS TO MEET NORTON. YOU AND YOUR BOYFRIEND CAN SUIT YOURSELVES.
FINE. JUST GIVE US A MO' TO GET DRESSED.
MINA, LAST NIGHT, WE WEREN'T LAUGHING AT YOU...
YES YOU WERE.
I SUPPOSE I SOUND LIKE I'M DESPERATELY TRYING TO STAY YOUNG. WELL, ALL RIGHT. I **AM**. WHAT'S THE ***ALTERNATIVE?***
WHAT'S GOING ON?
Mina, PLEASE...
THE ***ALTERNATIVE*** IS BEING FOSSILISED AS A VICTORIAN FREAK. FOREVER. ENDLESS LIFE IS STARTING TO ***GET*** TO ME, OKAY?
SO IS ***HADDO.*** I'M SCARED THAT SOMETHING BAD WILL HAPPEN TO US.
NOW, HURRY UP, IF YOU'RE COMING.
STONED
SOLD OUT

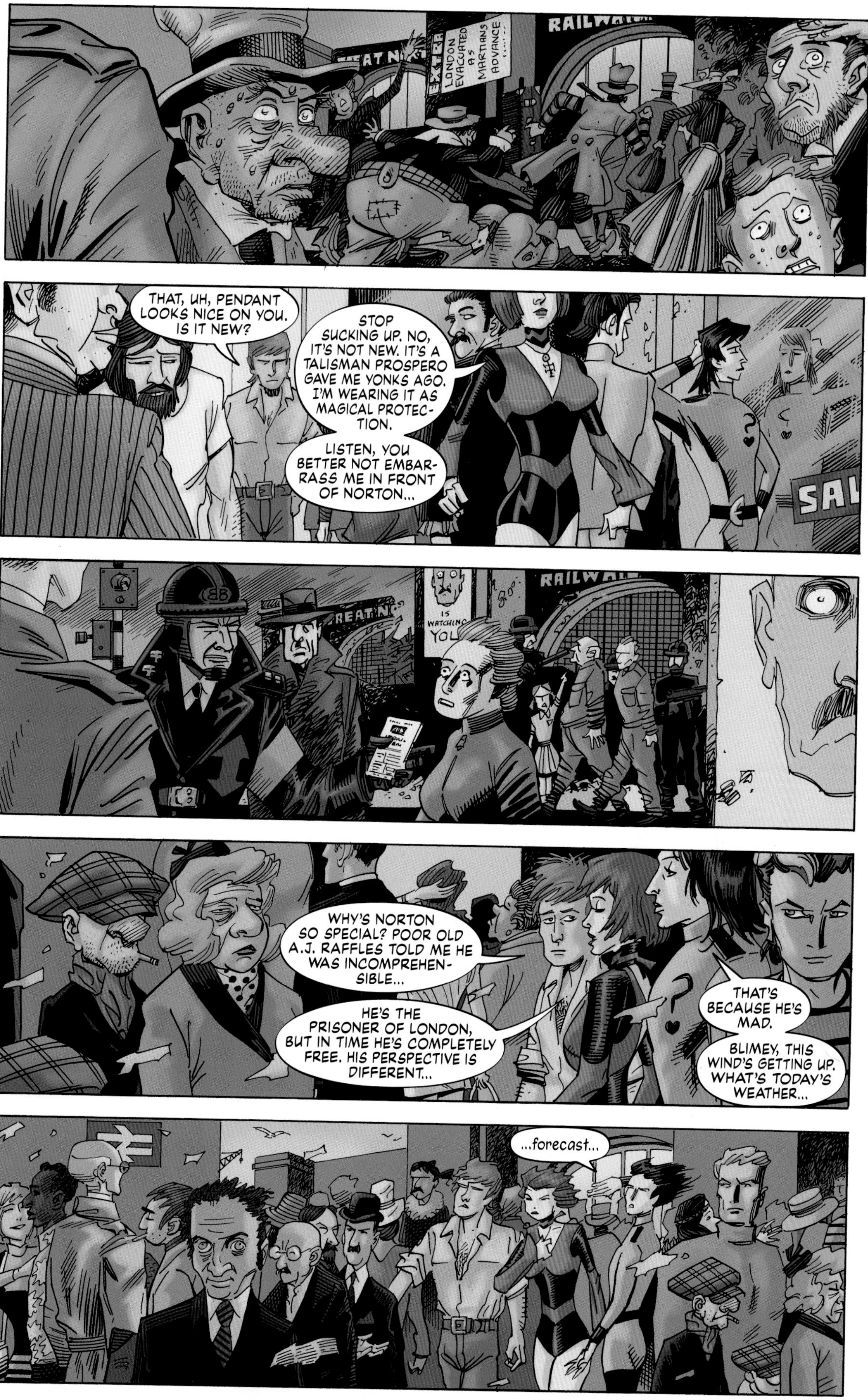
LONDON EVACUATED AS MARTIANS ADVANCE
THAT, UH, PENDANT LOOKS NICE ON YOU. IS IT NEW?
STOP SUCKING UP. NO, IT'S NOT NEW. IT'S A TALISMAN PROSPERO GAVE ME YONKS AGO. I'M WEARING IT AS MAGICAL PROTECTION.
LISTEN, YOU BETTER NOT EMBARRASS ME IN FRONT OF NORTON...
IS WATCHING YOU
WHY'S NORTON SO SPECIAL? POOR OLD A.J. RAFFLES TOLD ME HE WAS INCOMPREHENSIBLE...
HE'S THE PRISONER OF LONDON, BUT IN TIME HE'S COMPLETELY FREE. HIS PERSPECTIVE IS DIFFERENT...
THAT'S BECAUSE HE'S MAD.
BLIMEY, THIS WIND'S GETTING UP. WHAT'S TODAY'S WEATHER...
...forecast...

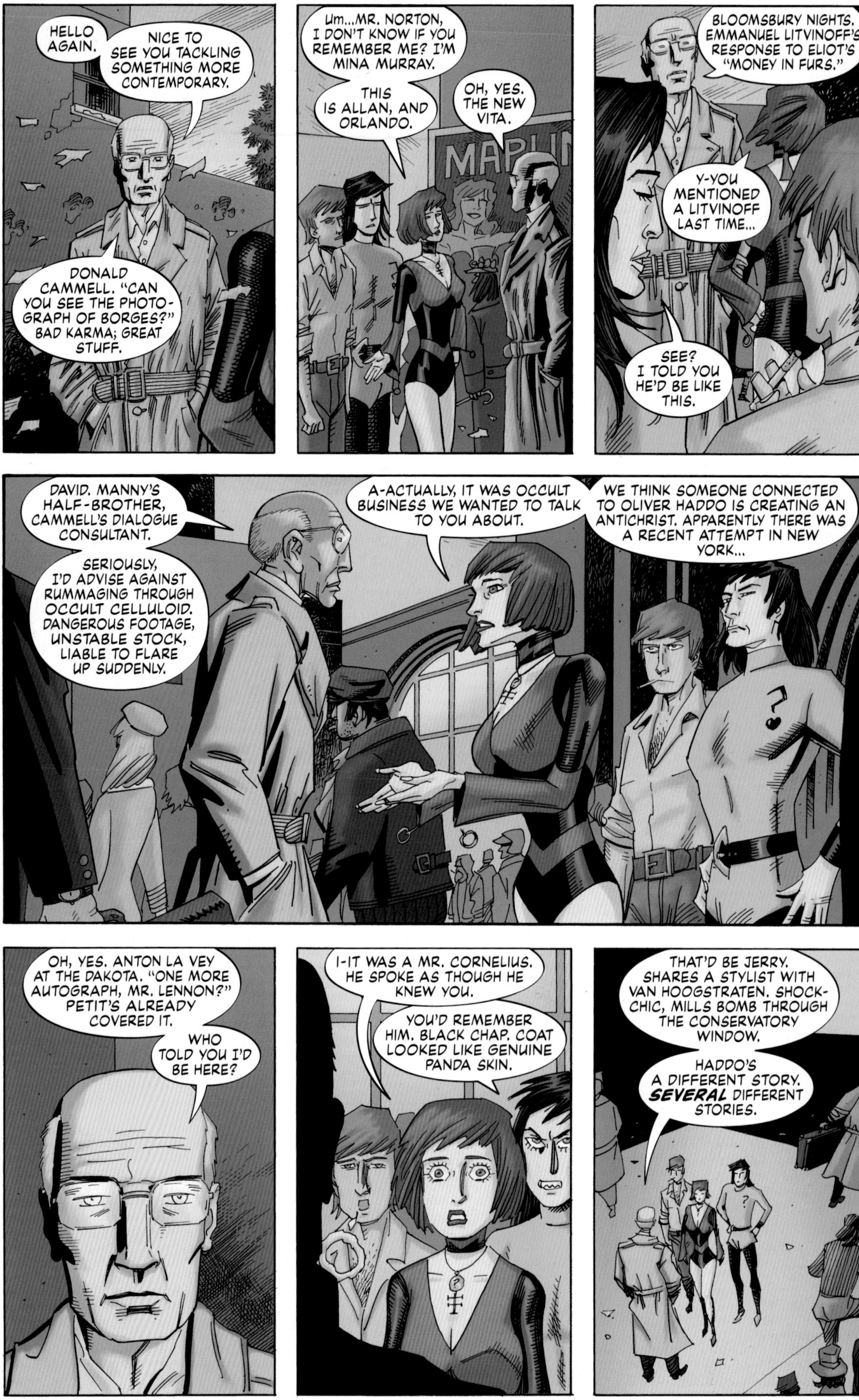
HELLO AGAIN.
NICE TO SEE YOU TACKLING SOMETHING MORE CONTEMPORARY.
DONALD CAMMELL. "CAN YOU SEE THE PHOTOGRAPH OF BORGES?" BAD KARMA; GREAT STUFF.
Um...MR. NORTON, I DON'T KNOW IF YOU REMEMBER ME? I'M MINA MURRAY.
THIS IS ALLAN, AND ORLANDO.
OH, YES. THE NEW VITA.
BLOOMSBURY NIGHTS. EMMANUEL LITVINOFF'S RESPONSE TO ELIOT'S "MONEY IN FURS."
Y-YOU MENTIONED A LITVINOFF LAST TIME...
SEE? I TOLD YOU HE'D BE LIKE THIS.
DAVID. MANNY'S HALF-BROTHER, CAMMELL'S DIALOGUE CONSULTANT.
SERIOUSLY, I'D ADVISE AGAINST RUMMAGING THROUGH OCCULT CELLULOID. DANGEROUS FOOTAGE, UNSTABLE STOCK, LIABLE TO FLARE UP SUDDENLY.
A-ACTUALLY, IT WAS OCCULT BUSINESS WE WANTED TO TALK TO YOU ABOUT.
WE THINK SOMEONE CONNECTED TO OLIVER HADDO IS CREATING AN ANTICHRIST. APPARENTLY THERE WAS A RECENT ATTEMPT IN NEW YORK...
OH, YES. ANTON LA VEY AT THE DAKOTA. "ONE MORE AUTOGRAPH, MR. LENNON?" PETIT'S ALREADY COVERED IT.
WHO TOLD YOU I'D BE HERE?
I-IT WAS A MR. CORNELIUS. HE SPOKE AS THOUGH HE KNEW YOU.
YOU'D REMEMBER HIM. BLACK CHAP. COAT LOOKED LIKE GENUINE PANDA SKIN.
THAT'D BE JERRY. SHARES A STYLIST WITH VAN HOOGSTRATEN. SHOCK-CHIC, MILLS BOMB THROUGH THE CONSERVATORY WINDOW.
HADDO'S A DIFFERENT STORY. **SEVERAL** DIFFERENT STORIES.

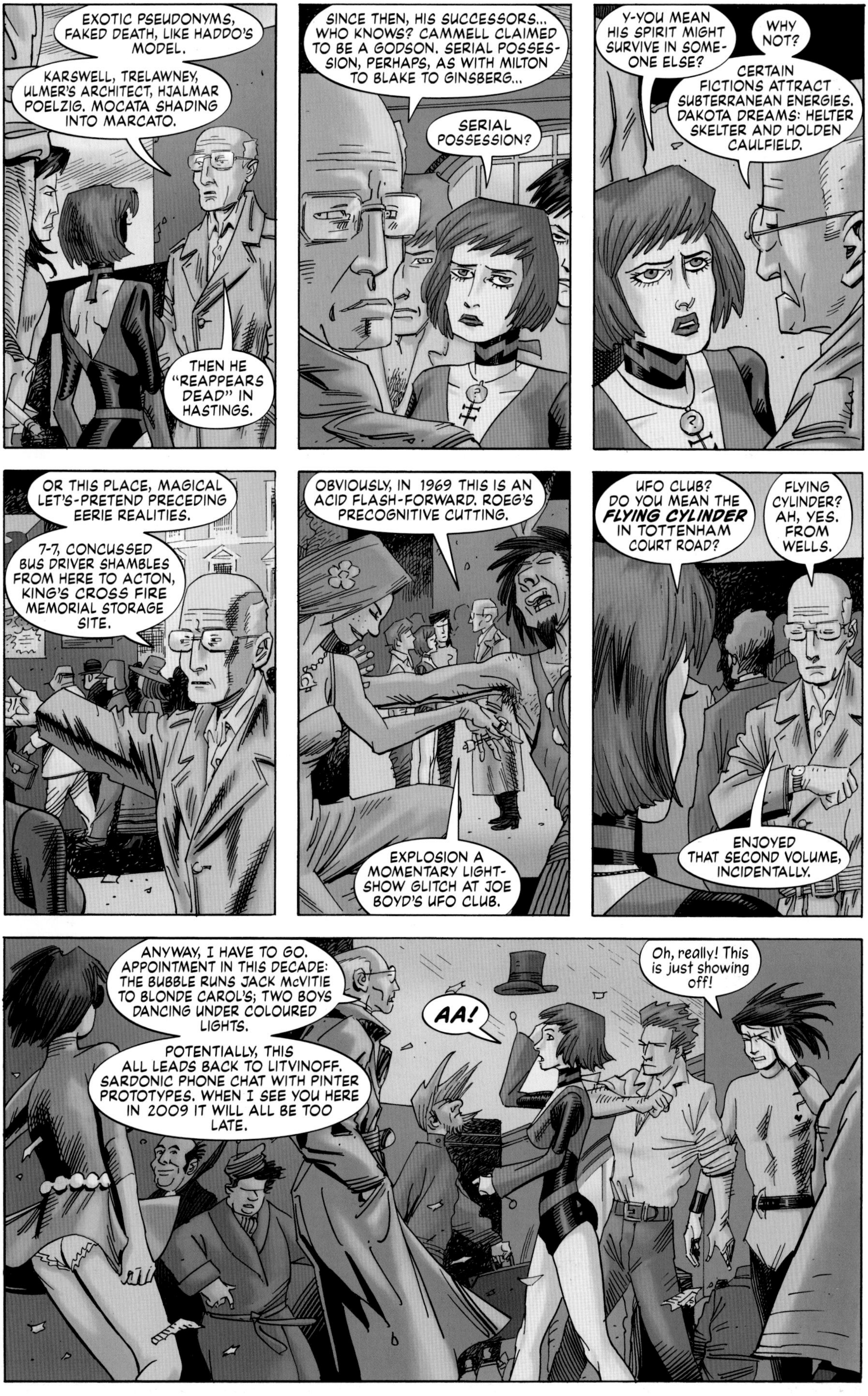
EXOTIC PSEUDONYMS, FAKED DEATH, LIKE HADDO'S MODEL.
KARSWELL, TRELAWNEY, ULMER'S ARCHITECT, HJALMAR POELZIG. MOCATA SHADING INTO MARCATO.
THEN HE "REAPPEARS DEAD" IN HASTINGS.
SINCE THEN, HIS SUCCESSORS... WHO KNOWS? CAMMELL CLAIMED TO BE A GODSON. SERIAL POSSESSION, PERHAPS, AS WITH MILTON TO BLAKE TO GINSBERG...
SERIAL POSSESSION?
Y-YOU MEAN HIS SPIRIT MIGHT SURVIVE IN SOMEONE ELSE?
WHY NOT?
CERTAIN FICTIONS ATTRACT SUBTERRANEAN ENERGIES. DAKOTA DREAMS: HELTER SKELTER AND HOLDEN CAULFIELD.
OR THIS PLACE, MAGICAL LET'S-PRETEND PRECEDING EERIE REALITIES.
7-7, CONCUSSED BUS DRIVER SHAMBLES FROM HERE TO ACTON, KING'S CROSS FIRE MEMORIAL STORAGE SITE.
OBVIOUSLY, IN 1969 THIS IS AN ACID FLASH-FORWARD. ROEG'S PRECOGNITIVE CUTTING.
EXPLOSION A MOMENTARY LIGHT-SHOW GLITCH AT JOE BOYD'S UFO CLUB.
UFO CLUB? DO YOU MEAN THE *FLYING CYLINDER* IN TOTTENHAM COURT ROAD?
FLYING CYLINDER? AH, YES. FROM WELLS.
ENJOYED THAT SECOND VOLUME, INCIDENTALLY.
ANYWAY, I HAVE TO GO. APPOINTMENT IN THIS DECADE: THE BUBBLE RUNS JACK McVITIE TO BLONDE CAROL'S; TWO BOYS DANCING UNDER COLOURED LIGHTS.
POTENTIALLY, THIS ALL LEADS BACK TO LITVINOFF. SARDONIC PHONE CHAT WITH PINTER PROTOTYPES. WHEN I SEE YOU HERE IN 2009 IT WILL ALL BE TOO LATE.
AA!
Oh, really! This is just showing off!

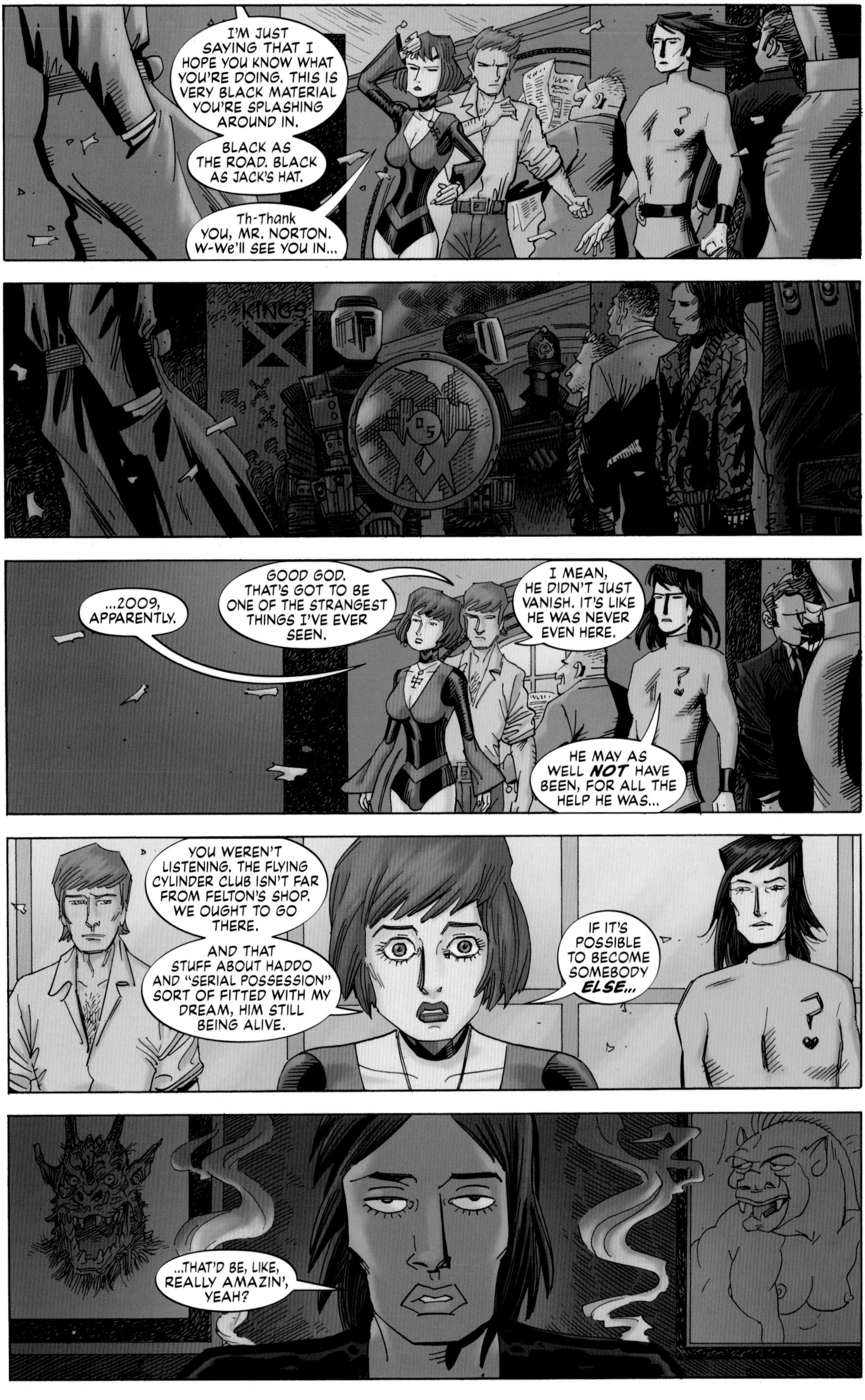
I'M JUST SAYING THAT I HOPE YOU KNOW WHAT YOU'RE DOING. THIS IS VERY BLACK MATERIAL YOU'RE SPLASHING AROUND IN.
BLACK AS THE ROAD. BLACK AS JACK'S HAT.
Th-Thank YOU, MR. NORTON. W-We'll SEE YOU IN...
KINGS
...2009, APPARENTLY.
GOOD GOD. THAT'S GOT TO BE ONE OF THE STRANGEST THINGS I'VE EVER SEEN.
I MEAN, HE DIDN'T JUST VANISH. IT'S LIKE HE WAS NEVER EVEN HERE.
HE MAY AS WELL **NOT** HAVE BEEN, FOR ALL THE HELP HE WAS...
YOU WEREN'T LISTENING. THE FLYING CYLINDER CLUB ISN'T FAR FROM FELTON'S SHOP. WE OUGHT TO GO THERE.
AND THAT STUFF ABOUT HADDO AND "SERIAL POSSESSION" SORT OF FITTED WITH MY DREAM, HIM STILL BEING ALIVE.
IF IT'S POSSIBLE TO BECOME SOMEBODY ***ELSE...***
...THAT'D BE, LIKE, REALLY AMAZIN', YEAH?

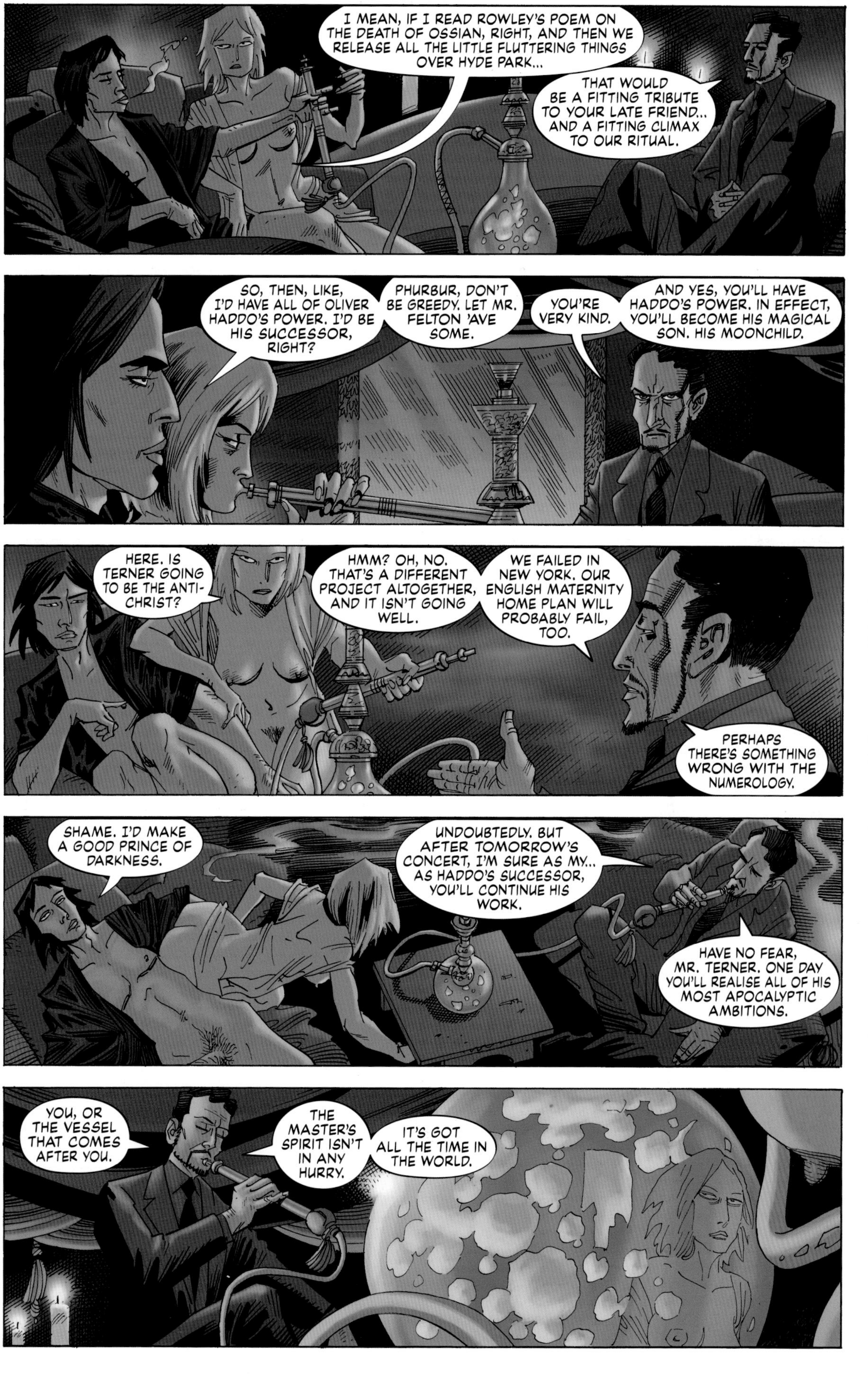
I MEAN, IF I READ ROWLEY'S POEM ON THE DEATH OF OSSIAN, RIGHT, AND THEN WE RELEASE ALL THE LITTLE FLUTTERING THINGS OVER HYDE PARK...
THAT WOULD BE A FITTING TRIBUTE TO YOUR LATE FRIEND... AND A FITTING CLIMAX TO OUR RITUAL.
SO, THEN, LIKE, I'D HAVE ALL OF OLIVER HADDO'S POWER. I'D BE HIS SUCCESSOR, RIGHT?
PHURBUR, DON'T BE GREEDY. LET MR. FELTON 'AVE SOME.
YOU'RE VERY KIND.
AND YES, YOU'LL HAVE HADDO'S POWER. IN EFFECT, YOU'LL BECOME HIS MAGICAL SON. HIS MOONCHILD.
HERE. IS TERNER GOING TO BE THE ANTI-CHRIST?
HMM? OH, NO. THAT'S A DIFFERENT PROJECT ALTOGETHER, AND IT ISN'T GOING WELL.
WE FAILED IN NEW YORK. OUR ENGLISH MATERNITY HOME PLAN WILL PROBABLY FAIL, TOO.
PERHAPS THERE'S SOMETHING WRONG WITH THE NUMEROLOGY.
SHAME. I'D MAKE A GOOD PRINCE OF DARKNESS.
UNDOUBTEDLY. BUT AFTER TOMORROW'S CONCERT, I'M SURE AS MY... AS HADDO'S SUCCESSOR, YOU'LL CONTINUE HIS WORK.
HAVE NO FEAR, MR. TERNER. ONE DAY YOU'LL REALISE ALL OF HIS MOST APOCALYPTIC AMBITIONS.
YOU, OR THE VESSEL THAT COMES AFTER YOU.
THE MASTER'S SPIRIT ISN'T IN ANY HURRY.
IT'S GOT ALL THE TIME IN THE WORLD.

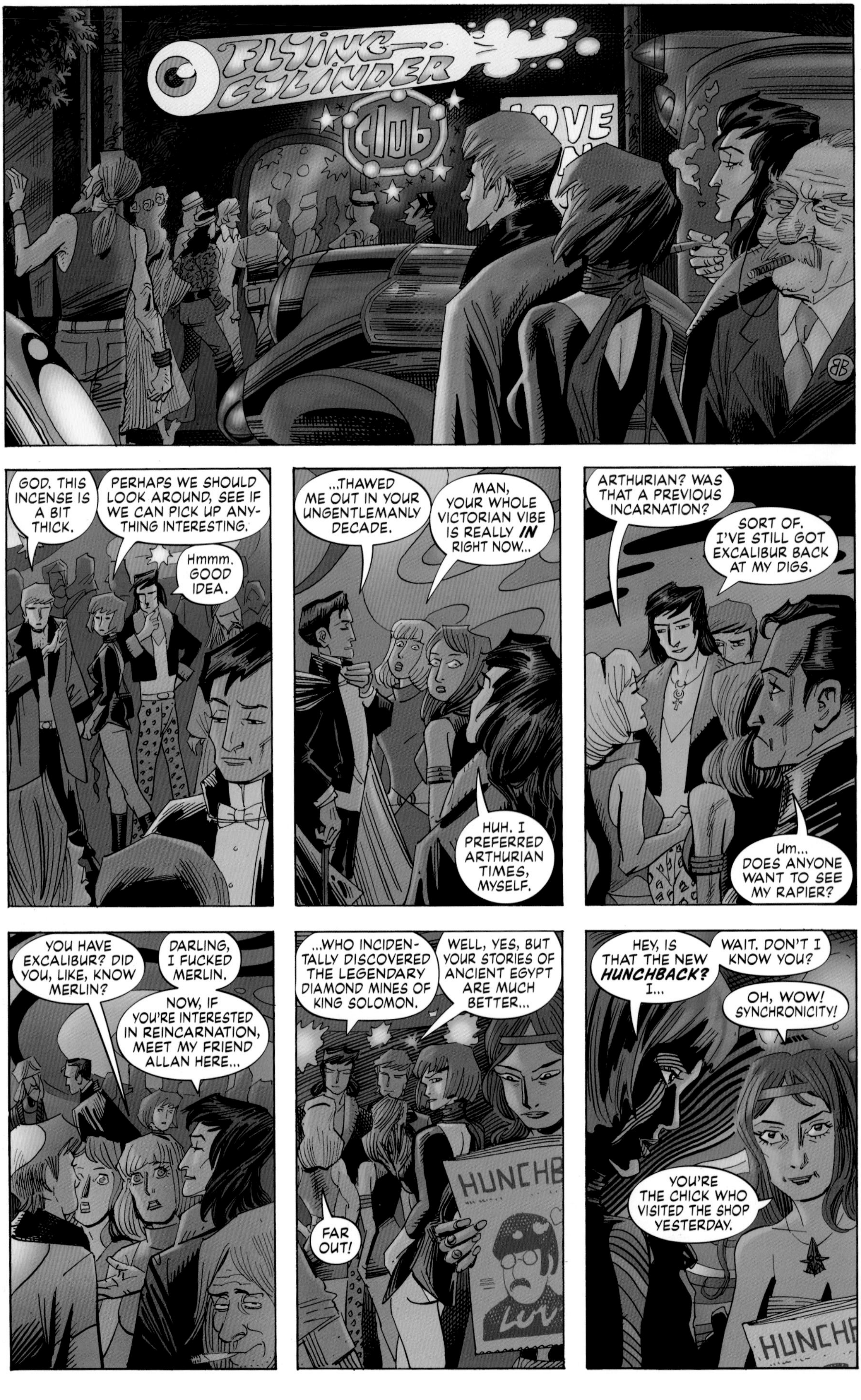
FLYING CYLINDER
club
LOVE
GOD. THIS INCENSE IS A BIT THICK.
PERHAPS WE SHOULD LOOK AROUND, SEE IF WE CAN PICK UP ANYTHING INTERESTING.
Hmmm. GOOD IDEA.
...THAWED ME OUT IN YOUR UNGENTLEMANLY DECADE.
MAN, YOUR WHOLE VICTORIAN VIBE IS REALLY IN RIGHT NOW...
HUH. I PREFERRED ARTHURIAN TIMES, MYSELF.
ARTHURIAN? WAS THAT A PREVIOUS INCARNATION?
SORT OF. I'VE STILL GOT EXCALIBUR BACK AT MY DIGS.
Um... DOES ANYONE WANT TO SEE MY RAPIER?
YOU HAVE EXCALIBUR? DID YOU, LIKE, KNOW MERLIN?
DARLING, I FUCKED MERLIN.
NOW, IF YOU'RE INTERESTED IN REINCARNATION, MEET MY FRIEND ALLAN HERE...
...WHO INCIDENTALLY DISCOVERED THE LEGENDARY DIAMOND MINES OF KING SOLOMON.
WELL, YES, BUT YOUR STORIES OF ANCIENT EGYPT ARE MUCH BETTER...
FAR OUT!
HUNCHB
HEY, IS THAT THE NEW HUNCHBACK? I...
WAIT. DON'T I KNOW YOU?
OH, WOW! SYNCHRONICITY!
YOU'RE THE CHICK WHO VISITED THE SHOP YESTERDAY.
HUNCHB

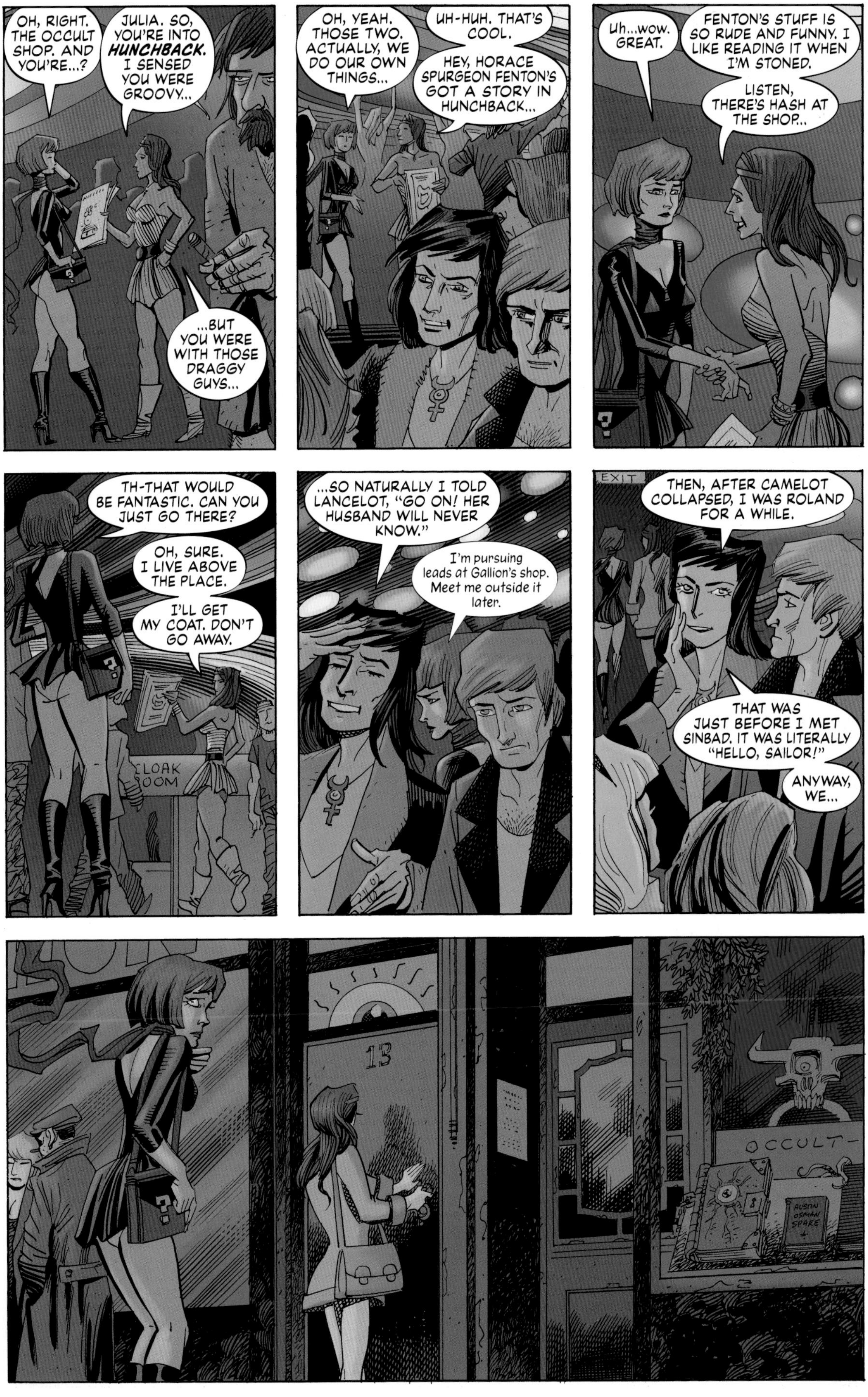
OH, RIGHT. THE OCCULT SHOP. AND YOU'RE...?
JULIA. SO, YOU'RE INTO HUNCHBACK. I SENSED YOU WERE GROOVY...
...BUT YOU WERE WITH THOSE DRAGGY GUYS...
OH, YEAH. THOSE TWO. ACTUALLY, WE DO OUR OWN THINGS...
UH-HUH. THAT'S COOL.
HEY, HORACE SPURGEON FENTON'S GOT A STORY IN HUNCHBACK...
Uh...wow. GREAT.
FENTON'S STUFF IS SO RUDE AND FUNNY. I LIKE READING IT WHEN I'M STONED.
LISTEN, THERE'S HASH AT THE SHOP...
TH-THAT WOULD BE FANTASTIC. CAN YOU JUST GO THERE?
OH, SURE. I LIVE ABOVE THE PLACE.
I'LL GET MY COAT. DON'T GO AWAY.
CLOAK ROOM
...SO NATURALLY I TOLD LANCELOT, "GO ON! HER HUSBAND WILL NEVER KNOW."
I'm pursuing leads at Gallion's shop. Meet me outside it later.
EXIT
THEN, AFTER CAMELOT COLLAPSED, I WAS ROLAND FOR A WHILE.
THAT WAS JUST BEFORE I MET SINBAD. IT WAS LITERALLY "HELLO, SAILOR!"
ANYWAY, WE...
13
OCCULT
AUSTIN OSMAN SPARE

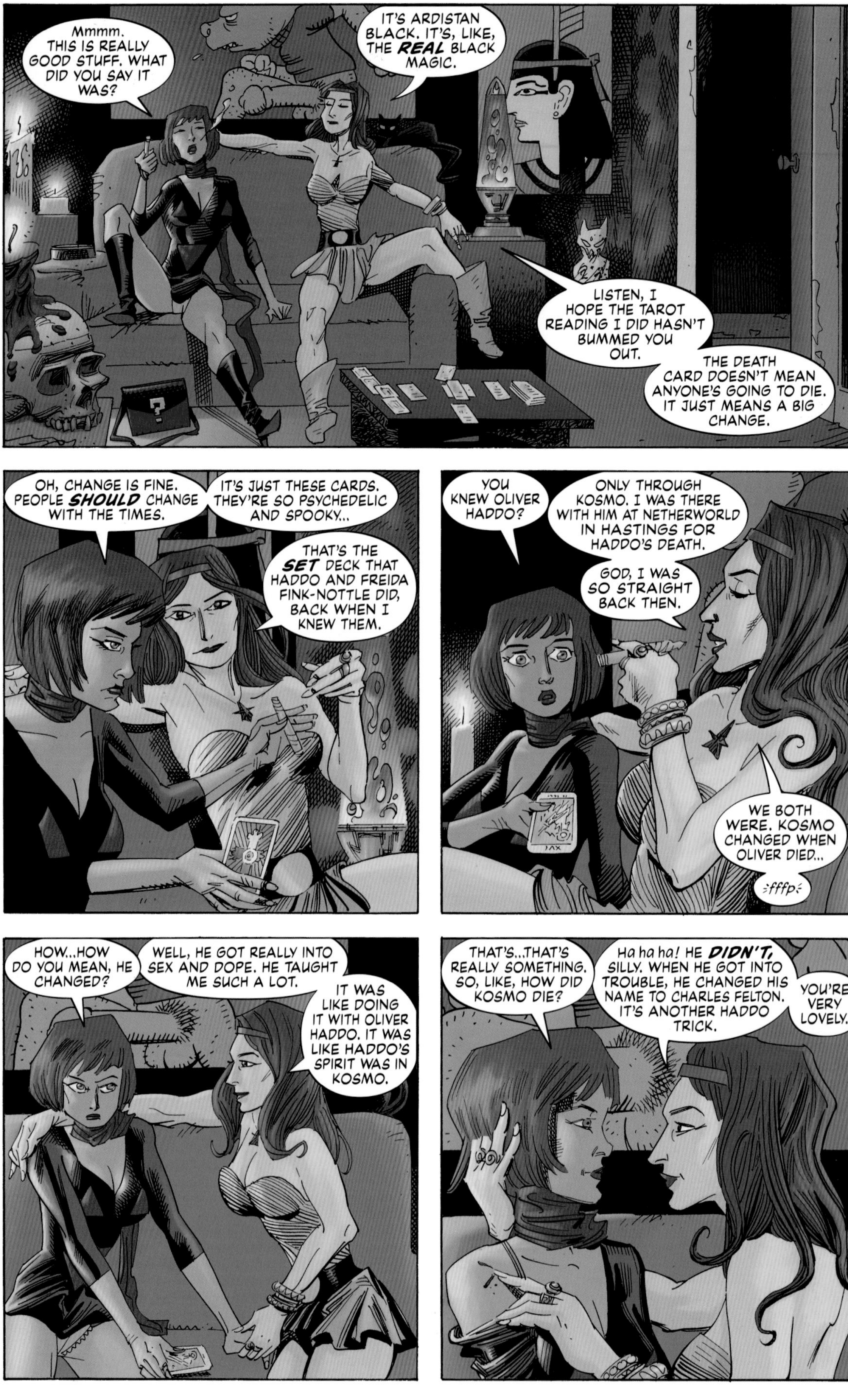

Mmmm. THIS IS REALLY GOOD STUFF. WHAT DID YOU SAY IT WAS?
IT'S ARDISTAN BLACK. IT'S, LIKE, THE ***REAL*** BLACK MAGIC.
LISTEN, I HOPE THE TAROT READING I DID HASN'T BUMMED YOU OUT.
THE DEATH CARD DOESN'T MEAN ANYONE'S GOING TO DIE. IT JUST MEANS A BIG CHANGE.
OH, CHANGE IS FINE. PEOPLE ***SHOULD*** CHANGE WITH THE TIMES.
IT'S JUST THESE CARDS. THEY'RE SO PSYCHEDELIC AND SPOOKY...
THAT'S THE ***SET*** DECK THAT HADDO AND FREIDA FINK-NOTTLE DID, BACK WHEN I KNEW THEM.
YOU KNEW OLIVER HADDO?
ONLY THROUGH KOSMO. I WAS THERE WITH HIM AT NETHERWORLD IN HASTINGS FOR HADDO'S DEATH.
GOD, I WAS SO STRAIGHT BACK THEN.
WE BOTH WERE. KOSMO CHANGED WHEN OLIVER DIED...
fffp
HOW...HOW DO YOU MEAN, HE CHANGED?
WELL, HE GOT REALLY INTO SEX AND DOPE. HE TAUGHT ME SUCH A LOT.
IT WAS LIKE DOING IT WITH OLIVER HADDO. IT WAS LIKE HADDO'S SPIRIT WAS IN KOSMO.
THAT'S...THAT'S REALLY SOMETHING. SO, LIKE, HOW DID KOSMO DIE?
Ha ha ha! HE ***DIDN'T,*** SILLY. WHEN HE GOT INTO TROUBLE, HE CHANGED HIS NAME TO CHARLES FELTON. IT'S ANOTHER HADDO TRICK.
YOU'RE VERY LOVELY.

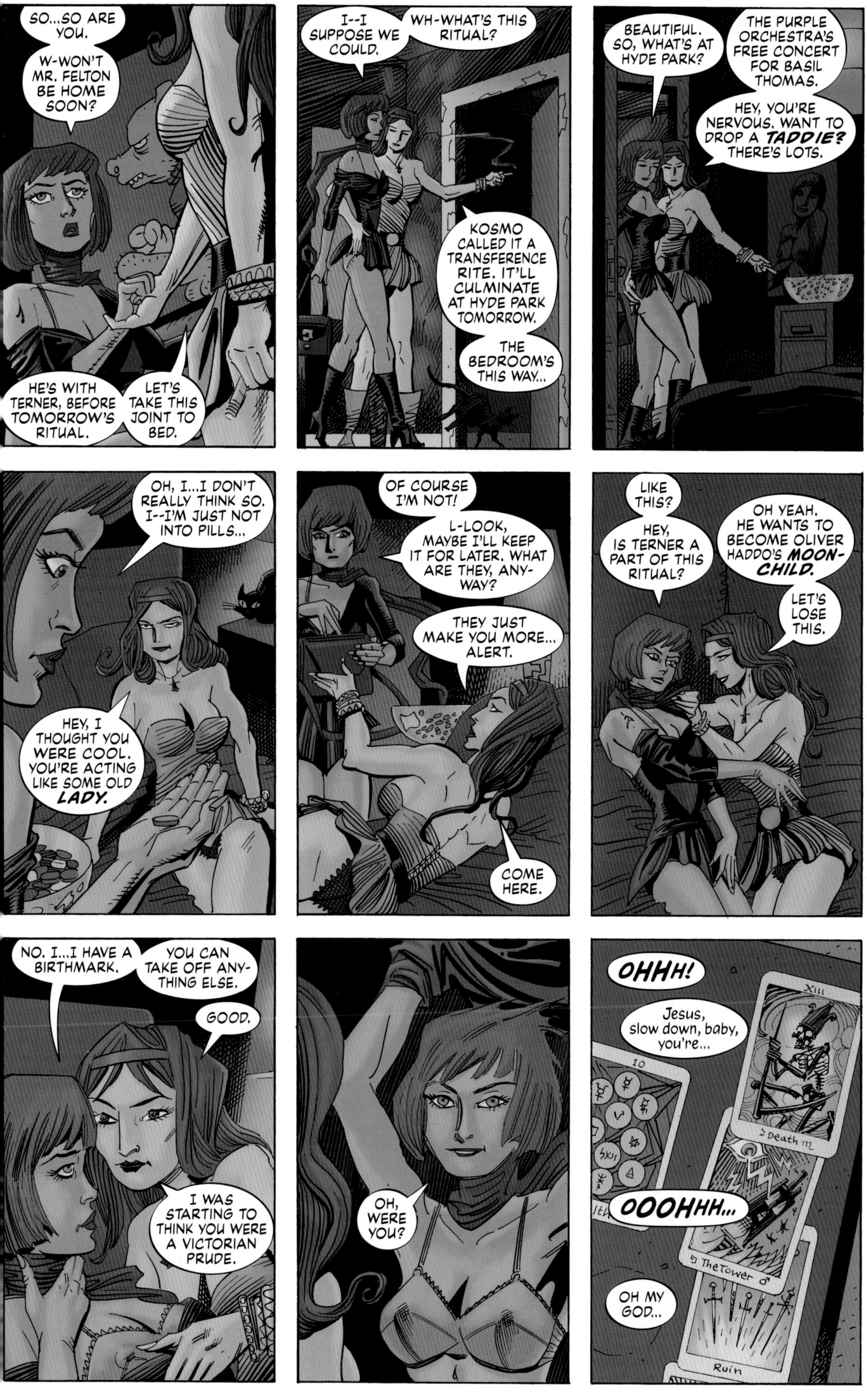
SO...SO ARE YOU.
W-WON'T MR. FELTON BE HOME SOON?
HE'S WITH TERNER, BEFORE TOMORROW'S RITUAL.
LET'S TAKE THIS JOINT TO BED.
I--I SUPPOSE WE COULD.
WH-WHAT'S THIS RITUAL?
KOSMO CALLED IT A TRANSFERENCE RITE. IT'LL CULMINATE AT HYDE PARK TOMORROW.
THE BEDROOM'S THIS WAY...
BEAUTIFUL. SO, WHAT'S AT HYDE PARK?
THE PURPLE ORCHESTRA'S FREE CONCERT FOR BASIL THOMAS.
HEY, YOU'RE NERVOUS. WANT TO DROP A **TADDIE?** THERE'S LOTS.
OH, I...I DON'T REALLY THINK SO. I--I'M JUST NOT INTO PILLS...
HEY, I THOUGHT YOU WERE COOL. YOU'RE ACTING LIKE SOME OLD **LADY.**
OF COURSE I'M NOT!
L-LOOK, MAYBE I'LL KEEP IT FOR LATER. WHAT ARE THEY, ANY-WAY?
THEY JUST MAKE YOU MORE... ALERT.
COME HERE.
LIKE THIS?
HEY, IS TERNER A PART OF THIS RITUAL?
OH YEAH. HE WANTS TO BECOME OLIVER HADDO'S **MOON-CHILD.**
LET'S LOSE THIS.
NO. I...I HAVE A BIRTHMARK.
YOU CAN TAKE OFF ANY-THING ELSE.
GOOD.
I WAS STARTING TO THINK YOU WERE A VICTORIAN PRUDE.
OH, WERE YOU?
OHHH!
Jesus, slow down, baby, you're...
XIII
Death
10
OOOHHH...
The Tower
OH MY GOD...
Ruin

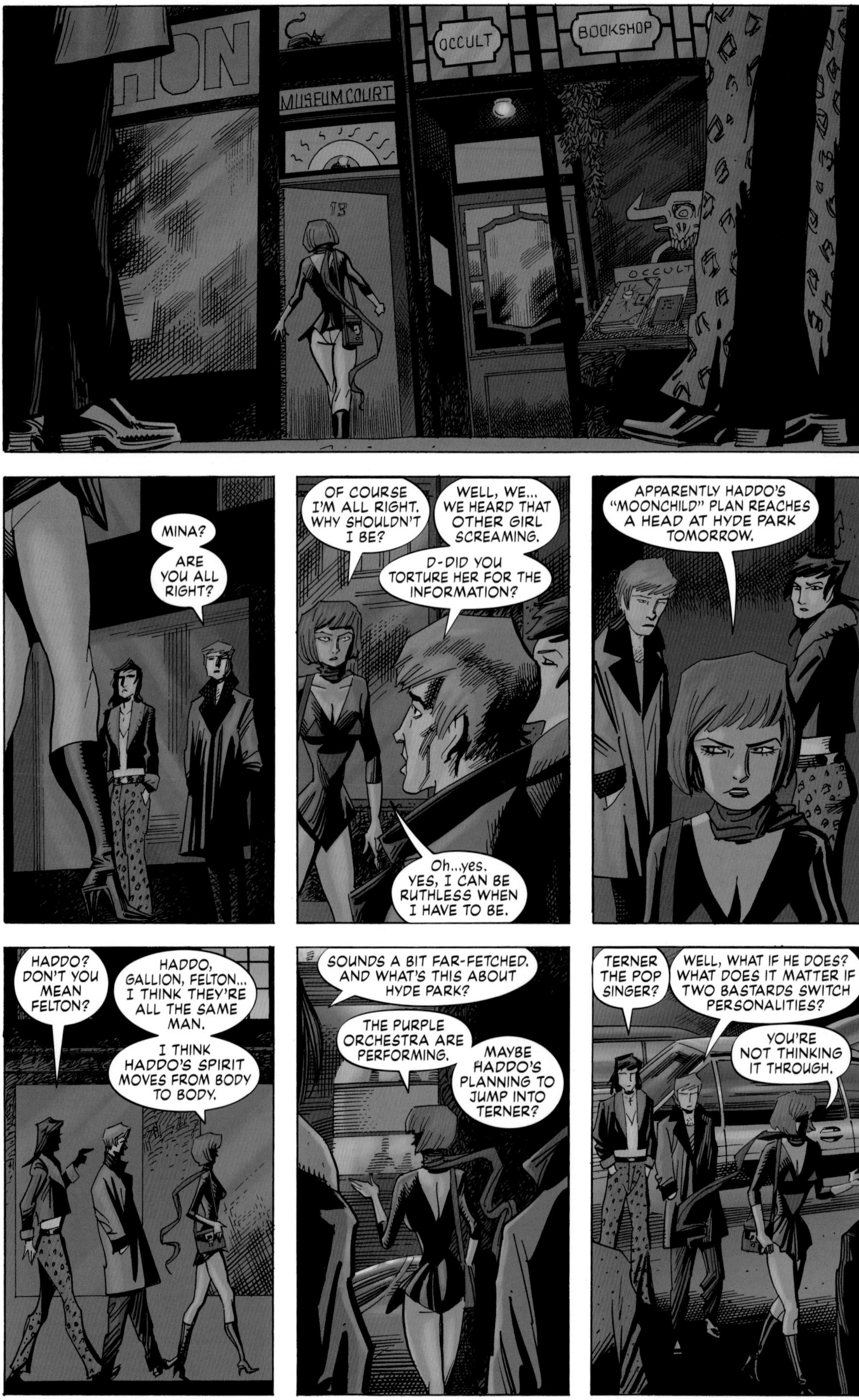
OCCULT
BOOKSHOP
MUSEUM COURT
13
OCCULT
MINA?
ARE YOU ALL RIGHT?
OF COURSE I'M ALL RIGHT. WHY SHOULDN'T I BE?
WELL, WE... WE HEARD THAT OTHER GIRL SCREAMING.
D-DID YOU TORTURE HER FOR THE INFORMATION?
Oh...yes. YES, I CAN BE RUTHLESS WHEN I HAVE TO BE.
APPARENTLY HADDO'S "MOONCHILD" PLAN REACHES A HEAD AT HYDE PARK TOMORROW.
HADDO? DON'T YOU MEAN FELTON?
HADDO, GALLION, FELTON... I THINK THEY'RE ALL THE SAME MAN.
I THINK HADDO'S SPIRIT MOVES FROM BODY TO BODY.
SOUNDS A BIT FAR-FETCHED. AND WHAT'S THIS ABOUT HYDE PARK?
THE PURPLE ORCHESTRA ARE PERFORMING.
MAYBE HADDO'S PLANNING TO JUMP INTO TERNER?
TERNER THE POP SINGER?
WELL, WHAT IF HE DOES? WHAT DOES IT MATTER IF TWO BASTARDS SWITCH PERSONALITIES?
YOU'RE NOT THINKING IT THROUGH.

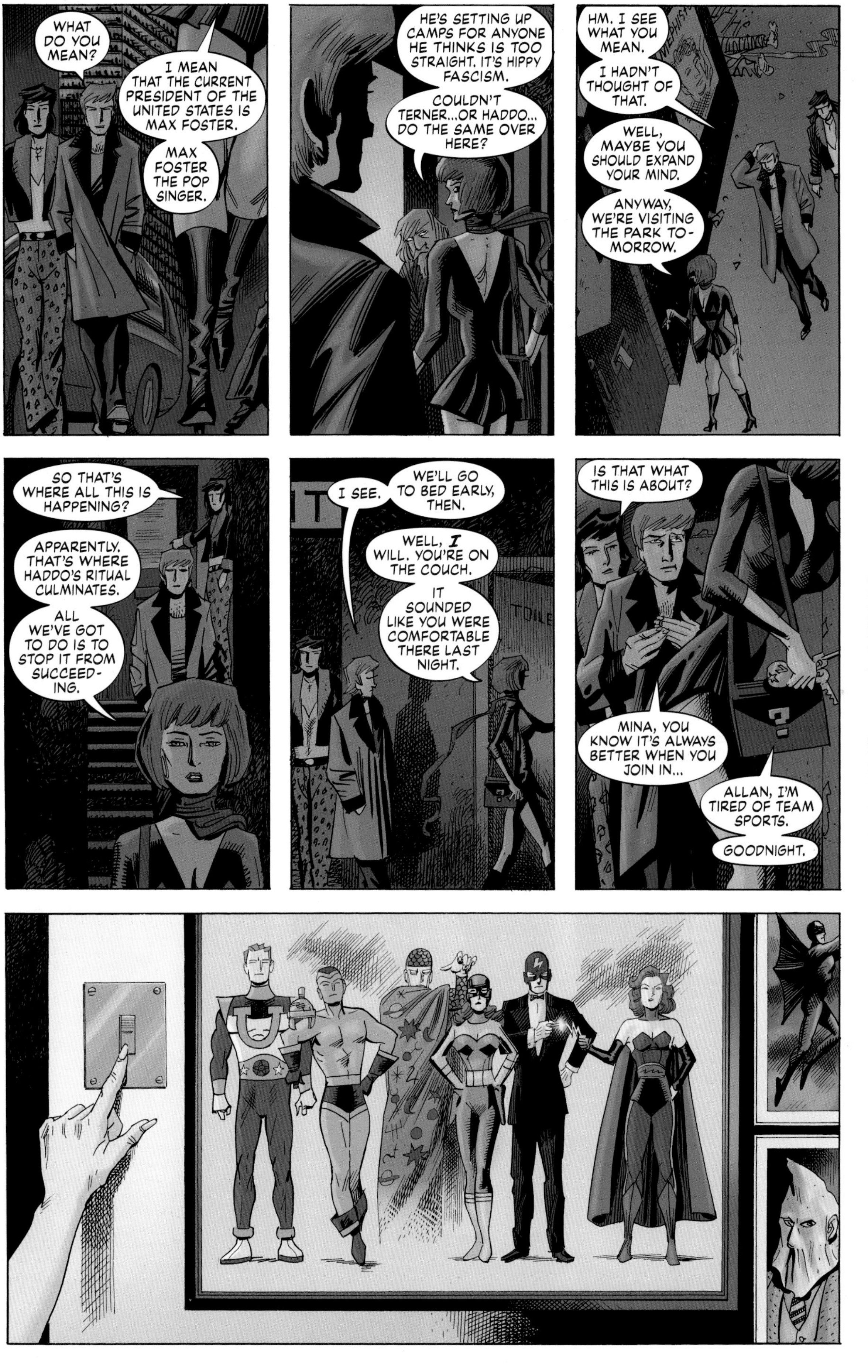
WHAT DO YOU MEAN?
I MEAN THAT THE CURRENT PRESIDENT OF THE UNITED STATES IS MAX FOSTER.
MAX FOSTER THE POP SINGER.
HE'S SETTING UP CAMPS FOR ANYONE HE THINKS IS TOO STRAIGHT. IT'S HIPPY FASCISM.
COULDN'T TERNER...OR HADDO... DO THE SAME OVER HERE?
HM. I SEE WHAT YOU MEAN.
I HADN'T THOUGHT OF THAT.
WELL, MAYBE YOU SHOULD EXPAND YOUR MIND.
ANYWAY, WE'RE VISITING THE PARK TO-MORROW.
SO THAT'S WHERE ALL THIS IS HAPPENING?
APPARENTLY. THAT'S WHERE HADDO'S RITUAL CULMINATES.
ALL WE'VE GOT TO DO IS TO STOP IT FROM SUCCEED-ING.
WE'LL GO TO BED EARLY, THEN.
I SEE.
WELL, ***I*** WILL. YOU'RE ON THE COUCH.
IT SOUNDED LIKE YOU WERE COMFORTABLE THERE LAST NIGHT.
IS THAT WHAT THIS IS ABOUT?
MINA, YOU KNOW IT'S ALWAYS BETTER WHEN YOU JOIN IN...
ALLAN, I'M TIRED OF TEAM SPORTS.
GOODNIGHT.

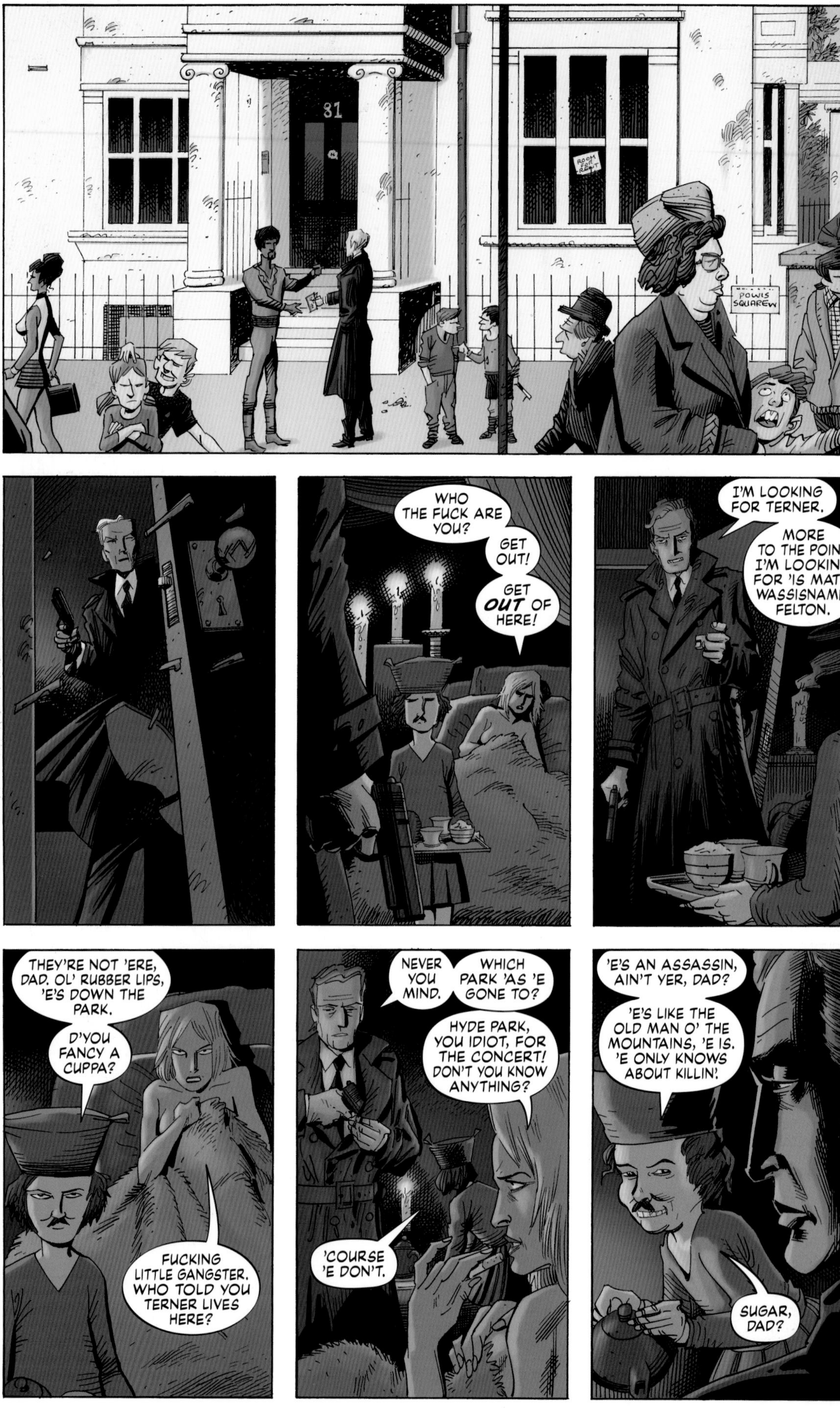
81
ROOM FOR RENT
POWIS SQUAREW
WHO THE FUCK ARE YOU?
GET OUT!
GET OUT OF HERE!
I'M LOOKING FOR TERNER.
MORE TO THE POINT I'M LOOKING FOR 'IS MATE, WASSISNAME, FELTON.
THEY'RE NOT 'ERE, DAD. OL' RUBBER LIPS, 'E'S DOWN THE PARK.
D'YOU FANCY A CUPPA?
FUCKING LITTLE GANGSTER. WHO TOLD YOU TERNER LIVES HERE?
NEVER YOU MIND.
WHICH PARK 'AS 'E GONE TO?
HYDE PARK, YOU IDIOT, FOR THE CONCERT! DON'T YOU KNOW ANYTHING?
'COURSE 'E DON'T.
'E'S AN ASSASSIN, AIN'T YER, DAD?
'E'S LIKE THE OLD MAN O' THE MOUNTAINS, 'E IS. 'E ONLY KNOWS ABOUT KILLIN'.
SUGAR, DAD?

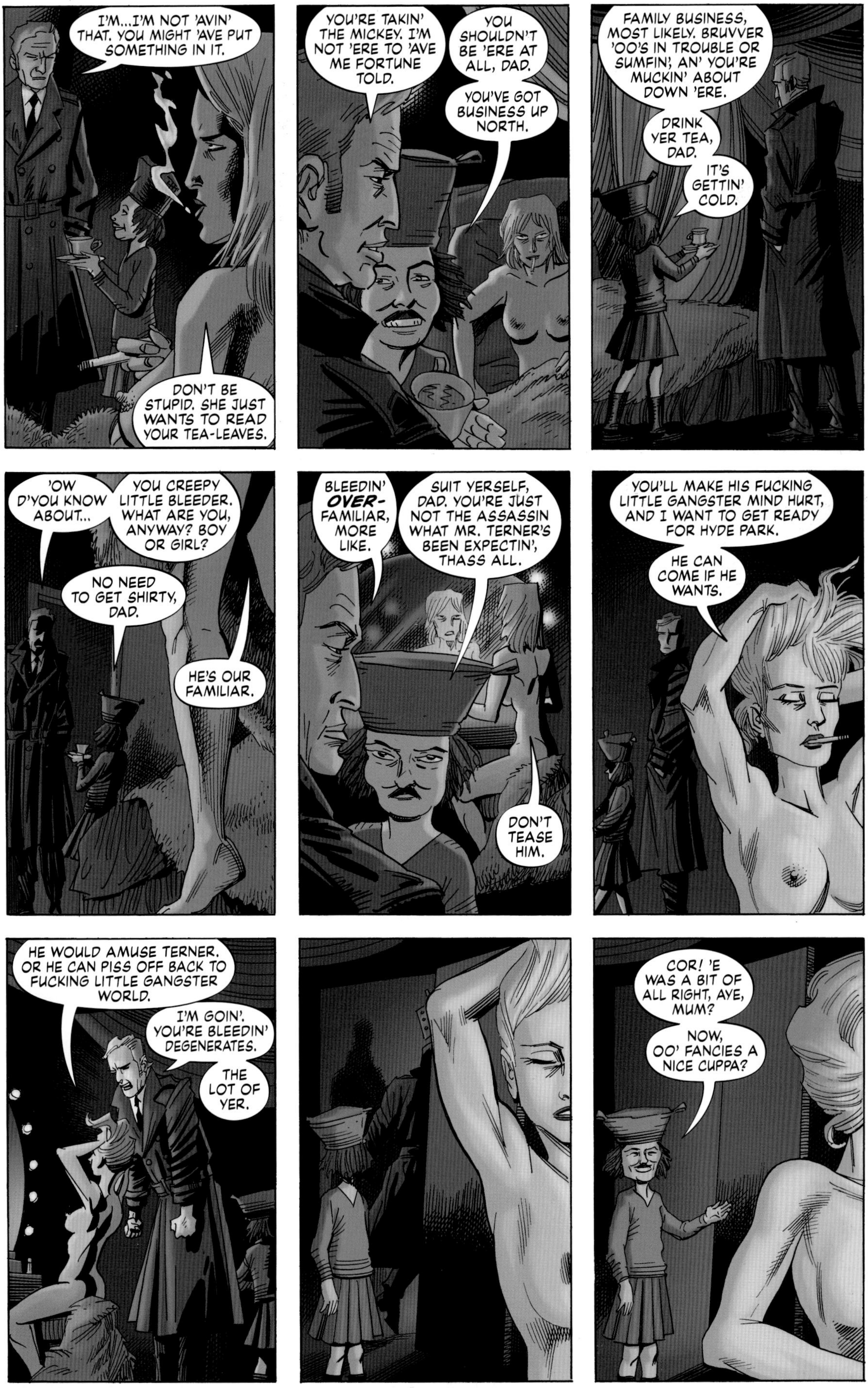
I'M...I'M NOT 'AVIN' THAT. YOU MIGHT 'AVE PUT SOMETHING IN IT.
DON'T BE STUPID. SHE JUST WANTS TO READ YOUR TEA-LEAVES.
YOU'RE TAKIN' THE MICKEY. I'M NOT 'ERE TO 'AVE ME FORTUNE TOLD.
YOU SHOULDN'T BE 'ERE AT ALL, DAD.
YOU'VE GOT BUSINESS UP NORTH.
FAMILY BUSINESS, MOST LIKELY. BRUVVER 'OO'S IN TROUBLE OR SUMFIN', AN' YOU'RE MUCKIN' ABOUT DOWN 'ERE.
DRINK YER TEA, DAD.
IT'S GETTIN' COLD.
'OW D'YOU KNOW ABOUT...
YOU CREEPY LITTLE BLEEDER. WHAT ARE YOU, ANYWAY? BOY OR GIRL?
NO NEED TO GET SHIRTY, DAD.
HE'S OUR FAMILIAR.
BLEEDIN' **OVER**-FAMILIAR, MORE LIKE.
SUIT YERSELF, DAD. YOU'RE JUST NOT THE ASSASSIN WHAT MR. TERNER'S BEEN EXPECTIN', THASS ALL.
DON'T TEASE HIM.
YOU'LL MAKE HIS FUCKING LITTLE GANGSTER MIND HURT, AND I WANT TO GET READY FOR HYDE PARK.
HE CAN COME IF HE WANTS.
HE WOULD AMUSE TERNER. OR HE CAN PISS OFF BACK TO FUCKING LITTLE GANGSTER WORLD.
I'M GOIN'. YOU'RE BLEEDIN' DEGENERATES.
THE LOT OF YER.
COR! 'E WAS A BIT OF ALL RIGHT, AYE, MUM?
NOW, OO' FANCIES A NICE CUPPA?

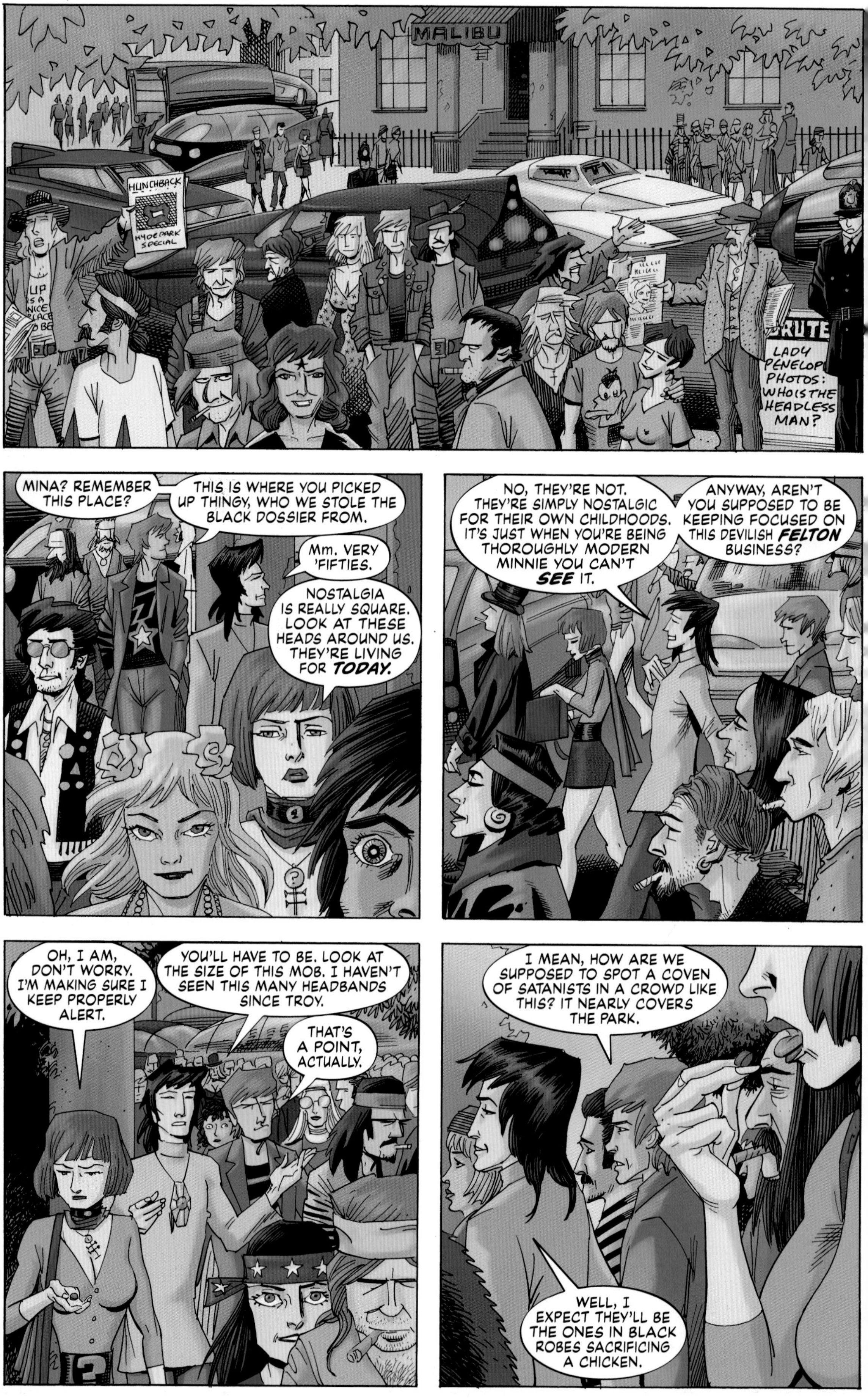
MALIBU
HUNCHBACK
HYDE PARK SPECIAL
BRUTE
LADY PENELOP
PHOTOS: WHO IS THE HEADLESS MAN?
MINA? REMEMBER THIS PLACE?
THIS IS WHERE YOU PICKED UP THINGY, WHO WE STOLE THE BLACK DOSSIER FROM.
Mm. VERY 'FIFTIES.
NOSTALGIA IS REALLY SQUARE. LOOK AT THESE HEADS AROUND US. THEY'RE LIVING FOR **TODAY.**
NO, THEY'RE NOT. THEY'RE SIMPLY NOSTALGIC FOR THEIR OWN CHILDHOODS. IT'S JUST WHEN YOU'RE BEING THOROUGHLY MODERN MINNIE YOU CAN'T **SEE** IT.
ANYWAY, AREN'T YOU SUPPOSED TO BE KEEPING FOCUSED ON THIS DEVILISH **FELTON** BUSINESS?
OH, I AM, DON'T WORRY. I'M MAKING SURE I KEEP PROPERLY ALERT.
YOU'LL HAVE TO BE. LOOK AT THE SIZE OF THIS MOB. I HAVEN'T SEEN THIS MANY HEADBANDS SINCE TROY.
THAT'S A POINT, ACTUALLY.
I MEAN, HOW ARE WE SUPPOSED TO SPOT A COVEN OF SATANISTS IN A CROWD LIKE THIS? IT NEARLY COVERS THE PARK.
WELL, I EXPECT THEY'LL BE THE ONES IN BLACK ROBES SACRIFICING A CHICKEN.

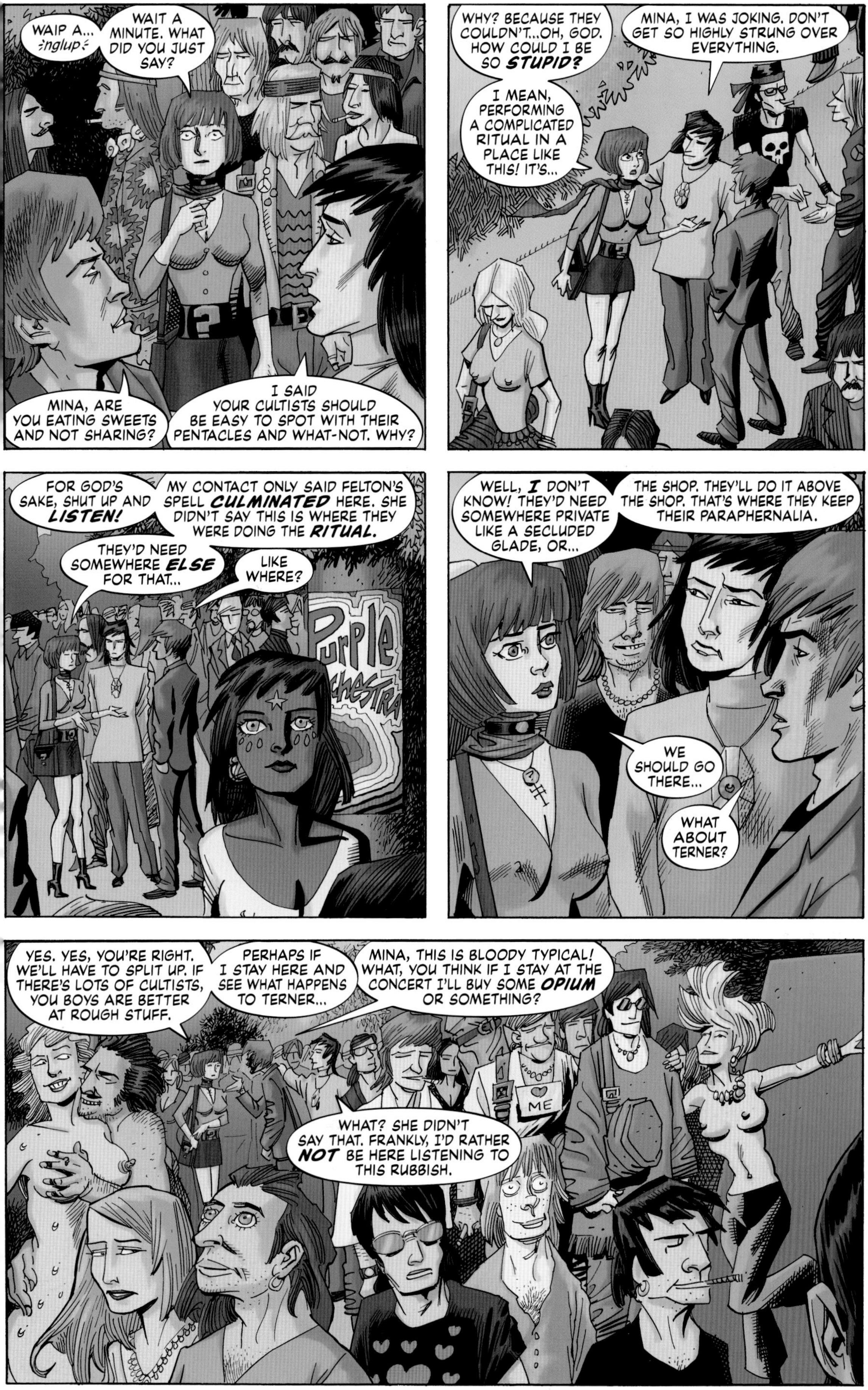
WAIP A... nglup
WAIT A MINUTE. WHAT DID YOU JUST SAY?
MINA, ARE YOU EATING SWEETS AND NOT SHARING?
I SAID YOUR CULTISTS SHOULD BE EASY TO SPOT WITH THEIR PENTACLES AND WHAT-NOT. WHY?
WHY? BECAUSE THEY COULDN'T...OH, GOD. HOW COULD I BE SO STUPID?
I MEAN, PERFORMING A COMPLICATED RITUAL IN A PLACE LIKE THIS! IT'S...
MINA, I WAS JOKING. DON'T GET SO HIGHLY STRUNG OVER EVERYTHING.
FOR GOD'S SAKE, SHUT UP AND LISTEN!
MY CONTACT ONLY SAID FELTON'S SPELL CULMINATED HERE. SHE DIDN'T SAY THIS IS WHERE THEY WERE DOING THE RITUAL.
THEY'D NEED SOMEWHERE ELSE FOR THAT...
LIKE WHERE?
Purple Orchestra
WELL, I DON'T KNOW! THEY'D NEED SOMEWHERE PRIVATE LIKE A SECLUDED GLADE, OR...
THE SHOP. THEY'LL DO IT ABOVE THE SHOP. THAT'S WHERE THEY KEEP THEIR PARAPHERNALIA.
WE SHOULD GO THERE...
WHAT ABOUT TERNER?
YES. YES, YOU'RE RIGHT. WE'LL HAVE TO SPLIT UP. IF THERE'S LOTS OF CULTISTS, YOU BOYS ARE BETTER AT ROUGH STUFF.
PERHAPS IF I STAY HERE AND SEE WHAT HAPPENS TO TERNER...
MINA, THIS IS BLOODY TYPICAL! WHAT, YOU THINK IF I STAY AT THE CONCERT I'LL BUY SOME OPIUM OR SOMETHING?
WHAT? SHE DIDN'T SAY THAT. FRANKLY, I'D RATHER NOT BE HERE LISTENING TO THIS RUBBISH.
ME

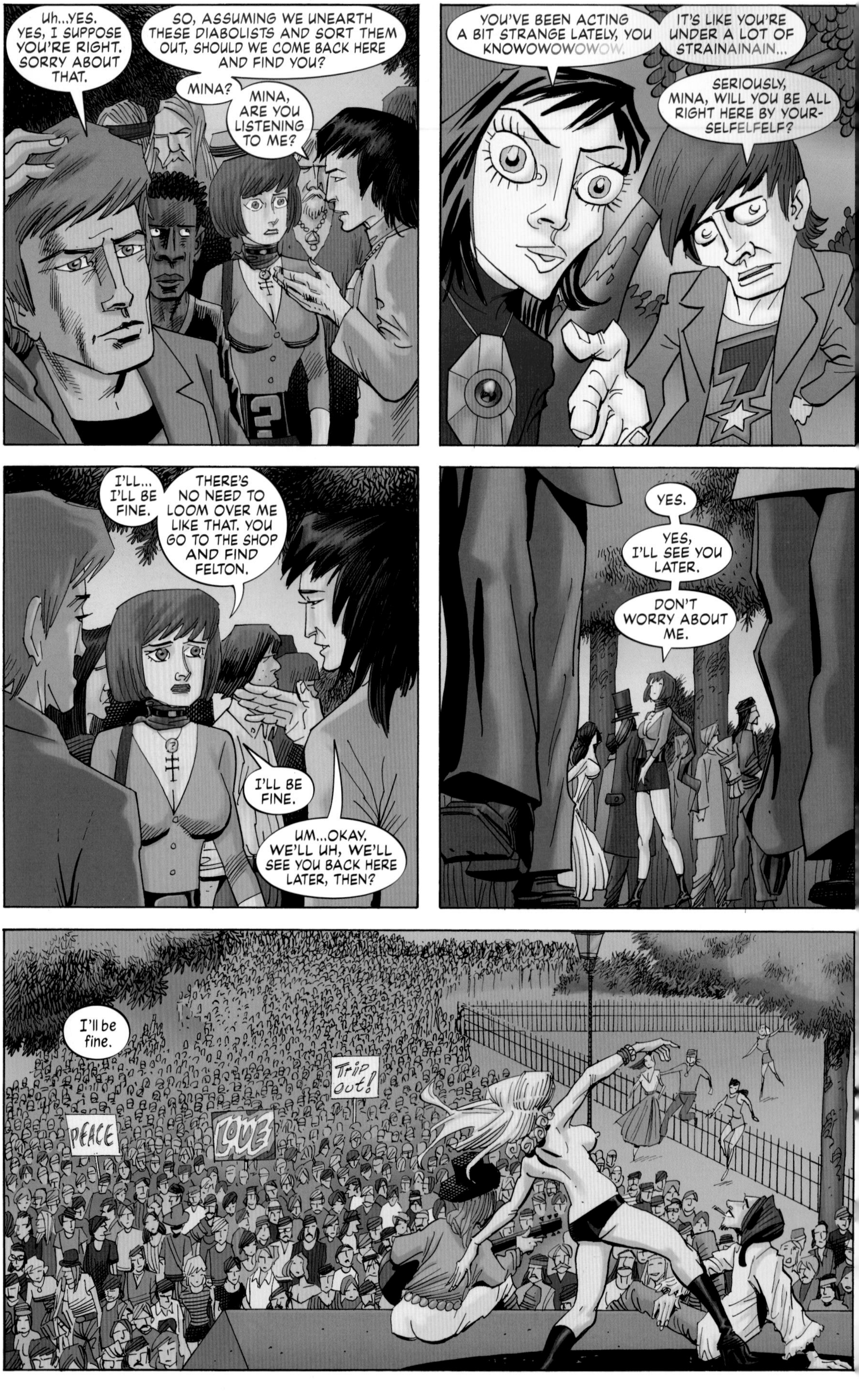
Uh...YES. YES, I SUPPOSE YOU'RE RIGHT. SORRY ABOUT THAT.
SO, ASSUMING WE UNEARTH THESE DIABOLISTS AND SORT THEM OUT, SHOULD WE COME BACK HERE AND FIND YOU?
MINA?
MINA, ARE YOU LISTENING TO ME?
YOU'VE BEEN ACTING A BIT STRANGE LATELY, YOU KNOWOWOWOWOWOW.
IT'S LIKE YOU'RE UNDER A LOT OF STRAINAINAIN...
SERIOUSLY, MINA, WILL YOU BE ALL RIGHT HERE BY YOUR-SELFELFELF?
I'LL... I'LL BE FINE.
THERE'S NO NEED TO LOOM OVER ME LIKE THAT. YOU GO TO THE SHOP AND FIND FELTON.
I'LL BE FINE.
UM...OKAY. WE'LL UH, WE'LL SEE YOU BACK HERE LATER, THEN?
YES.
YES, I'LL SEE YOU LATER.
DON'T WORRY ABOUT ME.
I'll be fine.
PEACE
LOVE
Trip out!

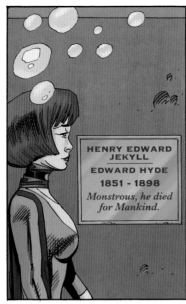

HENRY EDWARD
JEKYLL

EDWARD HYDE
1851 - 1898
*Monstrous, he died
for Mankind.*

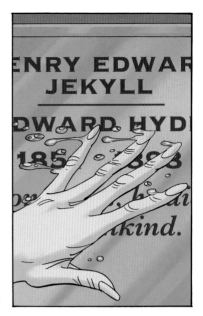

HEY, EASY,
MAN...

I'M SORRY.
SORRY.

HAS
EVERYONE
GOT THESE...
THINGS...?

WHOOPS...

ARE YOU OKAY,
LUVVVVVVVV?

SHE'S COOL. SHE'S
JUST TRIPPINGINGING.

LEAVE HER TO ENJOY
HERSELFELFELFELF.

PEACE,
SISTERISTER-
ISTERISTER...

YEAH.

YEAH, I'M
COOL. I'M JUST
TRICK...TRICKING...
I'M JUST
TRIPPING.

YEAH?
WELL, DON'T
LOOK 'ROUND OR
THAT BIG MONSTER
WILL FREAK YOU
OUT.

DON'T
TELL HER
THAT.

YOU JUST COME ON
AND SEE THE PURPLE
ORCHESTRA. THERE'S
NO MONSTER.

WHAT? HA HA.
WHAT ARE YOU
TALKING...

...ABOUT...

HEY,
LOOK COME
ONONONON...

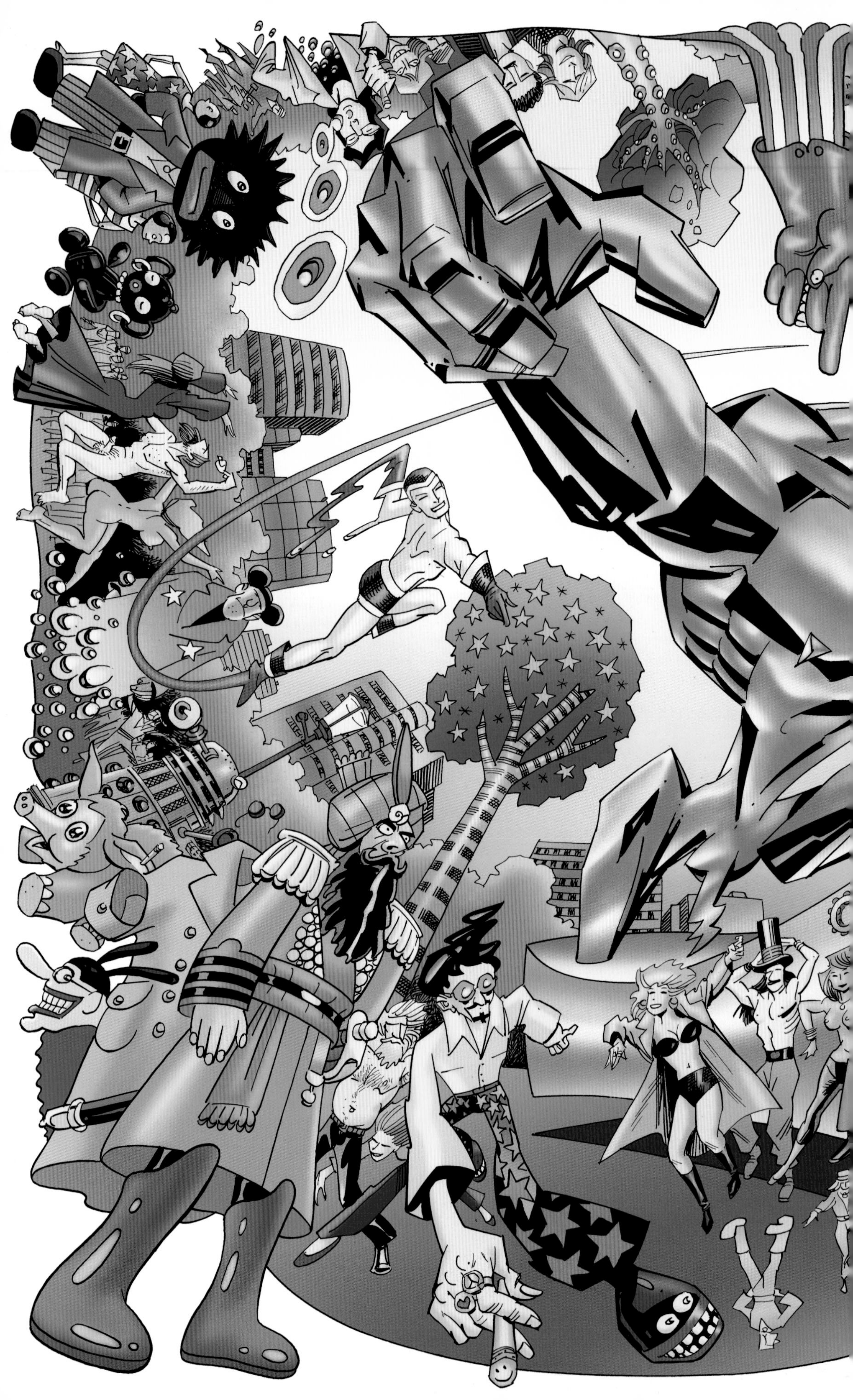

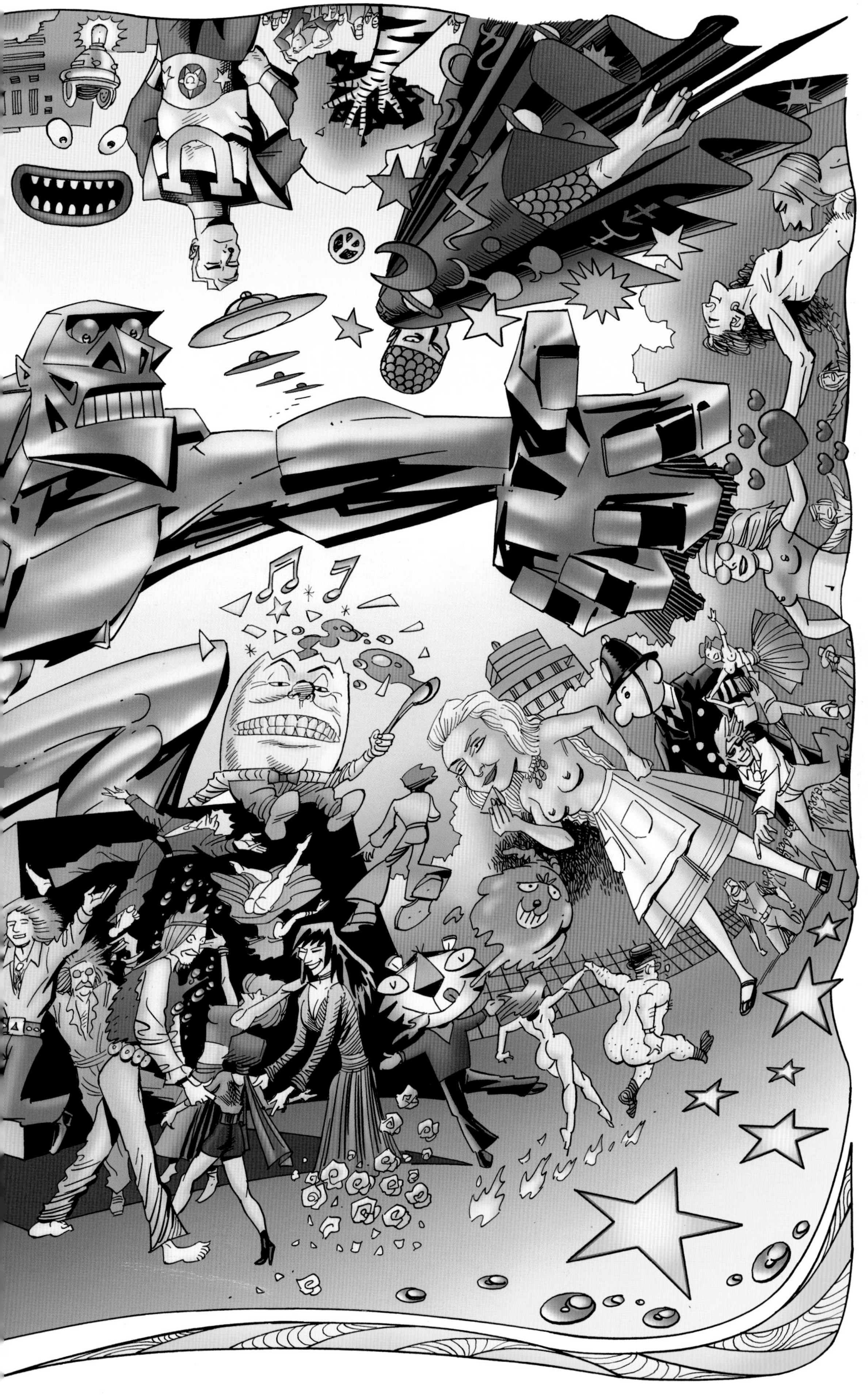

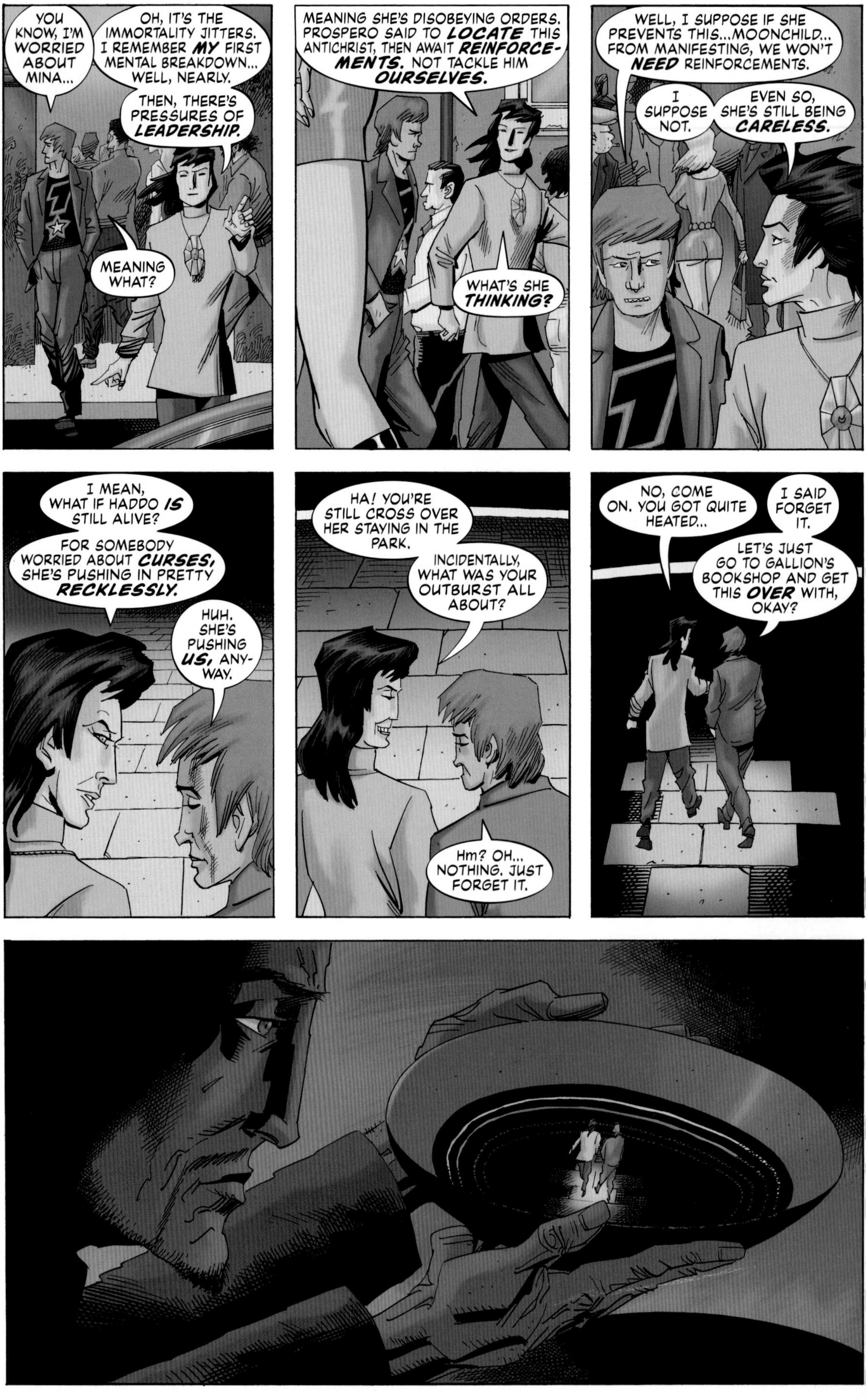
YOU KNOW, I'M WORRIED ABOUT MINA...
OH, IT'S THE IMMORTALITY JITTERS. I REMEMBER MY FIRST MENTAL BREAKDOWN... WELL, NEARLY.
THEN, THERE'S PRESSURES OF LEADERSHIP.
MEANING WHAT?
MEANING SHE'S DISOBEYING ORDERS. PROSPERO SAID TO LOCATE THIS ANTICHRIST, THEN AWAIT REINFORCEMENTS. NOT TACKLE HIM OURSELVES.
WHAT'S SHE THINKING?
WELL, I SUPPOSE IF SHE PREVENTS THIS...MOONCHILD... FROM MANIFESTING, WE WON'T NEED REINFORCEMENTS.
I SUPPOSE NOT.
EVEN SO, SHE'S STILL BEING CARELESS.
I MEAN, WHAT IF HADDO IS STILL ALIVE?
FOR SOMEBODY WORRIED ABOUT CURSES, SHE'S PUSHING IN PRETTY RECKLESSLY.
HUH. SHE'S PUSHING US, ANYWAY.
HA! YOU'RE STILL CROSS OVER HER STAYING IN THE PARK.
INCIDENTALLY, WHAT WAS YOUR OUTBURST ALL ABOUT?
Hm? OH... NOTHING. JUST FORGET IT.
NO, COME ON. YOU GOT QUITE HEATED...
I SAID FORGET IT.
LET'S JUST GO TO GALLION'S BOOKSHOP AND GET THIS OVER WITH, OKAY?

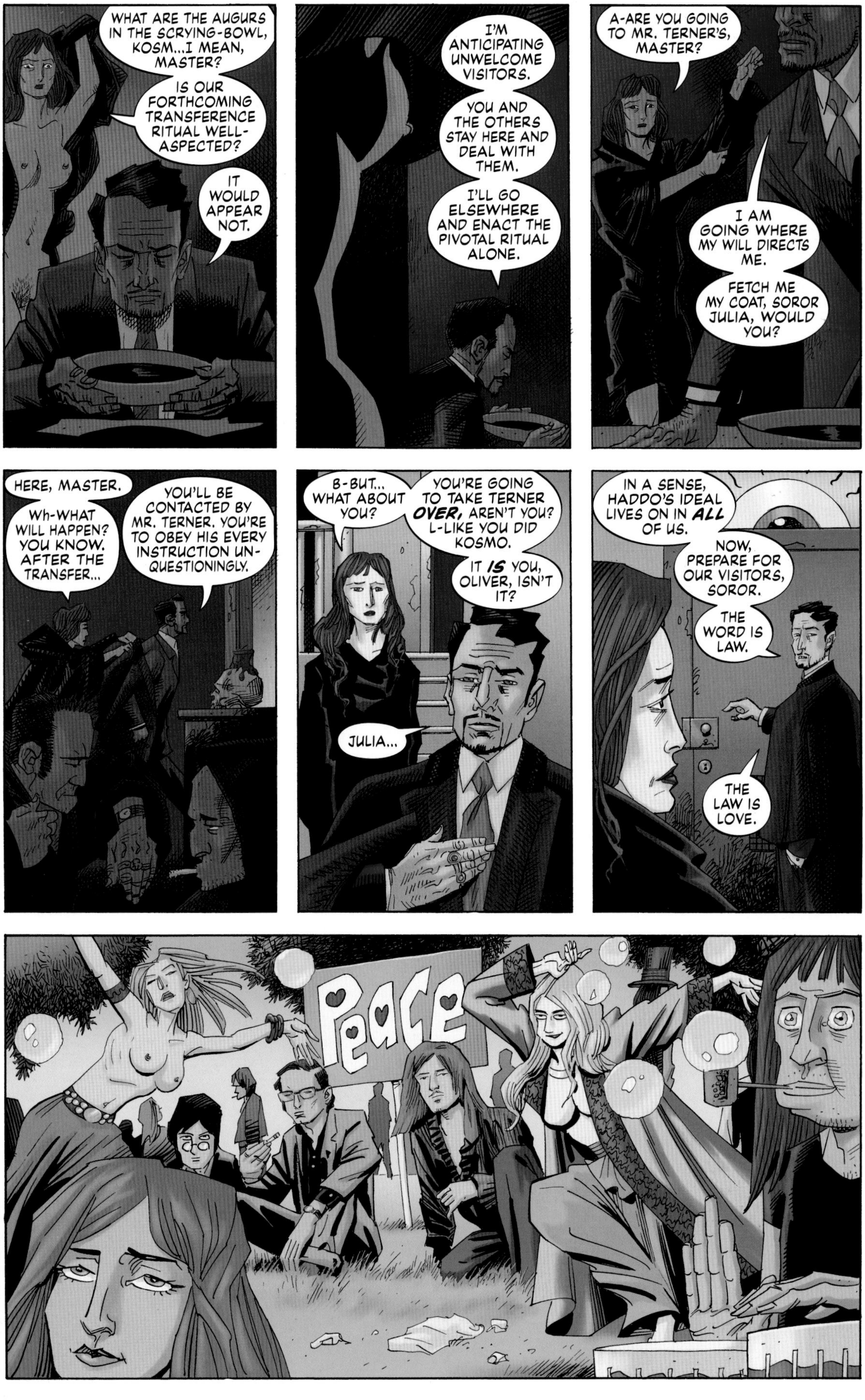
WHAT ARE THE AUGURS IN THE SCRYING-BOWL, KOSM...I MEAN, MASTER?
IS OUR FORTHCOMING TRANSFERENCE RITUAL WELL-ASPECTED?
IT WOULD APPEAR NOT.
I'M ANTICIPATING UNWELCOME VISITORS.
YOU AND THE OTHERS STAY HERE AND DEAL WITH THEM.
I'LL GO ELSEWHERE AND ENACT THE PIVOTAL RITUAL ALONE.
A-ARE YOU GOING TO MR. TERNER'S, MASTER?
I AM GOING WHERE MY WILL DIRECTS ME.
FETCH ME MY COAT, SOROR JULIA, WOULD YOU?
HERE, MASTER.
Wh-WHAT WILL HAPPEN? YOU KNOW. AFTER THE TRANSFER...
YOU'LL BE CONTACTED BY MR. TERNER. YOU'RE TO OBEY HIS EVERY INSTRUCTION UN-QUESTIONINGLY.
B-BUT... WHAT ABOUT YOU?
YOU'RE GOING TO TAKE TERNER *OVER,* AREN'T YOU? L-LIKE YOU DID KOSMO.
IT *IS* YOU, OLIVER, ISN'T IT?
JULIA...
IN A SENSE, HADDO'S IDEAL LIVES ON IN *ALL* OF US.
NOW, PREPARE FOR OUR VISITORS, SOROR.
THE WORD IS LAW.
THE LAW IS LOVE.
PEACE

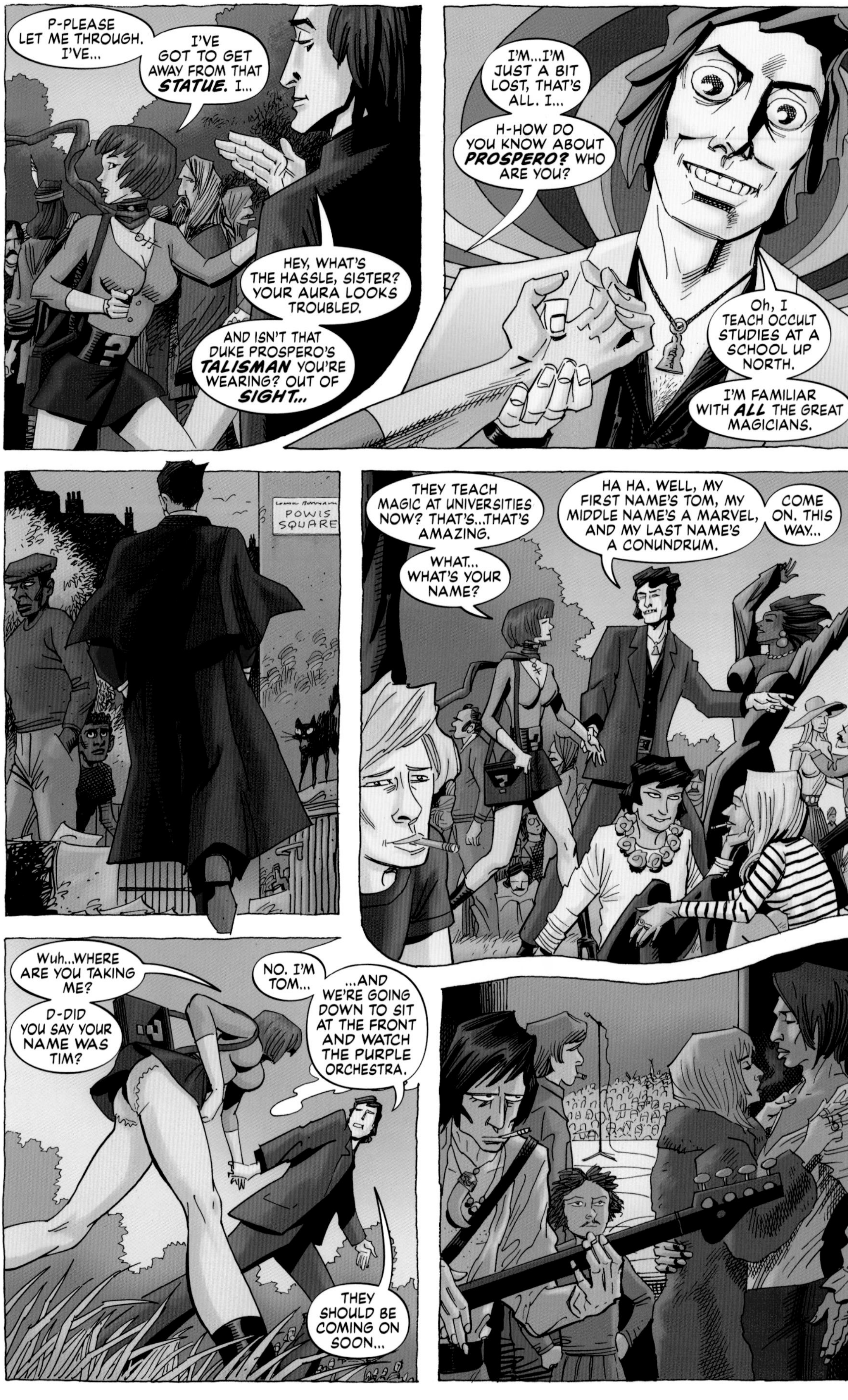
P-PLEASE LET ME THROUGH. I'VE...
I'VE GOT TO GET AWAY FROM THAT STATUE. I...
HEY, WHAT'S THE HASSLE, SISTER? YOUR AURA LOOKS TROUBLED.
AND ISN'T THAT DUKE PROSPERO'S TALISMAN YOU'RE WEARING? OUT OF SIGHT...
I'M...I'M JUST A BIT LOST, THAT'S ALL. I...
H-HOW DO YOU KNOW ABOUT PROSPERO? WHO ARE YOU?
Oh, I TEACH OCCULT STUDIES AT A SCHOOL UP NORTH.
I'M FAMILIAR WITH ALL THE GREAT MAGICIANS.
POWIS SQUARE
THEY TEACH MAGIC AT UNIVERSITIES NOW? THAT'S...THAT'S AMAZING.
WHAT... WHAT'S YOUR NAME?
HA HA. WELL, MY FIRST NAME'S TOM, MY MIDDLE NAME'S A MARVEL, AND MY LAST NAME'S A CONUNDRUM.
COME ON. THIS WAY...
Wuh...WHERE ARE YOU TAKING ME?
D-DID YOU SAY YOUR NAME WAS TIM?
NO. I'M TOM...
...AND WE'RE GOING DOWN TO SIT AT THE FRONT AND WATCH THE PURPLE ORCHESTRA.
THEY SHOULD BE COMING ON SOON...

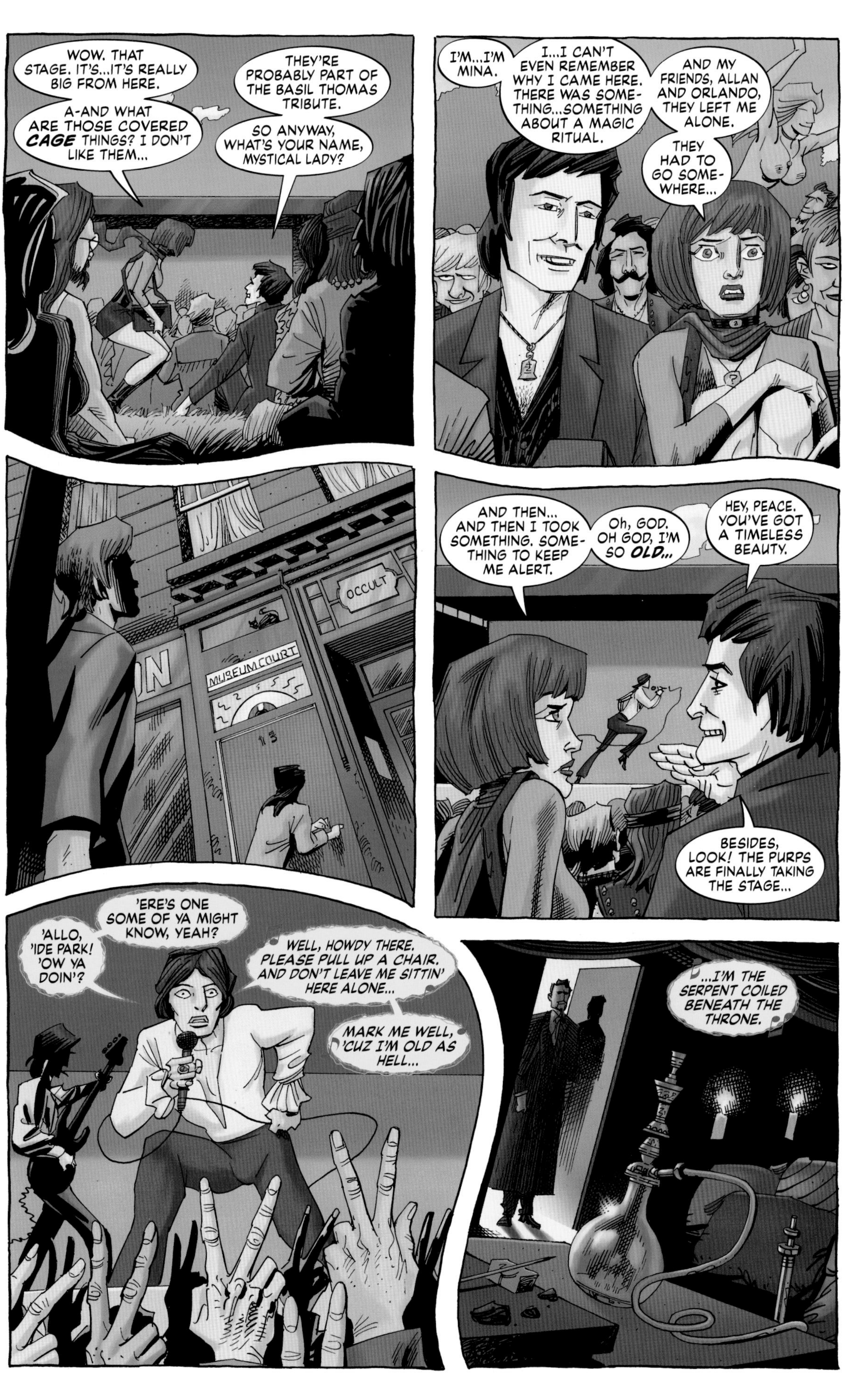
WOW. THAT STAGE. IT'S...IT'S REALLY BIG FROM HERE.
A-AND WHAT ARE THOSE COVERED CAGE THINGS? I DON'T LIKE THEM...
THEY'RE PROBABLY PART OF THE BASIL THOMAS TRIBUTE.
SO ANYWAY, WHAT'S YOUR NAME, MYSTICAL LADY?
I'M...I'M MINA.
I...I CAN'T EVEN REMEMBER WHY I CAME HERE. THERE WAS SOMETHING...SOMETHING ABOUT A MAGIC RITUAL.
AND MY FRIENDS, ALLAN AND ORLANDO, THEY LEFT ME ALONE.
THEY HAD TO GO SOMEWHERE...
OCCULT
MUSEUM COURT
AND THEN... AND THEN I TOOK SOMETHING. SOMETHING TO KEEP ME ALERT.
Oh, GOD. OH GOD, I'M SO OLD...
HEY, PEACE. YOU'VE GOT A TIMELESS BEAUTY.
BESIDES, LOOK! THE PURPS ARE FINALLY TAKING THE STAGE...
'ALLO, 'IDE PARK! 'OW YA DOIN'?
'ERE'S ONE SOME OF YA MIGHT KNOW, YEAH?
WELL, HOWDY THERE. PLEASE PULL UP A CHAIR. AND DON'T LEAVE ME SITTIN' HERE ALONE...
MARK ME WELL, 'CUZ I'M OLD AS HELL...
...I'M THE SERPENT COILED BENEATH THE THRONE.

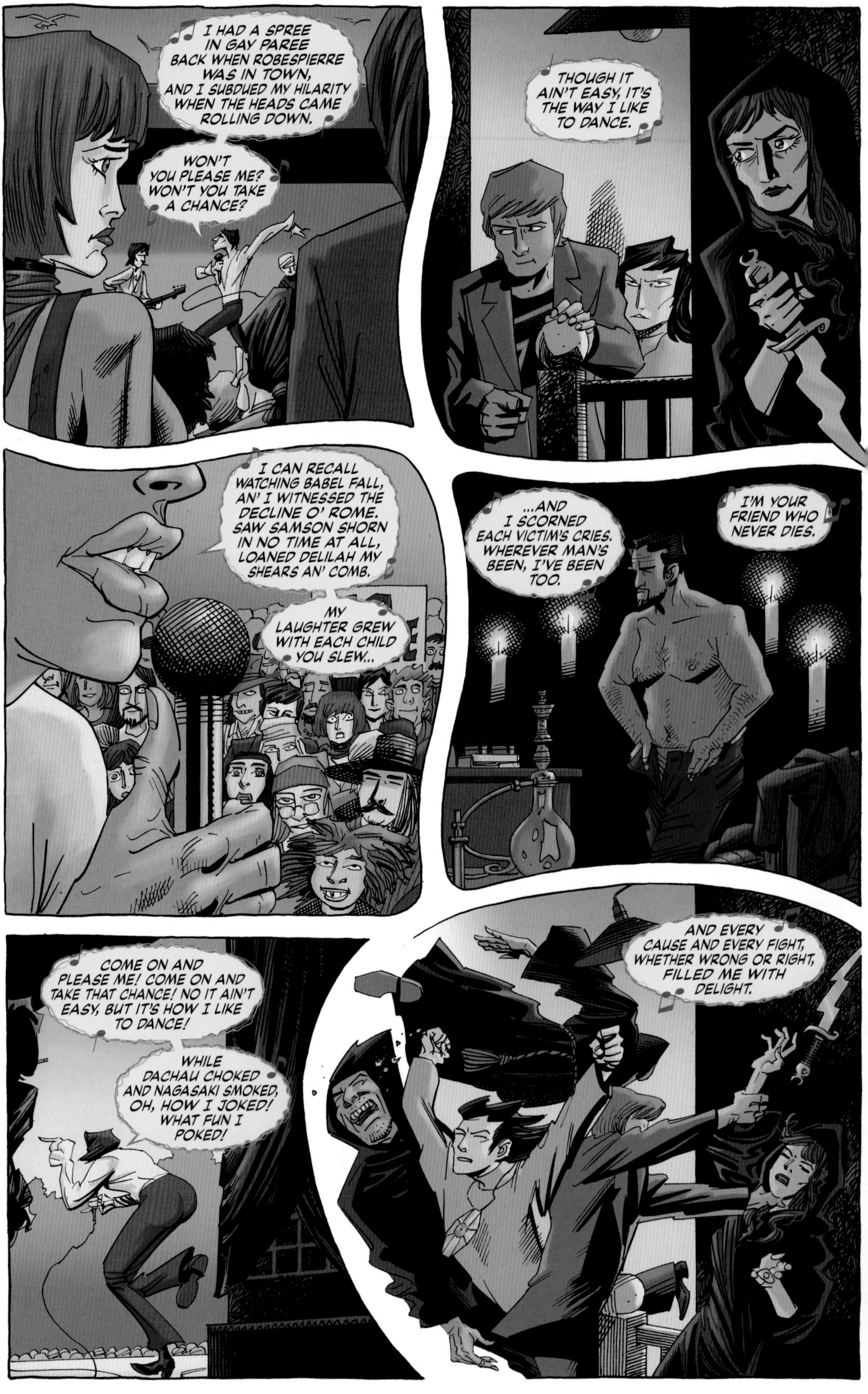
I HAD A SPREE IN GAY PAREE BACK WHEN ROBESPIERRE WAS IN TOWN, AND I SUBDUED MY HILARITY WHEN THE HEADS CAME ROLLING DOWN.
WON'T YOU PLEASE ME? WON'T YOU TAKE A CHANCE?
THOUGH IT AIN'T EASY, IT'S THE WAY I LIKE TO DANCE.
I CAN RECALL WATCHING BABEL FALL, AN' I WITNESSED THE DECLINE O' ROME. SAW SAMSON SHORN IN NO TIME AT ALL, LOANED DELILAH MY SHEARS AN' COMB.
MY LAUGHTER GREW WITH EACH CHILD YOU SLEW...
...AND I SCORNED EACH VICTIM'S CRIES. WHEREVER MAN'S BEEN, I'VE BEEN TOO.
I'M YOUR FRIEND WHO NEVER DIES.
COME ON AND PLEASE ME! COME ON AND TAKE THAT CHANCE! NO IT AIN'T EASY, BUT IT'S HOW I LIKE TO DANCE!
WHILE DACHAU CHOKED AND NAGASAKI SMOKED, OH, HOW I JOKED! WHAT FUN I POKED!
AND EVERY CAUSE AND EVERY FIGHT, WHETHER WRONG OR RIGHT, FILLED ME WITH DELIGHT.

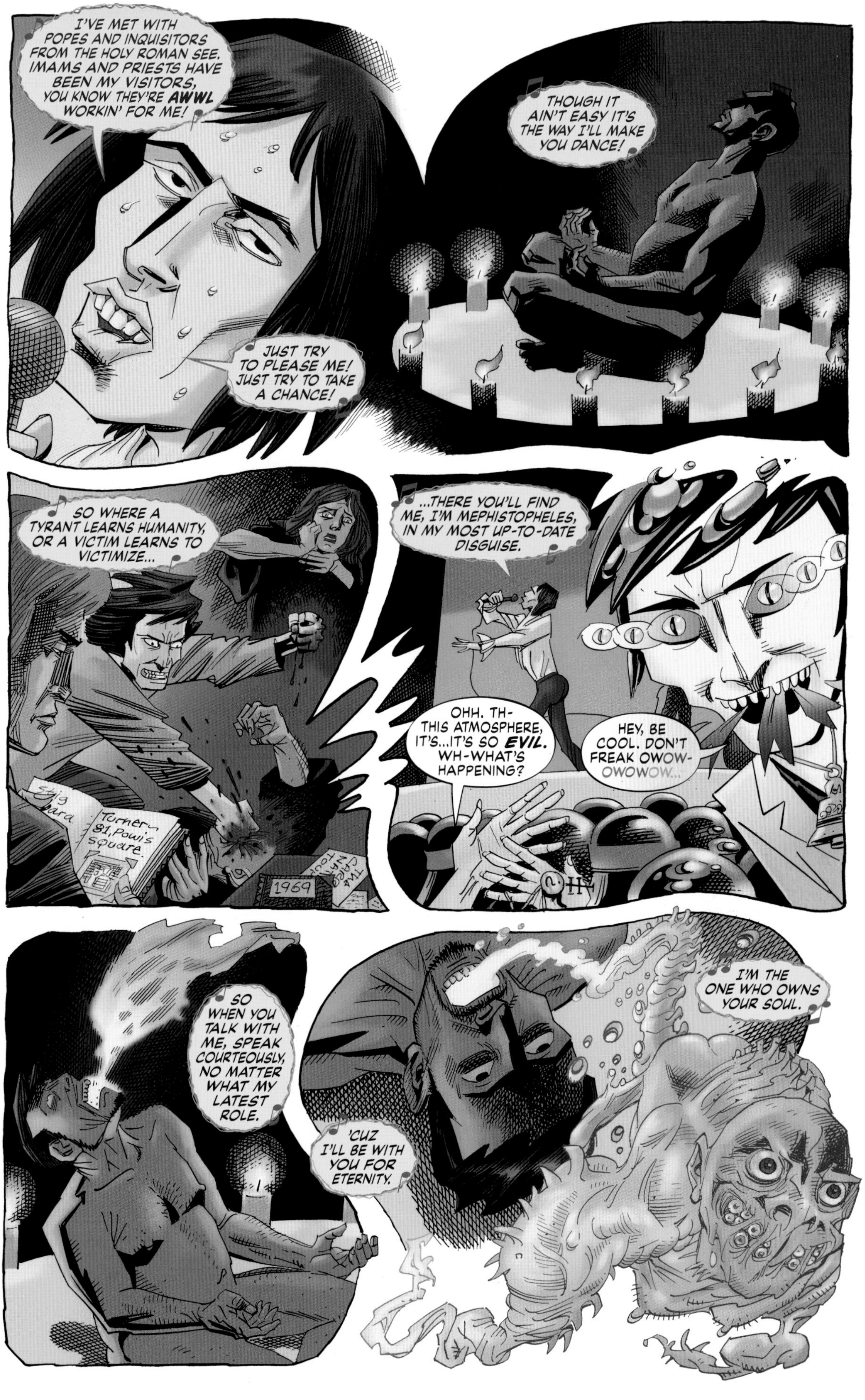
I'VE MET WITH POPES AND INQUISITORS FROM THE HOLY ROMAN SEE. IMAMS AND PRIESTS HAVE BEEN MY VISITORS, YOU KNOW THEY'RE AWWL WORKIN' FOR ME!
JUST TRY TO PLEASE ME! JUST TRY TO TAKE A CHANCE!
THOUGH IT AIN'T EASY IT'S THE WAY I'LL MAKE YOU DANCE!
SO WHERE A TYRANT LEARNS HUMANITY, OR A VICTIM LEARNS TO VICTIMIZE...
...THERE YOU'LL FIND ME, I'M MEPHISTOPHELES, IN MY MOST UP-TO-DATE DISGUISE.
OHH. TH- THIS ATMOSPHERE, IT'S...IT'S SO EVIL. WH-WHAT'S HAPPENING?
HEY, BE COOL. DON'T FREAK OWOW-OWOWOW...
SO WHEN YOU TALK WITH ME, SPEAK COURTEOUSLY, NO MATTER WHAT MY LATEST ROLE.
'CUZ I'LL BE WITH YOU FOR ETERNITY.
I'M THE ONE WHO OWNS YOUR SOUL.

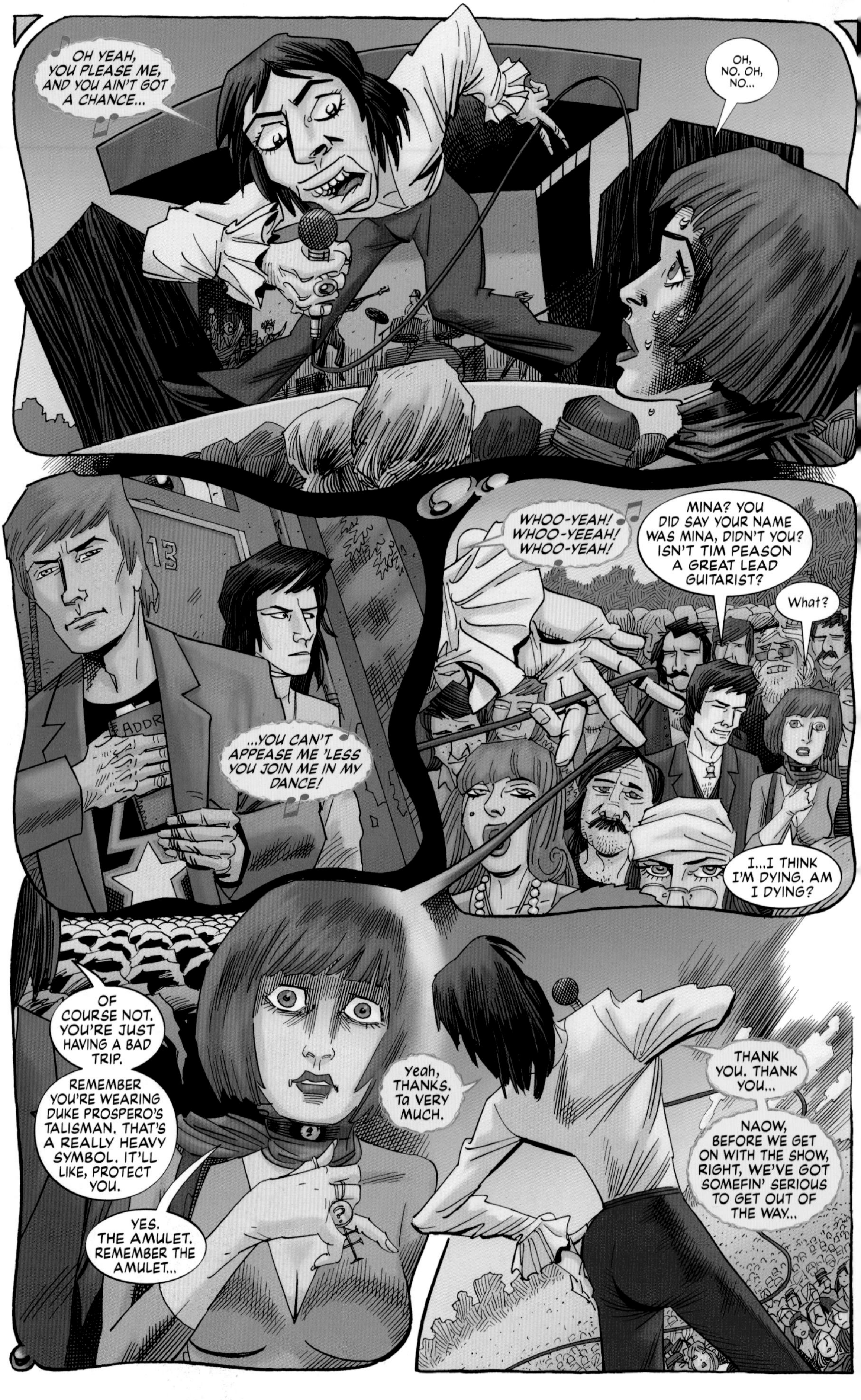
OH YEAH, YOU PLEASE ME, AND YOU AIN'T GOT A CHANCE...
OH, NO. OH, NO...
...YOU CAN'T APPEASE ME 'LESS YOU JOIN ME IN MY DANCE!
WHOO-YEAH! WHOO-YEEAH! WHOO-YEAH!
MINA? YOU DID SAY YOUR NAME WAS MINA, DIDN'T YOU? ISN'T TIM PEASON A GREAT LEAD GUITARIST?
What?
I...I THINK I'M DYING. AM I DYING?
OF COURSE NOT. YOU'RE JUST HAVING A BAD TRIP.
REMEMBER YOU'RE WEARING DUKE PROSPERO'S TALISMAN. THAT'S A REALLY HEAVY SYMBOL. IT'LL LIKE, PROTECT YOU.
YES. THE AMULET. REMEMBER THE AMULET...
Yeah, THANKS. Ta VERY MUCH.
THANK YOU. THANK YOU...
NAOW, BEFORE WE GET ON WITH THE SHOW, RIGHT, WE'VE GOT SOMEFIN' SERIOUS TO GET OUT OF THE WAY...

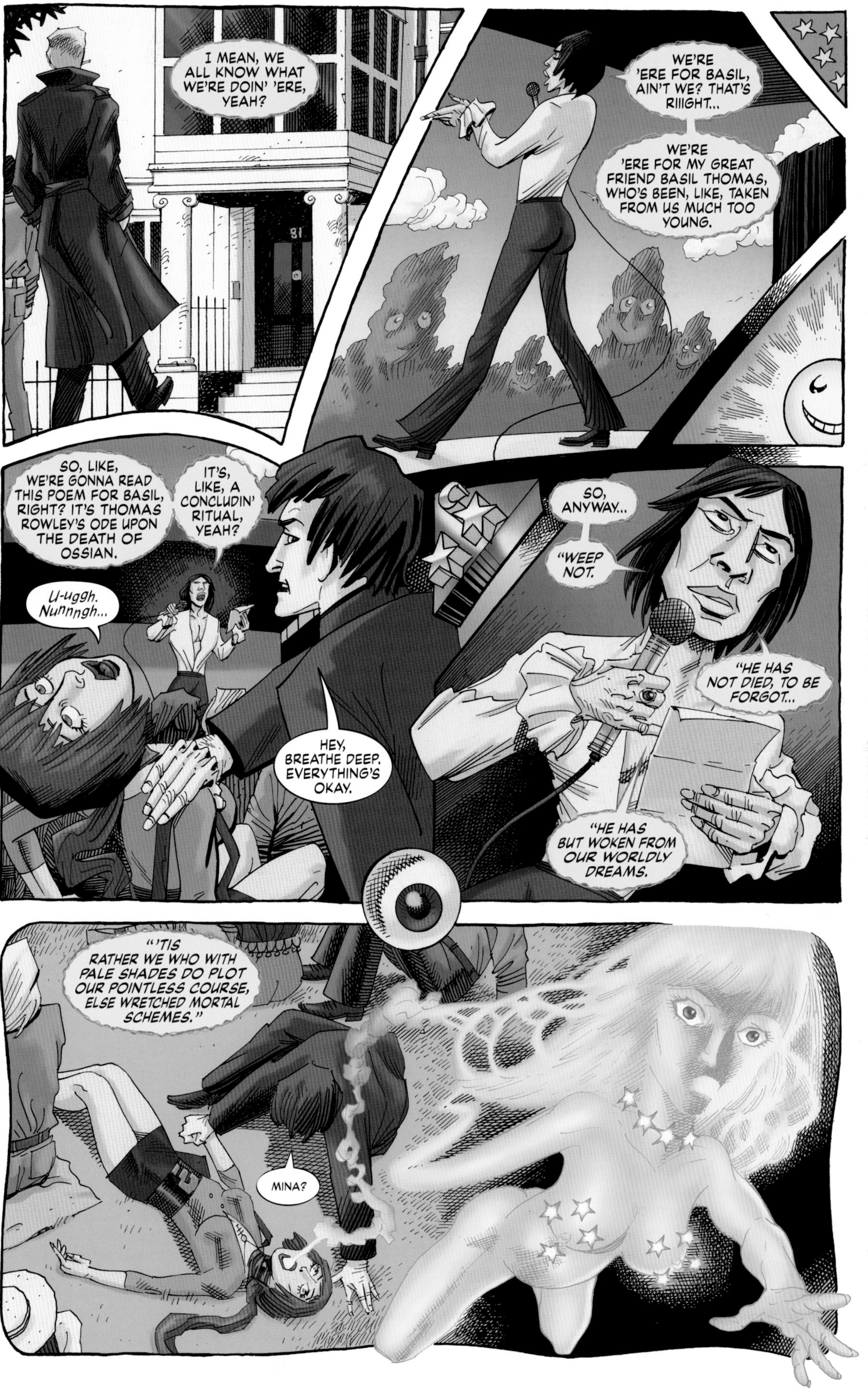
I MEAN, WE ALL KNOW WHAT WE'RE DOIN' 'ERE, YEAH?
WE'RE 'ERE FOR BASIL, AIN'T WE? THAT'S RIIIGHT...
WE'RE 'ERE FOR MY GREAT FRIEND BASIL THOMAS, WHO'S BEEN, LIKE, TAKEN FROM US MUCH TOO YOUNG.
SO, LIKE, WE'RE GONNA READ THIS POEM FOR BASIL, RIGHT? IT'S THOMAS ROWLEY'S ODE UPON THE DEATH OF OSSIAN.
IT'S, LIKE, A CONCLUDIN' RITUAL, YEAH?
U-uggh. Nunnngh...
HEY, BREATHE DEEP. EVERYTHING'S OKAY.
SO, ANYWAY...
"WEEP NOT.
"HE HAS NOT DIED, TO BE FORGOT...
"HE HAS BUT WOKEN FROM OUR WORLDLY DREAMS.
"'TIS RATHER WE WHO WITH PALE SHADES DO PLOT OUR POINTLESS COURSE, ELSE WRETCHED MORTAL SCHEMES."
MINA?

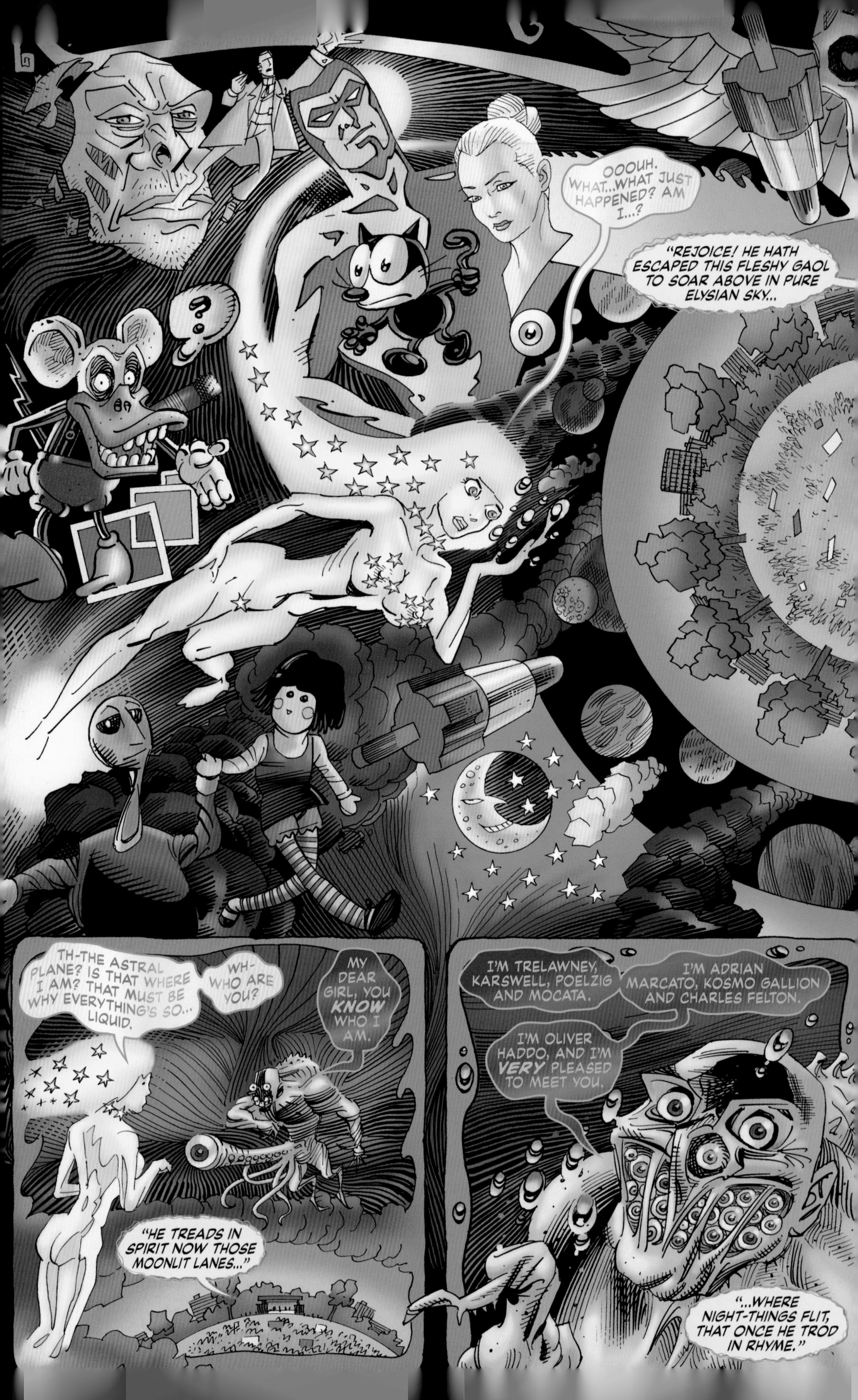
OOOUH. WHAT...WHAT JUST HAPPENED? AM I...?
"REJOICE! HE HATH ESCAPED THIS FLESHY GAOL TO SOAR ABOVE IN PURE ELYSIAN SKY...
?
TH-THE ASTRAL PLANE? IS THAT WHERE I AM? THAT MUST BE WHY EVERYTHING'S SO... LIQUID.
WH-WHO ARE YOU?
MY DEAR GIRL, YOU KNOW WHO I AM.
"HE TREADS IN SPIRIT NOW THOSE MOONLIT LANES..."
I'M TRELAWNEY, KARSWELL, POELZIG AND MOCATA.
I'M ADRIAN MARCATO, KOSMO GALLION AND CHARLES FELTON.
I'M OLIVER HADDO, AND I'M VERY PLEASED TO MEET YOU.
"...WHERE NIGHT-THINGS FLIT, THAT ONCE HE TROD IN RHYME."

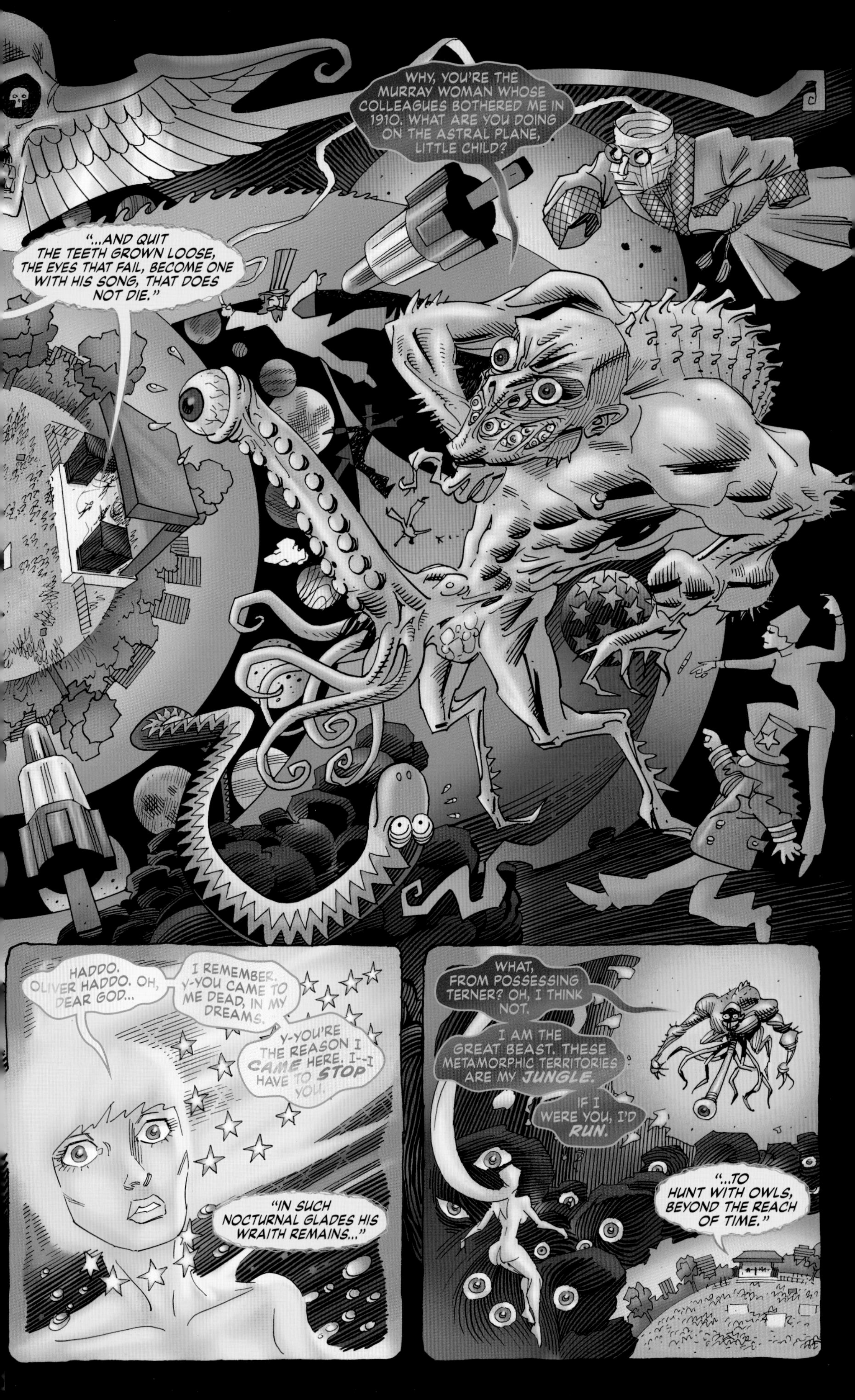
WHY, YOU'RE THE MURRAY WOMAN WHOSE COLLEAGUES BOTHERED ME IN 1910. WHAT ARE YOU DOING ON THE ASTRAL PLANE, LITTLE CHILD?
"...AND QUIT THE TEETH GROWN LOOSE, THE EYES THAT FAIL, BECOME ONE WITH HIS SONG, THAT DOES NOT DIE."
HADDO. OLIVER HADDO. OH, DEAR GOD...
I REMEMBER. Y-YOU CAME TO ME DEAD, IN MY DREAMS.
Y-YOU'RE THE REASON I CAME HERE. I--I HAVE TO STOP YOU.
"IN SUCH NOCTURNAL GLADES HIS WRAITH REMAINS..."
WHAT, FROM POSSESSING TERNER? OH, I THINK NOT.
I AM THE GREAT BEAST. THESE METAMORPHIC TERRITORIES ARE MY JUNGLE.
IF I WERE YOU, I'D RUN.
"...TO HUNT WITH OWLS, BEYOND THE REACH OF TIME."

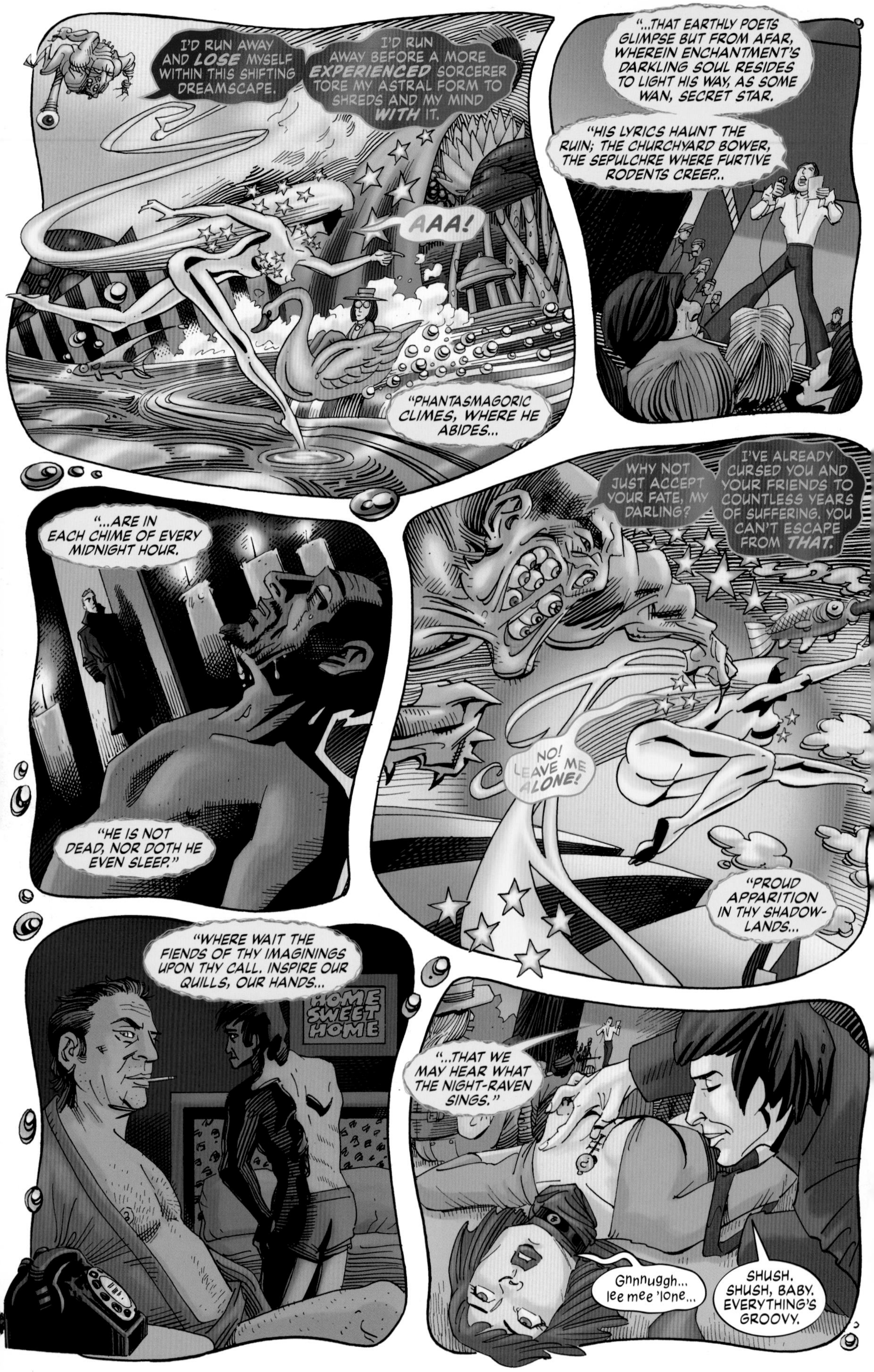
I'D RUN AWAY AND LOSE MYSELF WITHIN THIS SHIFTING DREAMSCAPE.
I'D RUN AWAY BEFORE A MORE EXPERIENCED SORCERER TORE MY ASTRAL FORM TO SHREDS AND MY MIND WITH IT.
AAA!
"PHANTASMAGORIC CLIMES, WHERE HE ABIDES...
"...THAT EARTHLY POETS GLIMPSE BUT FROM AFAR, WHEREIN ENCHANTMENT'S DARKLING SOUL RESIDES TO LIGHT HIS WAY, AS SOME WAN, SECRET STAR.
"HIS LYRICS HAUNT THE RUIN; THE CHURCHYARD BOWER, THE SEPULCHRE WHERE FURTIVE RODENTS CREEP...
"...ARE IN EACH CHIME OF EVERY MIDNIGHT HOUR.
"HE IS NOT DEAD, NOR DOTH HE EVEN SLEEP."
WHY NOT JUST ACCEPT YOUR FATE, MY DARLING?
I'VE ALREADY CURSED YOU AND YOUR FRIENDS TO COUNTLESS YEARS OF SUFFERING. YOU CAN'T ESCAPE FROM THAT.
NO! LEAVE ME ALONE!
"PROUD APPARITION IN THY SHADOW-LANDS...
"WHERE WAIT THE FIENDS OF THY IMAGININGS UPON THY CALL. INSPIRE OUR QUILLS, OUR HANDS...
HOME SWEET HOME
"...THAT WE MAY HEAR WHAT THE NIGHT-RAVEN SINGS."
Gnnnuggh... lee mee 'lone...
SHUSH. SHUSH, BABY. EVERYTHING'S GROOVY.

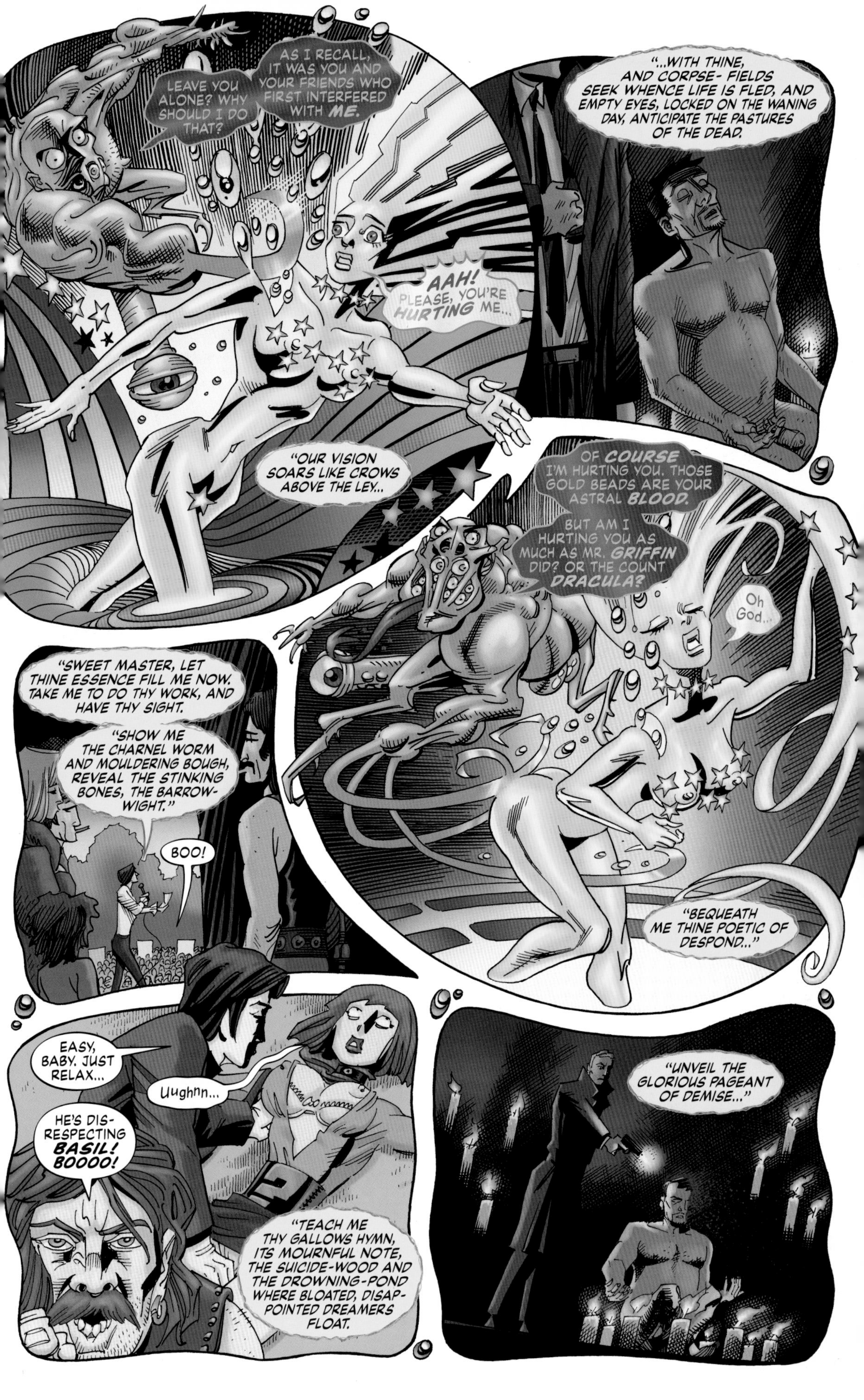

LEAVE YOU ALONE? WHY SHOULD I DO THAT?
AS I RECALL, IT WAS YOU AND YOUR FRIENDS WHO FIRST INTERFERED WITH ME.
AAH! PLEASE, YOU'RE HURTING ME...
"...WITH THINE, AND CORPSE- FIELDS SEEK WHENCE LIFE IS FLED, AND EMPTY EYES, LOCKED ON THE WANING DAY, ANTICIPATE THE PASTURES OF THE DEAD.
"OUR VISION SOARS LIKE CROWS ABOVE THE LEY...
OF COURSE I'M HURTING YOU. THOSE GOLD BEADS ARE YOUR ASTRAL BLOOD.
BUT AM I HURTING YOU AS MUCH AS MR. GRIFFIN DID? OR THE COUNT DRACULA?
Oh God...
"SWEET MASTER, LET THINE ESSENCE FILL ME NOW. TAKE ME TO DO THY WORK, AND HAVE THY SIGHT.
"SHOW ME THE CHARNEL WORM AND MOULDERING BOUGH, REVEAL THE STINKING BONES, THE BARROW-WIGHT."
BOO!
"BEQUEATH ME THINE POETIC OF DESPOND..."
EASY, BABY. JUST RELAX...
Uughnn...
HE'S DIS-RESPECTING BASIL! BOOOO!
"TEACH ME THY GALLOWS HYMN, ITS MOURNFUL NOTE, THE SUICIDE-WOOD AND THE DROWNING-POND WHERE BLOATED, DISAP-POINTED DREAMERS FLOAT.
"UNVEIL THE GLORIOUS PAGEANT OF DEMISE..."

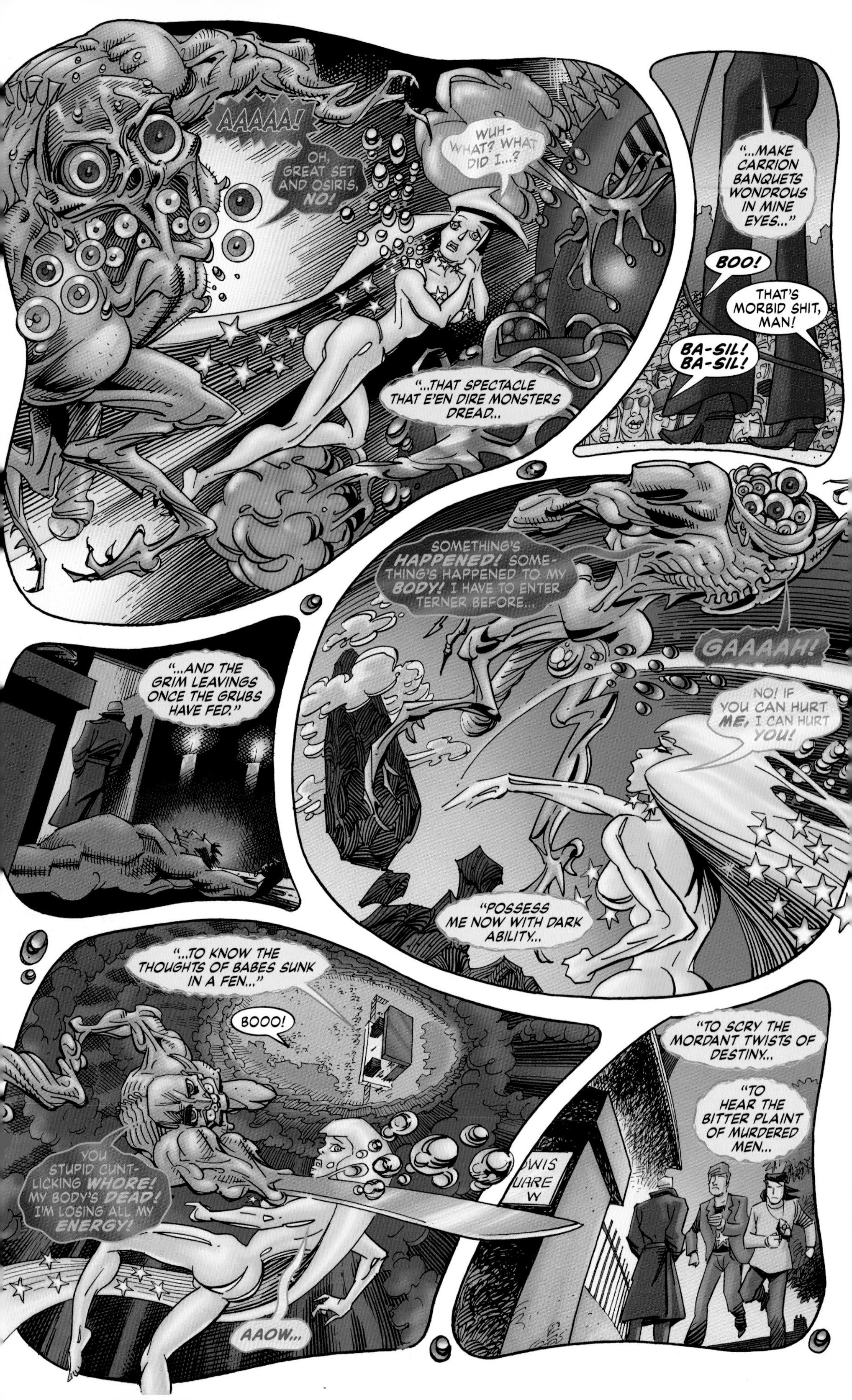
AAAAA!
OH, GREAT SET AND OSIRIS, NO!
WUH-WHAT? WHAT DID I...?
"...THAT SPECTACLE THAT E'EN DIRE MONSTERS DREAD...
"...MAKE CARRION BANQUETS WONDROUS IN MINE EYES..."
BOO!
THAT'S MORBID SHIT, MAN!
BA-SIL! BA-SIL!
"...AND THE GRIM LEAVINGS ONCE THE GRUBS HAVE FED."
SOMETHING'S HAPPENED! SOMETHING'S HAPPENED TO MY BODY! I HAVE TO ENTER TERNER BEFORE...
GAAAAH!
NO! IF YOU CAN HURT ME, I CAN HURT YOU!
"POSSESS ME NOW WITH DARK ABILITY...
"...TO KNOW THE THOUGHTS OF BABES SUNK IN A FEN..."
BOOO!
YOU STUPID CUNT-LICKING WHORE! MY BODY'S DEAD! I'M LOSING ALL MY ENERGY!
AAOW...
"TO SCRY THE MORDANT TWISTS OF DESTINY...
"TO HEAR THE BITTER PLAINT OF MURDERED MEN...

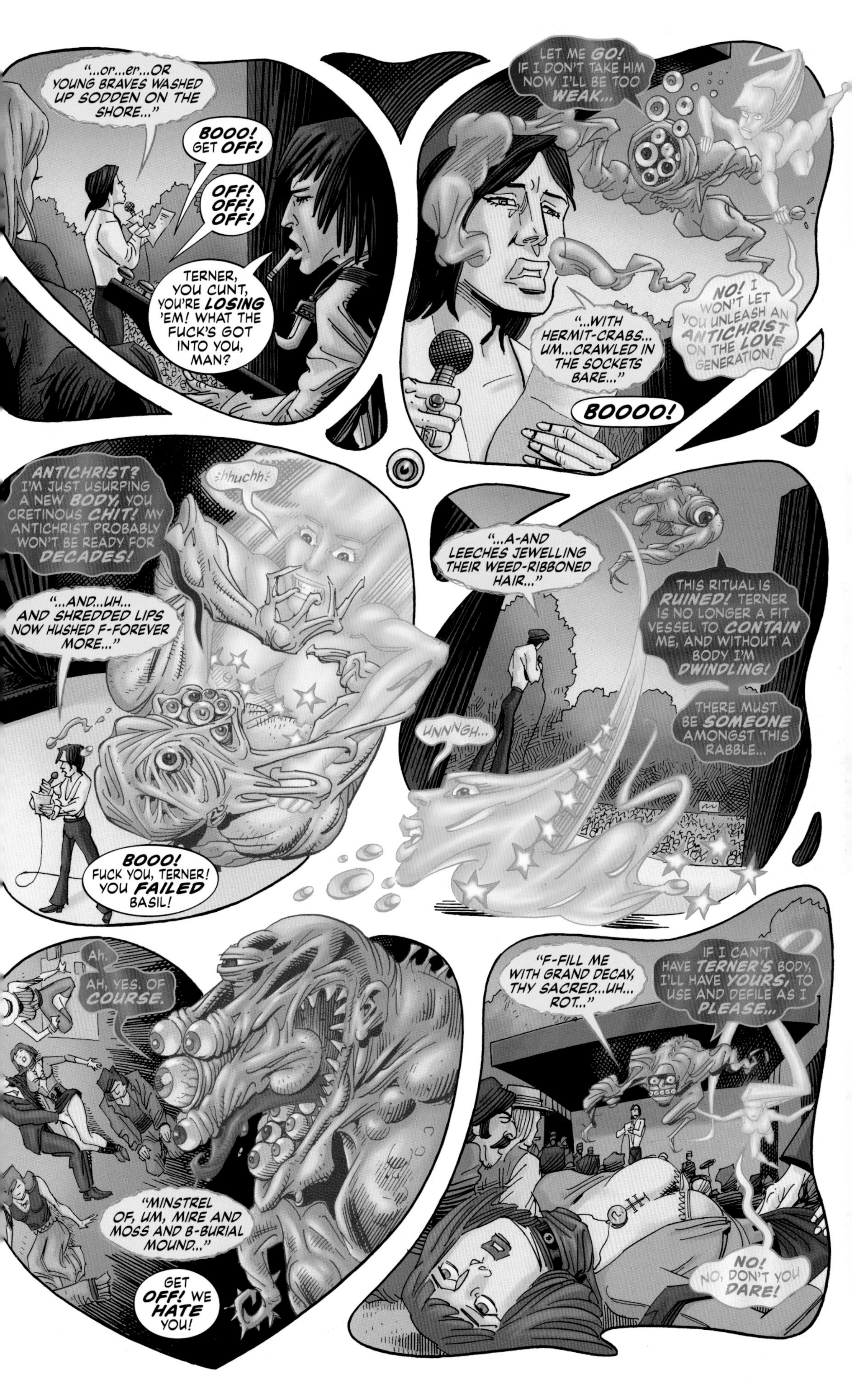
"...or...er...OR YOUNG BRAVES WASHED UP SODDEN ON THE SHORE..."
BOOO! GET OFF!
OFF! OFF! OFF!
TERNER, YOU CUNT, YOU'RE LOSING 'EM! WHAT THE FUCK'S GOT INTO YOU, MAN?
LET ME GO! IF I DON'T TAKE HIM NOW I'LL BE TOO WEAK...
"...WITH HERMIT-CRABS... UM...CRAWLED IN THE SOCKETS BARE..."
NO! I WON'T LET YOU UNLEASH AN ANTICHRIST ON THE LOVE GENERATION!
BOOOO!
ANTICHRIST? I'M JUST USURPING A NEW BODY, YOU CRETINOUS CHIT! MY ANTICHRIST PROBABLY WON'T BE READY FOR DECADES!
hhuchh
"...AND...UH... AND SHREDDED LIPS NOW HUSHED F-FOREVER MORE..."
BOOO! FUCK YOU, TERNER! YOU FAILED BASIL!
"...A-AND LEECHES JEWELLING THEIR WEED-RIBBONED HAIR..."
THIS RITUAL IS RUINED! TERNER IS NO LONGER A FIT VESSEL TO CONTAIN ME, AND WITHOUT A BODY I'M DWINDLING!
THERE MUST BE SOMEONE AMONGST THIS RABBLE...
UNNNGH...
Ah.
AH, YES. OF COURSE.
"MINSTREL OF, UM, MIRE AND MOSS AND B-BURIAL MOUND..."
GET OFF! WE HATE YOU!
"F-FILL ME WITH GRAND DECAY, THY SACRED...UH... ROT..."
IF I CAN'T HAVE TERNER'S BODY, I'LL HAVE YOURS, TO USE AND DEFILE AS I PLEASE...
NO! NO, DON'T YOU DARE!

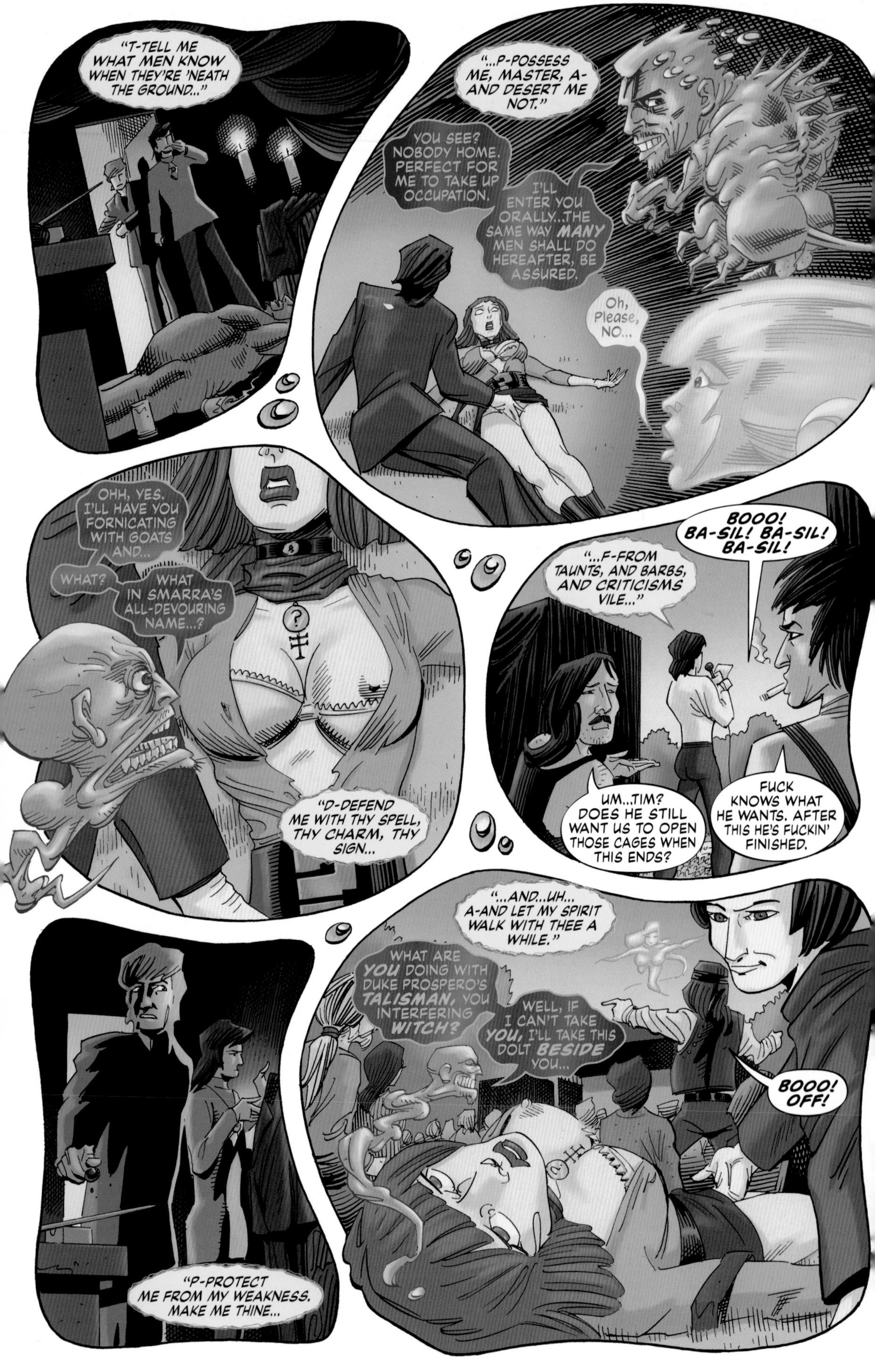
"T-TELL ME WHAT MEN KNOW WHEN THEY'RE 'NEATH THE GROUND..."
"...P-POSSESS ME, MASTER, A-AND DESERT ME NOT."
YOU SEE? NOBODY HOME. PERFECT FOR ME TO TAKE UP OCCUPATION.
I'LL ENTER YOU ORALLY...THE SAME WAY MANY MEN SHALL DO HEREAFTER, BE ASSURED.
Oh, Please, NO...
OHH, YES. I'LL HAVE YOU FORNICATING WITH GOATS AND...
WHAT?
WHAT IN SMARRA'S ALL-DEVOURING NAME...?
"D-DEFEND ME WITH THY SPELL, THY CHARM, THY SIGN...
"...F-FROM TAUNTS, AND BARBS, AND CRITICISMS VILE..."
BOOO! BA-SIL! BA-SIL! BA-SIL!
UM...TIM? DOES HE STILL WANT US TO OPEN THOSE CAGES WHEN THIS ENDS?
FUCK KNOWS WHAT HE WANTS. AFTER THIS HE'S FUCKIN' FINISHED.
"P-PROTECT ME FROM MY WEAKNESS. MAKE ME THINE...
"...AND...UH... A-AND LET MY SPIRIT WALK WITH THEE A WHILE."
WHAT ARE YOU DOING WITH DUKE PROSPERO'S TALISMAN, YOU INTERFERING WITCH?
WELL, IF I CAN'T TAKE YOU, I'LL TAKE THIS DOLT BESIDE YOU...
BOOO! OFF!

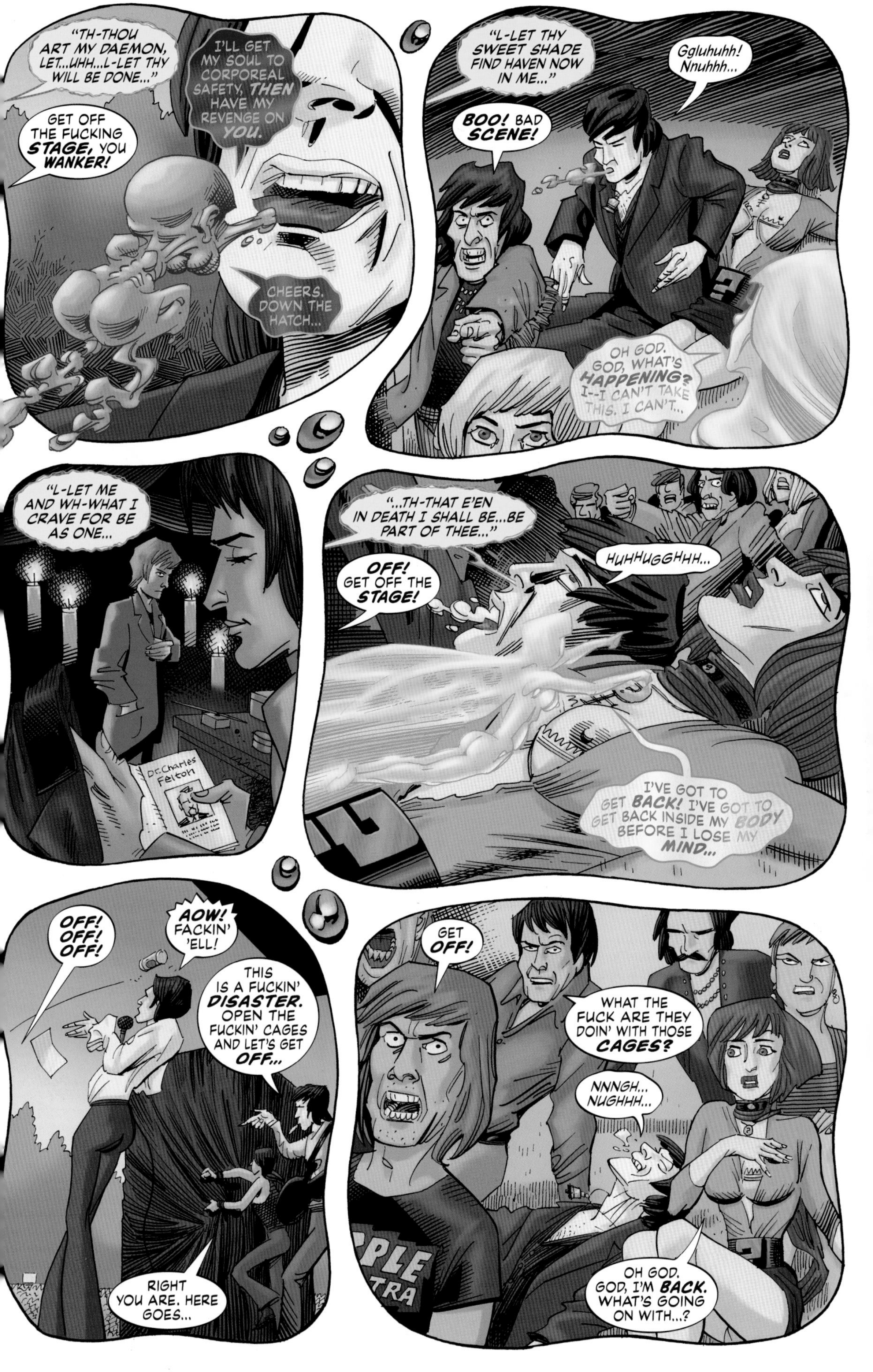
"TH-THOU ART MY DAEMON, LET...UHH...L-LET THY WILL BE DONE..."
I'LL GET MY SOUL TO CORPOREAL SAFETY, THEN HAVE MY REVENGE ON YOU.
GET OFF THE FUCKING STAGE, YOU WANKER!
CHEERS. DOWN THE HATCH...
"L-LET THY SWEET SHADE FIND HAVEN NOW IN ME..."
Ggluhuhh! Nnuhhh...
BOO! BAD SCENE!
OH GOD. GOD, WHAT'S HAPPENING? I--I CAN'T TAKE THIS. I CAN'T...
"L-LET ME AND WH-WHAT I CRAVE FOR BE AS ONE...
Dr. Charles Felton
"...TH-THAT E'EN IN DEATH I SHALL BE...BE PART OF THEE..."
HUHHUGGHHH...
OFF! GET OFF THE STAGE!
I'VE GOT TO GET BACK! I'VE GOT TO GET BACK INSIDE MY BODY BEFORE I LOSE MY MIND...
OFF! OFF! OFF!
AOW! FACKIN' 'ELL!
THIS IS A FUCKIN' DISASTER. OPEN THE FUCKIN' CAGES AND LET'S GET OFF...
RIGHT YOU ARE. HERE GOES...
GET OFF!
WHAT THE FUCK ARE THEY DOIN' WITH THOSE CAGES?
NNNGH... NUGHHH...
OH GOD. GOD, I'M BACK. WHAT'S GOING ON WITH...?

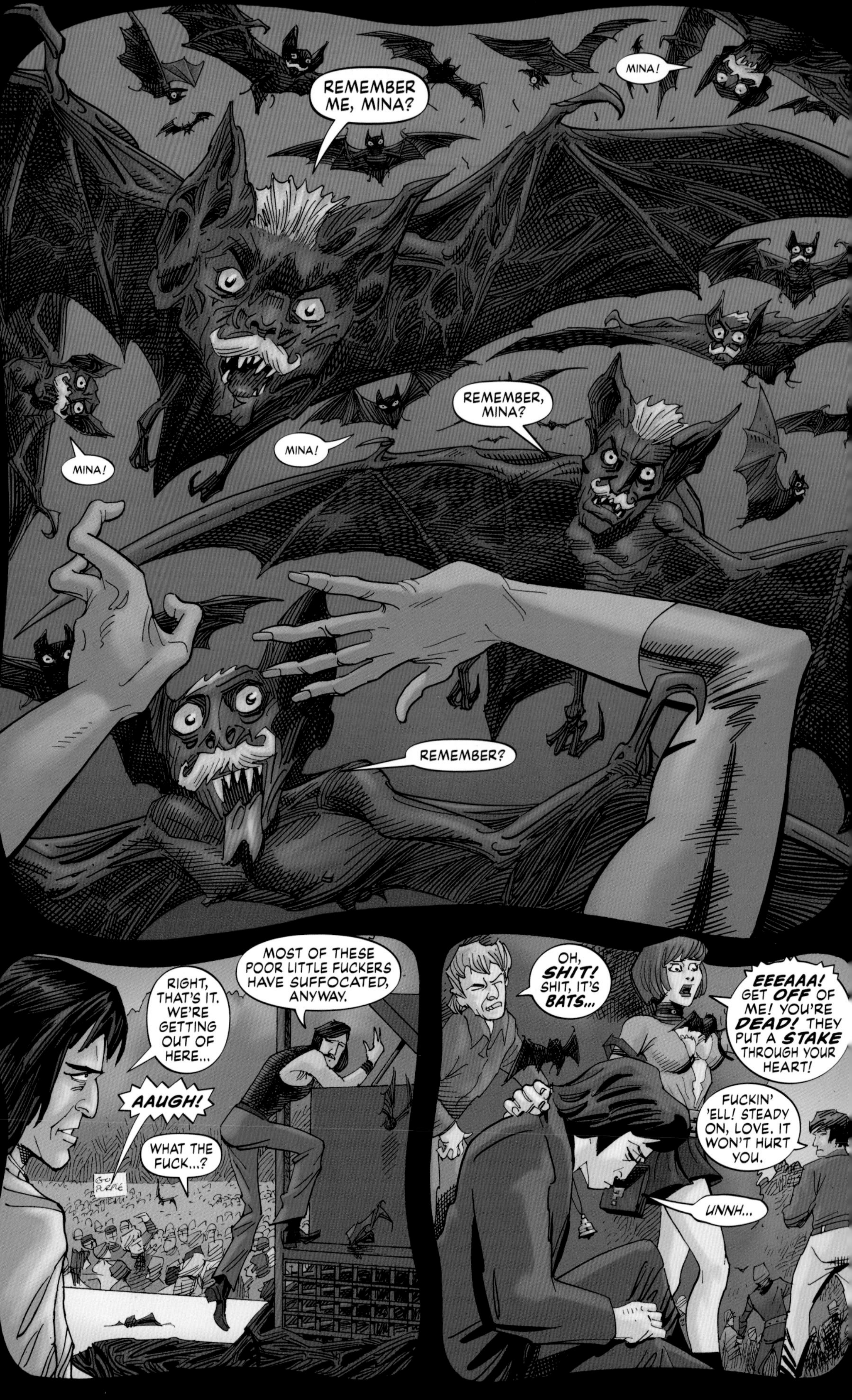
REMEMBER ME, MINA?
MINA!
REMEMBER, MINA?
MINA!
MINA!
REMEMBER?
RIGHT, THAT'S IT. WE'RE GETTING OUT OF HERE...
MOST OF THESE POOR LITTLE FUCKERS HAVE SUFFOCATED, ANYWAY.
AAUGH!
WHAT THE FUCK...?
OH, SHIT! SHIT, IT'S BATS...
EEEAAA! GET OFF OF ME! YOU'RE DEAD! THEY PUT A STAKE THROUGH YOUR HEART!
FUCKIN' 'ELL! STEADY ON, LOVE. IT WON'T HURT YOU.
UNNH...

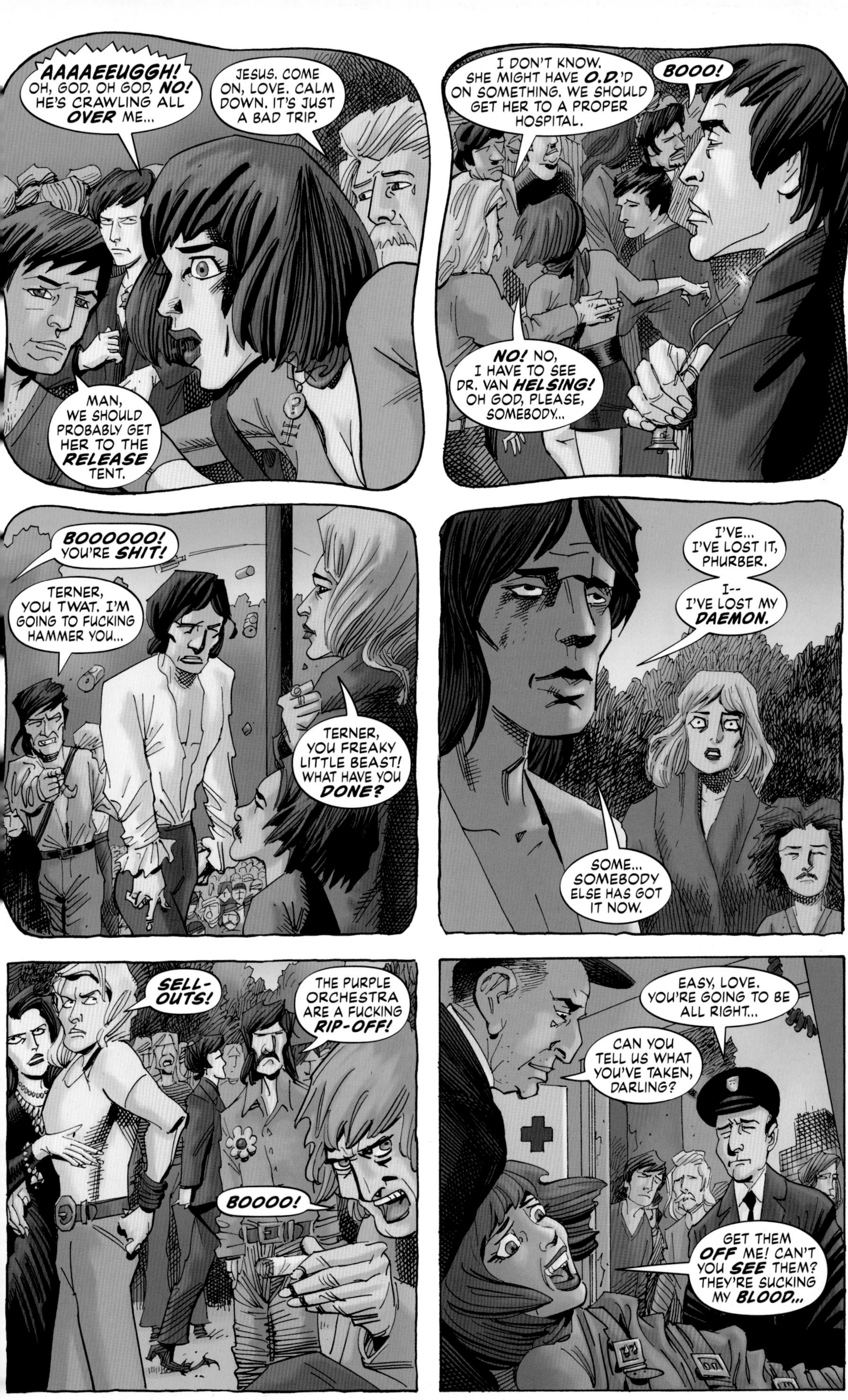
AAAAEEUGGH! OH, GOD. OH GOD, NO! HE'S CRAWLING ALL OVER ME...
JESUS. COME ON, LOVE. CALM DOWN. IT'S JUST A BAD TRIP.
MAN, WE SHOULD PROBABLY GET HER TO THE RELEASE TENT.
I DON'T KNOW. SHE MIGHT HAVE O.D.'D ON SOMETHING. WE SHOULD GET HER TO A PROPER HOSPITAL.
BOOO!
NO! NO, I HAVE TO SEE DR. VAN HELSING! OH GOD, PLEASE, SOMEBODY...
BOOOOOO! YOU'RE SHIT!
TERNER, YOU TWAT. I'M GOING TO FUCKING HAMMER YOU...
TERNER, YOU FREAKY LITTLE BEAST! WHAT HAVE YOU DONE?
I'VE... I'VE LOST IT, PHURBER.
I-- I'VE LOST MY DAEMON.
SOME... SOMEBODY ELSE HAS GOT IT NOW.
SELL-OUTS!
THE PURPLE ORCHESTRA ARE A FUCKING RIP-OFF!
BOOOO!
EASY, LOVE. YOU'RE GOING TO BE ALL RIGHT...
CAN YOU TELL US WHAT YOU'VE TAKEN, DARLING?
GET THEM OFF ME! CAN'T YOU SEE THEM? THEY'RE SUCKING MY BLOOD...

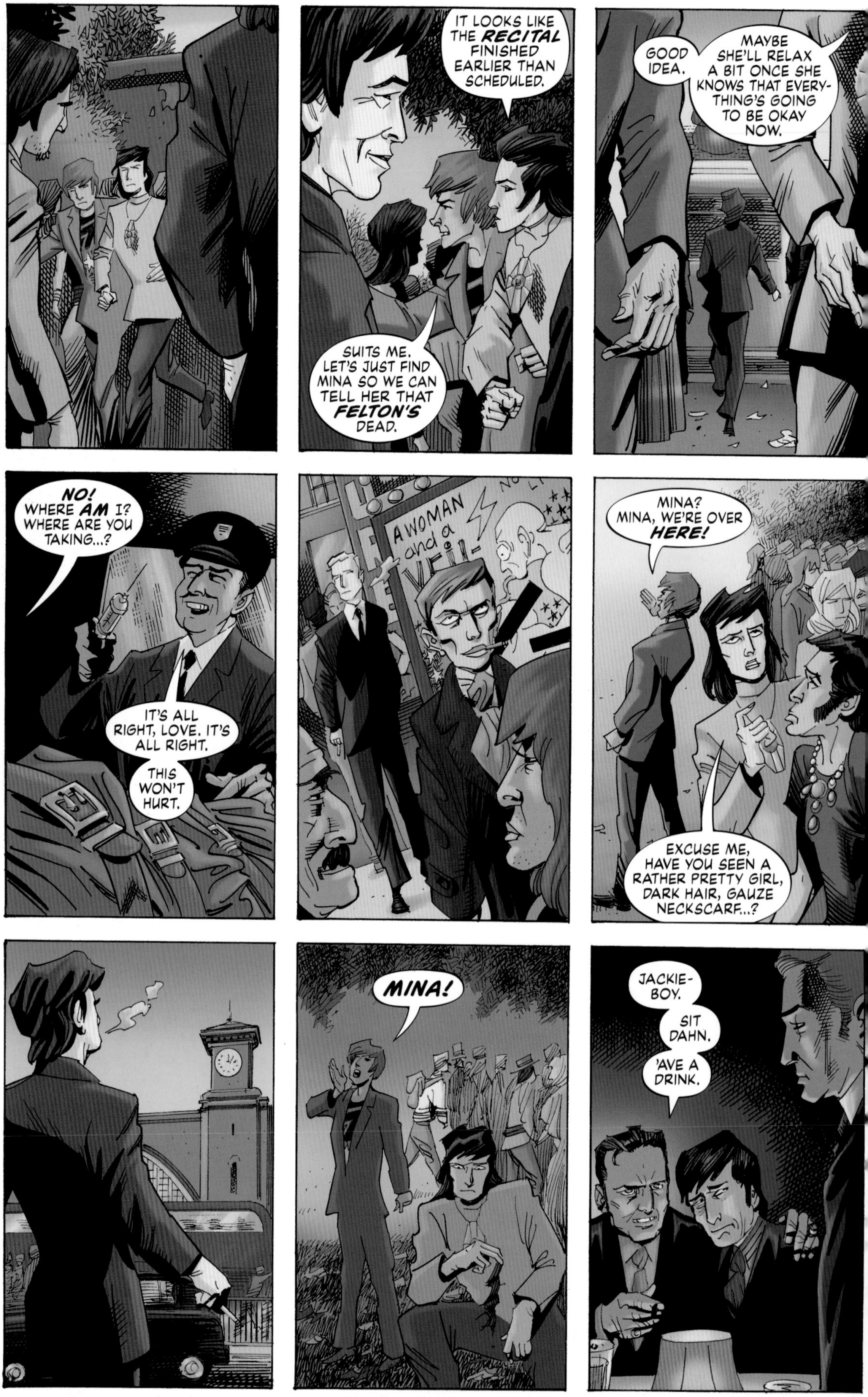
IT LOOKS LIKE THE RECITAL FINISHED EARLIER THAN SCHEDULED.
SUITS ME. LET'S JUST FIND MINA SO WE CAN TELL HER THAT FELTON'S DEAD.
GOOD IDEA.
MAYBE SHE'LL RELAX A BIT ONCE SHE KNOWS THAT EVERYTHING'S GOING TO BE OKAY NOW.
NO! WHERE AM I? WHERE ARE YOU TAKING...?
IT'S ALL RIGHT, LOVE. IT'S ALL RIGHT.
THIS WON'T HURT.
A WOMAN and a VEIL
MINA? MINA, WE'RE OVER HERE!
EXCUSE ME, HAVE YOU SEEN A RATHER PRETTY GIRL, DARK HAIR, GAUZE NECKSCARF...?
MINA!
JACKIE-BOY.
SIT DAHN.
'AVE A DRINK.

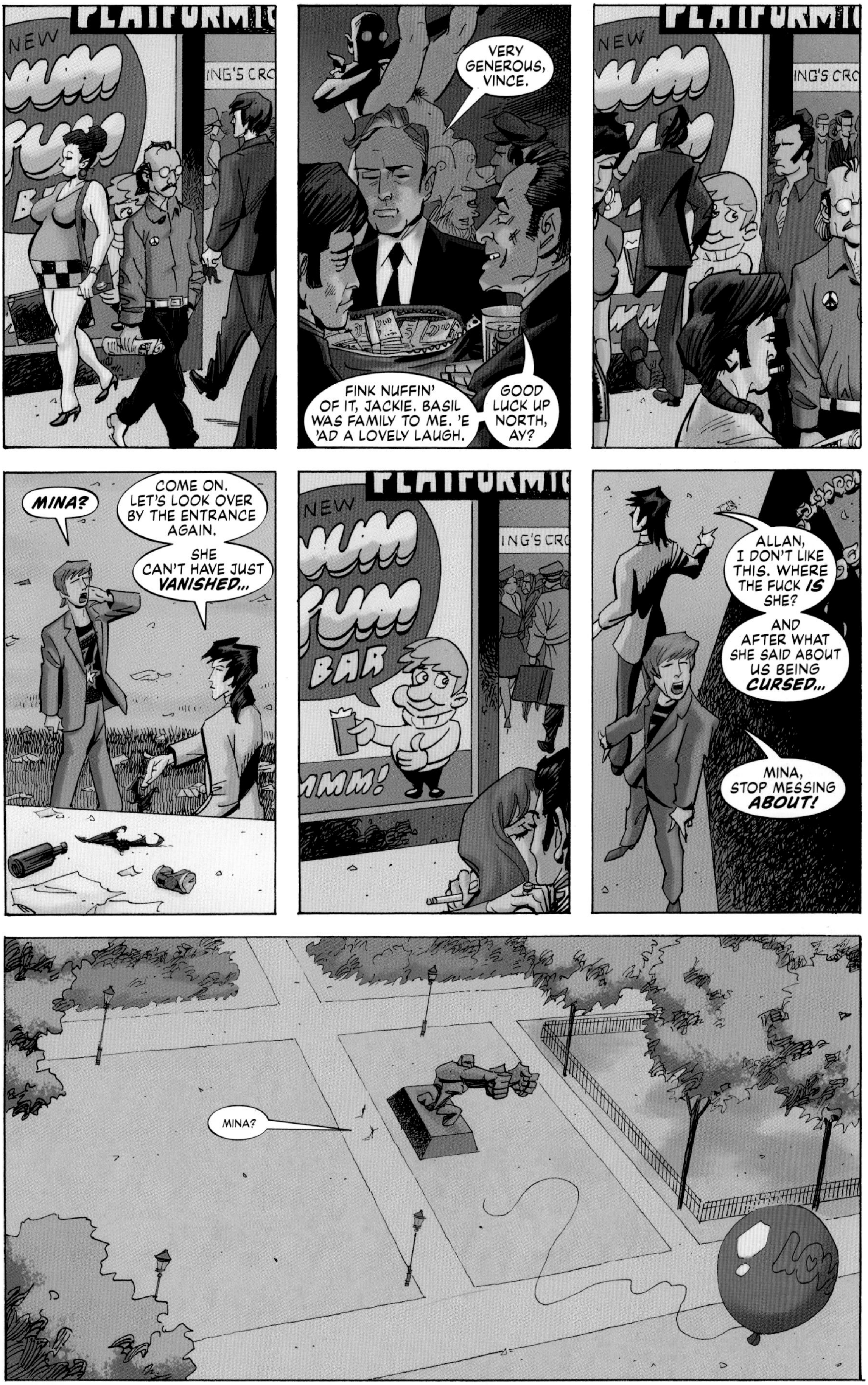
PLATFORMIC
NEW
ING'S CRO
VERY GENEROUS, VINCE.
FINK NUFFIN' OF IT, JACKIE. BASIL WAS FAMILY TO ME. 'E 'AD A LOVELY LAUGH.
GOOD LUCK UP NORTH, AY?
MINA?
COME ON. LET'S LOOK OVER BY THE ENTRANCE AGAIN.
SHE CAN'T HAVE JUST VANISHED...
BAR
ALLAN, I DON'T LIKE THIS. WHERE THE FUCK IS SHE?
AND AFTER WHAT SHE SAID ABOUT US BEING CURSED...
MINA, STOP MESSING ABOUT!
MINA?

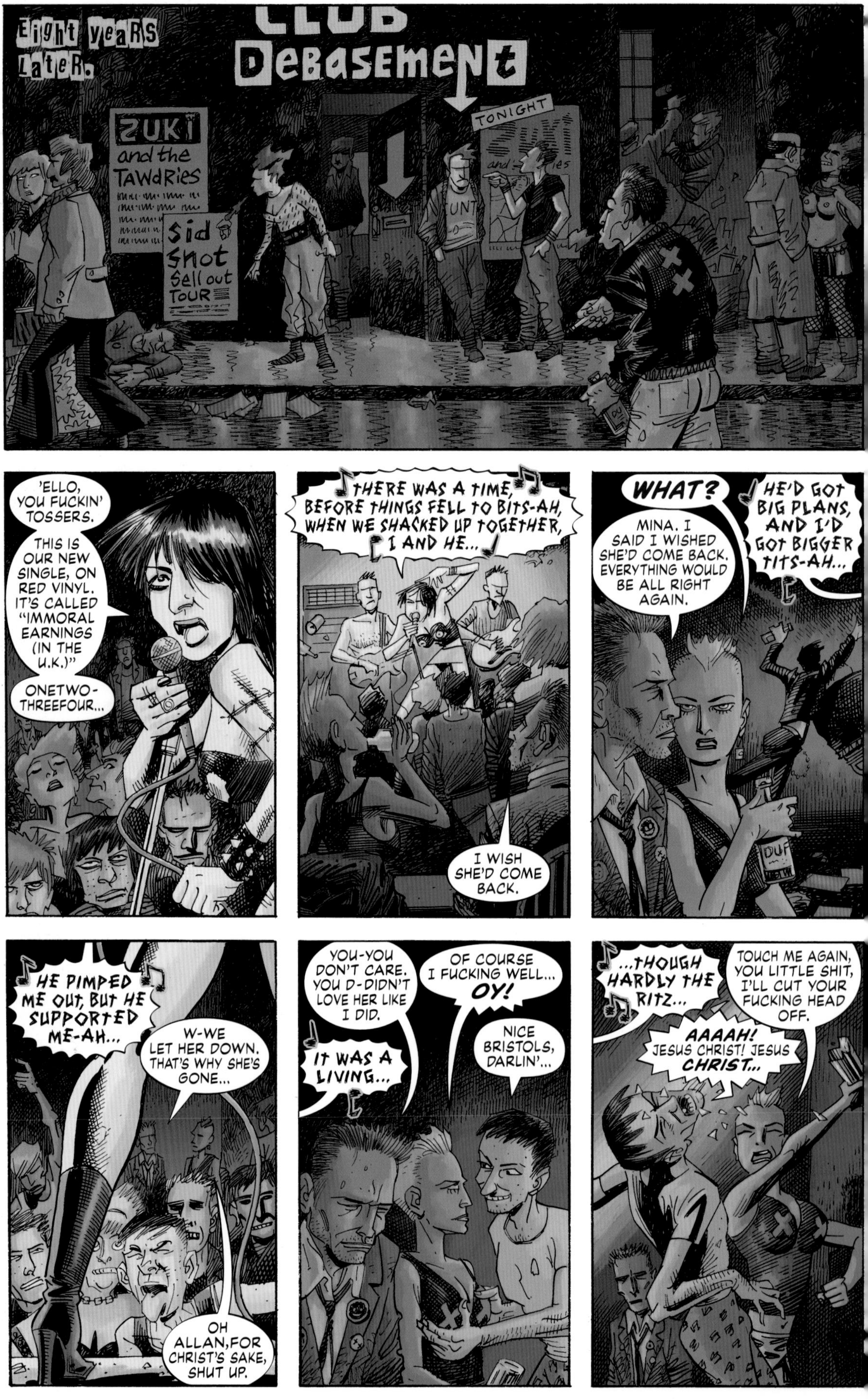
Eight years Later.
CLUB Debasement
ZUKI and the TAWDRIES
Sid Snot Sell out TOUR
TONIGHT
'ELLO, YOU FUCKIN' TOSSERS.
THIS IS OUR NEW SINGLE, ON RED VINYL. IT'S CALLED "IMMORAL EARNINGS (IN THE U.K.)"
ONETWO-THREEFOUR...
THERE WAS A TIME, BEFORE THINGS FELL TO BITS-AH, WHEN WE SHACKED UP TOGETHER, I AND HE...
I WISH SHE'D COME BACK.
WHAT?
HE'D GOT BIG PLANS, AND I'D GOT BIGGER TITS-AH...
MINA. I SAID I WISHED SHE'D COME BACK. EVERYTHING WOULD BE ALL RIGHT AGAIN.
HE PIMPED ME OUT, BUT HE SUPPORTED ME-AH...
W-WE LET HER DOWN. THAT'S WHY SHE'S GONE...
OH ALLAN, FOR CHRIST'S SAKE, SHUT UP.
YOU-YOU DON'T CARE. YOU D-DIDN'T LOVE HER LIKE I DID.
OF COURSE I FUCKING WELL... OY!
IT WAS A LIVING...
NICE BRISTOLS, DARLIN'...
...THOUGH HARDLY THE RITZ...
TOUCH ME AGAIN, YOU LITTLE SHIT, I'LL CUT YOUR FUCKING HEAD OFF.
AAAAH! JESUS CHRIST! JESUS CHRIST...

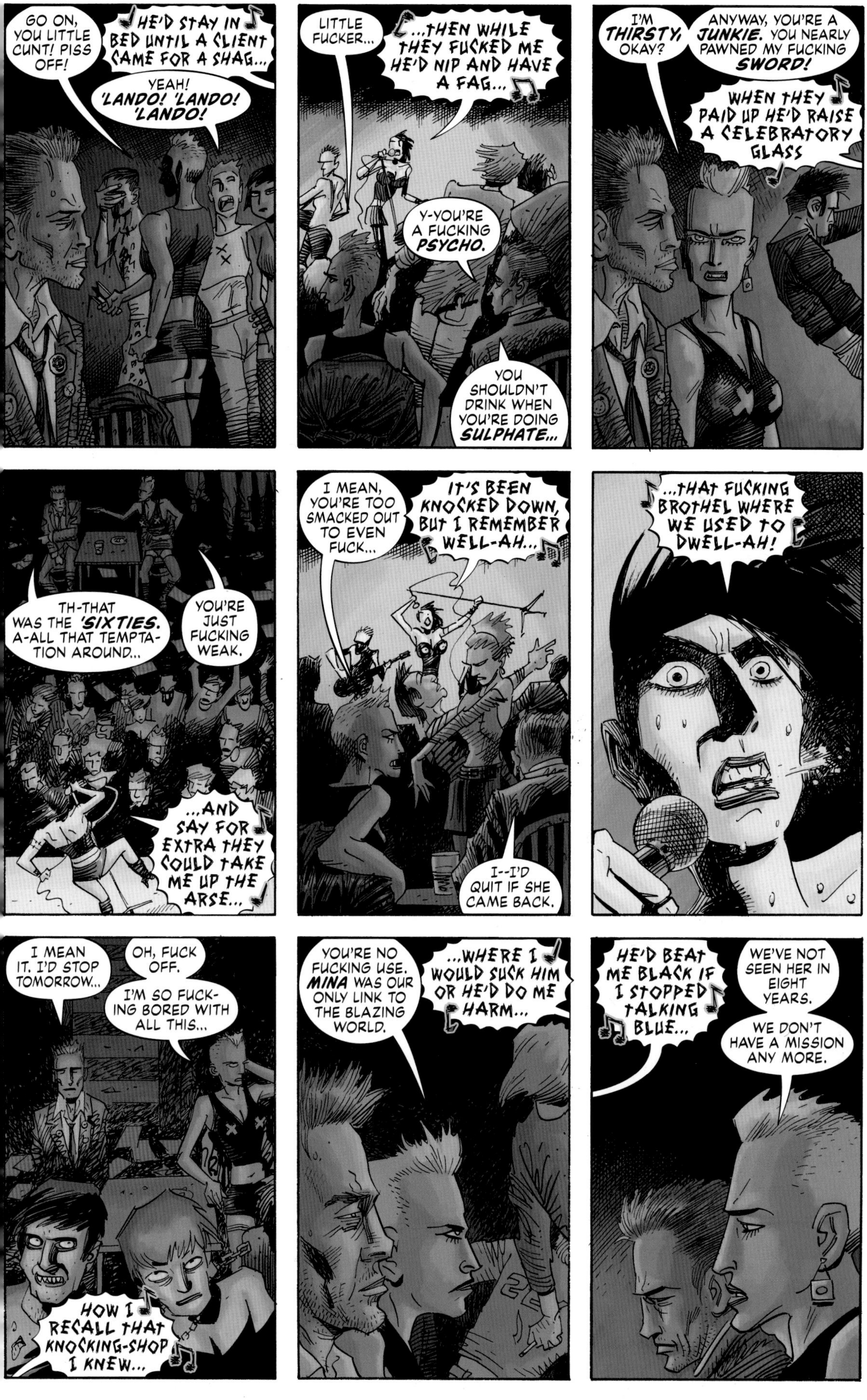
GO ON, YOU LITTLE CUNT! PISS OFF!
HE'D STAY IN BED UNTIL A CLIENT CAME FOR A SHAG...
YEAH! 'LANDO! 'LANDO! 'LANDO!
LITTLE FUCKER...
...THEN WHILE THEY FUCKED ME HE'D NIP AND HAVE A FAG...
Y-YOU'RE A FUCKING PSYCHO.
YOU SHOULDN'T DRINK WHEN YOU'RE DOING SULPHATE...
I'M THIRSTY, OKAY?
ANYWAY, YOU'RE A JUNKIE. YOU NEARLY PAWNED MY FUCKING SWORD!
WHEN THEY PAID UP HE'D RAISE A CELEBRATORY GLASS
TH-THAT WAS THE 'SIXTIES. A-ALL THAT TEMPTATION AROUND...
YOU'RE JUST FUCKING WEAK.
...AND SAY FOR EXTRA THEY COULD TAKE ME UP THE ARSE...
I MEAN, YOU'RE TOO SMACKED OUT TO EVEN FUCK...
IT'S BEEN KNOCKED DOWN, BUT I REMEMBER WELL-AH...
I--I'D QUIT IF SHE CAME BACK.
...THAT FUCKING BROTHEL WHERE WE USED TO DWELL-AH!
I MEAN IT. I'D STOP TOMORROW...
OH, FUCK OFF.
I'M SO FUCKING BORED WITH ALL THIS...
HOW I RECALL THAT KNOCKING-SHOP I KNEW...
YOU'RE NO FUCKING USE. MINA WAS OUR ONLY LINK TO THE BLAZING WORLD.
...WHERE I WOULD SUCK HIM OR HE'D DO ME HARM...
HE'D BEAT ME BLACK IF I STOPPED TALKING BLUE...
WE'VE NOT SEEN HER IN EIGHT YEARS.
WE DON'T HAVE A MISSION ANY MORE.

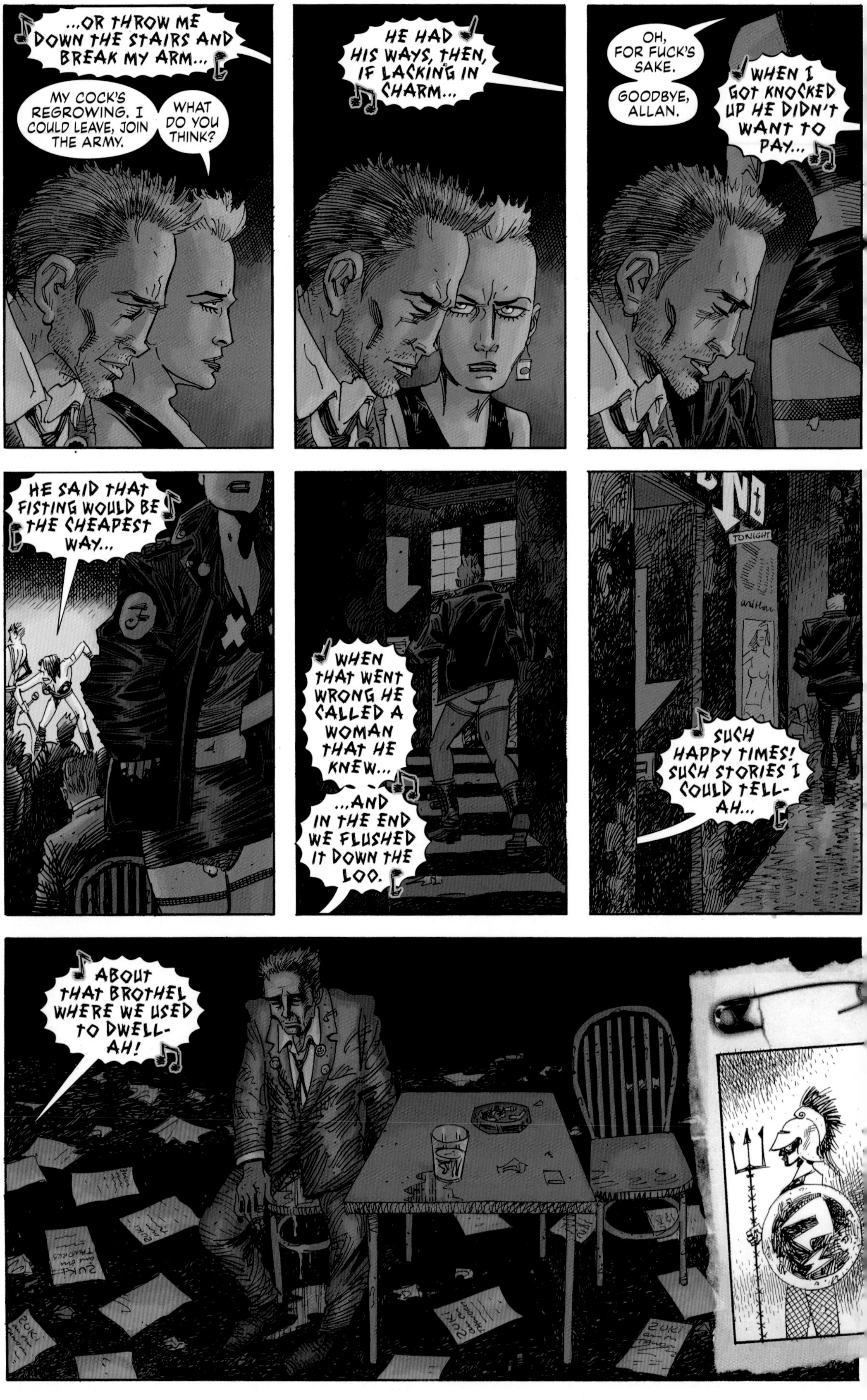
...OR THROW ME DOWN THE STAIRS AND BREAK MY ARM...
MY COCK'S REGROWING. I COULD LEAVE, JOIN THE ARMY.
WHAT DO YOU THINK?
HE HAD HIS WAYS, THEN, IF LACKING IN CHARM...
OH, FOR FUCK'S SAKE.
GOODBYE, ALLAN.
WHEN I GOT KNOCKED UP HE DIDN'T WANT TO PAY...
HE SAID THAT FISTING WOULD BE THE CHEAPEST WAY...
WHEN THAT WENT WRONG HE CALLED A WOMAN THAT HE KNEW...
...AND IN THE END WE FLUSHED IT DOWN THE LOO.
TONIGHT
SUCH HAPPY TIMES! SUCH STORIES I COULD TELL-AH...
ABOUT THAT BROTHEL WHERE WE USED TO DWELL-AH!

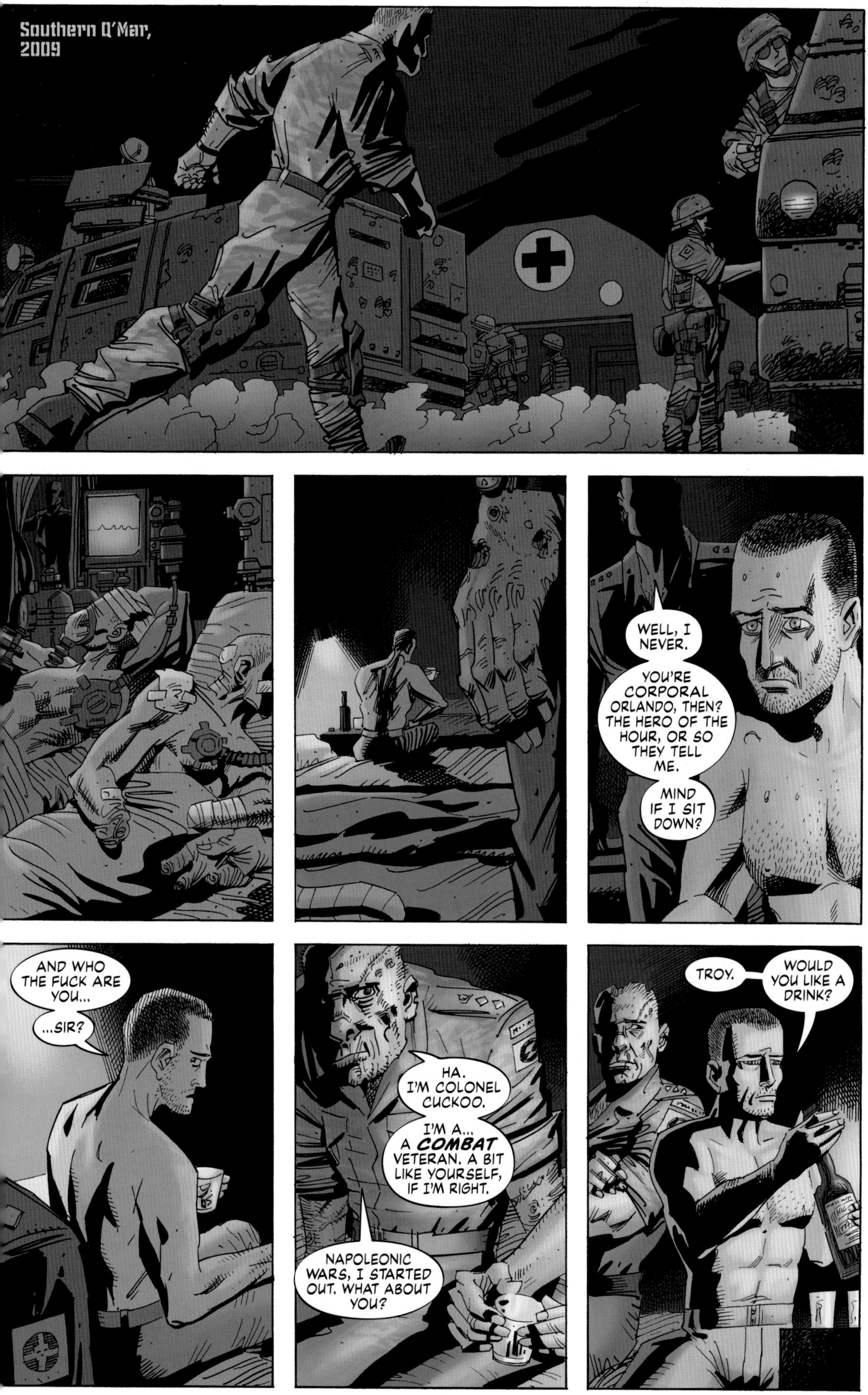

Southern Q'Mar, 2009
WELL, I NEVER.
YOU'RE CORPORAL ORLANDO, THEN? THE HERO OF THE HOUR, OR SO THEY TELL ME.
MIND IF I SIT DOWN?
AND WHO THE FUCK ARE YOU...
...SIR?
HA. I'M COLONEL CUCKOO.
I'M A... A COMBAT VETERAN. A BIT LIKE YOURSELF, IF I'M RIGHT.
NAPOLEONIC WARS, I STARTED OUT. WHAT ABOUT YOU?
TROY.
WOULD YOU LIKE A DRINK?

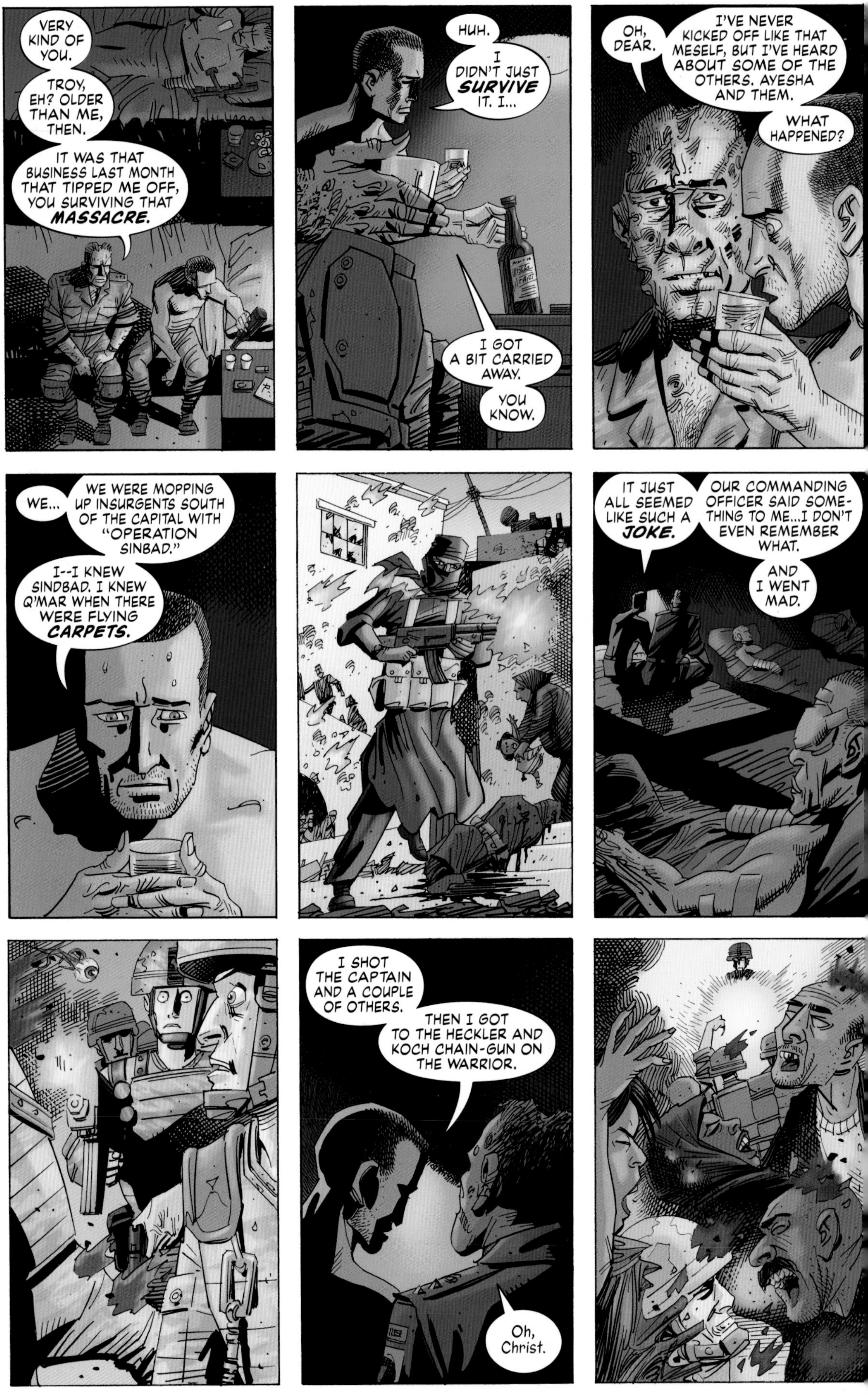
VERY KIND OF YOU.
TROY, EH? OLDER THAN ME, THEN.
IT WAS THAT BUSINESS LAST MONTH THAT TIPPED ME OFF, YOU SURVIVING THAT MASSACRE.
HUH.
I DIDN'T JUST SURVIVE IT. I...
I GOT A BIT CARRIED AWAY.
YOU KNOW.
OH, DEAR.
I'VE NEVER KICKED OFF LIKE THAT MESELF, BUT I'VE HEARD ABOUT SOME OF THE OTHERS. AYESHA AND THEM.
WHAT HAPPENED?
WE...
WE WERE MOPPING UP INSURGENTS SOUTH OF THE CAPITAL WITH "OPERATION SINBAD."
I--I KNEW SINDBAD. I KNEW Q'MAR WHEN THERE WERE FLYING CARPETS.
IT JUST ALL SEEMED LIKE SUCH A JOKE.
OUR COMMANDING OFFICER SAID SOME-THING TO ME...I DON'T EVEN REMEMBER WHAT.
AND I WENT MAD.
I SHOT THE CAPTAIN AND A COUPLE OF OTHERS.
THEN I GOT TO THE HECKLER AND KOCH CHAIN-GUN ON THE WARRIOR.
Oh, Christ.

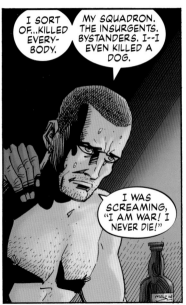

I SORT OF...KILLED EVERYBODY.

MY SQUADRON. THE INSURGENTS. BYSTANDERS. I--I EVEN KILLED A DOG.

I WAS SCREAMING, "I AM WAR! I NEVER DIE!"

THEY FOUND ME MUMBLING AMONGST ALL THE, YOU KNOW. THE BODIES.

THEY THINK I SURVIVED A MASSACRE. THEY'RE GIVING ME A MUH...

A-A MEDAL--※

STILL...

ENOUGH ABOUT ME, EH? THEY'RE FLYING ME HOME TOMORROW.

WHAT ABOUT YOU?

OH, I'LL BE ALL RIGHT.

THEY'RE SENDING US TO ARDISTAN AFTER WE'RE FINISHED HERE.

AFTER THAT, I EXPECT IT'LL BE KASHMIR OR SOMEWHERE.

ANYWAY, IT'S BEEN INTERESTING, TALKING TO YOU.

YOU LOOK AFTER YOURSELF. GET SOME REST, AND THAT.

I EXPECT I'LL SEE YOU NEXT WAR.

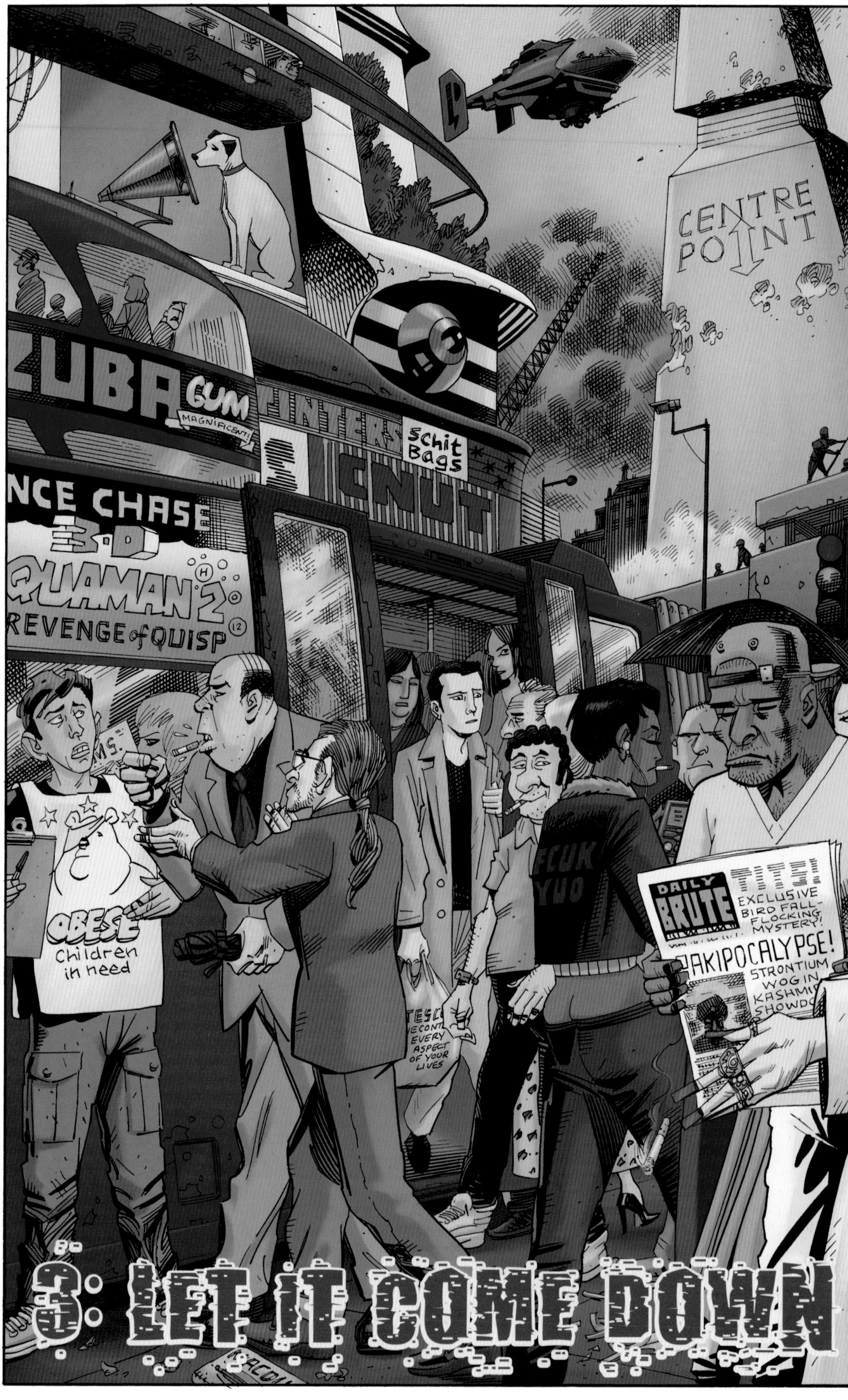

CENTRE POINT
UBA
GUM
MAGNIFICENT!
INTERS
Schit Bags
CNUT
NCE CHASE
3-D
QUAMAN 2
REVENGE of QUISP
OBESE
Children in need
FCUK YUO
TESCO
WE CONTROL EVERY ASPECT OF YOUR LIVES
DAILY BRUTE
TITS!
EXCLUSIVE
BIRD FALL-FLOCKING MYSTERY!
PAKIPOCALYPSE!
STRONTIUM WOG IN KASHMIR SHOWDOWN
3: LET IT COME DOWN

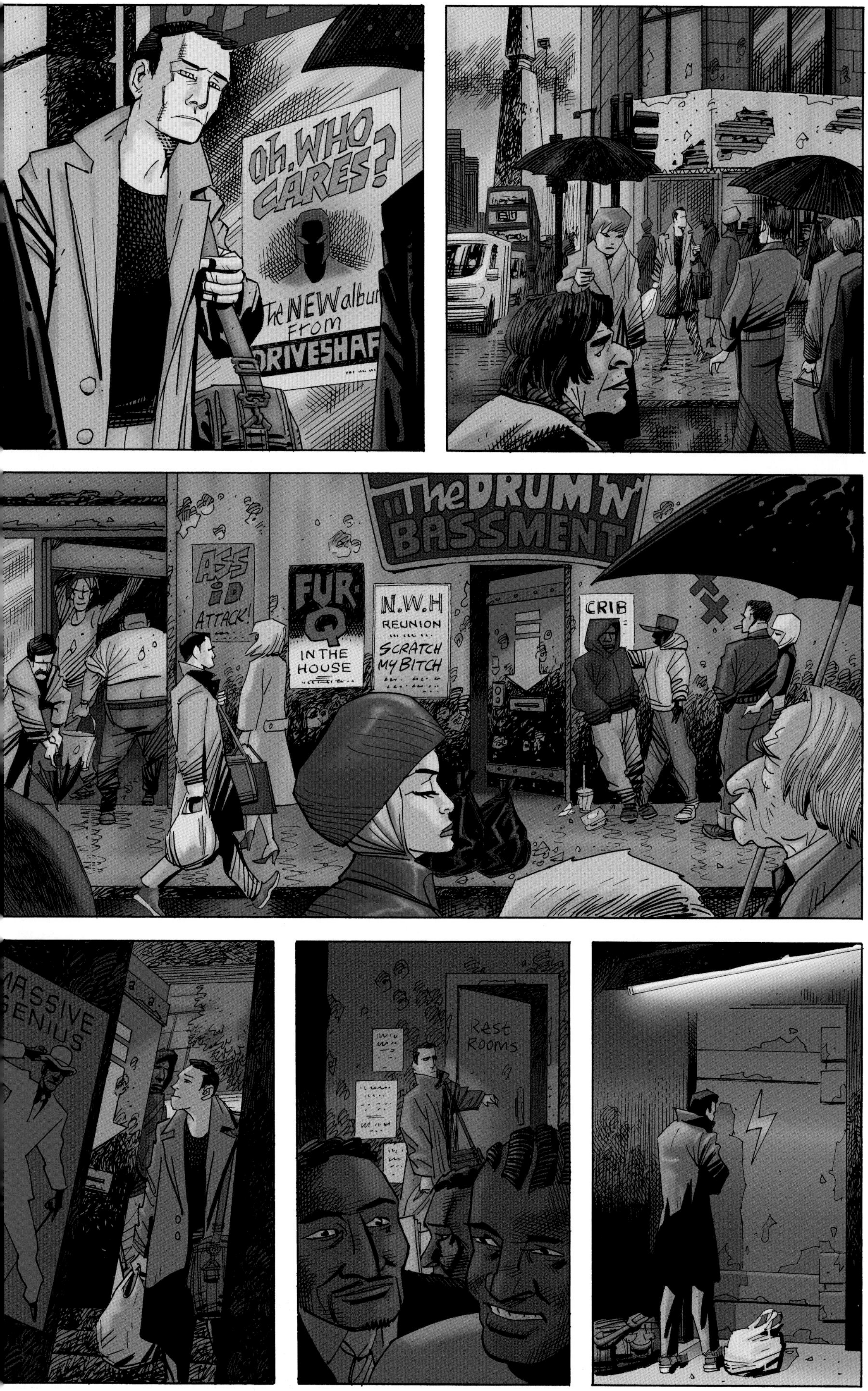

Oh. WHO CARES?
The NEW albu
From
DRIVESHAF
The DRUM 'N' BASSMENT
ASS iD ATTACK!
FUR-Q
IN THE HOUSE
N.W.H
REUNION
SCRATCH MY BITCH
CRIB
MASSIVE GENIUS
Rest Rooms

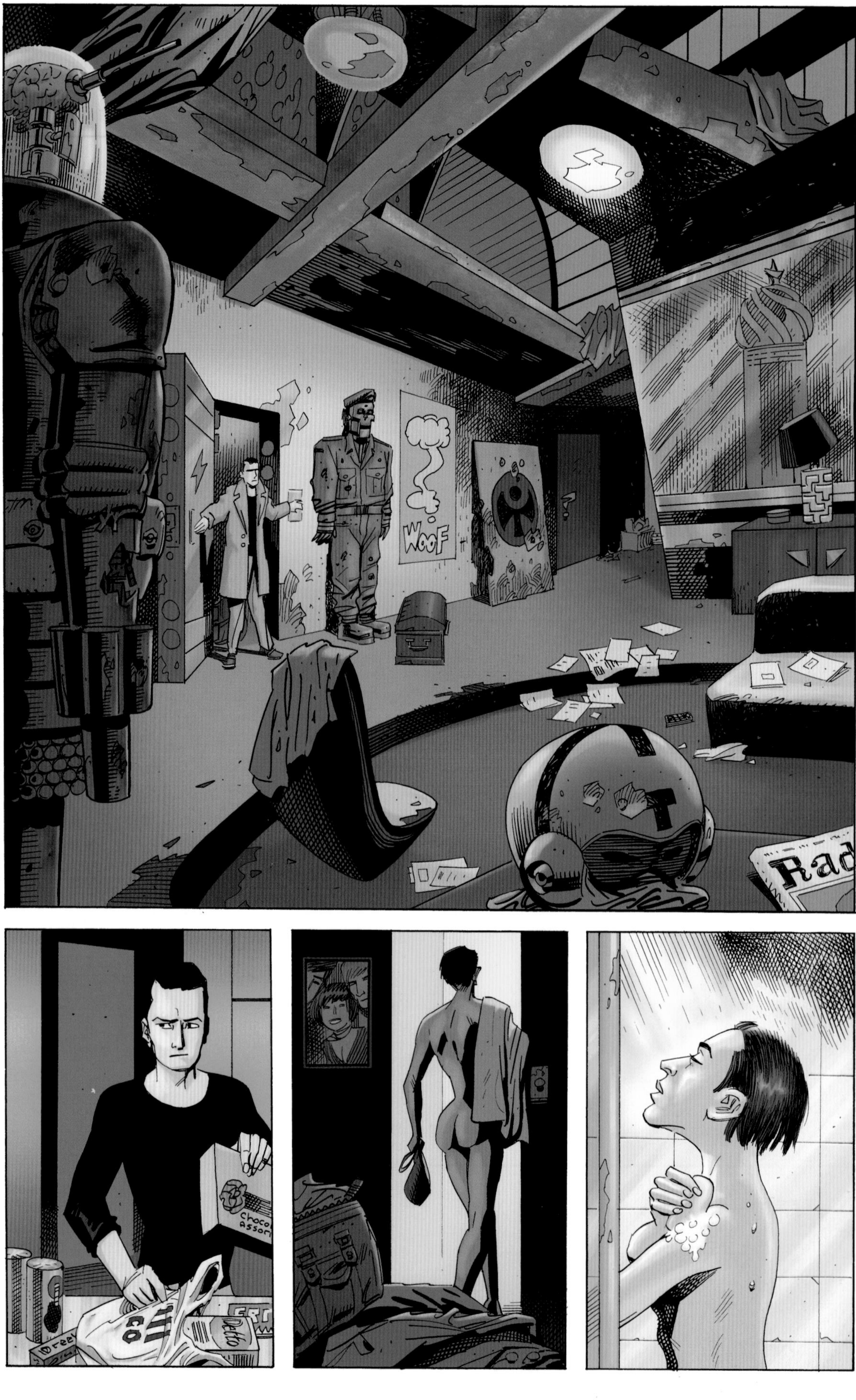
WOOF
Rad

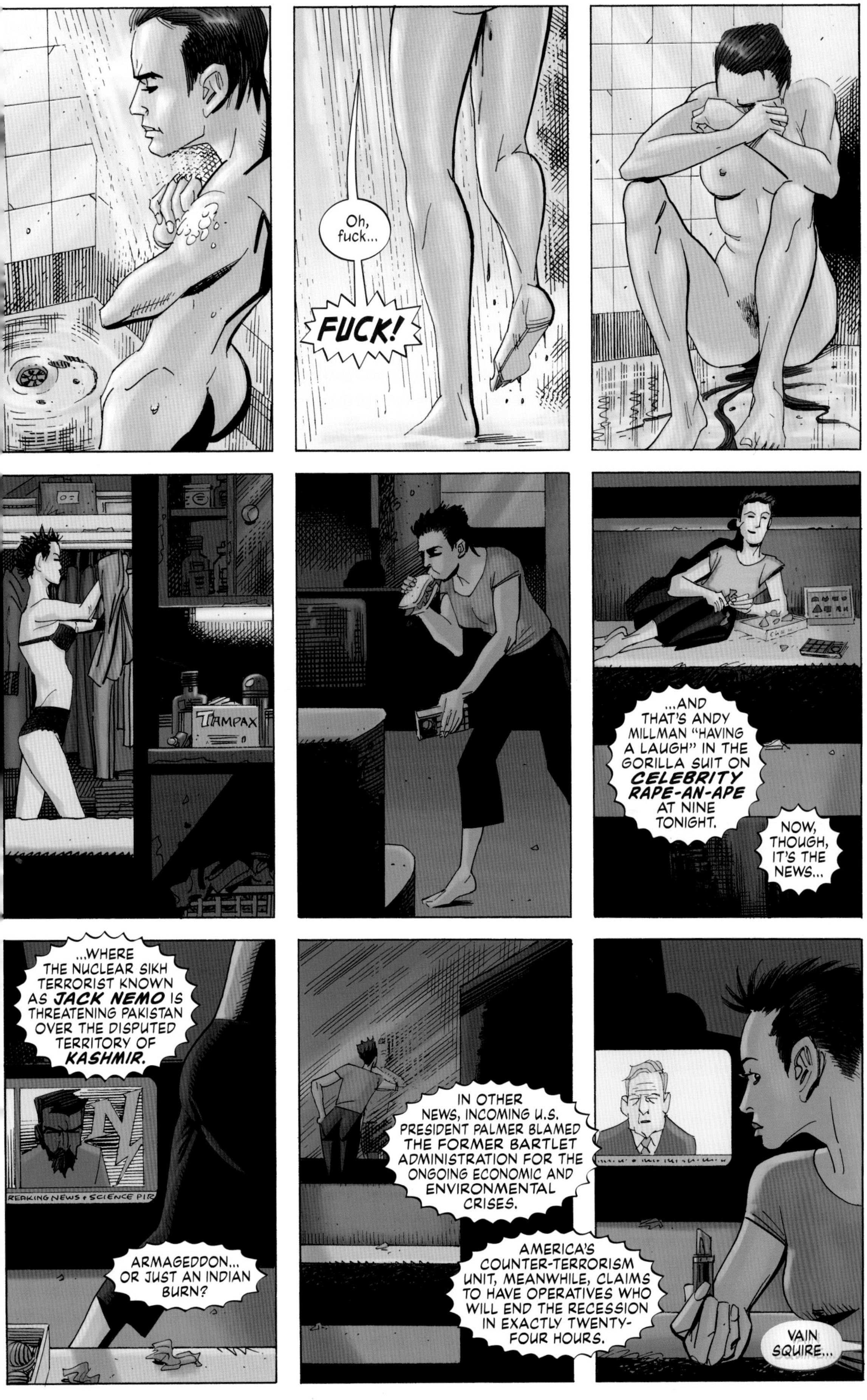
Oh, fuck...
FUCK!
TAMPAX
...AND THAT'S ANDY MILLMAN "HAVING A LAUGH" IN THE GORILLA SUIT ON CELEBRITY RAPE-AN-APE AT NINE TONIGHT.
NOW, THOUGH, IT'S THE NEWS...
...WHERE THE NUCLEAR SIKH TERRORIST KNOWN AS JACK NEMO IS THREATENING PAKISTAN OVER THE DISPUTED TERRITORY OF KASHMIR.
ARMAGEDDON... OR JUST AN INDIAN BURN?
IN OTHER NEWS, INCOMING U.S. PRESIDENT PALMER BLAMED THE FORMER BARTLET ADMINISTRATION FOR THE ONGOING ECONOMIC AND ENVIRONMENTAL CRISES.
AMERICA'S COUNTER-TERRORISM UNIT, MEANWHILE, CLAIMS TO HAVE OPERATIVES WHO WILL END THE RECESSION IN EXACTLY TWENTY-FOUR HOURS.
VAIN SQUIRE...

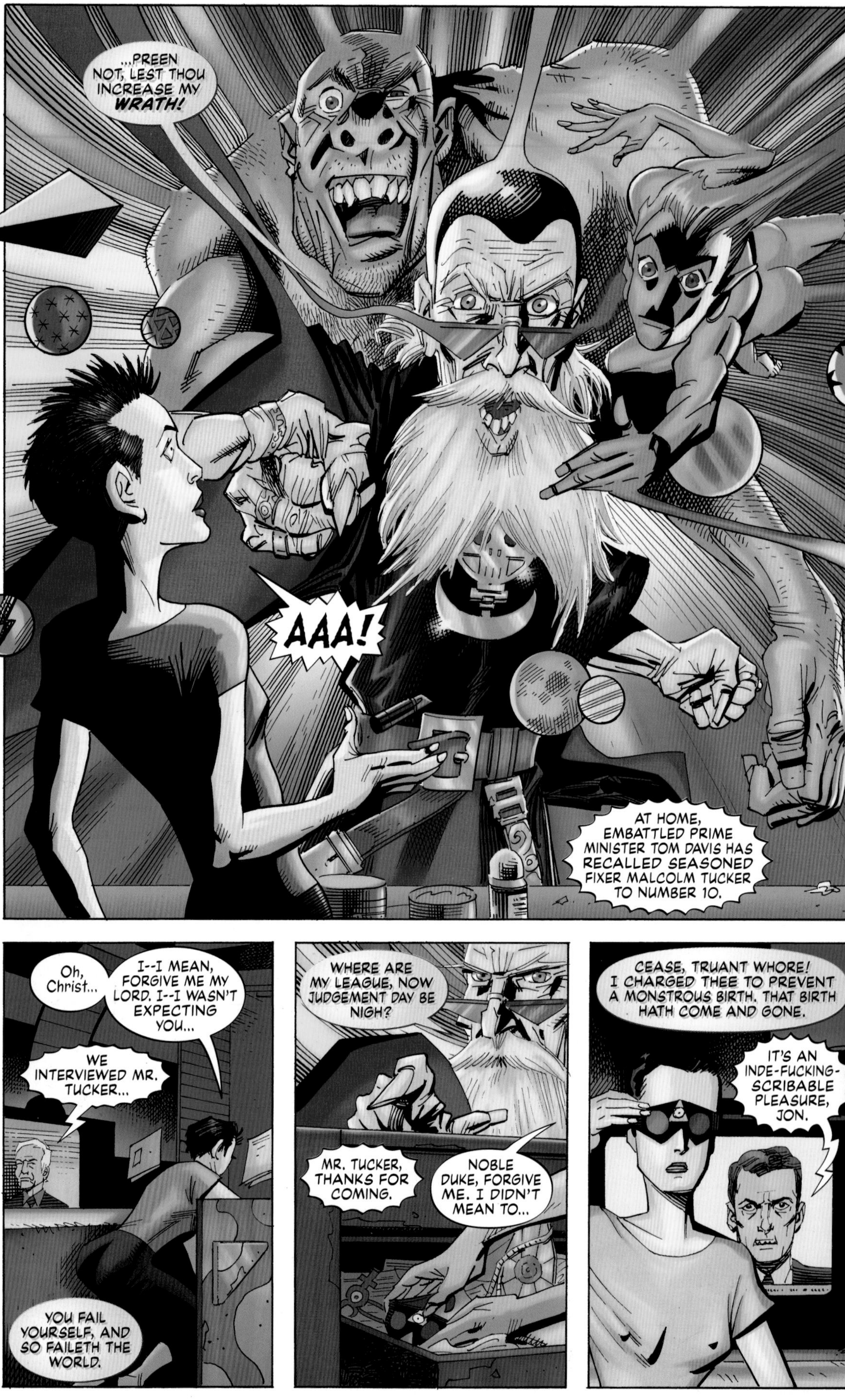

...PREEN NOT, LEST THOU INCREASE MY WRATH!
AAA!
AT HOME, EMBATTLED PRIME MINISTER TOM DAVIS HAS RECALLED SEASONED FIXER MALCOLM TUCKER TO NUMBER 10.
Oh, Christ...
I--I MEAN, FORGIVE ME MY LORD. I--I WASN'T EXPECTING YOU...
WE INTERVIEWED MR. TUCKER...
YOU FAIL YOURSELF, AND SO FAILETH THE WORLD.
WHERE ARE MY LEAGUE, NOW JUDGEMENT DAY BE NIGH?
MR. TUCKER, THANKS FOR COMING.
NOBLE DUKE, FORGIVE ME. I DIDN'T MEAN TO...
CEASE, TRUANT WHORE! I CHARGED THEE TO PREVENT A MONSTROUS BIRTH. THAT BIRTH HATH COME AND GONE.
IT'S AN INDE-FUCKING-SCRIBABLE PLEASURE, JON.

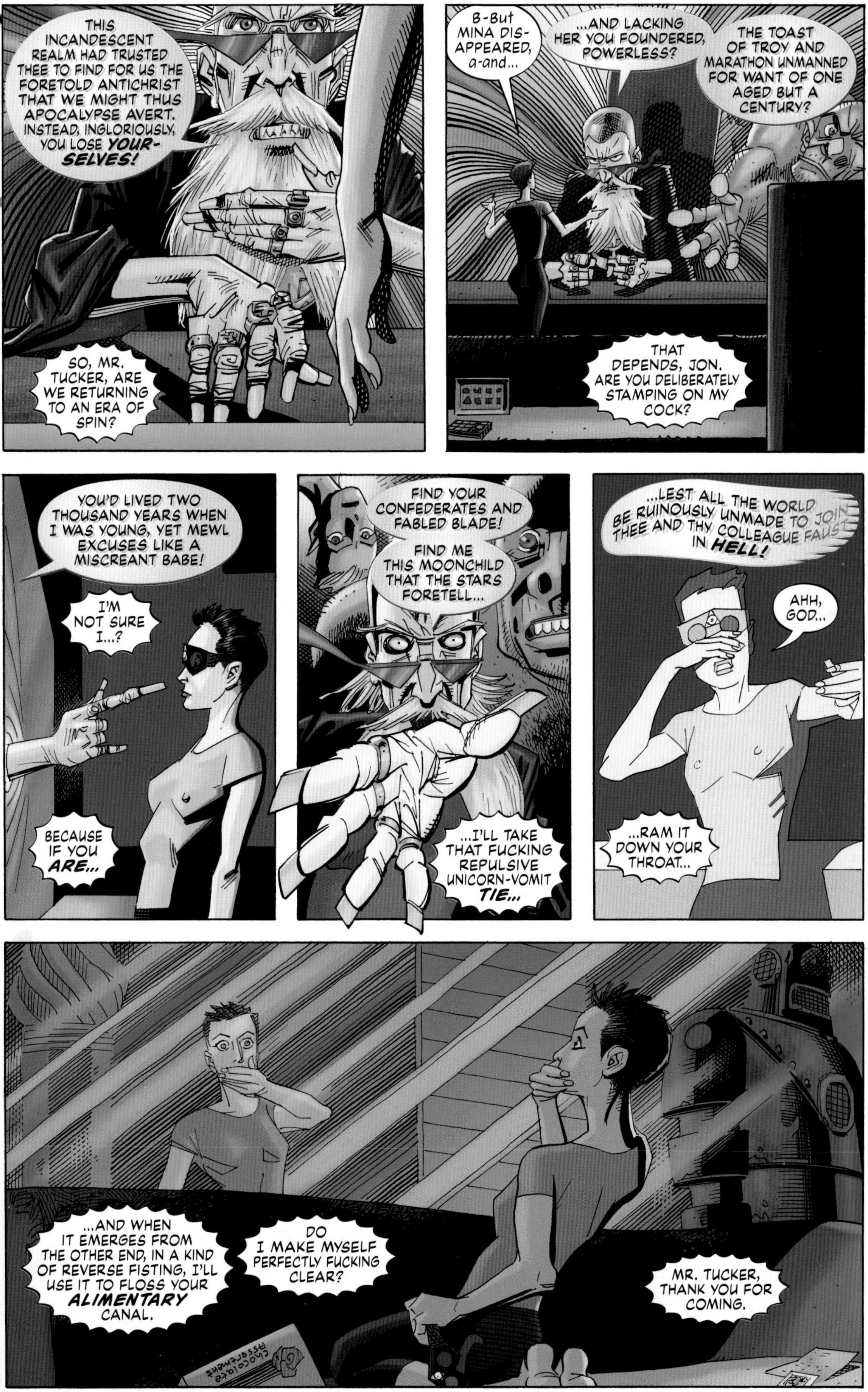
THIS INCANDESCENT REALM HAD TRUSTED THEE TO FIND FOR US THE FORETOLD ANTICHRIST THAT WE MIGHT THUS APOCALYPSE AVERT. INSTEAD, INGLORIOUSLY, YOU LOSE YOURSELVES!
SO, MR. TUCKER, ARE WE RETURNING TO AN ERA OF SPIN?
B-But MINA DISAPPEARED, a-and...
...AND LACKING HER YOU FOUNDERED, POWERLESS?
THE TOAST OF TROY AND MARATHON UNMANNED FOR WANT OF ONE AGED BUT A CENTURY?
THAT DEPENDS, JON. ARE YOU DELIBERATELY STAMPING ON MY COCK?
YOU'D LIVED TWO THOUSAND YEARS WHEN I WAS YOUNG, YET MEWL EXCUSES LIKE A MISCREANT BABE!
I'M NOT SURE I...?
BECAUSE IF YOU ARE...
FIND YOUR CONFEDERATES AND FABLED BLADE!
FIND ME THIS MOONCHILD THAT THE STARS FORETELL...
...I'LL TAKE THAT FUCKING REPULSIVE UNICORN-VOMIT TIE...
...LEST ALL THE WORLD BE RUINOUSLY UNMADE TO JOIN THEE AND THY COLLEAGUE FAUST IN HELL!
AHH, GOD...
...RAM IT DOWN YOUR THROAT...
...AND WHEN IT EMERGES FROM THE OTHER END, IN A KIND OF REVERSE FISTING, I'LL USE IT TO FLOSS YOUR ALIMENTARY CANAL.
DO I MAKE MYSELF PERFECTLY FUCKING CLEAR?
MR. TUCKER, THANK YOU FOR COMING.

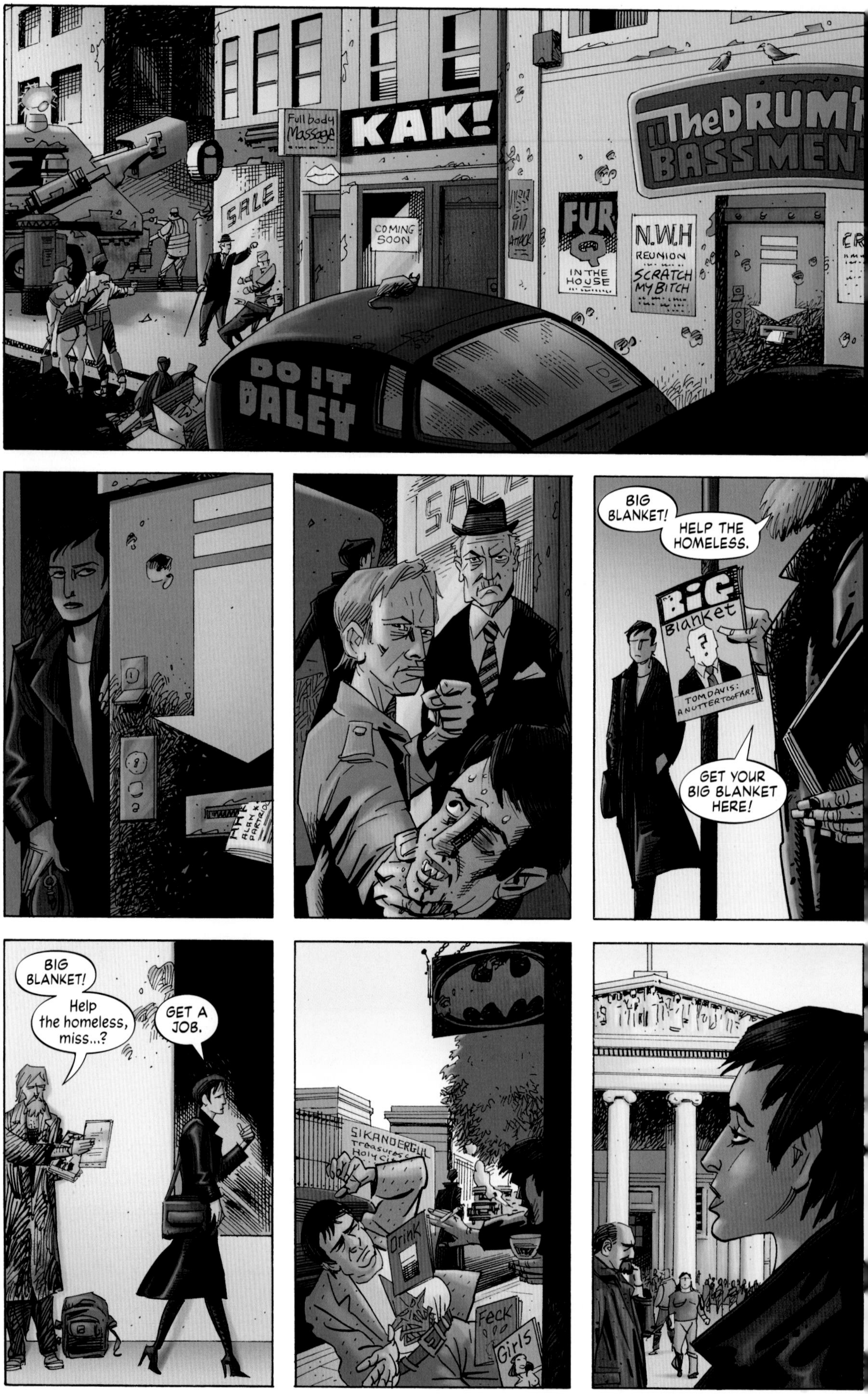
Full body Massage
KAK!
SALE
COMING SOON
FUR Q IN THE HOUSE
N.W.H REUNION SCRATCH MY BITCH
The DRUM'
BASSMEN
DO IT DALEY
BIG BLANKET!
HELP THE HOMELESS.
Big Blanket
TOM DAVIS: A NUTTER TOO FAR?
GET YOUR BIG BLANKET HERE!
BIG BLANKET!
Help the homeless, miss...?
GET A JOB.
Drink
Feck
Girls

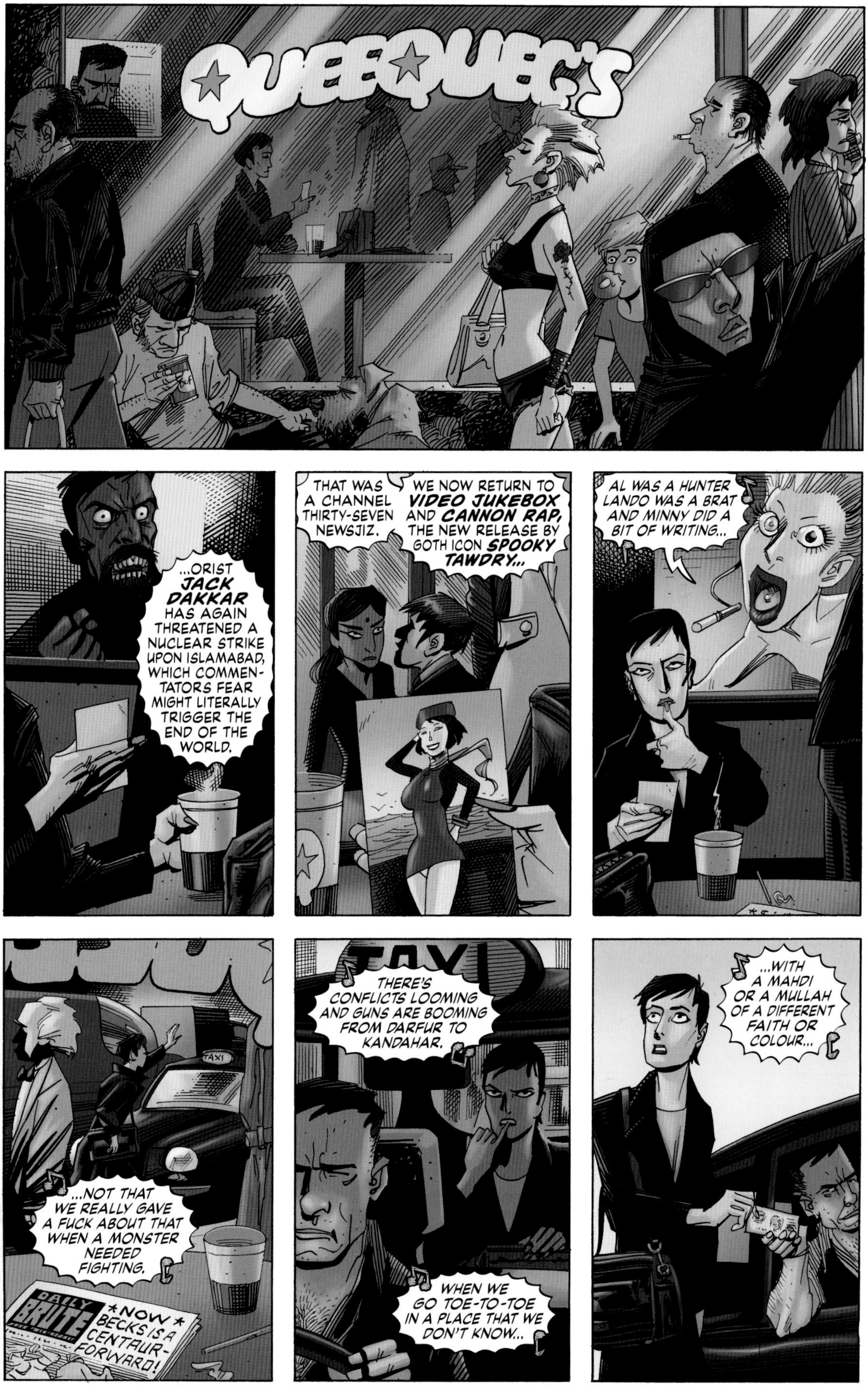
QUEEQUEG'S
...ORIST JACK DAKKAR HAS AGAIN THREATENED A NUCLEAR STRIKE UPON ISLAMABAD, WHICH COMMENTATORS FEAR MIGHT LITERALLY TRIGGER THE END OF THE WORLD.
THAT WAS A CHANNEL THIRTY-SEVEN NEWSJIZ.
WE NOW RETURN TO VIDEO JUKEBOX AND CANNON RAP, THE NEW RELEASE BY GOTH ICON SPOOKY TAWDRY...
AL WAS A HUNTER LANDO WAS A BRAT AND MINNY DID A BIT OF WRITING...
TAXI
...NOT THAT WE REALLY GAVE A FUCK ABOUT THAT WHEN A MONSTER NEEDED FIGHTING.
DAILY BRUTE
NOW BECKS IS A CENTAUR-FORWARD!
TAXI
THERE'S CONFLICTS LOOMING AND GUNS ARE BOOMING FROM DARFUR TO KANDAHAR.
WHEN WE GO TOE-TO-TOE IN A PLACE THAT WE DON'T KNOW...
...WITH A MAHDI OR A MULLAH OF A DIFFERENT FAITH OR COLOUR...

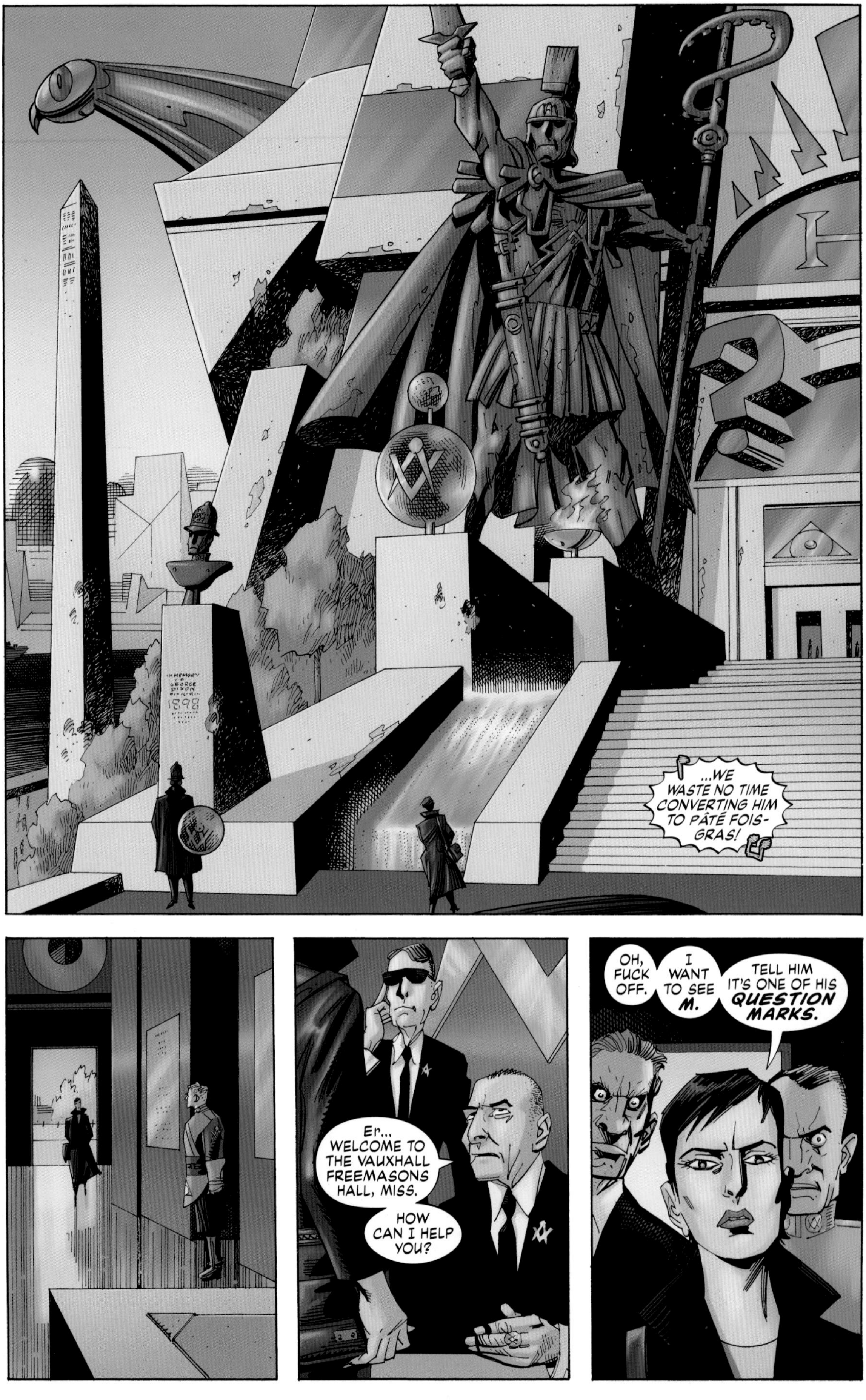
IN MEMORY
GEORGE
DIXON
1898
...WE WASTE NO TIME CONVERTING HIM TO PÂTÉ FOIS-GRAS!
Er... WELCOME TO THE VAUXHALL FREEMASONS HALL, MISS.
HOW CAN I HELP YOU?
OH, FUCK OFF.
I WANT TO SEE M.
TELL HIM IT'S ONE OF HIS QUESTION MARKS.

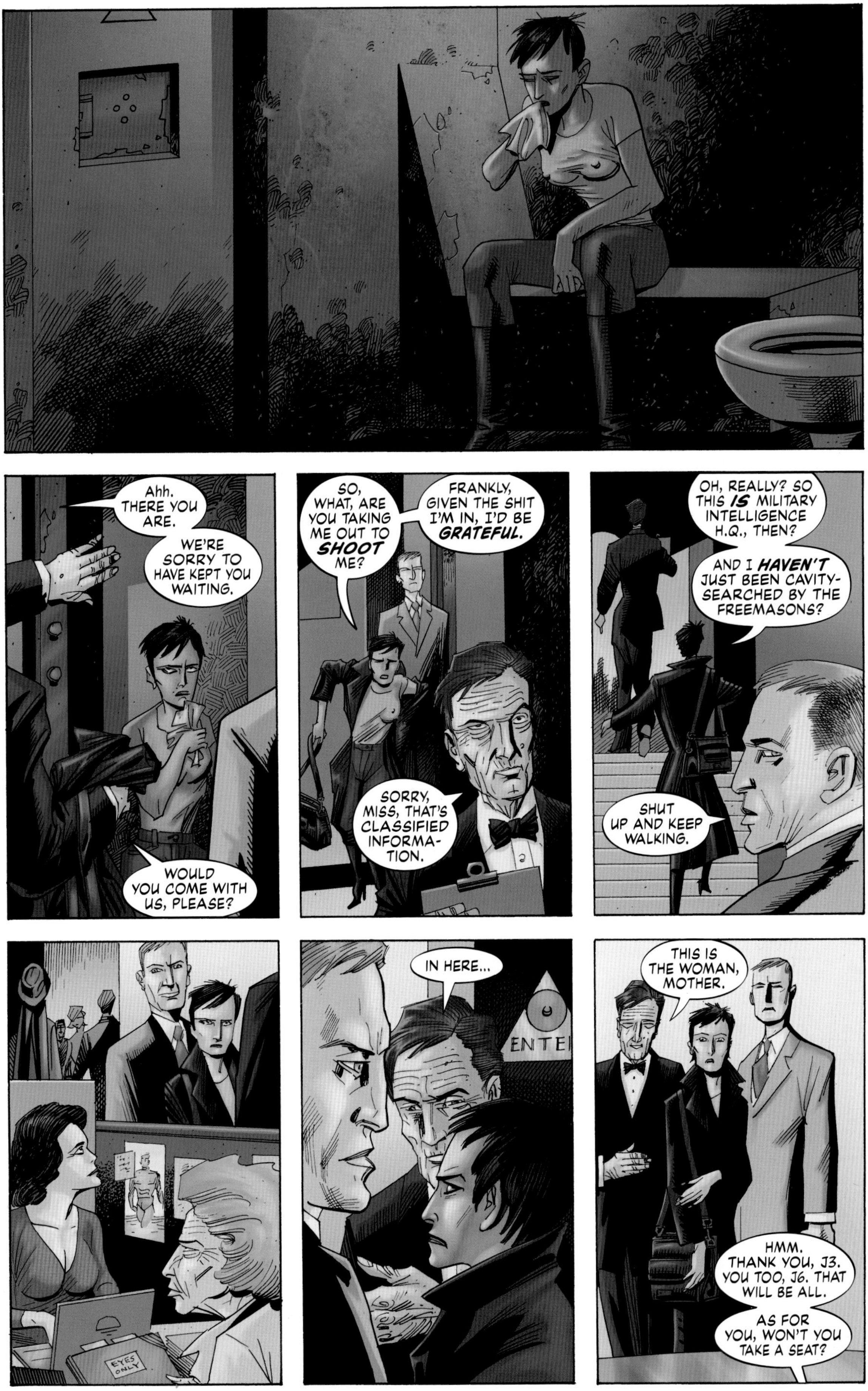

Ahh. THERE YOU ARE.
WE'RE SORRY TO HAVE KEPT YOU WAITING.
WOULD YOU COME WITH US, PLEASE?
SO, WHAT, ARE YOU TAKING ME OUT TO **SHOOT** ME?
FRANKLY, GIVEN THE SHIT I'M IN, I'D BE **GRATEFUL.**
SORRY, MISS, THAT'S CLASSIFIED INFORMATION.
OH, REALLY? SO THIS ***IS*** MILITARY INTELLIGENCE H.Q., THEN?
AND I ***HAVEN'T*** JUST BEEN CAVITY-SEARCHED BY THE FREEMASONS?
SHUT UP AND KEEP WALKING.
EYES ONLY
IN HERE...
ENTE
THIS IS THE WOMAN, MOTHER.
HMM. THANK YOU, J3. YOU TOO, J6. THAT WILL BE ALL.
AS FOR YOU, WON'T YOU TAKE A SEAT?

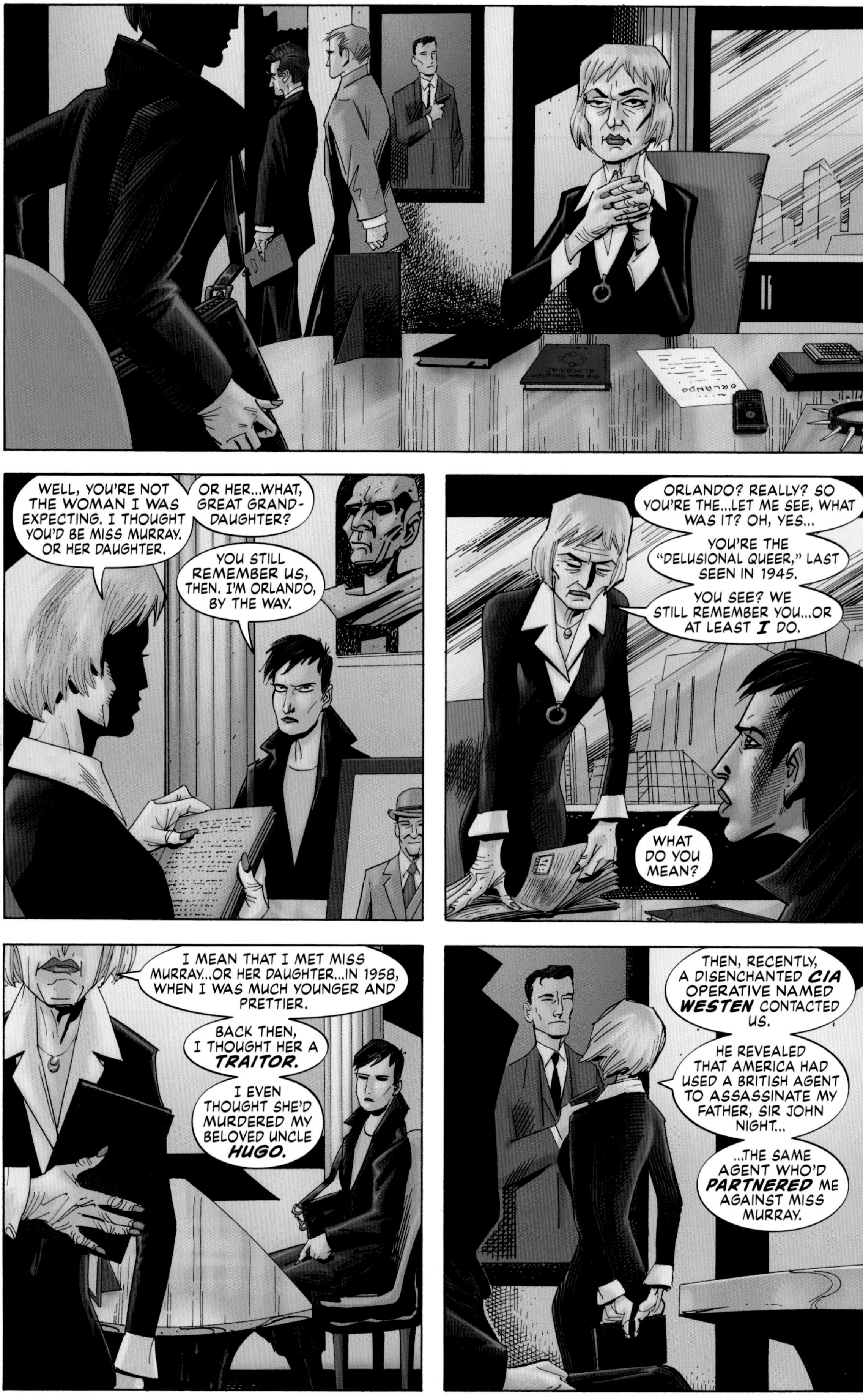

WELL, YOU'RE NOT THE WOMAN I WAS EXPECTING. I THOUGHT YOU'D BE MISS MURRAY. OR HER DAUGHTER.
OR HER...WHAT, GREAT GRAND-DAUGHTER?
YOU STILL REMEMBER US, THEN. I'M ORLANDO, BY THE WAY.
ORLANDO? REALLY? SO YOU'RE THE...LET ME SEE, WHAT WAS IT? OH, YES...
YOU'RE THE "DELUSIONAL QUEER," LAST SEEN IN 1945.
YOU SEE? WE STILL REMEMBER YOU...OR AT LEAST *I* DO.
WHAT DO YOU MEAN?
I MEAN THAT I MET MISS MURRAY...OR HER DAUGHTER...IN 1958, WHEN I WAS MUCH YOUNGER AND PRETTIER.
BACK THEN, I THOUGHT HER A **TRAITOR.**
I EVEN THOUGHT SHE'D MURDERED MY BELOVED UNCLE **HUGO.**
THEN, RECENTLY, A DISENCHANTED **CIA** OPERATIVE NAMED **WESTEN** CONTACTED US.
HE REVEALED THAT AMERICA HAD USED A BRITISH AGENT TO ASSASSINATE MY FATHER, SIR JOHN NIGHT...
...THE SAME AGENT WHO'D **PARTNERED** ME AGAINST MISS MURRAY.

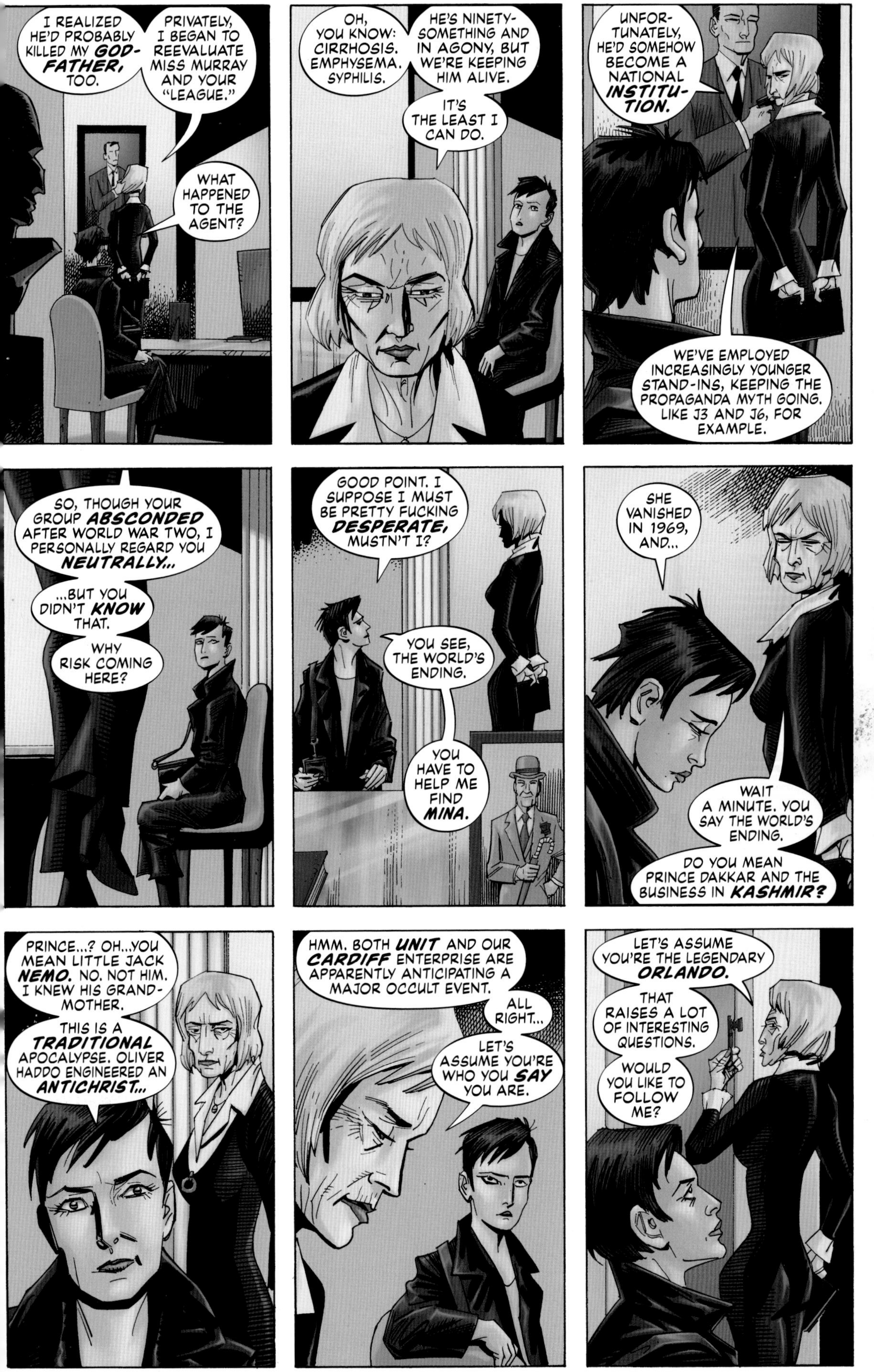
I REALIZED HE'D PROBABLY KILLED MY GODFATHER, TOO.
PRIVATELY, I BEGAN TO REEVALUATE MISS MURRAY AND YOUR "LEAGUE."
WHAT HAPPENED TO THE AGENT?
OH, YOU KNOW: CIRRHOSIS. EMPHYSEMA. SYPHILIS.
HE'S NINETY-SOMETHING AND IN AGONY, BUT WE'RE KEEPING HIM ALIVE.
IT'S THE LEAST I CAN DO.
UNFORTUNATELY, HE'D SOMEHOW BECOME A NATIONAL INSTITUTION.
WE'VE EMPLOYED INCREASINGLY YOUNGER STAND-INS, KEEPING THE PROPAGANDA MYTH GOING. LIKE J3 AND J6, FOR EXAMPLE.
SO, THOUGH YOUR GROUP ABSCONDED AFTER WORLD WAR TWO, I PERSONALLY REGARD YOU NEUTRALLY...
...BUT YOU DIDN'T KNOW THAT.
WHY RISK COMING HERE?
GOOD POINT. I SUPPOSE I MUST BE PRETTY FUCKING DESPERATE, MUSTN'T I?
YOU SEE, THE WORLD'S ENDING.
YOU HAVE TO HELP ME FIND MINA.
SHE VANISHED IN 1969, AND...
WAIT A MINUTE. YOU SAY THE WORLD'S ENDING.
DO YOU MEAN PRINCE DAKKAR AND THE BUSINESS IN KASHMIR?
PRINCE...? OH...YOU MEAN LITTLE JACK NEMO. NO. NOT HIM. I KNEW HIS GRANDMOTHER.
THIS IS A TRADITIONAL APOCALYPSE. OLIVER HADDO ENGINEERED AN ANTICHRIST...
HMM. BOTH UNIT AND OUR CARDIFF ENTERPRISE ARE APPARENTLY ANTICIPATING A MAJOR OCCULT EVENT.
ALL RIGHT...
LET'S ASSUME YOU'RE WHO YOU SAY YOU ARE.
LET'S ASSUME YOU'RE THE LEGENDARY ORLANDO.
THAT RAISES A LOT OF INTERESTING QUESTIONS.
WOULD YOU LIKE TO FOLLOW ME?

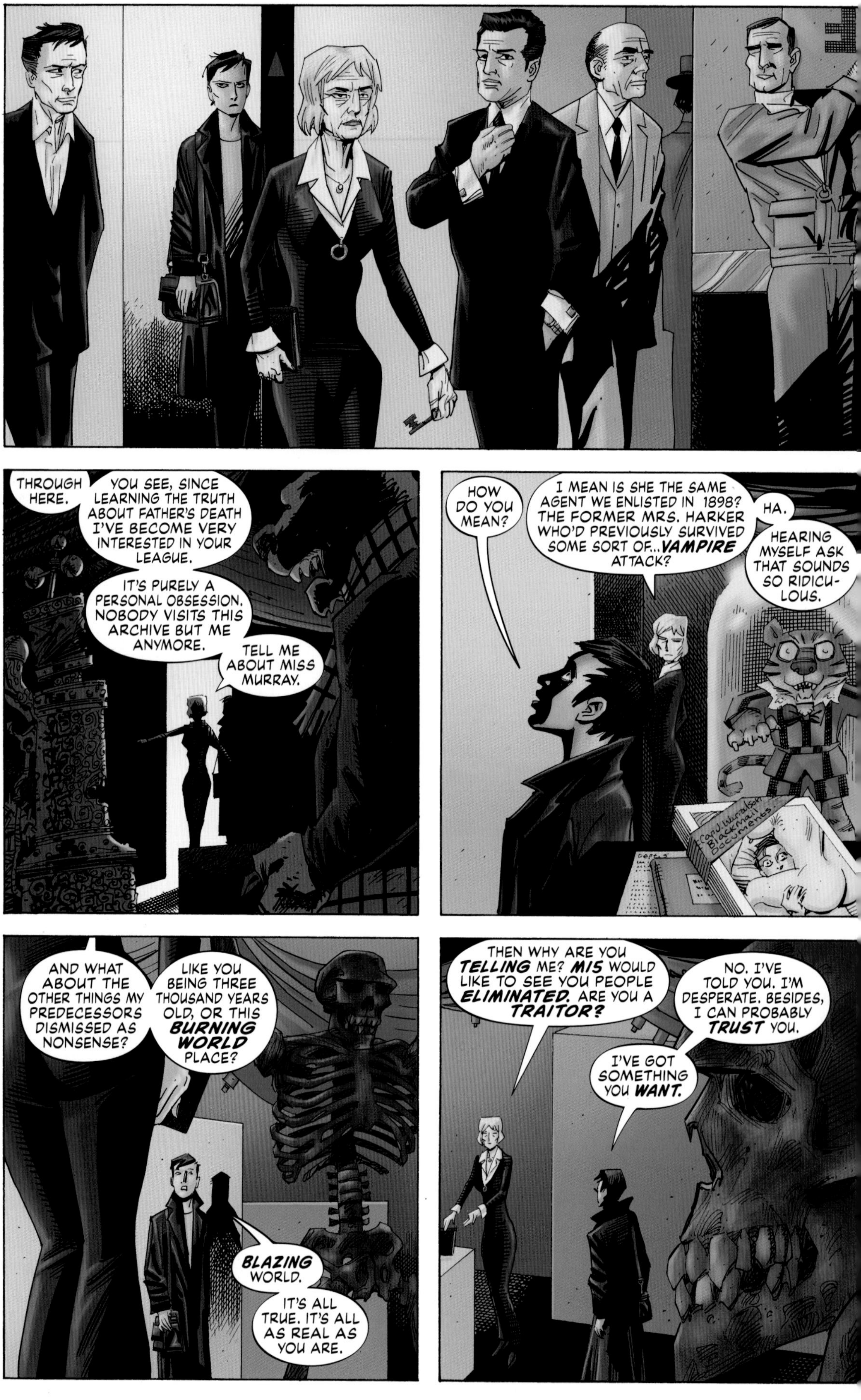
THROUGH HERE.
YOU SEE, SINCE LEARNING THE TRUTH ABOUT FATHER'S DEATH I'VE BECOME VERY INTERESTED IN YOUR LEAGUE.
IT'S PURELY A PERSONAL OBSESSION. NOBODY VISITS THIS ARCHIVE BUT ME ANYMORE.
TELL ME ABOUT MISS MURRAY.
HOW DO YOU MEAN?
I MEAN IS SHE THE SAME AGENT WE ENLISTED IN 1898? THE FORMER MRS. HARKER WHO'D PREVIOUSLY SURVIVED SOME SORT OF...*VAMPIRE* ATTACK?
HA.
HEARING MYSELF ASK THAT SOUNDS SO RIDICU-LOUS.
AND WHAT ABOUT THE OTHER THINGS MY PREDECESSORS DISMISSED AS NONSENSE?
LIKE YOU BEING THREE THOUSAND YEARS OLD, OR THIS *BURNING WORLD* PLACE?
BLAZING WORLD.
IT'S ALL TRUE. IT'S ALL AS REAL AS YOU ARE.
THEN WHY ARE YOU *TELLING* ME? *MI5* WOULD LIKE TO SEE YOU PEOPLE *ELIMINATED.* ARE YOU A *TRAITOR?*
NO. I'VE TOLD YOU. I'M DESPERATE. BESIDES, I CAN PROBABLY *TRUST* YOU.
I'VE GOT SOMETHING YOU *WANT.*

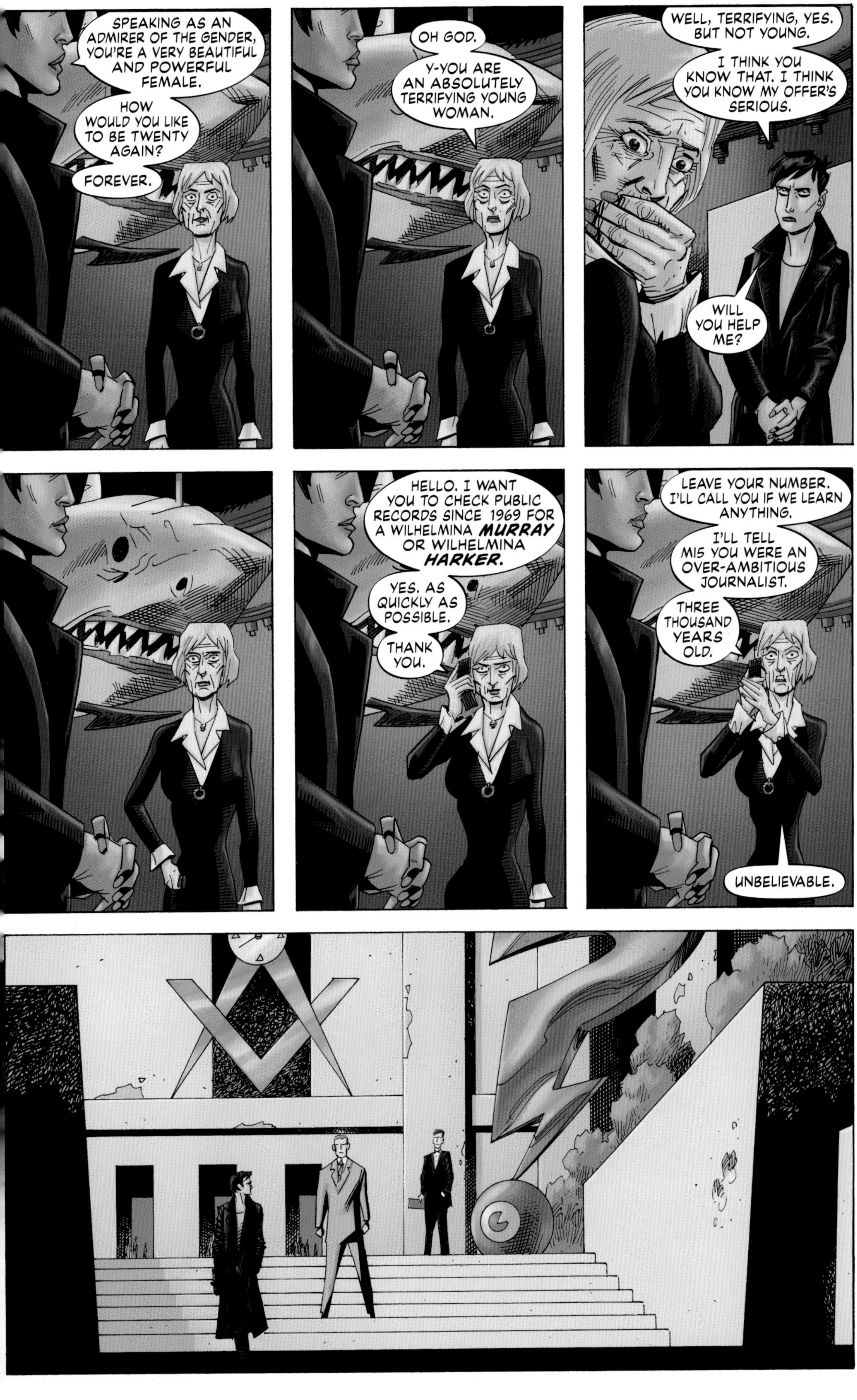
SPEAKING AS AN ADMIRER OF THE GENDER, YOU'RE A VERY BEAUTIFUL AND POWERFUL FEMALE.
HOW WOULD YOU LIKE TO BE TWENTY AGAIN?
FOREVER.
OH GOD.
Y-YOU ARE AN ABSOLUTELY TERRIFYING YOUNG WOMAN.
WELL, TERRIFYING, YES. BUT NOT YOUNG.
I THINK YOU KNOW THAT. I THINK YOU KNOW MY OFFER'S SERIOUS.
WILL YOU HELP ME?
HELLO. I WANT YOU TO CHECK PUBLIC RECORDS SINCE 1969 FOR A WILHELMINA **MURRAY** OR WILHELMINA **HARKER.**
YES. AS QUICKLY AS POSSIBLE.
THANK YOU.
LEAVE YOUR NUMBER. I'LL CALL YOU IF WE LEARN ANYTHING.
I'LL TELL MI5 YOU WERE AN OVER-AMBITIOUS JOURNALIST.
THREE THOUSAND YEARS OLD.
UNBELIEVABLE.

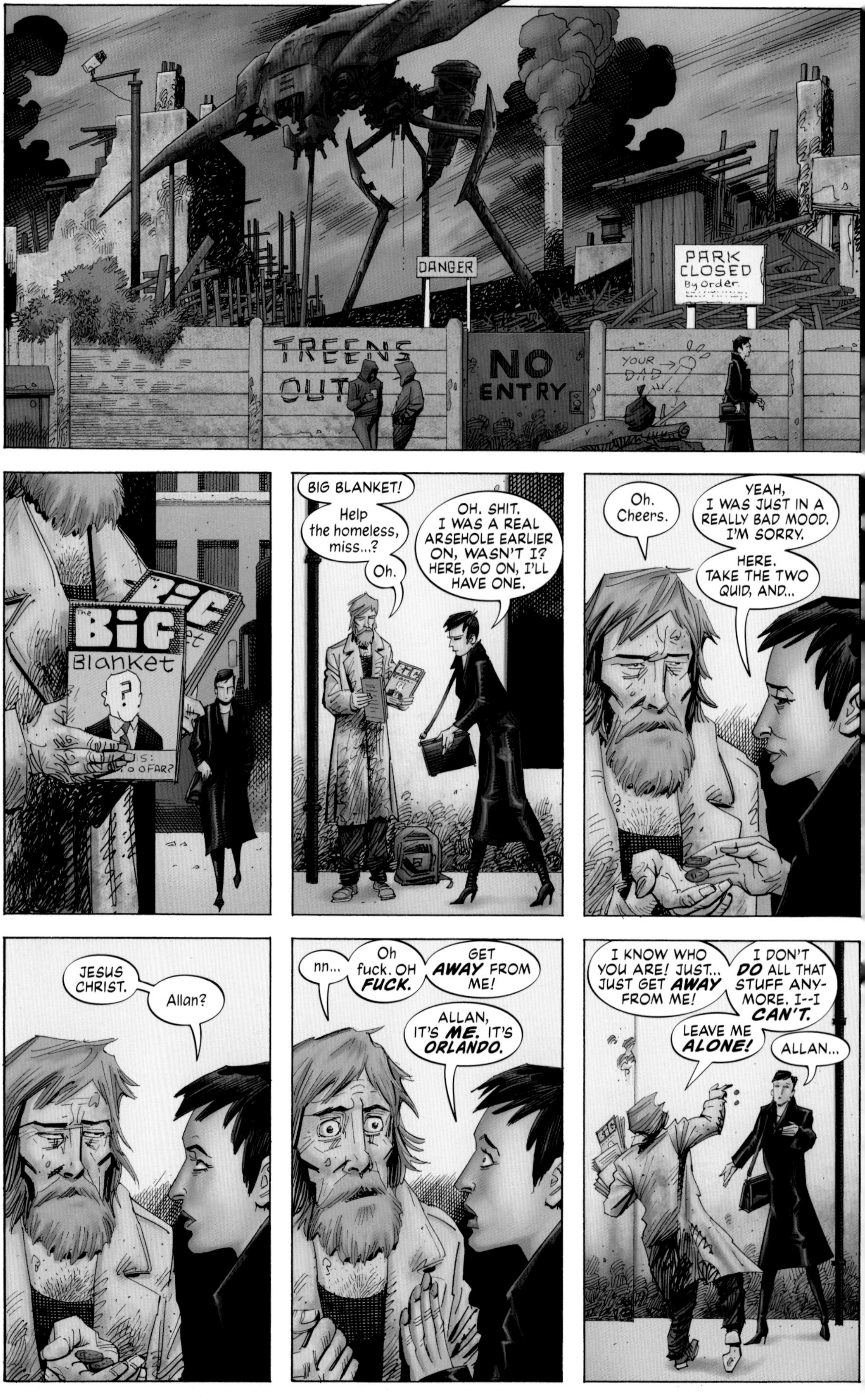
DANGER
PARK CLOSED By Order.
TREENS OUT
NO ENTRY
YOUR DAD
The BIG Blanket
BIG BLANKET!
Help the homeless, miss...?
Oh.
OH. SHIT. I WAS A REAL ARSEHOLE EARLIER ON, WASN'T I? HERE, GO ON, I'LL HAVE ONE.
Oh. Cheers.
YEAH, I WAS JUST IN A REALLY BAD MOOD. I'M SORRY.
HERE. TAKE THE TWO QUID, AND...
JESUS CHRIST.
Allan?
nn...
Oh fuck. OH FUCK.
GET AWAY FROM ME!
ALLAN, IT'S ME. IT'S ORLANDO.
I KNOW WHO YOU ARE! JUST... JUST GET AWAY FROM ME!
I DON'T DO ALL THAT STUFF ANY-MORE. I--I CAN'T.
LEAVE ME ALONE!
ALLAN...

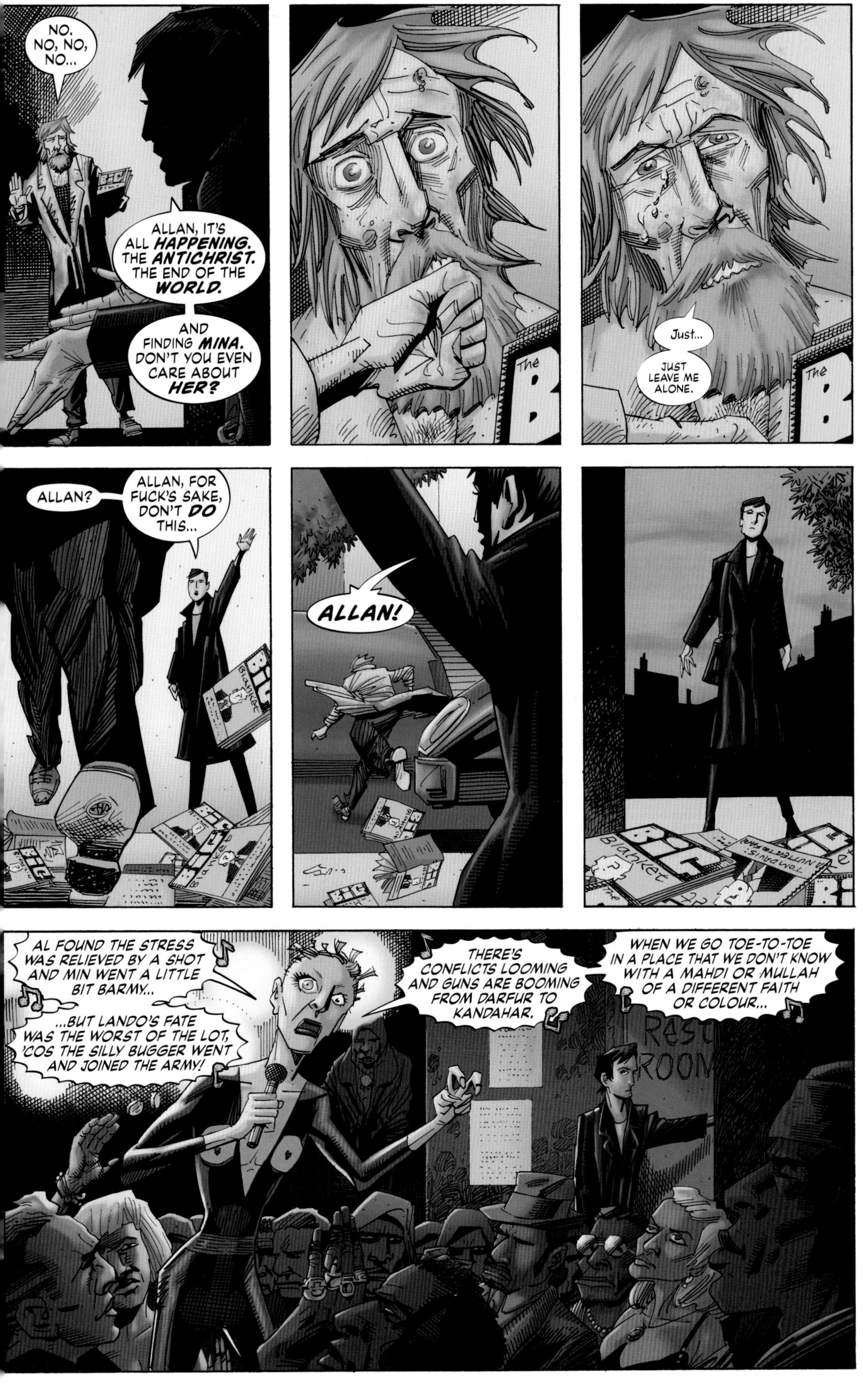
NO. NO, NO, NO...
ALLAN, IT'S ALL HAPPENING. THE ANTICHRIST. THE END OF THE WORLD.
AND FINDING MINA. DON'T YOU EVEN CARE ABOUT HER?
Just...
JUST LEAVE ME ALONE.
ALLAN?
ALLAN, FOR FUCK'S SAKE, DON'T DO THIS...
ALLAN!
AL FOUND THE STRESS WAS RELIEVED BY A SHOT AND MIN WENT A LITTLE BIT BARMY...
...BUT LANDO'S FATE WAS THE WORST OF THE LOT, 'COS THE SILLY BUGGER WENT AND JOINED THE ARMY!
THERE'S CONFLICTS LOOMING AND GUNS ARE BOOMING FROM DARFUR TO KANDAHAR.
WHEN WE GO TOE-TO-TOE IN A PLACE THAT WE DON'T KNOW WITH A MAHDI OR MULLAH OF A DIFFERENT FAITH OR COLOUR...

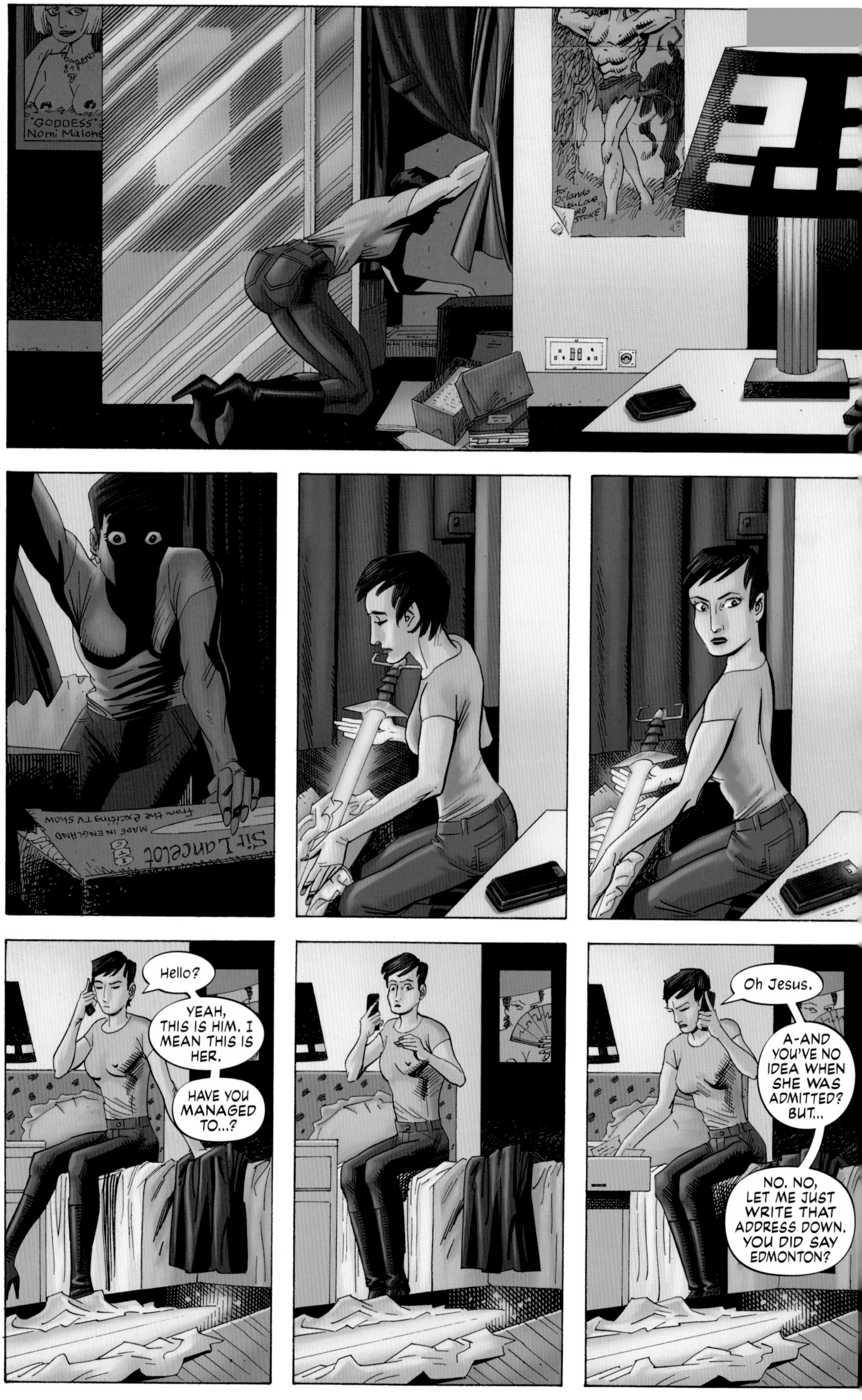
GODDESS
Nomi Malone
Sir Lancelot
MADE IN ENGLAND
from the exciting TV show
Hello?
YEAH, THIS IS HIM. I MEAN THIS IS HER.
HAVE YOU MANAGED TO...?
Oh Jesus.
A-AND YOU'VE NO IDEA WHEN SHE WAS ADMITTED? BUT...
NO. NO, LET ME JUST WRITE THAT ADDRESS DOWN. YOU DID SAY EDMONTON?

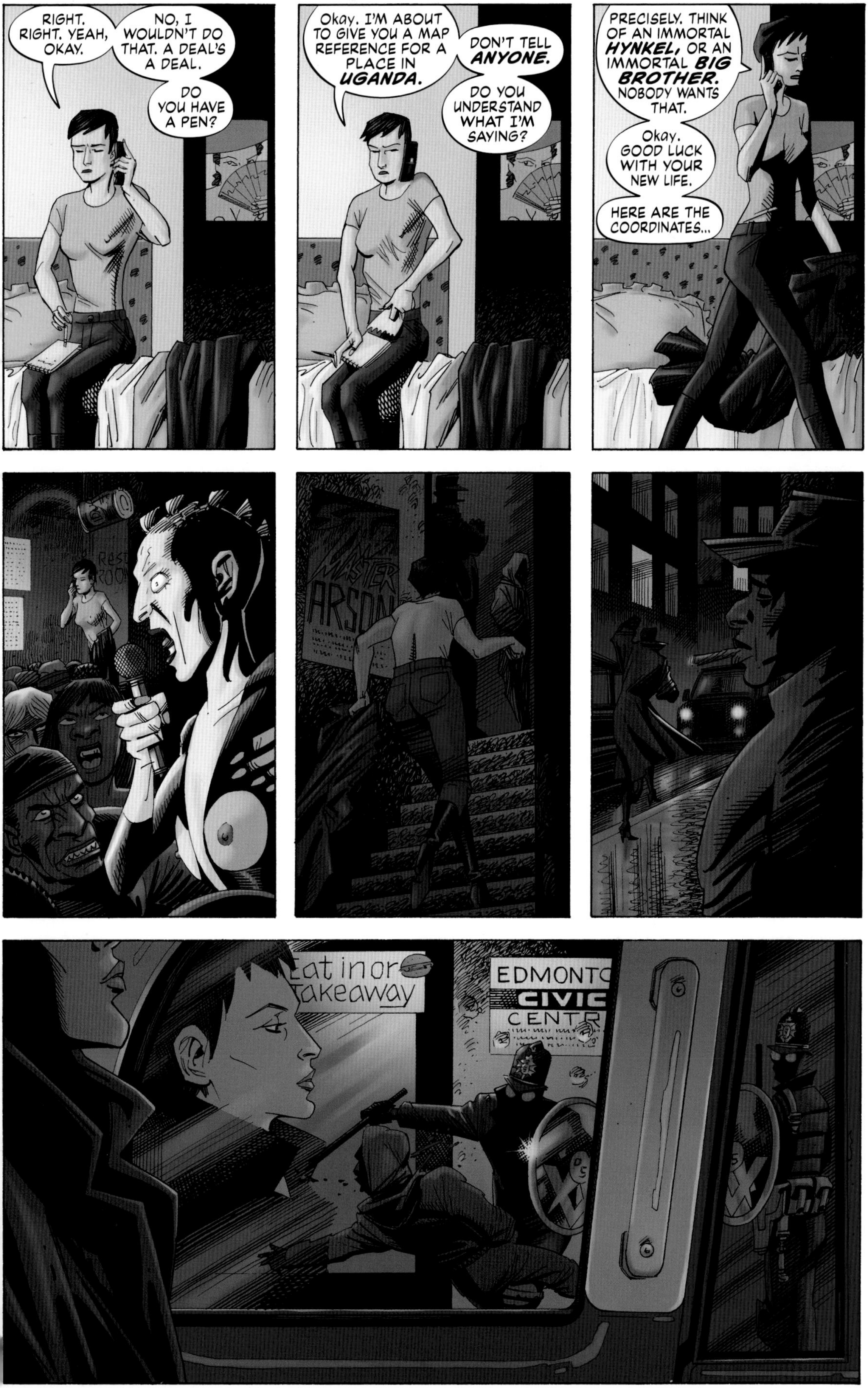
RIGHT. RIGHT. YEAH, OKAY.
NO, I WOULDN'T DO THAT. A DEAL'S A DEAL.
DO YOU HAVE A PEN?
Okay. I'M ABOUT TO GIVE YOU A MAP REFERENCE FOR A PLACE IN UGANDA.
DON'T TELL ANYONE.
DO YOU UNDERSTAND WHAT I'M SAYING?
PRECISELY. THINK OF AN IMMORTAL HYNKEL, OR AN IMMORTAL BIG BROTHER. NOBODY WANTS THAT.
Okay. GOOD LUCK WITH YOUR NEW LIFE.
HERE ARE THE COORDINATES...
REST ROOM
ARSON
Eat in or Takeaway
EDMONTO
CIVIC
CENTR

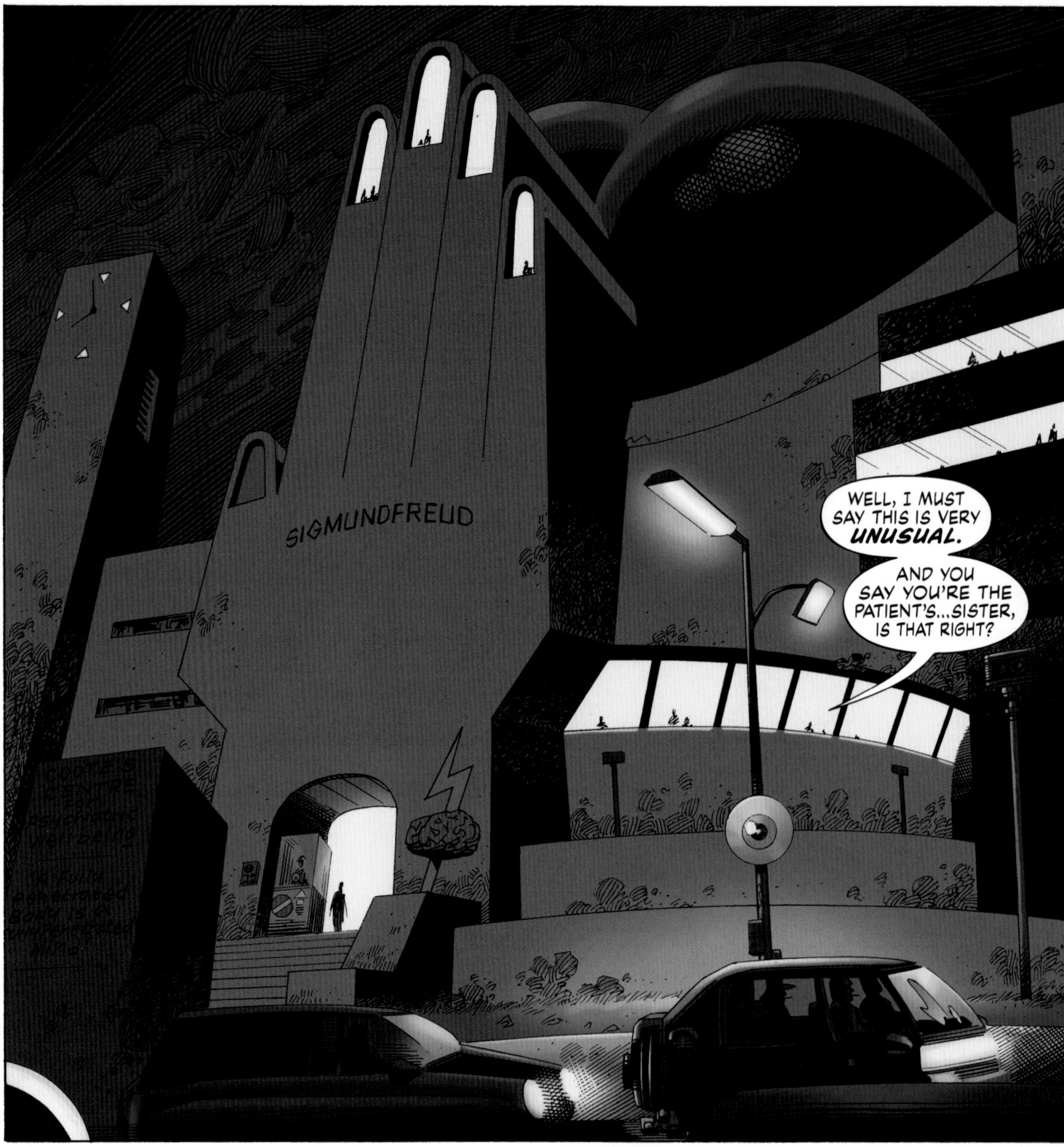
SIGMUNDFREUD
WELL, I MUST SAY THIS IS VERY ***UNUSUAL.***
AND YOU SAY YOU'RE THE PATIENT'S...SISTER, IS THAT RIGHT?

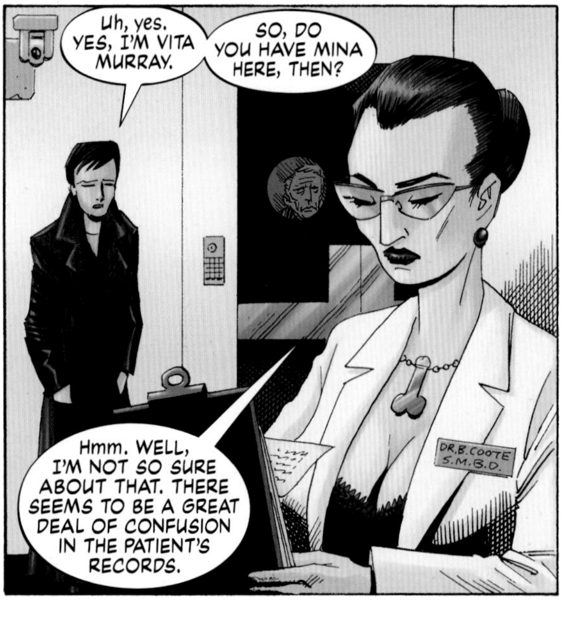
Uh, yes. YES, I'M VITA MURRAY.
SO, DO YOU HAVE MINA HERE, THEN?
DR.B.COOTE S.M.B.D.
Hmm. WELL, I'M NOT SO SURE ABOUT THAT. THERE SEEMS TO BE A GREAT DEAL OF CONFUSION IN THE PATIENT'S RECORDS.

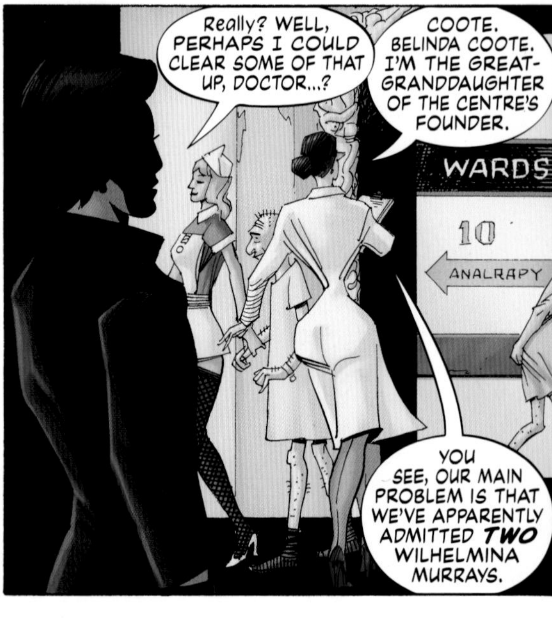
Really? WELL, PERHAPS I COULD CLEAR SOME OF THAT UP, DOCTOR...?
COOTE. BELINDA COOTE. I'M THE GREAT-GRANDDAUGHTER OF THE CENTRE'S FOUNDER.
WARDS
10
ANALRAPY
YOU SEE, OUR MAIN PROBLEM IS THAT WE'VE APPARENTLY ADMITTED ***TWO*** WILHELMINA MURRAYS.

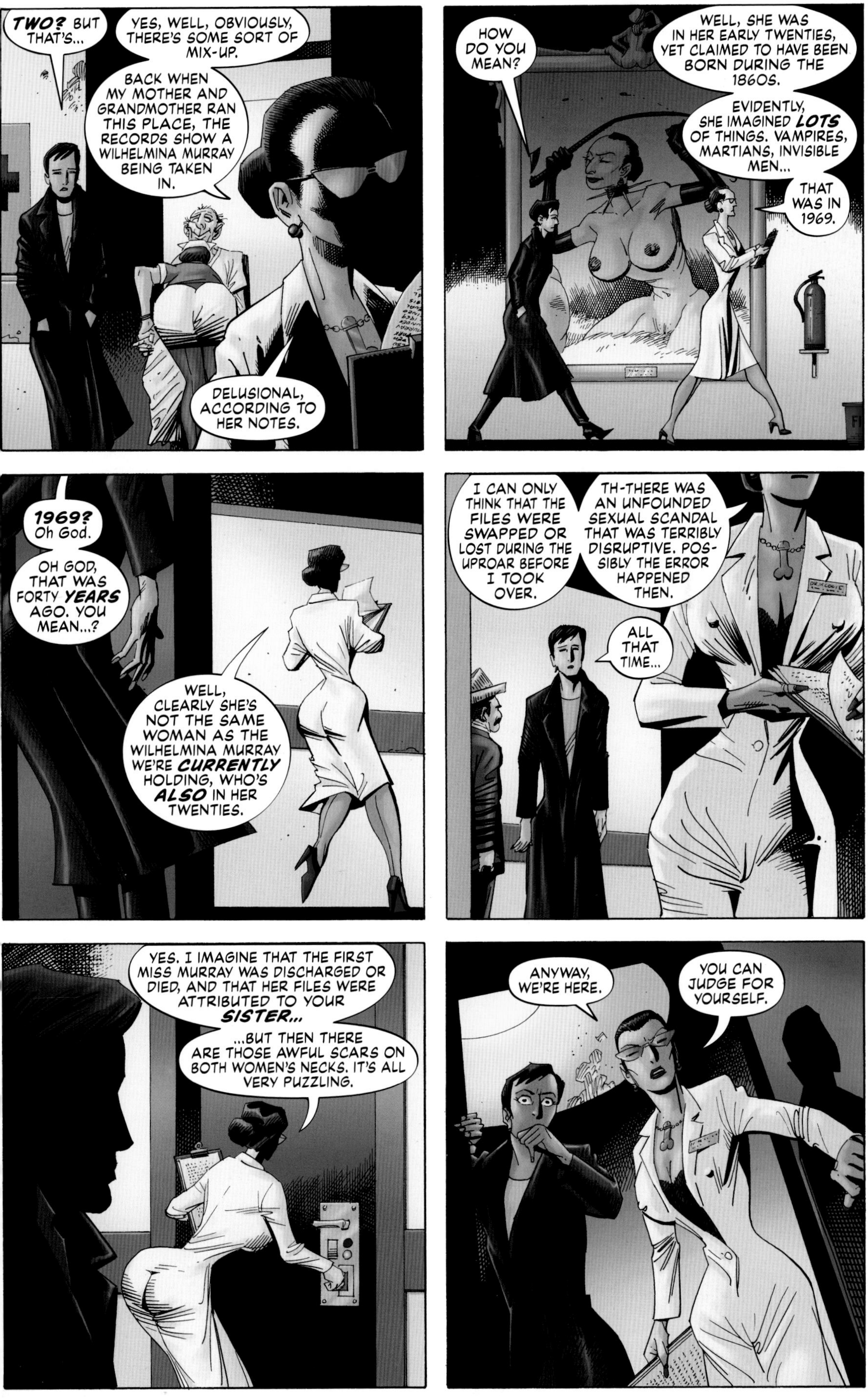
TWO? BUT THAT'S...
YES, WELL, OBVIOUSLY, THERE'S SOME SORT OF MIX-UP.
BACK WHEN MY MOTHER AND GRANDMOTHER RAN THIS PLACE, THE RECORDS SHOW A WILHELMINA MURRAY BEING TAKEN IN.
DELUSIONAL, ACCORDING TO HER NOTES.
HOW DO YOU MEAN?
WELL, SHE WAS IN HER EARLY TWENTIES, YET CLAIMED TO HAVE BEEN BORN DURING THE 1860S.
EVIDENTLY, SHE IMAGINED LOTS OF THINGS. VAMPIRES, MARTIANS, INVISIBLE MEN...
THAT WAS IN 1969.
1969? Oh God.
OH GOD, THAT WAS FORTY YEARS AGO. YOU MEAN...?
WELL, CLEARLY SHE'S NOT THE SAME WOMAN AS THE WILHELMINA MURRAY WE'RE CURRENTLY HOLDING, WHO'S ALSO IN HER TWENTIES.
I CAN ONLY THINK THAT THE FILES WERE SWAPPED OR LOST DURING THE UPROAR BEFORE I TOOK OVER.
TH-THERE WAS AN UNFOUNDED SEXUAL SCANDAL THAT WAS TERRIBLY DISRUPTIVE. POSSIBLY THE ERROR HAPPENED THEN.
ALL THAT TIME...
YES. I IMAGINE THAT THE FIRST MISS MURRAY WAS DISCHARGED OR DIED, AND THAT HER FILES WERE ATTRIBUTED TO YOUR SISTER...
...BUT THEN THERE ARE THOSE AWFUL SCARS ON BOTH WOMEN'S NECKS. IT'S ALL VERY PUZZLING.
ANYWAY, WE'RE HERE.
YOU CAN JUDGE FOR YOURSELF.

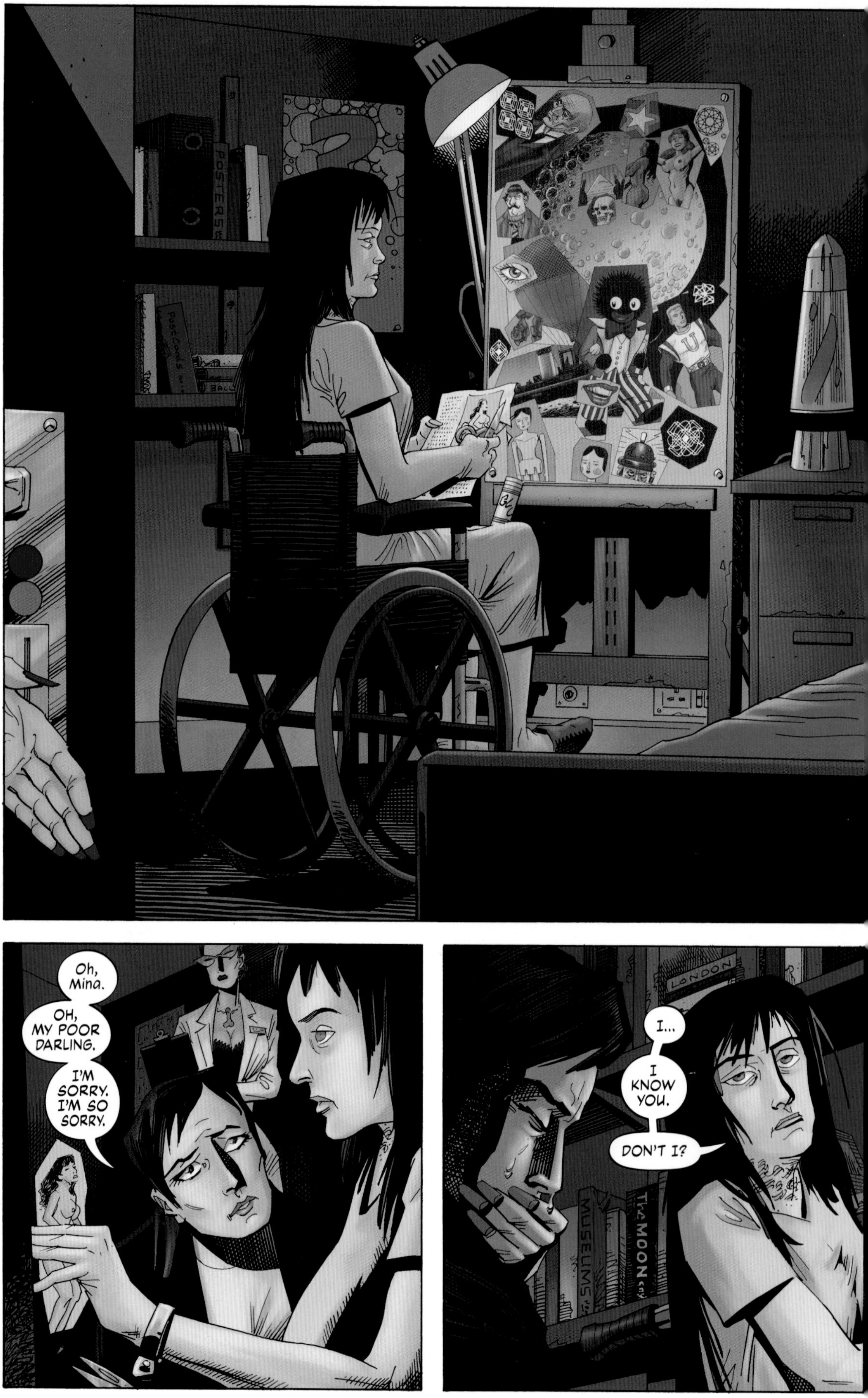
Oh, Mina.
OH, MY POOR DARLING.
I'M SORRY. I'M SO SORRY.
I...
I KNOW YOU.
DON'T I?

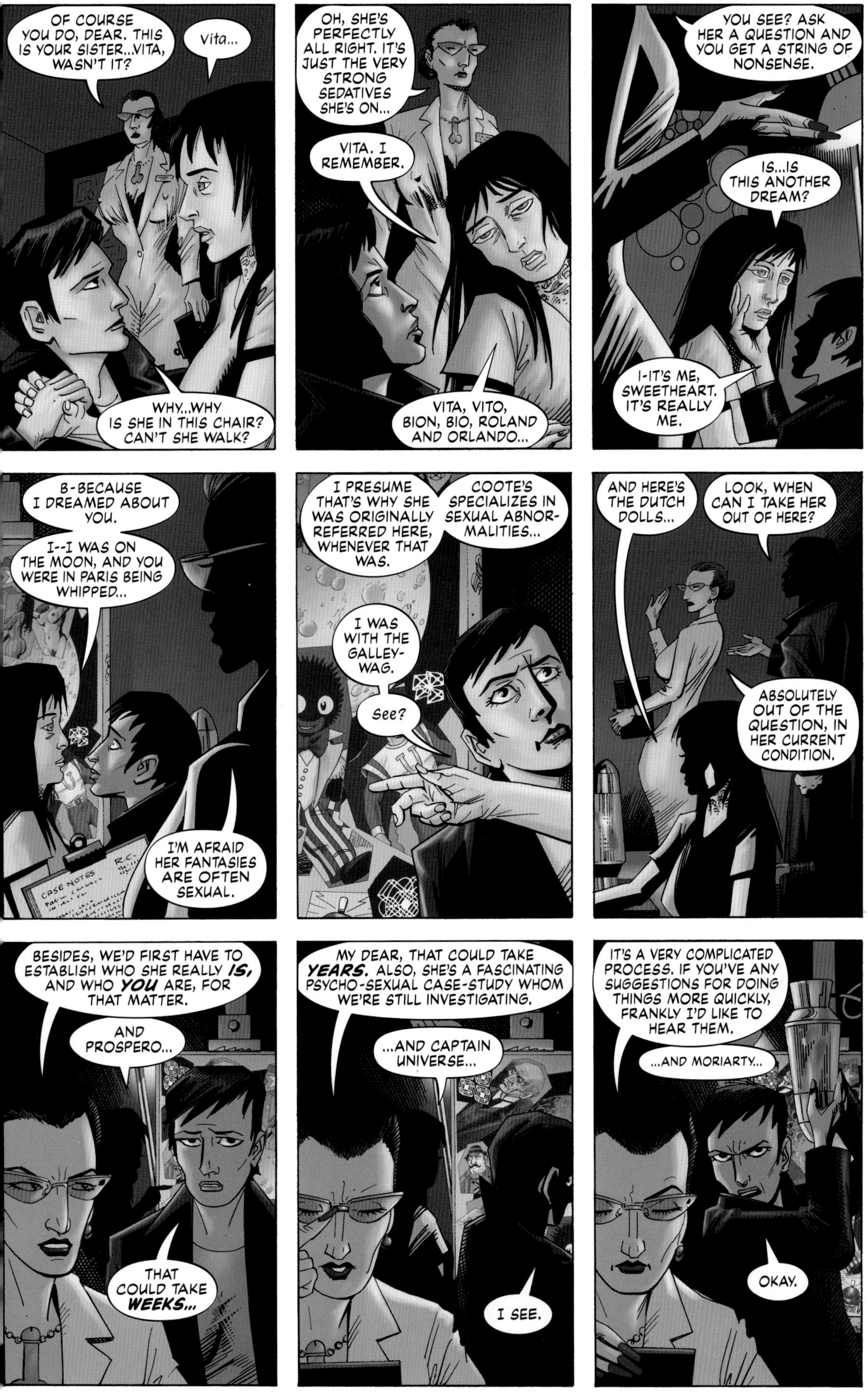
OF COURSE YOU DO, DEAR. THIS IS YOUR SISTER...VITA, WASN'T IT?
Vita...
WHY...WHY IS SHE IN THIS CHAIR? CAN'T SHE WALK?
OH, SHE'S PERFECTLY ALL RIGHT. IT'S JUST THE VERY STRONG SEDATIVES SHE'S ON...
VITA. I REMEMBER.
VITA, VITO, BION, BIO, ROLAND AND ORLANDO...
YOU SEE? ASK HER A QUESTION AND YOU GET A STRING OF NONSENSE.
IS...IS THIS ANOTHER DREAM?
I-IT'S ME, SWEETHEART. IT'S REALLY ME.
B-BECAUSE I DREAMED ABOUT YOU.
I--I WAS ON THE MOON, AND YOU WERE IN PARIS BEING WHIPPED...
I'M AFRAID HER FANTASIES ARE OFTEN SEXUAL.
CASE NOTES
R.C.
I PRESUME THAT'S WHY SHE WAS ORIGINALLY REFERRED HERE, WHENEVER THAT WAS.
COOTE'S SPECIALIZES IN SEXUAL ABNOR-MALITIES...
I WAS WITH THE GALLEY-WAG.
See?
AND HERE'S THE DUTCH DOLLS...
LOOK, WHEN CAN I TAKE HER OUT OF HERE?
ABSOLUTELY OUT OF THE QUESTION, IN HER CURRENT CONDITION.
BESIDES, WE'D FIRST HAVE TO ESTABLISH WHO SHE REALLY ***IS,*** AND WHO ***YOU*** ARE, FOR THAT MATTER.
AND PROSPERO...
THAT COULD TAKE ***WEEKS...***
MY DEAR, THAT COULD TAKE ***YEARS.*** ALSO, SHE'S A FASCINATING PSYCHO-SEXUAL CASE-STUDY WHOM WE'RE STILL INVESTIGATING.
...AND CAPTAIN UNIVERSE...
I SEE.
IT'S A VERY COMPLICATED PROCESS. IF YOU'VE ANY SUGGESTIONS FOR DOING THINGS MORE QUICKLY, FRANKLY I'D LIKE TO HEAR THEM.
...AND MORIARTY...
OKAY.

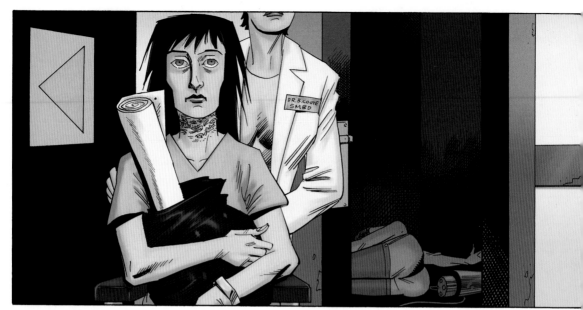

MIN IS IN BITS NOW, AL'S GONE UP IN SMOKE AND LANDO'S SEVERELY TWISTED.

BUT, TO BE FAIR, IF THEY COULDN'T TAKE A JOKE THEN THEY NEVER SHOULD HAVE BLOODY WELL ENLISTED!

THERE'S CONFLICTS LOOMING AND GUNS ARE BOOMING FROM DARFUR TO KANDAHAR.

METAL BAYONETS, THEY DON'T BEND: IT'S THE WORKER ON EACH END...

...SO IN EVERY BLITZ AND BATTLE IT'S THE COMMON FRONT-LINE CATTLE WHO IN BODY OR IN MIND GET TURNED TO PÂTÉ FOIE GRAS!

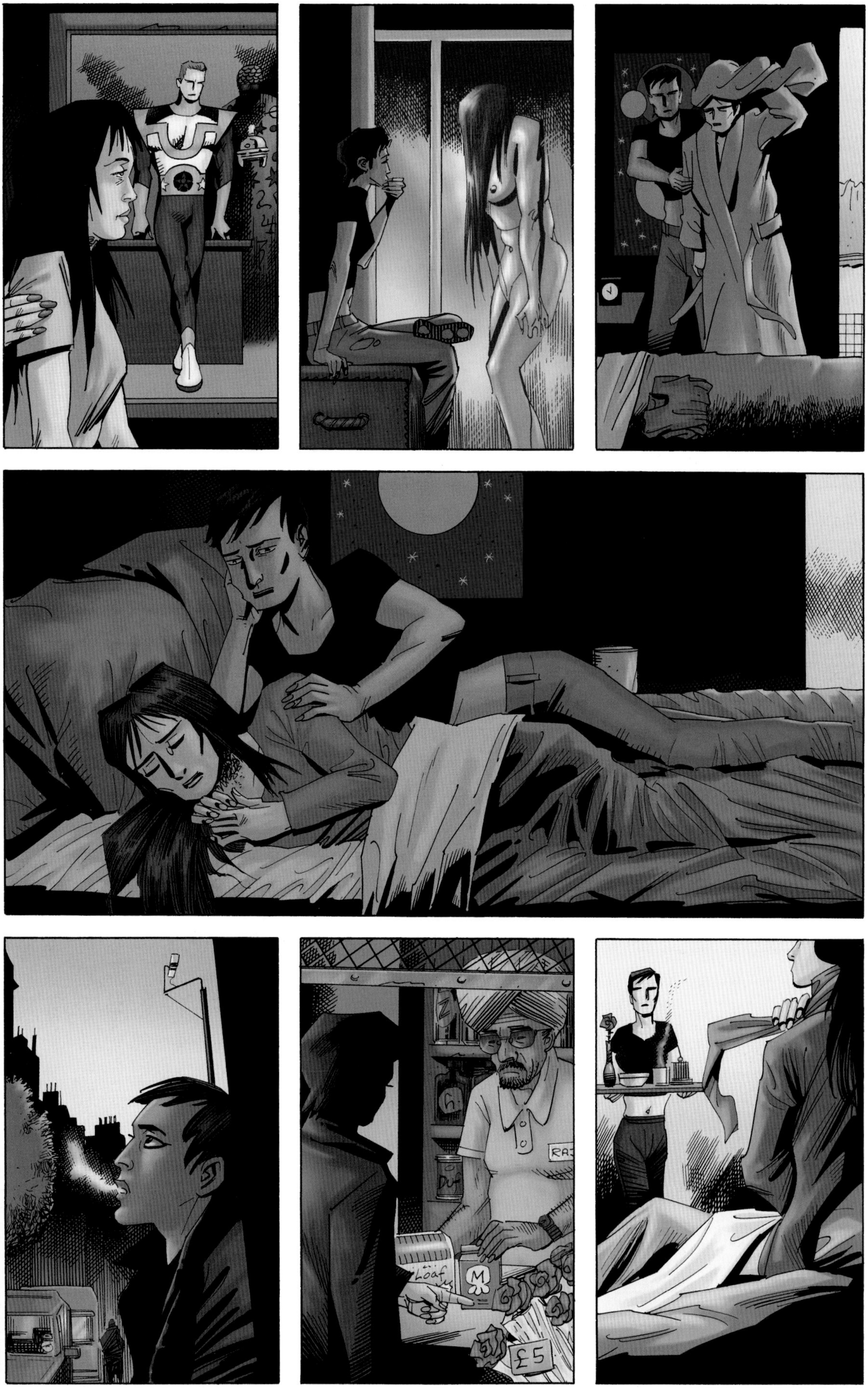
Loaf
£5

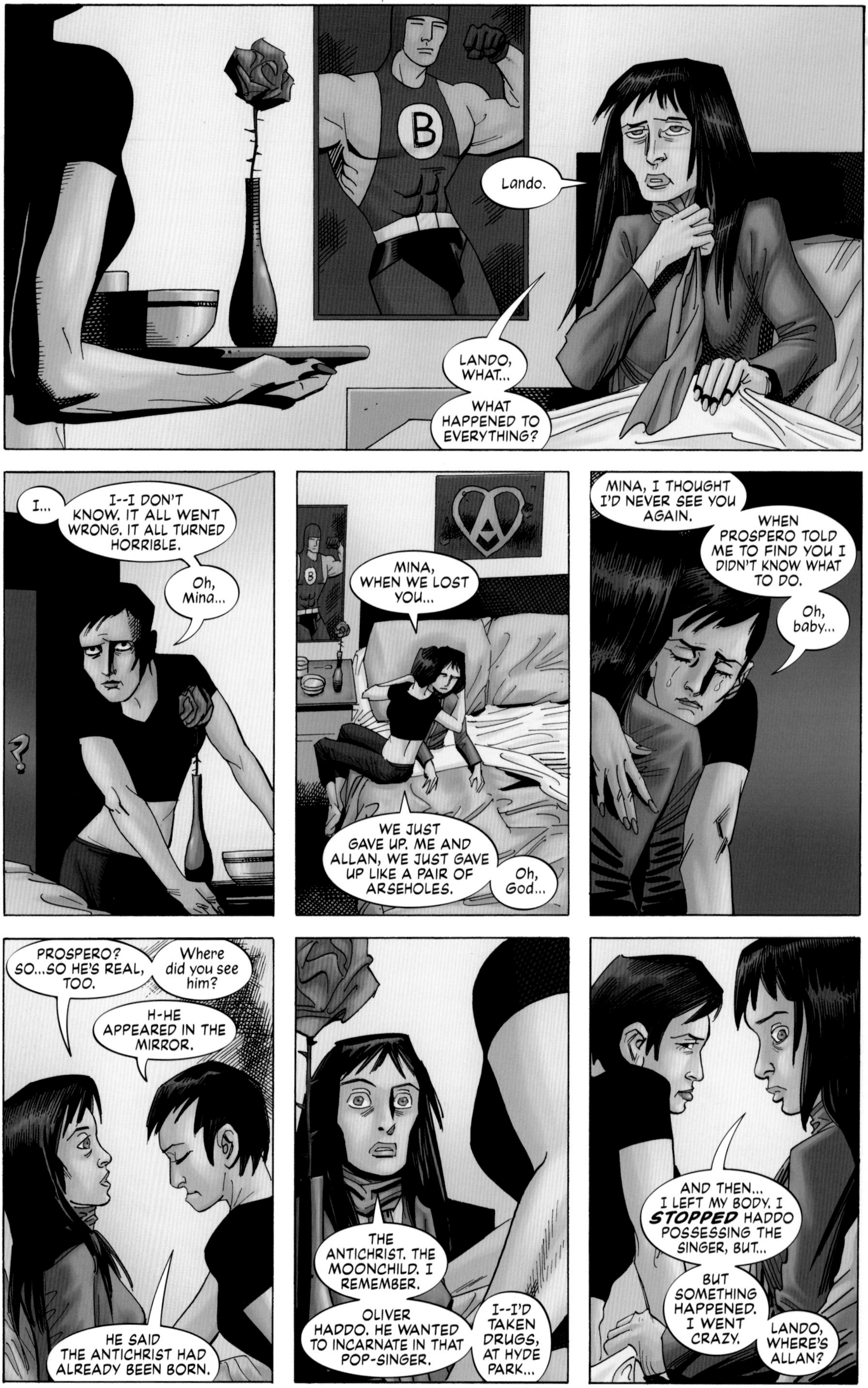
Lando.
LANDO, WHAT...
WHAT HAPPENED TO EVERYTHING?
I...
I--I DON'T KNOW. IT ALL WENT WRONG. IT ALL TURNED HORRIBLE.
Oh, Mina...
MINA, WHEN WE LOST YOU...
WE JUST GAVE UP. ME AND ALLAN, WE JUST GAVE UP LIKE A PAIR OF ARSEHOLES.
Oh, God...
MINA, I THOUGHT I'D NEVER SEE YOU AGAIN.
WHEN PROSPERO TOLD ME TO FIND YOU I DIDN'T KNOW WHAT TO DO.
Oh, baby...
PROSPERO? SO...SO HE'S REAL, TOO.
Where did you see him?
H-HE APPEARED IN THE MIRROR.
HE SAID THE ANTICHRIST HAD ALREADY BEEN BORN.
THE ANTICHRIST. THE MOONCHILD. I REMEMBER.
OLIVER HADDO. HE WANTED TO INCARNATE IN THAT POP-SINGER.
I--I'D TAKEN DRUGS, AT HYDE PARK...
AND THEN... I LEFT MY BODY. I STOPPED HADDO POSSESSING THE SINGER, BUT...
BUT SOMETHING HAPPENED. I WENT CRAZY.
LANDO, WHERE'S ALLAN?

H-HE'S SLEEPING ROUGH AND BACK ON HEROIN. HE STARTED SOON AFTER WE LOST YOU.

I--I BUMPED INTO HIM YESTERDAY.

HE RAN AWAY FROM ME.

PROSPERO TOLD ME TO FIND YOU BOTH BEFORE WE LOCATED THIS ANTICHRIST, BUT...

...ALLAN LOOKED DREADFUL. I--I THINK HE'S A LOST CAUSE.

NO.

NO, WE'LL FIND HIM. WE'VE GOT TO.

THIS BLOODY MEDICATION. I CAN'T THINK STRAIGHT.

RIGHT. OKAY. SORT MY HAIR OUT. FIND SOME CLOTHES...

MINA, YOU NEED REST.

I MEAN, WE MIGHT FIND ALLAN AT THE HOMELESS SHELTER, BUT FINDING THIS ANTICHRIST'S HOPELESS.

TH-THEN WE'LL ASK NORTON.

NORTON? MINA, HE NEVER MAKES ANY SENSE.

YES HE DOES. HE SAID HE'D SEE US IN 2009, WHEN IT WAS ALL TOO LATE.

AND NOW IT'S 2009, AND IT'S TOO LATE.

PLEASE HELP ME BRAID MY HAIR, WOULD YOU?

O-Or did I ask you that already?

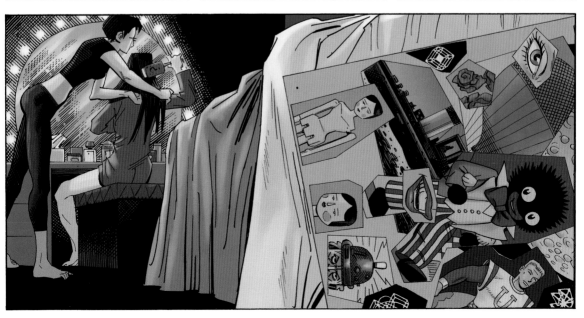

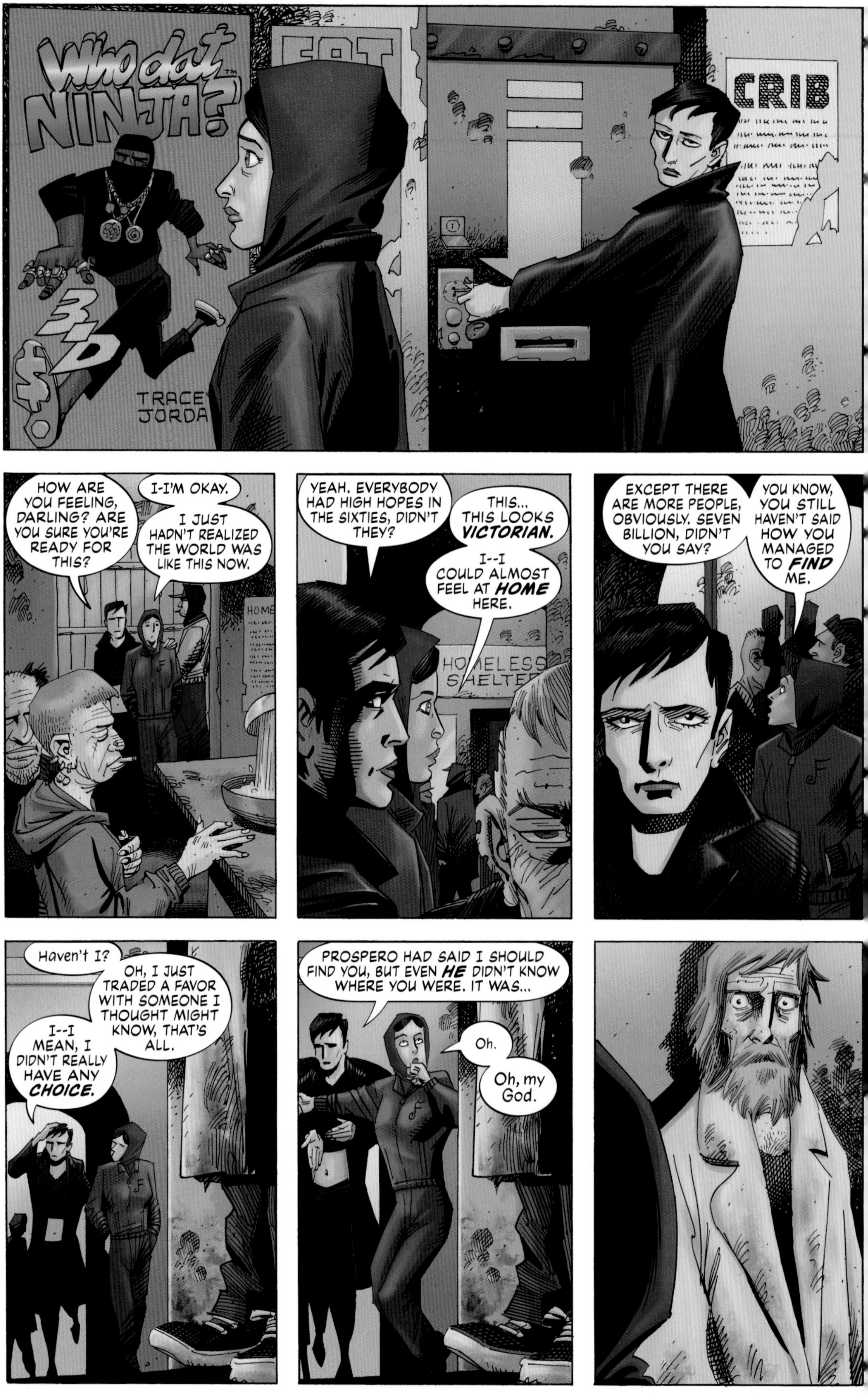

Who dat NINJA?™
3-D
$
TRACEY JORDA
CRIB
HOMELESS SHELTER
HOW ARE YOU FEELING, DARLING? ARE YOU SURE YOU'RE READY FOR THIS?
I-I'M OKAY.
I JUST HADN'T REALIZED THE WORLD WAS LIKE THIS NOW.
YEAH. EVERYBODY HAD HIGH HOPES IN THE SIXTIES, DIDN'T THEY?
THIS... THIS LOOKS VICTORIAN.
I--I COULD ALMOST FEEL AT HOME HERE.
EXCEPT THERE ARE MORE PEOPLE, OBVIOUSLY. SEVEN BILLION, DIDN'T YOU SAY?
YOU KNOW, YOU STILL HAVEN'T SAID HOW YOU MANAGED TO FIND ME.
Haven't I?
OH, I JUST TRADED A FAVOR WITH SOMEONE I THOUGHT MIGHT KNOW, THAT'S ALL.
I--I MEAN, I DIDN'T REALLY HAVE ANY CHOICE.
PROSPERO HAD SAID I SHOULD FIND YOU, BUT EVEN HE DIDN'T KNOW WHERE YOU WERE. IT WAS...
Oh.
Oh, my God.

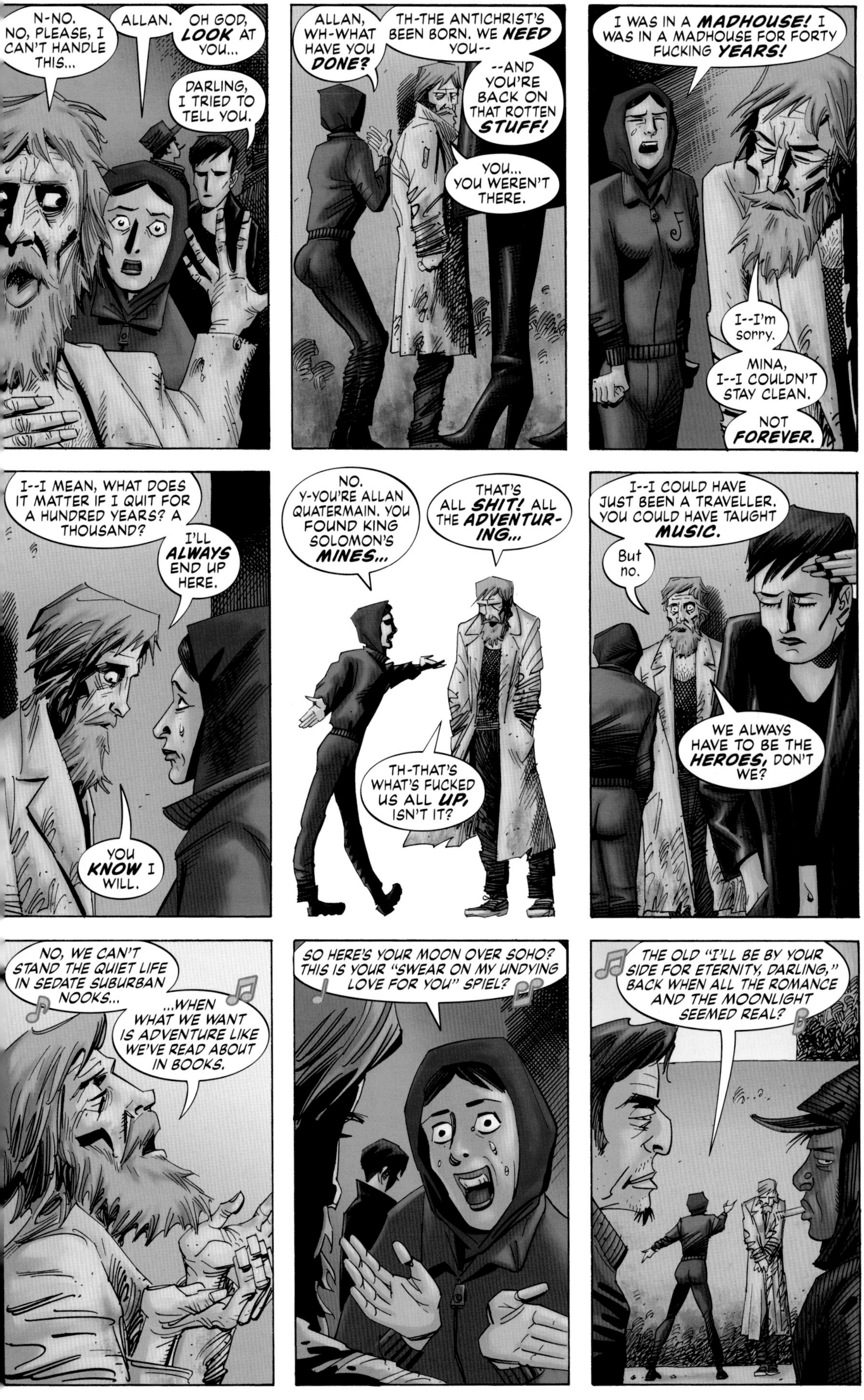
N-NO. NO, PLEASE, I CAN'T HANDLE THIS...
ALLAN.
OH GOD, LOOK AT YOU...
DARLING, I TRIED TO TELL YOU.
ALLAN, WH-WHAT HAVE YOU DONE?
TH-THE ANTICHRIST'S BEEN BORN. WE NEED YOU--
--AND YOU'RE BACK ON THAT ROTTEN STUFF!
YOU... YOU WEREN'T THERE.
I WAS IN A MADHOUSE! I WAS IN A MADHOUSE FOR FORTY FUCKING YEARS!
I--I'm sorry.
MINA, I--I COULDN'T STAY CLEAN.
NOT FOREVER.
I--I MEAN, WHAT DOES IT MATTER IF I QUIT FOR A HUNDRED YEARS? A THOUSAND?
I'LL ALWAYS END UP HERE.
YOU KNOW I WILL.
NO. Y-YOU'RE ALLAN QUATERMAIN. YOU FOUND KING SOLOMON'S MINES...
THAT'S ALL SHIT! ALL THE ADVENTURING...
TH-THAT'S WHAT'S FUCKED US ALL UP, ISN'T IT?
I--I COULD HAVE JUST BEEN A TRAVELLER. YOU COULD HAVE TAUGHT MUSIC.
But no.
WE ALWAYS HAVE TO BE THE HEROES, DON'T WE?
NO, WE CAN'T STAND THE QUIET LIFE IN SEDATE SUBURBAN NOOKS...
...WHEN WHAT WE WANT IS ADVENTURE LIKE WE'VE READ ABOUT IN BOOKS.
SO HERE'S YOUR MOON OVER SOHO? THIS IS YOUR "SWEAR ON MY UNDYING LOVE FOR YOU" SPIEL?
THE OLD "I'LL BE BY YOUR SIDE FOR ETERNITY, DARLING," BACK WHEN ALL THE ROMANCE AND THE MOONLIGHT SEEMED REAL?

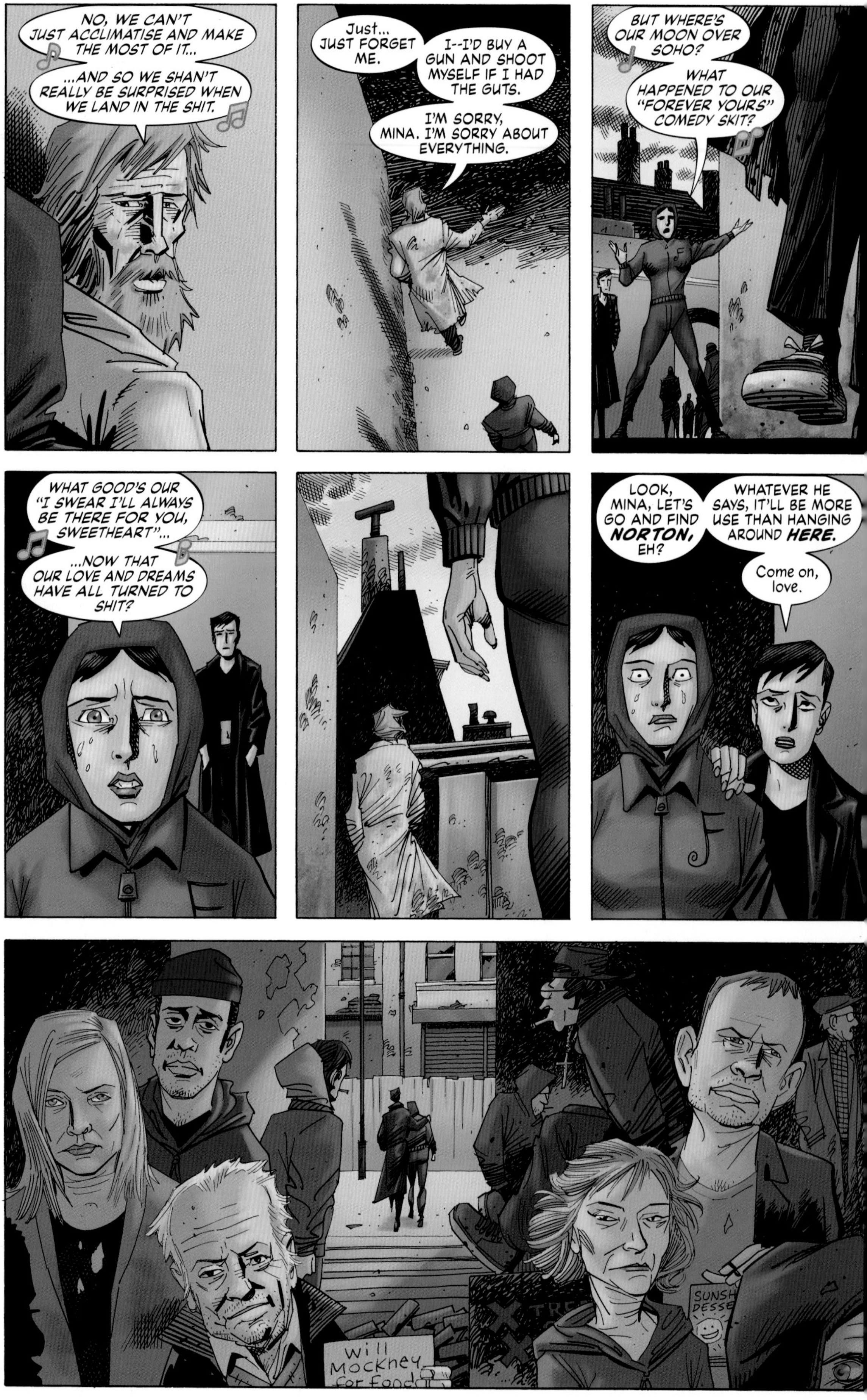
NO, WE CAN'T JUST ACCLIMATISE AND MAKE THE MOST OF IT...
...AND SO WE SHAN'T REALLY BE SURPRISED WHEN WE LAND IN THE SHIT.
Just... JUST FORGET ME.
I--I'D BUY A GUN AND SHOOT MYSELF IF I HAD THE GUTS.
I'M SORRY, MINA. I'M SORRY ABOUT EVERYTHING.
BUT WHERE'S OUR MOON OVER SOHO?
WHAT HAPPENED TO OUR "FOREVER YOURS" COMEDY SKIT?
WHAT GOOD'S OUR "I SWEAR I'LL ALWAYS BE THERE FOR YOU, SWEETHEART"...
...NOW THAT OUR LOVE AND DREAMS HAVE ALL TURNED TO SHIT?
LOOK, MINA, LET'S GO AND FIND NORTON, EH?
WHATEVER HE SAYS, IT'LL BE MORE USE THAN HANGING AROUND HERE.
Come on, love.
Will Mockney for Food

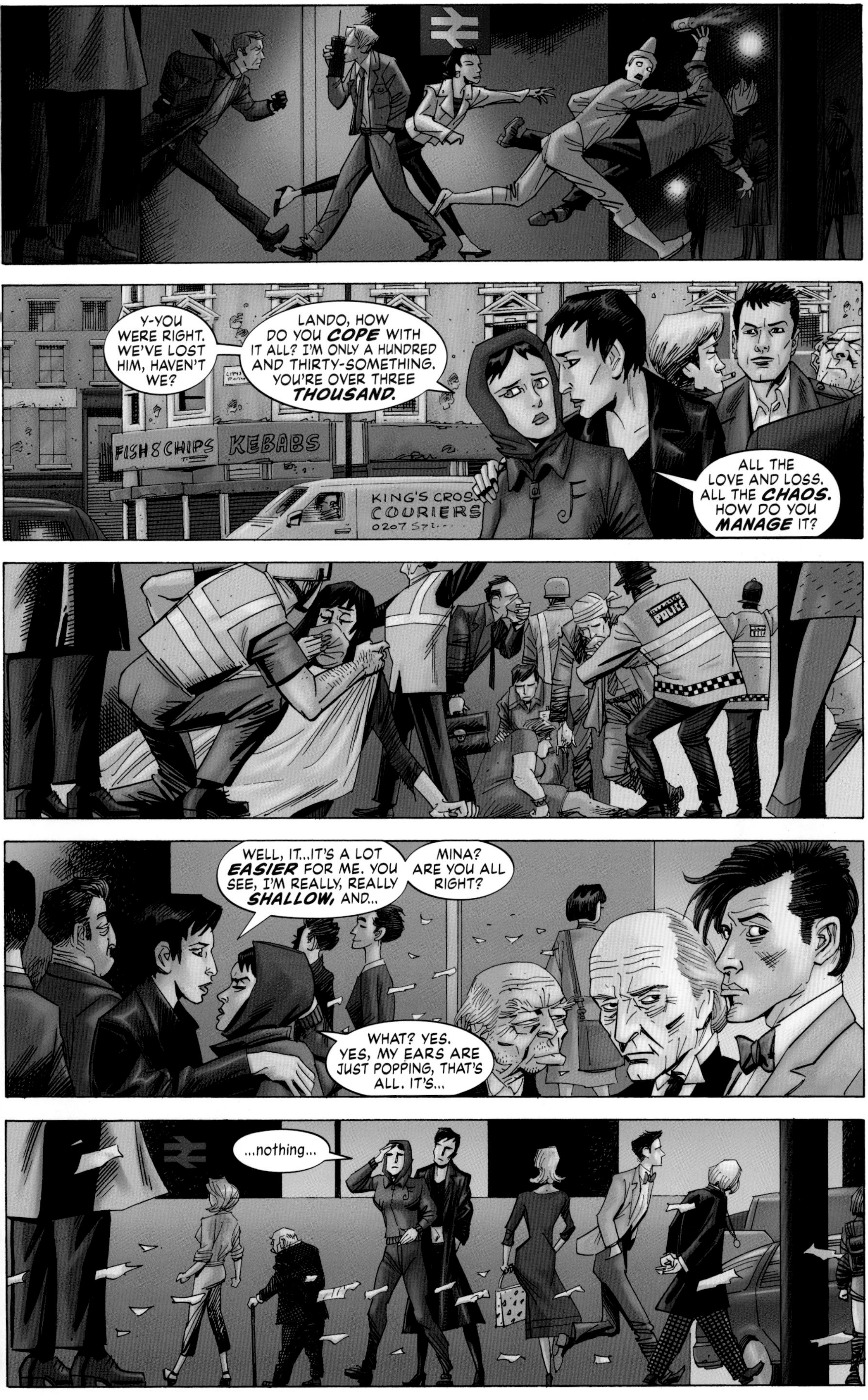
Y-YOU WERE RIGHT. WE'VE LOST HIM, HAVEN'T WE?
LANDO, HOW DO YOU COPE WITH IT ALL? I'M ONLY A HUNDRED AND THIRTY-SOMETHING. YOU'RE OVER THREE THOUSAND.
FISH & CHIPS
KEBABS
KING'S CROSS COURIERS
ALL THE LOVE AND LOSS. ALL THE CHAOS. HOW DO YOU MANAGE IT?
POLICE
WELL, IT...IT'S A LOT EASIER FOR ME. YOU SEE, I'M REALLY, REALLY SHALLOW, AND...
MINA? ARE YOU ALL RIGHT?
WHAT? YES. YES, MY EARS ARE JUST POPPING, THAT'S ALL. IT'S...
...nothing...

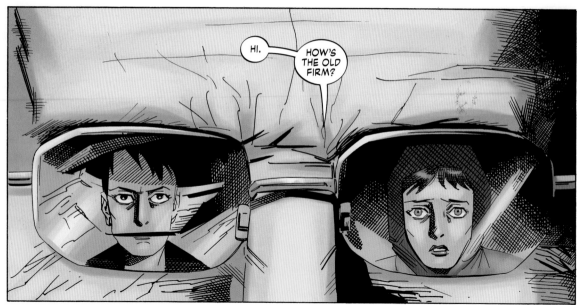

HI.

HOW'S THE OLD FIRM?

Not... NOT SO GOOD.

HADDO'S MOONCHILD'S BEEN BORN, AND... WELL, THERE'S NOT MUCH LEFT OF US.

IT'S TOO LATE. JUST LIKE YOU SAID.

I'M SORRY TO HEAR THAT.

Are you okay? SHOULD WE GET A CUP OF TEA OR ANY-THING?

NORTON, WE NEED *HELP*. *REAL* HELP.

FROM A SKELETAL NAZI DENTIST HAUNTING KING'S CROSS, SPOUTING VERBLESS SENTENCES? YOU MUST BE DESPERATE.

YOU'VE CERTAINLY CHANGED SINCE YOU FOUNDED LONDON HERE.

WH- WHAT?

YOU REMEMBER: GEOFFREY OF MONMOUTH'S CONFECTED ENGLISH HERITAGE. BRUTUS AT KING'S CROSS, NAMING THE CITY...

...TROY NOVANTUM.

I-IT HAPPENED *HERE*, DIDN'T IT? I'D *FOR-GOTTEN*...

A-AND AWAY FROM THE CEREMONY, I REMEMBER A MAN.

HE HAD LENSES OVER HIS EYES.

THAT WAS *YOU*.

WELL, LONDON'S FICTION *GERMINATES* HERE...

...AND IT'S HERE, IN AIDAN DUN'S *VALE ROYAL*, THAT IT FINDS ITS GROUND ZERO.

YOU MENTIONED HADDO'S MAGICAL CHILD.

LET'S GO INSIDE, SHALL WE?

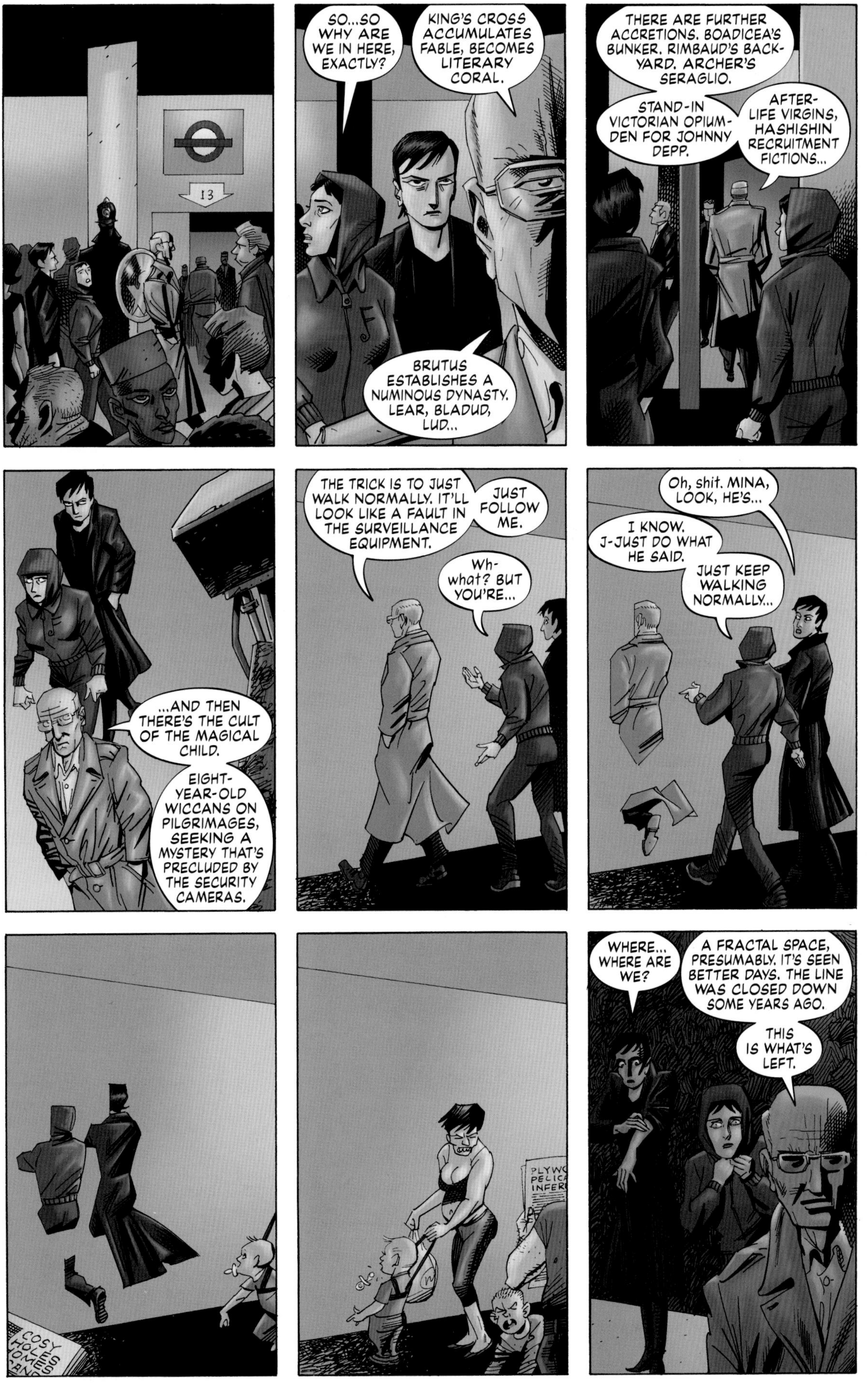
13
SO...SO WHY ARE WE IN HERE, EXACTLY?
KING'S CROSS ACCUMULATES FABLE, BECOMES LITERARY CORAL.
BRUTUS ESTABLISHES A NUMINOUS DYNASTY. LEAR, BLADUD, LUD...
THERE ARE FURTHER ACCRETIONS. BOADICEA'S BUNKER. RIMBAUD'S BACK-YARD. ARCHER'S SERAGLIO.
STAND-IN VICTORIAN OPIUM-DEN FOR JOHNNY DEPP.
AFTER-LIFE VIRGINS, HASHISHIN RECRUITMENT FICTIONS...
...AND THEN THERE'S THE CULT OF THE MAGICAL CHILD.
EIGHT-YEAR-OLD WICCANS ON PILGRIMAGES, SEEKING A MYSTERY THAT'S PRECLUDED BY THE SECURITY CAMERAS.
THE TRICK IS TO JUST WALK NORMALLY. IT'LL LOOK LIKE A FAULT IN THE SURVEILLANCE EQUIPMENT.
JUST FOLLOW ME.
Wh-what? BUT YOU'RE...
Oh, shit. MINA, LOOK, HE'S...
I KNOW. J-JUST DO WHAT HE SAID.
JUST KEEP WALKING NORMALLY...
COSY
HOLES
WHERE... WHERE ARE WE?
A FRACTAL SPACE, PRESUMABLY. IT'S SEEN BETTER DAYS. THE LINE WAS CLOSED DOWN SOME YEARS AGO.
THIS IS WHAT'S LEFT.

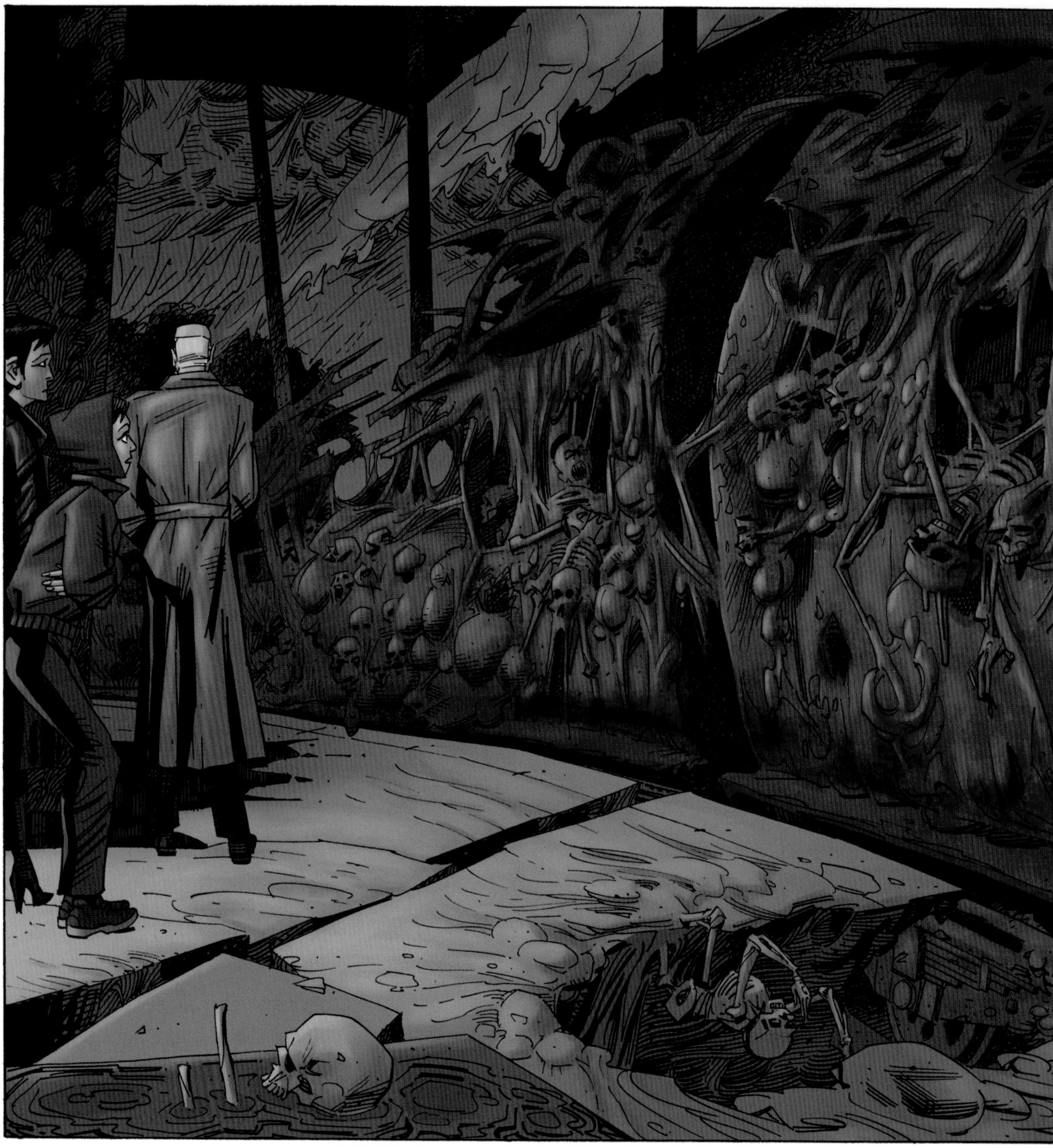

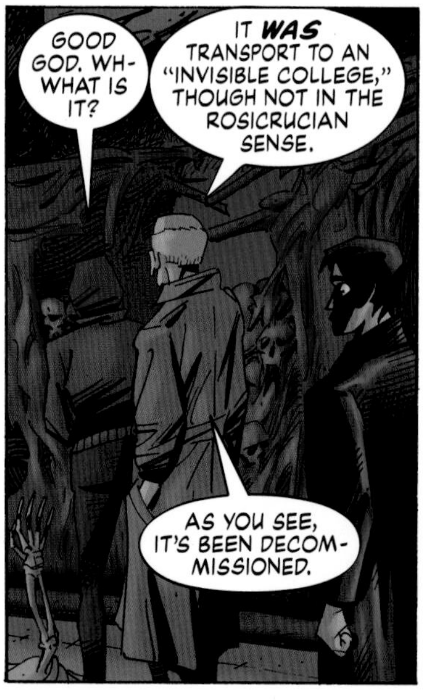
GOOD GOD. WH-WHAT IS IT?
IT WAS TRANSPORT TO AN "INVISIBLE COLLEGE," THOUGH NOT IN THE ROSICRUCIAN SENSE.
AS YOU SEE, IT'S BEEN DECOM-MISSIONED.

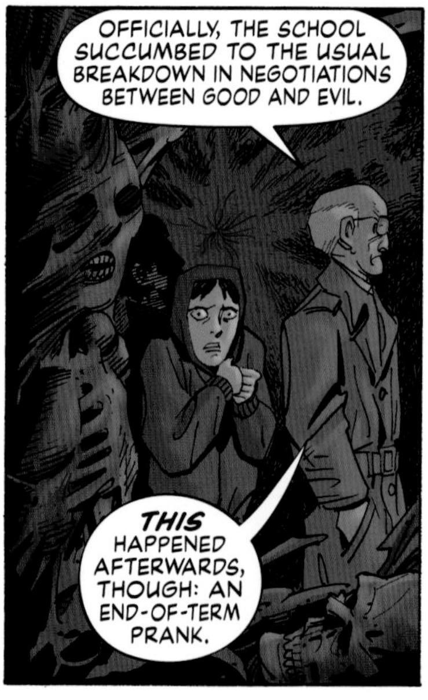
OFFICIALLY, THE SCHOOL SUCCUMBED TO THE USUAL BREAKDOWN IN NEGOTIATIONS BETWEEN GOOD AND EVIL.
THIS HAPPENED AFTERWARDS, THOUGH: AN END-OF-TERM PRANK.

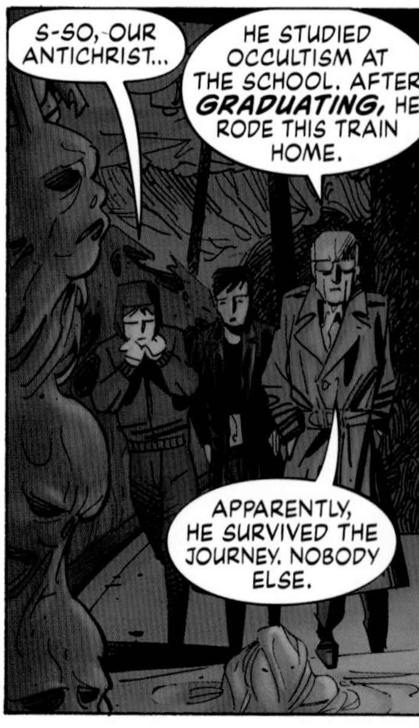
S-SO, OUR ANTICHRIST...
HE STUDIED OCCULTISM AT THE SCHOOL. AFTER GRADUATING, HE RODE THIS TRAIN HOME.
APPARENTLY, HE SURVIVED THE JOURNEY. NOBODY ELSE.

SO... SO ALL THESE *REMAINS*...

FELLOW PUPILS. CO-TRAVELLERS, OR THOSE UNLUCKY ENOUGH TO BE ON THE PLATFORM WHEN HE ROLLED IN.

COLLATERAL DAMAGE.

THAT... THAT MUST HAVE BEEN QUITE A SIGHT.

I--IS THE MOONCHILD STILL IN LONDON?

PERHAPS.

I SUPPOSE ANY SURVIVING SCHOOL RECORDS MIGHT TELL YOU.

W-WOULDN'T THAT MEAN GOING TO THE SCHOOL?

HOW WOULD WE *GET* THERE? THIS IS JUST WRECKAGE...

WELL, IT OBVIOUSLY WORKED WHEN IT ARRIVED.

BUT...I MEAN, THESE AREN'T PROPER CONTROLS.

I ASSUME IT RUNS ON SLOPPILY-DEFINED MAGICAL PRINCIPLES.

I'M SURE YOU TWO CAN HANDLE IT.

US TWO? AREN'T *YOU* COMING?

AFRAID NOT. I'M UNDER CITY-ARREST; HIGHLY SUSPECT SINCE MY HACKNEY BOOK.

AND UNFORTUNATELY, THE SCHOOL'S OUTSIDE *LONDON*.

THE INTERVENING MAGICAL LANDSCAPE IS HEAVILY FORESTED, REPORTEDLY. MYTHAGO WOODS, PERHAPS, OR CATLING'S VORRH.

IF I DON'T SEE YOU BEFORE THE APOCALYPSE, GOOD LUCK.

Oh fu... Oh fu... Oh fu... O fu... Oh fu...

AAAH! AAA AAA AA AAAH!

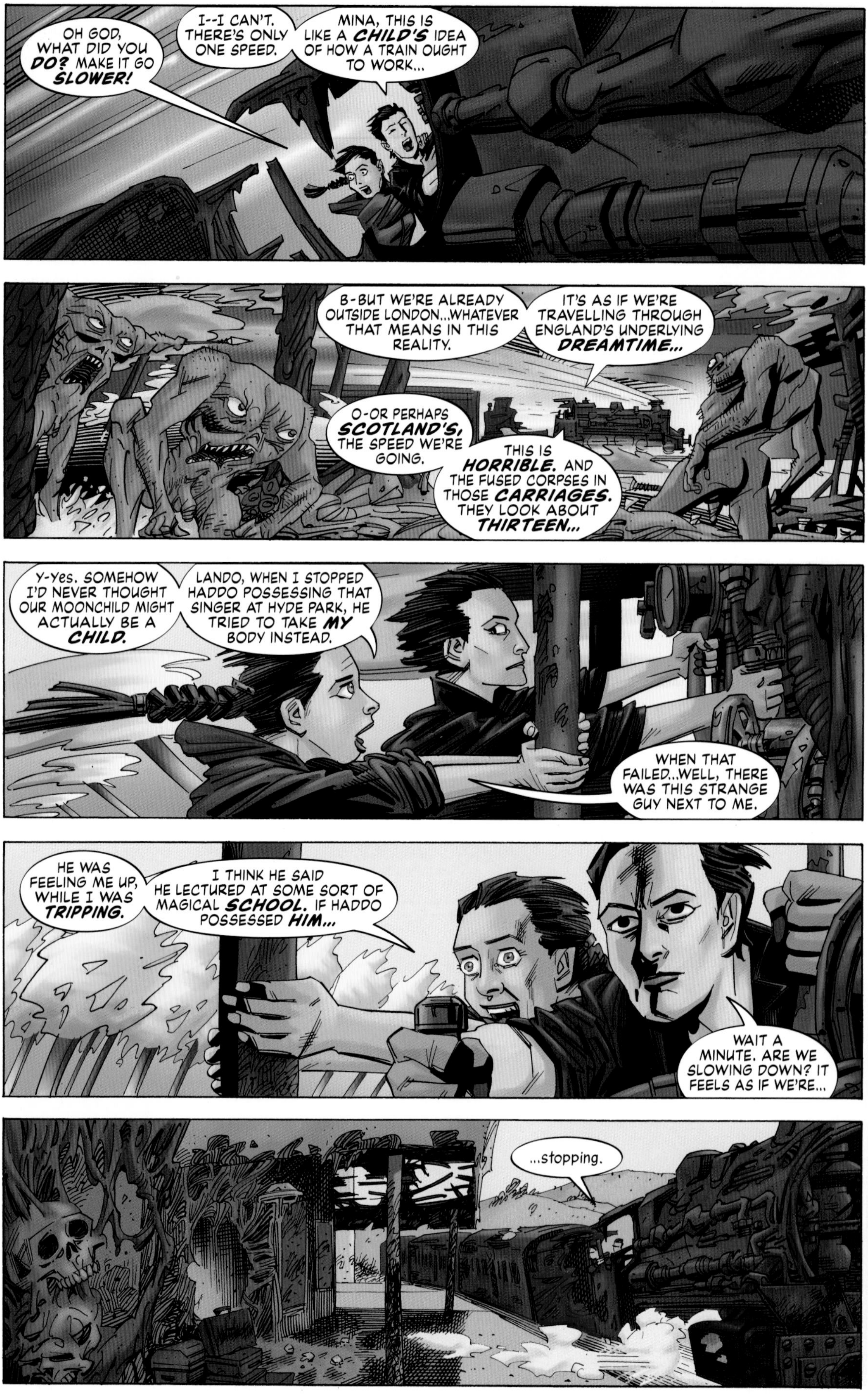
OH GOD, WHAT DID YOU DO? MAKE IT GO SLOWER!
I--I CAN'T. THERE'S ONLY ONE SPEED.
MINA, THIS IS LIKE A CHILD'S IDEA OF HOW A TRAIN OUGHT TO WORK...
B-BUT WE'RE ALREADY OUTSIDE LONDON...WHATEVER THAT MEANS IN THIS REALITY.
IT'S AS IF WE'RE TRAVELLING THROUGH ENGLAND'S UNDERLYING DREAMTIME...
O-OR PERHAPS SCOTLAND'S, THE SPEED WE'RE GOING.
THIS IS HORRIBLE. AND THE FUSED CORPSES IN THOSE CARRIAGES. THEY LOOK ABOUT THIRTEEN...
Y-Yes. SOMEHOW I'D NEVER THOUGHT OUR MOONCHILD MIGHT ACTUALLY BE A CHILD.
LANDO, WHEN I STOPPED HADDO POSSESSING THAT SINGER AT HYDE PARK, HE TRIED TO TAKE MY BODY INSTEAD.
WHEN THAT FAILED...WELL, THERE WAS THIS STRANGE GUY NEXT TO ME.
HE WAS FEELING ME UP, WHILE I WAS TRIPPING.
I THINK HE SAID HE LECTURED AT SOME SORT OF MAGICAL SCHOOL. IF HADDO POSSESSED HIM...
WAIT A MINUTE. ARE WE SLOWING DOWN? IT FEELS AS IF WE'RE...
...stopping.

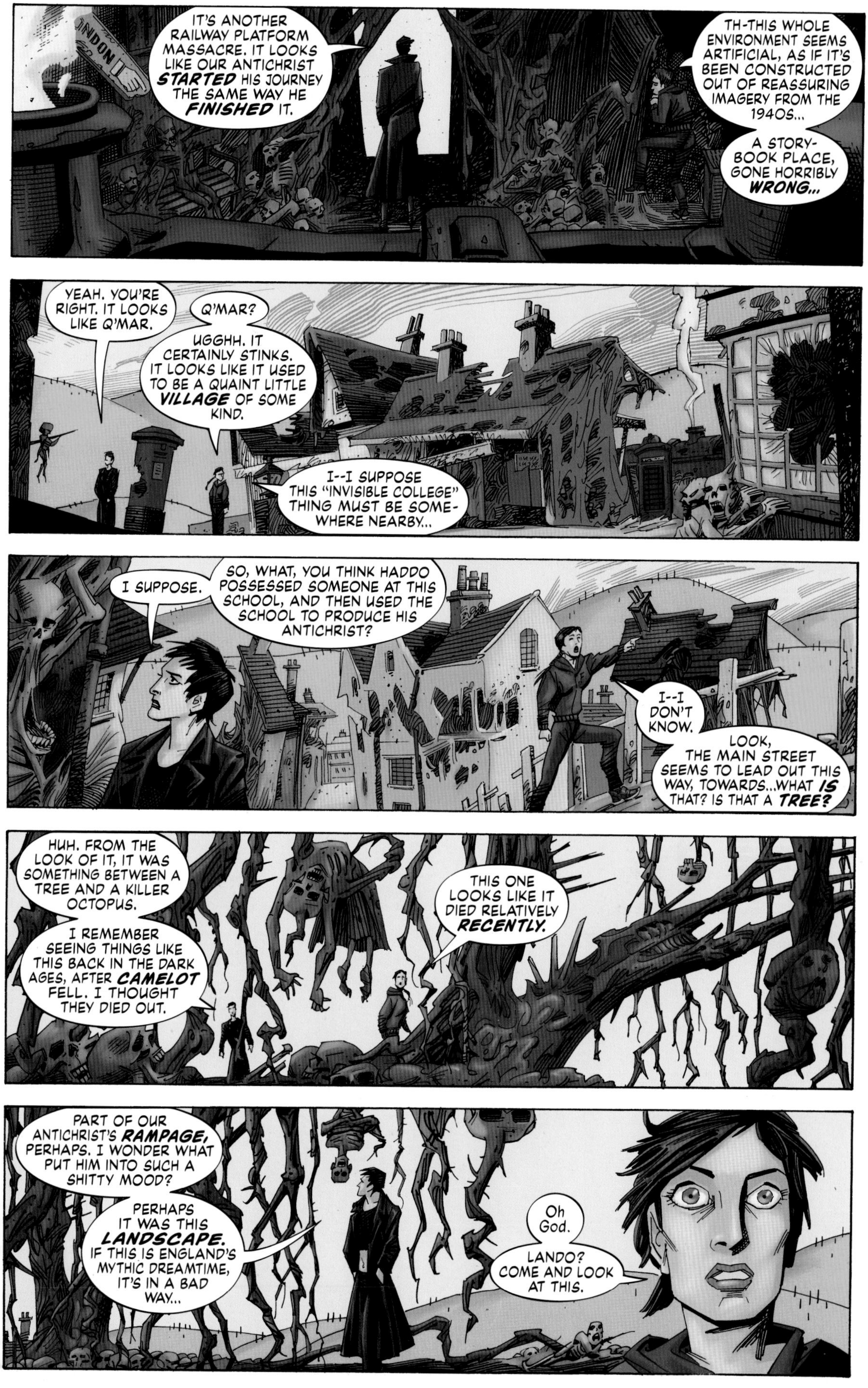
IT'S ANOTHER RAILWAY PLATFORM MASSACRE. IT LOOKS LIKE OUR ANTICHRIST ***STARTED*** HIS JOURNEY THE SAME WAY HE ***FINISHED*** IT.
TH-THIS WHOLE ENVIRONMENT SEEMS ARTIFICIAL, AS IF IT'S BEEN CONSTRUCTED OUT OF REASSURING IMAGERY FROM THE 1940S...
A STORY-BOOK PLACE, GONE HORRIBLY ***WRONG...***
YEAH. YOU'RE RIGHT. IT LOOKS LIKE Q'MAR.
Q'MAR?
UGGHH. IT CERTAINLY STINKS. IT LOOKS LIKE IT USED TO BE A QUAINT LITTLE ***VILLAGE*** OF SOME KIND.
I--I SUPPOSE THIS "INVISIBLE COLLEGE" THING MUST BE SOME-WHERE NEARBY...
I SUPPOSE.
SO, WHAT, YOU THINK HADDO POSSESSED SOMEONE AT THIS SCHOOL, AND THEN USED THE SCHOOL TO PRODUCE HIS ANTICHRIST?
I--I DON'T KNOW.
LOOK, THE MAIN STREET SEEMS TO LEAD OUT THIS WAY, TOWARDS...WHAT ***IS*** THAT? IS THAT A ***TREE?***
HUH. FROM THE LOOK OF IT, IT WAS SOMETHING BETWEEN A TREE AND A KILLER OCTOPUS.
I REMEMBER SEEING THINGS LIKE THIS BACK IN THE DARK AGES, AFTER ***CAMELOT*** FELL. I THOUGHT THEY DIED OUT.
THIS ONE LOOKS LIKE IT DIED RELATIVELY ***RECENTLY.***
PART OF OUR ANTICHRIST'S ***RAMPAGE,*** PERHAPS. I WONDER WHAT PUT HIM INTO SUCH A SHITTY MOOD?
PERHAPS IT WAS THIS ***LANDSCAPE.*** IF THIS IS ENGLAND'S MYTHIC DREAMTIME, IT'S IN A BAD WAY...
Oh God.
LANDO? COME AND LOOK AT THIS.

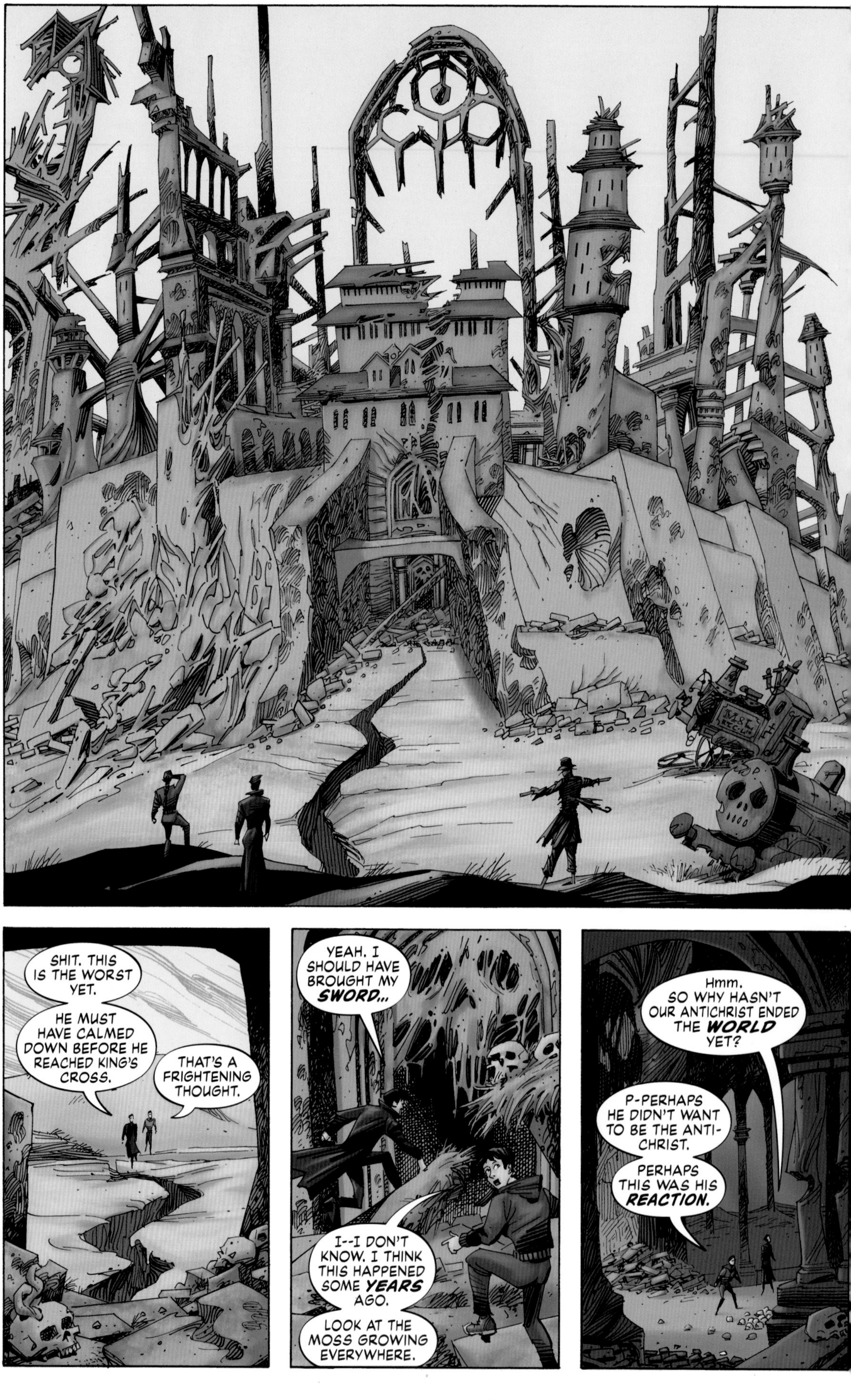
M&L
SHIT. THIS IS THE WORST YET.
HE MUST HAVE CALMED DOWN BEFORE HE REACHED KING'S CROSS.
THAT'S A FRIGHTENING THOUGHT.
YEAH. I SHOULD HAVE BROUGHT MY **SWORD...**
I--I DON'T KNOW. I THINK THIS HAPPENED SOME **YEARS** AGO.
LOOK AT THE MOSS GROWING EVERYWHERE.
Hmm. SO WHY HASN'T OUR ANTICHRIST ENDED THE **WORLD** YET?
P-PERHAPS HE DIDN'T WANT TO BE THE ANTI-CHRIST.
PERHAPS THIS WAS HIS **REACTION.**

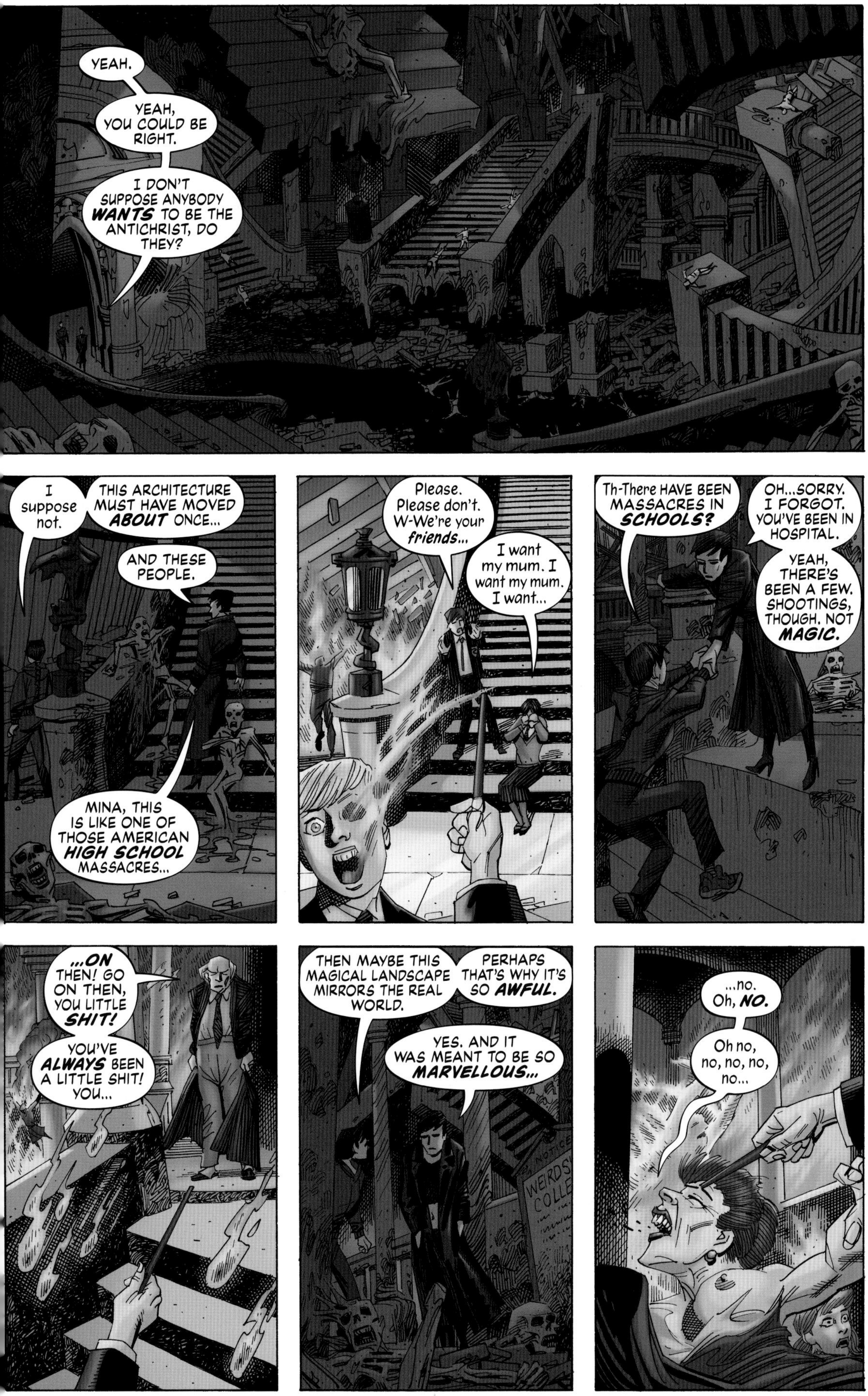

YEAH.
YEAH, YOU COULD BE RIGHT.
I DON'T SUPPOSE ANYBODY WANTS TO BE THE ANTICHRIST, DO THEY?
I suppose not.
THIS ARCHITECTURE MUST HAVE MOVED ABOUT ONCE...
AND THESE PEOPLE.
MINA, THIS IS LIKE ONE OF THOSE AMERICAN HIGH SCHOOL MASSACRES...
Please. Please don't. W-We're your friends...
I want my mum. I want my mum. I want...
Th-There HAVE BEEN MASSACRES IN SCHOOLS?
OH...SORRY. I FORGOT. YOU'VE BEEN IN HOSPITAL.
YEAH, THERE'S BEEN A FEW. SHOOTINGS, THOUGH. NOT MAGIC.
...ON THEN! GO ON THEN, YOU LITTLE SHIT!
YOU'VE ALWAYS BEEN A LITTLE SHIT! YOU...
THEN MAYBE THIS MAGICAL LANDSCAPE MIRRORS THE REAL WORLD.
PERHAPS THAT'S WHY IT'S SO AWFUL.
YES. AND IT WAS MEANT TO BE SO MARVELLOUS...
...no. Oh, NO.
Oh no, no, no, no, no...

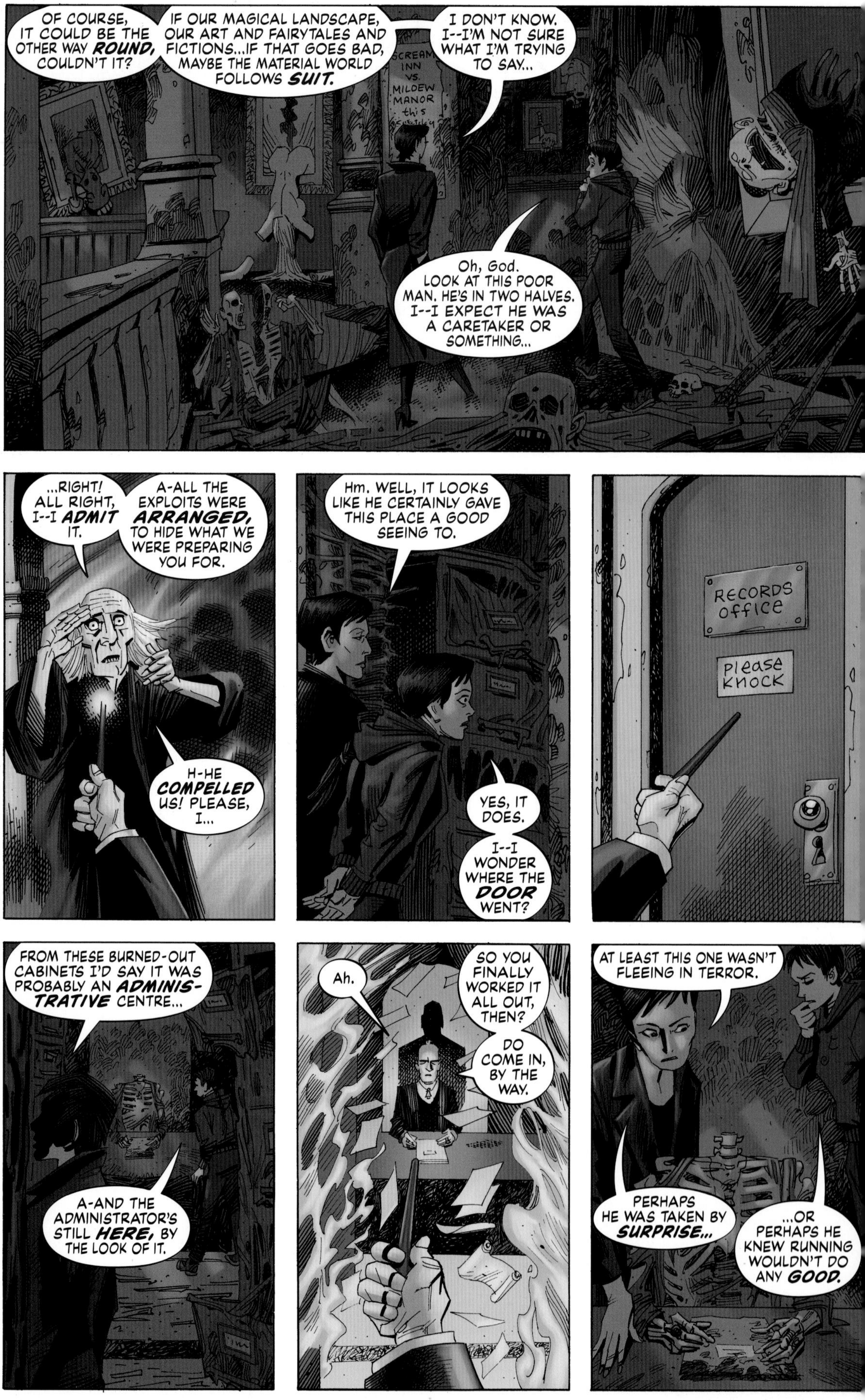
OF COURSE, IT COULD BE THE OTHER WAY ROUND, COULDN'T IT?
IF OUR MAGICAL LANDSCAPE, OUR ART AND FAIRYTALES AND FICTIONS...IF THAT GOES BAD, MAYBE THE MATERIAL WORLD FOLLOWS SUIT.
I DON'T KNOW. I--I'M NOT SURE WHAT I'M TRYING TO SAY...
SCREAM INN VS. MILDEW MANOR this
Oh, God. LOOK AT THIS POOR MAN. HE'S IN TWO HALVES. I--I EXPECT HE WAS A CARETAKER OR SOMETHING...
...RIGHT! ALL RIGHT, I--I ADMIT IT.
A-ALL THE EXPLOITS WERE ARRANGED, TO HIDE WHAT WE WERE PREPARING YOU FOR.
H-HE COMPELLED US! PLEASE, I...
Hm. WELL, IT LOOKS LIKE HE CERTAINLY GAVE THIS PLACE A GOOD SEEING TO.
YES, IT DOES.
I--I WONDER WHERE THE DOOR WENT?
RECORDS OFFICE
Please Knock
FROM THESE BURNED-OUT CABINETS I'D SAY IT WAS PROBABLY AN ADMINISTRATIVE CENTRE...
A-AND THE ADMINISTRATOR'S STILL HERE, BY THE LOOK OF IT.
Ah.
SO YOU FINALLY WORKED IT ALL OUT, THEN?
DO COME IN, BY THE WAY.
AT LEAST THIS ONE WASN'T FLEEING IN TERROR.
PERHAPS HE WAS TAKEN BY SURPRISE...
...OR PERHAPS HE KNEW RUNNING WOULDN'T DO ANY GOOD.

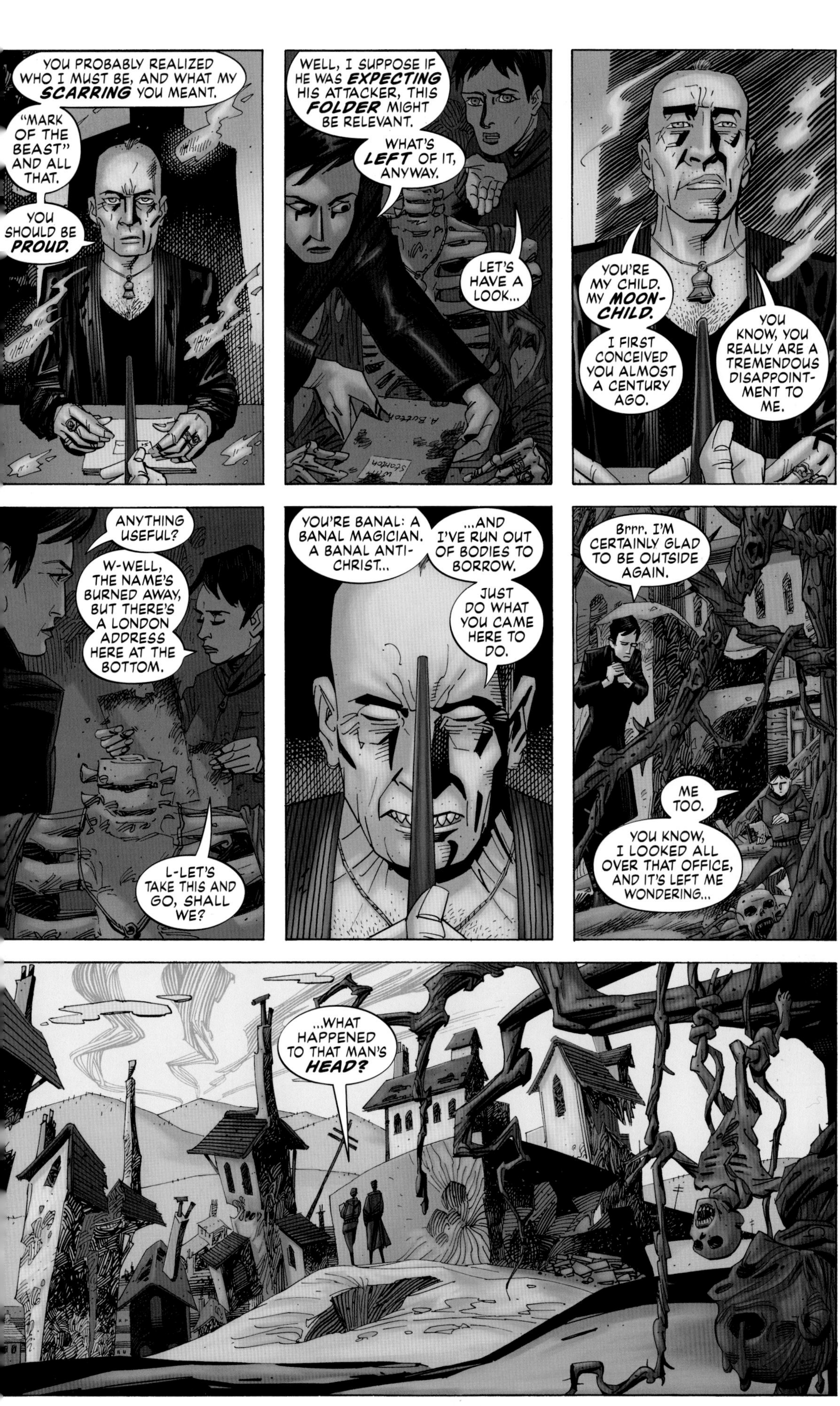

YOU PROBABLY REALIZED WHO I MUST BE, AND WHAT MY SCARRING YOU MEANT.
"MARK OF THE BEAST" AND ALL THAT.
YOU SHOULD BE PROUD.
WELL, I SUPPOSE IF HE WAS EXPECTING HIS ATTACKER, THIS FOLDER MIGHT BE RELEVANT.
WHAT'S LEFT OF IT, ANYWAY.
LET'S HAVE A LOOK...
A. Button
YOU'RE MY CHILD. MY MOON-CHILD.
I FIRST CONCEIVED YOU ALMOST A CENTURY AGO.
YOU KNOW, YOU REALLY ARE A TREMENDOUS DISAPPOINT-MENT TO ME.
ANYTHING USEFUL?
W-WELL, THE NAME'S BURNED AWAY, BUT THERE'S A LONDON ADDRESS HERE AT THE BOTTOM.
L-LET'S TAKE THIS AND GO, SHALL WE?
YOU'RE BANAL: A BANAL MAGICIAN. A BANAL ANTI-CHRIST...
...AND I'VE RUN OUT OF BODIES TO BORROW.
JUST DO WHAT YOU CAME HERE TO DO.
Brrr. I'M CERTAINLY GLAD TO BE OUTSIDE AGAIN.
ME TOO.
YOU KNOW, I LOOKED ALL OVER THAT OFFICE, AND IT'S LEFT ME WONDERING...
...WHAT HAPPENED TO THAT MAN'S HEAD?

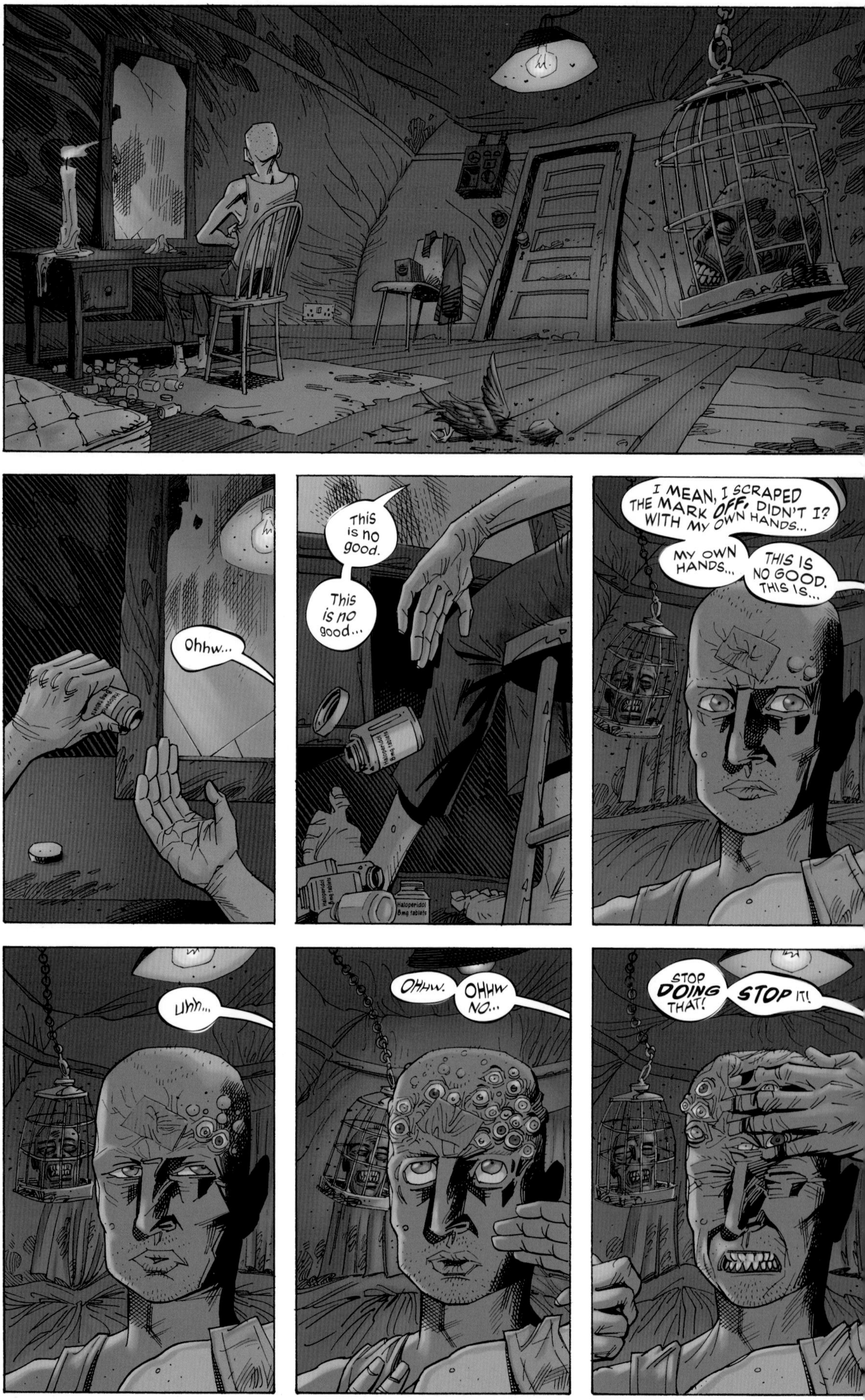
Ohhw...
This is no good.
This is no good...
Haloperidol 8mg tablets
I MEAN, I SCRAPED THE MARK OFF, DIDN'T I? WITH MY OWN HANDS...
MY OWN HANDS...
THIS IS NO GOOD. THIS IS...
Uhh...
OHHW.
OHHW NO...
STOP DOING THAT!
STOP IT!

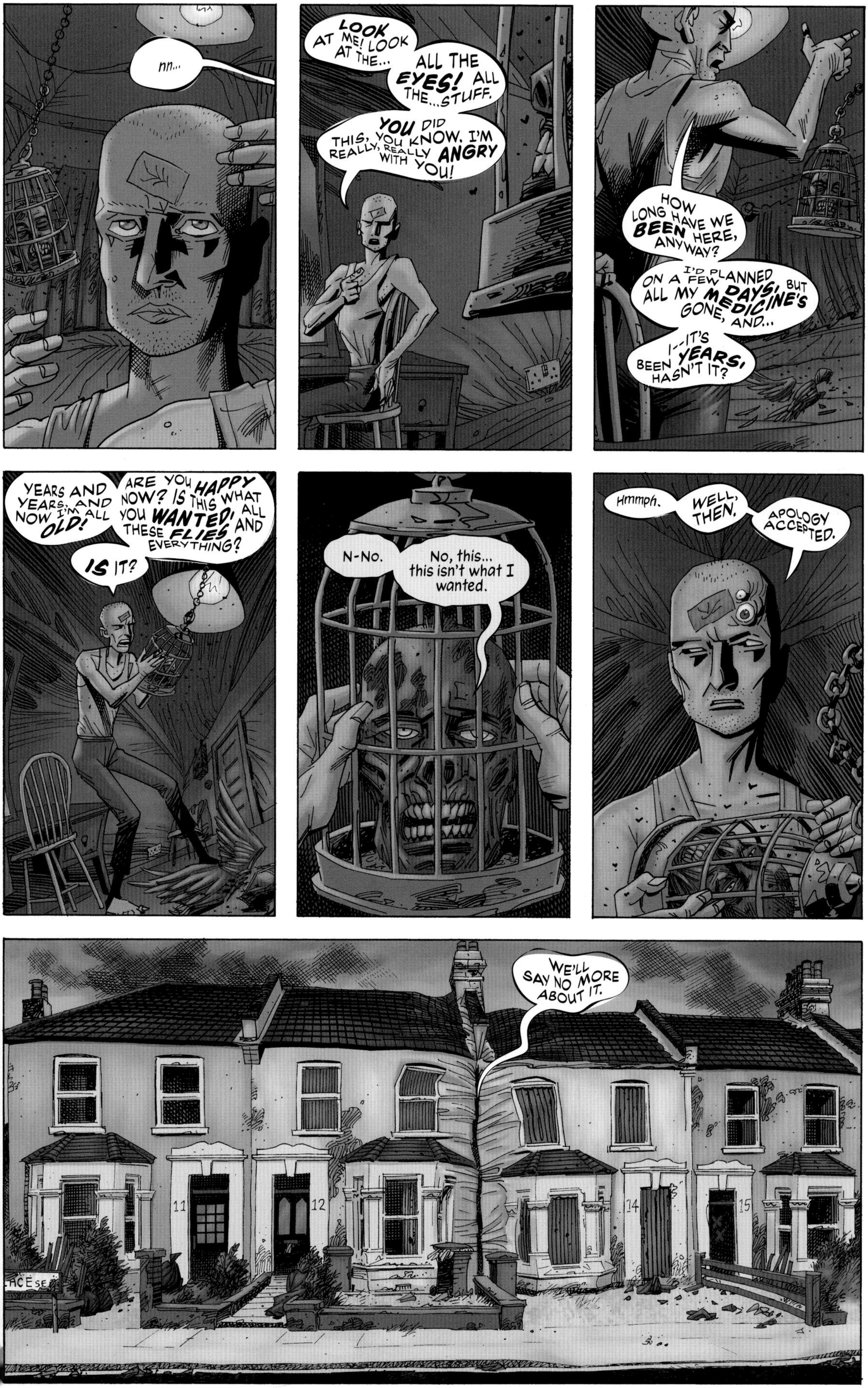
nn...
LOOK AT ME! LOOK AT THE...
ALL THE EYES! ALL THE...STUFF.
YOU DID THIS, YOU KNOW. I'M REALLY, REALLY ANGRY WITH YOU!
HOW LONG HAVE WE BEEN HERE, ANYWAY?
I'D PLANNED ON A FEW DAYS, BUT ALL MY MEDICINE'S GONE, AND...
I--IT'S BEEN YEARS, HASN'T IT?
YEARS AND YEARS, AND NOW I'M ALL OLD!
ARE YOU HAPPY NOW? IS THIS WHAT YOU WANTED, ALL THESE FLIES AND EVERYTHING?
IS IT?
N-No.
No, this... this isn't what I wanted.
Hmmph.
WELL, THEN.
APOLOGY ACCEPTED.
WE'LL SAY NO MORE ABOUT IT.
11
12
14
15

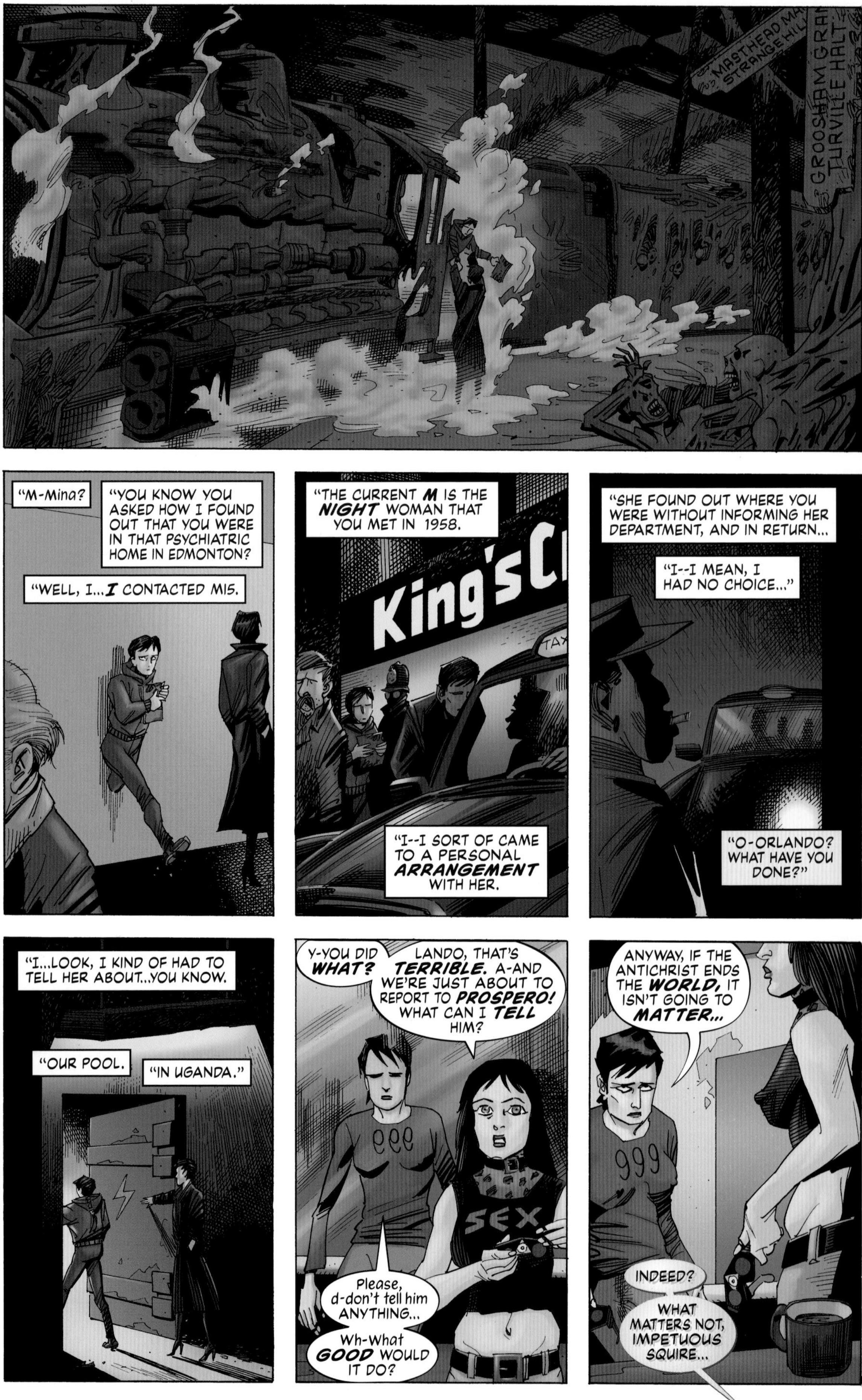
MASTHEAD MA
STRANGE HILL
GROOSHAM GRAN
TURVILLE HALT
"M-Mina?
"YOU KNOW YOU ASKED HOW I FOUND OUT THAT YOU WERE IN THAT PSYCHIATRIC HOME IN EDMONTON?
"WELL, I...I CONTACTED MI5.
"THE CURRENT M IS THE NIGHT WOMAN THAT YOU MET IN 1958.
King's C
"I--I SORT OF CAME TO A PERSONAL ARRANGEMENT WITH HER.
"SHE FOUND OUT WHERE YOU WERE WITHOUT INFORMING HER DEPARTMENT, AND IN RETURN...
"I--I MEAN, I HAD NO CHOICE..."
"O-ORLANDO? WHAT HAVE YOU DONE?"
"I...LOOK, I KIND OF HAD TO TELL HER ABOUT...YOU KNOW.
"OUR POOL.
"IN UGANDA."
Y-YOU DID WHAT?
LANDO, THAT'S TERRIBLE. A-AND WE'RE JUST ABOUT TO REPORT TO PROSPERO! WHAT CAN I TELL HIM?
Please, d-don't tell him ANYTHING...
Wh-What GOOD WOULD IT DO?
SEX
ANYWAY, IF THE ANTICHRIST ENDS THE WORLD, IT ISN'T GOING TO MATTER...
INDEED?
WHAT MATTERS NOT, IMPETUOUS SQUIRE...

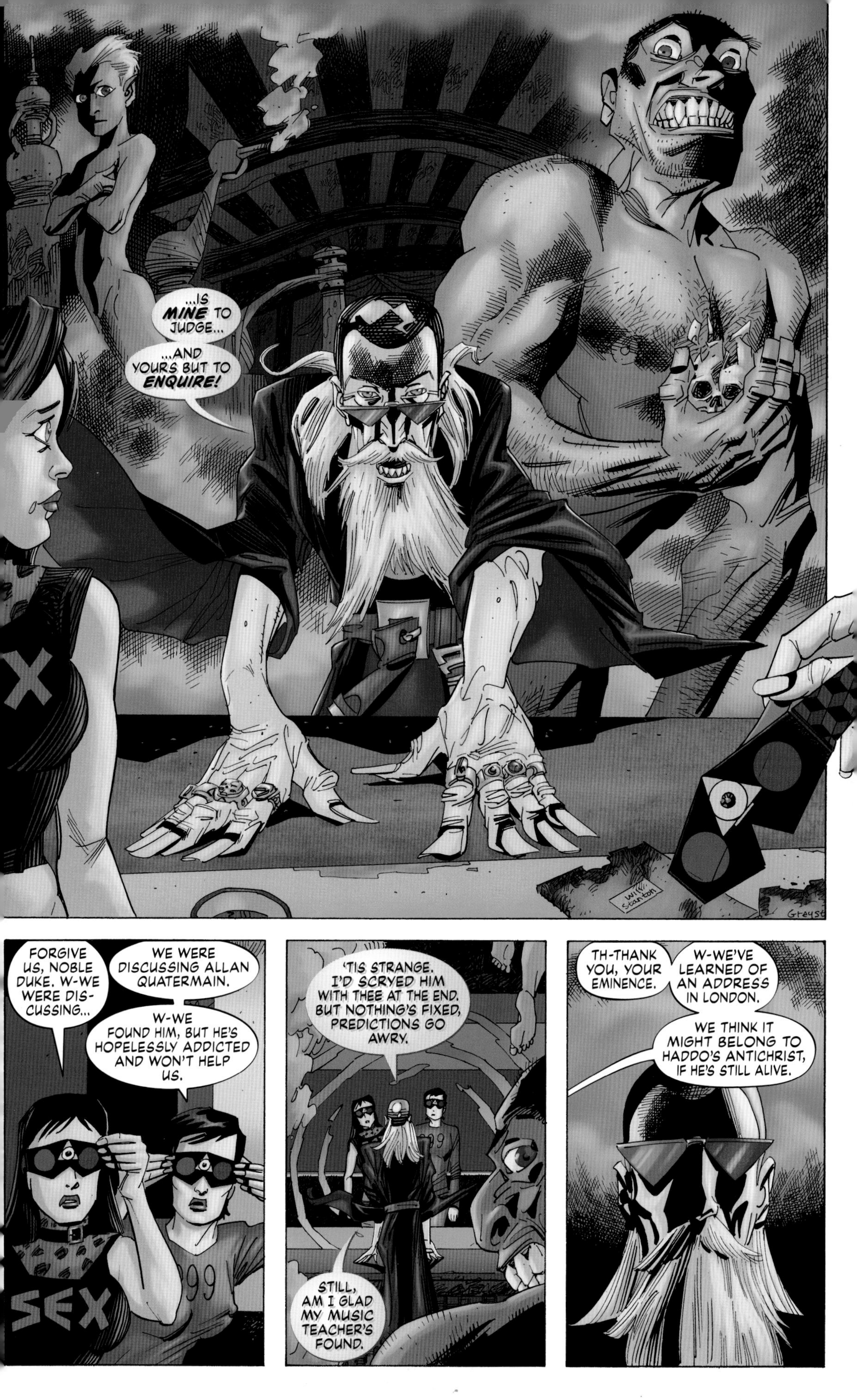
...IS MINE TO JUDGE...
...AND YOURS BUT TO ENQUIRE!
FORGIVE US, NOBLE DUKE. W-WE WERE DIS-CUSSING...
WE WERE DISCUSSING ALLAN QUATERMAIN.
W-WE FOUND HIM, BUT HE'S HOPELESSLY ADDICTED AND WON'T HELP US.
'TIS STRANGE. I'D SCRYED HIM WITH THEE AT THE END. BUT NOTHING'S FIXED, PREDICTIONS GO AWRY.
STILL, AM I GLAD MY MUSIC TEACHER'S FOUND.
TH-THANK YOU, YOUR EMINENCE.
W-WE'VE LEARNED OF AN ADDRESS IN LONDON.
WE THINK IT MIGHT BELONG TO HADDO'S ANTICHRIST, IF HE'S STILL ALIVE.

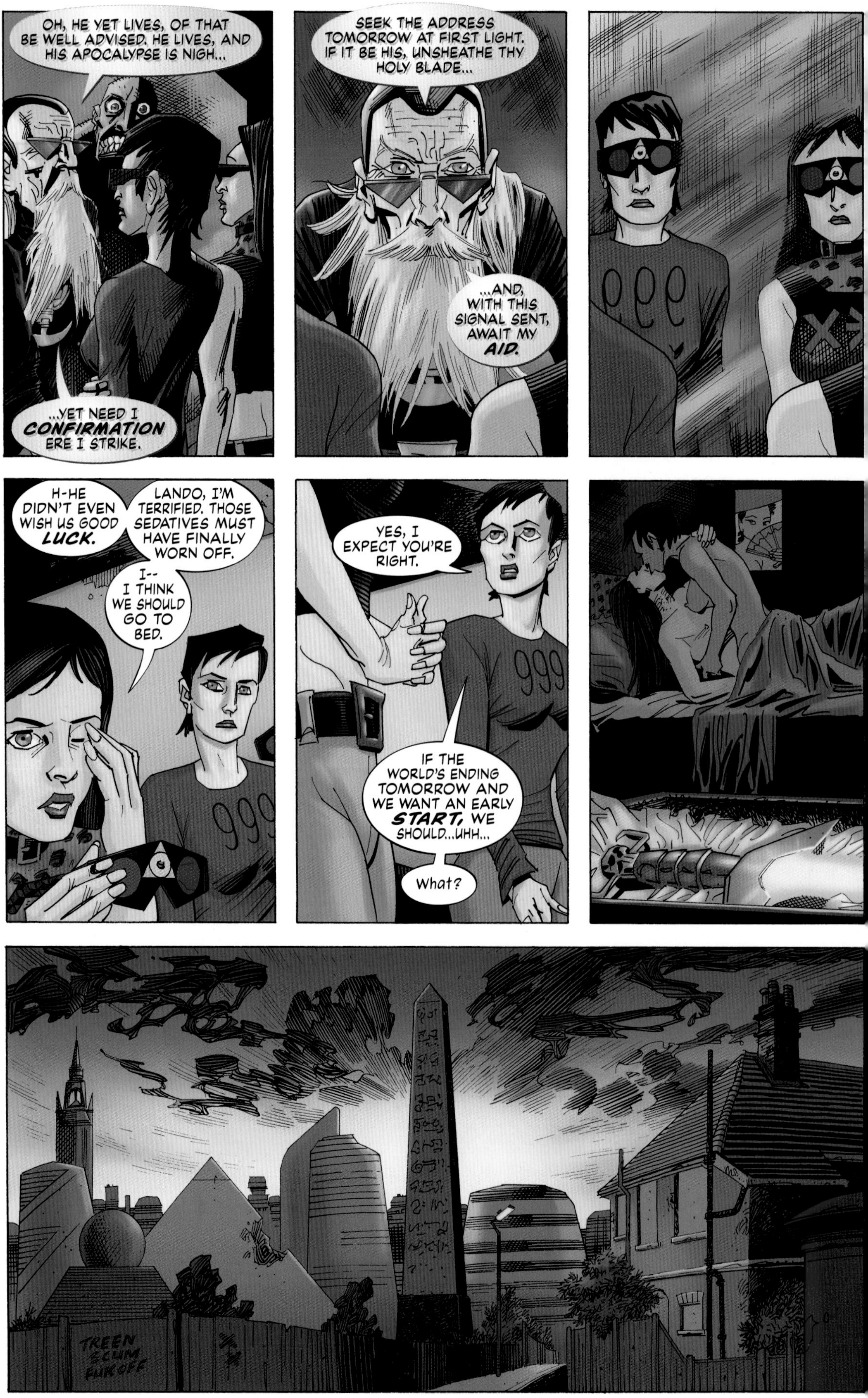
OH, HE YET LIVES, OF THAT BE WELL ADVISED. HE LIVES, AND HIS APOCALYPSE IS NIGH...
...YET NEED I CONFIRMATION ERE I STRIKE.
SEEK THE ADDRESS TOMORROW AT FIRST LIGHT. IF IT BE HIS, UNSHEATHE THY HOLY BLADE...
...AND, WITH THIS SIGNAL SENT, AWAIT MY AID.
H-HE DIDN'T EVEN WISH US GOOD LUCK.
LANDO, I'M TERRIFIED. THOSE SEDATIVES MUST HAVE FINALLY WORN OFF.
I-- I THINK WE SHOULD GO TO BED.
YES, I EXPECT YOU'RE RIGHT.
IF THE WORLD'S ENDING TOMORROW AND WE WANT AN EARLY START, WE SHOULD...UHH...
What?
TREEN SCUM FUK OFF

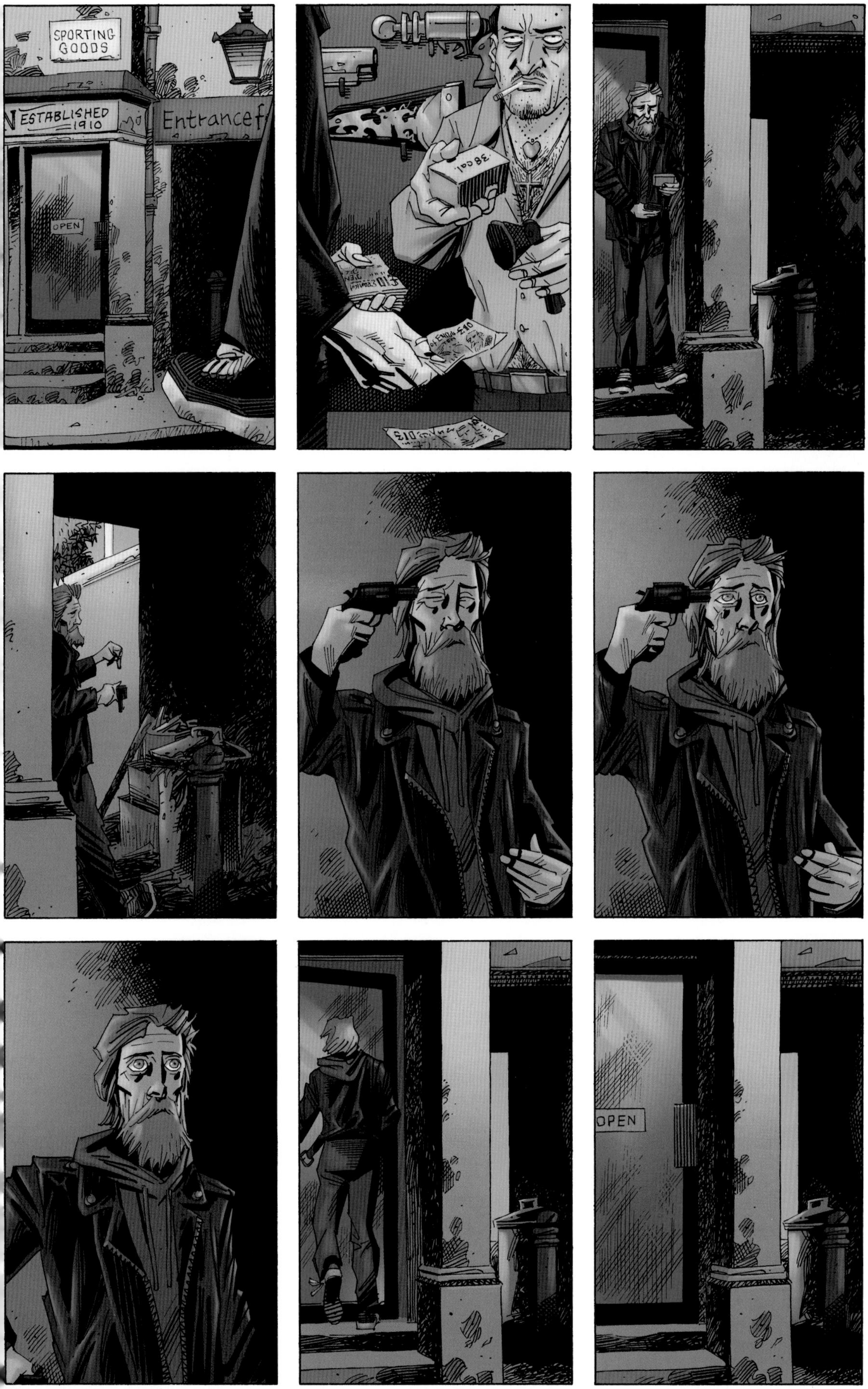
SPORTING GOODS
ESTABLISHED 1910
Entrance
OPEN
OPEN

W-WELL, THIS IS THE RIGHT *STREET*, BUT I CAN'T SEE THE HOUSE-NUMBER ANYWHERE.

LANDO, MOST OF THESE HOUSES LOOK *EMPTY*. HOW LONG HAS LONDON BEEN LIKE THIS?

IT'S THE RECESSION...NOT THAT I SUPPOSE IT MEANS MUCH ANYMORE, IF EVERYTHING'S ENDING.

I-IT'S NOT JUST THE *POVERTY*. PEOPLE WERE *DESPERATELY* POOR IN 1910, BUT AT LEAST THEY FELT THINGS HAD A *PURPOSE*.

HOW DID CULTURE FALL APART IN BARELY A HUNDRED *YEARS?*

BY BECOMING IRRELEVANT, SAME AS ALWAYS.

HAVE YOU SPOTTED THE HOUSE YET?

12

I--I THINK IT'S MORE TO DO WITH WHAT WE'RE *NOT* SPOTTING.

THESE HOUSES, THEY'RE NUMBERED CONSECUTIVELY ROUND THE CLOSE, BUT THERE'S ONE *MISSING*.

AND...IS IT MY EYES, OR IS ALL THE BRICKWORK SORT OF BENDING *INWARD* WHERE I'M STANDING?

I-IT LOOKS...

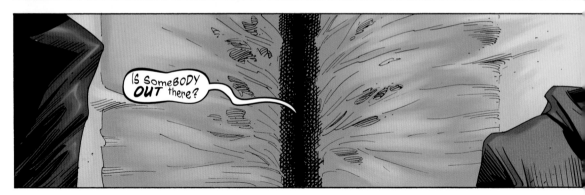

IS SOMEBODY *OUT* THERE?

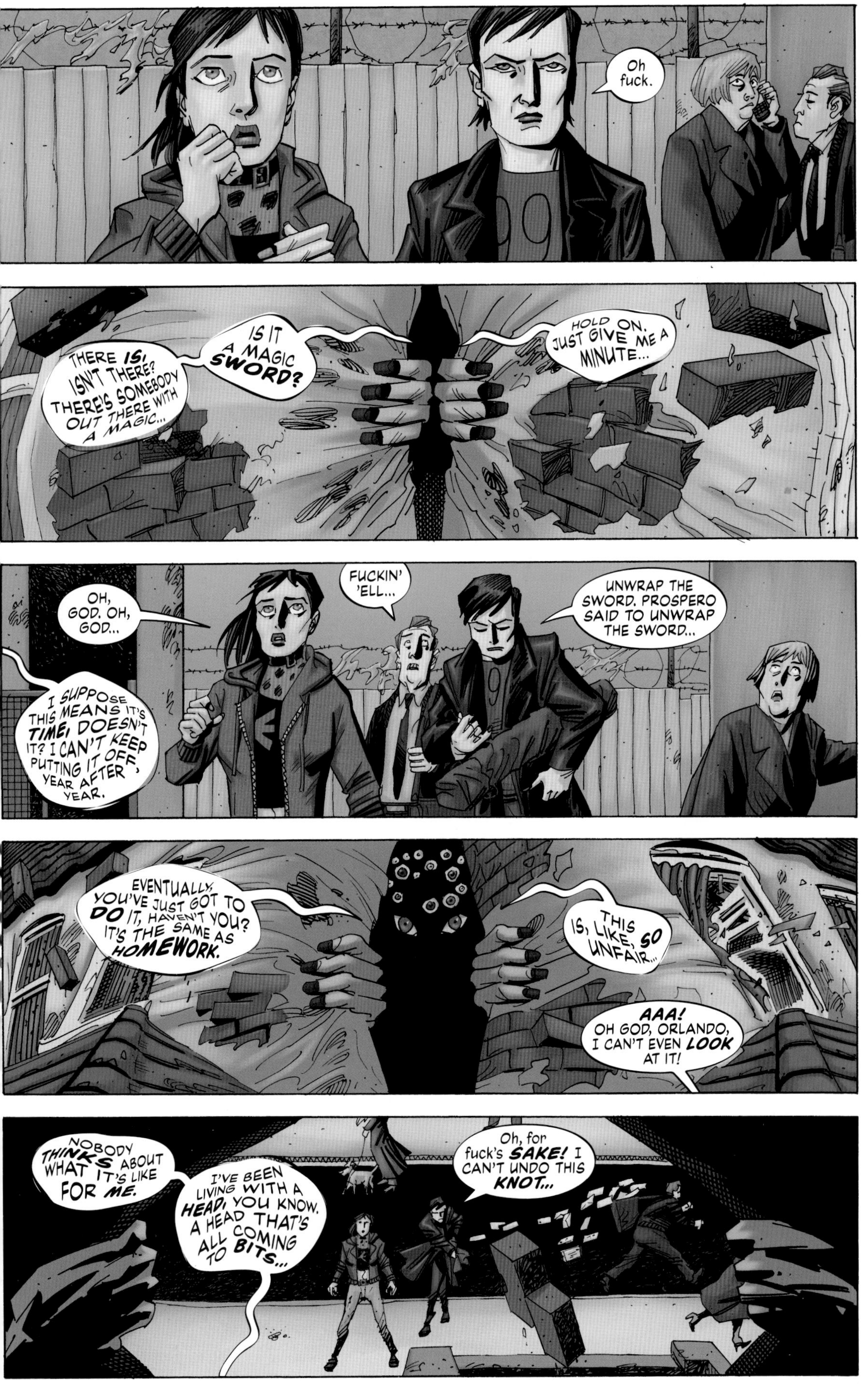
Oh fuck.
THERE IS, ISN'T THERE? THERE'S SOMEBODY OUT THERE WITH A MAGIC...
IS IT A MAGIC SWORD?
HOLD ON. JUST GIVE ME A MINUTE...
OH, GOD. OH, GOD...
FUCKIN' 'ELL...
UNWRAP THE SWORD. PROSPERO SAID TO UNWRAP THE SWORD...
I SUPPOSE THIS MEANS IT'S TIME, DOESN'T IT? I CAN'T KEEP PUTTING IT OFF, YEAR AFTER YEAR.
EVENTUALLY, YOU'VE JUST GOT TO DO IT, HAVEN'T YOU? IT'S THE SAME AS HOMEWORK.
THIS IS, LIKE, SO UNFAIR...
AAA! OH GOD, ORLANDO, I CAN'T EVEN LOOK AT IT!
NOBODY THINKS ABOUT WHAT IT'S LIKE FOR ME.
I'VE BEEN LIVING WITH A HEAD, YOU KNOW. A HEAD THAT'S ALL COMING TO BITS...
Oh, for fuck's SAKE! I CAN'T UNDO THIS KNOT...

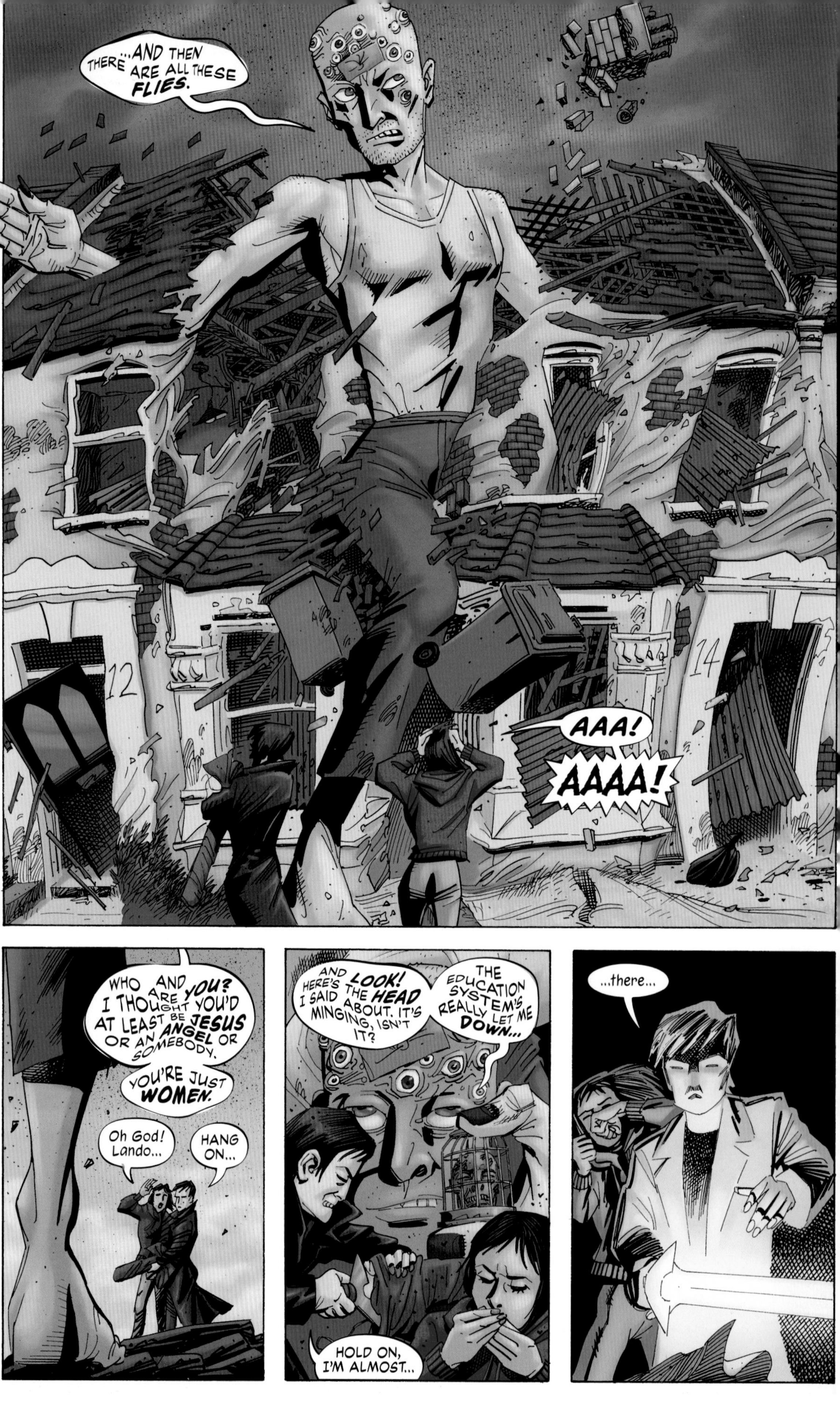
...AND THEN THERE ARE ALL THESE FLIES.
AAA!
AAAA!
WHO ARE YOU?
AND I THOUGHT YOU'D AT LEAST BE JESUS OR AN ANGEL OR SOMEBODY.
YOU'RE JUST WOMEN.
Oh God! Lando...
HANG ON...
AND LOOK! HERE'S THE HEAD I SAID ABOUT. IT'S MINGING, ISN'T IT?
THE EDUCATION SYSTEM'S REALLY LET ME DOWN...
HOLD ON, I'M ALMOST...
...there...

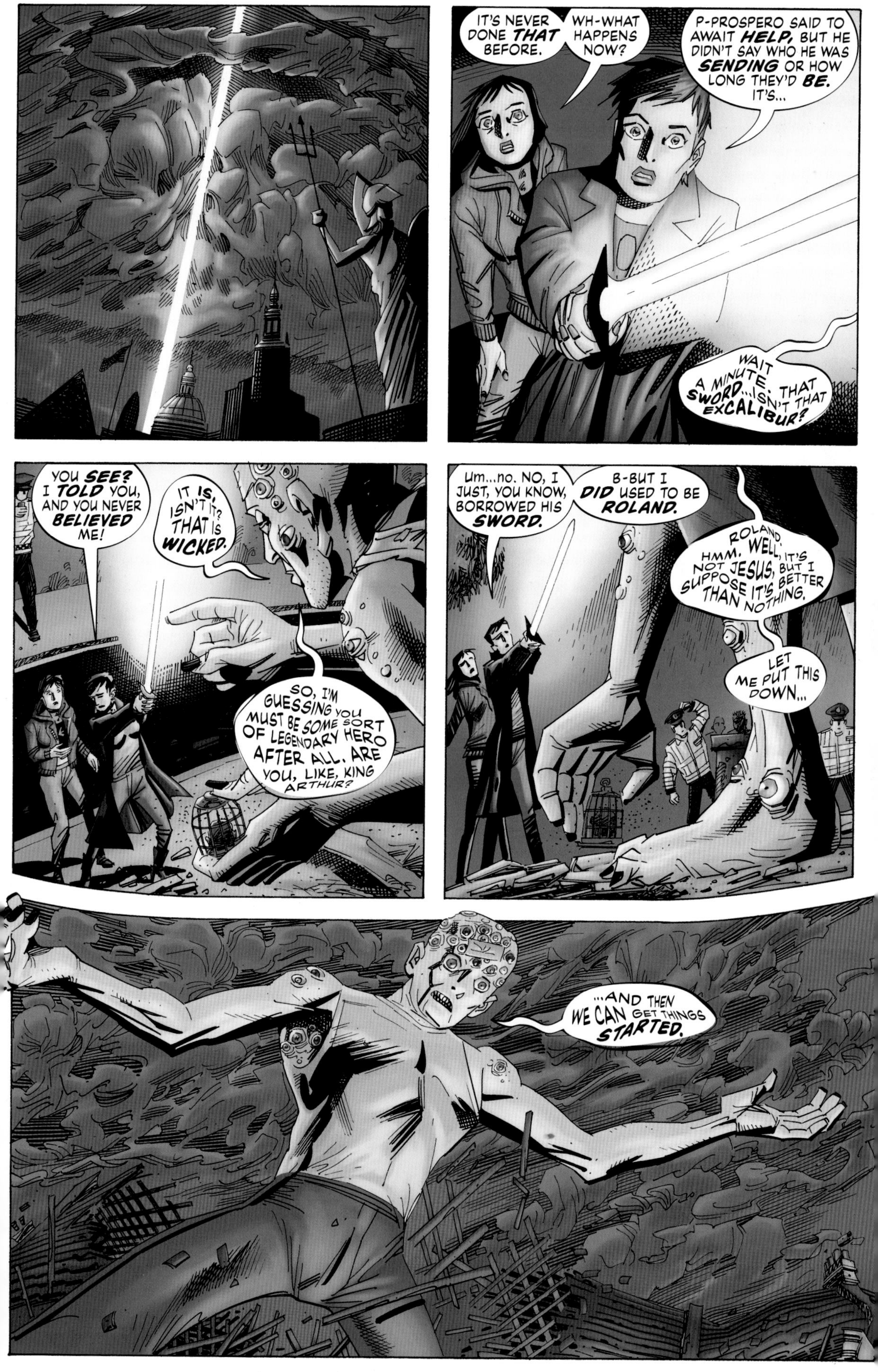
IT'S NEVER DONE THAT BEFORE.
WH-WHAT HAPPENS NOW?
P-PROSPERO SAID TO AWAIT HELP, BUT HE DIDN'T SAY WHO HE WAS SENDING OR HOW LONG THEY'D BE. IT'S...
WAIT A MINUTE. THAT SWORD...ISN'T THAT EXCALIBUR?
YOU SEE? I TOLD YOU, AND YOU NEVER BELIEVED ME!
IT IS, ISN'T IT? THAT IS WICKED.
SO, I'M GUESSING YOU MUST BE SOME SORT OF LEGENDARY HERO AFTER ALL. ARE YOU, LIKE, KING ARTHUR?
Um...no. NO, I JUST, YOU KNOW, BORROWED HIS SWORD.
B-BUT I DID USED TO BE ROLAND.
ROLAND. HMM. WELL, IT'S NOT JESUS, BUT I SUPPOSE IT'S BETTER THAN NOTHING.
LET ME PUT THIS DOWN...
...AND THEN WE CAN GET THINGS STARTED.

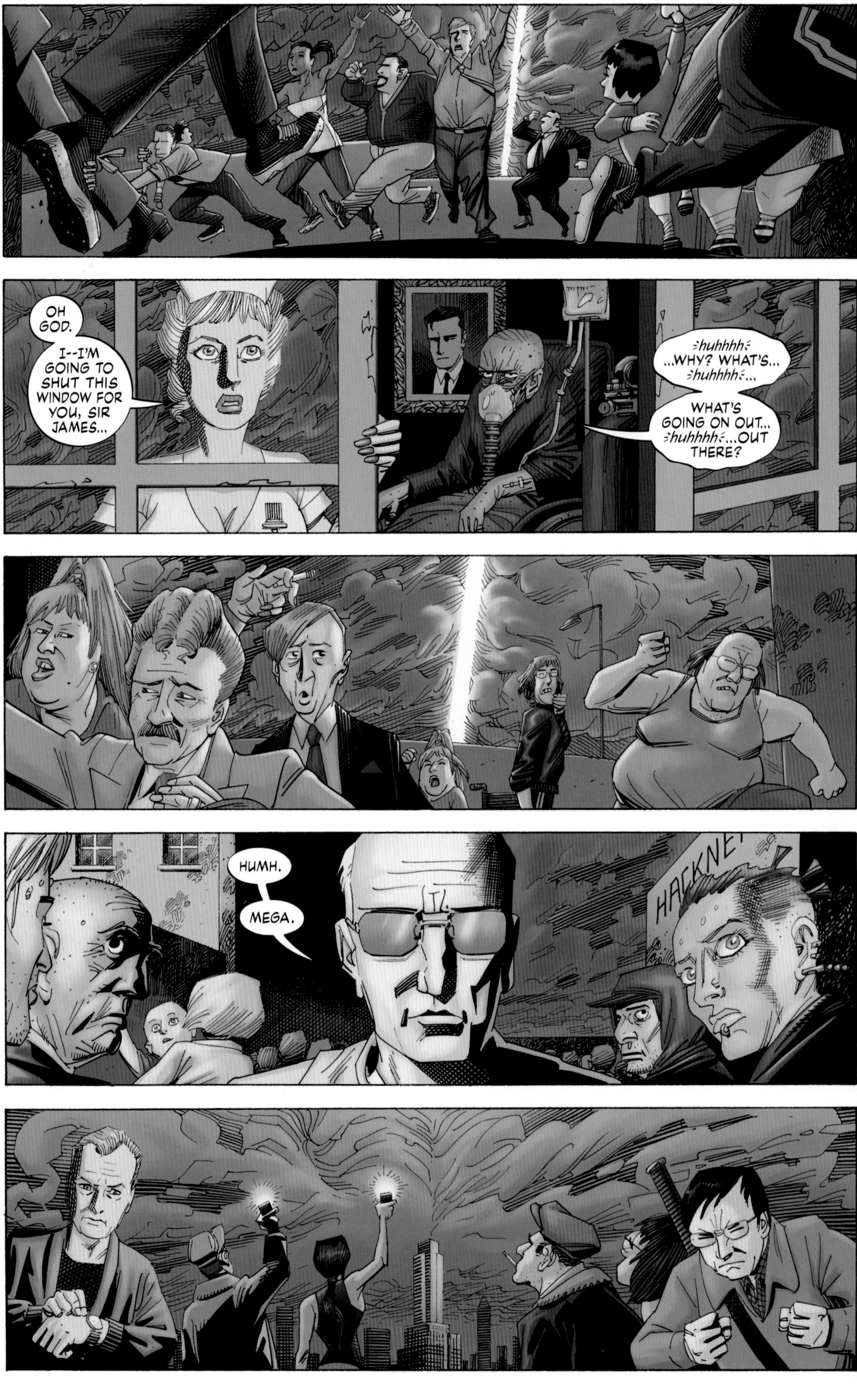
OH GOD.
I--I'M GOING TO SHUT THIS WINDOW FOR YOU, SIR JAMES...
huhhhh ...WHY? WHAT'S... huhhhh ...
WHAT'S GOING ON OUT... huhhhh ...OUT THERE?
HUMH.
MEGA.
HACKNEY

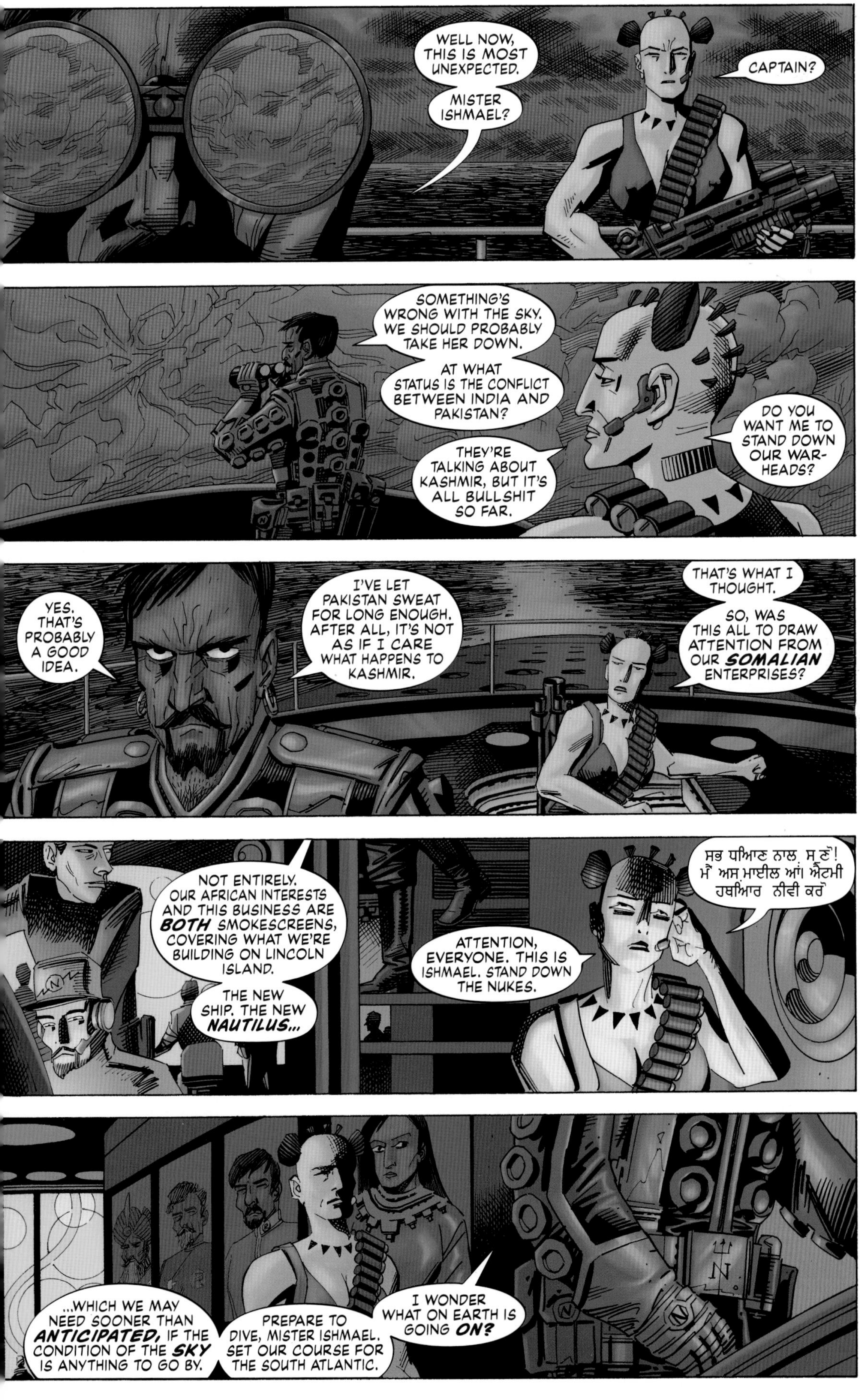
WELL NOW, THIS IS MOST UNEXPECTED.
MISTER ISHMAEL?
CAPTAIN?
SOMETHING'S WRONG WITH THE SKY. WE SHOULD PROBABLY TAKE HER DOWN.
AT WHAT STATUS IS THE CONFLICT BETWEEN INDIA AND PAKISTAN?
THEY'RE TALKING ABOUT KASHMIR, BUT IT'S ALL BULLSHIT SO FAR.
DO YOU WANT ME TO STAND DOWN OUR WAR-HEADS?
YES. THAT'S PROBABLY A GOOD IDEA.
I'VE LET PAKISTAN SWEAT FOR LONG ENOUGH. AFTER ALL, IT'S NOT AS IF I CARE WHAT HAPPENS TO KASHMIR.
THAT'S WHAT I THOUGHT.
SO, WAS THIS ALL TO DRAW ATTENTION FROM OUR **SOMALIAN** ENTERPRISES?
NOT ENTIRELY. OUR AFRICAN INTERESTS AND THIS BUSINESS ARE **BOTH** SMOKESCREENS, COVERING WHAT WE'RE BUILDING ON LINCOLN ISLAND.
THE NEW SHIP. THE NEW **NAUTILUS...**
ਸਭ ਧਿਆਨ ਨਾਲ ਸੁਣੋ! ਮੈਂ ਅਸ਼ਮਾਈਲ ਆਂ। ਐਟਮੀ ਹਥਿਆਰ ਨੀਵੀ ਕਰੋ
ATTENTION, EVERYONE. THIS IS ISHMAEL. STAND DOWN THE NUKES.
...WHICH WE MAY NEED SOONER THAN **ANTICIPATED,** IF THE CONDITION OF THE **SKY** IS ANYTHING TO GO BY.
PREPARE TO DIVE, MISTER ISHMAEL. SET OUR COURSE FOR THE SOUTH ATLANTIC.
I WONDER WHAT ON EARTH IS GOING **ON?**

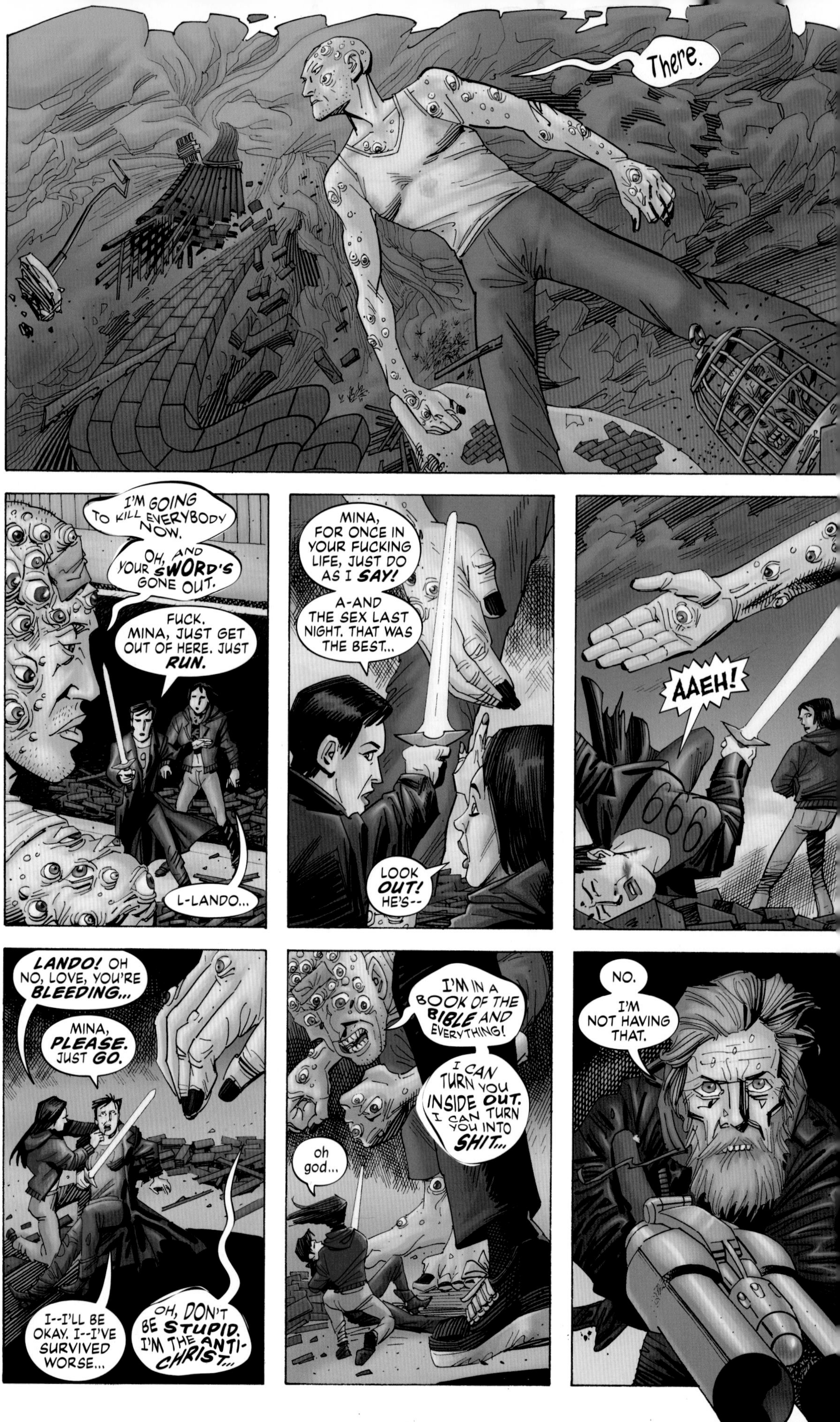
There.
I'M GOING TO KILL EVERYBODY NOW.
OH, AND YOUR SWORD'S GONE OUT.
FUCK. MINA, JUST GET OUT OF HERE. JUST RUN.
L-LANDO...
MINA, FOR ONCE IN YOUR FUCKING LIFE, JUST DO AS I SAY!
A-AND THE SEX LAST NIGHT. THAT WAS THE BEST...
LOOK OUT! HE'S--
AAEH!
LANDO! OH NO, LOVE, YOU'RE BLEEDING...
MINA, PLEASE. JUST GO.
I--I'LL BE OKAY. I--I'VE SURVIVED WORSE...
OH, DON'T BE STUPID. I'M THE ANTI-CHRIST...
I'M IN A BOOK OF THE BIBLE AND EVERYTHING!
I CAN TURN YOU INSIDE OUT. I CAN TURN YOU INTO SHIT...
oh god...
NO.
I'M NOT HAVING THAT.

...BLOODY THING. BLOODY FUCKING THING...

A-Allan?

ALLAN, WHAT ARE YOU DOING? W-WE THOUGHT YOU WERE...

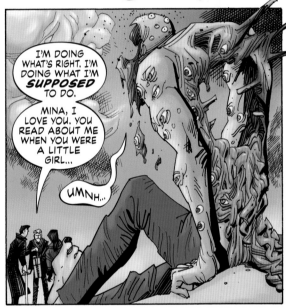

I'M DOING WHAT'S RIGHT. I'M DOING WHAT I'M **SUPPOSED** TO DO.

MINA, I LOVE YOU. YOU READ ABOUT ME WHEN YOU WERE A LITTLE GIRL...

UMNH...

...AND THAT'S WHO I **AM.** I'M **NOT** THIS FUCKING MESS. TH-THAT'S NOT HOW I WANT TO GO OUT.

I'M SOMEBODY **GOOD.** I'M ALLAN QUATERMAIN...

D-Darling, YOU...YOU DIDN'T NEED TO...

OH, SHIT. LOOK OUT. HE'S...

WHAT?

WHAT THE FUCK IS HE...?

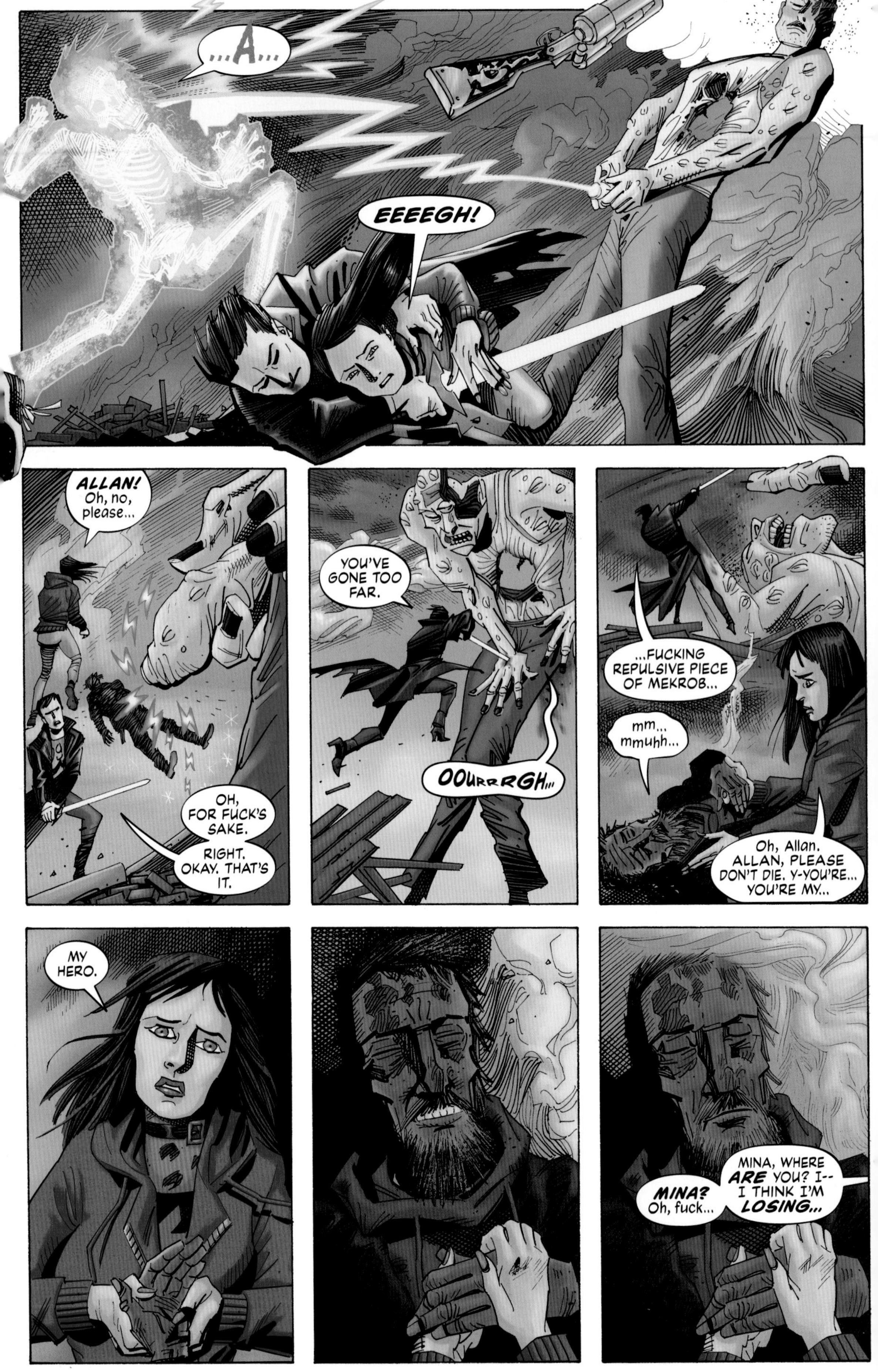
...A...
EEEEGH!
ALLAN! Oh, no, please...
OH, FOR FUCK'S SAKE.
RIGHT. OKAY. THAT'S IT.
YOU'VE GONE TOO FAR.
OOURRRGH...
...FUCKING REPULSIVE PIECE OF MEKROB...
mm... mmuhh...
Oh, Allan. ALLAN, PLEASE DON'T DIE. Y-YOU'RE... YOU'RE MY...
MY HERO.
MINA? Oh, fuck...
MINA, WHERE ARE YOU? I-- I THINK I'M LOSING...

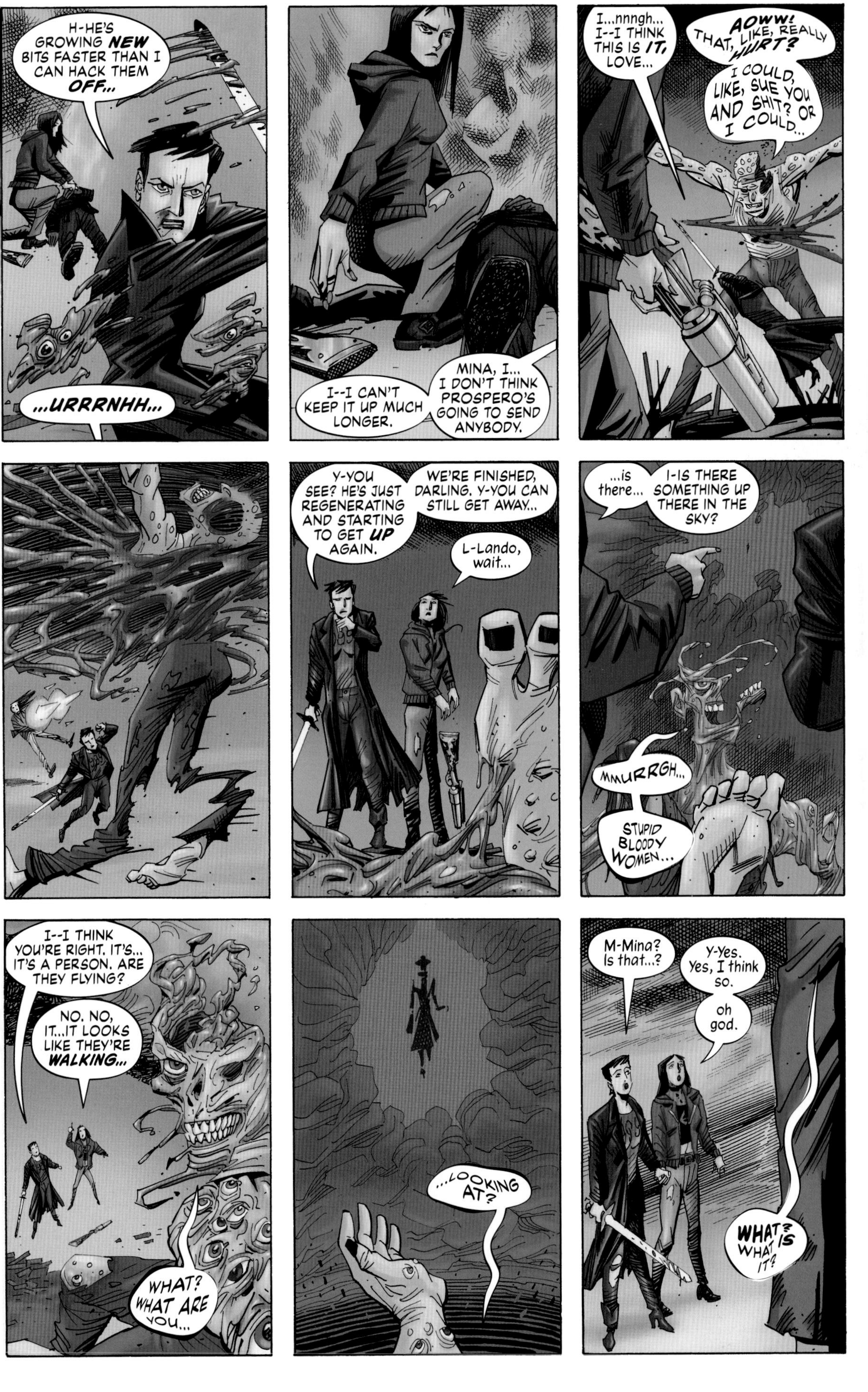

H-HE'S GROWING NEW BITS FASTER THAN I CAN HACK THEM OFF...
...URRRNHH...
I--I CAN'T KEEP IT UP MUCH LONGER.
MINA, I... I DON'T THINK PROSPERO'S GOING TO SEND ANYBODY.
I...nnngh... I--I THINK THIS IS IT, LOVE...
AOWW! THAT, LIKE, REALLY HURT?
I COULD, LIKE, SUE YOU AND SHIT? OR I COULD...
Y-YOU SEE? HE'S JUST REGENERATING AND STARTING TO GET UP AGAIN.
WE'RE FINISHED, DARLING. Y-YOU CAN STILL GET AWAY...
L-Lando, wait...
...is there...
I-IS THERE SOMETHING UP THERE IN THE SKY?
MMURRGH...
STUPID BLOODY WOMEN...
I--I THINK YOU'RE RIGHT. IT'S... IT'S A PERSON. ARE THEY FLYING?
NO. NO, IT...IT LOOKS LIKE THEY'RE WALKING...
WHAT? WHAT ARE YOU...
...LOOKING AT?
M-Mina? Is that...?
Y-Yes. Yes, I think so.
oh god.
WHAT? WHAT IS IT?

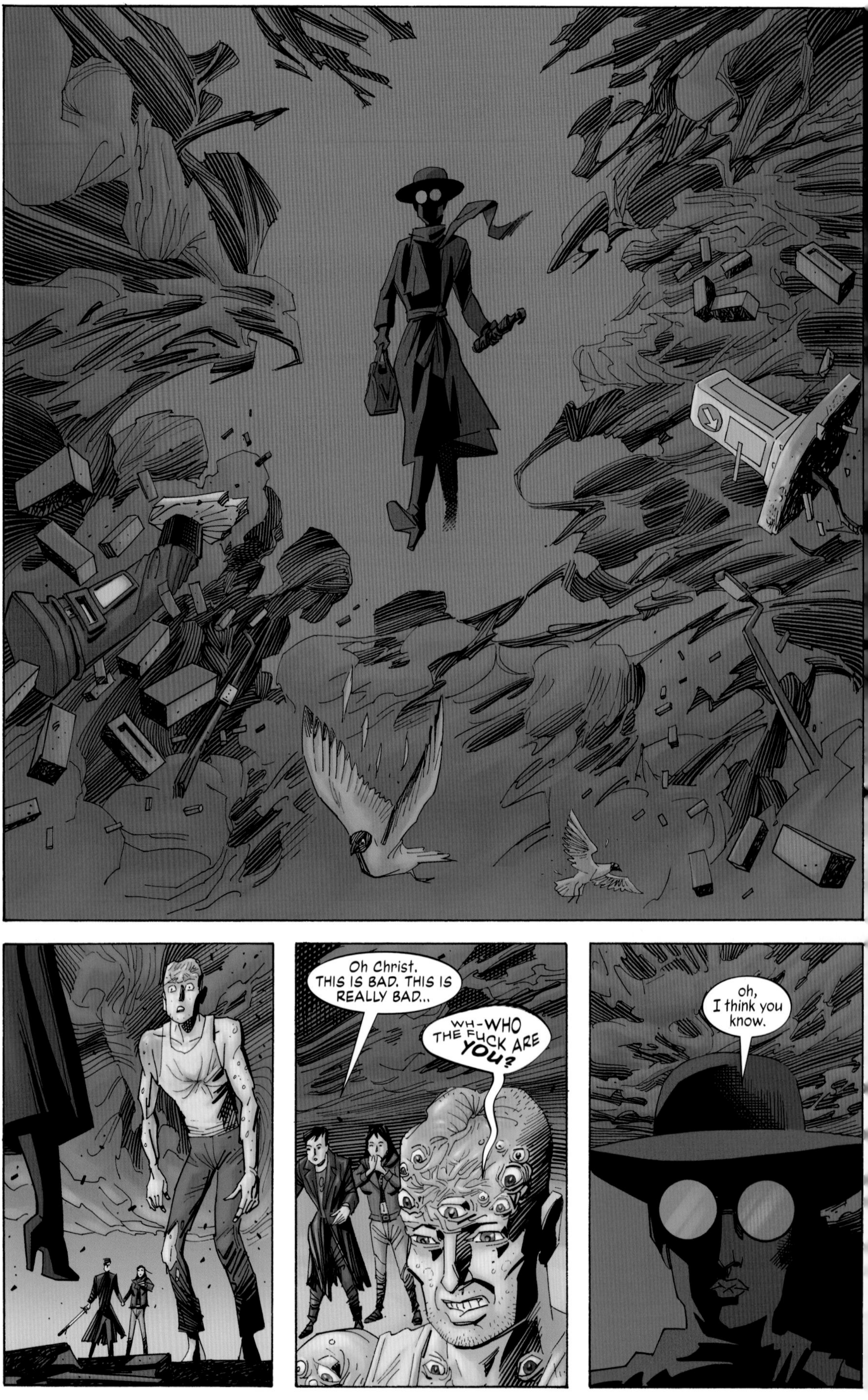
Oh Christ. THIS IS BAD. THIS IS REALLY BAD...
WH-WHO THE FUCK ARE YOU?
oh, I think you know.

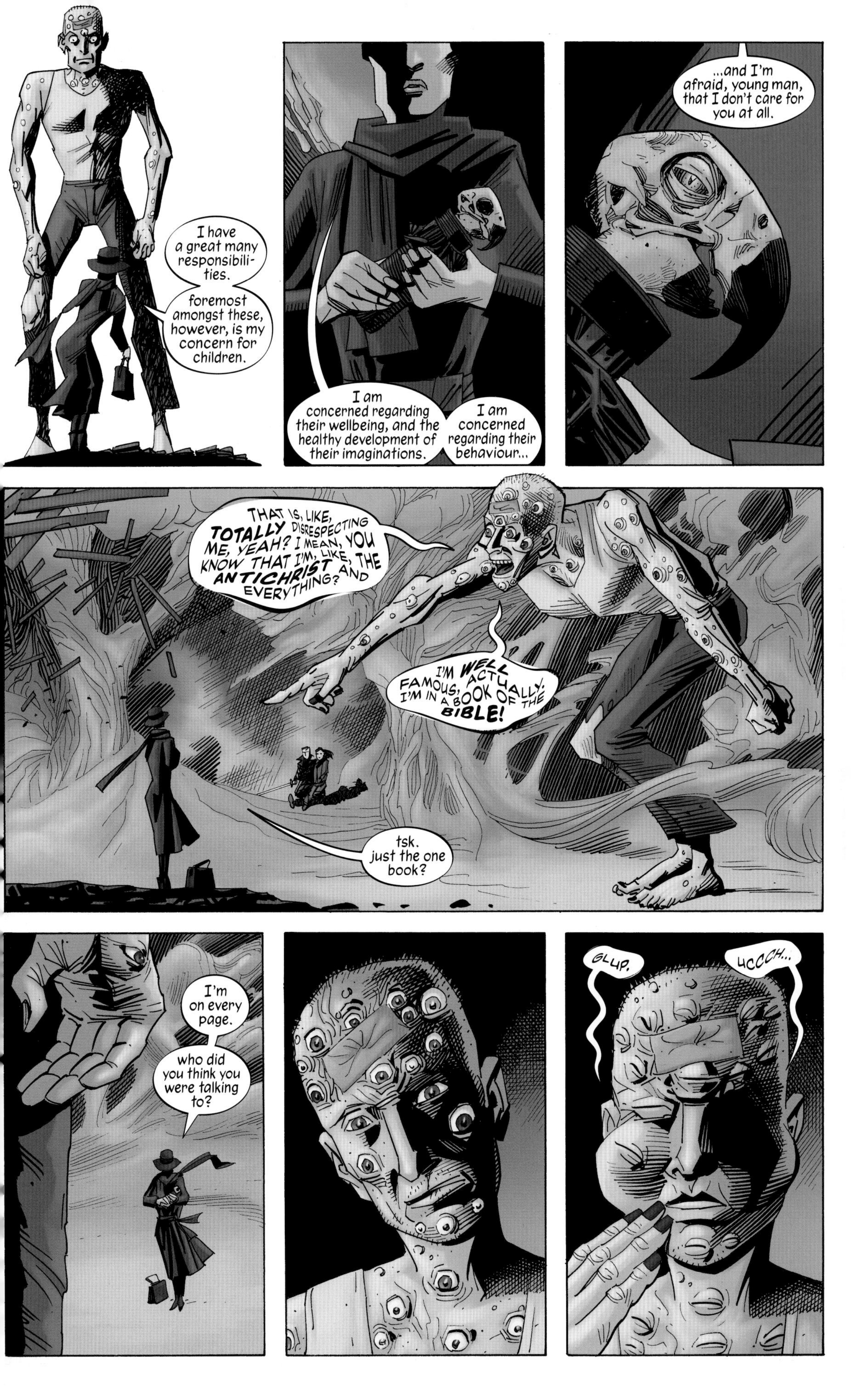
I have a great many responsibili-ties.
foremost amongst these, however, is my concern for children.
I am concerned regarding their wellbeing, and the healthy development of their imaginations.
I am concerned regarding their behaviour...
...and I'm afraid, young man, that I don't care for you at all.
THAT IS, LIKE, TOTALLY DISRESPECTING ME, YEAH? I MEAN, YOU KNOW THAT I'M, LIKE, THE ANTICHRIST AND EVERYTHING?
I'M WELL FAMOUS, ACTUALLY. I'M IN A BOOK OF THE BIBLE!
tsk. just the one book?
I'm on every page.
who did you think you were talking to?
GLUP.
UCCCH...

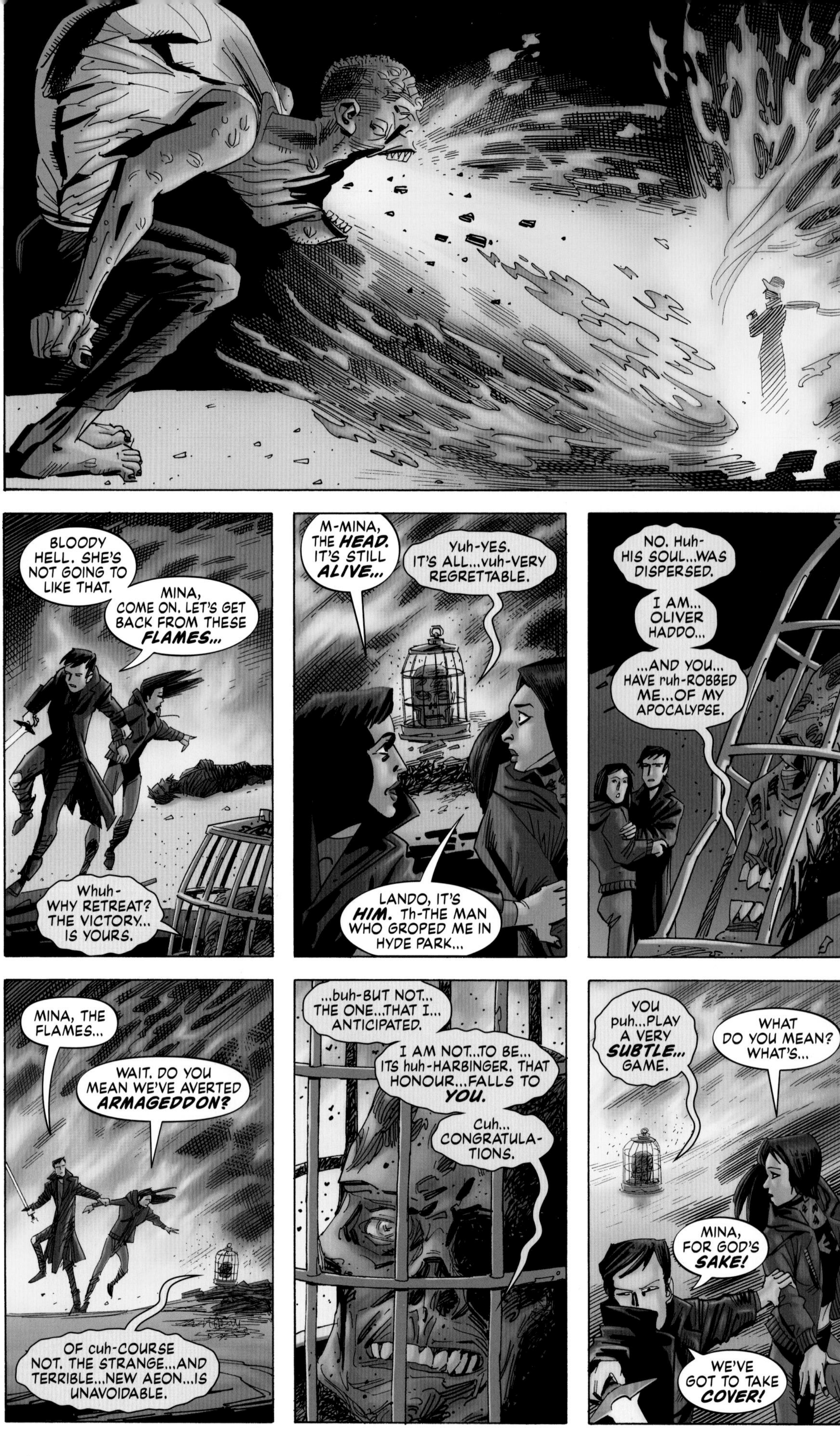
BLOODY HELL. SHE'S NOT GOING TO LIKE THAT.
MINA, COME ON. LET'S GET BACK FROM THESE FLAMES...
Whuh-WHY RETREAT? THE VICTORY... IS YOURS.
M-MINA, THE HEAD. IT'S STILL ALIVE...
Yuh-YES. IT'S ALL...vuh-VERY REGRETTABLE.
LANDO, IT'S HIM. Th-THE MAN WHO GROPED ME IN HYDE PARK...
NO. Huh-HIS SOUL...WAS DISPERSED.
I AM... OLIVER HADDO...
...AND YOU... HAVE ruh-ROBBED ME...OF MY APOCALYPSE.
MINA, THE FLAMES...
WAIT. DO YOU MEAN WE'VE AVERTED ARMAGEDDON?
OF cuh-COURSE NOT. THE STRANGE...AND TERRIBLE...NEW AEON...IS UNAVOIDABLE.
...buh-BUT NOT... THE ONE...THAT I... ANTICIPATED.
I AM NOT...TO BE... ITS huh-HARBINGER. THAT HONOUR...FALLS TO YOU.
Cuh... CONGRATULA-TIONS.
YOU puh...PLAY A VERY SUBTLE... GAME.
WHAT DO YOU MEAN? WHAT'S...
MINA, FOR GOD'S SAKE!
WE'VE GOT TO TAKE COVER!

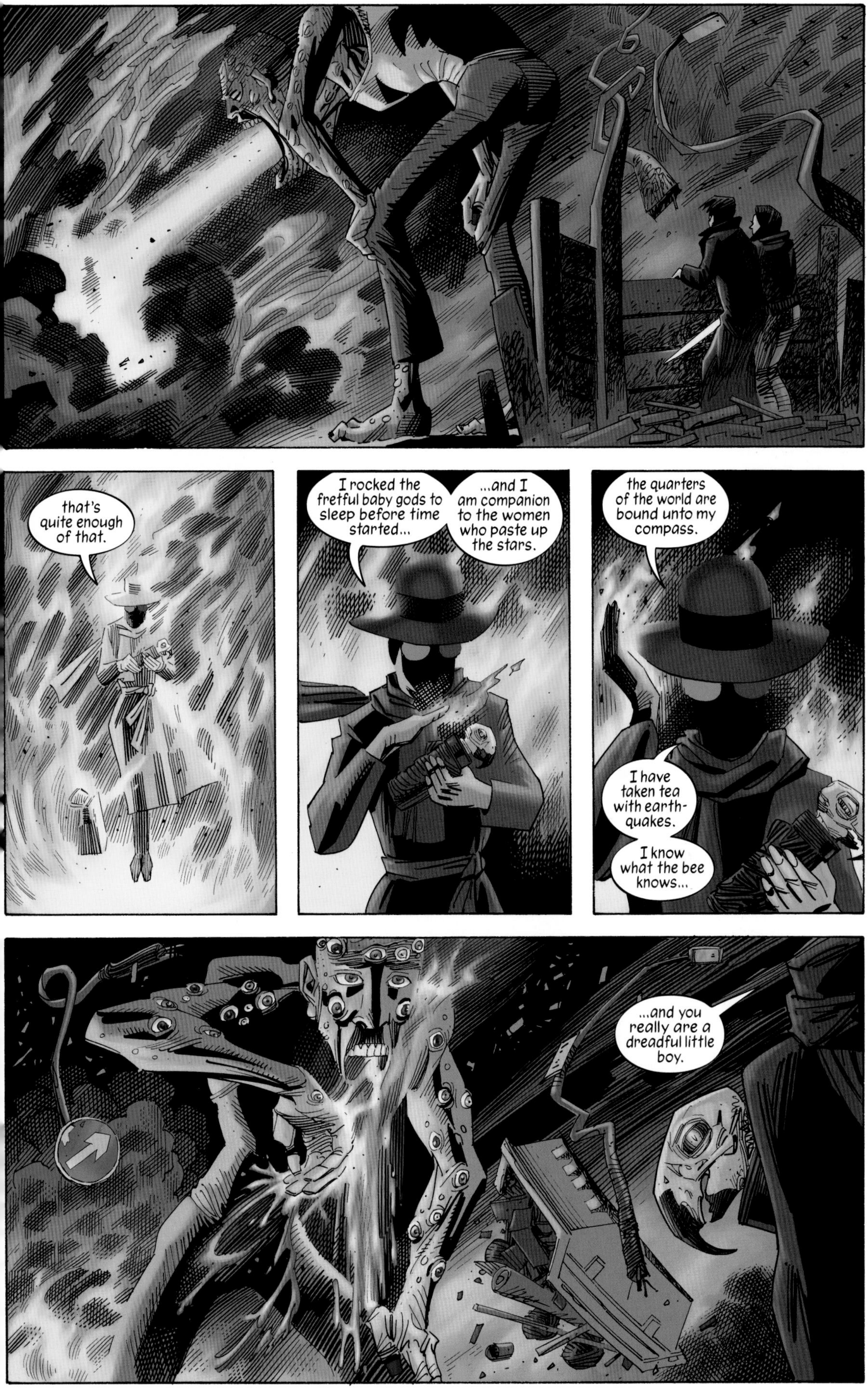
that's quite enough of that.
I rocked the fretful baby gods to sleep before time started...
...and I am companion to the women who paste up the stars.
the quarters of the world are bound unto my compass.
I have taken tea with earth-quakes.
I know what the bee knows...
...and you really are a dreadful little boy.

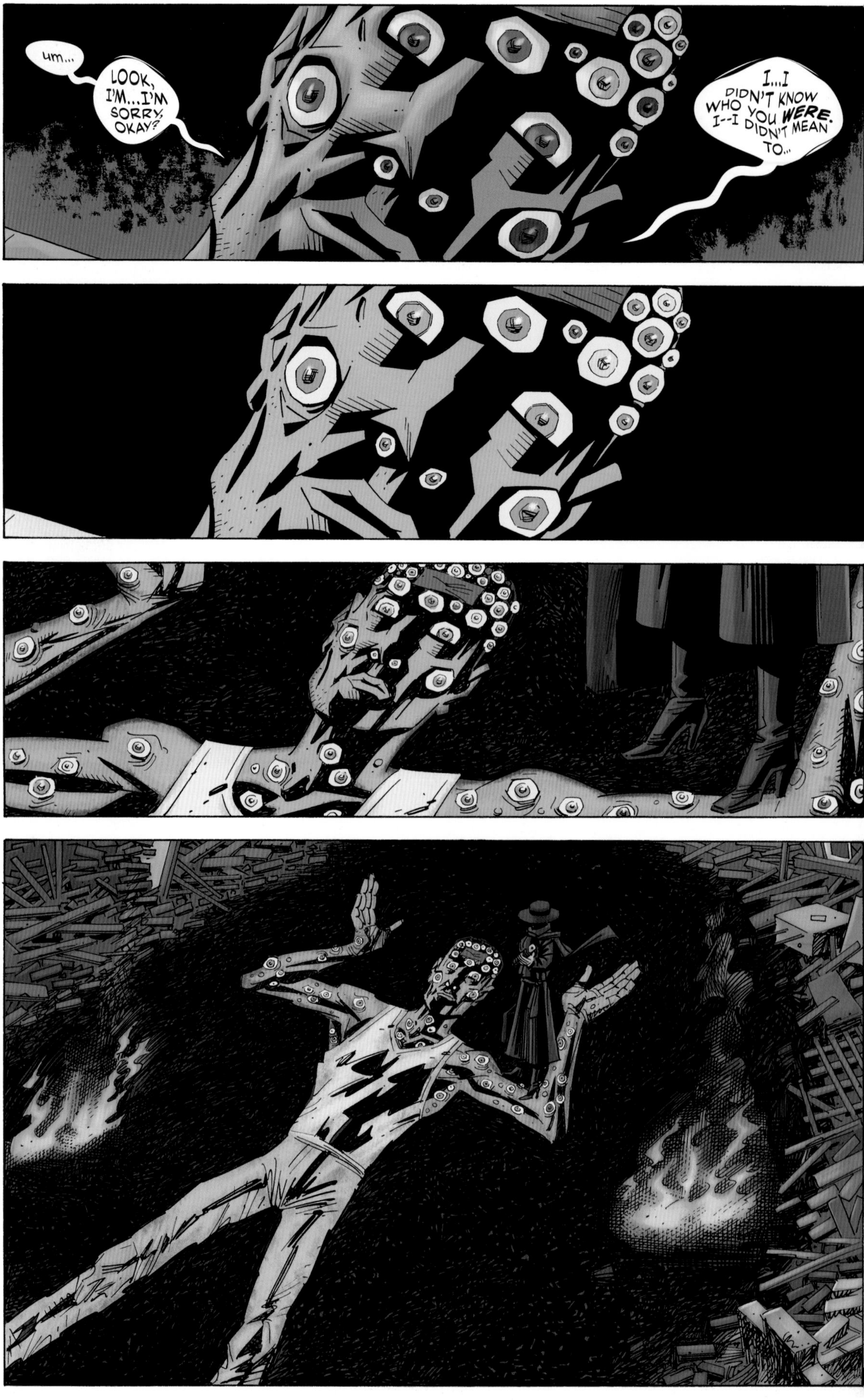
um...
LOOK, I'M...I'M SORRY, OKAY?
I...I DIDN'T KNOW WHO YOU WERE. I--I DIDN'T MEAN TO...

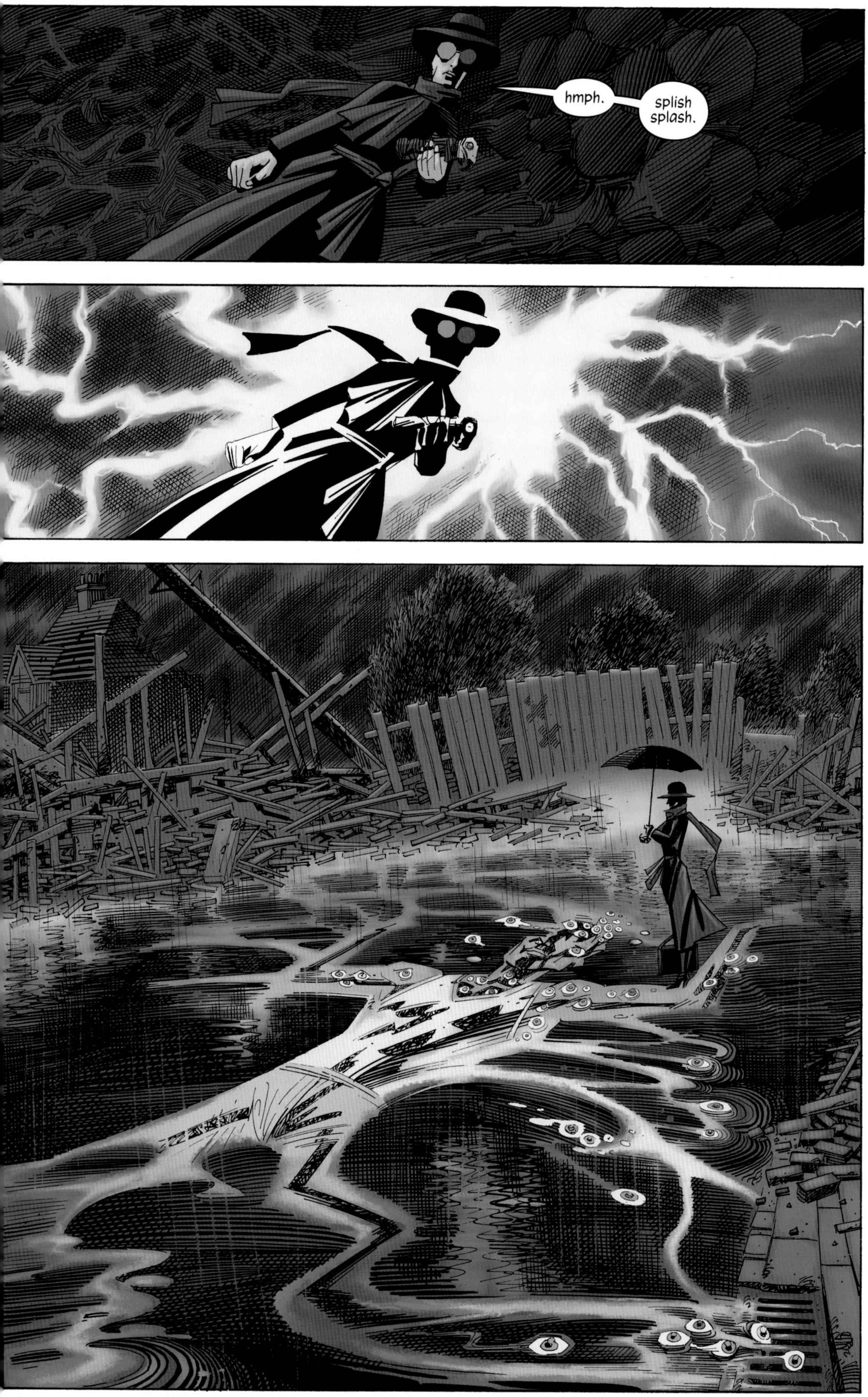
hmph.
splish splash.

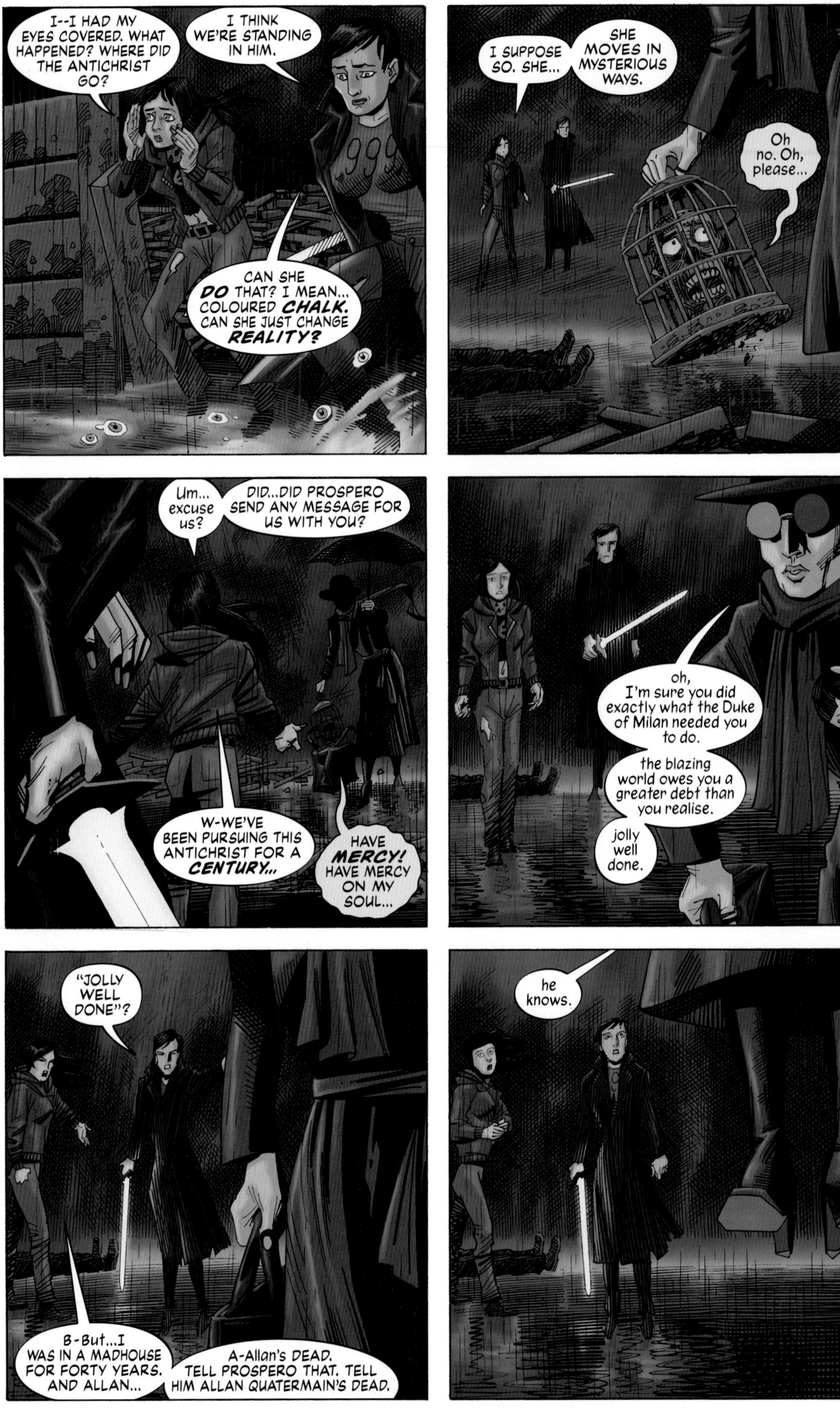
I--I HAD MY EYES COVERED. WHAT HAPPENED? WHERE DID THE ANTICHRIST GO?
I THINK WE'RE STANDING IN HIM.
CAN SHE **DO** THAT? I MEAN... COLOURED **CHALK.** CAN SHE JUST CHANGE **REALITY?**
I SUPPOSE SO. SHE...
SHE MOVES IN MYSTERIOUS WAYS.
Oh no. Oh, please...
Um... excuse us?
DID...DID PROSPERO SEND ANY MESSAGE FOR US WITH YOU?
W-WE'VE BEEN PURSUING THIS ANTICHRIST FOR A **CENTURY...**
HAVE **MERCY!** HAVE MERCY ON MY SOUL...
oh, I'm sure you did exactly what the Duke of Milan needed you to do.
the blazing world owes you a greater debt than you realise.
jolly well done.
"JOLLY WELL DONE"?
B-But...I WAS IN A MADHOUSE FOR FORTY YEARS. AND ALLAN...
A-Allan's DEAD. TELL PROSPERO THAT. TELL HIM ALLAN QUATERMAIN'S DEAD.
he knows.

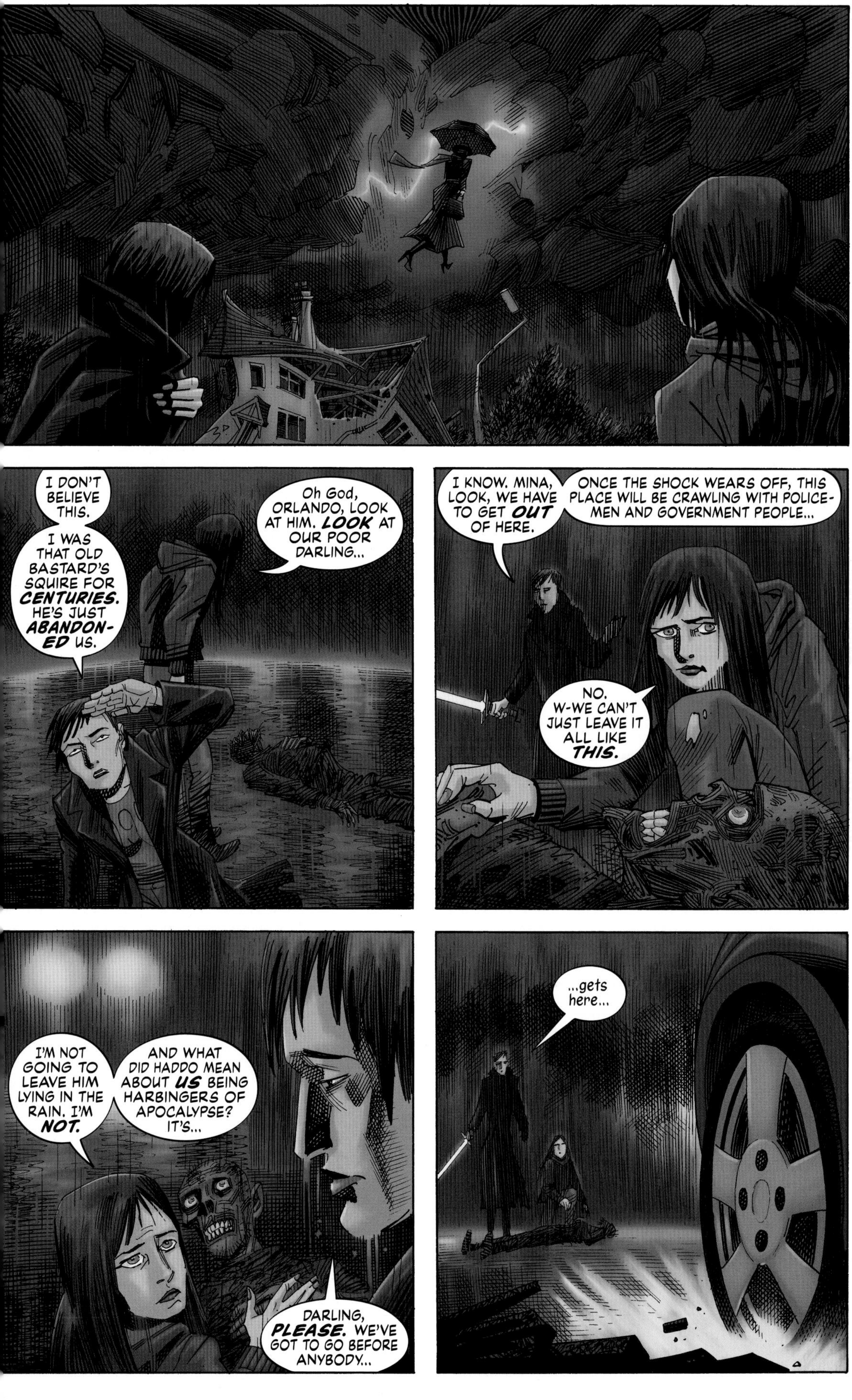

I DON'T BELIEVE THIS.
I WAS THAT OLD BASTARD'S SQUIRE FOR CENTURIES. HE'S JUST ABANDONED US.
Oh God, ORLANDO, LOOK AT HIM. LOOK AT OUR POOR DARLING...
I KNOW. MINA, LOOK, WE HAVE TO GET OUT OF HERE.
ONCE THE SHOCK WEARS OFF, THIS PLACE WILL BE CRAWLING WITH POLICEMEN AND GOVERNMENT PEOPLE...
NO. W-WE CAN'T JUST LEAVE IT ALL LIKE THIS.
I'M NOT GOING TO LEAVE HIM LYING IN THE RAIN. I'M NOT.
AND WHAT DID HADDO MEAN ABOUT US BEING HARBINGERS OF APOCALYPSE? IT'S...
DARLING, PLEASE. WE'VE GOT TO GO BEFORE ANYBODY...
...gets here...

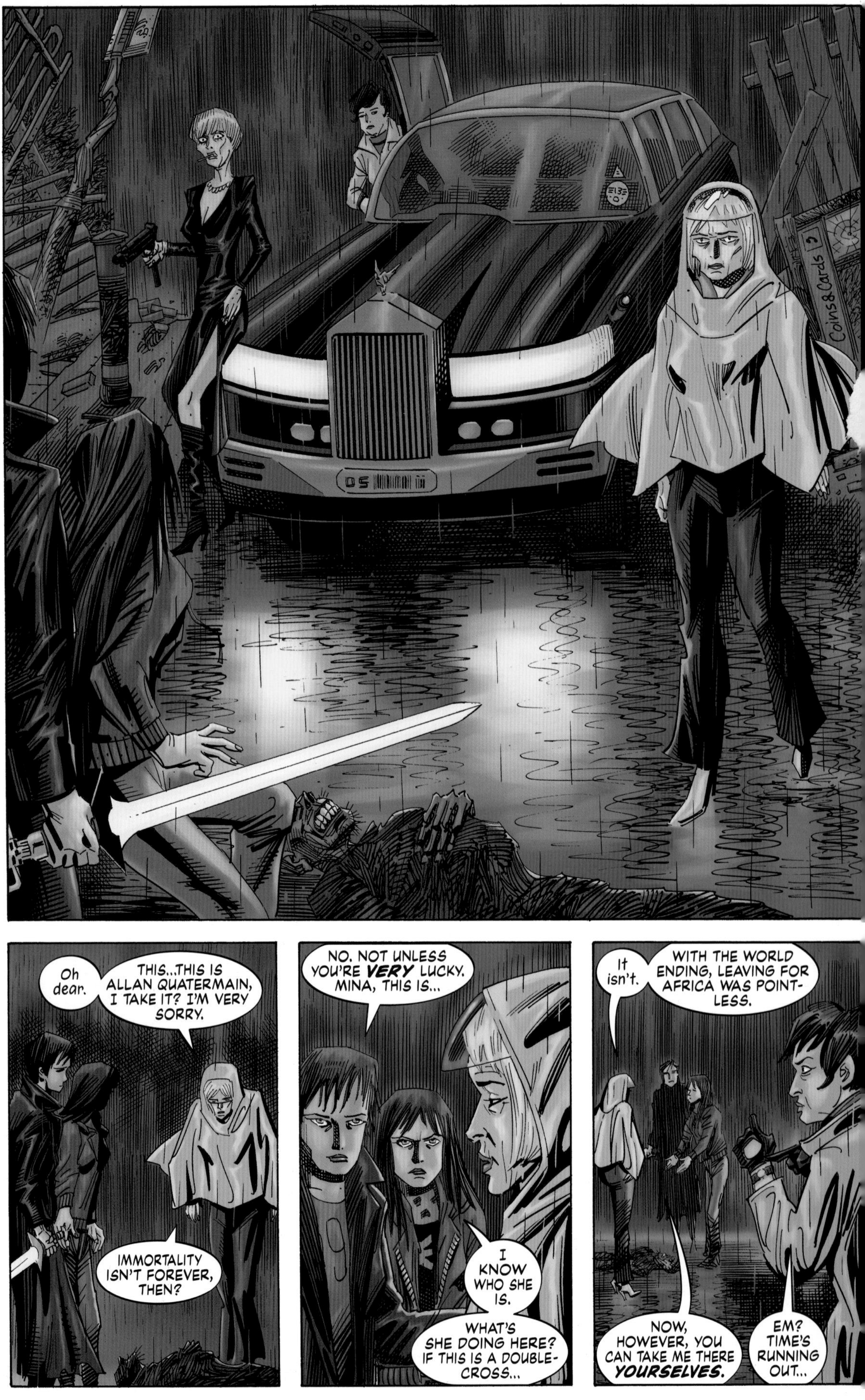
Coins&Cards
Oh dear.
THIS...THIS IS ALLAN QUATERMAIN, I TAKE IT? I'M VERY SORRY.
IMMORTALITY ISN'T FOREVER, THEN?
NO. NOT UNLESS YOU'RE VERY LUCKY. MINA, THIS IS...
I KNOW WHO SHE IS.
WHAT'S SHE DOING HERE? IF THIS IS A DOUBLE-CROSS...
It isn't.
WITH THE WORLD ENDING, LEAVING FOR AFRICA WAS POINTLESS.
NOW, HOWEVER, YOU CAN TAKE ME THERE YOURSELVES.
EM? TIME'S RUNNING OUT...

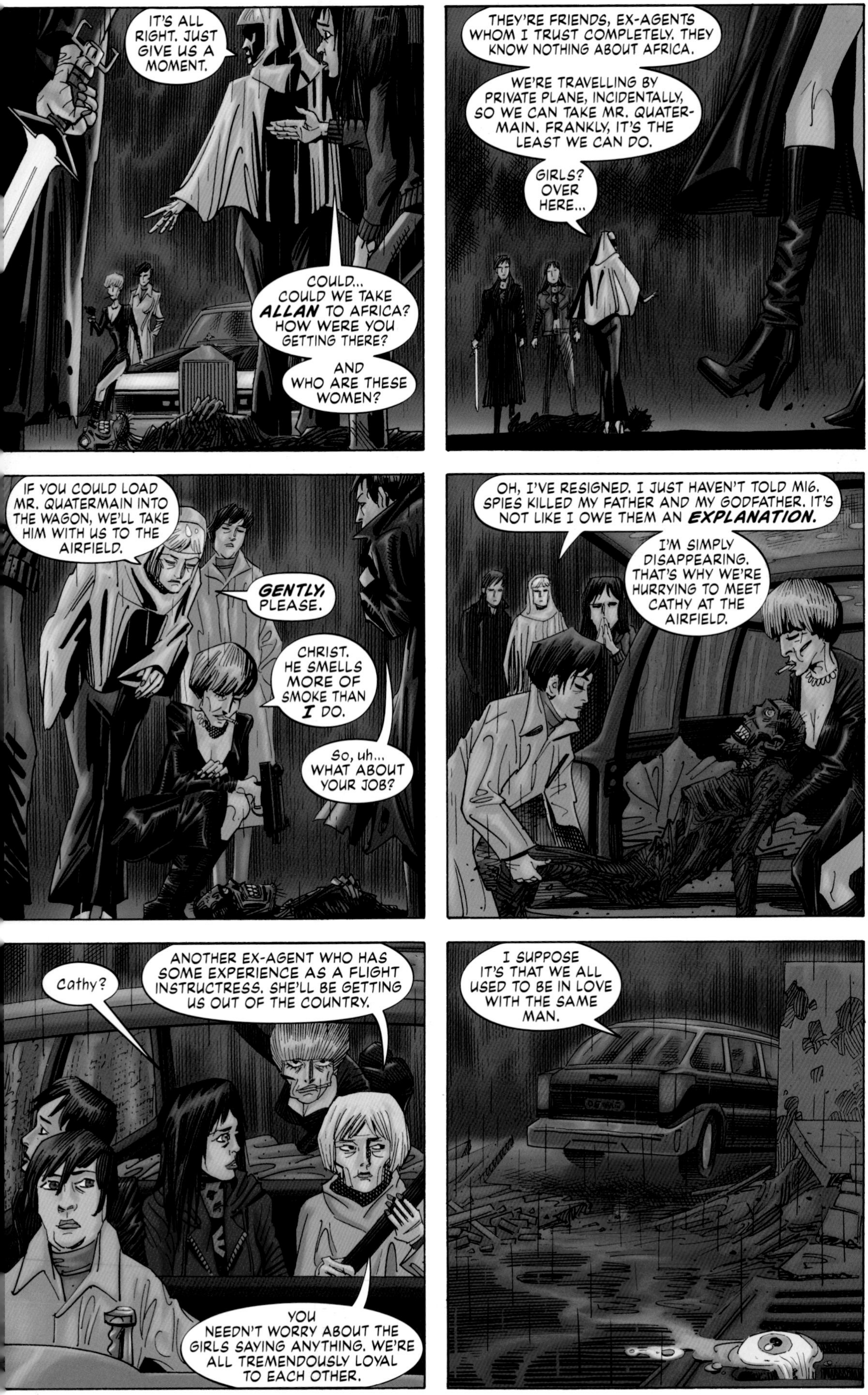

IT'S ALL RIGHT. JUST GIVE US A MOMENT.
COULD... COULD WE TAKE ALLAN TO AFRICA? HOW WERE YOU GETTING THERE?
AND WHO ARE THESE WOMEN?
THEY'RE FRIENDS, EX-AGENTS WHOM I TRUST COMPLETELY. THEY KNOW NOTHING ABOUT AFRICA.
WE'RE TRAVELLING BY PRIVATE PLANE, INCIDENTALLY, SO WE CAN TAKE MR. QUATERMAIN. FRANKLY, IT'S THE LEAST WE CAN DO.
GIRLS? OVER HERE...
IF YOU COULD LOAD MR. QUATERMAIN INTO THE WAGON, WE'LL TAKE HIM WITH US TO THE AIRFIELD.
GENTLY, PLEASE.
CHRIST. HE SMELLS MORE OF SMOKE THAN I DO.
So, uh... WHAT ABOUT YOUR JOB?
OH, I'VE RESIGNED. I JUST HAVEN'T TOLD MI6. SPIES KILLED MY FATHER AND MY GODFATHER. IT'S NOT LIKE I OWE THEM AN EXPLANATION.
I'M SIMPLY DISAPPEARING. THAT'S WHY WE'RE HURRYING TO MEET CATHY AT THE AIRFIELD.
Cathy?
ANOTHER EX-AGENT WHO HAS SOME EXPERIENCE AS A FLIGHT INSTRUCTRESS. SHE'LL BE GETTING US OUT OF THE COUNTRY.
YOU NEEDN'T WORRY ABOUT THE GIRLS SAYING ANYTHING. WE'RE ALL TREMENDOUSLY LOYAL TO EACH OTHER.
I SUPPOSE IT'S THAT WE ALL USED TO BE IN LOVE WITH THE SAME MAN.

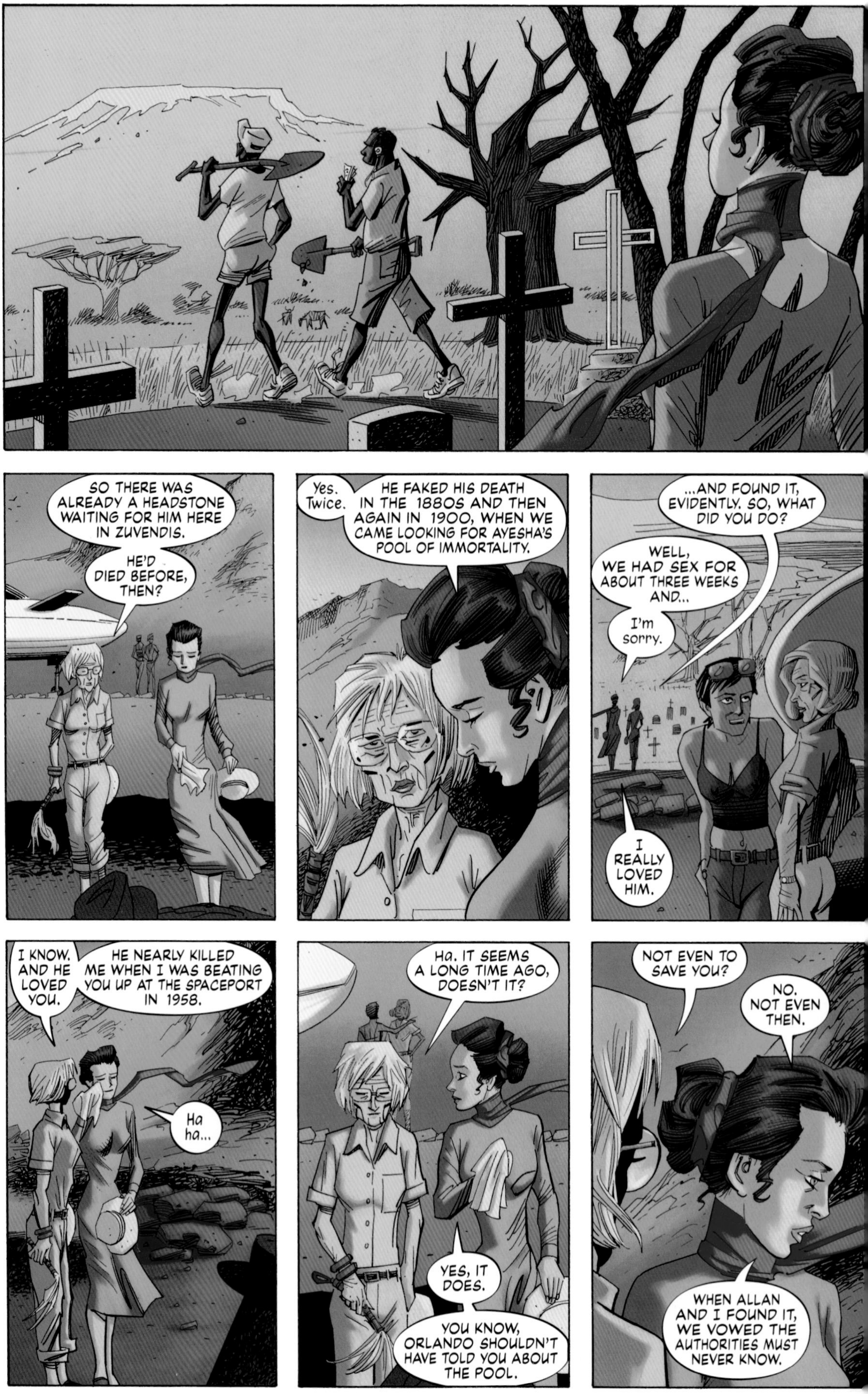
SO THERE WAS ALREADY A HEADSTONE WAITING FOR HIM HERE IN ZUVENDIS.
HE'D DIED BEFORE, THEN?
Yes. Twice.
HE FAKED HIS DEATH IN THE 1880S AND THEN AGAIN IN 1900, WHEN WE CAME LOOKING FOR AYESHA'S POOL OF IMMORTALITY.
...AND FOUND IT, EVIDENTLY. SO, WHAT DID YOU DO?
WELL, WE HAD SEX FOR ABOUT THREE WEEKS AND...
I'm sorry.
I REALLY LOVED HIM.
I KNOW. AND HE LOVED YOU.
HE NEARLY KILLED ME WHEN I WAS BEATING YOU UP AT THE SPACEPORT IN 1958.
Ha ha...
Ha. IT SEEMS A LONG TIME AGO, DOESN'T IT?
YES, IT DOES.
YOU KNOW, ORLANDO SHOULDN'T HAVE TOLD YOU ABOUT THE POOL.
NOT EVEN TO SAVE YOU?
NO. NOT EVEN THEN.
WHEN ALLAN AND I FOUND IT, WE VOWED THE AUTHORITIES MUST NEVER KNOW.

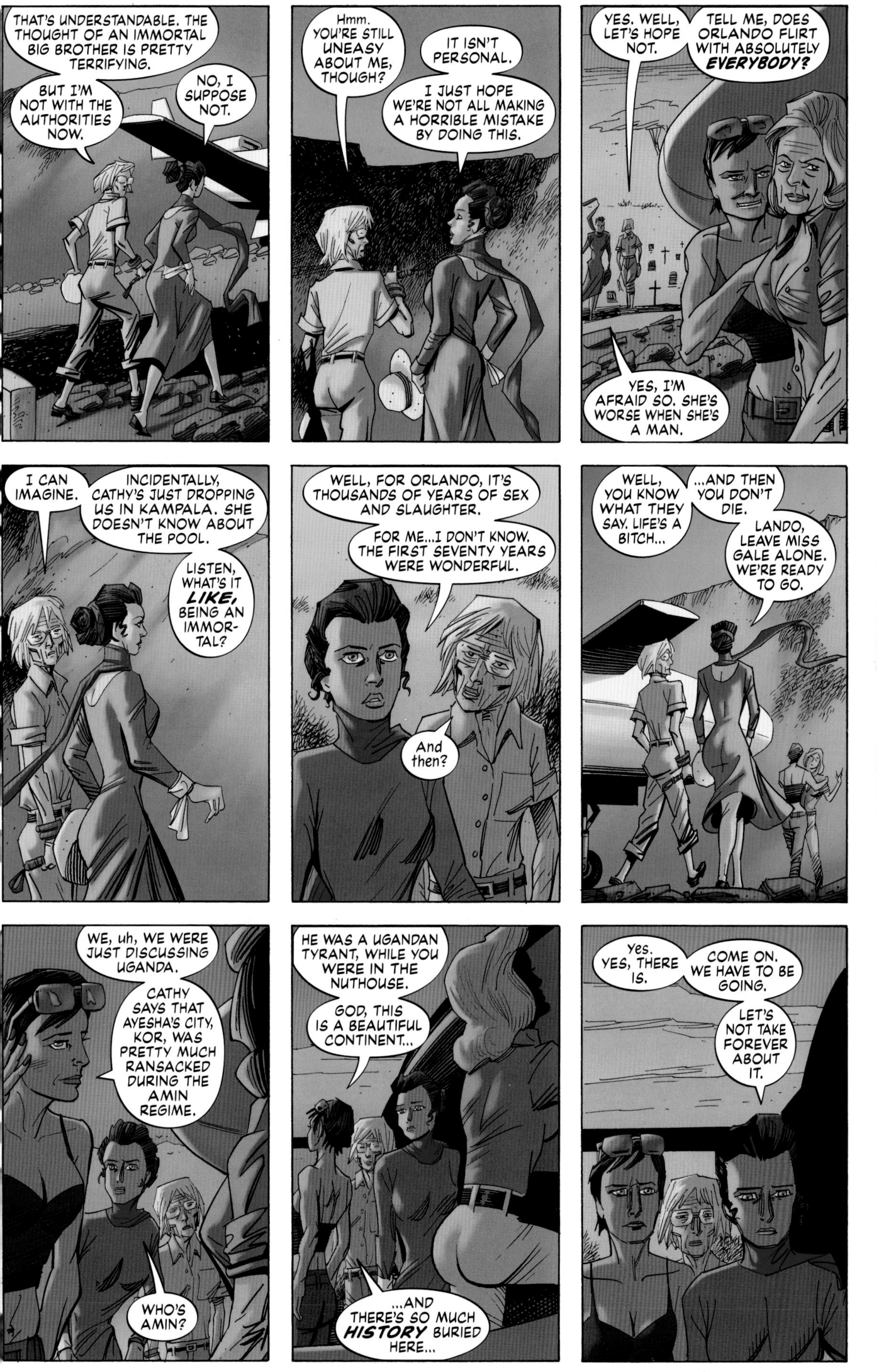
THAT'S UNDERSTANDABLE. THE THOUGHT OF AN IMMORTAL BIG BROTHER IS PRETTY TERRIFYING.
BUT I'M NOT WITH THE AUTHORITIES NOW.
NO, I SUPPOSE NOT.
Hmm. YOU'RE STILL UNEASY ABOUT ME, THOUGH?
IT ISN'T PERSONAL.
I JUST HOPE WE'RE NOT ALL MAKING A HORRIBLE MISTAKE BY DOING THIS.
YES. WELL, LET'S HOPE NOT.
TELL ME, DOES ORLANDO FLIRT WITH ABSOLUTELY *EVERYBODY?*
YES, I'M AFRAID SO. SHE'S WORSE WHEN SHE'S A MAN.
I CAN IMAGINE.
INCIDENTALLY, CATHY'S JUST DROPPING US IN KAMPALA. SHE DOESN'T KNOW ABOUT THE POOL.
LISTEN, WHAT'S IT *LIKE,* BEING AN IMMORTAL?
WELL, FOR ORLANDO, IT'S THOUSANDS OF YEARS OF SEX AND SLAUGHTER.
FOR ME...I DON'T KNOW. THE FIRST SEVENTY YEARS WERE WONDERFUL.
And then?
WELL, YOU KNOW WHAT THEY SAY. LIFE'S A BITCH...
...AND THEN YOU DON'T DIE.
LANDO, LEAVE MISS GALE ALONE. WE'RE READY TO GO.
WE, uh, WE WERE JUST DISCUSSING UGANDA.
CATHY SAYS THAT AYESHA'S CITY, KOR, WAS PRETTY MUCH RANSACKED DURING THE AMIN REGIME.
WHO'S AMIN?
HE WAS A UGANDAN TYRANT, WHILE YOU WERE IN THE NUTHOUSE.
GOD, THIS IS A BEAUTIFUL CONTINENT...
...AND THERE'S SO MUCH *HISTORY* BURIED HERE...
Yes. YES, THERE IS.
COME ON. WE HAVE TO BE GOING.
LET'S NOT TAKE FOREVER ABOUT IT.

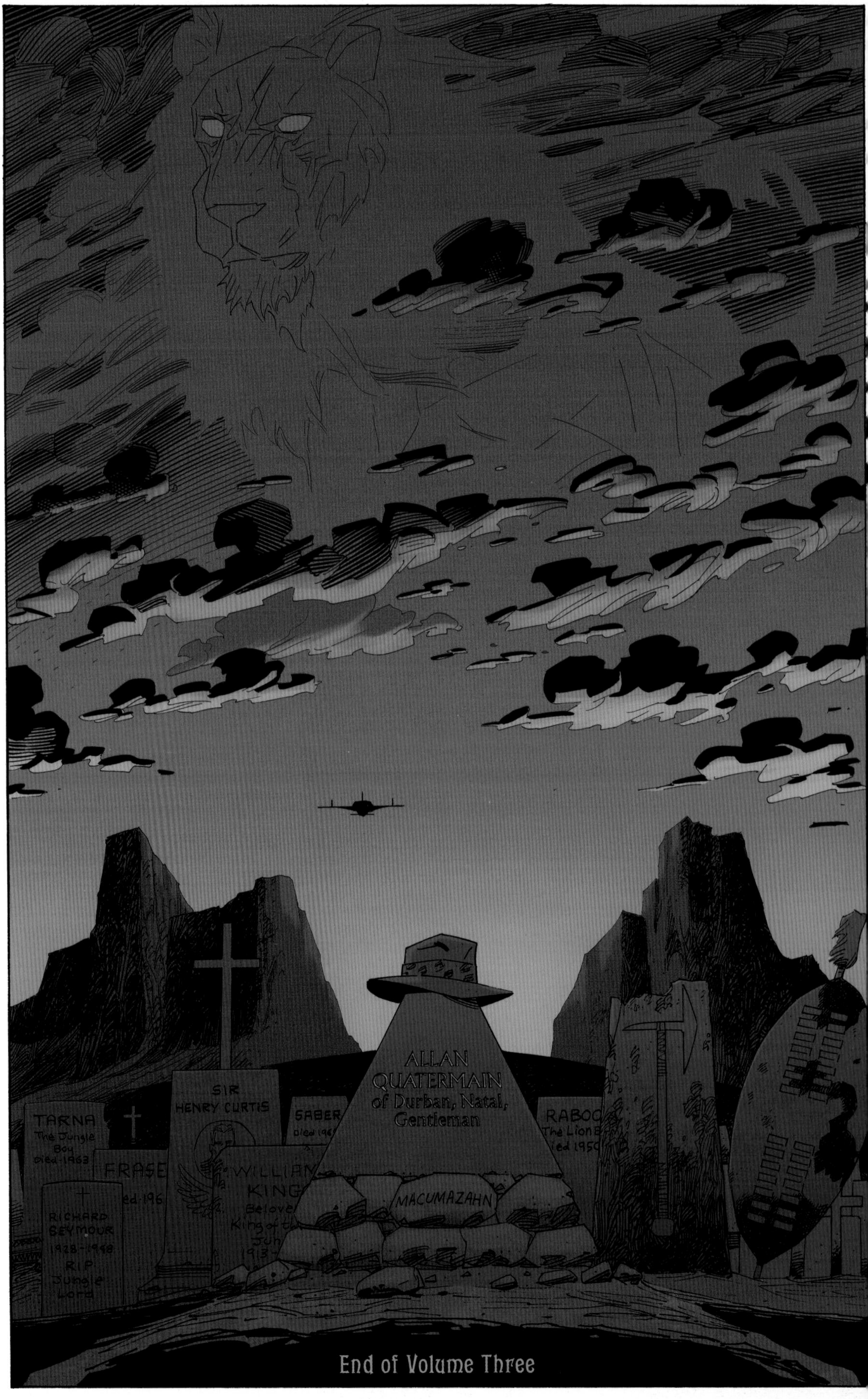
ALLAN QUATERMAIN of Durban, Natal, Gentleman
MACUMAZAHN
SIR HENRY CURTIS
TARNA The Jungle Boy Died 1963
RICHARD SEYMOUR 1928-1948 RIP Jungle Lord
SABER

End of Volume Three

— In Memoriam —
Mick Anglo
Emanuel Litvinoff
David Seabrook
Steve Moore

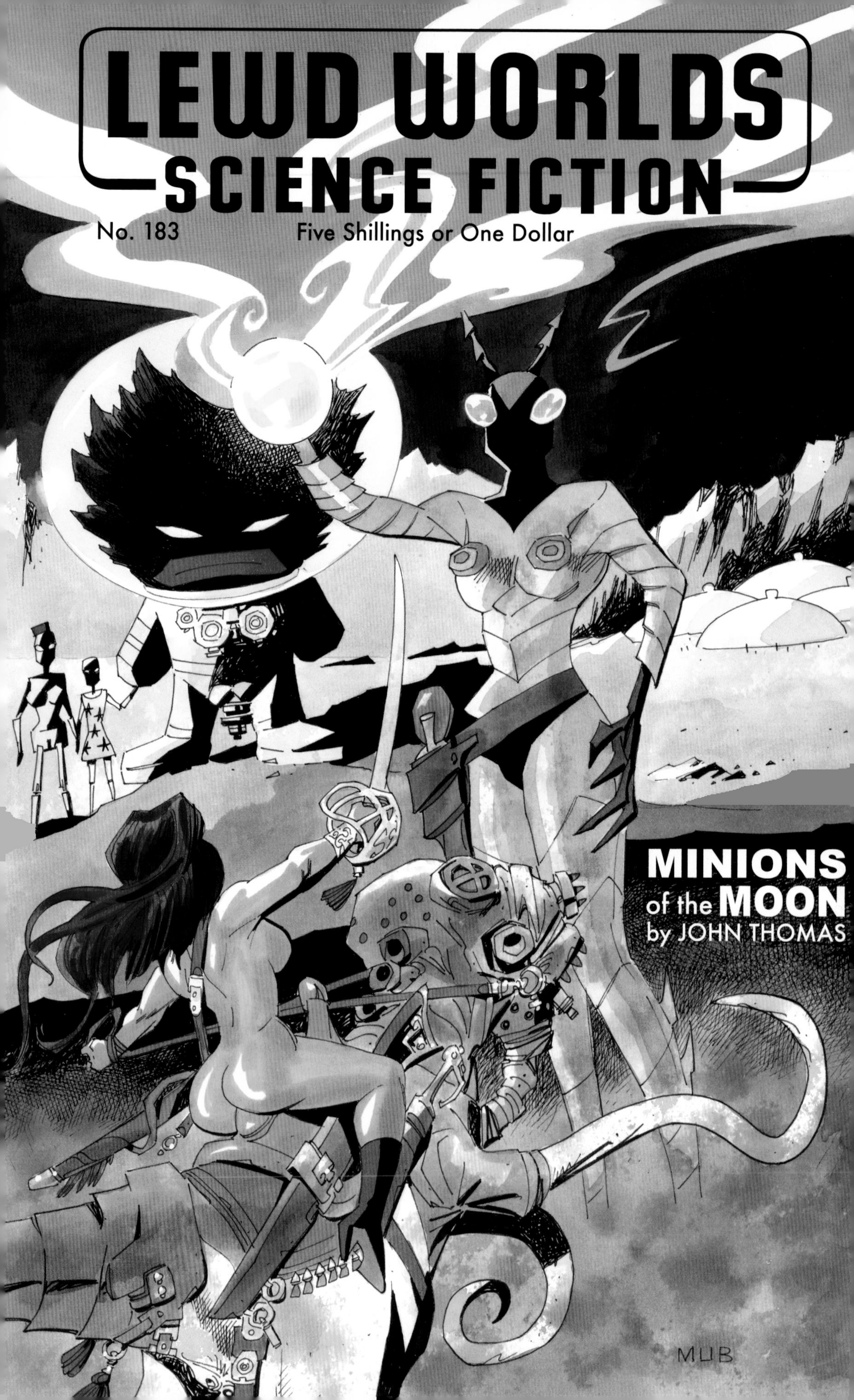
LEWD WORLDS
SCIENCE FICTION
No. 183
Five Shillings or One Dollar
MINIONS of the MOON
by JOHN THOMAS
MUB

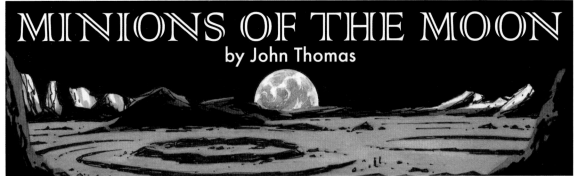

MINIONS OF THE MOON
by John Thomas

(Originally serialised in *Lewd Worlds Science Fiction*,
Ed. James Colvin, #183, 1969.)

Chapter One: Into The Limbus

The patient shouts and makes a fuss, is held down physically until the sedative they have attempted to re-fuse begins to take effect. Eventually the furious invective slurs and slobber drips down onto the restraining-jacket's shoulder. Everything breaks into disconnected words, which are dismantled further and reduced to grey, internal fog as consciousness recedes. The patient, by this point, cannot remember where they are, what year it is, or even their precise identity. The eyes slip out of focus, locked upon an icy full moon visible through the ward windows, or it might be the reflection of a light bulb.

Bio of Thebes, Abyssinia, 1236 BC:
Love amongst the Troglodytes

The sand a cooling talcum under her bare feet, she let the hunched and grunting elder lead her out by moonlight from the place where the immortals had their stinking burrows, their secluded town of holes there in the cloaca of humanity.

Bio had live amongst these sullen creatures for some four or five years, ever since she'd seen directions to their settlement carved deep into the rock surround of that strange pool, not far from Punt, filled with a blueness that was neither fire nor water. She had bathed there some nights after her escape from Egypt to East Africa upon an expedition, her abrupt departure brought about by the retraction and eventual inversion of her penis; the enlargement of her breasts. Become a woman she was beautiful, her salty comrades no more to be trusted, though in this she did not blame them. If she'd come across such loveliness a little earlier when she had been a boy, then Bio would have more than likely raped herself. With this in mind she'd fled west and had happened on the luminous lagoon of sapphire plasma, had immersed herself in the cold flames of the undying. On emerging, she had found the stone-etched diagram in the dark by sitting her wet rear upon it as she dried. Weeks later, following the carven map's instructions, she had come to Abyssinia and the pungent settlement of deathless and withdrawn near-animals who had, like she, swum in the azure mere of light, not far from Punt, at various remote points in antiquity. Bored, uncommunicative, these unkempt brutes mostly sat sunk in their pits and their own thoughts while they awaited a death that was clearly never going to arrive.

And yet she stayed there with them, chewed roots and ate grubs with them. She defecated in plain sight as they did and held conversations that were for the most part made of shrugs, sighs, or the raising of a straggly and trailing brow. The truth was that these torpid and subhuman demigods amazed her, filled her to the brim with awe at their solidity, their ancient stillness. They had the charisma not of men and women but of mountains, timeless features of the human landscape that had seen vast glaciers come and go, had heard the crash of fallen stars and stood as witness to uncountable extinctions. In their overpowering scent were untold centuries of cave-dark copulation, mammoth blood and jungle murder. Her current companion, said to be amongst the first of the immortals, was a large and very hairy male who walked upon his furry knuckle-bones almost as often as he did his feet. He sniffed and shuffled, leading her into the Abyssinian night.

He had some days before made her an offer by the means of gesture: he would show to her a great and sacred mystery, if she would let him mount her. This struck her as mythical rather than disagreeable and thus, with her consent, after a further hour of wading through sub-lunar silver they arrived at the appointed place, a desolate expanse of only rocks and fine-milled sand, where both would satisfy their curiosity.

She kneeled in the blonde pumice and he entered her, an act of great ferocity that nearly drove the breath from Bio yet which took but a few seconds to complete, unlike the man-beast's shuddering climax that went on and on until her thighs were trickling with primordial sperm, while both she and her lover howled into the constellations.

When they had rested, he drew her attention to the pieces of black stone about them in the white dust. Upon close inspection these were made from something she had not before encountered, a unique material that seemed to drink light, giving back no glitter or reflection. Some shards, furthermore, had smoothly crafted corners. Pinned beneath the detumescent primitive, she reached out with one hand to touch a midnight splinter.

Thoughts and images thrummed through her like a lightning-shock. Pre-human savages at time's dawn gaping in religious terror at the great square-cut black stone that stands there in their midst, the bravest creeping hesitantly forth to place a hand upon it. A cascade of information, fire and numbers, wheels and tools and weapons. Years later, its unfathomable work completed, the black block spontaneously shatters and is all but lost beneath the drifts of aeons…

She let the jet fragment tumble from her hand. Behind her, still inside her, the immortal cupped her face and lifted it. As though imparting a great secret, first he pointed to the sharp obsidian chips surrounding their joined bodies. Then he pointed to the moon.

Mina and Allan, Bloomsbury, 1910:
In the Wake of the Black Nautilus

He found her in their quarters at the museum, in its locked wing. She'd been crying, a release for all the dockside horrors of the afternoon, and when he sat down quietly beside her on their bed at first she shouted at him angrily, then cried some more.

'You didn't talk to her or see her eyes. They were so cold, and she was no more than fifteen years old. What can have happened to her that had killed her girlhood and replaced it with the mantle of her father? It wasn't the heads and slaughter that upset me half so much as that poor child, become a monster before she's become a woman.'

When he placed his arm protectively around her shoulders she at least did not flinch back from him, and they sat there in silence for some moments. He reflected that they were alone in the museum, in that vast space full of silent, ancient things. Orlando, after all the bloodshed on the wharf, had been much too excited to return to their headquarters and was very likely out carousing in the dives of the East End. Carnacki and the burglar Raffles, both in darker and more sober moods, had each retired home to their separate addresses and their highly individual lives. It was just him and Mina again now.

'Darling, I'm sorry for the mess we made of things with Haddo, and for all the stupid things that Lando said. We acted like a gang of idiots and everything went straight to hell as a result.'

She tilted back her head, and her jade eyes gazed up at him.

'It wasn't your fault. It would all have gone to hell as quickly if we'd done things my way. I was being unfair, blaming you. I think the truth of it is that I'm starting to feel overwhelmed by the enormity of knowing that we're going to live forever, like Orlando, ever since we took our dip in that Ugandan pool. It all seemed like a marvellous lark at first, like something from a fairy story, but just recently the thought of it has come to haunt me. I feel so small, Allan. I feel like I'm standing all alone upon the threshold of eternity. And if it's like this now, what will it be like in a hundred or a thousand years?"

He pulled her to him, stroking her black hair to soothe her, and to soothe himself. He knew exactly what she meant, had felt the same sense of unease since stepping from the blue fires of that strange African pool and finding himself young again, a strapping fellow in his early twenties with a lifetime's scars erased… or at least most of them. He'd found he still bore the faint signs of injuries sustained in boyhood, and of course the awful marks on Mina's throat had not been wiped away. Perhaps the blue fires had restored them to their prime, with any damages they had incurred prior to that point remaining unaffected? Allan didn't know. He only knew that he shared his beloved's apprehensions of their new immortal state, but had not managed to define those fears as clearly or succinctly as had she. He murmured to her and, again, it was as much to reassure himself as comfort her. About them was the dark of the museum, millennia deep.

'I've had the same thoughts, darling, but I promise you, you're not alone. If you're standing upon the threshold of eternity, then I'll be standing there beside you. Mina, you are everything to me. I love you and I promise you I always will.'

Her eyes still brimming, Mina favoured him with a sad smile.

'Always is a bigger word now than it was five years ago, my handsome hero. You may as well promise me the moon.'

He laughed, and gestured out through the tall windows of their bedroom at the bloated silver orb that hung like a Montgolfier balloon in the black heavens south of Oxford Street.

'What, that one? The one shining on the rotting cabbage leaves that choke the gutters along Berwick Street? The one that lights the drunk newspaper-writer's way from the Pillars of Hercules down to the Coach and Horses? Well, if that's the one you want, my love, then you shall have it. Upon my apparently eternal life, I hereby promise you the moon that's over Soho.'

Despite herself Mina was laughing with him now, her vision of the chilly, endless halls of Time beginning to recede, her dread abating. After all, perhaps Allan was right. Perhaps their love would be enough to outlast empires, outlast worlds. It seemed like long odds but it was at least a ray of hope that she could cling to, bright although remote and distant, like the gibbous satellite above the boozy brothels of that ancient neighborhood.

Allan and Orlando, Paris, 1964:
Her Long, Adorable Lashes

She lowered her subtly-painted eyes submissively while her demanding lover placed his hand upon her stockinged knee, there in the rear seat of a chauffer-driven limousine as it nosed through the outskirts of the intricately-textured city. It was a new game that they were playing, an experiment intended to enliven their extremely long relationship. Part of the game was that she should not call him by his name, and only speak when she was spoken to. In turn, he would refer to her only by her initial.

They were trying to continue the erotic European odysseys that they had read of in the journals of their 18th-century predecessors, and were travelling at present to a terribly exclusive gentlemen's establishment somewhere amongst the labyrinthine streets. Once they'd arrived, her lover would deliver her into a thrillingly demeaning form of sexual slavery, to be used and abused by the perverse members as they liked. Knowing them for descendants of the decadent aristocrats of Silling whom she'd heard her long-dead colleague Percy Blakeny speak of once, she shivered with a mixture of desire and dread to think of being owned by them, in that most intimate of manners. Sitting there beside her on the creaking leather rear seat of the car, so cold against her thighs, her lover turned and spoke, moving his hand along her sheer hose as he did so.

'It's a shame our mutual ladyfriend decided that she didn't want to travel with us, isn't it? It's almost as though she were making out that she's above this sort of thing, when we both know she isn't. Or at least, she's not when she's in the right mood, though it's been ages since that last occurred. I don't think that it's happened since that marvellous long night you showed us in the Blazing World, when we were just back from the wretched business that surrounded the Black Dossier, and that was, what, six years ago?'

His hand had by now reached beneath her dress's hem and was exploring at the lace-ensconced and sultry delta. She said nothing, but sat trembling with delight as he continued with his deceptively casual conversation. In the rear-view mirror she could see their silent driver's darting eyes as he watched while her lover fondled her.

'Of course, she's off having her own adventures with a lot of men and women in peculiar costumes, so I don't expect that ours would interest her. Quite frankly, I don't think her new secret society…"The Seven Stars," wasn't it called?…sounds half as interesting as the fraternity we're on our way to meet. Speaking of which, I've got a sudden urge to see your bottom, while it still officially belongs to me. Take off your underthings and give them to me, as a souvenir.'

Heart hammering, enflamed as much by her own harem-girl obedience as by the good-looking young man's deliberately gruff, commanding tone, she did as she was told. The chauffer's furtive eyes glinted lavisciously in the mirror as she lifted up her backside from the sticky seat and took down the requested items. Glimpsing her white rear, perfectly round as framed by the black stocking tops, her lover made the obvious lunar comparison. The car drove on and O. sat with her lovely eyelids lowered, staring at the automobile's carpeted interior, not daring to look up at him unless he asked her to.

Vull and Captain Universe, Stardust's Tomb, the Lesser Magellanic Cloud, 1964: Requiem for a Space-Wizard

The two super-adventurers, of whom but one was visible, stood framed by the stupendous airlock threshold of the hollow sun. The Captain, in his rose-and-primrose uniform, turned to the empty air beside him with a smile. Thanks to his absolute awareness of the cosmos, granted by the science-god Galileo, he could just make out the otherwise unseen form of his colleague standing next to him, the long cloak and the weird, shadowy helmet of Vull the Invisible picked out in flickering phosphorescent lines. From this translucent, shimmering mirage it was impossible to draw any conclusions as to Vull's identity, other than the impression of a slight and slender man whose age was indeterminate. Universe knew his friend to have been

thwarting evil-doers in the early 1930s, long before the Captain's own career had had its origin, and thus supposed that his companion must be in his fifties or his sixties. He clapped one hand on Vull's scrawny, cape-draped shoulder and asked the blank space for its opinion of the stunning infra-stellar headquarters that Captain Universe had taken from another costumed superman in planet-pulverising mortal combat.

'Well? What do you think? You must admit, it's a bit roomier than your Star Chamber down beneath Fitzrovia. The being who constructed it was a demented megalomaniac, of course, but since I redesigned the place I rather like it.'

Vull stood silent for a moment and then made reply, the deep and echoing tones issuing from nowhere with an almost electronic resonance around the edges of the sound. Universe wondered, and not for the first time, if his fellow hero might not be other than human, perhaps a sophisticated robot or a visitor come from some distant world.

'It's unbelievable. What are these funny rounded screens on stalks that seem to sprout from every surface? Are they your additions, or did they come with the property?'

The Captain, listening carefully to Vull's speech patterns, revised his opinion. The idiosyncrasies betrayed the speaker as an ordinary human rather than an android or a spaceman, but suggested that the senior member of The Seven Stars might be effeminate, which was to Universe's way of seeing things a more alarming possibility. Attempting to dispel this thoroughly unwelcome and surely uncharitable notion, he steered his invisible companion deeper into the astounding depths of the star-fortress as he answered.

'No, those are the former occupant's invention. They're a range of monitors or scanners that enabled him to view any location in the galaxy, including places in dimensions other than our own. One of them even looks into an utterly unheard-of astronomical phenomenon, a kind of hole or pocket in the fabric of space-time itself, inhabited by a grotesque thing that he called a "Headless Head-hunter." The blighter tried to throw me into it during our battle, but he wasn't quite as powerful as he thought he was. I left the view-screens where they were when I remodelled the remainder of this artificial star's interior. You never know when they might come in handy. Anyway, let me guide you around. I can show you the man himself, if you've a mind to see him.'

Again, the low, somehow electronic tones emerged from nothingness.

'I thought you said that he was dead. I thought you said you'd killed him.'

Leading his unseen guest over gleaming marble floors between spectacular and self-invented towers of inscrutable equipment or past huge and cryptic trophies from his own fantastic exploits, Universe gave an ambiguous shrug of his broad shoulders.

'It depends on what you mean by dead. You have to understand that this so-called Space Wizard was a brutal and sadistic monster. He preferred to punish adversaries with a fiendishly inventive range of living deaths, so that they could suffer eternally. I gave the power-crazed thug a taste of his own medicine, that's all.'

He gestured to the wall-sized portal made from foot-thick glass that their perambulations had been

leading to. There on the massive window's further side was what appeared to be a chamber filled with an unusually clear and transparent type of ice. Suspended as if floating at its centre was the freakish form of the defeated superman, an almost human entity some eight feet long from head to crown, clad in a skin-tight suit of lurid turquoise. It had far too many ribs and an abnormal musculature, with parts that were wildly disparate in their proportions. The exaggeratedly long head was topped with blonde hair that had frozen into spikes of an unnaturally bright yellow. While Vull stared in silence at the icebound giant, Captain Universe explained as best he could.

'The substance he's encased in is a frozen form of poly-water that he called Ice-9, and he had one or two unfortunates entombed within it when I tracked him back here to this lair for his last stand. I'll swear that he was drunk for that concluding showdown. You could smell the liquor on his breath and he was stumbling and uncoordinated, otherwise I doubt I could have thrown him into his own icy chamber of eternal torment quite as easily as was in fact the case.'

Once more there was a pause before the strange metallic voice made its enquiry.

'What were you fighting over? Were you working under the instruction of your employers at the United Nations?'

Captain Universe looked grim and shook his auburn head.

'The U.N. aren't the only force I answer to. My powers were given to me by a quintet of science-mystics who've transcended space and time, Pythagoras and Leonardo being counted in that number. These beings exist, along with other awesome presences, upon a level of reality beyond the confines of the mortal realm. Archimedes, Aristotle, and even more recent sub-atomic physicists such as the Swedish theoretician Borghelm. Our friend in the ice-block was attempting to force his way into that sublime elite, and I was given the command to stop him. It's that simple.'

Turning from the eerie exhibit, the pair walked back across the fake sun's cavernous interior, their conversation moving onto other matters.

'Vull, I'm sorry about how The Seven Stars worked out after our one and only victory against the 'Mass. I told my brother Jet about it and he was appalled. That thing might once have been one of his colleagues. Everyone feels bad about what happened.'

Vull, responding, sounded disappointed and yet philosophical.

'I know. I had high hopes for all of us, but now Mars Man and Satin have been forced to drop from sight along with all our other difficulties, I don't think it's possible to put things right. Besides, like you, I'm answerable to higher powers and currently have other matters to attend to. Could I ask you to return me to our home-world in your spaceship? More specifically, I need to rendezvous with representatives of the supernal forces that I mentioned at a ruined castle in the north of Scotland.'

Universe smiled and said he thought that it might be arranged.

It was, astonishingly, less than three days later that Vull stood upon the grassy slopes of crumbling Dunbayne Castle, watching for the halo-flash of rippling radiance high in the blue dome of the upper atmosphere that would mean Captain Universe's craft had broken the light-barrier and was on its way home towards the distant nebulae. When this had taken place, Vull sat upon the turf and waited for perhaps an hour or more before a wholly different means of transportation drifted into view above the northerly horizon. Even from this distance, the invisible adventurer could see the rising pink flecks that were a by-product of the pataphysically-constructed vessel's flower-powered engine.

Taking off the helmet of invisibility and startling some nearby sheep by suddenly appearing in their midst, Vull shook her long black hair down to her shoulders and awaited the arrival of the Rose of Nowhere.

Prospero and his operatives, the Blazing World, 1964: Coming Forth by Day

Over the ornamental root-garden there shone the thousand suns that give this realm its name. The tall and bearded figure in exquisite robes, born to Italian aristocracy some centuries before, peered through the jade and garnet lenses of his pince-nez at the company assembled on the ageless terraces before him. Four in number, they sat perched upon wide benches carved from single pieces of obsidian that had the staring eye motif which was the emblem of the Blazing World inlaid as a mosic of alabaster. In the star-crammed sky above, an Owl-man in a cut silk tunic screeched and swooped exuberantly.

Seated by herself on the bench closest to the magus was the marvellously wilful lady music-teacher, Wilhelmina Murray, who had so impressively commanded the third incarnation of that league he'd founded all those years ago. Clad in a single figure-hugging garment of jet black with cape and leather boots and gloves to match, she sat with an unusual bulb-topped helmet resting in her lap, gazing attentively at Prospero through goggles that had eyes of different colours, blankly staring discs of red and green.

The three remaining members of the band that the former Duke of Milan had lately summoned sat together on a separate couch of polished stone. These were two living wooden dolls named Peg and Sara Jane, along with the unnaturally squat and massive figure who was both their lover and commander. If this startling and yet engaging creature had a given name it was not known to the magician. Brought here to this dazzling fourth-dimensional domain by Queen Olympia of nearby Toyland, the wild-maned black aeronaut had introduced himself to Prospero as 'a cummun Galley-wag.' From this the wizard had surmised his guest to be perhaps an escaped slave, come from a hidden cosmos that was by some means concealed from ordinary scrutiny. That this supposed world and its occupants were formed from matter of far greater density than that which made the earthly plane was evidenced by the fine cracks appearing in the solid block of carved obsidian upon which the extra-terrestrial freebooter sat, his thick legs kicking idly, far too short to reach the ground. Being essentially organic in his nature despite the discrepancies of his material composition, the dark-matter buccaneer wore spectacles with mismatched lenses, like Miss Murray. His two literal playthings, on the other hand, were ani-manikins constructed on the principles established by the late Dr. Copelius and thus did not require the same corrective eyewear. Both clad in short summer dresses that appeared to have been fashioned from the flag of the United States, the two impossibly slim wooden figurines sat giggling and talking kittenishly to each other with trilling falsettos in a language which the magus recognised as Dutch. The conjuror's assembled crew were clearly growing restless as they waited for him to explain the reason for his urgent summoning. He cleared his throat, and then began.

'No doubt thou wouldst hear why I called thee hence: what grave calamity requires thine aid. Know then that this be not an earthly woe, but, rather, it afflicts another sphere.'

Prospero gestured with one ring-decked hand, heavy with chryosprase and tourmaline, and in the air before them there appeared a vision of an unmistakable pale orb against a field of sequinned night. The Galley-wag tilted his huge head quizzically.

'By the great quim o' singularity! Be that not your whirl's loon-lamp?'

The elderly mage and young music teacher felt as much as heard the creature's voice, with its inhumanly low register reverberating in their bellies and the marrow of their bones. Prospero nodded and, with one extended fingertip, touched the diaphanous and shimmering image in some half-a-dozen places, leaving a red dot of pulsing phosphorescence at each point of contact.

'Aye, ebon navigator of the void, it is the moon I conjure to plain sight. There, marked in crimson, see Earth's colonies, where fly the stiff and windless flags of France, of England, Germany, America. Yet are there conflicts in those cratered lands that are not born of earthly enmities. Two species native to that silv'ry ball have lately clashed together in a war which, ranging far across the lunar globe, endangers the terrestrial settlements. I fear that if these battles should persist, Earth's settlers shall be forced to relocate unto a certain area of that sphere where we wouldst rather that they ventured not, not until it is the appointed time there at the dawn of a new century. I charge thee to set sail, then, for night's jewel, there to placate these warring lunar tribes that our Blazing World's schemes go not awry.'

Miss Murray raised one black-gloved hand, and Prospero permitted her to speak.

'Most noble Duke, might I ask why my colleagues Allan and Orlando were not summoned to this meeting? Are they not to journey with us?'

The enchanter shook his head. Across the terraces, a sun that had a wry and sleepy smile was setting over diamond quays and ululating minarets.

'They undertake an amorous idyll in Europe's dens of pain and ecstasy, unwilling or unable to respond to all my imprecations and demands. I fear I know my former squire of old, lascivious and truant in her way, and hazard we shall see no more of her nor of thy youthful huntsman paramour until their lusty chase hath run its course.'

The music teacher, rising from her bench, pursed her lips disapprovingly.

'I see. Then we may as well board the Rose of Nowhere and make ready to embark as soon as possible. I bid you a good aeon, Prince of Necromancers.'

Prospero watched as the odd quartet walked off across the ornamental gardens, with the Galley-wag leaving behind him webs of crack and fracture on the paving stones in lieu of footprints. The twin doll-girls held hands as they skipped together with their flag-skirts flaring, chattering excitedly in Dutch, and only Wilhelmina Murray seemed disheartened. With her long cloak trailing mournfully and the outlandish helmet underneath her arm she strode away between fantastic topiaries. The magician gestured, and the evocation of the moon floating beside him fell apart into a billion scintillating motes. Chewing the ends of his moustache, he hoped that this was not an omen.

Mina and the Galley-wag, the Rose of Nowhere, 1964: Huckleberry Friends

Wearing the borrowed costume of a long-deceased Vull the Invisible she stood there on the deck, gripping the rail and marvelling that she could still respire although their boat had sailed beyond the thinnest reaches of Earth's upper atmosphere some half an hour before. Admittedly the air she breathed was scented heavily with roses, a by-product of the craft's unusual method of propulsion, but this was scarcely a hardship.

Behind them, her home planet was a stupefying opal while ahead was an infinity of ink where countless flakes of furnace-light hung in suspension. Somewhere down below, in the beguiling swirl and mottle of the blue world's cloud and ocean, she knew that her friends pursued their earthly lives as usual. Fathoms beneath the great sprawl of the sea, an ageing savage beauty known as Jenny Nemo would be lighting candles at the starboard shrine of her night-black submersible in memory of her late husband, the dependable Broad-Arrow Jack. Elsewhere within the seabed-grazing vessel, Jenny's daughter Hira would still be asleep in the next cabin to her own child, Jenny's grandson. Not yet six, Jack Dakkar was the fruit of an arranged dynastic union between his mother and the since-deceased air-pirate Armand Robur, a descendant of the more notorious Jean. Much as she'd liked the little boy when they had met, Mina could not help thinking that he represented a potentially explosive mix of lethal bloodstocks.

Then, of course, there were her other comrades. There was witty and ingenious Queen Olympia with her brooding consort in the snow-surrounded pocket of eternal summer known as Toyland. At their various secret bases or their alias day-jobs there were Captain Universe and the few other super-people who where left from Mina's recent incognito and foredoomed attempt to form a band of champions, while somewhere in the demimonde of Paris were her lovers, Allan and the pulchritudinous Orlando, hurling themselves into a debauch in an attempt to dull the dread that came with immortality.

Her reverie was interrupted by a doleful and protesting creak from the ship's black-material timbers,

somewhere close behind her. Turning, Mina found herself confronted by the Galley-wag. Like her, he had dispensed with the two-coloured spectacles now that they were no longer in the 4-D territories of the Blazing World, and the white saucers of his lidless eyes shone from the unreflective dark globe of his shaggy head as he addressed her formally, according to his own conventions.

'Bread and tits, resplendent swan of Peril! Does yer bezoms heave fer home?'

The subterranean pitch of his inhuman voice made the dark metal of the handrail hum in resonance. Mina smiled fondly as she ventured a reply in the same idiom.

'Bread and tits to *you,* brave rider on the night's starry pudendum. No, I wasn't homesick. I was thinking about all the people that we're leaving back on Earth, behind us. I suppose that I was feeling a bit…oh! I say, what's that, just off the port bow?'

The ethereal mariner swivelled his massive cranium to peer in the direction she had indicated. Mina noticed, quite irrelevantly, that he had a bottle tucked into the red sash of his belt. She fleetingly supposed this to be rum of an unworldly distillation. Something glittering approached them, tumbling through trans-planetary gloom and coruscating as it came, as though lit by its own internal fire.

'Why, by my tripes! It books to be a lantern-cadaver encubed in frusticles!'

As the trajectory of the revolving and illuminated mass began to take it under the ascending Rose of Nowhere, Mina gasped. It was a lump of ice, and at its heart was a contorted, black-clad corpse still clinging to a ball of greenish radiance. As the refrigerated mass rotated she found herself gazing into the eternally-unblinking, horror-stricken eyes of her late adversary, the depraved professor of mathematics, spymaster and criminal, James Moriarty. His gaunt features, locked in a last breathless scream, were under-lit by the crepuscular glow of the Cavorite clutched to his frozen breast. Then the corpse-satellite was gone, fallen away beneath their vessel to continue its unending orbit.

Hesitantly, still stunned by this unexpected meeting with her former foe, Mina communicated what she knew of the dead, icebound figure to her host. The Galley-wag gave a low, sympathetic growl that fractured a glass dial in his array of instruments.

'He sounds to be a noxic vile-guard, an' yer whirl's well rid o' hum. Now, wishin' no intrudence, I'd stamped herewards to bequire if you were wantin' blanket-company amid this wendless vastard of a night? I know as Sarey-Jane's taken a varnish to yer since you lost yer blondery, if you were in a mood fer sallymappin'. Alsewise, yer'd be wellcum bunked betwixt me an' the twin of 'um.'

Realising that she'd been politely propositioned and belatedly identifying the glass bottle jutting from the Galley-wag's red sash as being filled with linseed oil rather than an exotic rum, Mina felt both obscurely flattered and amused as she respectfully declined his invitation. Taking no offence, the baryonic buccaneer returned below decks to his greased and squeaking love-toys, leaving Mina with her thoughts and the indifferent canopy of stars. Ahead of them, beyond the Rose of Nowhere's shark-faced prow, a golf-ball moon inflated steadily across the next few hours until it filled the firmament from rim to rim.

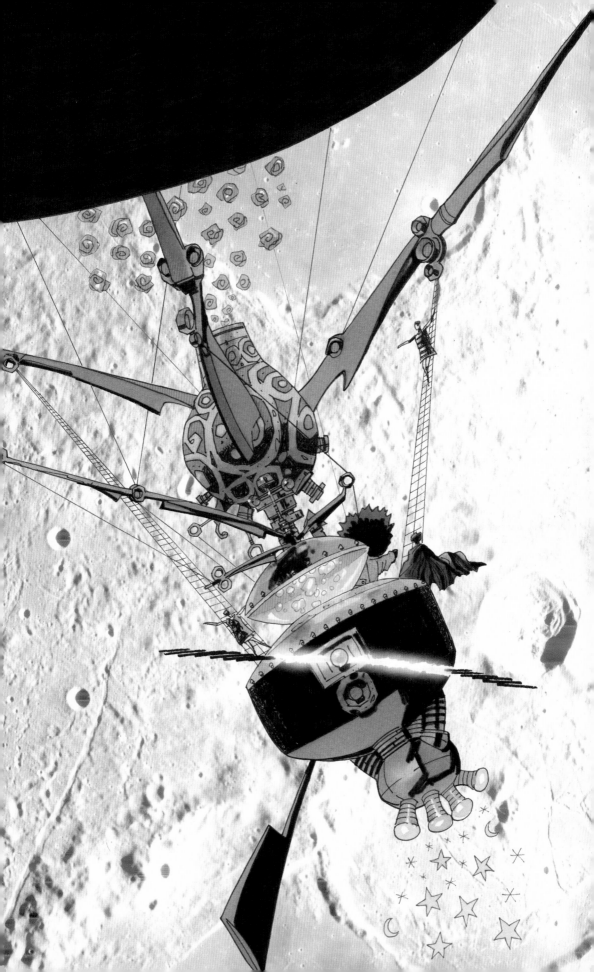

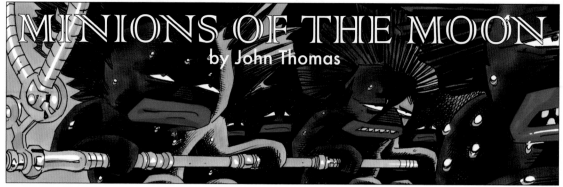

MINIONS OF THE MOON
by John Thomas

(Originally serialised in *Lewd Worlds Science Fiction*, Ed. James Colvin, #184, 1969.)

Chapter Two: The Distance From Tranquility

A tiny paper figure painstakingly cut from a jam-jar label and spread with adhesive paste is lodged unnoticed, stuck fast in the patient's straggly hair as they attempt to use the blunted plastic scissors despite fingers rendered numb and clumsy by repeated medication. Labouring obsessively on their collage, the patient has reduced all consciousness into a focused bead of present that refuses to acknowledge any past or future and therefore is spared even such basic existential questions as 'Where am I', much less 'How long have I been here?'

The clinic's proprietor, a woman doctor with what seem aggressively large breasts, stands at the patient's elbow and insists they take the first in that evening's procession of confounding medicines. The pill, dispersible in water, is served up in a small plastic cup. The patient gazes dully into this receptacle while the persistent doctor urges them to drink it down.

The small white tablet is disintegrating, fizzing into nothingness on its circumference and losing definition in the increasingly foggy liquid that surrounds it. It resembles the full moon in miniature, seen through obscuring cloud.

The Galley-wag, Black Matter Cosmos, circa 1896: Escape from Nowhere

As viewed by terrestrial eyes, the universe's fireball-dusted skin was all of it. The nine parts of its substance that were unaccounted for, its flesh and bones, remained concealed beneath this glittering epidermis. Thus invisible to human scrutiny, the core of the continuum existed as an unimaginably massive trans-galactic mountain range, a strangely-contoured topographic shape that hung unseen in stupefying folds millions of light-years deep. This was effectively the whole of spacetime, with the luminosities and nebulae known to mankind only cake-decorations on its surface.

Jackboy Sixty was, of course, not his true name… this was in actuality a finely modulated deep subsonic tone…but only a convenience bestowed on him by the pink masters, to distinguish him from all the other Jackboys that made up the blackboat's cargo. The pink masters had their origins in the star-pastures that were rumoured to exist upon those narrow margins of the cosmos said to somehow lie beyond the confines of this endless baryonic territory, this dark immensity that was the bulk of everything. In the phonetic language of

the masters…Jackboy Sixty had at first not recognised the bursts of separate, randomly pitched sounds as language but was learning rapidly in the characteristic manner of his kind…the vast atomic light that the pink humanoids originated from was known as 'Olodoria' or something similar, though some years later he would learn that in terrestrial astronomies it was referred to as 'Antares.' Here, then, was the home-world that had launched the blackboats into the dark guts of the continuum to trawl for sentient life as a commodity; as units to be sold upon the slave-blocks of the universe's flimsy, fiery surface.

The resourceful Jackboy, taken as an infant from his native planetoid in the night-system known as the Great Erebus Array, had realised some fifteen years into his captivity that the electro-shackle on his ankle had malfunctioned and could be removed during the sanctioned hours of sleep without alerting the pink masters. From that point on, whenever opportunity arose he'd quietly leave his fellow victims slumbering at their oars and make his way through the enormous galley's lightless innards to a disused storage hold that he'd discovered, empty and apparently unvisited due to the dangerously weak condition of the slave-ship's hull at this point, previously damaged by a hurtling blackball meteor and only partially repaired. For decades he had laboured in this secret chamber, navigating its dark contours by the bounce-back from his deep bass growl and handling work-tools by engulfing them in the soft substance of the pads with which his blunt arms terminated, until finally his magnificent folly was completed.

The escape craft nestled in a cradle of supporting struts, its all-important particle-sack hanging in limp folds across the vessel's upper surface. Jackboy Sixty knew that once he started the inflation process he'd have only moments before the tremendous loss of anti-particles leeched from the blackboat's drive was noticed, but knew also that he had no other option. Cranking round the wheel with a determined grunt he opened the gluino-valves and watched with satisfaction as the monstrous anti-matter bladder went into its primary then secondary expansion phases.

As he'd known it would, the bulkhead door of the abandoned cargo-hold abruptly hurtled inward on explosive bolts and two of the pink masters rushed into the chamber, jabbering in agitation. Jackboy Sixty recognised the taller of the pair as his own unit's whip-boss, a sadistic younger male named Kelger Vo, and knew that dozens of the compound-eyed and cerise-coloured slavers would be racing to assist their colleagues at that very moment. There would not be time for niceties.

The more diminutive of the two masters, a plump female that the naked and perspiring Jackboy thought was known as Vinvir Gu, had already pulled her control-wand from its holster and was levelling its tight beam of mind-scrambling micro-radiation at his over-sized and shaggy head. He whistled a shrill burst of hyper-sound, disintegrating the control-wand's crystal bulb, and then turned his attentions upon Kelger Vo. The wiry slaver, with his legs displayed unappetisingly by his short trousers, had realised the inefficacy of his comrade's control wand and was instead bringing out a much more daunting sonic weapon, this being the paralysing chime that would disrupt a nervous system's motor impulses and leave the target frozen in its tracks. Regretfully compressing his huge larynx, Jackboy Sixty first expressed a standing interference wave to cancel the vibrations of the gong-like apparatus and then went on to reduce both of the screaming galley-masters to flat puddles of undifferentiated protoplasm. By now, reinforcements were erupting through the chamber door with horror and surprise apparent in their wide, slack mouths and multi-faceted insectile eyes.

Stepping up to his makeshift vessel's steering wheel, he shouted down the cargo-hold's already weakened hull and was propelled out in a spore-burst of exploded debris and pink, twitching slaver bodies into the vast, unalleviated blackness of the baryonic cosmos. Navigating inexactly by the swelling thunder of approaching gravities or the dull roar of X-rays, Jackboy Sixty rode the howling dark out to its limits at velocities of such colossal magnitude that slowing down seemed an unlikelihood and stopping an impossibility. Bare-skinned and bellowing he clung tight to the rigging as his craft burst through into the rind of lights and galaxies, the shallow foam of spectacle that effervesced on the meniscus of the universe's giant midnight heart. Roaring at frequencies that stopped the dance of atoms and plunged temperatures towards a zero that was all but absolute, he fell into the blinding swirl of suns and worlds and magnetars. Nude and impossible in his fragmenting vehicle, he plummeted towards delirious adventure.

Mina, the Limbus of the Moon, 1964: Glass Shirts and Goose-Bones

Somewhere behind her she could hear the high-pitched chatter, all in Dutch, of the two giggling wooden automata as they assisted their intrepid captain with the mooring of The Rose of Nowhere there amongst the jagged molar rocks and grey dust-oceans of the moon. Picking her way carefully across the crunch and crumble of the powdery surface, Mina once again turned over in her tirelessly investigative mind the fact that she was breathing on the airless lunar satellite without respiratory apparatus; had in fact been breathing thus unaided on the deck of their improbable conveyance throughout the long trip from Earth. She was constructing a hypothesis based on the ancient anecdotal evidence of Baron Munchausen, apparently borne to the moon in a terrific waterspout. A waterspout, in Mina's understanding, was what happened when tornados touched upon the sea, and she conjectured an immense tornado that might stretch its whirling tunnel of tormented air across the empty void of space between her planet and its silvery companion.

That would not, of course, explain how there could be a stable atmospheric bubble clinging to the lunar landscape (where she thought that there was insufficient gravity for this to be achievable) nor yet how this precarious atmosphere might be replenished given the conspicuous lack of vegetation. She was still considering this seemingly intractable conundrum some few moments later when the toe of her black leather boot connected with an object partly buried in the finely-ground precipitate surrounding her. Upon inspection this turned out to be a rusting crown of what looked to be Anglo-Saxon origins, while a short distance further on she came across a single Argyle sock, some ballpoint pens, a wooden doll that might have been Elizabethan and a damaged violin, perhaps a Stradivarius. With mounting wonderment it dawned upon her that she must be situated in the fabled Limbus of the Moon, where all lost things were rumoured to accumulate. She thought her hypothetical tornado might at least provide a credible scientific means by which this curious displacement was accomplished, but as she traipsed further through the moon-sand with the squeals and answering growls of the Dutch dolls and their esteemed commander fading to inaudibility behind her, she discovered objects that did not appear to make an easy fit with any of her theories.

She found avian skeletons which she identified as those of geese, both wearing perished leather harnesses, and thought that they might be remainders from the fiercely-debated Godwin journey to the moon reputed to have happened long before Professor Cavor's mission, sometime in the late seventeenth century. She had, however, no such likely explanation for what seemed to be two broken halves of a suspiciously large tunic made entirely out of solid glass; for what appeared to be the decomposing head and thorax of a hippopotamus-sized ant, or for the tightly-furled Titanium-white suede of moss that she found covering one of the heftier lunar boulders. These seemed to be things that had originated on the moon rather than items snatched from a terrestrial source by some unproven interplanetary vortex. There were also faint impressions in the dust which she reluctantly concluded were prints made by the bare feet of women.

Lifting up her head she scanned the pearly ribbon of what seemed a far-too-close horizon, noticing the bubbling froths of dome that marked both the American and nearby British moon-bases, these settlements endangered by a war between two native lunar species which Mina had been instructed to prevent. Reasoning that the distant sealed environments suggested that the breathable pocket of atmosphere in which she was enclosed did not extend much further she elected to turn back, pulling her leather super-hero cloak about her in the icy climate as she trod through the ash-coloured dunes towards the tethered Rose of Nowhere and her waiting shipmates. It occurred to her that she was walking normally without the weightless, bouncing gait she'd heard described by other lunar voyagers. This tended to confirm her earlier observation that in lunar terms localised atmosphere implied localised gravity, although of course that didn't bring her any closer to an understanding of this baffling phenomenon or how it was supposed to work in scientific terms.

Later, over a frugal and yet filling meal of rations from the hyper-galleon's lockers, Mina and her shipmates did their best to formulate a plan of action. It was finally agreed that while the Galley-wag and his enthusiastic wooden harem would attempt to find out more about the warring native races, Mina would employ breathing equipment and her borrowed helmet of invisibility to more closely investigate the vulnerable terrestrial moon-bases which were threatened by the conflict. This decided, the black-matter buccaneer elected to recite a raucous shanty that described a week spent in what sounded like an ultra-spatial bordello, with which Sarah Jane and Peg clapped happily along.

'On my forst night a boxum humahedroid came ter me,
    With her ninth hole so deep t'were more a stringularity...'

Mina half listened to this listing of increasingly unfathomable and unlikely amorous encounters, usually involving topographically impossible erotic orifices or else sexual positions that could only be attained in higher mathematical dimensions. She mused briefly on a line that rhymed 'unnatural act' with 'tesseract', then turned her wandering attention to a starboard porthole where a clouded turquoise egg that she still found it difficult to think of as the Earth was at that moment slowly setting, all its tragedies and glories swallowed by the moon's bleakly vestigial skyline.

**The Galley-wag & the Frankenstein monster,
Arctic circle, 1896: Babes in Toyland**

He'd plunged through radiance incomprehensible to splinter his escape-craft on the icecaps of the first world that appeared to harbour any atmosphere conducive to survival. Waking in the ribcage wreckage of his crippled vessel, he had found himself sprawling amidst a silent swarm of airborne crystals that appeared to be composed of two parts hydrogen to one part oxygen, this mix existing in a hitherto undocumented frozen state. Shaking his head to clear the grogginess he found that he'd accumulated plump white ridges of the novel substance on the strangely-stiffened locks of his black mane. He also found himself surrounded by observers, stubby little bipeds with napped, yellowish-brown fur and glittering black eyes that at first glance seemed to be made from glass. The creatures, he observed, were clad in uniforms that had the bright extravagance of ceremonial costumes but which, viewed en masse, conveyed a strongly military impression. This impression was confirmed when, having realised that the former Jackboy was now conscious, all the fuzzy-textured beings simultaneously brought up hollow metal tubes which they directed at the new arrival, and which he deduced were some

archaic variety of weapon. He prepared to vent a low, disabling harmonic that he hoped would work on these bizarre bright-matter individuals, but was stayed from doing so by the appearance of a very different and much taller figure in his partly crystal-blinded field of vision.

This late entrant to the drama was a gangly and ectomorphic humanoid clad in what looked to be subdued formal attire surmounted by a grandiose cape of white fur held at the throat by an elaborate gold clasp. Where flesh was visible this was pale and translucent, so that an impression of the bones and musculature at work beneath the soapy skin was made disturbingly apparent. This sartorially splendid apparition gave a languid wave with one blanched hand at which the weapons of the short and furry regiment accompanying him were on the instant lowered. Stooping down so that his waxen and lugubrious countenance was brought into proximity with the escaped slave's own, he murmured a few indecipherable syllables which nonetheless seemed to be uttered in a questioning and sympathetic tone to which the prostrate baryonic mariner could only answer with a non-committal grunt and an ambiguous movement of his disproportionately large black cranium.

Though he discovered he was lapsing in and out of consciousness...presumably he'd greatly underestimated the enormous impact of his landing…in what seemed no time at all he and his incapacitated void-ship had been loaded onto separate low, flat wagons raised on huge blades that were pulled by the diminutive militia-animals across the slippery white expanse in which he'd seemingly arrived. After an indeterminable while the towers of an impressive architectural structure became visible through the obscuring whirl of frozen crystals, a great rearing palace built from simple shapes…blocks, pillars, arches…that were painted in a motley of bright primary colours. Being borne across some sort of gate that lowered to become a bridge and passing underneath a lofty wooden arch that was a beautiful deep emerald green were his last conscious memories for several days.

He woke to find himself in a resplendent bedchamber, almost entirely healed, where he was waited on by the small fleecy beasts who'd rescued him, albeit now dressed in a style less martial and presumably more suited to domestic serving duties. He was also visited by the tall, mournful being who'd commanded the aforesaid rescue, and by an extraordinary feminine automaton that after some few days he realised was his saviour's mate or perhaps lover. Within two weeks of commencing his confinement, his innate abilities with language had enabled him to undertake a dialogue with his unusual hosts and thus to learn more of the circumstances into which his improvised escape-craft had delivered him. It turned out that he and his ship were currently located at the north pole of a world which had the humble, self-effacing name of 'Dirt', this being the third major orbit-mass from a gigantic, crackling source of energy known as a sun; itself one of perhaps a hundred billion such that had arranged themselves into a vast and flat irregular ellipse that was referred to as a galaxy.

He also came to realise that his benefactors were by no means representative of this world's general inhabitants. The artificial female, whom it transpired was the queen of this strange polar region, had been made more than a century earlier by one of the predominating primate population, an unusually intelligent example of the species called Doctor Copelius. After a series of misfortunes this ingenious inventor had removed himself and his creation to this frozen wasteland, where he had proceeded to construct a whole civilisation of automata, entrusting them with the instructions for their own self-manufacture so that they might propagate themselves even in the event of his inevitable death. Ruling this secret clockwork realm was the doctor's original creation, whom he'd named 'Olympia.' Magnificently engineered and yet also possessed of an unsettling and icy sensuality, Olympia had a perfect and immobile doll-like countenance, a bosom and a cleavage that resembled some variety of typographical contrivance and a voice that chimed and tinkled in the manner of a wind-up musical device. The erstwhile Jackboy, having enjoyed naught but male companionship for several decades, found himself responding physically to the robotic regent but thought that to pursue such idle fancies might be inadvisable in light of the queen's evident relationship with the grave giant who'd found him injured out among the ice-fields, the dapper grotesque with skin like gelatine.

This brooding personage was not one of Copelius's marvellous mechanical confections, being artificial in a wholly different and perhaps more ghastly fashion altogether. As he told the story, he had been assembled from the body parts of diverse male cadavers and then somehow brought to life electrically by his ambitious 'father,' a one-time associate of the more elderly Copelius named Doctor Viktor Frankenstein. A string of tragedies had finally delivered this reanimated composite of other men to these northerly territories where he had discovered Toyland, as Olympia's principality was called, and the alluring mechanism who would soon become his bride. Due possibly to a shared masculine affinity it was this shambling Royal consort who instructed his inventive subjects to repair and modify the black star-sailor's craft, and also he who influenced his wife in her decision to provide the stranded voyager with a quintet of highly personable and vivacious wooden female manikins that had been engineered and modelled with the arts of love primarily in mind.

All things considered, he was starting to enjoy the idea of a cosmos with the lights on.

Mina, the American moon-colony, 1964:
A Long Way from Baltimore.

'No, see, this is very interesting. It's a documented fact that Kennedy Senior was running arms to Adenoid Hynkel during the war, but his son was an enthusiastic anti-fascist during the communist Thingmaker administration that followed. It just doesn't make sense that his assassin was a Red sympathiser. And then we hear these rumours about biological duplicates of Hynkel being reared in Brazil. Coincidence, my friend? I think not.'

Through the glass bubble of Pete Munch's helmet, his bespectacled and haggard face had the faintly superior and knowing look that made a growing number of his fellow moon-base operatives, Dave Rawls included, thoroughly dislike this wiry and persistent little man with his incessant idiot monologues concerning government conspiracy. The two men, Munch and Rawls, were working in the blue light of their thermite torches to repair one of the base's airlocks, damaged in the recent onslaught of gigantic moon-bugs that had so surprised the various lunar colonies. Even the Russian base had offered to share information in the hope of limiting the rampage of the monstrous insects before all of the terrestrial settlements were damaged or disrupted. Wearying of his companion's paranoid digressions, Rawls made an attempt to change the subject.

'Munch, if you don't mind, I'm getting sick of hearing all this shit. How 'bout you got a theory on where all these fucking giant ants are coming from? Now, that might be some fucking use.'

He instantly regretted asking his co-worker if he had a theory. Of course Pete Munch had a theory. There were rumours that the skinny self-styled intellectual liked to puff on the odd reefer with the niggers in the U.S. base's maintenance crew, and reefer-fiends have got a theory about everything.

'It's funny you should say that, Rawlsy, because it just so happens I do. You think about the moon, right? It was formed when a small planetoid crashed into the young Earth, billions of years ago. All of the debris from the impact gathered at the limits of Earth's field of gravity, where across the eons it coagulated into our moon, where we're standing now. But even back then, they've found fossils demonstrating that the Earth was home to primitive microbial life, surviving in conditions that are almost unimaginable. What if some of those tough micro-organisms got caught up in the exploding planetary wreckage that eventually congealed to form the moon? What if they'd evolved across the ages in the way that life evolved back home, but in a much different environment so that the most successful life-form is some kind of monster ant?'

Rawls wished he wasn't dressed up in his fishbowl helmet. Then he would have been at liberty to spit contemptuously. As it was, he had to settle for verbal disdain.

'Like I could give a shit. We've known about the moon-bugs since that limey Cavor's expedition came back from the moon without him in 1901. It's obvious they must have got here somehow. I don't care how. What I want to know is why they're suddenly attacking all Earth's lunar bases when we're not anywhere near their territory. I mean look at this! These fucking things got mandibles that cut through fucking steel! The fucking Baltimore Gun Club didn't plan for this.'

Munch nodded. All around, the pallid landscape stretched in silence to a black horizon.

'Well, I hear the Soviets believe the ants have got a rudimentary civilisation and even perhaps some kind of a religion. They say that the bugs' recent behaviour resembles violent uprisings on Earth…like Britain's Indian Mutiny…when people feel that their religious principles are somehow being violated. Boy, I wonder what an insect worships. Some kind of beetle Buddha, maybe?'

Pete Munch rambled on annoyingly, until his partner finally decided to just tune him out. As Rawls welded the airlock's sheared-through metal seal back into place his thoughts turned to the cute technician, Bayliss, who'd arrived here at the Pride of Baltimore moon colony with the last shuttle. Rawls had heard that Bayliss had a wife and son back home in Maryland, not that it necessarily meant anything: Dave Rawls was married with a kid as well, and he'd been blowing one of the administration guys from the main dome since he first got here. Men were lonely up here on the moon. Some of them even went insane and suffered from mirages of moon-pussy, naked women running through the brilliant lunar dust, slow-motion titties bouncing in the piss-weak gravity. Give pretty-boy Bayliss a few weeks of that and he'd be partying with Dave Rawls in the rover-hangars…

As lost in his erotic reverie as Munch was in his endlessly unreeling speculative discourse on insect theology, Rawls failed to notice the procession of small boot-prints that were forming magically in the soft pumice only a few feet away, heading off from the American dome-complex and into the empty lunar wastes. Through the receivers of her stolen helmet of invisibility, Mina had heard enough. She waded on towards her rendezvous with only rising plumes of dust to mark her passage.

The Galley-wag and company, above the moon, 1964: Skulls and Amazons

A thin film of translucent grey was slithering across the crater floor some several hundred feet below, cast by The Rose of Nowhere as she glided high above the lunar surface on her mission of reconnaissance. While Peg and Sarah Jane applied themselves to the great steering-wheel, their dark commander stood beside the rail and trained his huge light-drinking eyes upon the barren landscape crawling by beneath them. The remarkable black-matter privateer who'd once been known as Jackboy Sixty had already noted two or three intriguing incongruities in his appraisal of the reputedly lifeless satellite, and deep within his neuron-dense and disproportionately massive brain he was engaged in trying to connect these disparate impressions into a coherent narrative, attempting not to be distracted by the casually salacious chatter of his wooden women.

He had steered his marvellous balloon-boat past the nest of gentle swellings that were moon-hills and had seen the teeming city-hive of the clearly distressed and angry Selenites. Like unusually agitated armoured cars the giant insects milled in a belligerent confusion on the edges of a 'market square' arrangement at the centre of their colony, carefully avoiding a conspicuously empty spot right in the middle of this open area as if it were some kind of recently-denuded holy ground. Watching the urgent and incessant semaphore of the unsettled arthropods' antennae, the lost son of the Great Erebus Array had come to the conclusion that if the six-legged monsters had communicated by the means of sound rather than pheromones he would be hearing enraged bellows and wails of incredulous bereavement from the furiously churning mob. He'd idly wondered what could have upset them so.

Journeying on, occasionally squinting at the night sky through an astrolabe more to impress the Dutch dolls than for any practical considerations, he had reached a wide expanse that seemed to him to be possessed of an anomalously bumpy texture, so that he turned down The Rose of Nowhere's burners and descended to perhaps ten feet above the slumbering albino dunes for a closer inspection. At close range, he'd been bewildered to discover that the landscape's goose-bumped grain when viewed from overhead was at this lower altitude resolved into a field of what looked very much like human skulls. Locking the wheel into a pre-set automatic course, even the two womanikins ceased their squeaky flirtation long enough to join their baryonic lover at the rail and gaze in silent fascination at this ghastly spread of brittle egg-shell relics, bleaching there in the reflected Earthlight.

Fearing at first that this morbid spectacle betrayed some massacre of Earthling colonists, it had been the

sheer number of the fleshless craniums which had convinced him that this could not be the case. There were at least two or three thousand of them, far too many to have vanished unremarked from the terrestrial moon-bases, and unless he was mistaken in his understanding of human anatomy all of the skulls were male. Did this imply that there was currently or had once been a human population on the moon that had not come here from Miss Murray's twentieth-century home planet? Reasoning that if this plane of death's-heads were a lunar cemetery or ossuary then that would suggest some form of major settlement nearby, he'd lifted up into the higher reaches of the star-sprayed firmament once more and glided on across those silver pastures, acne-scarred by meteorites.

Only when he had ventured some leagues further and had stumbled on the sprawling acreage of alabaster moss, the grazing alien livestock and, most trenchantly, the citadel of naked women did he feel it would be prudent to return The Rose of Nowhere to her moorings and consult with his human accomplice as to how they should proceed in these combustible, outrageous circumstances.

Mina, Mysta and Maza, the moon, 1964: Give Me the Moonlight, Give Me the Girls…

Only when the skull-fields first came into view over the starboard bow did she reluctantly believe the tale the Galley-wag had told her when he and the dolls had taken her aboard after their rendezvous in the moon's Limbus. The pale bulbs with staring, empty sockets called to mind a probably-apocryphal report she'd come across some decades previously of a so-called 'honeymoon in space,' where the adventuring young couple had described a field of skulls here on Earth's orbiting companion. This connection, although anecdotal, did at least suggest a precedent for the bone carpet above which The Rose of Nowhere drifted

onward through the dark. Mina had no such explanation, though, for the immense moss-garden when
they reached it, or for the odd fauna that were feeding
there. She rapidly identified the chalk-white growth as
being the same species that she'd previously noticed
near their landing-site, and thought that in these
quantities it might explain the intermittent presence of
an atmosphere…though not what kept that atmosphere
from drifting into space when the moon's gravity was
patently inadequate to do so. Then, of course, there
were the animals.

These were exotic almost to the point of being
comical. A herd of piglet-creatures that communicated
in low whistles and whose hides gave the impression they'd somehow been knitted were all clustering
around a wavering giant worm or salamander which
appeared to be secreting a clear, broth-like fluid that
the lunar swine found nourishing. Nearby a smaller
group of very different animals were nibbling contentedly at the lush pelt of moss, these having skins
that were predominately black albeit marked with a
distinctive pattern of white polka-dots. After observing
them for a few moments, Mina also noticed that these
black-and-white things seemed to possess an innate
ability to change their shape. There were at least three
or four other species present on the fleecy lunar veldt,
including a variety of plump yet brightly-patterned bird
whose stubby and vestigial-looking wings were nonetheless sufficient to propel it through the low-gravity
heavens.

Just beyond these fields of what were obviously
beasts reared as food they found the citadel that Mina
had until then thought to be either a bawdy joke or an
idyllic sexual fancy of her shaggy-haired companion.
Its towers and boulevards were thronged with stunning amazons, all naked save for the occasional cape,
sword-belt or wrought silver helmet and all with eyes
fixed inquisitively on the Galley-wag's extraordinary
vessel as, at Mina's signal, it descended cautiously towards what seemed to be the city's central plaza where
a statuesque reception party waited.

Given the inherent strangeness of the situation, Mina barely blinked when it transpired that
the beguiling lunar nudes had an impressive grasp of
English and, apparently thanks to a radio transmitter
situated up in the high Andes, fluent Spanish. Mina
and her party were escorted to an opalescent chamber
where the Galley-wag sat with an ornate cushion in his
lap, as Mina later realised to conceal the generous tu-
mescence that their hostesses' nudity had instantly oc-
casioned, and there met with two astonishingly lovely
women whom it seemed were high-ranked representatives of this remarkable all-female populace, a brunette
evidently known as Mysta and a blonde named Maza.
These conversed both amiably and willingly, although
the tale that they recounted was alarming.

Countless centuries ago, the women's native
race had been a great civilisation that existed near
the universe's rim, developing amongst those oldest
first-formed suns until an unavoidable catastrophe…a
deadly ray-emitting star known as a gamma-burster…
had threatened to sterilise their entire galaxy. Migrat-
ing to the inner cosmos, the ancestors of these women
and their erstwhile mates had settled on Earth's moon
in the terrestrial Neolithic period, discovering that
some zones had workable gravity caused by incred-
ibly dense obelisks of black material that had been
buried on the lunar satellite for unknown reasons by
a similarly unknown agency, sometime in the remote
primordial past. They'd introduced their oxygen-
producing moss and livestock, far from the native
ant-like creatures they'd discovered here, establishing
a thriving colony that had branched off at least twice
to investigate the possibilities for humanoid survival
on both Mars and Venus. Here upon the moon, their
enclave had been a utopia until just sixty-three years
earlier. Until the plague.

This plague, which Mina realised guiltily had co-
incided with Professor Cavor's 1901 lunar expedition,
had killed every last male in the colony, accounting
for the lawn of polished skulls. The bereaved females,
though of great longevity in human terms, had no
more than a century to find some means of making
themselves pregnant before even the youngest amongst
them would be past child-bearing age. Luckily, they
had recently found a solution in the form of a vacuum-
preserved and frozen human male cadaver which, it
was believed, might very well provide a source of still-
viable sperm. Ironically, the means of their salvation
was discovered in the midst of the indigenous moon-
insects, where it seemed to have no function save as
an object of veneration. It was most regrettable, Mysta
agreed, that their removal of the body had provoked
such a warlike reaction from the Selenites. And yet,
as Maza went on to enquire, given the women's dire
predicament, what else were they to do?

Even as the two lunar beauties led her and her
shipmates down to the refrigerated chamber where
the freeze-dried specimen of masculinity was held in
storage, Mina felt the fateful fragments of the puzzle
falling ominously into place somewhere within her
reeling mind. Before the bulkhead chamber doors
were opened in an icy cloud of crystallising vapour,
she knew just what she would see.

There in the bluish artificial light, rigid as the sar-
cophagus of an Egyptian king, stood a corpulent figure
that she had last met in better health almost seventy
years before. With cricket cap frost-welded to his head
and the fate of a species in his ice-encrusted loins, the
dead eyes of Professor Selwyn Cavor stared plaintively
through the rising billows of sub-zero condensation
into Mina's own.

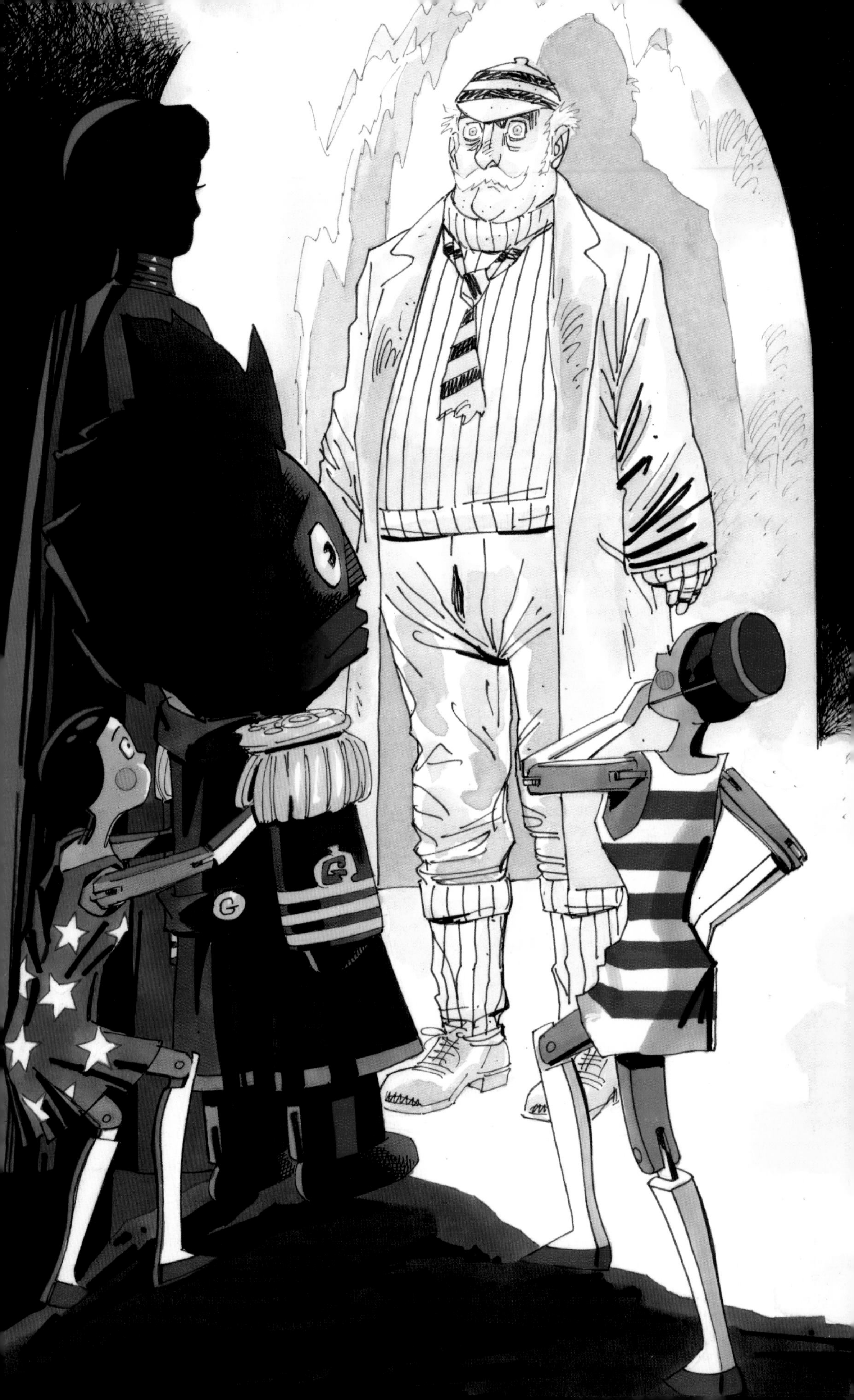

MINIONS OF THE MOON
by John Thomas

(Originally serialised in *Lewd Worlds Science Fiction*, Ed. James Colvin, #185, 1969.)

Chapter Three: Saviours

Wheels locked in place, the patient's chair will clearly not be going anywhere. Through an obscuring cumulus of sedatives the notion percolates that these hours are officially allotted to art therapy, the inmates formally encouraged in the reconstruction of their smashed identities from paper, glue and pre-emptively blunted crayons. Listlessly the patient makes pretence at working on a cut-and-paste collage, uselessly adding and subtracting elements simply to foster the appearance of continued work upon a project that in actuality was finished months ago.

If it were thought to be complete there is the danger that it might be taken off by the administrators and exhibited as if the product of a gifted four year-old, with subsequent demands upon the patient to start work on something new. In fact, the thought of more creative toil is actively upsetting. All those hours of careful labour had nothing to do with therapeutic self-expression, but had everything to do with ordinary self-preservation.

The assembled picture is the patient's sole escape hatch. It has long been glaringly apparent, even in their fog of pharmaceutics, that they are forgotten by an outside world which they in turn must struggle to remember. There will be no saviour swooping to their rescue, this they are convinced of. No way out, save through the portal they have patiently constructed. Sitting there before the angled drawing board it's possible to let the disinfectant-scented corridors melt into nothingness. It's possible to step, like a true lunatic, into a paper landscape flooded with both memory and meaning.

The immobile wheelchair provides no impediment. The patient walks unfettered in a private realm of dust, and hush, and silver...

Cavor and the Selenites, the moon, 1901:
A Cricket-Cap of Thorns

This self was not a self that any sapient biped could have recognised as such. Not predicated on a discrete individual awareness, it was rather the emergent property of an insensate multitude. Lacking for a conceptual equivalent to 'I' or 'We' the nebulous sense of identity had instead coalesced about a core of 'This', a delicately balanced semiotic scent-trace that was not even a word. Almost an entity, this self inhabited a sparse reality comprised of little more than an olfactory map, a pheromonal grid across which the ten thousand chitin-plated engines representing its material corpus acted out their sorties and retrievals. Now, however, the stench-diagram that was its world seemed torn to incoherent fragments as this self attempted desperately to process unfamiliar data; to contain a new and shattering information.

From the point of view of the marooned professor, naturally, the situation was less complex and more readily explained, albeit equally upsetting: having ordered his companions to return to Earth without him in their vessel coated by his marvellous metallic paste, he now faced the inevitable consequences of his selfless sacrifice. As black and lustrous as obsidian, as big as tractors, the unreasoning lunar insects crowded down the narrow rock channel towards him, clambering across their comrades' backs and crushing them to gory splinters in a single-minded rush on their objective. The jet foliage of their antennae twitched and trembled as though in an absent breeze, danced as though to a rhapsody inaudible. Mandibles scissored with a sound like stropping butchers' knives and Selwyn Cavor had the dismal realisation that he'd been backed to the very edge of this particular anomalous patch of the satellite's terrain, which somehow harboured near-terrestrial gravity and atmosphere. One more retreating step would take his spindly-limbed and bulbous body, clad in only jacket, britches, scarf and comically-perched hat into a zone of freezing suffocation that was nonetheless preferable to those advancing jaws, like clashing scimitars. His last breath soured by the now-overwhelming tang of formic acid, he pulled his cap firmly down and then did what he had to.

This self halted in its several dozen tracks. The complicated fragrance-pattern it had been pursuing seemed to suddenly collapse, subsiding to an inert pool of signal which was motionless, the sharpness of the odour fading rapidly on a steep gradient that this self usually associated with an irrevocable and almost instantaneous loss of heat. A knowledge vast and terrible began to crystallise within the net of sensory impressions that were this self's only apprehension of the universe, an ominous assemblage of unprecedented notions that the reeling horde-mind struggled to assimilate.

The swiftly cooling perfume-profile sprawled unmoving at its myriad feet was, this self sensed, a very different and perhaps even a more developed category of self that came from elsewhere. Elsewhere, as defined by this self, was a place beyond its charted atlas of aromas and therefore effectively beyond material existence as that term was understood by the compound intelligence. Further to this, the strange chemical outline of the creature lying still and prone before this self had previously been accompanied by two more scent-shapes of a similar morphology which had by some means since departed past the range of sensory apprehension. Inconceivably, the three intruders had appeared to be autonomous rather than three components of a rival self; a that self. With their evident capacity for somehow organising matter into new forms, such as the containing shell that they'd come here from elsewhere in, it was apparent that these hereto unimaginable non-collective entities were of a higher order of complexity and had arrived here from a consequently higher plane of being. The celestial trinity had left one of their number here, perhaps with the intent of educating and illuminating this self, elevating the perceptions of its colony-awareness to their own exalted altitudes of consciousness. And now this self had driven that redeemer to its death.

A new bouquet began to register in its accustomed fragrance-palette, having notes of awe with undertones of terror and eternity. This self had caught its first whiff of religion.

Mina & the Galley-wag, the Amazon moon-city, 1964: A Harsh Mistress

Mina watched in dismal fascination as the fiery-eyed nude studies that made up the lunar cavalry led out their pale and raucous saurian steeds from a capacious subterranean stable onto the moon's sunlit fields of dust. The fitting of perhaps a thousand ornate silver bridles made a music of deceptive delicacy, starkly punctuated by aggressive reptile shrieks, and the adventuress wondered despairingly how things had reached this sorry state, the very conflict she'd been sent here with the Blazing World's instructions to prevent. The female myrmidons, part of a colony migrated from the universe's rim innumerable aeons since, had lost the male component of their species to a relatively recent plague. Facing extinction without any ready method of fertilisation, they'd resorted to appropriating the remains of stranded lunar pioneer Professor Selwyn Cavor, hoping to extract the late explorer's frozen sperm and thereby propagate their way out of the current crisis. Catastrophically, however, the professor's frosted cadaver had seemingly become an object of religious veneration to the selfsame creatures that had killed him, monstrous insects native to the planetoid and known only as Selenites. These giant arthropods were sure to want their idol back, with the ferocious amazons determined that they shouldn't have it. The forthcoming war, which seemed inevitable now, would put at risk the moon's many terrestrial colonies and force the humans to seek safer habitats in areas of the satellite to which the Blazing World would rather that they did not venture, or at least not yet. Forestalling this eventuality had been her task, at which Mina had proven a conspicuous failure.

Nearby the dark-matter buccaneer whose *Rose of Nowhere* had transported her to this precarious sphere stood with his gawping wooden cabin-girls as keen spectator to the naked army's martial preparations. Dish-sized pupils eagerly drank in every salacious detail of the various straddlings and mountings as the Galley-wag kept up the flimsiest pretence at conversation with one of the women's leaders, a translucently complexioned blonde named Maza. This entirely spurious discourse was effected solely for the purposes of keeping the impatient warrior queen within the baryonic pirate's prurient and appreciative vicinity for as long as was feasible.

'By my endrenching spurt, 'tis as mammariable a fluck of butter-backs as I have hairto wetnessed! Be they mostpartly cumpliable about the slidey-ride, in yer herpinion?'

Such English as Maza had acquired from scattered wireless broadcasts was quite clearly insufficient to the task of fathoming the extra-solar privateer's impenetrable patois. Making the erroneous assumption that her visitor's enquiry must pertain to the bipedal lunar lizards rather than their riders, the imperious moon-queen tossed her white-gold mane dismissively as she replied. Her intonations had a faintly Spanish lilt, no doubt as a result of the stentorian radio transmitter in the Andes previously cited as a source of the unearthly amazons' linguistic expertise.

'The Nak-Kar are a breed somewhere between your own world's dino-saurians and the briefly-reigning giant flightless birds that followed them. Though distantly related to the stubby-winged and brightly-patterned moon-fowl that you have observed amongst our livestock, the Nak-Kar are a much larger and more vicious strain that are ideal as battle-animals. Some think that nothing save their presence keeps at bay the solitary perverted giant who observes all our doings from afar.'

At this the corsair of the starless abyss tipped his barrel-sized head to one side inquisitively.

'I cannaught remagine whyfor anybawdy might engoarge in such a hinterprize.'

Seemingly unfamiliar with the whole idea of disingenuousness, Maza shook her long platinum locks in sympathy with the freebooter's evident incomprehension.

'Nor can I. He was already here when we Lunites first landed many generations since. He keeps to his own lunar neighbourhood, that bluish atmospheric pocket barely visible upon the west horizon. Bald and perhaps four of your Earth metres tall, his only task is seemingly to loiter in an inappropriately skimpy bathrobe, looking on unblinkingly as we perform our daily regimen of military exercises. We refer to him as 'the voyeur'. His is a very different species from our own, or otherwise we would have sought to use his seed in our repopulation strategy. It scarcely need be said that only similar considerations have discouraged us from harvesting your own genetic matter.'

Here the former galley-captive blinked inscrutably and shrugged.

'Waal, let us not dismess my genie-trickle matter so unpheromoniously. I'll grunt yer it's a menstruous inprodability, but I'd pit all me beef and thunder to the attemptation...'

Mina, gazing bleakly at the snapping, squawking ocean of albino dragons and their lance or cutlass-wielding riders, suddenly shook off her trance of lacerating self-recrimination.

'Wait a minute. If you're so convinced that human sperm will do the trick, why haven't you abducted any of the males from the terrestrial moon-bases that are within your reach? From what I know of earthmen they'd most probably consider it a blessing, rather than a violation.'

Maza ventured a small, mournful smile.

'Then they would be aware of us as something other than a wistful myth or a moon-addled fantasy. They would investigate us and then after that, if earthly history is anything to go by, they would subjugate us or destroy us. Better that our tribe fade to extinction for the want of men than suffer such indignities. I fear that your Professor Cavor is our best and only hope, and be assured that we shall fight to the last woman to retain possession of his body. It is true; the native Selenites outnumber us by more than ten to one. Despite superior intellects and greater martial talents we may not survive the coming conflict, but what other option do we have?'

The erstwhile music teacher was still wondering if Selwyn Cavor had ever anticipated that one day women would fight over his body when a perturbation at the corner of her vision captured her attention. The horizon to the south, though icy cold, seemed suddenly to shimmer as if through the curtain of a heat haze. A black, teeming heat haze. Maza too had noticed this phenomenon and called out to her sister-monarch Mysta, mounted at the head of the assembled reptile-riders, in a language that to Mina's ear had vowel-sounds and inflections that were very similar to Cantonese. As Mysta passed on these instructions to the mounted warriors about her, her blonde sibling turned back to their otherworldly guests and with her eyes as sere and unforgiving as an arctic winter offered a translation.

'Be at once to arms. To arms, and to the death. They're coming.'

The Baltimore Fun Club, American moon-colony, 1964: Moonbeams, Home in a Jar

The sun's last rays, beguiling as they sloped across the base's largely unused rear equipment hangar, were as colourless and pallid as its first. Taking a deep pull on the smouldering and pungent stick of tea, Pete Munch supposed that was the aspect of his lunar tour of duty that he'd found it hardest to adjust to: no blue skies by day without an atmosphere to scatter solar radiance, and likewise no red at sunset. Nothing except spangled darkness over the horizon, any time of day or night. This monochrome existence, he reflected, must be what it's like to be a character out of a television show. He pictured himself in a sitcom with his straggly hair bobbed and a starched white apron, raising one plucked eyebrow at his screen husband's ineptitude, and was immediately wracked with mirth that noisily propelled the sweet

smoke from his flaring nostrils in a series of volcanic bursts. Guilty about the wastage, he held out the reefer in one waving hand for the next man in line to take a hit.

Shaking his head in condescending pity, maintenance crew supervisor Cyrus Pemberton retrieved the spindly offering from between Pete Munch's nicotine-stained fingers, with his languid and yet piercing ivory gaze remaining fixed upon the watery-eyed and coughing senior engineer.

'Hey, Munch, are you sure that you're not a relative of that Norwegian painter guy? That picture of the scream he did is pretty much how I imagine you looked as a baby. No offence.'

While Pemberton took businesslike sips on the sizzling marijuana cigarette, the third of the self-styled Baltimore Fun Club members present in the hangar for the lunar sundown grinned and went on cleaning his high-voltage plasma rifle. Senior charge-hand Marlon Little had the lean build of a dancer and the lethal reputation of a cobra, one of those who had enlisted as a way out of Baltimore's blacker and, inevitably, poorer neighbourhoods. No-one belittled Marlon Little.

'Well, shit. Pemberton, how come a natural New York Times art critic like yourself is up here on the fuckin' moon? You oughtta be back Earthside, bumping up negro intelligence statistics.'

The charge-hand's immediate superior regarded Little with the heavy-lidded and unblinking languor of a hopped-up basilisk, his eyes like yellow warning lanterns through the rising fumes.

'Might I remind you that I'm up here supervising a whole bunch of trigger-happy niggers like yourself? Take two demerits, and I'm docking you a week's pay for the insubordination, plus your general lack of ruliness...' This last touch was too much for even Pemberton. He passed the joint to Little in a mutual barrage of giggles, while Pete Munch attempted to get back in on the conversation.

'Marlon, if you're such a gunslinger, how come you're playing with that sissy plasma rifle?'

Little studied Munch with narrow-eyed disdain while he held down his lungful of the moon-grass. Finally he blew a swirling nebula into the swiftly disappearing sunrays.

'Munch, I thought you pasty motherfuckers just about invented physics? You go lettin' loose with some pump-action number up here on the moon, that scrawny white ass gonna be in orbit.'

The attendant image which this conjured, the bespectacled and hangdog engineer endlessly circling the lunar satellite bearing a smoking shotgun and a look of pained surprise, had all three of them laughing. As the woefully-depleted twist of burning gage returned to him, Pete Munch drew in a scorching breath and gazed contentedly out through the foot-thick screens of flexiglass over a pockmarked reach of taut-stretched shadows and declining light. Membership of the Fun Club, for which he had naturally provided the obscurely witty name, was one of the chief perks of his eighteen-month lunar stint. The hydroponic weed they clandestinely grew up here in the neglected antechambers of *The Pride of Baltimore* was dynamite, and Munch could tell that both his colleagues thought of him as hipper than the average white guy. He was pretty sure they found his frequent monologues on jazz instructive and informative rather than patronising and insufferable for all of their good-natured, ribbing protests to the contrary. He could identify, and figured they appreciated that.

The moon-hemp, though, a hefty mason-jar full of

the stuff, was twice as strong as anything he'd tried in Maryland. He loved the way it made his neurons twinkle in a blissful, shimmering wave and how his every random thought instantly sprouted ornate coral fronds of imagery, especially in an eye-tricking lunar dusk such as the one that now confronted him. He hadn't even known until he got here that the moon had dusks and days and nights. He hadn't realised that it was rotating, with its revolutions timed uncannily so that the same face always looked away from Earth. Twilight transformed the vista to a luminescent ambiguity in which, when suitably intoxicated, anything could be imagined. Now, for instance, with the pot enhancing Munch's visionary capabilities, he conjured a phantasmagoric tableau from the random mottling of shine and shade that stained the distant dunes. Astounded by his own capacity to visualise...maybe he should have been a beatnik artist after all...he pictured an exquisite diorama which even a Coleridge might find difficult to better. Through his mind's eye galloped a delirious and erotic cavalcade of naked women, *Stagman* centrefolds astride fierce alabaster monsters with the waning light become a glinting constellation on their lifted lances, silver helmets and barbaric ornaments. It was a shame, in many ways, that such a fine creative mind as his was being wasted in the engineering corps where there was no-one to appreciate its treasures...

'Munch, I have to ask, are you dead from the hairstyle down by any chance? I mean, you're sitting here just grinning, looking smug. Can't you see all that crazy shit that's going on out there?'

Startled, the neurasthenic ferret of a man spun round to face Cy Pemberton with wild, disoriented eyeballs circling like frantic goldfish in the bowls of his prescription lenses.

'Uh...yes. Yes, I can. Jesus, can you? Fuck!'

Pemberton glared pointedly at Munch in lieu of answer. Marlon Little, shuffling the packing crate he sat on to command a better view of the unscheduled nude revue outside, put down his plasma rifle to give an appreciative whistle at the universe and all of its surprising bounties.

'Huh. You know what's funny? We the only motherfuckers seein' this shit. Everybody else is in the recreation unit watchin' some Montana Wildhack picture what my cousin tells me only got about three titty-shots in the whole thing.'

Having just managed to convince himself that he was looking at some kind of interplanetary incident rather than evidence of his own limitless imagination, Pete Munch was incredulous.

'Gentlemen, we're standing on a scientific threshold of discovery! For God sake, this is man's first glimpse of a whole new civilisation, and you're counting up the boobies? What we've got to do is alert base command, then work out how we're going to accurately write this up...'

Little was laughing openly by now and even the disdainful Pemberton seemed tickled.

'Munch, my man, you have to be aware that your own reputation on the base is, shall we say, hardly a level-headed one. And as for me and Mr. Little here, you may have noticed that we're black. So, say we enter a report about how we saw naked ladies riding big white newts over the moon-hills from this hangar that we're not supposed to be in, let alone be growing dope in, what do you imagine to be the most likely repercussions?' Clearly not expecting a reply, the maintenance chief let his mocking and appraising gaze slide from the speechless engineer back to the Folies Bergère carnage going on beyond the viewport.

'So, no. We ain't writing this one up. Damn. You know what, I wish I had some popcorn.'

And with that the Fun Club settled back to watch the fun.

Mina, the Galley-wag & Maza, *The Rose of Nowhere,* 1964: A Moonlight Flit

'You interfering witch,' snarled Maza. 'Do you even understand what you are doing?'

Clad in Vull's concealing helmet of invisibility and poised behind the furious lunar regent with a similarly unseen 'dagger' (actually a metal slide-rule) pressed against the struggling monarch's windpipe, Mina was beginning to suspect she had disastrously misunderstood the whole delirious situation and therefore elected to keep quiet. Ahead of and below *The Rose of Nowhere* as it slid through the extraterrestrial gloom she could make out the vanguard of the Lunite cavalry, a scything arc of argent weaponry and smooth marmoreal flesh that sliced into the tidal wall of black and gleaming giant ants, approaching from the opposite direction like enraged and scuttling caviar.

As soon as Maza's sister and co-ruler Mysta had charged out of the moon-city with her mounted cohort to engage with the onrushing Selenites, Mina's sequence of actions (far too desperate and impulsive to be called a plan) had simply blossomed into being fully-formed, like Athena from Zeus's brow albeit with little sign of that goddess's wisdom or divine assurance. Switching on her misappropriated helmet at a setting where the light-deflecting headgear was itself not visible, she'd whipped her slide-rule from its pouch and tackled the fair-haired moon-empress from behind, pressing the harmless instrument against her startled captive's throat and hissing threateningly in Maza's ear.

'Now, listen carefully. Nobody else can see or hear me, and the blade that you can feel is razor-sharp. You're going to do exactly as I say, and if you even think of raising an alarm I'll slit your gizzard. Nod once if you understand me.'

Maza, even less certain than Mina as to what a gizzard was, had made a tiny inclination of her head, her carmine lips set in a tight and angry line. Compelled thus, the nude beauty had allowed her unseen captor to frog-march her to those vaults beneath the soaring Lunite towers and battlements, accompanied by the Dutch dolls and their anomalous commander who'd all seemed just as bewildered as the lunar potentate herself by this bizarre turn of events. The amazons on guard outside the icy subterranean storage chambers had been ordered by their sovereign to unlock their frigid cellar and then help transport its contents to the Galley-wag's extraordinary sky-boat, never noticing their leader's look of helpless rage or the strained quality her intonations had, much less that she'd left two distinct and separate sets of footprints in the all-pervading lunar dust behind her.

Now, as Mina gazed down anxiously across her captive's shoulder and *The Rose of Nowhere's* starboard rail at the horrific fever-vision of a conflict going on below, she was less sure of her frantically improvised agenda than she'd even been at the scheme's outset. The determined former Mrs. Harker's only certainty was that she must do something to avert this species-threatening disaster, a conviction which a brief glance at the seething battlefield beneath their hovering vehicle served only to entrench: she saw the chestnut-haired Valkyrie Mysta wheel her screaming mount about into a charge, dipping her lance to pierce the thorax of a rearing insectile aggressor and then letting the impaled and squirming behemoth's forward momentum carry it above her head in a slow arc through the slight gravity, to land as pulp and twitching fragments in her wake. Mina watched helplessly as elsewhere in the murderous melee one of the shrieking Nak-Kar lizard-stallions toppled sideways, one leg bitten through by bone-shearing ant mandibles with the result that both the screeching reptile and its luckless fallen rider were at once torn to unrecognisable and gory shreds by the attendant horde of milling Selenites. Swallowing hard, Mina made her attempt to seize the moment.

'Most Resplendent Boson of the Ultimate,' she solemnly intoned, employing a bedizened honorific of the kind she knew that her black-matter comrade favoured. 'We must be about the lowering of our bounty; on stout ropes for preference and to a prudent fifteen feet above the skirmish. Also, would you have some manner of loud-hailing instrument for our reluctant guest to utilise?'

The being previously known as Jackboy Sixty scratched his monstrous head as he considered. **'Waal, there moot be some ferriety o' hullering-trumpet that I can loquate, if yer'll alaw me bit a merement. Minewheel, Peg and Sarey-Jane shall drangle the refrigerbaited cargo to a scrutably frost-rating dipth below our zippelin, as yer surgist.'**

The wooden women, with their striped or spangled dresses standing out like stiff flags in some non-existent moon-breeze, set about a winching-down of the rope-cradled object that their captain had instructed them to lower. At the same time their ebon superior emerged from the aft locker with an item which resembled a hand-held trombone augmented by mysterious valves and other, less identifiable components. He held this device up to their angry prisoner and to the faint heat-pattern that his massive extra-human eyes could just make out standing behind the fuming matriarch, tilting his shaggy cranium to one side quizzically, awaiting a response from Mina.

'Give Queen Maza here the megaphone or whatever you call it. Now, your Majesty, you're going to recite the words I whisper to you, and if you can manage that convincingly I promise there's a way that this can be made right without the need for further slaughter. If you cannot manage that, however, then your lifeless body will be flung unceremoniously to that heaving mass of Selenites beneath us. Just do as you're told, and we shall see what happens.'

But what happened was a great surprise to everyone, especially the author of the strategy.

Mysta, Cavor & the Selenites, the moon, 1964: A Sea of Crises

This self halted instantaneously in its multitude of tracks. Somehow suspended in the odourless expanse that hung above the pungent markers and meridians of its awareness-field were the characteristic acid reek and the distinctive sugar-codes which signified the slain redeemer. Visibly, a wave of eerily coordinated motion rippled through its thousands of antennae as these realigned to point in one direction, like black compass-needles swinging inexorably towards a single north.

For Mysta, standing in the stirrups of her blanched and flightless dragon, stained with insect-juice up to her elbows, the effect was as immediate and as bewildering. The scurrying battalion were, with horrible simultaneity, frozen to perfect immobility save for their feelers that all trembled now towards a point above the carnage and behind her, forcing the moon-warrior to wheel her snarling Nak-Kar steed about so that she too might view the source of the disturbance.

In the glittering black above the battlefield, the strange balloon-boat of their recent visitors was drifting as though upon some aetheric tide, and dangling beneath it was the bluish-grey form of the Lunites' chosen posthumous sperm-donor, headgear frost-fused with his fraying scalp. More startling still from Mysta's point of view was the appearance of her own beloved sister, Maza, standing at the vessel's rail all by herself and calling to the combatants below, aided by some arcane variety of speaking-apparatus. It was to the hypothetical aural distortions of this instrument that Mysta readily attributed the note of strangled tension in her sibling's voice as she addressed the multitude.

'Hear me, my people! Cease your attack. We are returning that which is the totem of our insect neighbours to the place from where we first removed it. We expect them to abandon their hostilities and follow us, and I beseech you not to use this opportunity to injure them. Instead, withdraw to our own fortress and await my imminent return. When we have made full restitution to the Selenites, my friends aboard this craft have promised me that they will next locate a suitable replacement for the seed-source that we have relinquished, and that in a day or so we shall be back amongst you with the promised offering. Mysta, rule wisely in my absence. I'll be with you soon.'

With that the curiously-decorated airboat floated off towards the planetoid's horizon, while the Lunite women's insect adversaries crawled after it en masse, in ordered ranks and at a reverential pace that made it seem as if they were embarked upon some monstrous and inhuman pilgrimage. Obeying Maza's parting wishes, Mysta turned her puzzled cavalry about and led the subdued legion back to the tall spires and pastures of their own encampment, all the while trying to banish from her mind the anxious undercurrent there had been in Maza's clipped inflections and the trapped look in her sister's eyes. She only hoped that their peculiar guests would keep their promise, and that she had not just witnessed the surrender of the only thing which stood between her people and extinction.

Mina and company, the Amazon moon-city, days later: The Sins of the Father

Maza almost pealed with joy as she crushed Mina to her bosom in a hug of gratitude, while the dark-matter corsair and his Dutch dolls looked on jealously. Her platinum hair gleaming in the soft reflected earthlight, the moon-queen expressed her thanks for the ninth time that evening.

'Truly, you and your companions are our saviours. I trust you will forgive the harsh words that we had when I thought you my captor, just before the wisdom of your scheme was made apparent to me. You are neither she-dog nor flat-chested, and I herewith render my apologies. When you returned the frozen corpse of your former acquaintance to the Selenites and then continued on with me aboard in the direction of your native planet, I did not know what to think. But then you showed me the replacement sperm-source that you'd promised, and I understood. My people's prayers were answered, and without potentially annihilating war against the native insect-kind. How can we possibly repay this act of great beneficence?'

The visibly excited Galley-wag was clearly just about to offer his lascivious ideas as to the nature of a suitable reward when Mina thought to intervene. They were all sitting at a banquet table laden down with fresh-cooked moonbirds, shorn of their Easter-egg plumage and then lightly broiled. The centrepiece was one of the black and white spotted metamorphic bipeds that the travellers had earlier seen grazing on the moss-fields just outside the lunar city, crouching roasted on a salver with some form of local fruit stuffed in its mouth. Gesturing to the feast, Mina deflected any thought of further reimbursement, to the obvious annoyance of her lusty pirate colleague.

'Oh, this generous spread is all the thanks we need, your Majesty. With war between the Lunites and the

Selenites averted, the black obelisks which you suggested were responsible for this sphere's intermittent gravity will not be unearthed by terrestrial explorers until such time as my masters wish, thus serving my ends admirably. How is the work with your new donor going, incidentally? I shouldn't mind a last look at him before we embark for our home planet, if that was at all convenient.'

And so it was that soon thereafter Mina found herself in what appeared to be a brightly lit Lunite laboratory somewhere within the city's labyrinthine bowels. Amazon beauties with mask-like expressions busied themselves with pipettes and Petri dishes round the naked cadaver upon its central slab. Their ministrations were already clearly at an advanced stage, and Maza smiled with satisfaction.

'See! We have already managed to extract a myriad of viable spermatozoa and have fertilised a number of donated eggs successfully. Soon, all the moon will be alive with our new benefactor's children. And you say he was a brilliant man; a great professor like our previous donor?'

Mina nodded, studiedly avoiding the accusing glare of her black-matter cohort as he stood beside her, silently berating her for her economy with what he knew to be the truth.

'Yes. The professor was a famous mathematician of tremendous intellect and capability. I can only imagine what a moon-reared generation of his offspring will be like, but, anyway, I'm sure that everything will turn out for the best.'

Voice cracking slightly on the last words of her declaration, caught out in a lie, Mina discovered that her gaze was locked upon the dead stare of the late James Moriarty, dark eyes knowing and sardonic, even in demise. She shuddered inwardly, and wondered what undreamt-of future tribulations she had set in motion here.

What great and monstrous eclipse?

The patient gazes fixedly at their collage, lost in its mesmerising detail. Through an obfuscating ground-fog of incessant medication the idea persists that in these random scraps of glued-together imagery are to be found the scattered fragments of the inmate's past, the shards of their misplaced identity: a minstrel-costumed racial slur clipped from the label on a jar of marmalade; a fine-hatched chapbook illustration that depicts a melodrama villain clinging to a glass ball of unearthly radiance; wooden dolls and naked women and behind it all a full and risen moon, the emblematic flag of lunacy.

So caught up is the patient in their faltering attempt to reconstruct a personality from paste and paper that at first they do not notice the return of the large-breasted doctor, nor the fact that the physician is accompanied by a visitor. This latter party is now crouching by the patient's wheelchair, murmuring in husky female tones that somehow permeate the soporific haze.

'Oh, Mina. Oh, my poor darling. I'm sorry. I'm so sorry.'

Gradually, unhurriedly, the patient's head turns from the patchwork masterpiece to study their first caller in what must be nearly forty years. Outside, through a North London night, the hectic world proceeds towards its end and in the brown blur of an urban firmament no stars are visible, nor over Soho is there any moon.

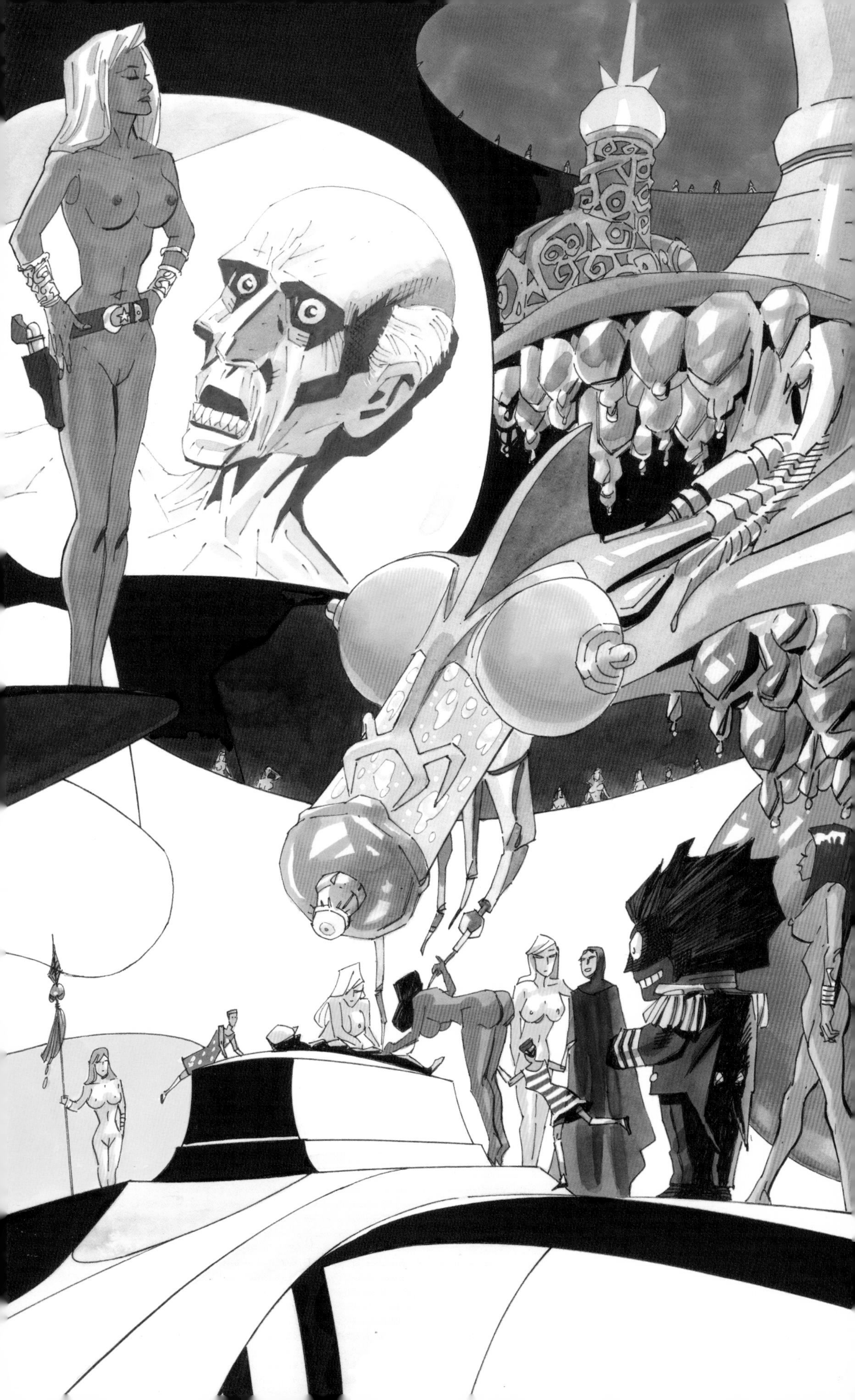

COVER GALLERY

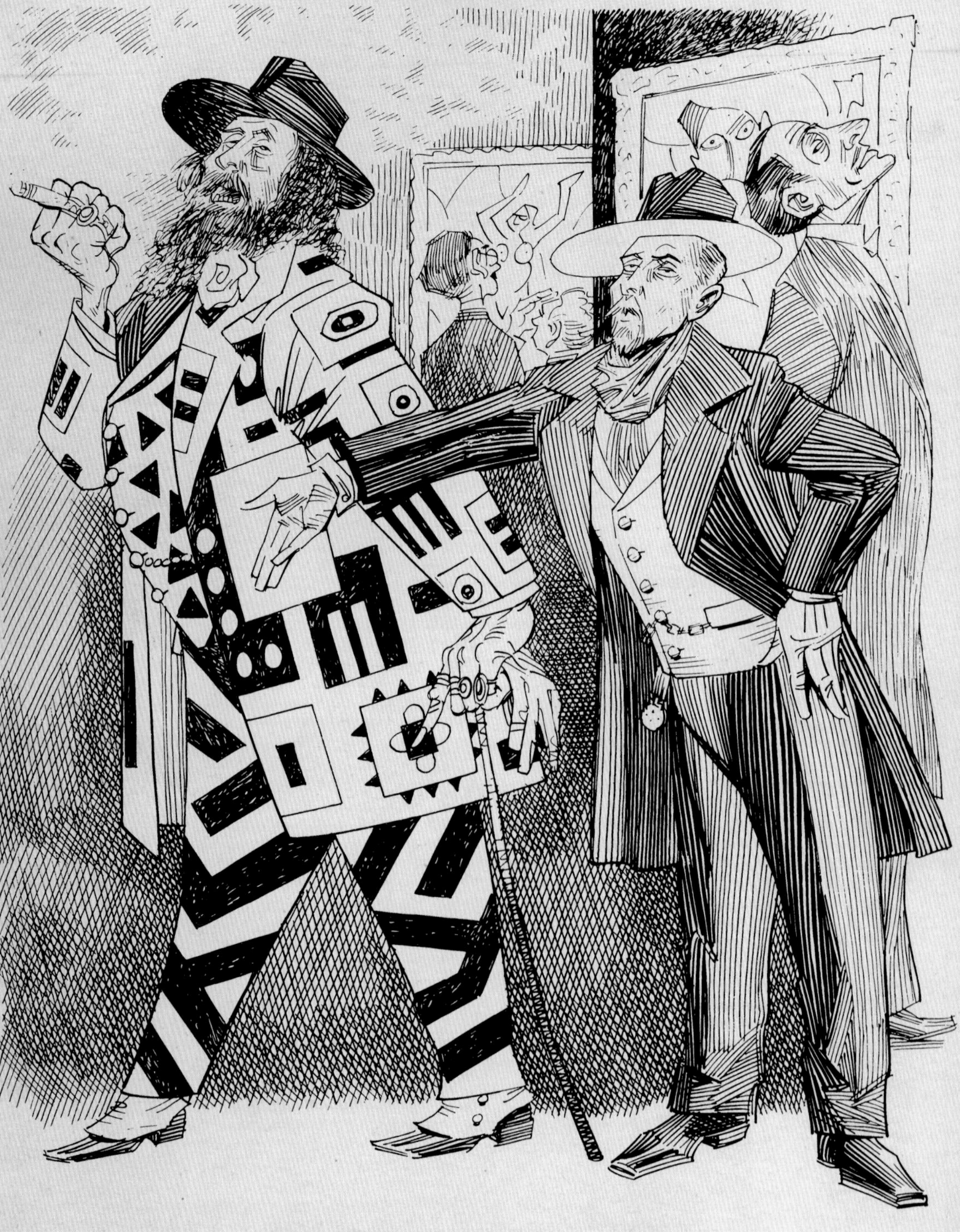

ROGUES IN THE GALLERY.

ALAN MOORE (Author and dandy). **"They say TODD KLEIN designed this tat and spun his calligraphic skills on it."**
KEVIN O'NEILL (Artist and probably Irish). **"To be sure, BEN DIMAGMALIW'S colouring gilds the lily an' all."**
AMERICAN PUBLISHER (Eavesdropping). **"Those foolish fops will work for scraps."**

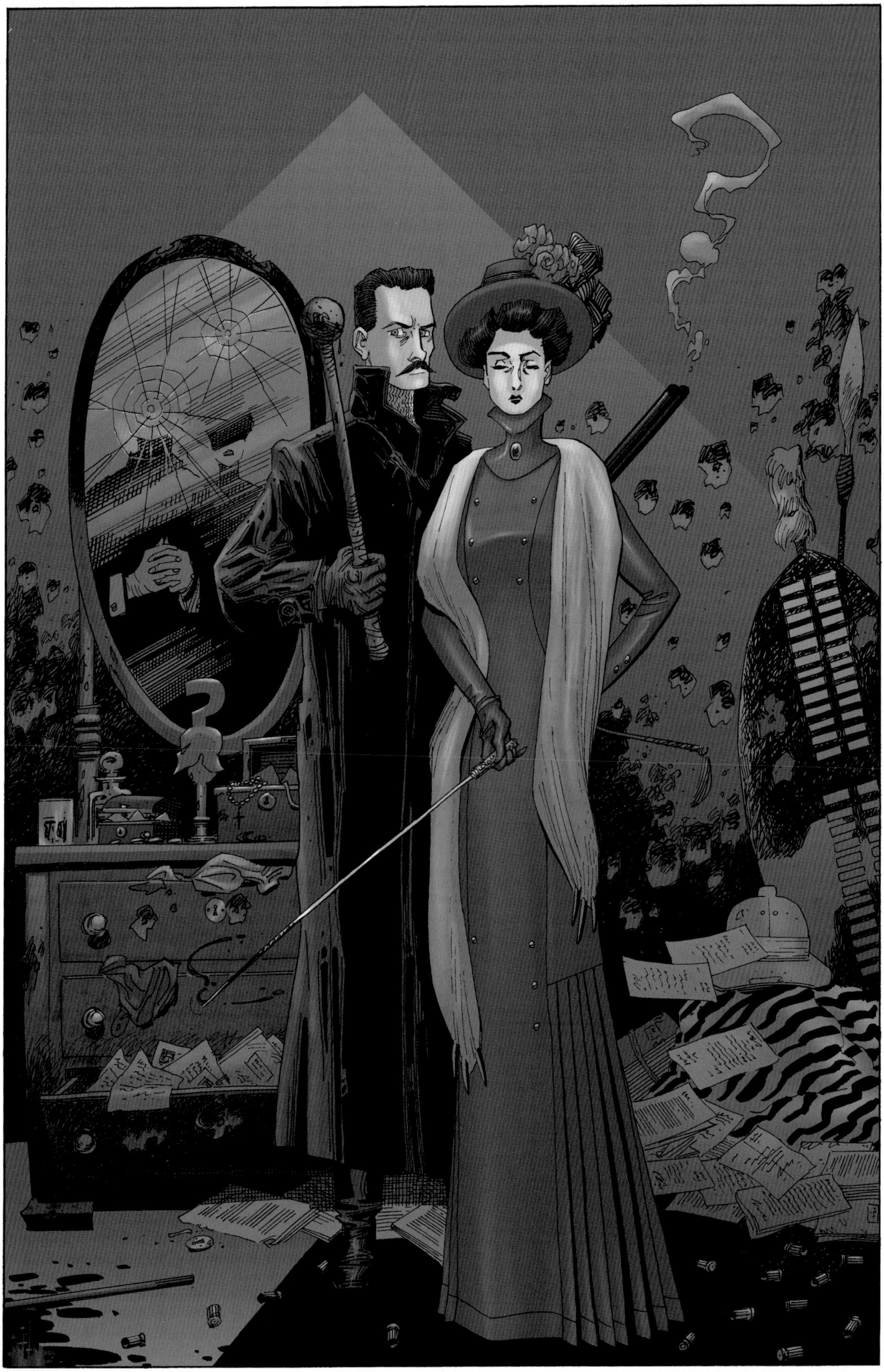

Promotional art for Volume III presentation, San Diego circa 2003.
(The Black Dossier project went into production first, delaying Volume III.)

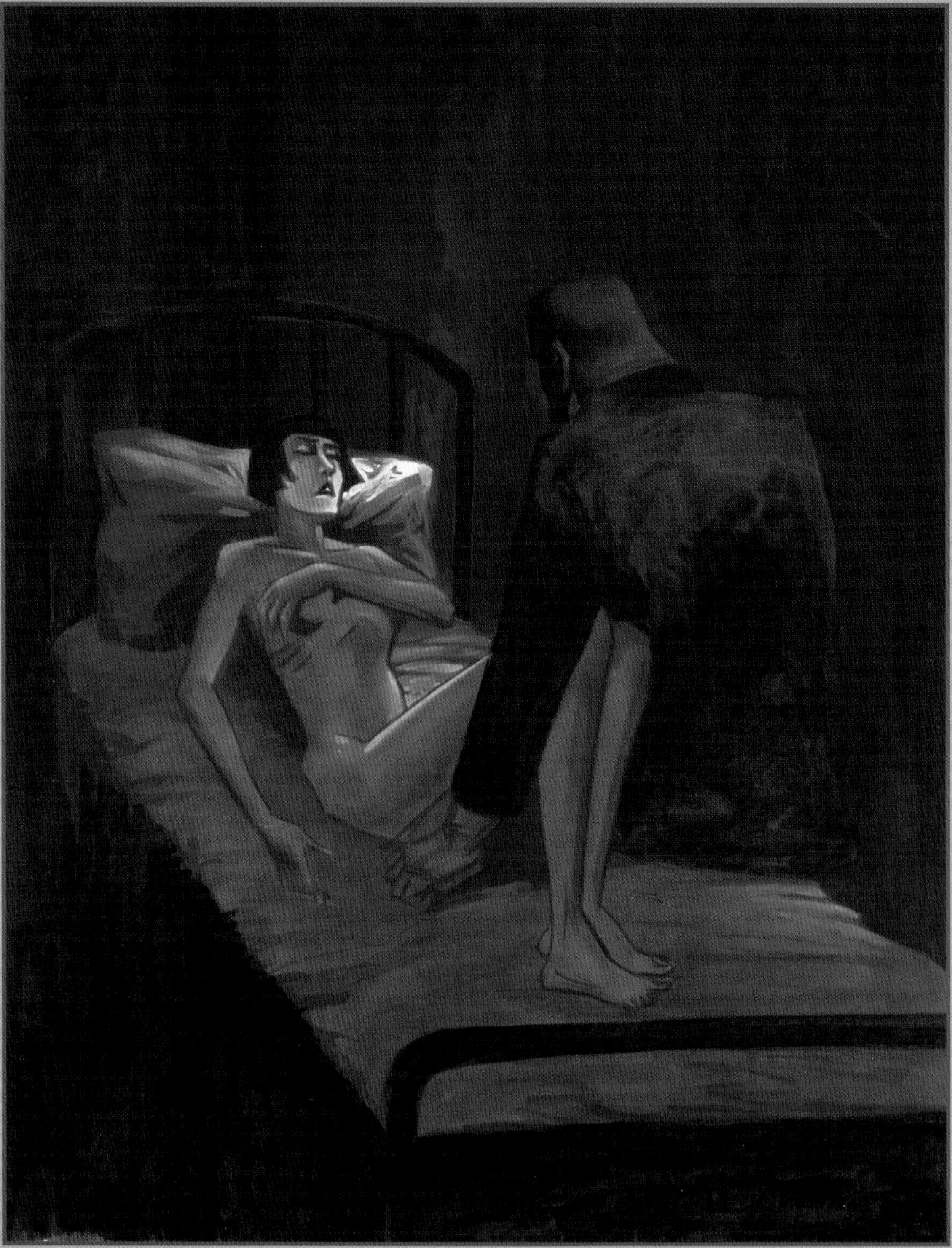

Robin Yaldwyn *"What Now?"* c. 1910-1911
The Copper Foundation, Copper Art Gallery

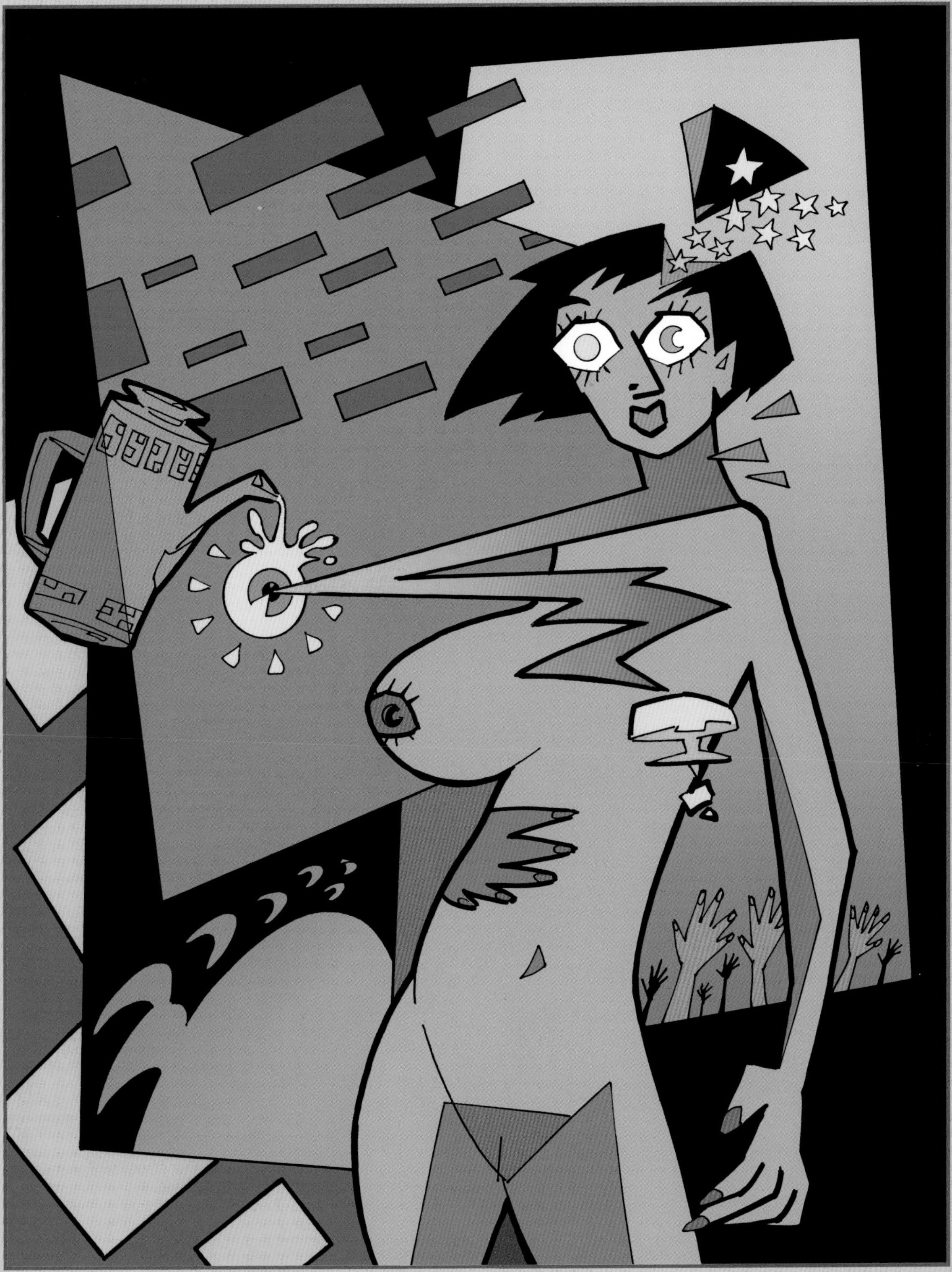

Paul Ashby "Hyde Park" c. 1969
Crichton Gallery, Bond Street, London

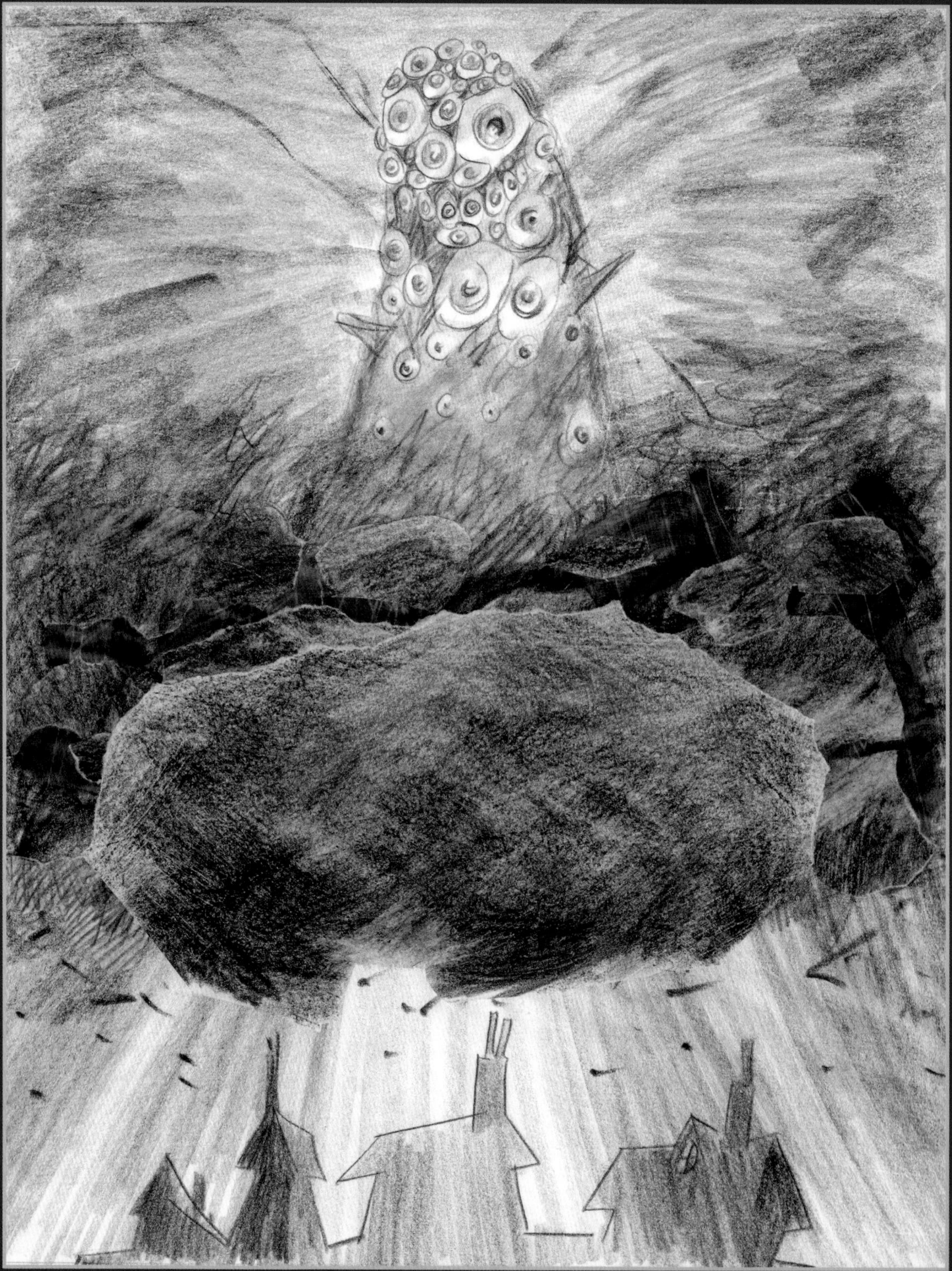

Michael Glass "What 15Peter20 Told Me" c. 2009
Coote's Centre Archive

Original cover devised for the BAO Publishing Italian Edition,
La Lega Degli Straordinari Gentlemen - Century.

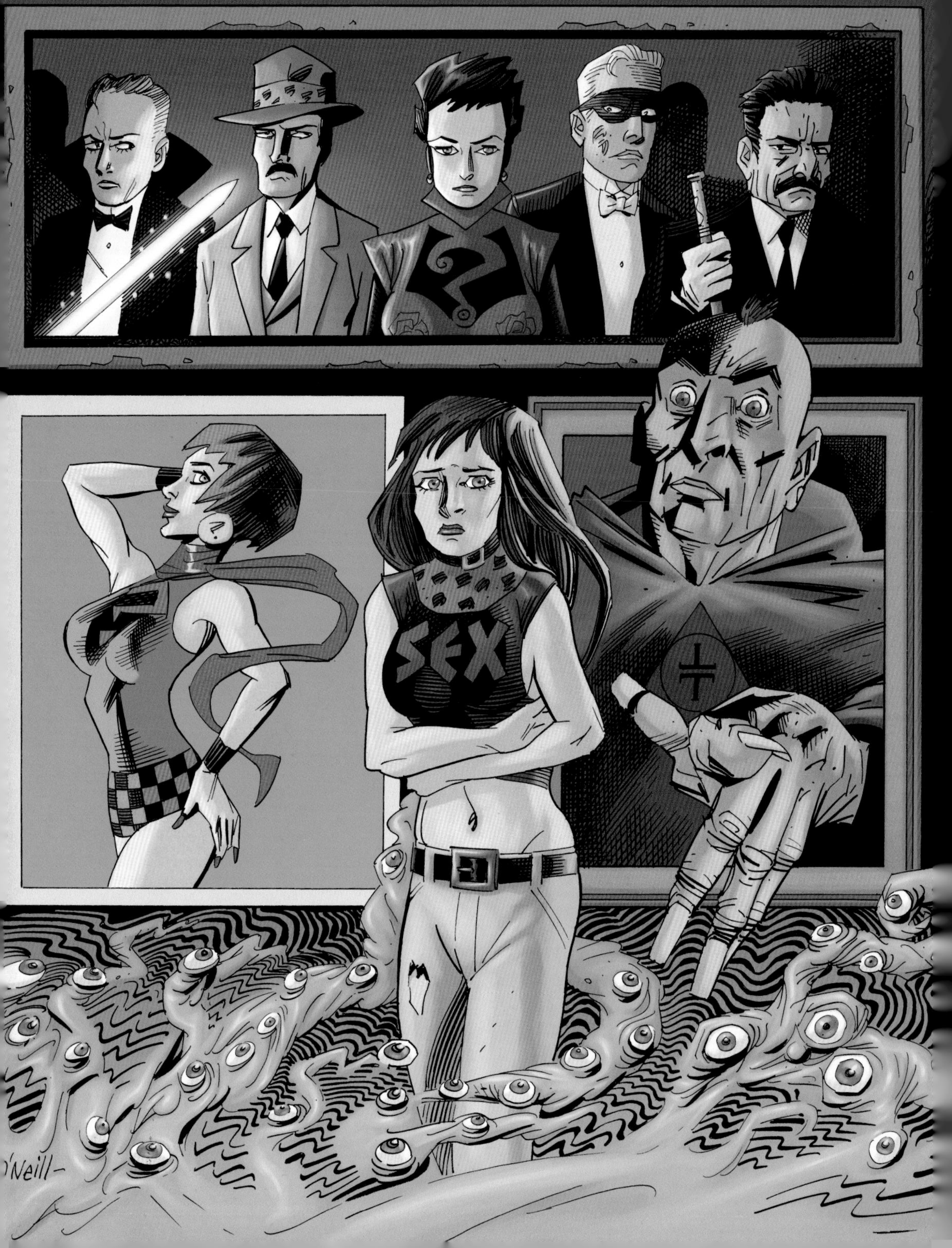
SEX

The LEAGUE of EXTRAORDINARY GENTLEMEN
CENTURY: 1910™

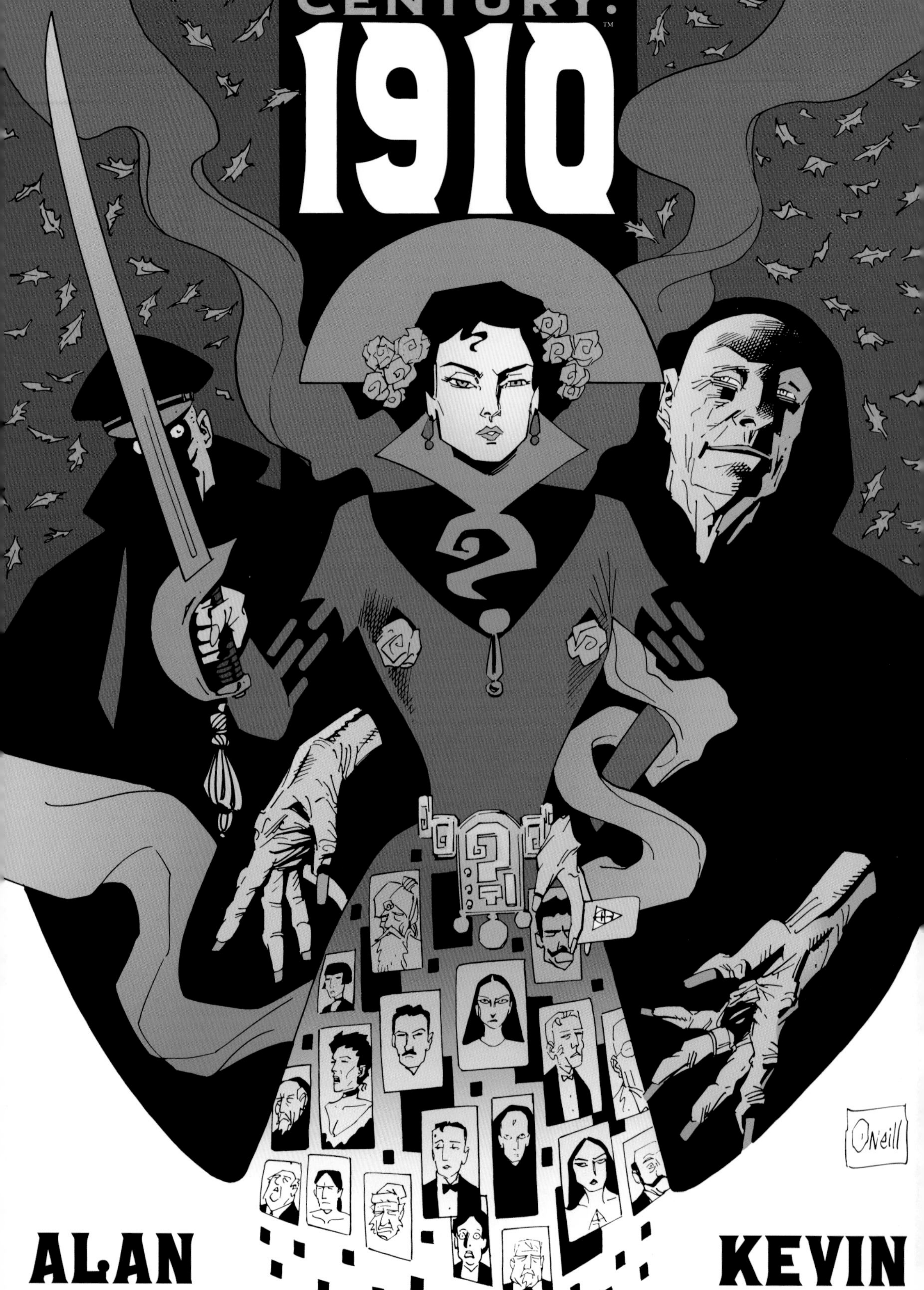
O'Neill

ALAN MOORE

KEVIN O'NEILL

THE LEAGUE OF EXTRAORDINARY GENTLEMEN™
ALAN MOORE
CENTURY:
1969™
KEVIN O'NEILL
O'Neill

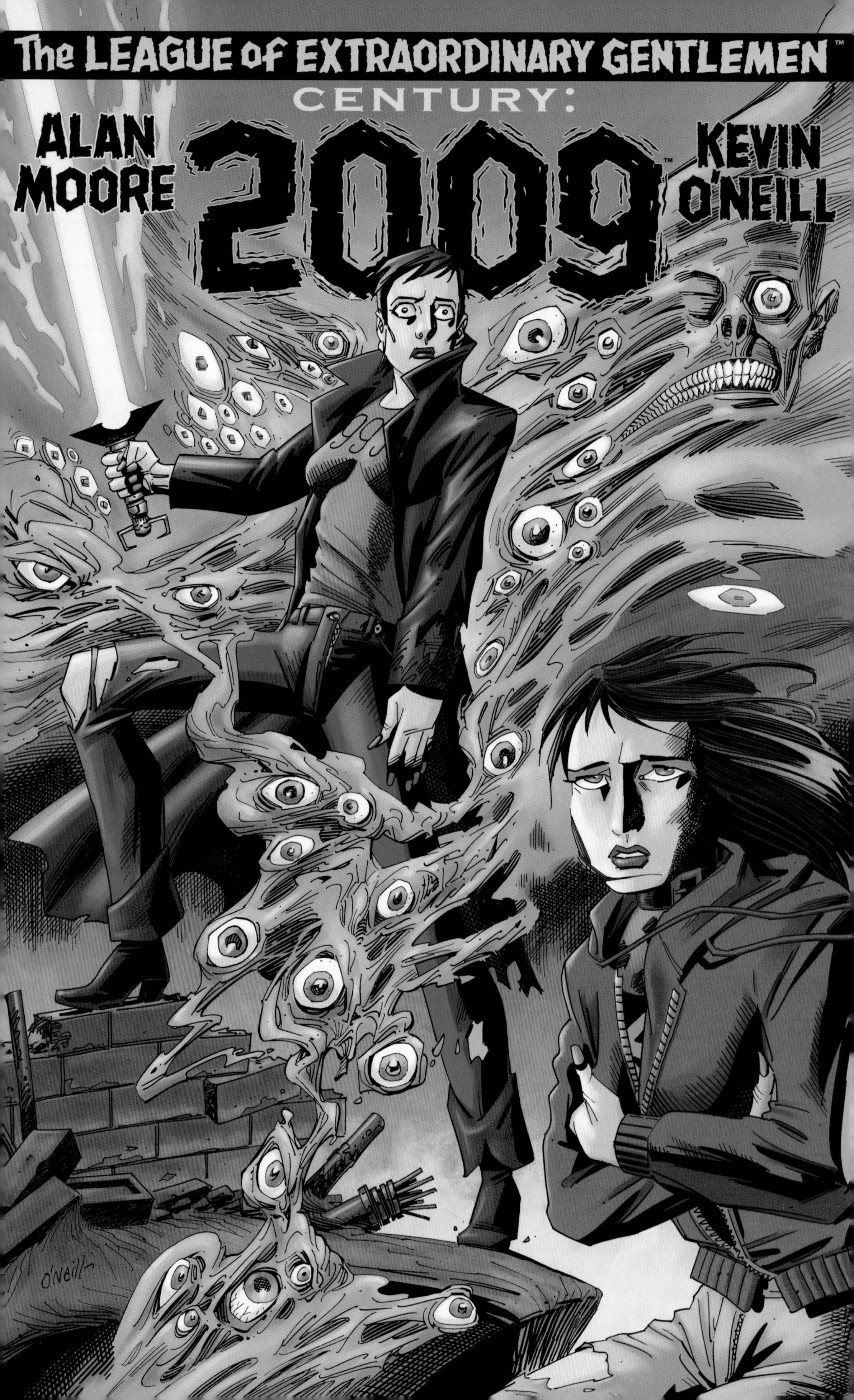
The LEAGUE of EXTRAORDINARY GENTLEMEN™
CENTURY:
ALAN MOORE
2009™
KEVIN O'NEILL
O'Neill

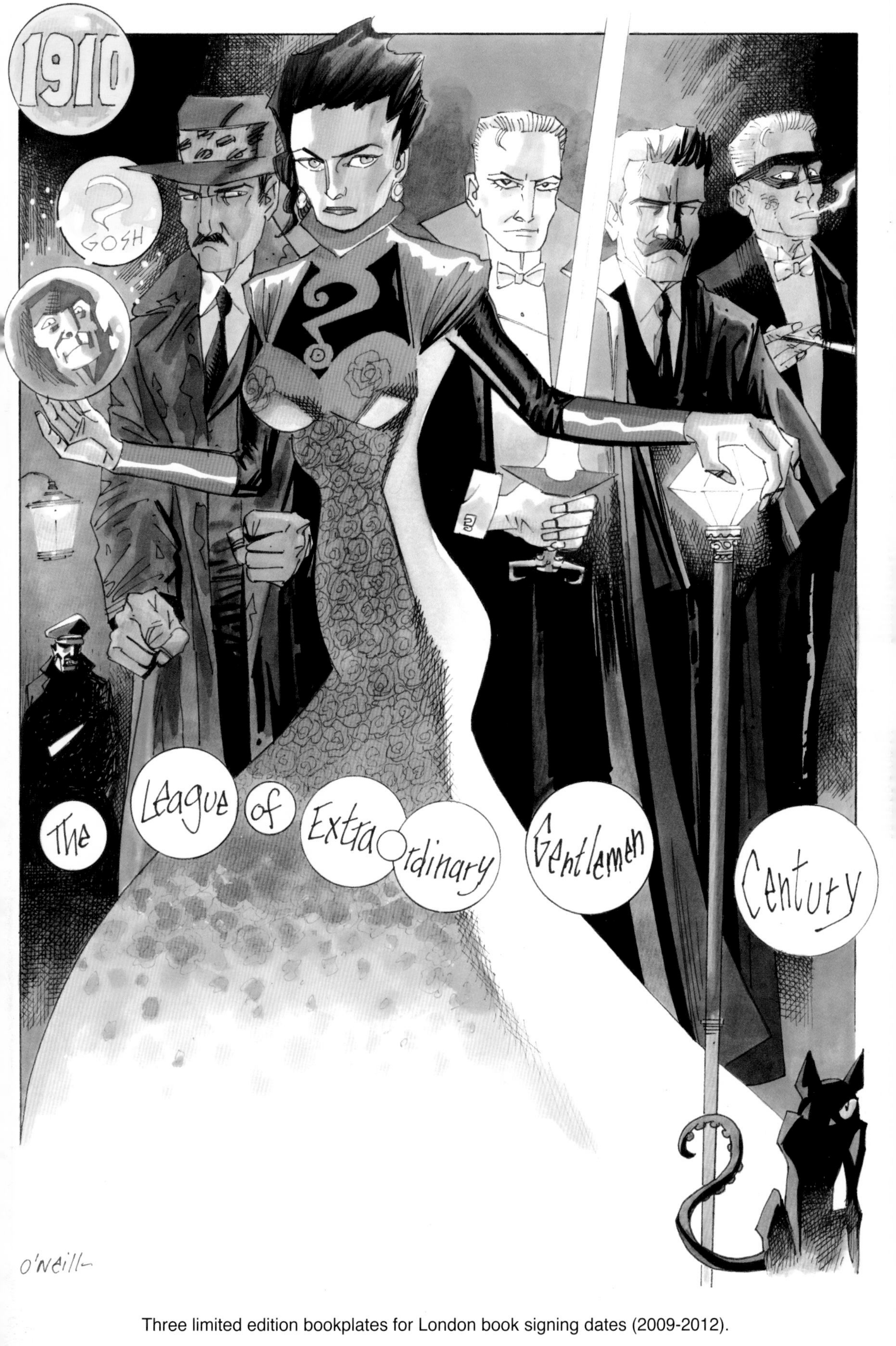
1910
GOSH
The League of Extraordinary Gentlemen
Century
O'Neill

Three limited edition bookplates for London book signing dates (2009-2012).

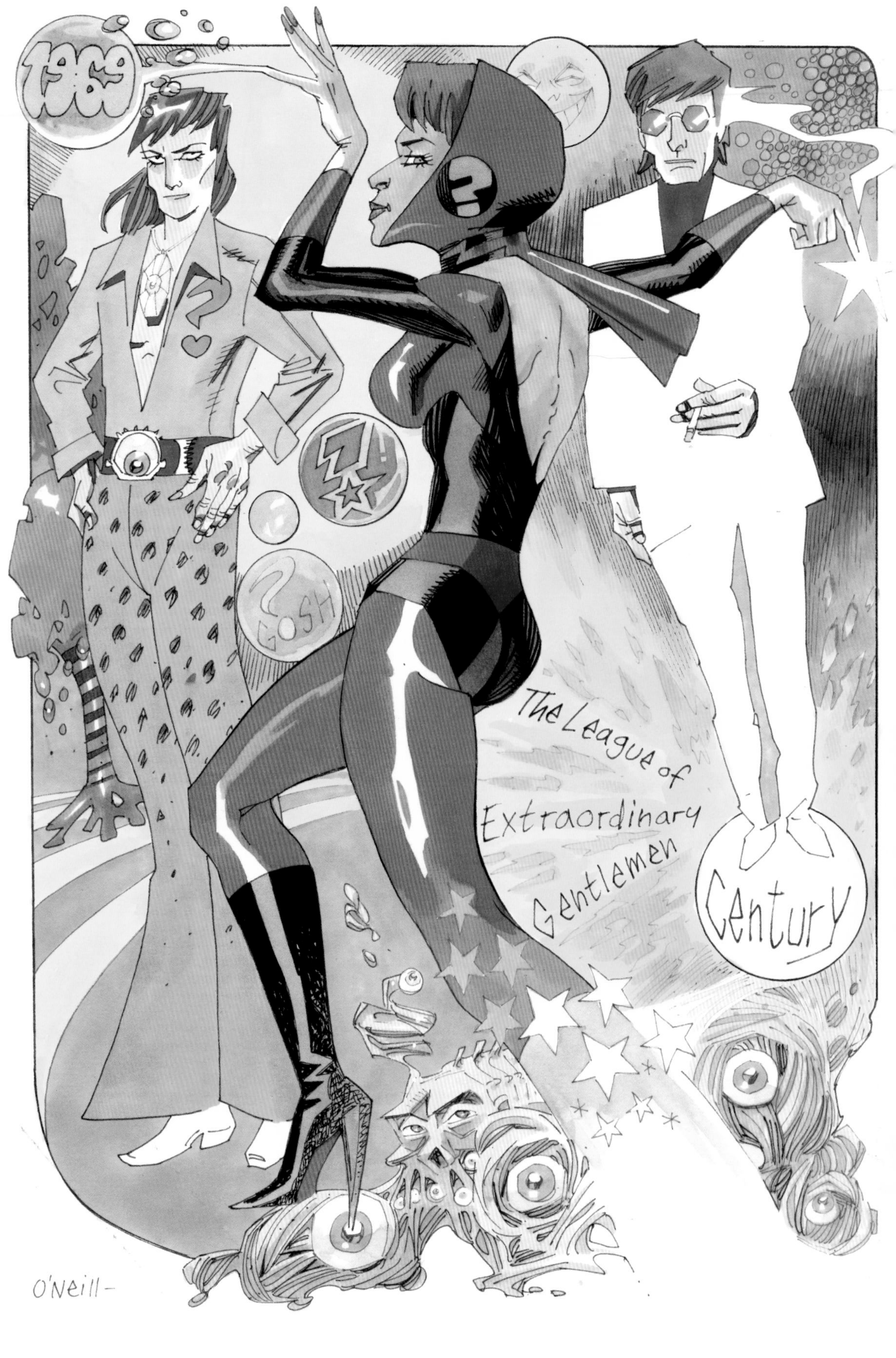

1969
?!
GOSH
The League of Extraordinary Gentlemen
Century
O'Neill

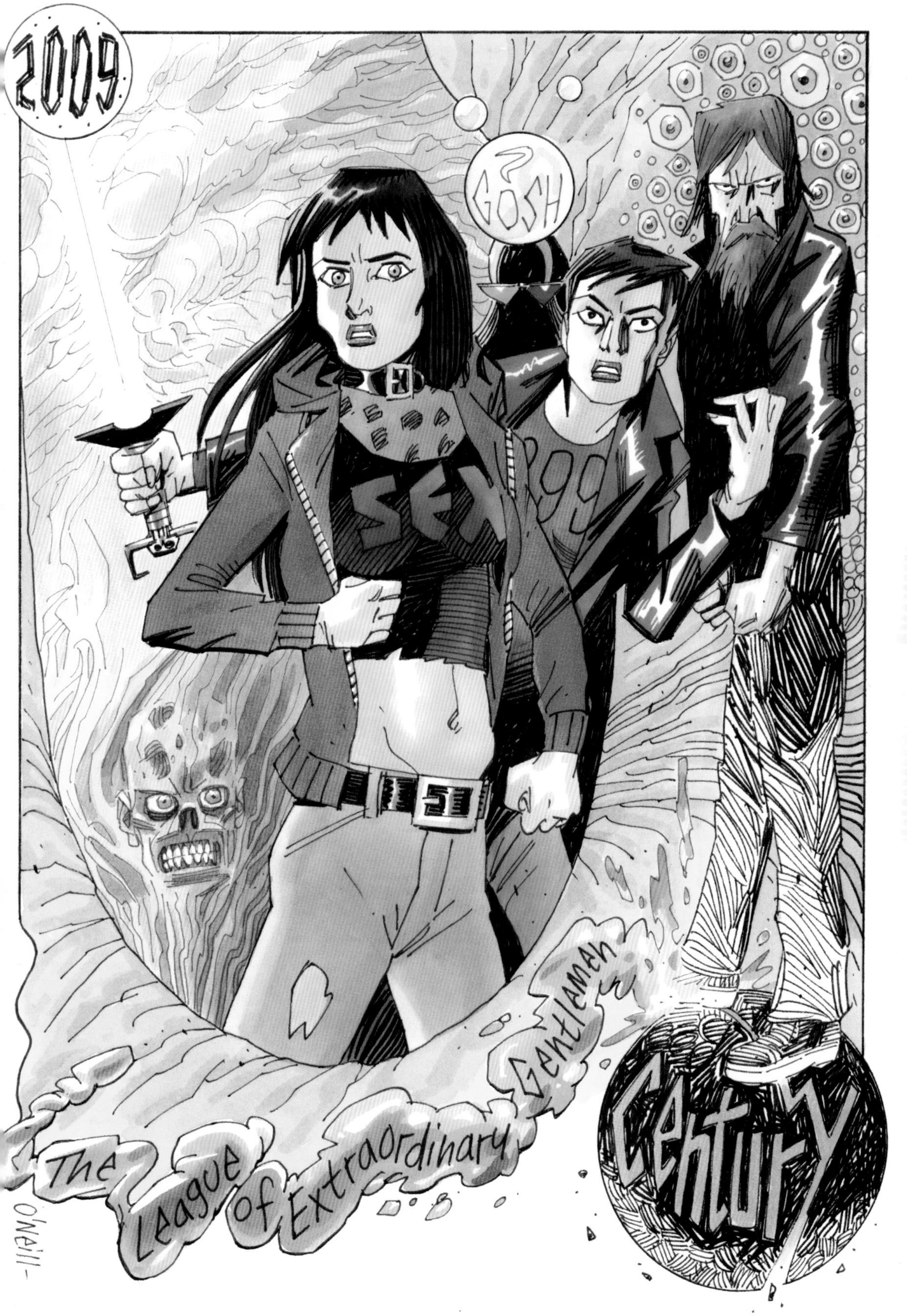
2009
?
GOSH
The League of Extraordinary Gentlemen
Century
O'Neill

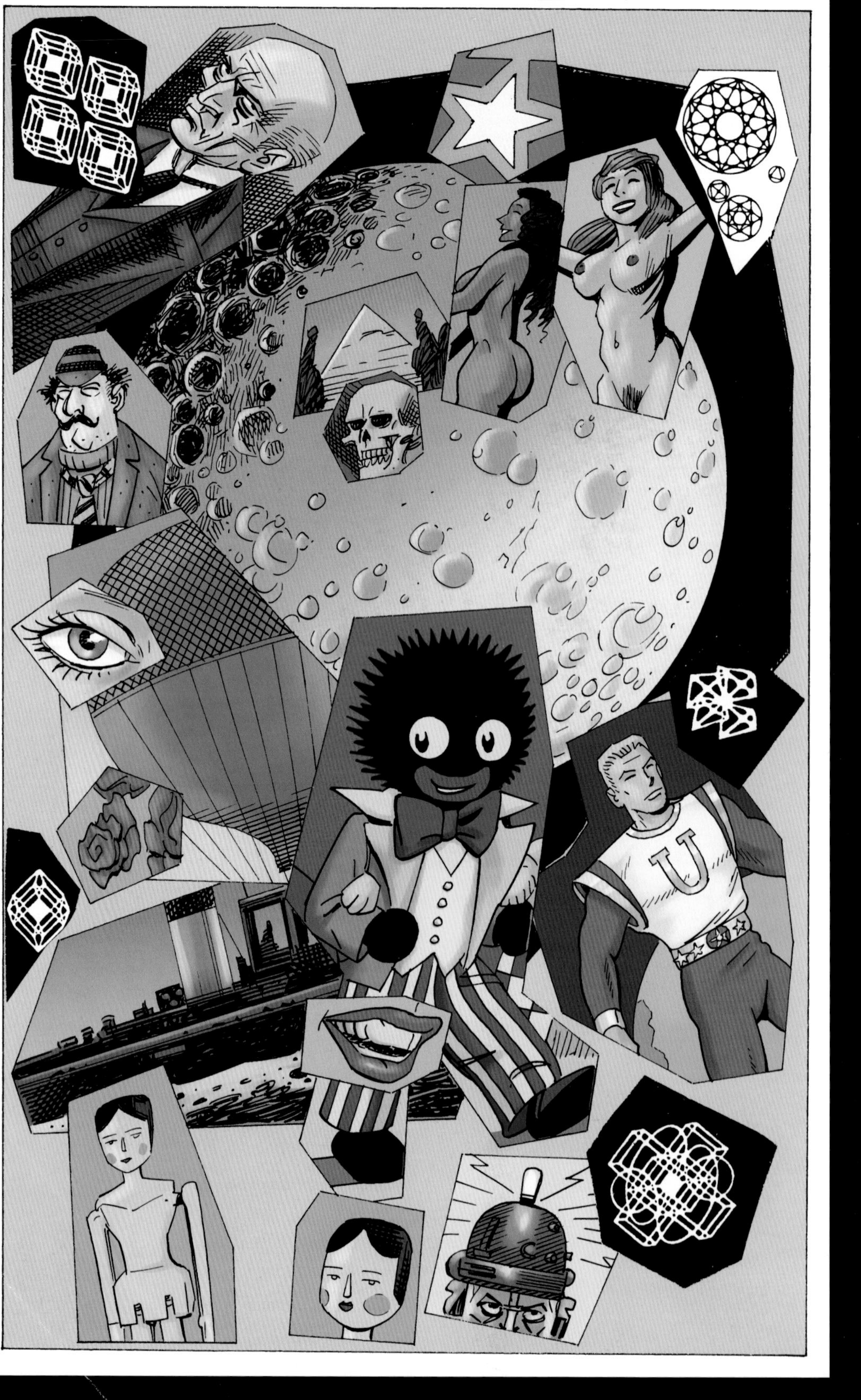